Windows® 2000 Server Secrets®

Harry M. Brelsford

IDG Books Worldwide, Inc.
An International Data Group Company

Foster City, CA ♦ Chicago, IL ♦ Indianapolis, IN ♦ New York, NY

Windows® 2000 Server Secrets®

Published by
IDG Books Worldwide, Inc.
An International Data Group Company
919 E. Hillsdale Blvd., Suite 400
Foster City, CA 94404
www.idgbooks.com (IDG Books Worldwide Web site)

Library of Congress Catalog Card Number: 99-068328

ISBN: 0-7645-4620-1

Printed in the United States of America

10 9 8 7 6 5 4 3 2 1

1B/SZ/RR/ZZ/FC

Distributed in the United States by IDG Books Worldwide, Inc.

Distributed by CDG Books Canada Inc. for Canada; by Transworld Publishers Limited in the United Kingdom; by IDG Norge Books for Norway; by IDG Sweden Books for Sweden; by IDG Books Australia Publishing Corporation Pty. Ltd. for Australia and New Zealand; by TransQuest Publishers Pte Ltd. for Singapore, Malaysia, Thailand, Indonesia, and Hong Kong; by Gotop Information Inc. for Taiwan; by ICG Muse, Inc. for Japan; by Intersoft for South Africa; by Eyrolles for France; by International Thomson Publishing for Germany, Austria and Switzerland; by Distribuidora Cuspide for Argentina; by LR International for Brazil; by Galileo Libros for Chile; by Ediciones ZETA S.C.R. Ltda. for Peru; by WS Computer Publishing Corporation, Inc., for the Philippines; by Contemporanea de Ediciones for Venezuela; by Express Computer Distributors for the Caribbean and West Indies; by Micronesia Media Distributor, Inc. for Micronesia; by Chips Computadoras S.A. de C.V. for Mexico; by Editorial Norma de Panama S.A. for Panama; by American Bookshops for Finland.

For general information on IDG Books Worldwide's books in the U.S., please call our Consumer Customer Service department at 800-762-2974. For reseller information, including discounts and premium sales, please call our Reseller Customer Service department at 800-434-3422.

For information on where to purchase IDG Books Worldwide's books outside the U.S., please contact our International Sales department at 317-596-5530 or fax 317-596-5692.

For consumer information on foreign language translations, please contact our Customer Service department at 800-434-3422, fax 317-596-5692, or e-mail rights@idgbooks.com.

For information on licensing foreign or domestic rights, please phone +1-650-655-3109.

For sales inquiries and special prices for bulk quantities, please contact our Sales department at 650-655-3200 or write to the address above.

For information on using IDG Books Worldwide's books in the classroom or for ordering examination copies, please contact our Educational Sales department at 800-434-2086 or fax 317-596-5499.

For press review copies, author interviews, or other publicity information, please contact our Public Relations department at 650-655-3000 or fax 650-655-3299.

For authorization to photocopy items for corporate, personal, or educational use, please contact Copyright Clearance Center, 222 Rosewood Drive, Danvers, MA 01923, or fax 978-750-4470.

Windows® 2000 Server Secrets®

ABOUT IDG BOOKS WORLDWIDE

Welcome to the world of IDG Books Worldwide.

IDG Books Worldwide, Inc., is a subsidiary of International Data Group, the world's largest publisher of computer-related information and the leading global provider of information services on information technology. IDG was founded more than 30 years ago by Patrick J. McGovern and now employs more than 9,000 people worldwide. IDG publishes more than 290 computer publications in over 75 countries. More than 90 million people read one or more IDG publications each month.

Launched in 1990, IDG Books Worldwide is today the #1 publisher of best-selling computer books in the United States. We are proud to have received eight awards from the Computer Press Association in recognition of editorial excellence and three from Computer Currents' First Annual Readers' Choice Awards. Our best-selling *...For Dummies®* series has more than 50 million copies in print with translations in 31 languages. IDG Books Worldwide, through a joint venture with IDG's Hi-Tech Beijing, became the first U.S. publisher to publish a computer book in the People's Republic of China. In record time, IDG Books Worldwide has become the first choice for millions of readers around the world who want to learn how to better manage their businesses.

Our mission is simple: Every one of our books is designed to bring extra value and skill-building instructions to the reader. Our books are written by experts who understand and care about our readers. The knowledge base of our editorial staff comes from years of experience in publishing, education, and journalism — experience we use to produce books to carry us into the new millennium. In short, we care about books, so we attract the best people. We devote special attention to details such as audience, interior design, use of icons, and illustrations. And because we use an efficient process of authoring, editing, and desktop publishing our books electronically, we can spend more time ensuring superior content and less time on the technicalities of making books.

You can count on our commitment to deliver high-quality books at competitive prices on topics you want to read about. At IDG Books Worldwide, we continue in the IDG tradition of delivering quality for more than 30 years. You'll find no better book on a subject than one from IDG Books Worldwide.

John Kilcullen
Chairman and CEO
IDG Books Worldwide, Inc.

Steven Berkowitz
President and Publisher
IDG Books Worldwide, Inc.

Eighth Annual Computer Press Awards 1992

Ninth Annual Computer Press Awards 1993

X
WINNER

Tenth Annual Computer Press Awards 1994

Eleventh Annual Computer Press Awards 1995

IDG is the world's leading IT media, research and exposition company. Founded in 1964, IDG had 1997 revenues of $2.05 billion and has more than 9,000 employees worldwide. IDG offers the widest range of media options that reach IT buyers in 75 countries representing 95% of worldwide IT spending. IDG's diverse product and services portfolio spans six key areas including print publishing, online publishing, expositions and conferences, market research, education and training, and global marketing services. More than 90 million people read one or more of IDG's 290 magazines and newspapers, including IDG's leading global brands — Computerworld, PC World, Network World, Macworld and the Channel World family of publications. IDG Books Worldwide is one of the fastest-growing computer book publishers in the world, with more than 700 titles in 36 languages. The "...For Dummies®" series alone has more than 50 million copies in print. IDG offers online users the largest network of technology-specific Web sites around the world through IDG.net (http://www.idg.net), which comprises more than 225 targeted Web sites in 55 countries worldwide. International Data Corporation (IDC) is the world's largest provider of information technology data, analysis and consulting, with research centers in over 41 countries and more than 400 research analysts worldwide. IDG World Expo is a leading producer of more than 168 globally branded conferences and expositions in 35 countries including E3 (Electronic Entertainment Expo), Macworld Expo, ComNet, Windows World Expo, ICE (Internet Commerce Expo), Agenda, DEMO, and Spotlight. IDG's training subsidiary, ExecuTrain, is the world's largest computer training company, with more than 230 locations worldwide and 785 training courses. IDG Marketing Services helps industry-leading IT companies build international brand recognition by developing global integrated marketing programs via IDG's print, online and exposition products worldwide. Further information about the company can be found at www.idg.com.

1/24/99

Credits

Acquisitions Editor
Jim Sumser

Development Editors
Kurt Stephan
Jennifer Rowe
Brian MacDonald

Technical Editor
James R. Kiniry, Jr.

Copy Editors
Chandani Thapa
Victoria Anne Lee
Lauren Kennedy

Project Coordinator
Linda Marousek

Graphics and Production Specialists
Mario Amador
Stephanie Hollier
Jude Levinson
Ramses Ramirez

Quality Control Specialist
Chris Weisbart

Book Designer
Drew Moore

Illustrators
Shelley Norris
Karl Brandt

Proofreading and Indexing
York Production Services

Cover Design
Deborah Reinerio

About the Author

Harry M. Brelsford, MCSE, MCT, CNE, CLSE, CNP, MBA, is a contributing editor at *Microsoft Certified Professional Magazine*, for which he pens the regular online column, "Windows 2000 Foundations." He is a practicing network consultant in the Seattle, Washington area, where he specializes in Microsoft BackOffice projects. Harry is an instructor in the online MCSE program at Seattle Pacific University, a Microsoft AATP. He has published over 100 technology and business articles in numerous magazines, and is a founding member of the BackOffice Professionals Association (BOPA) in Redmond, Washington. A life-long learner, Harry earned his MBA from the University of Denver in 1986. When time allows, Harry enjoys cross-country skiing and sailing with his family in the Pacific Northwest. You can contact him at `harryb@nwlink.com` or `www.nwlink.com/~harryb`.

To Kristen, my wife and the mother of our Geoffrey Sailor and Harry Skier! You were truly there, whether you knew it or not, typing each key, writing each page, and reviewing each draft with me. You made contributions to this book in a *billion* ways. And let's not forget dear Mom, Diane Brelsford, who ultimately made everything possible for me.

Foreword

Making the decision to install Windows 2000 Server is really just the first step in yet another long, challenging journey you face as a network administrator. That's why you'll want to take Harry Brelsford, who's been there, along with you.

If you're a network professional responsible for deploying, supporting, and maintaining this new and highly complex product, you know that running MAKEBOOT.EXE to create those first setup disks is just the beginning. What comes after that is a huge need for hands-on knowledge — far beyond what's available from Microsoft sources.

Harry Brelsford knows what it means to sit in front of a server and install a Microsoft product, then support and maintain it for demanding customers after the fact. His expertise as a consultant and his years of in-the-field experience as a practicing network administrator are reflected in this book.

I've worked with Harry since shortly after the launch of *Microsoft Certified Professional Magazine* in early 1995, so I know that he's been out there in the trenches right along with the rest of you. He's both a contributing editor to the magazine and an MCSE — further proof that he understands Microsoft technology in general and Microsoft Windows in particular.

The title of the book says it all. The "secrets" about Windows 2000 Server inserted throughout the book are truly that: little-known tips and tricks for saving time and increasing productivity, tested by someone who's worked extensively with both Windows NT and Windows 2000 Server in the field.

If you need further proof of Harry's real-world expertise, take a look at the table of contents. Only someone who really understands Windows 2000 Server would know that you won't get far without solid knowledge of TCP/IP — hence Part II is devoted to the topic.

And only somebody who's done plenty of installations, troubleshooting, and support calls would include extensive information on third-party tools that will be useful in many Windows 2000 Server installations. If you're not using some of these now, perhaps this information will be an eye-opener about what's out there, and can save you time and hassle. And you'll also want to take a look at Harry's coverage of optimization and troubleshooting — much of it information that I haven't seen anywhere else.

If you're not familiar with Windows 2000 Server yet but are eyeing it with interest, this is the perfect book to show you the richness and complexity of the product, from someone who enjoys working with it. You won't find marketing spiels or product apologies here. Instead, you'll get useful, professional information, all of it written in Harry's inimitable style.

It's tough to stay on top of new product releases from Microsoft, but this book is a timely one. In fact, as I read through the diverse topics covered, I thought over and over, "What a great article idea for the magazine!" Harry's been brightening the pages of *MCP Magazine* for years with his knowledge, insights, and wit. Spend some time with this book and let him give you a true insider's coaching on Windows 2000 Server.

Linda Briggs
Editor-in-Chief, *Microsoft Certified Professional Magazine*
September 1999

Preface

Welcome! *Windows 2000 Server Secrets* is a book based on Microsoft's latest release of its successful network operating system. It is a book unlike many others on the shelf. It is a collection of secrets gathered in the trenches from my 10+ years of experience as a computer professional. This book is about having "been there, done that, and still doing it daily" with networking, and specifically Windows 2000 Server. And with its quippy delivery, it is both a reference book and a summer-vacation-at-the-beach kind of read.

Why use this book? Can't you just read a user manual and trade journal story about Windows 2000 Server? I can give you at least eight reasons to purchase this book today:

- **Expectation management.** Windows 2000 Server is in its infancy as far as network operating systems go. And while my (and your) enthusiasm is most likely very high for this product, we need to remain realistic about what Windows 2000 Server can do today and what it'll likely deliver on tomorrow. As often as possible, I draw out areas in Windows 2000 Server where you should proactively manage your expectations.
- **Windows 2000 Server transition and planning.** The adage "proper planning prevents poor performance" clearly applies to Windows 2000 Server today. By getting your Windows 2000 Server house in order up front with help from this book, you'll have more success when you enhance, upgrade, and expand your network later on for whatever reason. Transition and planning is a recurring theme that spans the entire book.
- **Windows 2000 Server.** It's now time! Simply stated, it's *now* time to start using Windows 2000 Server. You've waited long enough, riding the emotional rollercoaster waiting for Windows 2000 Server to arrive. It has arrived, and this book is focused on deployment. No more talk about what will be. The talk is about what is.
- **MCSE certification tips.** This book is written by a practicing MCSE. Hey, I've taken those demanding exams over the years (sometimes more than once). May my well-placed MCSE insights enable you to pass your exams sooner rather than later. And don't forget the Windows 2000 Server MCSE track is very different from past MCSE operating system tracks. In fact, if you're a Windows NT 4.0 MCSE, you will need to re-certify on Windows 2000 Server.
- **TCP/IP.** This is a timeless topic that you can never get enough of. Mastering TCP/IP is one of the fastest ways to achieve greatness in the Windows 2000 Server community. I am especially proud of my discussion on DNS in Chapter 6. DNS is an area I highly recommend you master immediately, because it has assumed a core role in Windows 2000 Server. TCP/IP is covered from cradle to grave in Part II, "TCP/IP."

- **Performance analysis.** Like TCP/IP, this topic doesn't have an expiration date. In fact, the more experienced you become with Windows 2000 Server, the more important performance analysis becomes. Too often, you learn performance analysis in a crisis, but hopefully you'll read Part VI, "Optimizing Windows 2000 Server" before that day arrives. Truth be told, I initially wrote this section for my own benefit because I just could not find great books on the market that adequately addressed performance analysis issues, such as Performance Monitor logging and Network Monitor packet analysis. I hope you will benefit from my efforts in this area.
- **Third-party solutions.** Another motivating factor in writing this book was my use of the Microsoft Official Curriculum (MOC) and other Microsoft-centric texts as a practicing MCT. The MOC is a great first step for getting certified. But the MOC has not and will probably never highlight third-party solutions that we experienced network professionals like to use (and often must use) to keep our networks humming and our stakeholders singing. In that spirit, I serve up deft discussions on the use of third-party applications, utilities, and tools such as NessSoft's PingPlotter. Let's face it — too many books on the shelves are written myopically about Microsoft networking solutions, such as Windows 2000 Server, in a vacuum. Most of us, however, supplement Windows 2000 Server with a variety of third-party applications, utilities, and tools. My book reflects this real-world paradigm.
- **Real-world attitude.** Speaking of the real world, I've committed my waking hours, both day and night, to write this book for you as one of you. By day, I'm an MCSE consultant who is typing commands, rebooting servers, and downloading drivers. At night, when I'm not training future MCSEs as an instructor, I morph into a scratch writer, brining you the tools to navigate your network in the new Windows 2000 Server world. I'm not just a technology writer, and because of that, this book is unique when compared against many others. And perhaps most important of all, I don't have a staff of writers doing the dirty work for me. The buck stops here.

Introducing Windows 2000 Server

Many of us likened the arrival of Windows 2000 Server to the pathetic main characters in Samuel Beckett's *Waiting for Godot* who wait and wait for Godot. Fortunately, for you and I, Godot has arrived at long last. It was worth the wait. On all counts, Microsoft has delivered with Windows 2000 Server a network operating system that is mature beyond its days (maybe that's why it took so long to get it out the door!).

But don't be lulled into thinking that Windows 2000 Server doesn't have its own high need for attention. While you're not dealing with an infant here, more often than not you're dealing with a toddler. At times, you can let Windows 2000 Server run wild without a great deal of concern. Other times it must be disciplined. The Windows 2000 Server wisdom contained within these covers will help you understand these differences.

With the first release of Windows 2000 Server (see Figure P-1), you will find yourself assuming the role of a parent. In other words, you're the proud parent of a new network operating system. Congratulations! And while this book doesn't recite Microsoft's Windows 2000 Server's user manual, consider this book a "what to expect when you're raising a network operating system" supplement. Stick with me on this Windows 2000 Server "secrets" journey and I can promise you'll feel a wonderful sense of accomplishment. You will learn how to use this product in the real world and feel empowered to implement Windows 2000 Server in ways that weren't even anticipated by the developers at Microsoft.

Figure P-2: Microsoft Management Console

What Is Windows 2000 Server?

Microsoft has positioned Windows 2000 Server as a robust, reliable, and secure network server operating system, with an emphasis on providing directory services and running applications. It is a 29 million-line, 32-bit operating system that participates in a "true" server scenario, that of the Active Directory/domain security model. And don't overlook its easy-to-use, Windows 98-like graphical user interface (GUI). The Windows 2000 Server interface is already appreciated by other NOS crowds such as seasoned NetWare administrators!

Beneath the pretty face, Windows 2000 Server is a huge, powerful network operating system. Needless to say, Windows 2000 Server is too big for any one individual to completely master. At the enterprise level, it is common to see Windows 2000 Server job classes divided so that one person is responsible for managing only part of the Windows 2000 Server. And while some would say you're just a cog in the enterprise wheel, in reality, you're on the front line of Windows 2000 Server, seeing it deployed as the masters at Microsoft intended.

As many of you know the basics of Windows 2000 Server, or at least I assume you do, you won't be acting as a feature creature in this or other chapters. But I will attempt to help define the Windows 2000 Server paradigm in this book. This includes:

- Lightweight Directory Access Protocol (LDAP)-based Active Directory (see Chapters 11 and 12)
- Different types of Windows 2000 Server such as Professional (Chapter 14) and Advanced Server and Datacenter (Chapter 15)
- New domain structure based on the industry standard Domain Name System (DNS) server (Chapter 6)
- Robust security based on the Kerberos Internet standard (Chapter 13)

TCP/IP paradigm shift

Clearly, Windows 2000 Server extends the use of the TCP/IP protocol suite "paradigm shift" that started with Windows NT Server 3.51. Microsoft has not only embraced the TCP/IP de facto standard for network and internetworking protocols but, I submit, with Windows 2000 Server, they've mastered it. The paradigm shift I speak of relates to Microsoft using TCP/IP because of its worldwide acceptance, its open standards (something lacking in IPX/SPX), and its routable nature (something that's missing in NetBEUI). And because the Internet uses the TCP/IP protocol suite, Microsoft's TCP/IP paradigm shift was also Microsoft's Internet paradigm shift — but more on that in a moment.

The default network protocol in Windows 2000 Server, TCP/IP is automatically installed when you set up Windows 2000 Server (discussed in Chapter 2). And while you may continue using other network protocols such as NetBEUI and IPX/SPX, you have fewer and fewer reasons to do so.

With the TCP/IP protocol suite, Windows 2000 Server is a true enterprise-level network server that conforms to the conventional thinking of the Internet. In order for you to exploit the vast resources of the Internet on your Windows 2000 Server network, it is critical that you use the TCP/IP protocol suite. By reading the chapters in Part II, "TCP/IP," you will have the opportunity to master this protocol. The information in Part II may be the most important part of this book. But whatever your motivations and viewpoints, mastering TCP/IP is a smart move on your climb to Windows 2000 Server guru status.

Internet paradigm shift

The release of Windows 2000 Server represents Microsoft's continued shift in its business mission from its traditional LAN and desktop view of computing to Internet-based. Many of the improvements that Microsoft has introduced in Windows 2000 Server, such as the Internet Connection Wizard, have dramatically increased Internet functionality. This is also apparent with Microsoft's further integration between Internet Explorer (IE) and the operating system. Eat your heart out, U.S. Justice Department!

Windows 2000 Server Zen

With the release of Windows 2000 Server, network professionals are starting a long journey toward ultimately mastering Microsoft's new generation of network operating systems. But there are many smart reasons for introducing Windows 2000 Server in your organization today.

- **Learning Curve Analysis.** Windows 2000 Server has a new look and feel. That said, you can now exhale a sigh or relief; the GUI changes between Windows NT Server 3.5*x* and Windows NT Server 4.0 were more dramatic than those you'll discover in Windows 2000 Server. In some ways, you already know Windows 2000 Server better than you might think. One example of this is the Microsoft Management Console (MMC) shown in Figure P-2. If you have ever installed the Windows NT Server 4.0 Option Pack, you've most likely encountered the MMC. If not, don't worry; it's easy to work with and is discussed several times in this book.
- **Applications compatibility testing.** Early adopters will jump on the first opportunity to test critical business applications for basic compatibility with Windows 2000 Server. Don't believe me? Look no further than my good client Jack, who is the MIS manager at a chain of athletic clubs in the Pacific Northwest. Jack is already testing the membership check-in program for Windows 2000 Server compatibility.
- **Driver compatibility testing.** Second only to application testing will be the need to test software drivers for common and legacy hardware devices. Do these devices run on Windows 2000 Server or not? Such an answer is critical for the landscape architect at a Northwest landscaping firm hoping to print blueprints from an old HP Plotter via Windows 2000 Server.
- **Planning purposes (Active Directory design).** The upstream planning process is reason enough to deploy Windows 2000 Server sooner rather than later. One such Windows 2000 Server planning area is Active Directory (covered in Chapters 11 and 12).
- **Cultural reengineering and acceptance.** You may be interested to know that a recent keynote address at a Windows 2000 conference (summer 1999) brought to my attention that Windows 2000 Server, in particular Active Directory, will be 20 percent hard work and 80 percent politics at

the enterprise level. I suspect that you will encounter similar, non-computer dynamics in your organization as well.

- **Get the show on the road.** Enough already. We've waited years for Windows 2000 Server. The time is now to start mastering it.

And there are several ways to introduce Windows 2000 Server in your organization before it is truly ready to throw the switch. The following list goes from silly to serious so as not to ignore the breadth of the Windows 2000 Server community.

- **Basement Weekend Warrior.** Like the ham radio operator of the 1960s and 1970s, the Windows 2000 Server basement weekend warrior is learning Windows 2000 Server with the idea of introducing it into the company when appropriate. These are the self-studying types. Bless their hearts.
- **Skunk Works.** To draw on a term floated in the 1980s, within every company considering Windows 2000 Server, there are network administrators and engineers operating just under the radar screen. These individuals, heroes in the eyes of many, are sneaking Windows 2000 Server into the work place, one installation at a time.
- **MCSE Alibis.** Repeat the refrain: "I'm getting certified." Many early Windows 2000 Server installations are being undertaken more for the benefit of the certification candidate than the employers. Whatever works.
- **Coexistence.** On a more serious note: Early adopters are successfully and correctly asserting that Windows 2000 Server should be introduced into the organization today to test for compatibilities.
- **Throw the dog in the water.** What the hell: go for it. This is the straight up approach. Or the "Just do it" Nike approach. Here, Windows 2000 Server is introduced today in the organization. No questions asked.

However, it is important to remember that, like beef and fine wine, an NOS should be aged to perfection before use. Using an NOS before its time is certainly not recommended and would be considered foolish among qualified and experienced network professionals. One of my earliest experiences with Windows NT Server 4.0 might be applied to today's Windows 2000 Server product. Eager to deploy Windows NT Server 4.0 after only its first service pack (SP1) had been released, I successfully convinced a client not to deploy Windows NT Server 3.51 with its Service Pack 5 (SP5). Needless to say, this mistake was serious in a real production environment. Early releases of Windows NT Server 4.0 were just that: early. Perhaps I was seduced more by the attractive interface and less by the stability of its predecessor at the SP5 level. If I had to do it again, I would have taken a more conservative approach in the early days of Windows NT Server 4.0 and deployed Windows NT Server 3.51 (SP5) first.

The point is this. Start using Windows 2000 Server today, as it's finally here and ready to go. But for goodness' sake, use it first in a test lab or test network before deployment on production servers. By following a disciplined game plan, you'll avoid failures in deploying Windows 2000 Server in your organization.

The MCSE

Many readers are pursuing the Microsoft Certified Professional designation known as Microsoft Certified Systems Engineer (MCSE). As a practicing MCSE, I know the journey you are on. In general, I have emphasized topics such as TCP/IP and performance analysis that benefit MCSE candidates seeking to pass the grueling certification exams. Where possible, I offer secrets that are MCSE exam-specific. I've been there and done that. I hope I can help you get there too!

The dramatic increase in the popularity of the MCSE designation occurred before the appearance of Windows 2000 Server. A few of us even started and obtained our MCSEs during the Windows NT Server 3.*x* era. Many friends joined us during the Windows NT Server 4.0 era. And many more peers will join us as MCSEs in the Windows 2000 Server lifecycle. It's a good thing! Designing, installing, implementing, and managing Windows 2000 Server is enough work for everyone. And mastering such tasks is not only a key aspect of the MCSE program, but also the underlying emphasis of this book.

This book is not necessarily written for the newly arrived NT professional. In fact, it is assumed you have worked with Windows 2000 Server before and are seeking to improve your Windows 2000 Server-specific skill set. Hence the numerous notes, tips, and (of course) secrets.. Simply stated, this is not a rewrite of the user manual or the resource kit. I believe you will welcome and appreciate this approach.

Are You Ready for This Book?

To fully enjoy this book, you must, at a minimum, have a keen interest in Windows 2000 Server. Add computer-related work experience, network certifications, degrees, and training, and you'll get even more benefit from reading and using this book. In short, you will derive from this book what you put into it. Those with less networking experience may be the ones to utter "wow" and "cool" the loudest and longest. The gurus can always benefit from revisiting many tried-and-true network management methods presented herein. And I think the gurus will benefit greatly from my inclusion of several real-world, third-party matters, such as non-Microsoft tools that extend the reach of Windows 2000 Server.

How This Book Is Organized

I have organized the book into six parts, as follows:

- **Part I: Introduction, Planning, Setup, and Implementation.** It is here that I present, in a sincere and honorable way, the steps for installing Windows 2000 Server. I say "sincere and honorable" because here, as throughout the book, I go to great lengths to avoid recasting the user manuals that ship with Windows 2000 Server. Rather, in addition to providing the installation basics you must follow, I offer supplemental secrets at every installation and implementation turn in the road.
- **Part II: TCP/IP.** Enough said. This important topic is, of course, worthy of its own book, but I strive to integrate core TCP/IP topics into the discussion of Windows 2000 Server. I think you will especially enjoy the DNS, troubleshooting, Internet, and VPN discussions. And no, I don't recount for you the history of the Internet, starting with the Department of Defense (I'm sure you already have books that do that).
- **Part III: Windows 2000 Server Administration.** This section could have been titled "Real-World, Day-to-Day Windows 2000 Server." I took my own experiences, validated by a group of peers, and created a list of the 12 most likely Windows NT Server-related tasks you will perform each day. The result? See Chapter 9, "The Daily Dozen." Monthly and annual matters are presented as a baker's dozen list and are covered in Chapter 10, which also offers compelling insights into a network vision.
- **Part IV: Active Directory and Security.** Clearly this was too large a topic for a single chapter, so I turned it into an entire section. The two critical dimensions of Active Directory are covered: planning and implementation.
- **Part V: All In the Family.** Windows 2000 Server doesn't stand alone as the only Microsoft networking solution. There are several flavors of Windows 2000 Server, including Professional, Advanced, and Datacenter Server. These flavors are sampled in this section. And amazingly, for many smaller businesses, good old Small Business Server (yes, based on Windows NT Server 4.0) remains the best solution in today's Windows 2000 world (consider this your first secret in the book). Small Business Server is covered from A to Z in Chapter 16.
- **Part VI: Optimizing Windows 2000 Server.** Here, you will find the secrets to improving the performance of your Windows 2000 Server network. Topics include basic quantitative analysis (MBA-style), Performance Monitor, and the advanced use of Network Monitor. You will also greatly benefit from the secrets and insights into Windows 2000 Server troubleshooting. Troubleshooting topics include troubleshooting hands-on approaches, methodologies, tools, and resources. If some of my tips save you even just one hour of network downtime, might I suggest this book has more than paid back the price you bought it for.

In addition, third-party applications discussed in the book are available, in trial version, on the companion CD-ROM — see Appendix D for more information.

Conventions Used in This Book

I use five icons throughout this book. You should know their meaning before proceeding:

The Secret icon underscores why we're here. Secrets are the foundation of this book; they are little-known timesavers, productivity gainers, and other proprietary Swiss Army knife-type workarounds you might like to know as a Windows 2000 Server professional.

Notes are more widely known tidbits of information, factoids, trivia, and the like.

Tips fall somewhere between Secrets and Notes. While important, tips are typically less tasty than Secrets. Got it?

Caution is used to warn of possible danger. It is a yellow light advising you to slow down and think. Perhaps a red light is approaching faster than you think.

A Cross-Reference is used to tie together common topics in themes that occur in several places within the book. It's your opportunity to learn more about something in another chapter.

Tell Us What You Think

A book about Windows 2000 Server necessarily assumes some of the "behaviors" of Windows 2000 Server, right? By that, I mean that you've probably thought of ways in which Windows 2000 Server could be improved. Likewise, as you read and refer to this book, you'll undoubtedly think of ways in which this book could be improved.

That said, both IDG Books Worldwide and I want to hear from you. Please register your book online at the IDG Books Worldwide Web site (at `my2cents.idgbooks.com`) and give us your feedback. If you are interested in communicating with me directly, send e-mail to `harryb@nwlink.com`. Bear with me; I'll try to answer your e-mails within a few business days. Hey — when you're a practicing Windows 2000 Server professional, things sometimes get a little crazy!

Acknowledgments

No author is an island, although many of us live on 'em. Behind the title and author's name on the cover, there is a supporting cast that contributed to the production of this book.

First and foremost are the contributing writers who assisted with bits and pieces of this book. They are Steve Crandall, Kevin Kocis, and Dawn Casey. And, of course, there is the wonderful Jim Kiniry, the technical editor for this work.

Second is the support team at IDG Books Worldwide, who worked double-time to get this book out on the market for your benefit. Thanks in particular to Jim Sumser, Jennifer Rowe, Kurt Stephan, Chandani Thapa, Brian MacDonald, Victoria Lee, and Lauren Kennedy. (Needless to say, there are many other cast members at IDG Books whom I've overlooked — thanks again!)

Third, kindly join me in acknowledging my portfolio of consulting clients who have provided unlimited contributions to this book. Without them, I would be "secretless in Seattle," and this book would have suffered greatly as a result.

Fourth, please recognize those rare and special individuals we all have in our lives. For me, that includes not only my extended family on both sides, but also a whole host of mentors who have helped pave my road in life. To Stumpy Faulkner, former President of Jack White Company in Anchorage, Alaska, who gave me my first computer job. And thanks to countless others, including one of the best bosses I ever had, Barry MacKechnie. And finally, without the hardware support from Compaq in Redmond, Washington, my attempts to create complex Windows 2000 Server network scenarios would have been futile. Thanks guys!

Whew! Enjoy the book!!!

Contents at a Glance

Contents

Part I

Introduction, Planning, Setup, and Implementation

Chapter 1

Windows 2000 Server Planning

In This Chapter

- Windows 2000 Server planning
- Software planning issues
- Hardware planning issues
- Service providers involved in Windows 2000 Server deployment

Planning your Windows 2000 Server implementation involves several aspects, some of which you may not have considered. We'll start with the physical site and end with the people involved (not that people come last by any means).

Physical Site

Too often, Windows 2000 Server specialists give belated attention to the physical site at which they'll be installing the Windows 2000 Server. In past network builds over the years, I've been stuck at 11 p.m. on a Sunday evening, unable to move an attorney's large oak desk, counting the hours until the Monday morning stampede. I had overlooked a basic feature of the physical site, and that mistake was costly. As you implement Windows 2000 Server, you'll need to pay attention not only to the technical infrastructure and hardware and software resources, but also to the physical layout of the site.

Media infrastructure

Before you begin installation, ask whether the cabling is in place or whether both the cabling and the installation service have been ordered. Have you "tested" the cabling if you are using existing cabling on your Windows 2000 Server network? A simple handheld cable tester will save you a little of the pain and agony that I've suffered from seemingly ideal cabling that in reality is faulty.

OK, so you don't have a $5,000 Fluke cable tester handy. You can easily test a cable run for basic "fitness" with a hub, a laptop with a network adapter, and cabling. Having a buddy and two cheap walkie-talkie handheld radios will help as well. First, set up the hub in the wiring or server closet/storage area and attach it to the patch panel via patch cables. Second, hit the floor with a live laptop and a network adapter (typically in the form of a dongle hanging from a PC card). Test each and every LAN wall jack to make sure that you are "green lighting" back at the hub. You have now completed a very basic cabling test at the physical level. Oh, and put the buddy and walkie-talkies to work so that you don't need to run back and forth between laptop and hub too many times when performing this test.

As-builts

Before assuming responsibility for a site or performing a server conversion (typically from NetWare to Windows NT Server these days!), insist on completing a computer system as-built of the site (see Figure 1-1). If you know something about the construction industry, you are certainly no stranger to the term *as-built.* An as-built in real estate is a drawing that shows everything at a site: building, fixtures, improvements, and so on. It is similar to an X ray at the doctor's office. An X ray shows everything you have. A computer system as-built drawing likewise provides a snapshot view of your existing hardware and software resources.

A doctor relies on the X rays as a here-and-now view of your "system" in order to make the correct medical decisions. You should do the same with your computer system prior to implementing Windows 2000 Server. How do I create the as-built drawings? I simply perform a technical walkthrough of the site armed with a handheld Dictaphone. Later, at the office, I transcribe my notes, much like a doctor does, to create my as-built drawing using Visio (a popular network diagramming product).

By insisting on creating a computer system as-built as an early planning step for Windows 2000 Server implementations, you can avoid the typical problem of missing a few details along the way, such as not having a JetDirect card for the HP printer you plan to reuse. In part because of my upfront reliance on as-built drawings, I've served up more competitive network installation project bids, but more important, I've done a better job of managing my client's expectations. That's resulted in higher client satisfaction survey results!

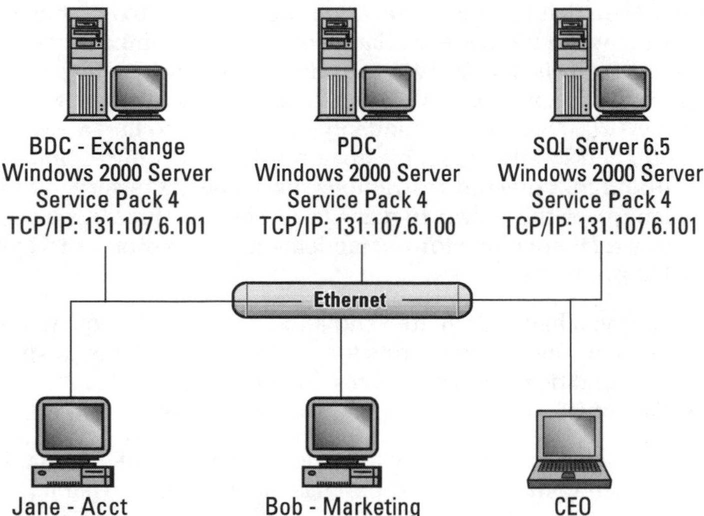

Figure 1-1: A sample computer network as-built drawing

Physical infrastructure

Consider the condition of the physical plant in which the network will reside. Is it newer office space with few concerns about dust, heat, and other basics? Or is this a working environment such as a front office/manufacturing facility combination? Different environments will necessitate different strategies. The physical infrastructure may determine what type of machines you place on the network. I'm seeing manufacturing sites readily accept Windows Terminal Server vis-á-vis Windows NT Server 4.0 as a low-cost and durable computing solution for less-than-ideal conditions. And the physical infrastructure can determine how I treat the implementation from a personal comfort perspective. At the downtown legal firm in the glass tower, I wear nothing but suits and ties. A visit to the Windows 2000 Server network at the construction company means a golf shirt and shorts.

Trust me when I say this: Be sure that all surface spaces, such as table tops, desks, and shelves, are at least 12" away from the wall or could be easily moved if necessary. I've stopped entire Windows NT Server conversions because immovable objects stood between myself, the server, and power outlets. That gets expensive at $125 to $200 per hour!

Be sure to use that last pre-installation walk-through to establish that sufficient power outlets are available for all of the components associated with your Windows 2000 Server, including spare outlets for plugging in your laptop for performing CD-ROM-based research. It's funny how an installation of Windows 2000 Server can suddenly compel you to find answers via your Microsoft TechNet CDs. Also, it's not a bad idea to confirm that a telephone jack (without PBX dial-out restrictions) exists near the server. Even if you don't plan to use the server to manage communications, it's a good idea to have a free telephone line for the modem on your laptop or to call vendor product support lines.

Ensure that you have adequate ventilation so that both you and the server don't overheat. One of my secrets for surviving summer is to spend lots of time in air-conditioned server rooms. In large enterprise-level installations, things like sufficient power, telephone jacks, and ventilation are a given.

With the conclusion of your walk-through, you've finished your site survey and are armed to make the best purchasing decisions possible.

Remember that your as-builts, site surveys, and walk-throughs should allow you to right-size your Windows 2000 Server installation. From this exercise, you create your Windows 2000 Server purchase specifications. Purchasing too much — that is, buying your way out of trouble — is as great an IT management sin as purchasing too little or forgetting critical components.

Server Hardware

Network professionals and MCSE-types working with Windows 2000 Server enjoy working with technology from two dimensions: hardware and software. One side can't be separated from the other. Conversely, developers and MCSD-types are typically concerned with only the software side. And don't overlook the service providers and people you will need to implement your Windows 2000 Server-based network. I haven't, and I discuss these critical team players later in this chapter.

Let's discuss hardware first. Your commitment to hardware is up front (that is, early on in the life cycle of your Windows 2000 Server network). It is important to make good decisions in the beginning because the hardware is going to be with you for some time. It's certainly no fun to go back to the boss and ask for more. With hardware purchases, you typically get just one chance to ask for what you want.

The actual server that will run Windows 2000 Server should, of course, be a server-class machine if at all possible. We're primarily concerned with five areas when right-sizing a server for a Windows 2000 Server installation: processor, memory, network subsystem, server internals, and disk storage.

Processor

Beware of Intel advertisements in trade journals that might give you a bad case of processor envy. Yes, the processor is very important. But right-sizing your Windows 2000 Server environment means that you understand how the file server will be used. Plain old file and print server-type environments aren't as dependent on processor power as client/server environments. Saving a document to a network shared storage area is very different from running one or more Microsoft BackOffice components on your Windows 2000 Server machine. If you don't believe me, run this very basic processor utilization test if you'd like to observe first-hand the differences between a Windows 2000 Server that behaves as a file and print server and one that behaves as an application server. First, right-click the Windows 2000 Server taskbar so that the secondary menu is displayed. Then, with the Performance tab sheet selected in Task Manager, observe the graphical display of the processor utilization rate (see Figure 1-2).

Interestingly, if you're not running BackOffice or similar major applications on this Windows 2000 Server machine, you will probably see what I see: a processor utilization rate in the single digits or low teens. Thus, it may not be wise for you to spend your funds on a super-expensive four-way processor solution such as a high-end Compaq server. Next, if you have any major client/server or server-based applications installed on your machine, launch these applications and create user activity. You should observe a significant increase in the processor activity as displayed by Task Manager. If this second set of conditions, running busy server applications, is the world you live in, then you are really running an applications server and you may benefit from additional processing power.

Note that I discuss Task Manager and a range of performance measures later in Part VI of this book, "Optimizing Windows 2000 Server."

You may be interested to know that in writing this book, I opted for dual-processor machines (a Dell server and a Compaq workstation). My reasoning? Getting a book out on time is a mission-critical endeavor for me and I needed the extra power of a dual-processor environment to keep me on schedule!

That said, of course you should strive to purchase the best processor (Pentium II-class) that you can afford. If anything, purchasing the best processor you can today will help extend the useful life of your server 48, 60, or even 72 months from now, when you implement demanding server-based applications that need power beyond your immediate needs.

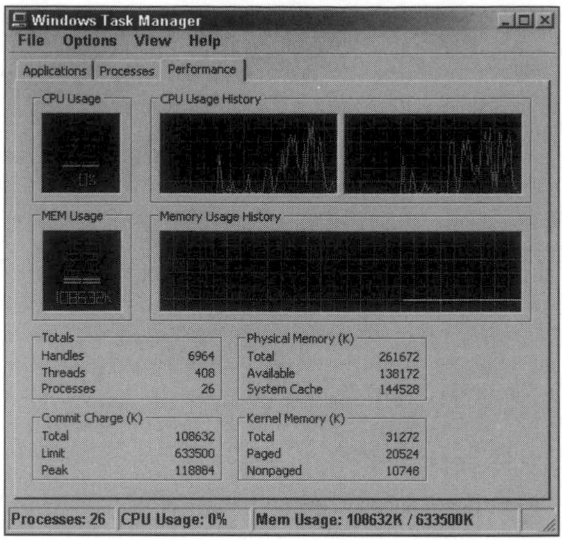

Figure 1-2: The Performance tab sheet in Task Manager

In fact, I'm planning to right-size my smaller and medium-sized Windows 2000 Server client sites with dual-processor Compaq Proliant/Prosignia or Dell PowerEdge servers below the $5,000 price range (as of late 1999). Why dual-processor motherboards? By purchasing this motherboard architecture today, even with a single processor, I have "engineered" the future into this Windows 2000 Server machine. By adding a second processor at a future date, be it to accommodate new applications or for some other reason, we will dramatically extend the life of this server and improve its performance for a relatively small outlay of funds (a second server-class top-of-the-line Intel processor can typically be purchased for under $1,000).

Tip

Purchasing a dual processor-capable server today with a single processor on board allows you to do one other thing: ride the processor price yield curve. The law of technology is that processing power doubles every 18 months, and processor prices decrease in relation to this law. So by deferring for several months the outlay of funds needed to double the processing power of your computer, you effectively ride the processor pricing yield curve. That means you could take advantage of a lower total price to double your system power at a future date. That's smart IT management.

The option of adding a second processor at a future date has been a very compelling component of my presentation to clients. I'm typically working with business decision makers who need to hear the "business case" for purchasing name-brand server-class machines that are dual processor-capable.

Another argument allows me to prevail at this planning stage. By looking more closely at the needs of my client, I can often easily see that Windows 2000 Server is being introduced into the organization to allow the introduction of some "killer" business application that, more likely than not, is based on Microsoft SQL Server.

A prime example of this is Great Plains Dynamics — SQL version (a.k.a. e-Enterprise). Such a high-powered accounting application enables management to get information via reports that they've never had before, such as sales by Internet domain name. Great Plains Dynamics only runs on Windows NT Server or Windows 2000 Server (and only on the Intel platform). My typical installation for a Great Plains Dynamics customer includes a dual-processor server such as one in the Dell PowerEdge line. Because the introduction of Windows 2000 Server into organizations such as these also affects several other "systems" (for instance, it affords the opportunity to convert from Word Perfect to Microsoft Office 2000), the Great Plains Dynamics installation usually follows two to three months after the Windows 2000 Server machine has been deployed and tested. See my discussion earlier in this chapter about deploying Windows 2000 Server as soon as possible in your organization. That is because organizations like to get the new networks up and running with everyone happy prior to introducing Great Plains Dynamics. It's a smart move.

That three-month delay allows my clients to enjoy a price reduction of $100 to $200 on the second processor because prices are typically adjusted downward each month by resellers when it comes to hardware. When working with small and medium-sized sites, that's the kind of good news that I want to deliver. It's also another example of riding the processor pricing yield curve!

Memory

The more memory, the better (of course!). Here there is, in my humble opinion, a one-to-one return for each dollar spent on RAM. Windows 2000 Server loves RAM. So if you're faced with hardware trade-offs, RAM is one option that you should trade up. Doubling your RAM on a Windows 2000 server will noticeably improve performance, especially when you are running memory-intensive applications at the server such as Microsoft SQL Server. You will recall that this is, in part, because RAM acts as primary memory on the machine. It's very fast. Hard disk-based storage acts as secondary memory, which is slower. And even though we can fool Windows 2000 Server into thinking life is good and that we have much more RAM than we really do via a large paging file, there's nothing like an abundance of real RAM.

Be sure to consult a bona fide hardware technician as you consider what type of memory to add to your Windows 2000 Server machine. I've made the mistake of ordering the wrong type of RAM memory for older machines, clones, and the like. To the naked eye, parity and nonparity RAM chips look very much alike. The same is true of DRAM and SRAM memory. Be aware of these issues in your planning stage.

I am hereby officially recommending that any Windows 2000 Server installation have a minimum of 256MB of RAM memory.

Network subsystem

Of course, a 100MB network card using the PCI architecture is preferable to a 10MB ISA-based card. The rule here clearly is to implement the fastest network components possible. No brainer. The "hidden cost" that I've confronted head-on with clients seeking counsel on the choice of 100MB versus 10MB isn't the explicit cost of the network adapter card. Heck, a 10/100 PCI-based network adapter card from 3COM can be had for under $100.

The real cost of going to 100MB, in my experience, involves other network components, such as a 100MB hub, a 10/100 dual-speed hub, or a switch. Whereas I can purchase a 10MB hub for pennies (say an eight-port hub for under $100), a 100MB hub may cost more than three times that amount. For smaller clients, the ones who gripe over $20 backup tapes, the additional network speed isn't considered valuable.

Want to be a true hero at a relatively low cost? Then consider adding a second NIC card to boost network subsystem performance. Remember that the job of the network adapter card is essentially to convert the parallel electronic data stream from the internal bus architecture of the computer to a serial format that is placed onto network media (which may consist of twisted pair cabling). Talk about an obvious bottleneck — reducing data from a parallel to serial format!

Adding a second network adapter card will be most beneficial in file servers. Here I am thinking of large file transfers such as 20MB AutoCAD files. That's a lot of information to be sent as serial data! A second network adapter card works wonders here.

Server internals

You may or may not be a strong hardware person. Perhaps you are and you've purchased this book to learn more about the software side of Windows 2000 Server (if so, you've come to the right place). But remember that the network equation is easily 50 percent hardware and 50 percent software. It takes two to tango on the Ethernet. That said, how can you hope to make the most appropriate decisions regarding the server's internal architecture?

To cut to the chase and learn the difference between ISA, EISA, and SCSI (and their various forms), I suggest that you select the Networking Essentials MCSE certification text from IDG Books Worldwide. The book *Networking Essentials MCSE Study Guide* by Jason Nash (ISBN: 0-7645-3177-8) is over 500 pages of good stuff relating to networking fundamentals. Specifically, you can sharpen your understanding of server "internals."

Disk storage

Essentially, disk storage implementations can be poor, adequate, or superior.

- **Poor design.** Poor design takes two forms.
  - The first involves single hard drives in a machine. In my experience, this occurs when an older machine is being used as a Windows 2000 Server machine, and that machine only has one hard drive. Perhaps the machine dates back to an era when storage space was relatively expensive, resulting in a generation of single hard drive machines. Another case is when off-the-shelf workstations are used as Windows 2000 Server machines. Your average Dell or Gateway workstation is designed for the end user and usually ships with a single hard disk (although typically it will have multiple partitions). A single hard drive implementation has no fault tolerance.
  - The second scenario that I call poor design relates to spanned hard drives. Here again, this most likely involves an older machine that has been converted from an older version of NetWare or a desktop operating system into a machine running Windows 2000 Server. Because storage is cheap, many network administrators take the path of least resistance and simply daisy-chain additional storage devices to the server to satisfy increased space needs. A spanned drive implementation has no fault tolerance.

  Either of the two examples just offered suggest poor planning, and perhaps the parties involved are saving a few dollars today, but in a foolhardy manner.
- **Adequate design.** Adequate storage solutions include mirroring and duplexing. Here, one hard disk is an exact copy of the other. If these two hard disks share the same controller card, the solution is known as *mirroring*. If the two hard disks have separate controllers, the solution is known as *duplexing* (which is technically better than mirroring, although hard disk controllers fail far less often than hard disks). Mirroring is a common solution, but expensive. In order to have 10GB of usable storage space, you would need to purchase two hard disks of 10GB each (for a total purchase of 20GB). The result is a 50 percent utilization ratio, which is costly.
- **Superior design.** A superior storage design is RAID-based. Here, a redundant array of inexpensive disks (RAID) work as a team to provide maximum performance and usable space at the lowest possible costs. A RAID solution using RAID 5 (the most common RAID solution) requires at least three hard disks (and more often five or more). Each disk both stores data and includes a parity or recalculation zone area. The parity zone maintains just enough information about the other disks so that if one of the disks fails, the missing data from the failed member can be rebuilt according to information provided by other RAID member disks. The total storage available is much higher than with mirroring. For

example, if you had a five-disk RAID array totaling 10GB of space, then 8GB would be usable. Here, one-fifth of the total storage is dedicated to the parity zone.

To find the space used by the parity zone in a RAID scenario, just take the inverted fraction of the number of disks. For example, a five-disk RAID array may be expressed as 5 / 1 = 5. Thus, the parity area is 1 / 5 = .20 or 20 percent. Further, that means that 80 percent of the disk space is usable for storing data. This information might be useful as you prepare for the Networking Essentials exam as part of the MCSE track.

A hardware-based RAID solution managed by the server is greatly preferred over having Windows 2000 Server managing the RAID solution. That's because you take advantage of the "smart" disk subsystem by allowing it to manage the RAID function. You avoid taxing the Windows 2000 Server operating system with additional RAID management overhead.

A RAID-based storage solution is only slightly more expensive than mirroring. Add to that higher performance with read activity in which the server employs multiple read head I/O, and RAID appears to be a very attractive storage solution. The next time you are pricing storage, get bids for both mirroring and RAID and see for yourself.

Name brands versus clones

One final comment on planning your hardware: Remember that you are asking Windows 2000 Server to act as the foundation for your company's information infrastructure. And like any foundation, if it is off-center, everyone that follows will have to "shim" their layer to make it fit, much as shims are used in a house when the foundation isn't level.

The kind of hardware that you purchase will make a difference in how your network infrastructure performs in the long run. Name brands such as Compaq, Dell, and IBM tend to be rock-solid and reliable. These machines typically have better "plumbing" than cheaper clones from your uncle's computer shop. Better plumbing might take the form of larger fans or two power supplies. And the organizations that support your server tend to be more reliable when trouble strikes. Support is certainly IBM's historical claim to fame.

Clones, on the other hand, will typically run Windows 2000 Server with few problems initially (that is, if the installation was successful). But more than one client who insisted on saving a few dollars and purchasing a clone PC to use as a network server machine has called a year later looking for Joe, the clone-maker. Needless to say, Joe has found the love of his life and moved to Bora-Bora.

At the enterprise level, it has been my experience that clones aren't considered in the server farm mix. In fact, many name brands are eliminated from consideration for two major reasons (although I'm sure there are more). First, name brands such as IBM, Compaq, and Dell have superior server hardware management applications that others don't. With Compaq, this includes the SmartStart and Insight Manager applications. These management applications not only assist in the configuration of your servers during setup, but more important, they mitigate server downtime in a crisis by directing your efforts to failed server components. This management capability is rarely available in clones, or even in some of the name brands you might think would know better. So server hardware management applications are a huge reason for selecting well-known name brand servers over other alternatives.

The second criterion for many firms when deciding on a server is the hardware manufacturer's support network, something I touched on earlier. Take a well-known Western U.S. auto parts retailer with 110 stores in locations both large and small. Few hardware manufacturers could support all of these locations within a four-hour callback period. In fact, the only organization that I've seen consistently provide this level of support is IBM. Not the cheapest server solution, but for organizations with far-flung operations, perhaps the best.

So for what it's worth, don't save a few dollars and mistakenly purchase the cheapest clone on the market as your Windows 2000 Server machine. In fact, my firm has been known to turn down network consulting business because a client didn't want to purchase a name-brand server. That alone has proven to be an early warning sign of problems ahead.

Software

We now get to one of my favorite topics: software. In the summer of 1999, as I explained the future "greatness" of Windows 2000 Server to business decision makers (the ones who write the checks), the inevitable line of questioning comparing Windows 2000 Server to other network operating systems started early. The debate can actually be cut short if you think smart. Businesses really are implementing one network solution or another because of the applications that they need to run. In fact, such thinking is often part of the Introduction to Computers lecture at any college. First you find the applications that you need. Then you find a computer and operation system that will run the applications.

If this rule holds true for you, then you want to heed the underlying trend present today in the business software market. ISVs are beating a path to the Windows 2000 community. In fact, many businesses are now finding that the next release of their favorite business software is only available on Microsoft platforms such as Windows 2000 Server and Windows NT Server. The often-heard phrase, "We no longer support our product on NetWare," is the sound of money to this MCSE!

It's the software, stupid! Don't forget, this mantra will not only drive Windows 2000 Server's growth, but is a fundamental tenet of any successful technology implementation.

Service Providers

Any successful Windows 2000 Server deployment requires the involvement of others. These parties are listed here in the order in which you should consider contacting them (based on observed delays such as service delivery).

1. **Telephone company.** Clearly, you can never order your telephone company-related service(s) too early. Even an extra business telephone line can take weeks to arrive. And if you're implementing a WAN, sometimes the service requests are measured in months. Make the telephone company your first call.
2. **ISP.** Internet service providers (ISPs) need sufficient lead time to order your domain name or switch your domain name.
3. **Cabling.** Although the cabling team may complete their work in a day or two, depending on the size of your network, these critical players are often scheduled weeks in advance. An early call is necessary so that you can book your work dates.
4. **Outside subject-matter experts.** Although we consultants believe we can respond rapidly to your call, such is not always the case. The more time we have to work with you on a project, the better job we can do, because we'll be less rushed, have more time to prepare and conduct research, and ultimately charge you less.
5. **Hardware/software resellers.** Don't wait until the last moment to order your hardware and software.

In 1999, hardware resellers such as Dell are experiencing backlogs averaging two weeks on servers. I predict this backlog will grow in late 1999 as the year 2000 approaches and many businesses upgrade their systems to eliminate motherboard BIOS problems.

People

Don't forget the people involved as you plan for a successful Windows 2000 Server implementation. At least three groups need your attention: managers, administrators, and users. Maintaining contact with the people in all these groups is essential for a smooth implementation. Management should be kept informed and happy at all times. They write the checks for your project! Who are the administrators and how much do they need to know? Remember to make the membership of this club (administrators) exclusive. It is a very powerful group. Keeping the users satisfied will ultimately make or break a successful Windows 2000 Server implementation. Make sure your users can print and save files, use e-mail, and generally trust the system.

Tip

The planning phase of the project is the best time to arrange for end user training on the new Windows 2000 Server-based network. And take my advice — have a real trainer perform the training at your organization. We MCSE-types sometimes look foolish trying to train end users on networking basics (logons, printing, saving) and e-mail (using Microsoft Outlook 2000).

Key contact list

As part of your planning activities, be sure to create a list of key contacts (telephone numbers, e-mail addresses). Allow up to six telephone numbers per key contact for main office, private office, home, cellular, pager, and fax.

Loose Ends

I've grouped everything in this section as loose ends to consider addressing as you implement Windows 2000 Server in your organization.

General

Even experienced network professionals need to "stick to the knitting," or stay focused when implementing a Windows 2000 Server network. That includes reviewing the following points and, as necessary, completing the tasks called for. Admittedly, creating drive mappings isn't terribly exciting or difficult, but the failure to do so is extremely embarrassing. For that reason, I share the following general points:

- **Drive mappings.** Try to create your drive mappings in advance, and get end-user sign-offs for the drives. Why? Some vendors want to use specific drive letters. Other vendors cannot use UNC naming for drives and need a drive letter assigned.
- **The ISVs' unique needs.** Anything is possible in this category. Some accounting software vendors can only use TCP/IP and not IPX/SPX. Other accounting software vendors require Registry modifications (Great Plains). Some ISVs will provide you with lengthy network installation manuals that you should peruse in advance (Timberline's 60-pager is a record in my book).
- **User security.** Use a whiteboard to create a security map showing which users have what rights. And how do you enforce security: logon, shares, NTFS-based security, or other ways (logon machine and hour restrictions)?

- **Naming conventions.** Plan for machine names, share names, printer names, and user names in advance. Don't find yourself installing Windows 2000 Server before you think of the basics. Otherwise you're bound to overlook something, resulting in a substandard network.

Keep names as short as possible and avoid using separators. When you are referring to a shared resource or mapping a drive, a short name is always preferred to a long name. Shorter names are, at a minimum, easier to spell.

- **Keep it simple starting out (KISSO).** Use the simplest Windows 2000 Server directory and domain structure possible. Many inexperienced people working with network operating systems such as Windows 2000 Server create far too much "stuff" because MCSE textbooks taught them to do so!
- **Reseat cards.** When building the server, look under the hood and reseat the interface cards (modem, network adapter, sound, hard disk controller). These cards may have come loose on the long journey from the computer manufacturing facility. Avoid the mistakes I made, such as when I found an unseated network adapter card only after I'd nearly completed a network operating system installation (reaching the point when you specify the network adapter driver).
- **Create the utility partition.** Sometimes when looking at the work of others, I've seen name-brand servers such as Compaq lacking the hidden utility partition that you should create during server setup. With Compaq, the SmartStart tool allows you to access useful drivers, run system tests, and register cards. Be sure to create the hidden utility partition before you start installing Windows 2000 Server. Each server vendor has its own utilities (for instance, Dell's is called Server Assistant).

Existing networks

If you are introducing Windows 2000 Server into an existing network, you should consider the following points:

- **Existing Windows NT Server domains.** If you plan to add a Windows 2000 Server to an existing Windows NT-based network, deciding the role of each server is critical. Will Windows 2000 Server act as a member server or a domain controller?
- **NetWare.** This venerable operating system is frequently converted to Windows NT Server. Several issues exist regarding conversions from NetWare and NT/NetWare coexistence. These are discussed during the course of this book.
- **Macintosh.** It is likely the Macintosh community will embrace Windows 2000 Server as a file and print server, but not as an application server. That's because Macintosh-related support, when installed on Windows 2000 Server, provides robust file sharing and printer support. However, native Macintosh applications can't run on a Windows 2000 Server.

- **UNIX.** Out-of-the-box support for UNX connectivity to Windows 2000 Server will need to be fortified by third-party enhancements such as NFS clients. Natively, Windows 2000 Server doesn't have strong UNIX support.

Summary

In this chapter, we covered these topics:

- Windows 2000 Server planning issues
- Evaluating your existing network before upgrading
- Testing your existing software for compatibility with Windows 2000 Server
- Upgrading your hardware to support Windows 2000 Server
- Coordinating the service providers on your Windows 2000 Server project

Chapter 2

Installation and Implementation

In This Chapter

- Making Windows 2000 Server setup disks
- Installing Windows 2000 Server
- Using alternate Windows 2000 Server installation methods
- Completing Windows 2000 Server implementation tasks
- Deploying a Windows 2000 Server test lab

Perhaps you've already raced ahead and installed Windows 2000 Server on your machine. If so, is this chapter for you? You bet it is. Why? For a couple of reasons. First, have you ever reached the end of a journey or process and decided that if you had the chance to do it over again, you would do it differently? You bet! This chapter provides a fresh perspective on installing Windows 2000 Server and is perhaps that missing viewpoint you've been seeking to confront your existing Windows 2000 Server installation.

I also wrote this chapter assuming that, with one or two Windows 2000 Server installations under your belt, you can benefit from another look at the installation process so that you might make both major and minor course corrections in your future Windows 2000 Server installations. Perhaps you've already learned a thing or two from your initial Windows 2000 Server installations. Might I be so bold as to suggest that spending a few hours with this chapter will allow you to learn even more? For example, my painfully detailed installation steps enable you to readily see points of failure should you have a Windows 2000 Server installation go south on ya.

If you're new to Windows 2000 Server, this chapter is mandatory reading. In fact, to the extent time allows, read this chapter before installing Windows 2000 Server. Like a sailor who studies his charts before casting off, you won't be learning your map while you are under sail. It's truly a case of proper preparation to prevent poor performance.

Creating Windows 2000 Server Setup Disks

The first step in the Windows 2000 Server setup process is to use MAKEBOOT.EXE to create the four setup disks. This program is found in the MAKEBOOT folder on the Windows 2000 Server CD-ROM.

You will need to run MAKEBOOT.EXE from an existing machine running a 32-bit operating system such as Windows 2000 Server, Windows 2000 Professional, Windows NT Server, Windows NT Workstation, Windows 98, or Windows 95. The point is that you clearly can't run MAKEBOOT.EXE on a new machine that you haven't installed Windows 2000 Server on, because that is the goal you are seeking to reach in this chapter!

STEPS:

To make Windows 2000 setup disks

Step 1. From a command prompt or Run dialog box, launch MAKEBOOT.EXE.

Step 2. You will see the following text. When asked about which floppy drive to copy the image to, enter the appropriate drive letter, such as A or B. When entering the drive letter, there is no need to enter a colon (:), even though that is the standard convention used when communicating a drive letter (for example, A:). Hit Enter.

```
This program creates the setup boot disks for Microsoft Windows 2000.
To create these disks, you need to provide four blank, formatted,
high-density disks.
Please specify the floppy drive to copy the image to:
```

Step 3. You will be prompted to insert four disks that will become the Windows 2000 Server setup boot disk and disks 2, 3, and 4, respectively. You will be prompted by the following on-screen menus.

```
Insert one of these disks into drive A:. This disk will become the
Windows 2000 Setup Boot Disk. Press any key when you are ready.
Insert one of these disks into drive A:. This disk will become the
Windows 2000 Disk #2. Press any key when you are ready.
Insert one of these disks into drive A:. This disk will become the
Windows 2000 Disk #3. Press any key when you are ready.
Insert one of these disks into drive A:. This disk will become the
Windows 2000 Disk #4. Press any key when you are ready.
```

You are now ready to start the Windows 2000 Server setup process.

The old way (that is, in Windows NT Server 4.0) of making setup disks, using `Winnt.exe`, no longer works with Windows 2000 Server. You must use the `MAKEBOOT.EXE` approach.

Windows 2000 Server Setup Process

The big moment has arrived. Essentially, you will do a four-floppy swap, insert a CD-ROM, reboot a couple of times and everything is complete. Right? Well, sorta. By strict definition, you could say, at this point you've set up Windows 2000 Server. But of course, so much more awaits you, such as the matters discussed over the next several hundred pages of this book. But first things first. Let's install Windows 2000 Server by following the next 40 steps (literally).

The Windows 2000 Server installation can be divided into three major categories: character-based setup, graphical user interface (GUI) setup, and the configuration phase (see Figure 2-1). These three phases can be mapped to the different steps you are about to undertake, as seen in Table 2-1.

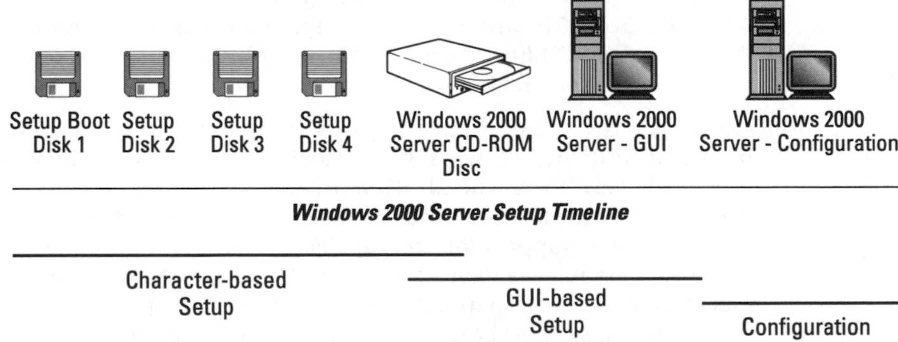

Figure 2-1: Overview of Windows 2000 Server installation

Table 2-1 Windows 2000 Server Setup Phases

Phase	*Section*
Character-based Setup	Section A
GUI Setup	Section B
Configuration	Section C

STEPS:

Section A — Character-based setup

Step 1. Be sure that your machine is ready for the installation of Windows 2000 Server: All hardware components are attached. You have created any background system partitions (for example, Dell Server Assistant and its utility partition). You've installed a network adapter card. Your machine is attached to a network. The power cable is attached to the machine. Perhaps most importantly, the drive boot order is such that the machine will boot from drive A: (which is where I'm assuming you will place your Windows 2000 Server setup floppy disks).

Step 2. Insert the Windows 2000 Server boot disk in the floppy drive and turn on the power to the machine. The machine will boot from this diskette. You will see the following message:

```
Setup is inspecting your computer's hardware configuration.
```

Step 3. The Windows 2000 Setup screen appears. It is a blue-colored, character-based setup screen with the words "Windows 2000 Setup" in white text in the upper left-hand corner. Note this is a "good" blue screen, not the evil blue screens you see when a system crashes.

You are given the opportunity at this point to press F6 to install third-party drivers or RAID array drivers. If you elect to do this now, you must have the drivers on diskettes as the CD-ROM drive has not been detected yet (and is unavailable). This is typically done when the operating system doesn't have on-board driver support for your device(s). One such example occurs when manufacturers release devices, such as RAID storage arrays, well after the operating system has shipped. Needless to say, the operating system developers, in all their great wisdom, can't anticipate the driver needs of future, non-existent devices. You'll have to supply such a driver.

Messages quickly appear at the bottom of the Windows 2000 Setup screen as the setup process continues. This is normal and represents the loading of basic drivers and resources. Two kinds of resources are loaded between Windows 2000 Server Setup Disk #1 and Windows 2000 Server Setup Disk #2:

- Machine Identification Data
- Windows 2000 Executive

Step 4. When you see the following message, insert the Windows 2000 Server Setup Disk #2 and press Enter.

```
Please insert the disk labeled Windows 2000 Server Setup Disk #2 into
Drive A:.
     *     Press ENTER when ready.
```

Step 5. The setup process continues and the following resources are loaded:

- Hardware Abstraction Layer
- multi(0)disk(0)rdisk(0)partition(0)
- Windows Configuration Data
- Setup Font
- Locale-Specific Data
- Windows 2000 Setup
- PCI Bus Driver
- ACPI Plug & Play Bus Driver
- ISA Plug & Play Bus Driver
- ACPI Embedded Controller Driver
- IEEE 1394 Bus OHCI Compliant Port Driver
- PCMCIA Support
- PCI IDE Bus Driver
- Intel IDE Bus Driver
- Mount Point Manager
- Volume Manager
- Partition Manager
- Floppy Drive Support
- Dynamic Volume Support (dmload)
- Dynamic Volume Support (dmio)
- IEEE 1394 SBP2 Port Driver
- Open Host Controller
- Universal Host Controller
- Generic USB Hub Driver
- Human Interface Parser
- Serial Port Driver
- Serial Port Enumerator
- Video Drivers
- XT/AT or Enhanced Keyboard (83-104 keys)
- USB Keyboard
- Keyboard Driver
- SCSI Port Driver

Continued

STEPS:

Section A — Character-based setup *(continued)*

Step 6. When you see the following message, insert the Windows 2000 Server Setup Disk #3 and press Enter.

```
Please insert the disk labeled Windows 2000 Server Setup Disk #3 into
Drive A:.
    *     Press ENTER when ready.
```

Step 7. The following resources will load:

- Compaq Drive Array
- IDE CD-ROM ATAPI 1.2/PCI IDE Controller
- NCR 53C710
- Adaptec AHA-154x series
- Adaptec AHA-151x series
- Adaptec AHA-2920 series
- Symbios Logic C8100
- BusLogic SCSI Host Adapter
- Adaptec AHA 2940
- Mylex DAC 690
- QLogic PCI SCSI Host Adapter
- AMD PCI SCSI Controller/Ethernet Adapter
- BusLogic FlashPoint
- Compaq 32-bit Fast Wide SCSI 2IE
- Emulax LP 6000 Fibre Channel
- QLogic QLA2100 64-Bit PCI Fiber Channel
- AdvanSys SCSI Host Adapter
- AdvanSys 3550 Ultra Wide SCSI
- AMI Ultra Wide SCSI
- AMI Megaraid RAID Adapter
- Compaq Fibre Channel Host Controller
- Diamond Multimedia System SCSI Host Adapter
- Initio
- QLogic ISP 1240
- M-Systems Flash Disk Adapter
- JNI Fiber Channel Adapter

- Adaptec AHA-2940/U2/AIC 7890
- IBM Server RAID Adapter
- Symbios Logic C8xx PCI SCSI Host Adapter
- Symbios Logic C896

Step 8. When you see the following message, insert the Windows 2000 Server Setup Disk #4 and press Enter.

```
Please insert the disk labeled Windows 2000 Server Setup Disk #4 into
Drive A:.
     *     Press ENTER when ready.
```

Step 9. The following resources will load.

- Dynamic Volume Support (dmboot)
- Floppy Disk Driver
- SCSI CD-ROM Driver
- SCSI Disk
- SCSI Floppy Disk
- FAT File System
- Windows NT File System (NTFS)
- CD-ROM File System

A message reading "Setup is starting Windows 2000" will appear. This is a fundamental milestone, as it represents the first attempt to actually "start" the underlying operating system. This message will remain on your screen for five to seven minutes.

Another friendly blue screen will briefly appear that communicates the kernel is loading, along with a message at the bottom of the screen that a keyboard driver is being loaded.

It is possible at this point that you will experience a setup failure. That's because the operating system is attempting to start and use the drivers and resources loaded from the past several steps, and all hell may well break loose. You may receive the following setup-related Stop message:

```
*** STOP: 0X0000001E (0XC0000006,0X8046C8C,0X00000000,0X4850C98C)
KMODE_EXCEPTION_NOT_HANDLED
*** Address 804E6C8C base at 80400000, DateStamp 37741730 -
ntorkrnl.exe
```

If this is the first time you've seen this Stop error screen, restart your computer. If this screen appears again, follow these steps:

Check to be sure that you have adequate disk space. If a driver is identified in the Stop message, disable the driver or check with the manufacturer for driver updates. Try changing video adapters.

Continued

STEPS:

Section A — Character-based setup *(continued)*

Check with your hardware vendor for any BIOS updates. Disable BIOS memory options such as caching or shadowing. If you need to use Safe Mode to remove or disable components, restart your computer, press F8 to select Advanced Startup Options, and then select Safe Mode.

Refer to your *Getting Started* manual for more information on troubleshooting Stop errors.

You are advised to double-check your computer configuration and make sure it conforms to the Windows 2000 Hardware Compatibility List (HCL). If you perform a reinstall following the advice of the Stop message, consider hitting F6 at Step 3 (above).

When I've received such an Stop message as part of the Windows 2000 Server setup process, I've worked around it by creating a 100MB FAT partition on my destination hard disk using a bootable MS-DOS system disk that contains FDISK and FORMAT. After creating such a partition, restart the Windows 2000 Server setup process and it should work fine.

Step 10. A Windows 2000 Server setup screen, similar to the following, will now appear. Press Enter to continue.

```
Windows 2000 Server Setup
Welcome to Setup.
This portion of the Setup program prepares Microsoft(r) Windows
2000(tm) to run on your computer.
*     To setup Windows 2000 now, press ENTER.
*     To repair a Windows 2000 installation, press R.
*     To quit Setup without installing Windows 2000, press F3.
ENTER=Continue   R=Repair   F3=Quit
```

Step 11. The next screen will ask that you insert the Windows 2000 Server CD-ROM disk.

```
Insert the CD labeled:
Windows 2000 Server CD-ROM
into your CD-ROM drive.

*     Press ENTER when ready

F3 = Quit     ENTER = Continue
```

Step 12. The Windows 2000 Licensing Agreement, all eight screens, will appear (only one screen at a time though). Click the PgDn key on your keyboard to read the license and press F8 to accept the terms and conditions.

Step 13. The next screen, shown here, allows you to configure your drive space into partitions.

```
Windows 2000 Server Setup
The following list shows the existing partitions and
unpartitioned space on this computer.

Use the UP and DOWN arrow keys to select an item in the list.
To set up Windows 2000 on the selected item, press ENTER.
To create a partition in the unpartitioned space, press C.
To delete the selected partition, press D.

8715 MD Disk at Id 0 on bus 0 on aic78u2
     Unpartitioned space      3000 MB
     D: FAT (VOLUME1)         2000 MB ( 1471 MB free)
     E: FAT (VOLUME2)         2000 MB ( 1471 MB free)
     Unpartitioned space      1715 MB

ENTER = Install C = Create Partition F3 = Quit
```

Note the preceding drive space information will vary depending on your unique situation. In this example, type C to create a partition on the 3GB unpartitioned space. You will be taken to a Create partition screen where you may specify the size of the new partition.

```
Windows 2000 Server Setup
You asked Setup to create a new partition on
8715 MB Disk 0 at Id 0 on bus 0 on aic78u2.
To create the new partition, enter a size below and press ENTER.
To go back to the previous screen without creating the partition,
press ESC.

The minimum size for the new partition is:     1 megabytes (MB)
The maximum size for the new partition is:     3000 megabytes (MB)
Create partition of size (in MB):              3000

ENTER = Create  ESC = Cancel
```

When creating a partition, the default size of the partition will always be the total size of the unpartitioned space you are seeking to partition (for example, 3GB). You may change this value to reflect a partition size that is smaller than the total size of the unpartitioned space.

If you wanted to delete existing partitions, you would select the partition to delete and press D. You would then be taken to two confirmation screens which both confirm you want to delete this partition.

Step 14. After creating the partition, you will be returned to the following screen that allows you to continue your Windows 2000 Server installation.

```
Windows 2000 Server Setup
The following list shows the existing partitions and
unpartitioned space on this computer.
```

Continued

STEPS:

Section A — Character-based setup *(continued)*

```
Use the UP and DOWN arrow keys to select an item in the list.
To set up Windows 2000 on the selected item, press ENTER.
To create a partition in the unpartitioned space, press C.
To delete the selected partition, press D.

8715 MD Disk at Id 0 on bus 0 on aic78u2
     C: New (Unformatted)          3000 MB
     D: FAT (VOLUME1)              2000 MB ( 1471 MB free)
     E: FAT (VOLUME2)              2000 MB ( 1471 MB free)
     Unpartitioned space           1715 MB

ENTER = Install C = Create Partition F3 = Quit
```

You would now press Enter to continue the installation.

Step 15. The following screen requesting you to format the partition appears. Make your selection and press Enter.

```
Windows 2000 Server Setup
The partition you selected is not formatted. Setup will now
format the partition.

Use the UP and DOWN arrow keys to select the file system you want, and
then press ENTER.

If you want to select a different partition for Windows 2000, press
ESC.

     Format the partition using the NTFS file system
     Format the partition using the FAT file system

ENTER = Continue   ESC = Cancel
```

Be sure to format the file system as NTFS to take advantage of many advanced Windows 2000 features, the least of which is enhanced security. This advice is somewhat different from the Windows NT Server 4.0 days when you could find many authorities that suggested you install the Windows NT Server operating system on a FAT partition.

The following screen will appear, displaying the progress of the formatting operation.

```
Please wait while Setup formats the partition
C: New (Unformatted)  3000MB
on 8715 MB Disk 0 at Id 0 on bus 0 on aic78u2.

Setup is formatting...
```

Step 16. After formatting, the following screen will appear regarding the examination of your hard disks.

```
Please wait while Setup examines your disks. This may take several
minutes depending on the size of your disks.
```

Step 17. After the disk(s) have been examined and passed with flying colors, the following screen will appear as Windows 2000 Server prepares to copy disks from the CD-ROM disk to the hard disk that will have Windows 2000 Server installed on it.

```
Creating a list of files to be copied...
```

The next screen reads:

```
Please wait while Setup copies files to the Windows 2000 Installation
folders. This may take several minutes to complete.
```

At this point, Setup will copy numerous files with the following file extensions:

- .inf
- .dll
- .exe
- .sys
- .axa
- .bas
- .hlp
- .chg
- .chm
- .msi
- .enu
- .ttf

Step 18. After the files have copied, the next screen that appears facilitates the initialization of Windows 2000 Server. Your base Windows 2000 configuration will be saved at this point.

```
Please wait while Setup initializes your Windows 2000 configuration.
```

Another screen follows that confirms the character-based portion of Setup is complete.

```
This portion of Setup has been completed successfully.

If there is a floppy disk in Drive A:, remove it. To restart your
computer, press ENTER. When your computer restarts, Setup will
continue. Your computer will reboot in XXX seconds.
```

Continued

STEPS:

Section A — Character-based setup *(continued)*

Step 19. The computer reboots, and the character-based start menu created by the `BOOT.INI` file is briefly displayed. This start menu doesn't have a countdown timer that allows you to pause the start-up. That timer will appear on the start menu after the complete installation of Windows 2000 Server. Windows 2000 Server is started and an automatic logon is performed.

STEPS:

Section B — GUI-based setup

Step 1. This is the start of the graphical user interface (GUI) portion of the Windows 2000 Server setup phase. The Windows 2000 Server Setup screen that is displayed says, "Welcome to the Windows 2000 Setup Wizard. This wizard installs Windows 2000 Server on your computer. The wizard needs to gather information about you and your computer to setup Windows 2000 properly." You will click Next to continue.

Step 2. The next screen of the Windows 2000 Setup Wizard displayed communicates that devices are being installed. It is here that device detection occurs as part of the setup. Note this device detection and installation process will take several minutes.

It is likely your monitor will flicker on and off at least once as part of the video device driver testing process. This is normal.

Step 3. The Regional Settings screen will appear. This allows you to set the language for your machine. After adjusting your settings, click Next to continue.

You can fix a possible Windows 2000 Y2K problem at this point. Select the Customize button and pick the Date tab sheet from Regional Options. Set the Short date format to mm/dd/yyyy (you will note it was set to mm/dd/yy by default). Setting the short date to four positions in the year field (yyyy) allows you to bring older Microsoft programs such as Access 2.0 into Y2K compliance.

Step 4. The Personalize Your Software screen will appear. You will have the opportunity to input name and organization. Click Next.

Step 5. The Licensing Mode screen will appear. Select between Per Server or Per Seat licensing modes. Make a selection and click Next.

With Per Server licensing, each connection must have its own client access license (CAL). With Per Seat licensing, each computer must have its own CAL. I typically pick Per Seat as my licensing choice so any computer can log on to any server at any time with regard to connection license issues.

Step 6. The Computer Name and Administrator Password screen appears. Provide a computer name and Administrator password, and click Next.

Make your life easy and select a short computer name. Not only is a short name easier to remember, but it's also easier to spell and type.

Step 7. The Windows 2000 Components screen appears, allowing you to add or remove components. Make your selections and click Next. The available components to add include the following:

- Certificate Services
- Internet Information Services (IIS)
- Management and Monitoring Tools
- Message Queuing Services
- Microsoft Indexing Service
- Microsoft Script Debugger
- Networking Services
- Other Network, File, and Print Services
- Remote Installation Services
- Remote Storage
- Terminal Services
- Terminal Services Licensing

During the initial setup of Windows 2000 Server, I suggest that you install only those services you will initially need. Other services can be installed as needed at a future date. It's much easier to troubleshoot a bad installation that is a skinny installation (that is, has fewer services installed).

Step 8. On the next screen (Date and Time Settings), provide the correct time and date. Click Next.

Step 9. The Networking Settings screen appears. It is here that you install software that allows you to communicate with other computers and the Internet. Click Next. You will be instructed to wait while Windows 2000 Server installs networking components.

Continued

STEPS

Section B — GUI-based setup *(continued)*

Step 10. Another Networking Settings screen appears. You will select between installing Typical or Custom settings. Make your selection and click Next. If you aren't sure which selection to make, choose Typical for now. Click Next. Note the network adapter card is automatically detected at this stage.

The Typical setting includes the Client for Microsoft Networks, File and Print Sharing for Microsoft Networks, and TCP/IP transport protocol configured for automatic addressing.

Step 11. A variety of status messages will appear as the Windows 2000 Server networking components are installed and activated. These messages will vary depending on the components you elected to install. This step requires no interaction from you.

Step 12. A screen will appear announcing that Setup must complete a final list of tasks. These final tasks perform the following actions:

- Start menu items
- Register components
- Saves settings
- Remove any temporary files used

Each of the preceding tasks will be highlighted via an arrow on your screen as the task is being completed.

Step 13. Finally, you will receive a screen that says you are completing the Windows 2000 Setup Wizard. Click Finish to restart the machine.

You should remove the Windows 2000 Server CD-ROM disk at this time (before the reboot).

STEPS:

Section C — Configuration setup

Step 1. After the machine restarts, press Ctrl-Alt-Delete to logon as the Administrator.

Step 2. The Windows 2000 Configure Your Server screen is displayed, offering congratulations (see Figure 2-2). Here you will select whether your machine will be the only server or one of many servers on the network. Make the appropriate selection and click Next.

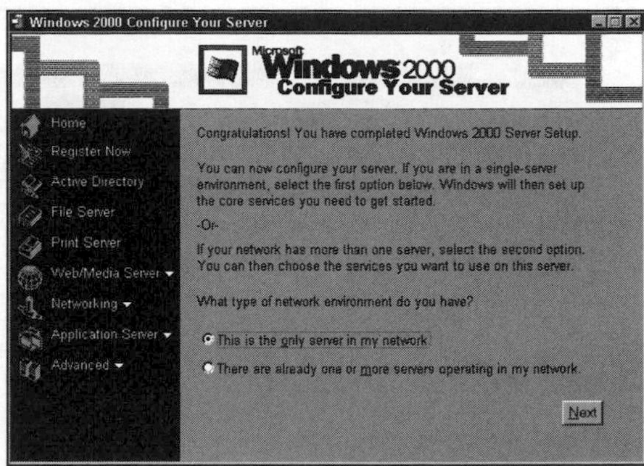

Figure 2-2: Windows 2000 Configure Your Server — Congratulations screen

Step 3. If you selected only your machine to be on a network, the next screen communicates that the machine will be configured as a domain controller (see Figure 2-3). Active Directory, DHCP, and DNS will be configured. Click Next.

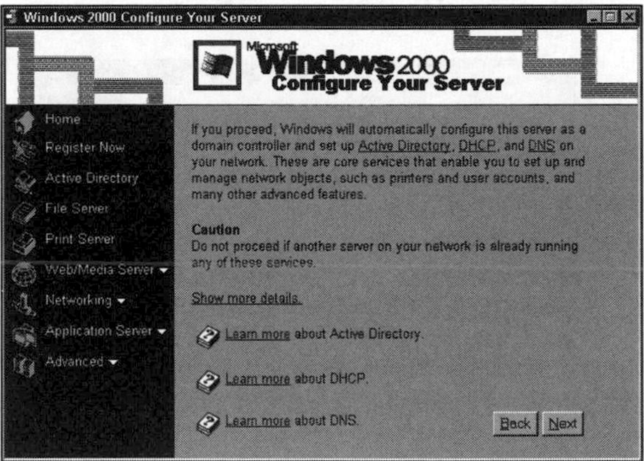

Figure 2-3: Configure machine as domain controller with Active Directory, DHCP, and DNS

Step 4. Provide the Active Directory and domain controller information requested on the next screen (Figure 2-4). Note the Preview of Active Directory domain name will automatically be completed. Click Next.

Continued

STEPS:

Section C — Configuration setup *(continued)*

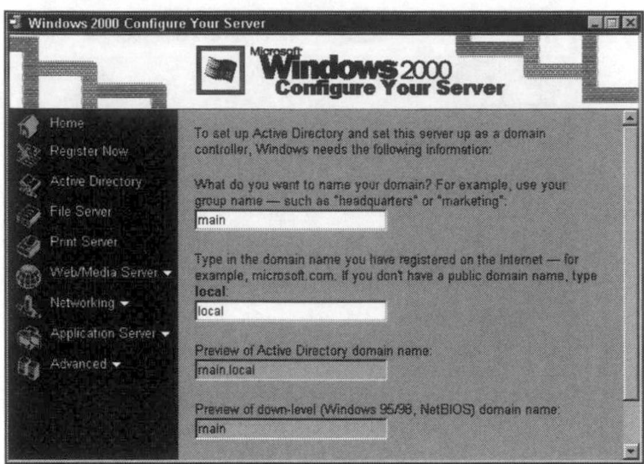

Figure 2-4: Provide domain name

Step 5. The next screen notifies you that additional configuration tasks, taking several minutes, will now start (Figure 2-5). Afterwards, the machine will restart and the Configure Server screen will appear again.

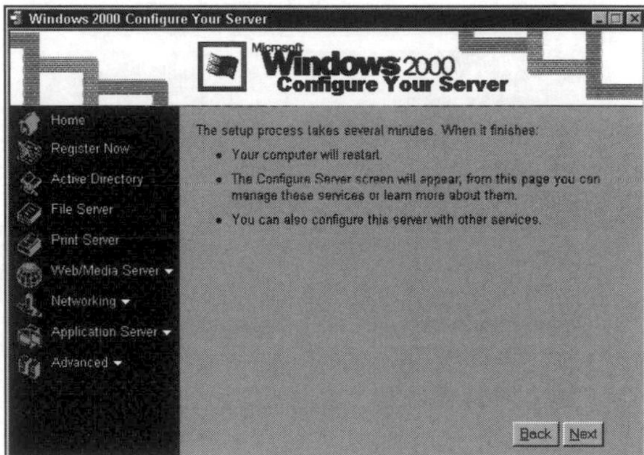

Figure 2-5: Finishing Setup

You will observe the following activities:

- The Active Directory Installation Wizard will run in unattended mode (Figure 2-6).
- Numerous services will be configured, such as Internet Information Server (IIS), COM+, and Management and Monitoring Tools.

- You will be asked to insert the Windows 2000 Server CD-ROM in the CD-ROM drive of your machine (you removed this earlier during the setup process).
- The machine will reboot.

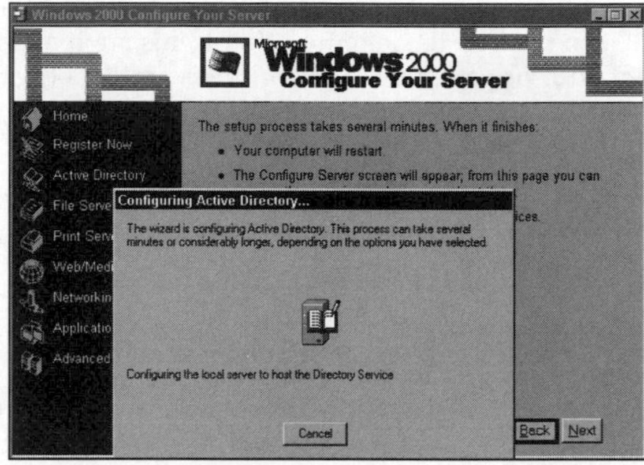

Figure 2-6: Configuring Active Directory

Step 6. After the machine reboots and you log on, you will be greeted with the Windows 2000 Configure Your Server screen again (see Figure 2-7). You will be advised that you need to configure a static IP address and authorize the DHCP service for the Active Directory, DNS, and DHCP configurations to be completed. You will recall that you did not provide a static IP address earlier in the installation process by selecting Typical in the Network Settings screen. Open the DHCP Manager as instructed and authorize the DHCP service (by selecting Authorize from the All Tasks menu). After configuring DHCP, click OK.

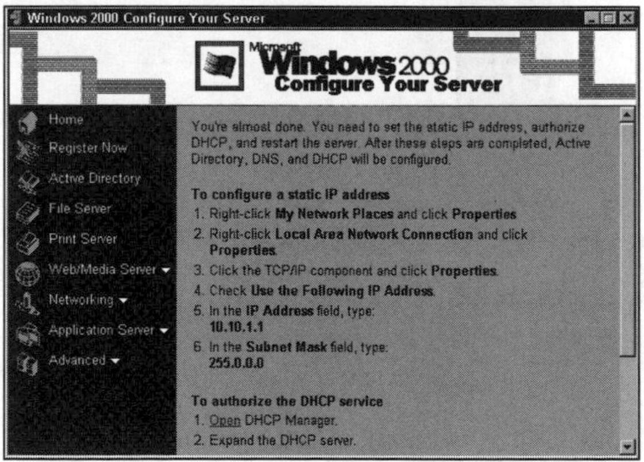

Figure 2-7: Configure static IP and authorize DHCP

Continued

STEPS:

Section C — Configuration setup *(continued)*

Windows 2000 Server automatically creates a 10.0.0.*x* private network as its DHCP scope. You will need to modify this if you intend to have a different IP addressing schema for your private network, such as real Internet addresses. You will also need to reconfigure other items such as the DHCP scope options to reflect your private network IP address settings (again, if the addresses vary from the suggested 10.0.0.*x* settings).

Step 7. Reboot your machine for these additional configuration settings to take effect. This is accomplished by selecting Restart from the Shut Down menu (even though you would expect to see Reboot as the menu choice).

This reboot will likely take longer than other Windows 2000 Server reboots you experience. That's because many final settings are being applied.

Step 8. The standard Configure Your Server screen (see Figure 2-8) appears when you log on. Unless disabled, this screen will always appear when you log on to your Windows 2000 Server machine.

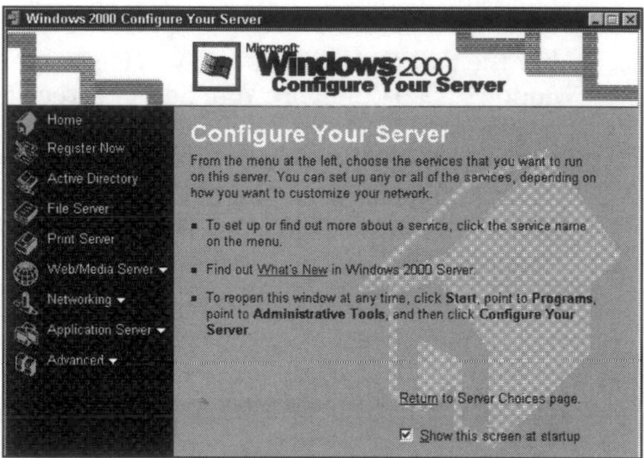

Figure 2-8: Standard Windows 2000 configuration startup screen

The Configure Your Server screen is very useful for learning Windows 2000 Server. The objects in the left pane provide steps and information for configuring basic system components. These objects are reviewed in detail in the "Fully Implementing Windows 2000 Server" section.

Alternate Setup Methods

There are several different ways to set up your Windows 2000 Server environment. These range from installing Windows 2000 Server over a network to disk duplication approaches. I'll explore each approach over the next few pages. Note that the prevailing paradigm concerning alternative setup methods is that of automation. In most cases, the need to consider an alternative setup method is to save time.

Network installation

Installing Windows 2000 Server over a network is very similar to how it was done in the Windows NT Server days. The Windows 2000 Server source files are placed in a shared folder or share point and accessed by hosts on the network. You then run `WINNT.EXE` or `WINNT32.EXE` from the host on which you are attempting to install Windows 2000 Server.

You're on your own when it comes to getting the host to access the shared folder containing the Windows 2000 Server setup files. That is, you need to make the network connection happen. Note that you can still create a client setup disk under Windows NT Server 4.0. Use Network Client Administrator found in Administrator Tools (Common). That provides a basic logon and allows you to connect and launch the Windows 2000 Server setup files. Other possibilities include installing another operating system on the host, such as Windows 98, to facilitate basic network connectivity.

Note that installing Windows 2000 Server over a network is sans setup disks. Call it doing your part to save the world's supply of 3.5" floppy disks. The environmental movement thanks you.

Automated installations

One cool tool found in the Windows 2000 Server Resource Kit is Setup Manager (see Figure 2-9). Setup Manager allows you to efficiently create an answer file, titled `unattended.txt`, for automating the installation of Windows 2000 Server on additional machines. You can think of Setup Manager as your smart scripting editor.

Figure 2-9: Setup Manager

Setup Manager is typically used to create or edit answer files. Answer files for Windows 2000 Professional and Server are titled `unattended.txt`. For the Remote Installation Services, the answer file is titled `remboot.sif`. Setup Manager creates `sysprep.inf` as the answer file for use by the System Preparation Tool. These different answer file options are displayed in Figure 2-10.

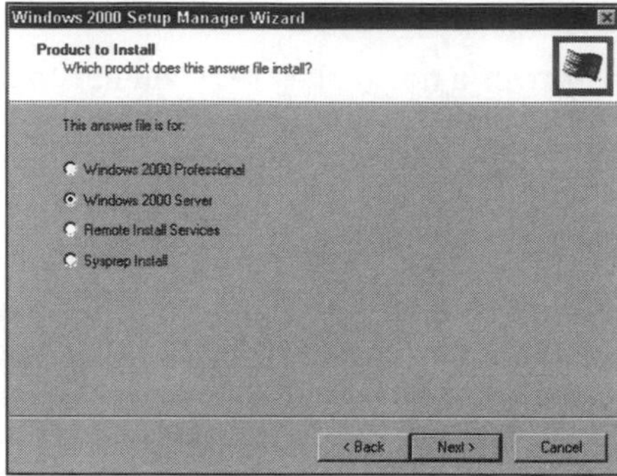

Figure 2-10: Answer file types

When running System Manager, you will specify the type of user interaction required by an installation (see Figure 2-11). This is a very handy feature for allowing limited customization during an automated installation process.

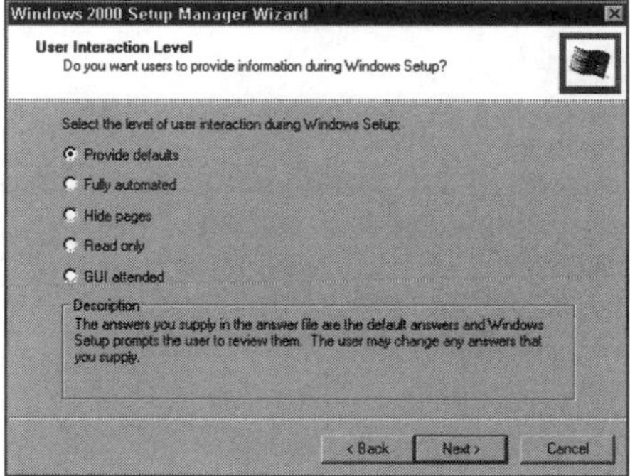

Figure 2-11: User Interaction Level

The Setup Manager will ask you to provide (or not provide) the following information to create an answer file:

- Name
- Organization
- CD Key
- Licensing Mode

- Computer Names
- Administrator Password
- Display Settings
- Network Settings
- Join a Domain
- Time Zone
- Additional Settings (optional) such as Telephony, Regional Settings, Installation Folder, Printers, Run Once commands (such as `.bat` files), Distribution Folder, Additional Mass Storage Drivers, Hardware Abstraction Layer, end of setup commands to run, OEM branding.

One of the key differences between using an answer file (that is, `unattend.txt`) via Setup Manager and Disk Duplication (discussed next) involves the Hardware Abstraction Layer (HAL). Whereas the Setup Manager enables you to create an answer file that allows you to specify a different HAL so you can efficiently set up different types of machines, the Disk Duplication method demands that the HAL on the destination machine be exactly the same as the original machine (same with mass storage controllers).

You can even set up Windows 2000 Server domain controllers via answer files, with one small twist. After automatically installing Windows 2000 Server on another machine using an answer file, you will need to run the `dcpromo` command on the newly minted machine.

Disk duplication

You must first have exactly identical machines. Once that basic requirement has been met, disk duplication is extremely efficient. The disk duplication process is quite simple, using the following steps.

STEPS:

Disk duplication

Step 1. Create the "perfect" Windows 2000 Server you want to replicate. That includes the correct OS configuration and properly installed applications.

Step 2. Run the System Preparation Tool (`sysprep.exe`) on the "perfect" machine to prepare the disk for duplication.

One of the main jobs of the System Preparation Tool is to remove computer-specific information such as security identifier codes (SIDs). Unique SIDs are created on the destination machines automatically when the image is deployed.

Continued

STEPS:

Disk duplication *(continued)*

Step 3. Reboot the "perfect" machine.

Step 4. Use a third-party disk imaging tool such as Ghost to create a gold code or master disk image.

Step 5. Deploy this image to exactly identical machines as needed.

Remote installations

Psst! Want an efficient way to install Windows 2000 Professional on a fleet of workstation-level computers? Use the Remote Installation Services (RIS) feature in Windows 2000 Server.

You will need to manually install RIS on your Windows 2000 Server via the Add/Remove Software applet in Control Panel if you didn't install it when you built your Windows 2000 Server machine. Before RIS can be installed, there are three prerequisite network services that must be running on your Windows 2000 Server: DNS Server, DHCP Server, and Active Directory.

RIS must be installed on an NTFS shared volume that is not on the same disk as Windows 2000 Server.

Not only can you roll out Windows 2000 Professional to a group of workstations with ease, but RIS both eliminates hardware-specific images (meaning machines don't need to be identical) and runs Plug and Play detection during each setup.

The client machine must support RIS. These machines typically include Net PCs (thin clients), EPROM-based network adapter card-based computers (computers that can log on to the RIS server using the Pre-Boot Execution Environment boot ROM), or computers running a remote installation boot disk (perhaps the simplest of all).

For the MCSEs amongst us, consider attending Microsoft Official Curriculum course 1563, "Deploying Microsoft Windows 2000 Professional with IntelliMirror," to master RIS.

Setup Workarounds and Troubleshooting

Earlier in the chapter I mentioned that you could create a 100MB FAT partition on your machine if you're having trouble installing Windows 2000 Server after the fourth setup diskette. That is true. But there are other things you can do as well to solve the installation problems. One technique I used on that old clone server I bought from my country friend Joe, which wouldn't even accept a standard Windows 2000 installation straight up, was to do an upgrade from an existing operating system. Witness this. Time after time, the machine had failed to install Windows 2000 Server correctly. When I installed Windows NT Workstation and upgraded to Windows 2000 Server, it worked wonderfully!

A few comments about troubleshooting a Windows 2000 Server installation. You should consider any or all of the following if you have a failed Windows 2000 Server installation on your hands.

- Bad Media. Was the CD-ROM Disc dimpled? If so, call Microsoft and get new Windows 2000 Server media delivered to you.
- Unsupported CD-ROM drive. Talk about shades of the early Windows NT Advanced Server 3.1 days. Back then, unsupported CD-ROMs drives were a major problem. That was in large part due to the high costs of SCSI CD-ROM drives. Perhaps you remember that there was a little-known method of installing Windows NT Server from an unsupported CD-ROM drive, but that it couldn't be accessed again (a major problem when trying to perform an emergency repair). But enough of ancient history. Today, the problem of unsupported drives isn't as great, but it's always a possibility. My advice? Double-check the Hardware Compatibility List (HCL).
- Insufficient disk space. This is a common problem when installing Windows 2000 Server. You simply don't have enough disk space to complete the setup operation.
- Failed services. If a predecessor service fails to start, then successor services won't start. This is a common cause of failed installations.

Fully Implementing Windows 2000 Server

A few final steps remain before you can confidently say that you've completed the setup and implementation of your Windows 2000 Server. Depending on your situation, these steps may vary. And after you've configured your Windows 2000 Server, I suggest you fully test it (perhaps for months) before deploying it in a production environment. Trust me on that one, and follow the guidelines at the end of this section for creating a Windows 2000 Server test lab.

Upon logon, the Windows 2000 Configure Your Server screen will appear unless you explicitly disable it (something you will want to do after seeing it time and time again). The left pane displays a variety of options that are extremely useful in configuring your Windows 2000 Server for action (see Figure 2-12).

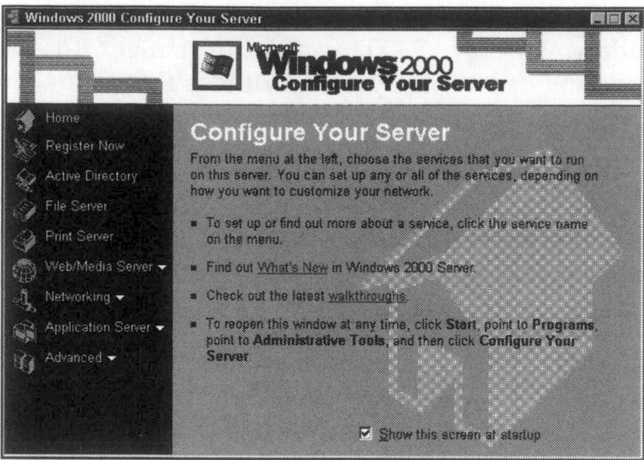

Figure 2-12: Configure Your Server screen

In Table 2-2, I explain the significance of each left panel selection. I highly recommend you make use of these options while learning Windows 2000 Server.

Table 2-2 Configure Your Server Options

Option	*Description*
Home	This is the Configure Your Server page seen in Figure 2-12.
Register Now	This option enables you to register your copy of Windows 2000 Server.
Active Directory	This screen will tell you if Active Directory is or is not installed on your computer. Additional links to manage user accounts, group settings, and learn more about Active Directory are provided.
File Server	This option enables you to manage shared folders.
Print Server	This option launches the Add Printer Wizard and allows you to manage printers.
Web/Media Server	This option enables you to manage IIS and streaming media server.
Networking	This option enables you to manage DHCP, DNS, Remote Access, and Routing.
Application Server	This option enables you to manage group policy, IntelliMirror, component services, terminal services, database server-related functions, and e-mail server-related functions.
Advanced	This option enables you to install the Windows 2000 Administration Tools on a client computer to facilitate remote management.

One configuration issue touched in passing earlier in this chapter was "dcpromo," which stands for domain controller promotion. This tool is used to promote member servers into domain controller roles. Use this tool with care.

Testing Windows 2000 Server

Testing is a key factor in the success of your Windows 2000 implementation project. If you currently do not have a lab, it is important to begin developing a plan to create one as early as possible. A testing lab, for all intents and purposes, refers to an actual network segregated from the corporate LAN. Your lab needs to focus on thorough testing based on realistic scenarios (such as a test environment based on your production environment). The lab is important because it is required early in the planning phase of a Windows 2000 Server deployment project to learn about the product, concepts, and developing solutions. Or in other words, no Windows 2000 Server implementation is complete without first having passed muster in the test lab. Get it!

Reasons for a test lab

At first glance, the reason for a test lab is obvious. Testing, right? No problem. (Dr. Frankenstein thought it was no problem, either...) There are several reasons for setting up a test lab, ranging from low opportunity costs to establishing a "regret minimization framework" (to borrow the words of Jeff Bezos, the founder of Amazon.com).

Lower opportunity costs

A test lab provides non-production impact — the opportunity to test hardware and software without impacting your user community. In this environment, you and your project team can verify your assumptions about Windows 2000 Server, reveal deployment issues, and optimize your rollout design – not to mention inherit a wealth of information about the latest Windows operating system. Imagine achieving all this without impacting your corporate network! This is very important, particularly if you discover your hardware or software does not function optimally under Windows 2000 Server. You wouldn't want to upgrade your manager's computer only to find that half of her hardware is inoperable. Not a great first impression of Windows 2000 Server.

Documentation verification

Another reason for configuring a test lab is documentation verification. For my lab, I followed the *Windows 2000 Beta 3 Training Kit* from Microsoft Press. This allowed me to learn the various features of Windows 2000 Server in a smaller lab before implementing the features on a larger scale. In doing this, I was also able to verify Microsoft's documentation. In addition, third-party companies use different software, hardware, and networking equipment. In your current administrative environment, you should have documentation outlining various installation procedures including setups and configurations. Well, that documentation may change under Windows 2000 Server. As a direct result, you will be able to standardize configurations and create new documentation.

Regret minimization framework

A final reason for developing a test lab is the opportunity to reduce the chance for errors and minimize downtime in the production environment. Reducing errors is known as regret minimization framework. Because your experiences in the lab have provided you with the opportunity to learn and troubleshoot various scenarios and create new documentation (including scripts and revised deployment processes), the chances for error are significantly minimized — as well as workstation and server downtime. The test lab will more than pay for itself with reduced support and redeployment costs in contrast to poorly tested solutions. You will have the opportunity to resolve issues such as the following in the lab:

- Hardware incompatibilities
- Software incompatibilities
- Interoperability and performance
- Operational or deployment inefficiencies
- Limited knowledge of Windows 2000 Server technologies
- Domain and network design issues

If you experience any of these problems in your Windows 2000 Server test lab, you will have the opportunity to design contingency plans, optimize deployment scenarios, and develop administrative procedures that will more effectively manage time and costs in your production environment.

Planning your test lab

Planning is the biggest key to creating a successful testing lab. Without a plan, control and direction of your test lab will prove difficult. A well-designed test lab will provide a controlled environment for testing throughout the project life cycle — from learning the new technology to identifying hardware and software incompatibilities and fine-tuning the implementation process.

Research

The first step in developing your Windows 2000 Server test lab plan is research. You can research the various aspects of Windows 2000 Server by downloading a wealth of information from Microsoft's Web site — everything from the new features of Windows 2000 Server to walk-throughs, white papers, and deployment planning. Also, investigate resources available from Microsoft Press. I mentioned earlier the *Windows 2000 Beta 3 Training Kit*, which is a book published by Microsoft Press. Lastly, you can find a significant number of newsgroups sponsored by Microsoft focusing on Windows 2000 Server. Postings in these newsgroups identify issues raised by other administrators, and may offer you some solutions as your test lab progresses.

Training

The second step in planning is proper training. Members being considered for your test team should receive the necessary training. To find a local Certified Technical Educational Center (CTEC), call (800) 727-3351 in the United States and Canada, and (206) 635-2233 outside these areas. Microsoft has designed courses focusing on various facets of Windows 2000 Server, ranging from topical upgrades to revamping domain architecture. These courses may prove invaluable if you are considering a significant corporate upgrade or rollout. TechNet is another great training resource, with features on Windows 2000 Server. TechNet is available online at `www.microsoft.com/technet`. A CD subscription is also available for an additional fee.

Goal establishment

The next step is establishing goals. The key to establishing goals is to align your lab goals with management's goals. One of your main goals should be to determine the return on investment of your test lab. Budget considerations are always a critical issue with management. Identify the major areas where your lab will provide future returns. These may be in the form of time and effort savings as well. Include the following in your savings estimates:

- Cleaner implementations
- Operational efficiencies
- Automated administration
- Remote administration
- Consolidating testing areas (if others exist for other purposes)
- Early hands-on training

All of these considerations will provide significant future returns. If you have a help desk that tracks trouble tickets or issues, be sure to use their metrics as a base for your calculations. You will need to compile a spreadsheet documenting projected cost savings based on your organization's costs associated with the factors listed previously. Make sure you work with management to address concerns about your current infrastructure and devise tests accordingly. Lab goals should coincide with company goals.

Other goals for your test lab should include the following:

- Revised documentation
- Revised administration procedures
- Protocol standardization
- Standard user configurations (disk imaging)

If your IT group has been operating with work instructions or standard operating procedures (SOP), you're ahead of the game. If not, you should start documenting your administrative procedures. These may include topics such as software and hardware installation and configuration, administrative operating procedures such as account creation, backup procedures, network management, maintenance procedures — the list goes on. Documentation is critical, as it expands the knowledge base in your support group. Windows 2000 Server is a large and complicated operating system. Sharing knowledge among your team members about its many features is imperative to its successful implementation.

Goals such as standardizing protocols and user configurations will alleviate additional network congestion as well as administrative intervention. Obviously you should focus on TCP/IP as your main protocol. Try to eliminate the need for NetBIOS, Appletalk, NFS, IPX, and so on, as you implement Windows 2000 Server. This may not be completely attainable, but try to implement TCP/IP solutions wherever possible. Also consider the goal of creating a standard disk image for your organization (if you haven't already), including system policies, user rights, and administrative access. By standardizing the appearance and functionality of your clients, less intervention and support will be necessary, and support will be streamlined. If you work with a larger organization that includes research and/or development departments, standardization may prove difficult. In such cases, focus on developing standards for 80 percent of your population.

One question you may ask yourself is whether or not your organization requires a test lab for Windows 2000 Server. The answer should be a resounding "Yes." However, the scale and testing criteria may vary widely depending on the amount of services you are looking to implement, as well as the nature of your company's business.

Lab procedures

After setting your lab goals, develop procedures for your lab. The procedures range from identifying team roles to developing a test plan.

First, establish a test team, including a lead person who will maintain contact with management and present status updates. Make sure the team leader possesses strong communication skills and interacts well with management. Also, consider sponsorship from a management person outside your IT group who can provide helpful, neutral support.

Next, work with the team to create a test plan that includes lab design, methodology, resources, schedules, and pass/fail criteria. When designing your lab, you will need to assess your current environment as well as your proposed environment.

Lab design

Lab design is critical to the success of your project. You will want to develop a safe and adequate lab design for future considerations. Your lab design should also be meaningful. That is, the lab design should be similar to your real world network. If you don't use Macintosh computers at your site, then avoid testing Macintoshes in your test lab, eh?

Methodology

Methodology includes the what, how, and why of testing Windows 2000 Server. Identify what features of Windows 2000 Server you will be evaluating. Document how you will go about testing those features, and then provide your reasoning for testing them. In most cases, there is a strong business need to test certain features. You should also identify pass/fail criteria in addition to functionality. Knowing whether or not your test has succeeded is critical.

Keep in mind that your lab should support tests for the following:

- All implemented services
- Hardware compatibility
- Deployment processes
- Client interoperability
- Compatibility with production environment

Another methodology step is to develop a tracking system. I suggest and have used a lab log in the form of a spreadsheet or database, where you can track your testing progress. Set up manual logs describing the current status of the computer/hardware/software at each testing station. This way, if other members of your test team get interrupted, you have a snapshot of their progress. Make sure this information gets entered into the spreadsheet or database. This will assist with error reproducibility and troubleshooting later in your testing. There are many ways to devise a tracking system. Make sure you design a system beneficial to your team.

Resources

The test plan should include considerations such as lab location and accessibility, scheduling for inventory and testing priorities, hardware and software to be utilized in the lab environment, and individual assignments. Make sure you isolate the test lab from the rest of your production network. If you must provide a connection to the corporate network, plan for ways to regulate and control access and a way to quickly disconnect if necessary. You should also consider designing router configurations to protect your corporate network so that testing with multihomed systems in the lab won't negatively impact production users and processes.

Assign asset tags or bar code stickers to all lab equipment for identity and security purposes. Also, enable security logs on the systems and establish login/logout protocol.

Schedule

Establishing a project schedule may prove challenging. As you really don't know what kind of roadblocks you will encounter on your lab journey, setting a schedule may prove a bit complicated. Start by prioritizing your lab goals. Identify which lab goals are business critical and start with those. Determining if your computer systems are Windows 2000-compliant should be one of the goals at the top of your list. You may need to work with management when prioritizing (if you haven't already). When estimating time frames for testing, estimate conservatively. Add at least 25 percent to your approximate time frames to allot for unforeseen dilemmas. And don't be anxious to condense time frames if you later find you are ahead of schedule. You may need the time later in your testing.

Pass/fail metrics

When finalizing your project schedule, build in some checkpoints and metrics. It's important to monitor your progress and be able to present to management some concrete information. Checkpoints will enable you to step back and analyze your time frames, your pass/fail rate, as well as your logs and other documentation. As a result, you will be able to create metrics from your logs and provide presentation material for management. If you see, for example, that 50 percent of your hardware or software does not meet the Windows 2000 criteria, those metrics need to be conveyed to management as soon as possible. This may affect how soon your company will be able to upgrade. It is a good idea to create a presentation explaining your findings and call a meeting for management. Regular audits by non-IT individuals will ensure that procedures are being followed properly.

Testing resources

Your current environment will determine hardware resources for your lab. If you are part of a WAN configuration, you will obviously need more hardware than a single-site configuration would. Let's start by looking at Microsoft's three-phase recommended lab development process (see Figure 2-13).

The design and building phases will change as your knowledge increases and new requirements evolve from your testing. Use this flow chart to determine your need to redesign and rebuild various features of your test lab.

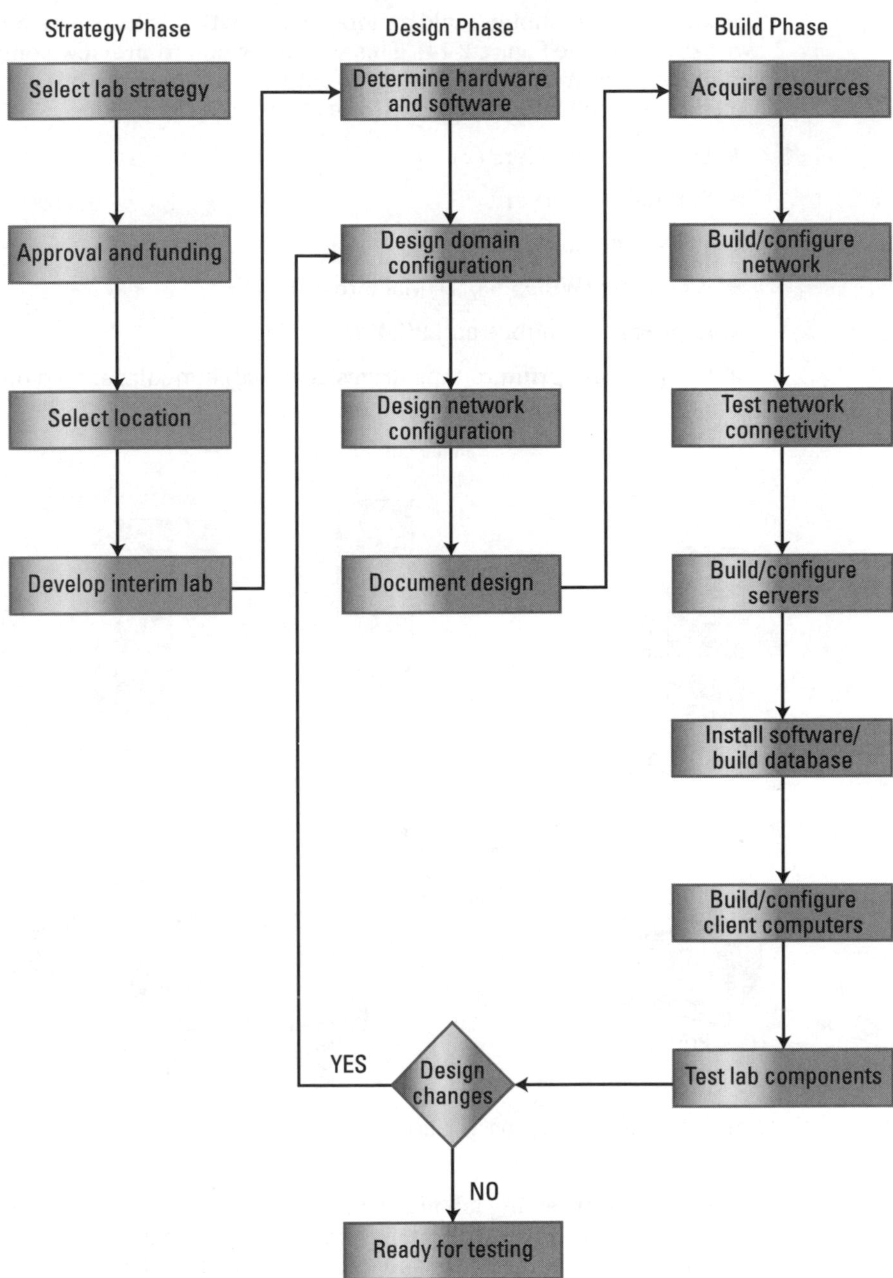

Figure 2-13: Lab development process

For starters, you should build an interim lab with a few servers and workstations (see Figure 2-14). This will allow you to preview some of the initial facets of Windows 2000 Server until your high-end lab is set up. Consider the following hardware for a starter configuration:

- Domain controllers (2)
- Standalone server
- WAN simulator/router
- All clients (Win95/98/NT/Macintosh/UNIX)
- Laptops (for mobile and PCMCIA testing)
- Peripherals (printers/tape drives/removable media, and so on)

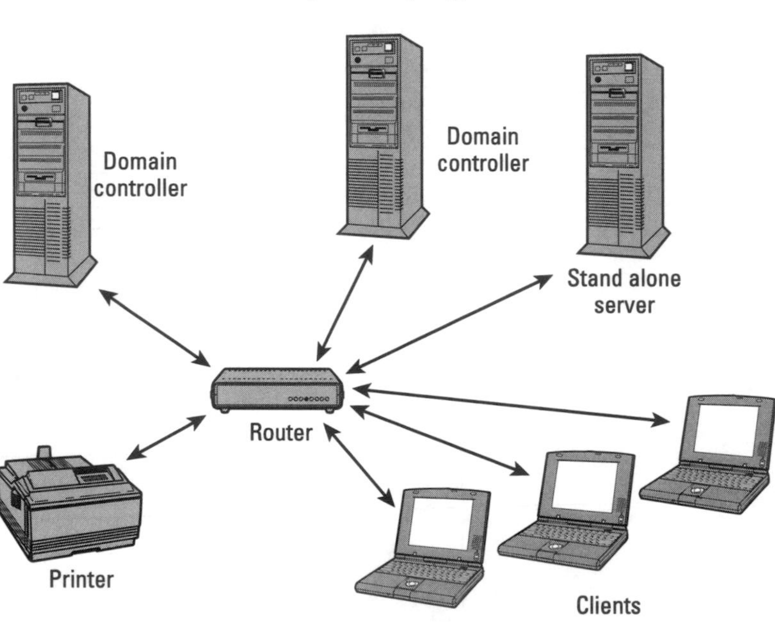

Figure 2-14: Sample lab configuration

Remember, your testing lab needs to be representative of your current environment. Configure your units exactly as they exist in your user community. Set up a primary and backup domain controller, a file and print server or Web server, and configure your clients. Give strong consideration to imaging an existing backup domain controller and testing an upgrade to Windows 2000 Server.

It is important to consider the quantity of tests that will be performed when determining necessary resources. Too many testing configurations may prove to be costly and can limit testing efforts. Your team will need to decide which testing configurations are necessary for qualitative results.

For testing purposes, inventory all your hardware and software. This may be quite a task, particularly if you're part of a large organization or you have never completed an audit. For example, you may discover that your company uses every modem model on the market. If this is the case, standardization is important to ease administration. Depending on the outcome of your testing, you may want to consider standardizing hardware such as PCMCIA cards, modems, NICs, and video and multimedia cards. In terms of software, include all applications currently used in your environment. This includes custom and proprietary software, which may experience the more difficulty upgrading to Windows 2000 Server than other third-party applications. As I mentioned earlier, focus on business-critical applications, such as e-mail, remote access, and Internet software.

If your organization is not staffed for test lab support, you may need to consider additional consultant resources. Consultants should not be as involved in the planning process as they should be in the implementation and testing arenas. Focus on the less critical tasks for your consultants.

Remember, your test lab must focus on users as well as administrators. While making an effort to ensure administration is eased, remember that user support accounts for a large portion of IT's costs. Focusing on making their computer tasks easier and user-friendlier should be top priority.

Budget

Budgeting for a test lab can be a challenging process. Many managers outside IT/MIS departments may consider lab environments for research and development purposes, not for IT purposes. As a result, funding for such a lab may be limited. Of course, you have already presented all the good news about Windows 2000 Server to management — lower TCO (total cost of ownership), non-production impact on future testing (in addition to Windows 2000 Server testing), and so on. You can assist with budget concerns by being creative in your approach to getting test lab equipment.

One option is purchasing identical hardware through auctions. A variety of Web sites now feature auctions that include wide ranges of hardware, software, and networking equipment. While this may be an economical option, finding comparable hardware to your current environment may be an issue. There may also be the question of quality or history of the machine.

Another budget option is leasing. Leasing has become increasingly popular, particularly short-term leasing, focusing on the life cycle of computers. This can be an attractive choice if you are able to cycle some of the computers into production following your testing (I would suggest, however, retaining several in your test environment). Leasing is also appealing to managers not looking to spend capital on testing equipment. Spreading out the cost can be beneficial.

A final option is renting. However, renting costs tend to be fairly high, because companies offering this service need to keep the computers in circulation. Unlike the leasing option, the renting company will eat the cost if they can't rent out the units. As a result, costs tend to be significantly higher, by as much as two to three times. Still, for short-term testing solutions, this may be a good option.

Other considerations

As with any kind of testing, environment, security, data integrity and disaster recovery are critical. You should address these concerns when designing your test lab. Make sure your lab is in a locked or restricted area accessible only to team members and necessary personnel. Don't set up a lab in an open office or cubicle when security can be compromised. Consider setting up in a climate-controlled environment similar to your server room. (Actually, if there is considerable space in your server area, this is an ideal place!) Make sure the lab area is cool, static- and dust-free. Carpeted areas should be avoided at all costs as they produce far too much static electricity.

In terms of disaster recovery, be sure you employ several uninterruptible power supplies (UPS) with the proper wattage to support your test environment, as well as regularly updated emergency repair disks (ERDs) and automatic system recovery (ASR) disks, as they are referred to in Windows 2000 Server.

In terms of general safety, install a smoke detector and a sprinkler system or fire extinguisher. Your lab should provide room to roam. Keep walking areas free of wires, cables, and hubs. This is a common sight in some test labs I've been in, and needs to be avoided at all costs.

Testing Specifics

I've spent several pages casting the vision of a Windows 2000 Server testing environment. I now want to get more specific and provide a list of hardware and software components that should be tested. Also found in this discussion are different testing scenarios.

Hardware testing

Prior to testing your hardware, complete a thorough inventory of all hardware currently in your environment. For computer testing, your units should be ACPI-compliant, particularly laptops. Their components should also be included in the Windows 2000 Server hardware compatibility list (HCL). Your hardware list should include such items as the following:

- Modems and PCMCIA cards
- Tape drives
- Video cards
- Sound/multimedia cards
- SCSI cards
- Printers
- Other peripheral devices

Along with your inventory, document the URLs of popular vendor sites that may post updated Windows 2000 Server drivers for their hardware. Download the drivers to a local server for future testing. Some plug-and-play hardware may require manual configurations under Windows 2000 Server, so it's important to have updated drivers. Also, test Universal Serial Bus (USB) functionality on your units.

Remember that your hardware testing should focus on setting a standard for moving forward.

Software testing

Software testing should follow the same guidelines as hardware. After conducting an inventory, you may find several applications and executables designed for platform-specific purposes. These applications may need to be upgraded or replaced depending on their functionality. Once again, document the vendor URL for software upgrades and patches.

When you begin testing software, focus on the business-critical applications first. As I mentioned earlier, e-mail, remote access, and Internet applications, as well as your office suite, should fall into this category. Test deployment scenarios of your software which include the following:

- Clean installation
- Upgrade for Windows 9*x*, NT
- Via SMS or other remote installation
- Imaging (such Symantec Ghost and Microsoft's Sysprep)
- Windows Installer
- Uninstallation

If your software encounters errors in any of your deployment scenarios, you will need to contact the vendor or Microsoft for resolution.

When testing software, develop a process for testing. For example, when testing the compatibility of application documents, consider the following process:

1. Open a new document.
2. Apply a template and enter data.
3. Save and print file.
4. Send file as mail attachment.
5. Open file on another client and print.

In any case, make sure your process is representative of your user base. What do your users do?

LAN and WAN considerations

As your test lab grows beyond the scope of a few machines, you will want to prepare for higher-ended situations. Implementing expanded services on your servers and growing your lab network will be the next step in testing Windows 2000 Server. Use the same services and configurations that you will use when you deploy to your user environment. If you are running DNS, DHCP, or WINS, set these up for testing in your lab. Set up your domain controllers as replicas of your production domain controllers, including copies of the SAM database. If you are planning to implement Active Directory, make certain you have met with management to discuss name space conventions moving forward. Your test lab servers provide a great starting ground for your future domain model. Test roaming profiles at this stage if you are considering them. Offline user data management is a great service for portables running Windows 2000 Server — test this feature as well. Testing mixed domain models is another option at this stage. You will want to verify and assess how NT4 servers function with Windows 2000 Server domain controllers. Also, verify your server upgrade or migration process.

Testing results

Remember, an important key to a successful test lab is documentation, and that includes documenting results. I've seen results documented several different ways, including using the journal and note entries in Microsoft Outlook 2000, posting on Web pages, and even printing out and storing in a notebook. Without results, you and your company's management may have a difficult time considering an upgrade to Windows 2000 Server. Make sure your documentation provides quantitative and qualitative results. The more measurable information you provide for a presentation, the better your transition to Windows 2000 Server will be. Be sure to distribute a hard copy of all your testing results to your team, management, and your non-IT sponsor. A final presentation to management should top off your lab efforts.

Summary

Installing and implementing Windows 2000 Server correctly is essential to having a properly functioning network. This chapter presented the installation process as well as alternate installation methods. Implementing issues, such as testing your Windows 2000 Server installation, are discussed.

- Step-by-step instructions for installing Windows 2000 Server
- When to use alternative Windows 2000 Server installation methods
- Windows 2000 Server implementation issues
- Testing your Windows 2000 Server installation

Part II

TCP/IP

Chapter 3

Implementing TCP/IP

In This Chapter

- Defining TCP/IP
- Microsoft's implementation of TCP/IP
- A detailed analysis of TCP
- A detailed analysis of IP
- Windows Sockets: a definition and the application
- Three parts of Internet addressing: the IP address, subnet mask, and default gateway
- Windows 2000 Server basic routing

Have you ever wondered what the payoff was from years of US military expenditures? Was it $200 wrenches and other doodads publicly highlighted by former Senator William Proxmire and his "Golden Fleece" awards? No, two of the great payoffs from the huge military buildup that have spanned generations are Transmission Control Protocol/Internet Protocol (TCP/IP) and the Internet itself. Not only has TCP/IP become a de facto standard for internetworking, it is also the default protocol for Windows 2000 Server.

As I prepared this chapter, I promised myself that I wouldn't drone on about the history of the Internet, Request for Comments (RFCs), and other historical hooey that has been covered in far too many books. In fact, I make two assumptions: First, that you are not a *newbie*—you know the definition of TCP/IP and have other thicker and more technical resources dedicated specifically to TCP/IP. And second, that perhaps like me, you have trouble sitting still when the going gets boring; if the presentation of TCP/IP (which can be very dry) isn't exciting, you will drift away and miss the finer points about TCP/IP that are important to catch. Call it attention deficit disorder, but you have my assurance that I'll cut to the chase and tell you what you need to know about using TCP/IP with Windows 2000 Server. This said, I'd like to take just a few pages to set the foundation for our TCP/IP discussion.

About TCP/IP

Although TCP/IP's popularity can in part be traced to darn good publicity, it is also an efficient routable protocol that is robust enough to perform well on large corporate networks. Network engineers now favor TCP/IP because it is scalable from the smallest node (a single workstation running TCP/IP for dial-up Internet access) to a local area network (LAN) and even a worldwide enterprise wide area network (WAN). Developers know that TCP/IP has an important role in their lives as they develop client/server WinSock-compliant applications at the upper layers of the OSI model.

Remember the golden rule for TCP/IP: It's a good fit, and you can say one size truly fits all when discussing protocols.

So important is TCP/IP that a grassroots movement has arisen within the MCSE certification community, claiming TCP/IP should be included as a core exam for the MCSE track. And this claim is with good reason. Perhaps no greater paradigm shift has occurred in network computing than the early- to mid-90s shift to the Internet and use of the TCP/IP protocol. Not only did the move to the Internet catch many (including Microsoft) off guard, but the rapid acceptance of the TCP/IP protocol left more than one from the Novell camp (and the IPX world) briefly concerned about their job prospects.

The standard-bearer

Transmission Control Protocol/Internet Protocol (TCP/IP) has emerged as the standard protocol for not only networked personal computers but also standalone computers that access the Internet. Close to celebrating its 30th birthday, TCP/IP was developed in 1969, at the height of the antiwar protests against the Department of the Defense. It was part of the experiment that created ARPANET, which became the Internet as we know it.

The key point to remember about TCP/IP is that it is routable, scalable, connects unlike systems via FTP and Telnet, and is designed for use with WANs (or internets). Equally important today, don't forget that TCP/IP is designed for use with the Internet.

Additionally, TCP/IP is an "enabling," or foundation technology that not only supports Internet connectivity but also Point to Point Protocol (PPP), Point to Point Tunneling Protocol (PPTP) and Windows Sockets. PPP and PPTP are discussed later in this book.

Uppercase "Internet" refers to the global Internet that millions use and enjoy. Lowercase "internet" refers to a private WAN that is connected via routers.

Developers can rejoice because Microsoft's implementation of TCP/IP supports the Windows Sockets interface, a Windows-based implementation of the Berkeley Sockets interface for network programming (a widely used standard). Developers and users alike can also rejoice because Microsoft's TCP/IP protocol suite in Windows 2000 Server is older and wiser. Back in the old NT days, did you ever have to reinstall TCP/IP because it had somehow become mysteriously corrupted? Did the Dynamic Host Configuration Protocol (DHCP) ever fail you? You bet! This iteration of the TCP/IP protocol stack, which was revised for Windows 2000 Server, is greatly welcomed; developers (in general) and users will find that Microsoft's TCP/IP is a robust, scalable cross-platform client/server framework, which grants them success.

By committee: Requests for Comments

A popular saying in professional basketball in the late 1990s is "We win by committee." That is, everyone contributes to the effort. Well, you can say everyone has contributed to the effort to develop the TCP/IP protocol suite, and more importantly, everyone has contributed to the effort to maintain it. The contributions are in the form of Requests for Comments (RFCs), and the RFC documents go a long way toward helping both developers and network engineers understand the TCP/IP protocol suite and the Internet itself. And unlike those who are media shy, those of us who spend significant time in the TCP/IP community are very interested in "comments" related to implementing TCP/IP.

The standards setting process is managed by the Internet Activities Board (IAB). This is a committee that is responsible not only for setting Internet standards but also controlling the publication of RFCs. Two groups are governed by the IAB: the Internet Engineering Task Force (IETF) and the Internet Research Task Force (IRTF). Whereas the IRTF coordinates all TCP/IP research projects and the like, the IETF focuses on Internet problems and solutions. RFCs are officially published by the IETF with input from the parent organization (IAB), the IRTF, and contributors such as you and me.

In fact, anyone in the networking and development communities can contribute to the TCP/IP standard-making process. Just submit a document as an RFC to the IETF. Crazy? You bet. But it's true. The RFC that you submit might just cut the mustard and become published after extensive editorial review, testing, and consensus among the powers that be.

Secret

Many companies in the software and technology fields contribute significant resources to have their implementations of protocols and other networking and developer features adapted as standards by industry boards such as the IETF. Although it is possible to contribute to the TCP/IP RFC process, in reality, this world consists mainly of corporate-level software engineers from companies such as HP, IBM, and Microsoft. Standards implemented via the consensus method in place for TCP/IP RFCs have survived a very political process (and not necessarily of the Justice Department-variety).

Likewise, a manufacturer may elect to implement certain RFCs and ignore others. Table 3-1 shows the full set of RFCs that make up Microsoft's implementation of the TCP/IP protocol suite.

Table 3-1 Request for Comments Supported by Microsoft's TCP/IP Protocol Stack

RFC	*Title*
768	User Datagram Protocol (UDP)
783	Trivial File Transfer Protocol (TFTP)
791	Internet Protocol (IP)
792	Internet Control Message Protocol (ICMP)
793	Transmission Control Protocol (TCP)
816	Fault Isolation and Recovery*
826	Address Resolution Protocol (ARP)
854	Telnet Protocol (TELNET)
862	Echo Protocol (ECHO)
863	Discard Protocol (DISCARD)
864	Character Generator Protocol (CHARGEN)
865	Quote of the Day Protocol (QUOTE)
867	Daytime Protocol (DAYTIME)
894	IP over Ethernet
919, 922	IP Broadcast Datagrams (broadcasting with subnets)
950	Internet Standard Subnetting Procedure*
959	File Transfer Protocol (FTP)
1001, 1002	NetBIOS Service Protocols
1034, 1035	Domain Name System (DNS)
1042	IP over Token Ring
1055	Transmission of IP over Serial Lines (IP-SLIP)
1112	Internet Group Management Protocol (IGMP)
1122, 1123	Host Requirements (communications and applications)
1134	Point to Point Protocol (PPP)
1144	Compressing TCP/IP Headers for Low-Speed SerialLinks
1157	Simple Network Management Protocol (SNMP)
1179	Line Printer Daemon Protocol
1188	IP over FDDI
1191	Path MTU Discovery

RFC	Title
1201	IP over ARCNET
1231	IEEE 802.5 Token Ring MIB (MIB-II)
1332	PPP Internet Protocol Control Protocol (IPCP)
1333	PPP Authentication Protocol
1518	An Architecture for IP Address Allocation with CDIR*
1519	Classless Inter-Domain Routing (CDIR)*
1533	DHCP Options and BOOTP Vendor Extensions
1534	Interoperations between DHCP and BOOTP
1541	Dynamic Host Configuration Protocol (DHCP)
1542	Clarifications and Extensions for the Bootstrap Protocol
1547	Requirements for Point to Point Protocol (PPP)
1548	Point to Point Protocol (PPP)
1549	PPP in High-Level Data Link Control (HDLC) Framing
1552	PPP Internetwork Packet Exchange Control Protocol (IPXCP)
1553	IPX Header Compression
1570	Link Control Protocol (LCP) Extensions

The RFCs listed with an asterisk (*) in Table 3-1 are new additions to Windows 2000 Server versus its predecessor, Windows NT Server 4.0.

Windows 2000 Server also incorporates the functionality of the following draft RFCs that are unnumbered at this time:

- NetBIOS Frame Control Protocol (NBFCP)
- PPP over ISDN
- PPP over X.25
- Compression Control Protocol

If you want to track RFC activity in the TCP/IP and Internet communities, point your browser to review the IAB-published quarterly memo titled "IAB Official Protocol Standard." Here you will receive the current RFC status for each "protocol" in the TCP/IP protocol suite. You may also download the RFCs from this site.

The IAB home page may be found at `www.iab.org`. (Figure 3-1) To be honest, those

who are newer to Windows 2000 Server may not be as interested in RFC and visiting the IAB home page as those who have worked in the industry for longer periods of time. Why? My observation is that the longer you've been working with networks, the more interested you are in expanding your horizons beyond just the Windows 2000 Server NOS. If this is true, then RFCs are a great place to start that expansion.

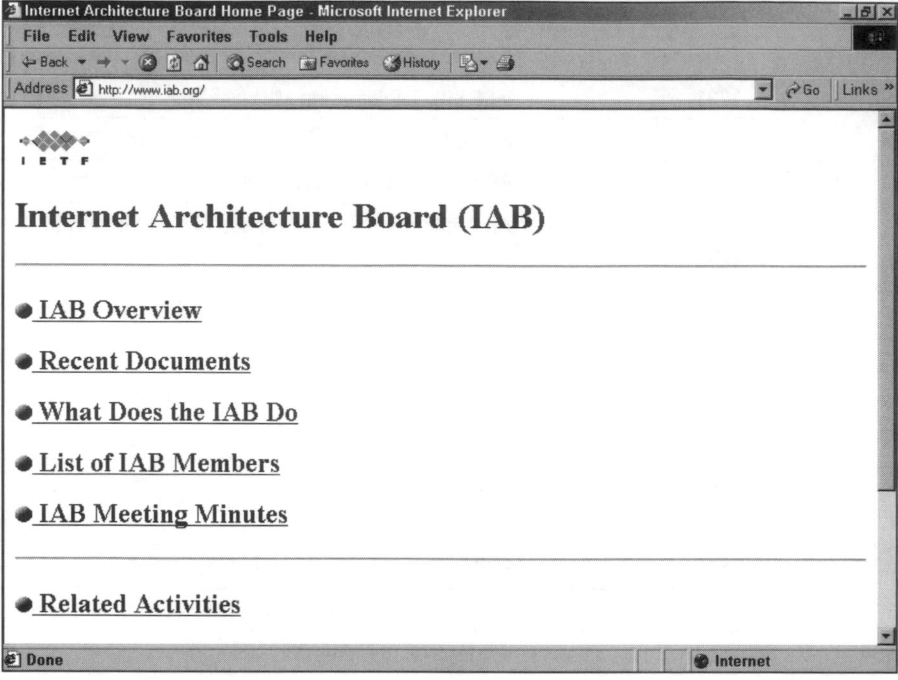

Figure 3-1: The IAB home page

To obtain RFCs via FTP, go to the following FTP sites:

```
NIS.NSF.NET
NISC.JVNC.NET
VENERA.ISI.EDU
WUARCHIVE.WUSTL.EDU
SRC.DOC.IC.AC.UK
DS.INTERNIC.NET
NIC.DDN.MIL
```

It's a suite, not just a protocol

It's essential to understand that TCP/IP is a protocol suite that spans several layers of the OSI model. It is incorrect to think of TCP/IP as a protocol in a singular sense; it's not just a networking layer protocol. In fact, TCP/IP doesn't even map well to the OSI model because it's based on an alternate networking-model called the *DOD model* (that's DOD for Department of Defense). It is also known as the Internet Protocol Suite. Where the OSI model has seven layers, the DOD model has four layers that map to the seven layers of the OSI model, as shown in Figure 3-2.

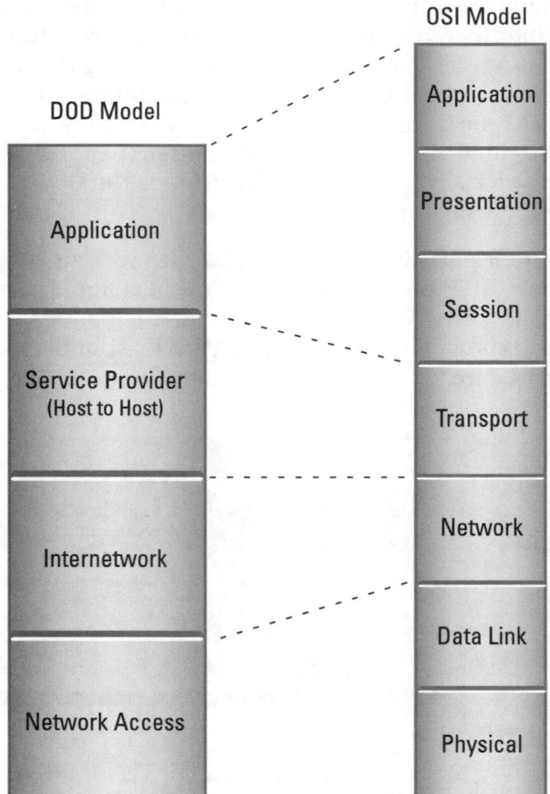

Figure 3-2: The DOD and OSI protocol models

It is interesting to note the following:

- The DOD application layer maps to the upper three layers of the OSI model (application, presentation, and session). This is where you find TCP/IP applications such as *Telnet.* It is also the home of Windows Sockets and NetBIOS.
- The transport layer is simple. The DOD model and the OSI model map directly to each other. Here is where TCP and UDP reside. *Tip:* Remember that TCP is connection-oriented and guaranteed; UDP is connectionless and doesn't guarantee delivery.
- The DOD "Internet" layer maps directly to the OSI network layer. Here you find IP, ARP, ICMP, and so on.
- The network interface is at the bottom of the DOD model. This layer maps to the OSI's data link and physical layers.

The DOD model provides a comparative framework for understanding T CP/IP in contexts other than the OSI model. That is clear from the points just covered. But, as an MCT instructor, I still enjoy hearing the predictable question, "How does it apply to me?" from my MCSE students. Granted, certification students quickly lose interest in a subject if they can't see its relevance. Regarding the DOD discussion, you can see that TCP/IP packets captured on a Windows 2000 Server network reference the DOD model (see the Ethernet Type line in Figure 3-3).

Basically, it is important to understand the underlying models that can be used to describe the TCP/IP protocol suite and how it is implemented. When you work with peers from the Windows 2000 Server community, you will find that they assume you know this stuff. If you don't at least understand the basics, you'll quickly be lost in the proverbial ether.

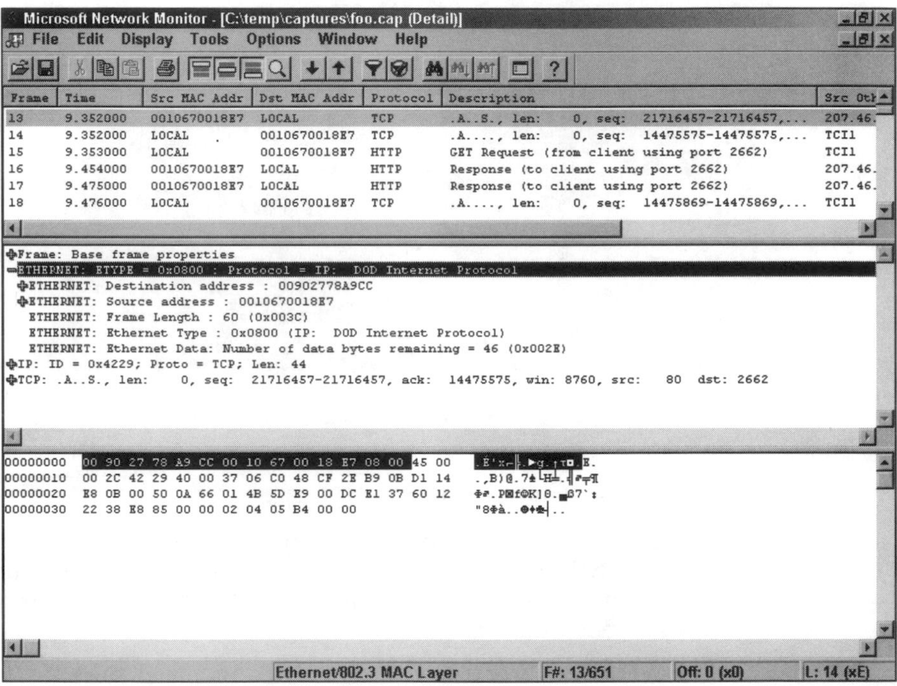

Figure 3-3: A reference to the DOD model in a packet capture

Comparing TCP/IP to operating systems

Unfortunately, one thing neither the OSI or DOD model will do for you is conceptually map TCP/IP to the underlying operating system on your computer. This is because both the OSI and DOD models are oriented to explain communications models via a layering approach. A "ring" model describes the world of operating systems, starting basically with the Kernel (see Figure 3-4).

With the operating system ring model, note that the Kernel is in Ring 0 and applications run in Ring 3. Do you know what the difference between running code in Ring 0 and in Ring 3 is? *Hint:* Ring 3 has protected memory space for applications and Ring 0 is very fast!

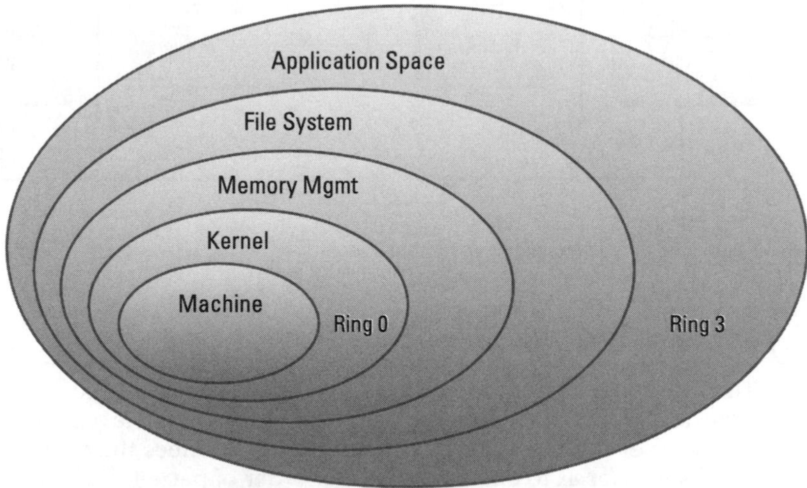

Figure 3-4: The operating system ring model

A Look at the Protocols

As with a large American farm family, every member or protocol in the TCP/IP protocol suite has a job. These family members contribute to the greater whole — the communication between hosts on a network. And as with a large family, each protocol lives on a certain floor in the house. This was shown previously when the TCP/IP protocol suite was mapped to both the OSI model and the DOD Model. At each layer of the DOD model (see Figure 3-5), data is treated differently, which is similar to the OSI model.

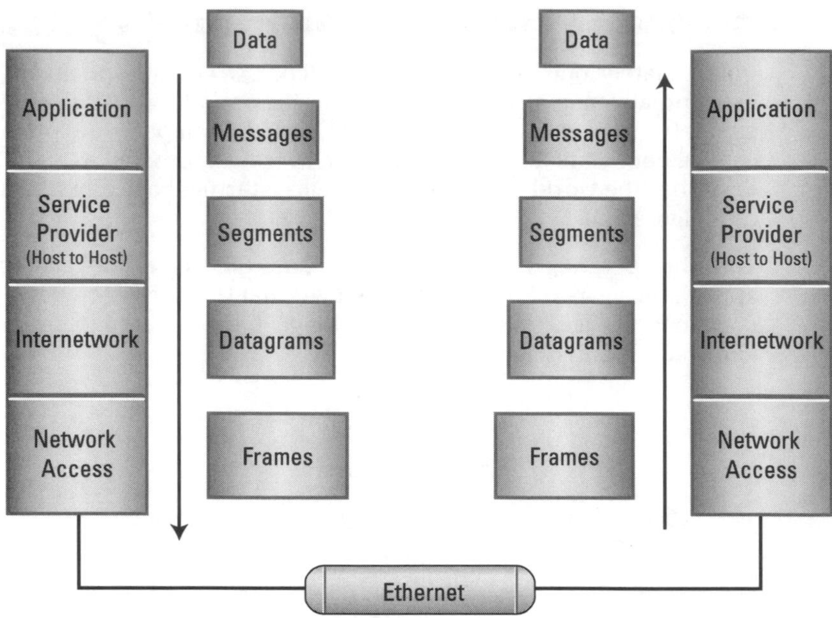

Figure 3-5: DOD layering and communications

Transmission Control Protocol

The most common protocol used today at the transportation level, Transmission Control Protocol (TCP) provides a reliable, connection-oriented delivery service on top of IP. TCP not only guarantees the delivery of packets, but goes so far as to ensure the proper order of packets. A checksum feature assures that the packet header and data are accurate. If these are not accurate or a packet is otherwise faulty or lost, TCP assumes responsibility for retransmitting the packet. Because TCP is reliable, it is a good upper-level member of the TCP/IP protocol suite to use for client/server applications and for important or critical services such as messaging. In short, TCP is the transport layer protocol of choice for session-oriented transmissions. In Figure 3-6, frames 3–5 show the three-way handshake that is the signature of ACK-based communications involving TCP. Packet 4 is both a response and an acknowledgment. Packet 5 is an acknowledgment that acknowledges packet 4. So many packets, so little bandwidth!

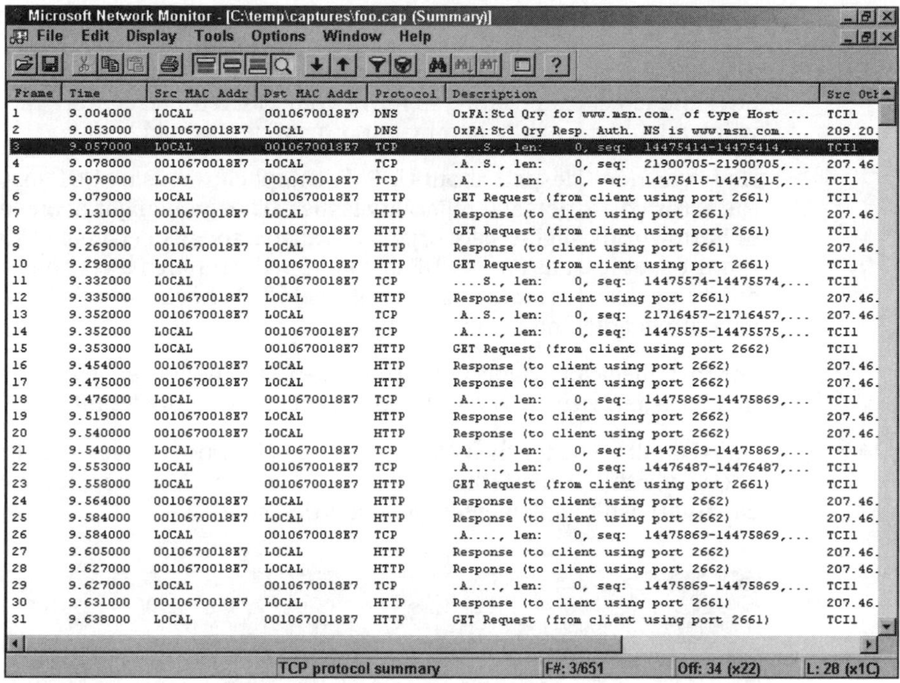

Frame	Time	Src MAC Addr	Dst MAC Addr	Protocol	Description	Src Oth
1	9.004000	LOCAL	0010670018E7	DNS	0xFA:Std Qry for www.msn.com. of type Host ...	TCI1
2	9.053000	0010670018E7	LOCAL	DNS	0xFA:Std Qry Resp. Auth. NS is www.msn.com....	209.20.
3	9.057000	LOCAL	0010670018E7	TCP	....S., len: 0, seq: 14475414-14475414,...	TCI1
4	9.078000	0010670018E7	LOCAL	TCP	.A..S., len: 0, seq: 21900705-21900705,...	207.46.
5	9.078000	LOCAL	0010670018E7	TCP	.A...., len: 0, seq: 14475415-14475415,...	TCI1
6	9.079000	LOCAL	0010670018E7	HTTP	GET Request (from client using port 2661)	TCI1
7	9.131000	0010670018E7	LOCAL	HTTP	Response (to client using port 2661)	207.46.
8	9.229000	LOCAL	0010670018E7	HTTP	GET Request (from client using port 2661)	TCI1
9	9.269000	0010670018E7	LOCAL	HTTP	Response (to client using port 2661)	207.46.
10	9.298000	LOCAL	0010670018E7	HTTP	GET Request (from client using port 2661)	TCI1
11	9.332000	LOCAL	0010670018E7	TCP	....S., len: 0, seq: 14475574-14475574,...	TCI1
12	9.335000	0010670018E7	LOCAL	HTTP	Response (to client using port 2661)	207.46.
13	9.352000	0010670018E7	LOCAL	TCP	.A..S., len: 0, seq: 21716457-21716457,...	207.46.
14	9.352000	LOCAL	0010670018E7	TCP	.A...., len: 0, seq: 14475575-14475575,...	TCI1
15	9.353000	LOCAL	0010670018E7	HTTP	GET Request (from client using port 2662)	TCI1
16	9.454000	0010670018E7	LOCAL	HTTP	Response (to client using port 2662)	207.46.
17	9.475000	0010670018E7	LOCAL	HTTP	Response (to client using port 2662)	207.46.
18	9.476000	LOCAL	0010670018E7	TCP	.A...., len: 0, seq: 14475869-14475869,...	TCI1
19	9.519000	0010670018E7	LOCAL	HTTP	Response (to client using port 2662)	207.46.
20	9.540000	0010670018E7	LOCAL	HTTP	Response (to client using port 2662)	207.46.
21	9.540000	LOCAL	0010670018E7	TCP	.A...., len: 0, seq: 14475869-14475869,...	TCI1
22	9.553000	LOCAL	0010670018E7	TCP	.A...., len: 0, seq: 14476487-14476487,...	TCI1
23	9.558000	LOCAL	0010670018E7	HTTP	GET Request (from client using port 2661)	TCI1
24	9.564000	0010670018E7	LOCAL	HTTP	Response (to client using port 2662)	207.46.
25	9.584000	0010670018E7	LOCAL	HTTP	Response (to client using port 2662)	207.46.
26	9.584000	LOCAL	0010670018E7	TCP	.A...., len: 0, seq: 14475869-14475869,...	TCI1
27	9.605000	0010670018E7	LOCAL	HTTP	Response (to client using port 2662)	207.46.
28	9.627000	0010670018E7	LOCAL	HTTP	Response (to client using port 2662)	207.46.
29	9.627000	LOCAL	0010670018E7	TCP	.A...., len: 0, seq: 14475869-14475869,...	TCI1
30	9.631000	0010670018E7	LOCAL	HTTP	Response (to client using port 2661)	207.46.
31	9.638000	LOCAL	0010670018E7	HTTP	GET Request (from client using port 2661)	TCI1

Figure 3-6: TCP/IP frame capture

As with life, using TCP has tradeoffs. A primary tradeoff from implementing TCP is that the acknowledgment process increases network traffic. Think of it as active listening in a group-counseling scenario. Each participant tells his or her story and someone in the group is responsible for repeating the information shared by the participants back to the group. If you've been in a group-counseling scenario, you know what I mean. Well, this form of acknowledgment certainly slows down the overall speed of communications but, arguably, it does increase the quality of the communication (the repetition exercise is a form of acknowledgment). Similarly, with the network, these acknowledgments (ACKs) effectively slow down the network but, of course, increase reliability.

User Datagram Protocol

Meet TCP's evil brother, who is unreliable to say the least. User Datagram Protocol (UDP), which operates at the transport layer in the DOD model as TCP does, offers connectionless-oriented service without delivery or sequencing guarantees.

UDP has long been a favorite method for transporting multimedia information such as video and sound. Think about it. If you are using CUSEEME on the Internet and an occasional frame is dropped, it's really not a big deal (it would have the effect of appearing to lower your video frame capture rate). The video might look a little bumpy but otherwise it would be fine.

However, don't despair about UDP. The application using UDP may handle the error correction and reliability issues. Thus you might achieve the best of both worlds: higher network data transfer speeds because ACKs are not required, at least as far as UDP is concerned, and high-level applications enforcing acknowledgments. An optional UDP checksum value can also validate header and data integrity.

For this checksum value setting, see the UDP Checksum field under the UDP header when viewing UDP-related packets in Network Monitor.

The default value for the UDP Checksum is 0 or not active (see Figure 3-7), as shown via the Display Filter of Network Monitor. Of course, if the checksum capability isn't implemented, it is of little use.

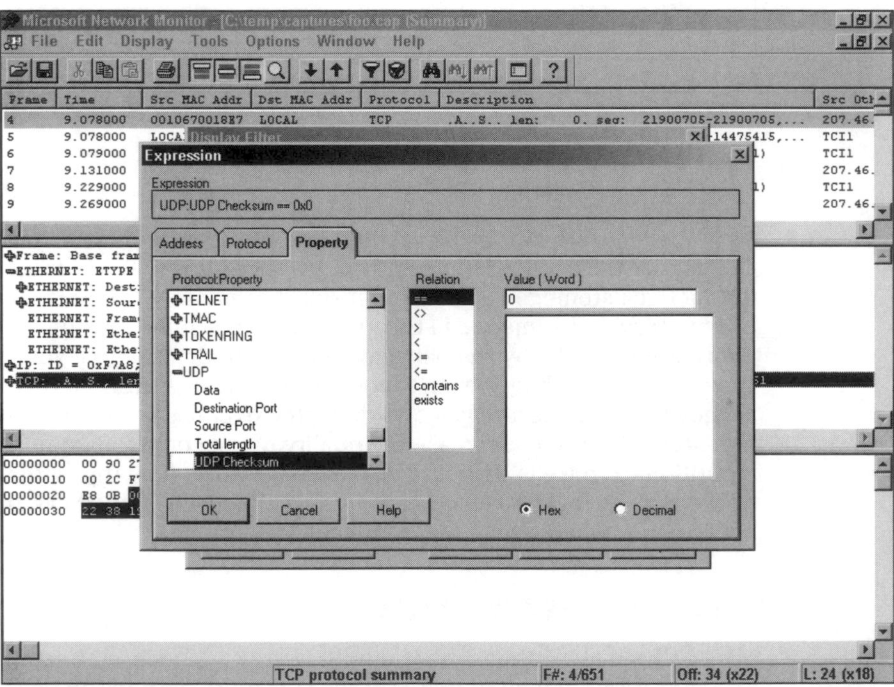

Figure 3-7: The default value for the UDP checksum

In Figure 3-8, UDP is being used and the checksum value is 0XCA58. This checksum value will vary from packet to packet — it is packet unique. A checksum may be your best ally when you attempt to debug a network communication issue surrounding UDP.

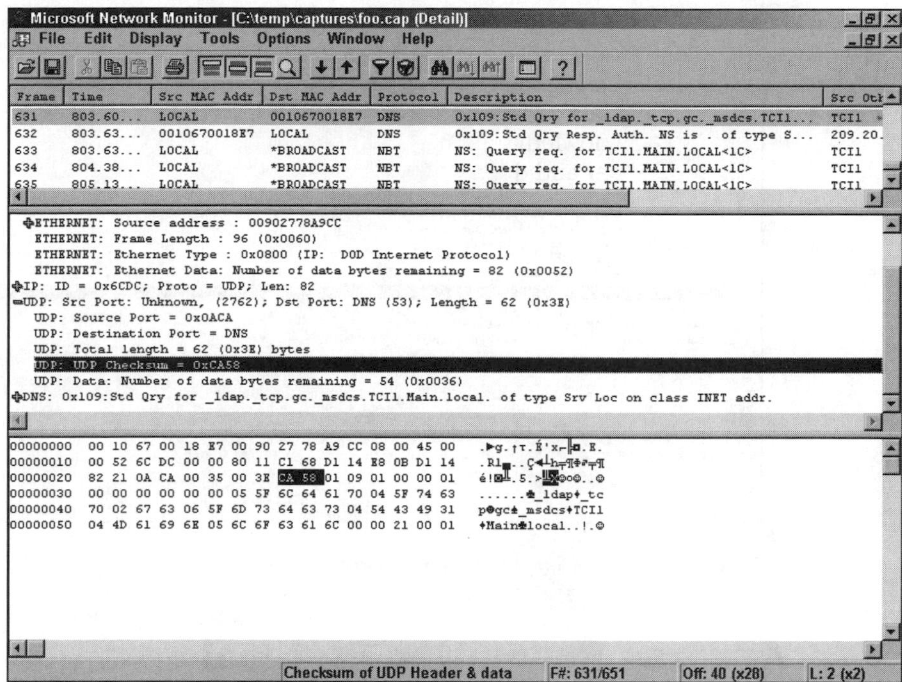

Figure 3-8: The UDP checksum value

Internet Protocol

Essentially Internet Protocol (IP) provides packet delivery for all of the other protocols within the TCP/IP protocol suite. Computer data under the auspices of IP communications is treated to a best-effort, connectionless delivery system. There is no guarantee that IP packets will arrive at their destination or in order. The checksum feature, shown in Figure 3-9 as value 0x525B, relates only to the integrity of the IP header.

So what, you ask, is the connection between IP and TCP? Well, TCP provides the guarantee; IP offers us the world in terms of addressing. IP provides the routing information necessary so that data may be passed from one host to another. IP also assists in the fragmentation and reassembly of packets. This is accomplished by imposing rules to which routers adhere.

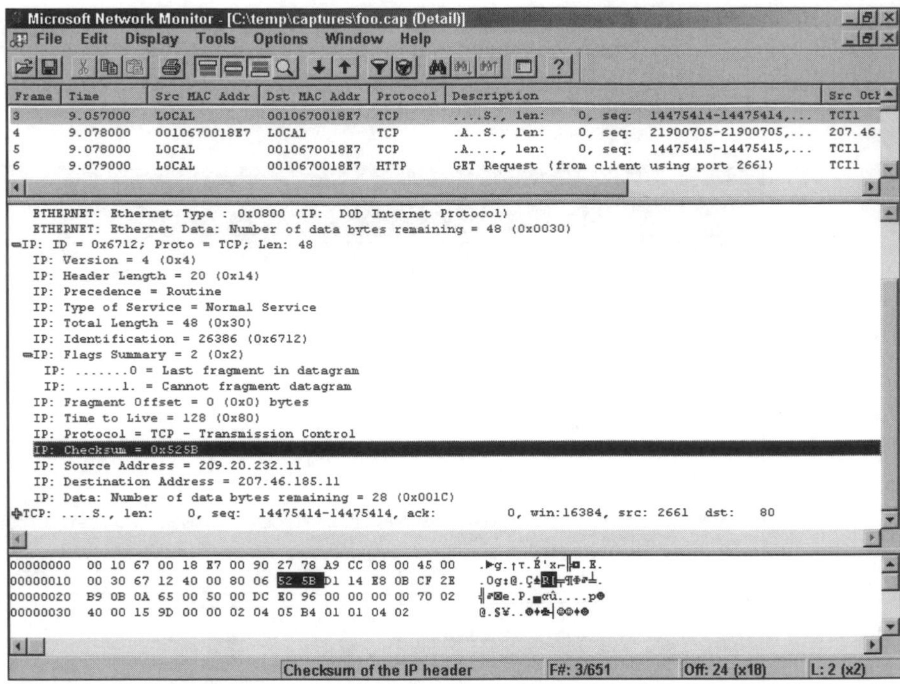

Figure 3-9: The IP section of a data packet on a network

Address Resolution Protocol

Although it is not directly tied to the transport of data and although it is not seen by users and applications, Address Resolution Protocol (ARP) can be considered a maintenance protocol that is important in its support of the TCP/IP protocol suite. Basically, the sending host must somehow map the destination IP address to its respective MAC address (physical hardware address). This is because network communications, at the physical level, look like the diagram in Figure 3-10.

The physical address is acquired by IP via the broadcast of a special inquiry packet (ARP request packet). Because it is a broadcast packet, it is evaluated by all ARP-enabled system on the local IP subnet. The node that "owns" the IP address being queried replies and reports its MAC address to the original sender in an ARP reply packet. This sequence is shown in Figure 3-11.

Frame 543 shows the initiation of the ARP polling process. Notice the Target's Hardware Address is empty but the Target's Protocol Address is displayed as 209.20.232.1. Remember that you are trying to resolve the target's hardware address to its IP address. This is the first step in that process.

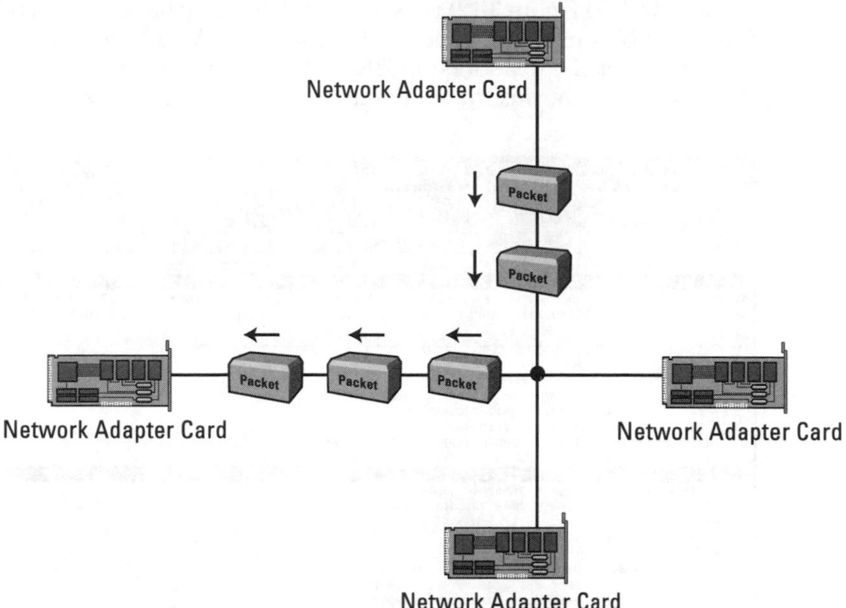

Figure 3-10: A packet traveling between network adapters

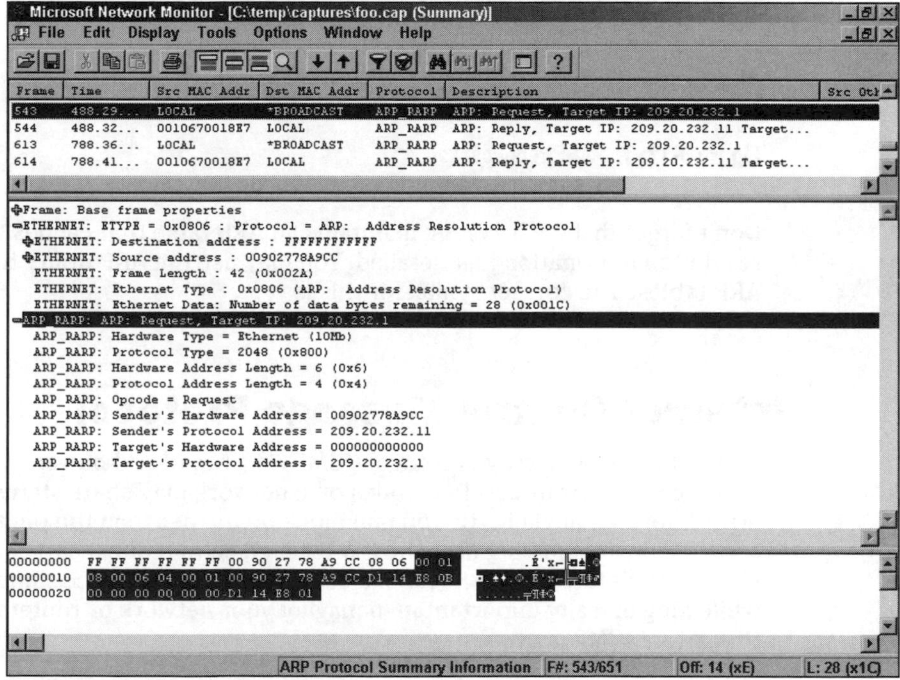

Figure 3-11: The ARP request packet

Frame 544 (see Figure 3-12) presents the ARP reply packet. Here the target of frame 543 becomes the sender and reports its MAC address as 00902778A9CC, thus resolving the IP address of 209.20.232.11. This information is returned to the computer that was the sender in frame 543 and is the target in frame 544.

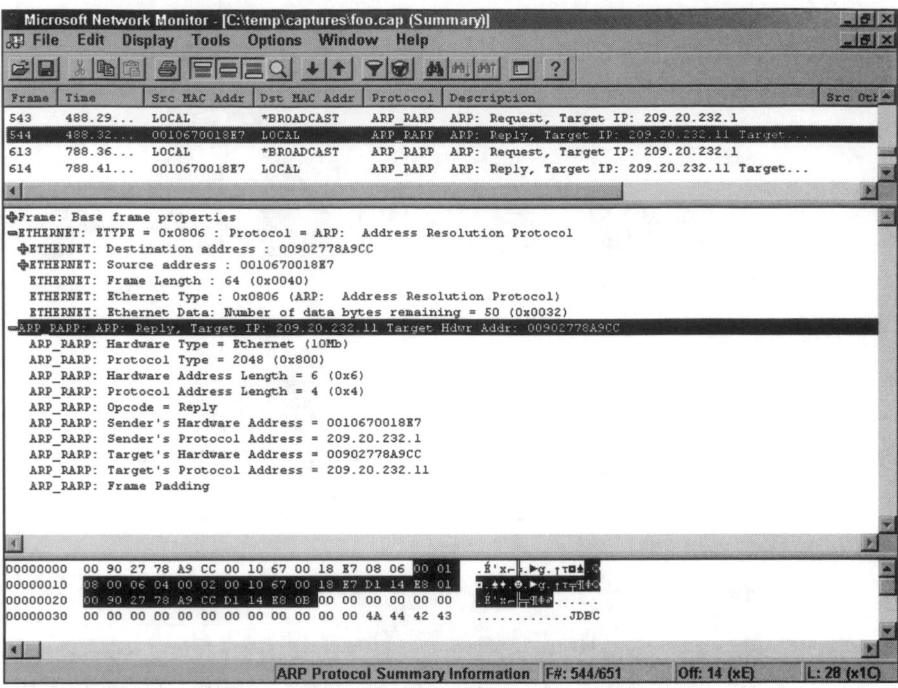

Figure 3-12: The ARP reply packet

Don't forget that each system maintains an ARP table that caches the type of resolution information just detailed. You may use the ARP utility to view the ARP tables. The correct syntax for this is:

```
C:>arp -a
```

Internet Control Message Protocol

Internet Control Message Protocol (ICMP) is a bread-and-butter "maintenance" protocol. Two nodes on a network may share status and error information via ICMP. You must look no further than the ping utility to see ICMP in action. Ping uses the ICMP-based echo request and echo reply packets to detect if a specific IP-based network node is functioning. Thus, while ping is really important in managing your network or routers, it's safe to say that ICMP is even more so.

The ICMP packet (packet 7) shown in Figure 3-13 initiates the echo command from IP address 131.107.2.214 to 131.107.2.210.

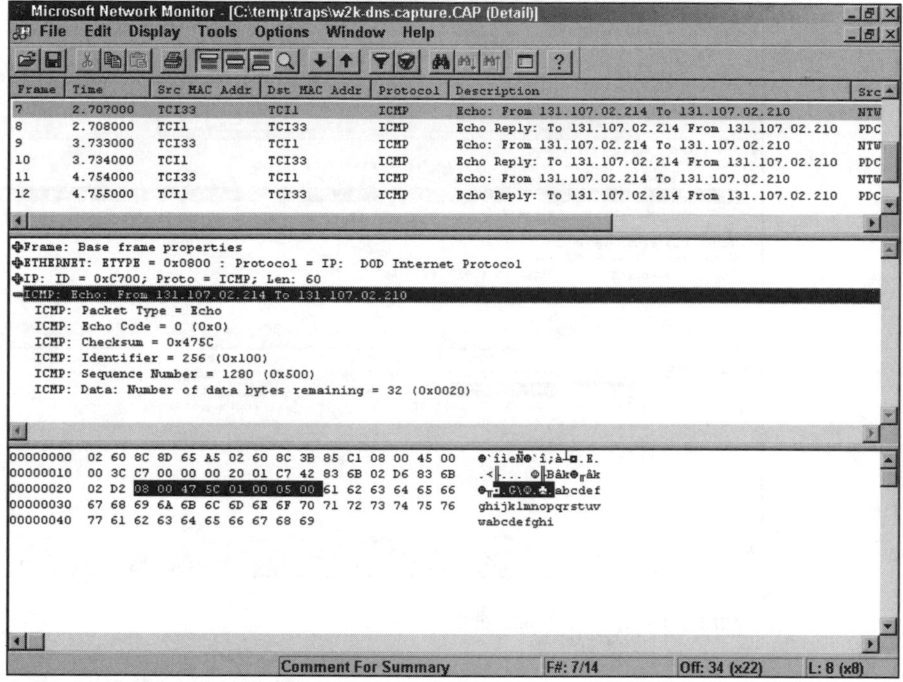

Figure 3-13: The ICMP packet 7

The ICMP packet (packet 8) shown in Figure 3-14 shows the echo reply from IP address 131.107.2.210 to 131.107.2.214.

ICMP is required in each and every IP network implementation.

Internet Group Management Protocol

Yet another maintenance protocol, Internet Group Management Protocol (IGMP) is similar to ICMP in that it provides a method that dictates how devices can share and report status information on an IP network. Interestingly, IGMP uses *multicasting* (a form of broadcasting) to communicate with all devices contained in the membership of a multicast group. This group is displayed in the Group Address field shown in Figure 3-15. Notice the Group Address option displays the NetBIOS name of all machines detected on the subnet.

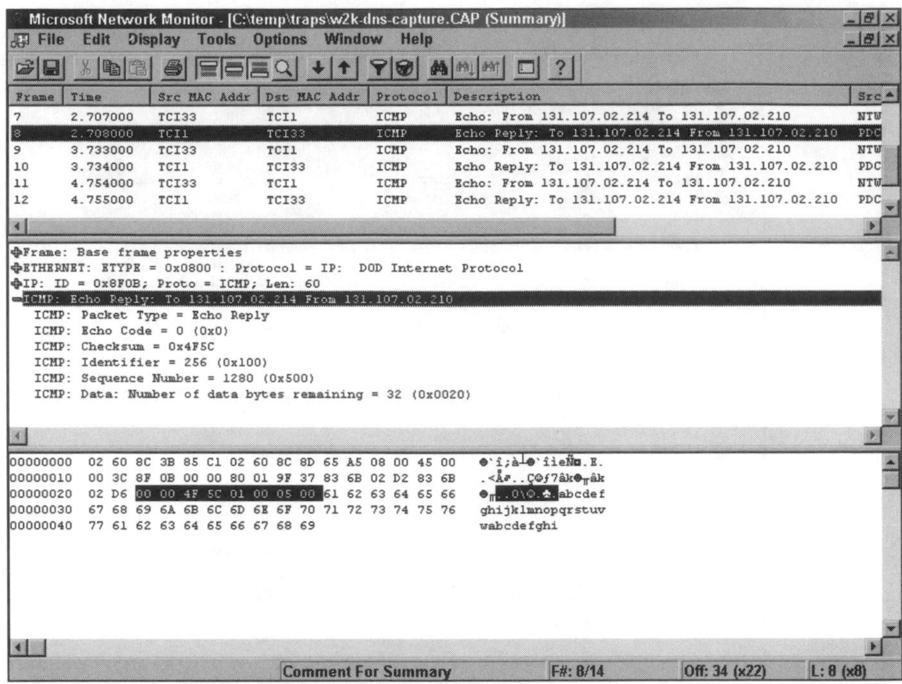

Figure 3-14: The ICMP packet 8

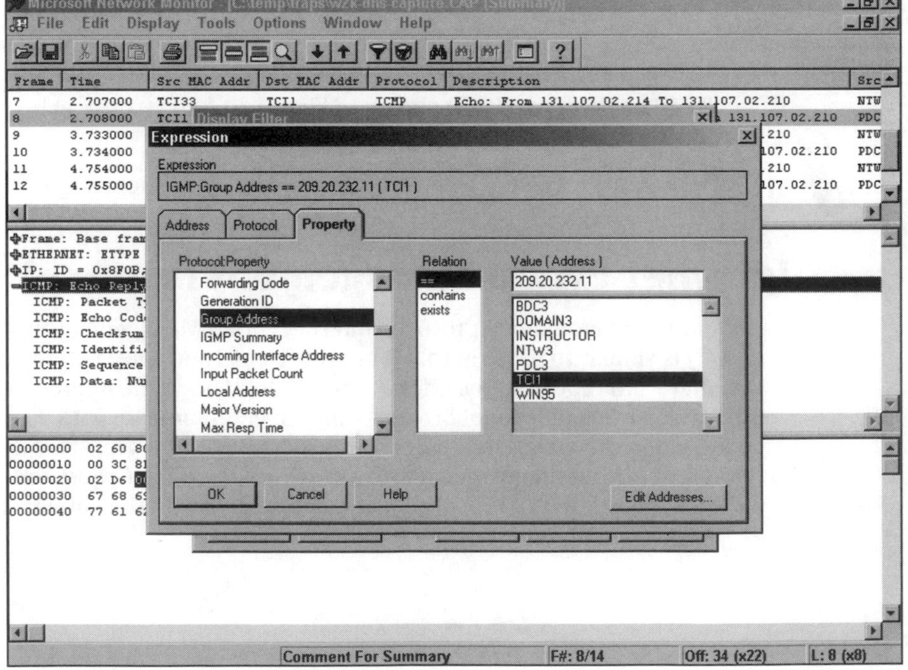

Figure 3-15: IGMP protocol properties

Your router must be configured to allow multicasting to permit IGMP-based packets to pass through.

Simple Network Management Protocol

Simple Network Management Protocol (SNMP) is a management protocol that facilitates the exchange of information from SNMP devices on the network. Routers, hubs, and bridges can all be SNMP devices, depending on the device you use.

Be careful about paying the SNMP tax unless you really need this functionality. The SNMP tax is the incremental cash outlay you will incur to purchase a device that is SNMP-enabled rather than one that is not. A perfect example is a DSU. Here the SNMP tax can amount to several hundred dollars or more depending on the DSU model. Note that Windows 2000 Server has limited SNMP management capabilities that are available via Management Information File (MIF) interpretation in System Management Server (SMS), a Microsoft BackOffice component. You will typically use a specific SNMP management device, such as a high-end HP Open View–based solution.

What Is the Microsoft TCP/IP Protocol Suite in Windows 2000 Server?

Earlier I said that even Microsoft missed the early signs of the TCP/IP revolution. This is true. Those of us who rushed out to purchase and install Windows NT Advanced Server 3.1 will recall that the default protocol was NetBEUI. This changed with the Windows NT Server 3.5*x* releases; first IPX and then TCP/IP became the default protocol for Windows NT Server. As many say about Microsoft, they got it right on the third try.

Another sign of Microsoft's late arrival to the TCP/IP party was that it had zero presence in the early days of the commerce use of the Internet. Early arrivals to the Internet were using such things as FTP, Gopher, and Mosaic browsers. Microsoft didn't have a contribution until Pearl Harbor Day 1995 when Bill Gates issued an internal memo proclaiming Microsoft the new Internet company. And they haven't missed a beat since then. In fact, as you shall see, the TCP/IP protocol suite included with Windows 2000 Server includes several features that improve both its performance and its reliability.

Specifically, the TCP/IP protocol stack included with Windows 2000 Server has the following features:

- **Core TCP/IP.** Support for core TCP/IP protocols, including TCP, IP, User Datagram Protocol (UDP), Address Resolution Protocol (ARP), and Internet Control Message Protocol (ICMP). This TCP/IP protocol suite implementation dictates how computers communicate and how networks interconnect.

- **Network programming support.** Support for network programming interfaces such as Windows Sockets, remote procedure calls (RPC), NetBIOS, and network dynamic data exchange (Net DDE).
- **TCP/IP connectivity utilities.** Basic connectivity utilities found in Microsoft's TCP/IP protocol suite that enable Windows 2000 users to interact with different systems such as UNIX.
- **LPR.** "Server" side of TCP/IP printing for UNIX clients. Prints a file to a host running the Lpdsvc service. Note that "lpd" is line printer daemon in the UNIX community.
- **FINGER.** Can obtain system information from a remote computer that supports the TCP/IP Finger server.
- **FTP.** Enables the bidirectional transfer of files between a Windows 2000 computer and another host running FTP server software.
- **RCP.** Remote Copy Protocol. Copies files between a Windows 2000 computer and a host server running the RCP service (which is a UNIX utility).
- **REXEC.** Remote Execution. Runs a process on a remote computer.
- **RSH.** Remote Shell. Runs commands on a server running the RSH service (which is a UNIX utility).
- **Telnet.** Provides terminal emulation to a TCP/IP host running Telnet server software.

Tip

Telnet is your best friend in the TCP/IP world when working with WANs. There is perhaps no better test than to Telnet into a distant server and check e-mail. Telnet is a better test than a simple ping because Telnet runs more as an application. For example, just because you can ping a distant location doesn't mean that you can Telnet into the site. As you will discover, Telnet is incredibly valuable for managing your routers and DSUs.

- **Tftp.** Provides bidirectional file transfers between a Windows 2000 computer and a TCP/IP host running TFTP server software. Communicates via messaging using UDP instead of TCP.
- **Diagnostic utilities.** TCP/IP diagnostic utilities to detect, resolve, and prevent TCP/IP networking problems.
- **ARP.** Resolves hardware or MAC addresses to IP addresses.
- **Hostname.** Returns the computer host name for authentication by the RCP, RSH, and REXEC utilities.
- **IPConfig.** Similar to winipcfg in Windows 95/98 but, quite frankly, not as robust. Part of the problem is that IPConfig is still character-based and its reports are somewhat limited. By contrast, winipcfg is GUI-based and more pleasant to work with.
- **Lpq.** Obtains the status of a print queue on a host running LPD service.

- **Nbtstat.** Returns a list of NetBIOS computer names that have been resolved to IP addresses.
- **Netstat.** Returns TCP/IP protocol session information.
- **Ping.** Tests connectivity and verifies configurations.
- **Route.** Modifies or returns the local routing table.

Route can be used to set up a static route. A static route is extremely valuable in certain conditions. If you work with multiple subnets and multiple routers, it's likely you will learn this command.

- **Tracert.** Displays the path taken by a packet to its destination host. Here again, you will use this utility extensively in your TCP/IP travels. Tracert is frequently employed when resolving possible WAN failures or router configuration errors.
- **Internet support.** Support for Internet, internet, and intranet-based computers. This support includes:
  - **Internet Information Server.** Used for Web publishing and administration
  - **Dynamic Host Configuration Protocol (DHCP).** Used for automatically configuring TCP/IP network nodes
  - **Windows Internet Naming Service (WINS).** Used for dynamically registering and querying NetBIOS computer names
  - **Domain Name System (DNS).** Service used for registering and querying DNS domain names
  - **TCP/IP printing.** Used for accessing UNIX-defined printers or network printers directly connected via a network adapter card (such as HP's JetDirect card, which now uses TCP/IP printing; as an aside, HP's JetDirect card used the DLC protocol almost exclusively back in the "old days.")

A common mistake Window 2000 Server newbies make is to overload the services required to effectively manage and optimize their network. TCP/IP printing services are often loaded without any reason. I suspect this occurs during setup because they look like the kind of services one should "just load." Know your services and don't overload your Windows 2000 Server unnecessarily.

  - **Simple Network Management Protocol (SNMP) agent.** Remote management of your Windows 2000 computer is possible by loading this service and using a management tool such as HP Open View. SNMP support is also included for DHCP and WINS servers with Microsoft's TCP/IP protocol stack.
  - **Simple Protocols.** Simple protocols to respond to simple requests — Microsoft's TCP/IP protocol suite enables Windows 2000 to respond to computers that request and support the following: Character Generator, Daytime, Discard, Echo, and Quote of the Day.

- **Path MTU Discovery.** Provides the capability to determine the datagram size for all routers between Windows 2000–based computers and other computers on the WAN.
- **Internet Group Management Protocol (IGMP).** Microsoft TCP/IP supports IGMP. It is typically used by workgroup software products at the upper layers of the OSI model.

Many of these TCP/IP utilities and commands are discussed at length in Chapter 5.

The TCP/IP Settings in Windows 2000 Server

Where are the Windows 2000 TCP/IP settings stored? In the Windows 2000 Registry, of course! Typically modified via GUI-based applications such as the Local Area Connection Properties property sheet — General tab sheet, basic TCP/IP configuration parameters are fairly straightforward. However, what about modifying parameters such as Time to Live (TTL)? The TTL value is either 128 seconds or 128 hops, depending on which comes first (see Figure 3-16). It is effectively the number of routers that a packet may pass through before being discarded.

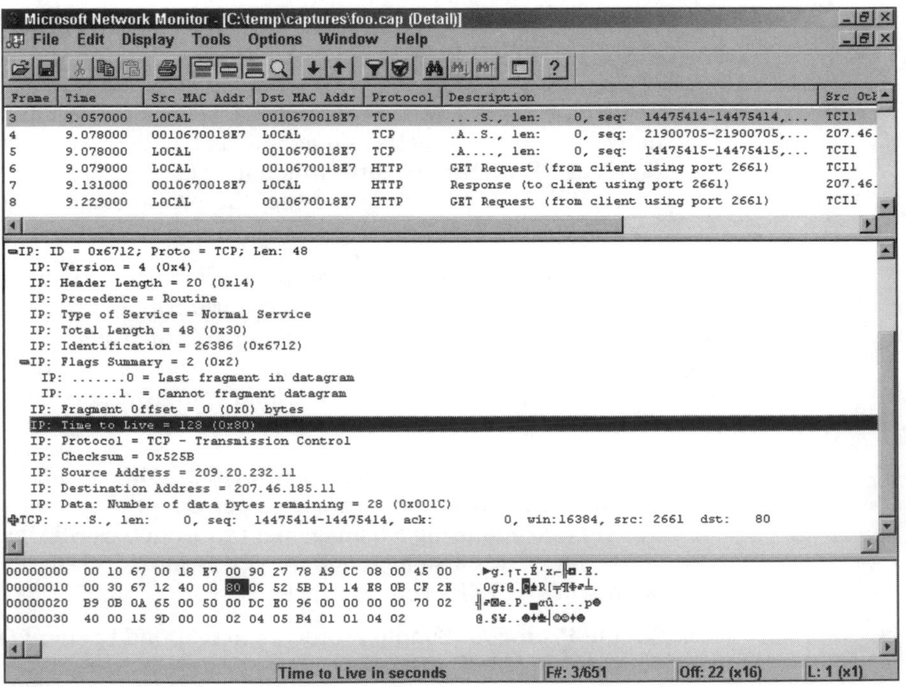

Figure 3-16: The TTL value

Many TCP/IP parameters may only be modified via the Registry. Quite frankly, most TCP/IP parameters are configured under the Parameters key found via `HKEY_LOCAL_MACHINE\SYSTEM\CurrentControlSet\Services\Tcpip`. The Parameters subkey (see Figure 3-17) houses most of the important TCP/IP configuration parameters that you should be concerned with.

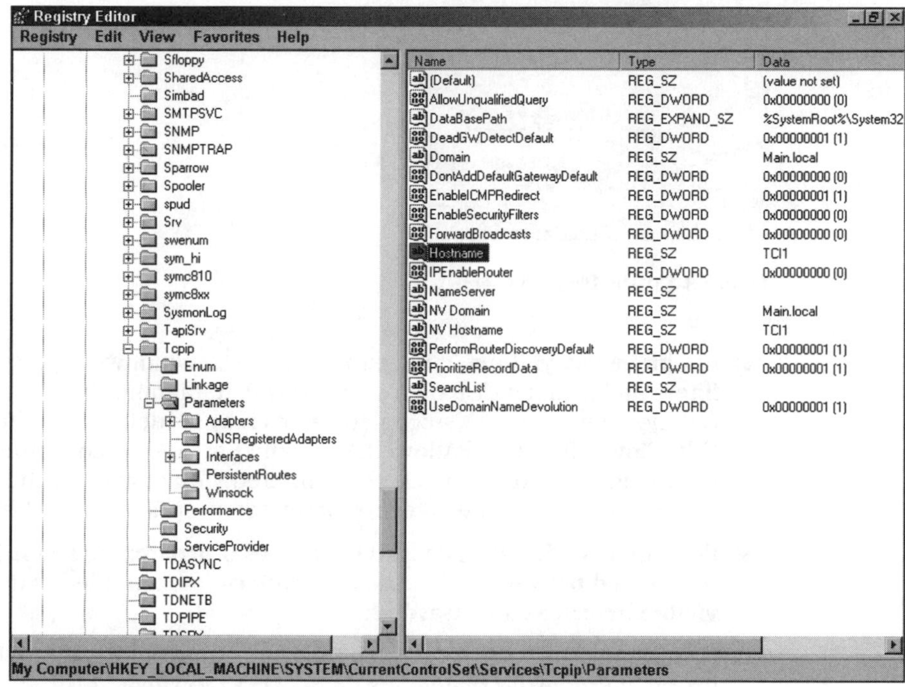

Figure 3-17: The Parameters subkey

Here are important existing values within the Parameters subkey:

- **DataBasePath. Used by the Windows Sockets interface, it specifies the path to such standard Internet database files as HOSTS, LMHOSTS, networks, and protocols.**
- **Domain. The domain entry you make in the TCP/IP Protocol Properties dialog box on the DNS tab sheet (see Figure 3-18). This value is used by the Windows Socket interface. The Domain is the name of the Internet domain that your computer belongs to. As you know, a domain is nothing more than a group name that has computers associated with it.**

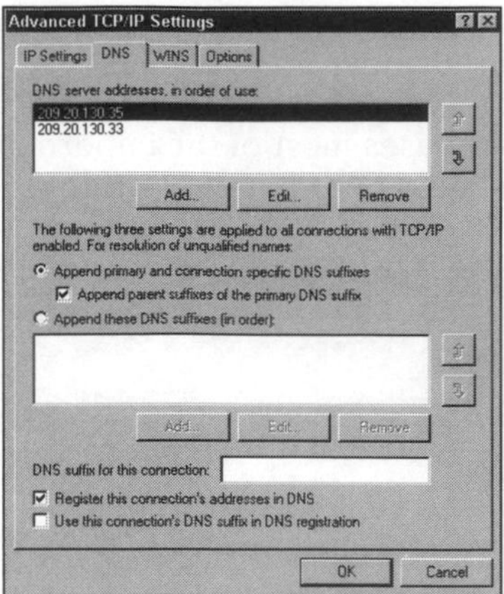

Figure 3-18: The DNS tab sheet

- **EnableSecurityFilters.** If the entry value is 1, Windows 2000 Server filters all incoming UDP datagrams, raw IP datagrams, and TCP SYNs (connection requests). Accepted values may be defined via these keys: UdpAllowedPorts, TCPAllowedPorts, and RawIpAllowedProtocols. Interestingly, incoming packets are filtered with respect to the local computers. Packets destined for other computers are not filtered.
- **ForwardBroadcasts. Entry that specifies if broadcasts should be forwarded between two or more adapters. The enabled state has visible broadcasts forwarded.**
- **Hostname.** The name entered in the Host Name field in the TCP/IP Protocol Properties dialog box on the DNS tab sheet. It is the DNS host name of the system. Whenever a Windows Sockets application issues the hostname command, this name is returned.
- **IPEnableRouter. A value of 1 indicates that the system can route IP packets between the networks it is connected to. Packets are not routed if the value is 0.**
- **NameServer. Lists the DNS servers that will resolve names when queried by Windows Sockets.**

Secret

This value overrides the value in the DhcpNameServer value field (a value supplied to DHCP clients via a scope).

- **SearchList. Lists domain name suffixes to try when an unsuffixed name cannot be resolved by using DNS. This information is used by the Windows Sockets interface.**
- **Adding Registry Values.** Other values that you may add to `HKEY_LOCAL_MACHINE\SYSTEM\CurrentControlSet\Services\Tcpip\Parameters` are:

- **ArpCacheLife.** Specifies how long entries will remain in the ARP cache table. An entry remains in the ARP table until it expires or until the table entry is reused.
- **DefaultTTL.** The default Time to Live (TTL) value found in the header of outgoing IP packets. TTL is the number of seconds that an IP packet can live on a network without reaching its destination.
- **KeepAliveInterval.** Calculates the interval between keep-alive retransmissions until a response is received. Basically calculates the wait until the next keep-alive transmission. After the number of transmissions specified in TcpMaxDataRetransmissions are unanswered, the connection aborts.
- **KeepAliveTime.** Specifies the interval that TCP sends a keep-alive packet to verify a connect is still intact.
- **TcpMaxConnectRetransmissions.** The number of times TCP retransmits a connect request before aborting its attempts. Interestingly, this value is doubled with each attempt from its default of three seconds.
- **TcpMaxDataRetransmissions.** The number of times a data segment will be retransmitted by TCP before aborting.
- **TcpNumConnections.** The maximum number of open TCP connections that can occur simultaneously.
- **TcpTimedWaitDelay.** Determines how long a connection stays in a wait state, known as TIME_WAIT, before being closed.
- **TcpUseRFC1122UrgentPointer.** Defines how TCP defines urgent. "1" is based on RFC 1122. "0" or no entry in the Registry uses the "mode" from Berkeley-derived BSD systems.

A Day in the Life of a TCP/IP Packet

Remember the famous photo essay book *A Day in the Life of America*, which showed a snapshot of life in America? It was interesting and introspective. I thought you might enjoy getting into the details of a day in the life of a packet in a similar manner. As stated in RFC 791, which relates to the IP portion of the packet:

> The implementation of a protocol must be robust. Each implementation must expect to interoperate with others created by different individuals. While the goal of this specification is to be explicit about the protocol, there is the possibility of differing interpretations. In general, an implementation must be conservative in its sending behavior, and liberal in its receiving behavior. That is, it must be careful to send well-formed datagrams, but must accept any datagram that it can interpret.

When you get down to packet analysis, you are often left thinking that it's amazing this stuff works as well as it does. That said, many have asked over the years—just how do you read a TCP/IP packet? Well, this is how you do it!

IP

First, examine the IP portion of the TCP/IP network packet because it comes first in the packet (see Figure 3-19).

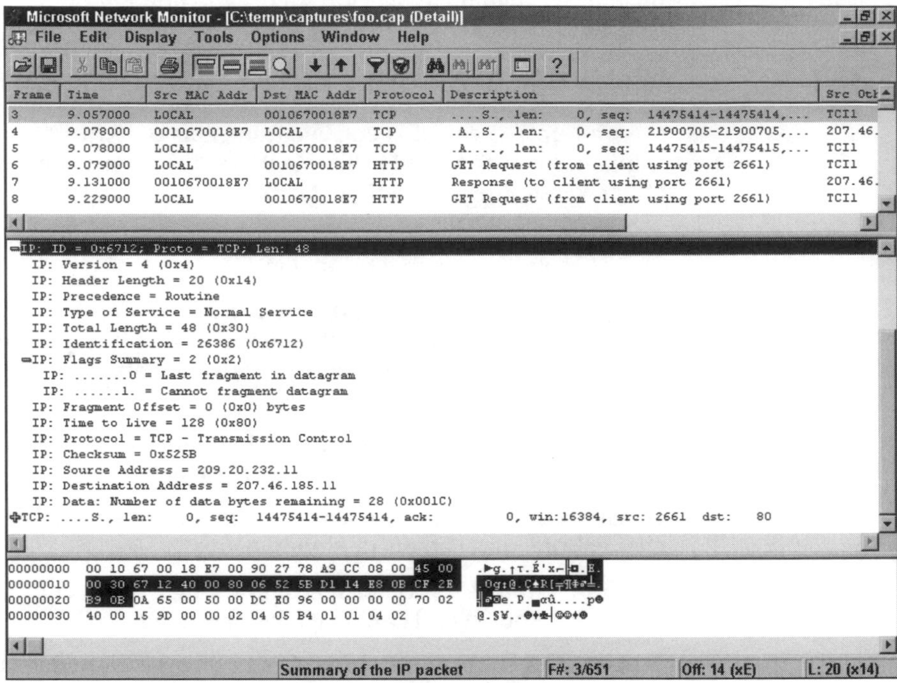

Figure 3-19: The IP portion of a TCP/IP network packet

As you will discover, by breaking down the IP portion into its discrete components, the analysis is actually easier than it looks. Contrast that to looking at the packet as a whole. That view can be a little overwhelming. The following list starts with the version setting.

- **Version: 4 bits.** The Version field indicates the format of the internet header. As you can see in Figure 3-19, this is Version 4.
- **Internet Header Length (IHL): 4 bits.** Internet Header Length is the length of the internet header in 32-bit words and it points to the beginning of the data. The minimum value for a correct header is 5.
- **Type of Service: 8 bits.** The Type of Service provides an indication of the abstract parameters of the quality of service desired. These parameters are used to guide the selection of the actual service parameters when transmitting a datagram through a particular network. Several networks offer service precedence, which treats high-precedence traffic as more important than other traffic (generally by accepting only traffic above a

certain precedence at times of high load). An example of this might be some of the newer networking technologies, such as ATM, that enable you to set priorities for different traffic. With ATM, the major choice is a three-way tradeoff among low delay, high reliability, and high throughput.

The information in Table 3-2 is shown as subcategories underneath the IP:Service Type = 0 (0X0) field.

Table 3-2 IP Service Type Information

Bit	*Description*
Bits 0–2:	Precedence
Bit 3:	0 = normal delay; 1 = low delay
Bits 4:	0 = normal throughput; 1 = high throughput
Bits 5:	0 = normal reliability; 1 = high reliability
Bits 6–7:	Reserved for future use

The use of the delay, throughput, and reliability indications may increase the cost (in some sense) of the service. In many networks, better performance for one of these parameters is coupled with worse performance for another.

- **Precedence.** The type of service is used to specify the treatment of the datagram during its transmission through the internet system. Example mappings of the Internet type of service to the actual service provided on networks such as AUTODIN II, ARPANET, SATNET, and PRNET are given in "Service Mappings." The sample packet in Figure 3-19 shows "Routine." Table 3-3 provides the list of precedence options.

Table 3-3 Precedence Values

Value	*Description*
111	Network Control
110	Internetwork Control
101	CRITIC/ECP
100	Flash Override
011	Flash
010	Immediate
001	Priority
000	Routine

The Network Control precedence designation is intended only for use within a network. The actual use and control of that designation is up to each network. The Internetwork Control designation is intended only for use by gateway control originators. If the actual use of these precedence designations is of concern to a particular network, it is the responsibility of that network to control the access to, and use of, those precedence designations.

- **Total Length: 16 bits.** Total Length is the length of the datagram, measured in octets, including internet header and data. This field allows the length of a datagram to be up to 65,535 octets. Such long datagrams are impractical for most hosts and networks. All hosts must be prepared to accept datagrams of up to 576 octets, whether they arrive whole or in fragments. It is recommended that hosts only send datagrams larger than 576 octets if they have assurance that the destination is prepared to accept the larger datagrams.

  The number 576 has been selected so that a reasonable-sized data block can be transmitted in addition to the required header information. For example, this size permits a data block of 512 octets plus a 64-octet header to fit in a datagram. The maximal internet header is 60 octets, and a typical internet header is 20 octets; this provides a margin for headers of higher-level protocols.

- **Identification: 16 bits.** This is an identifying value assigned by the sender to aid in assembling the fragments of a datagram.
- **Flags: 3 bits.** In our same packet, the settings are "Last fragment in datagram" and "Cannot fragment datagram." Here are the possible flag settings:
  - Bit 0–5: reserved; must be zero
  - Bit 6: (DF) 0 = May Fragment; 1 = Don't Fragment
  - Bit 7: (MF) 0 = Last Fragment; 1 = More Fragments
- **Fragment Offset: 13 bits.** This field indicates where in the datagram this fragment belongs. The fragment offset is measured in units of eight octets (64 bits). The first fragment has offset zero.
- **Time to Live: 8 bits.** This field indicates the maximum time the datagram is permitted to remain in the internet system. If this field contains the value zero, then the datagram must be destroyed. This field is modified in internet header processing. The time is measured in units of seconds, but given that every module that processes a datagram must decrease the TTL by at least one (even if it processes the datagram in less than a second), the TTL must be thought of only as an upper bound on the time a datagram may exist. The intention is to cause undeliverable datagrams to be discarded, and to bound the maximum datagram lifetime.
- **Protocol: 8 bits.** This field indicates the next-level protocol used in the data portion of the internet datagram.

- **Header Checksum: 16 bits.** This is a checksum on the header only. Because some header fields change (as does Time to Live), the header checksum is recomputed and verified at each point that the internet header is processed.

  The checksum algorithm is: *The checksum field is the 16-bit ones complement of the ones complement sum of all 16-bit words in the header.* In English, it's a calculated value similar to a cyclical redundancy check to ensure that the data packet has "integrity."
- **Source Address: 32 bits.** This is the source address.
- **Destination Address: 32 bits.** This is the destination address.
- **Options: variable.** The options may appear or may not appear in datagrams. As you can see, none appear in our sample data packet. They must be implemented by all IP modules (host and gateways). What is optional is their transmission in any particular datagram, not their implementation.
- **Padding: variable.** The internet header padding is used to ensure that the internet header ends on a 32-bit boundary. The padding is zero.

And with that, give yourself a round of applause as you've reached the end of the detailed IP packet discussion. Now, onward to TCP.

TCP

It's time for the details about TCP. TCP is that part of the TCP/IP protocol suite that resides in the middle OSI layers. Its primary responsibilities include assuring reliable delivery by maintaining a connection-oriented session between sender and receiver (see Figure 3-20).

This list, which breaks down the TCP portion of a packet, starts with the source setting.

- **Source Port: 16 bits.** The source port number is the port value of the sender.
- **Destination Port: 16 bits.** The destination port number is the port value of the receiver.
- **Sequence Number: 32 bits.** This is the sequence number of the first data octet in this segment (except when SYN is present). If SYN is present, the sequence number is the initial sequence number (ISN) and the first data octet is ISN + 1.
- **Acknowledgment Number: 32 bits.** If the ACK control bit is set, this field contains the value of the next sequence number the sender of the segment is expecting to receive. Once a connection is established, this is always sent.

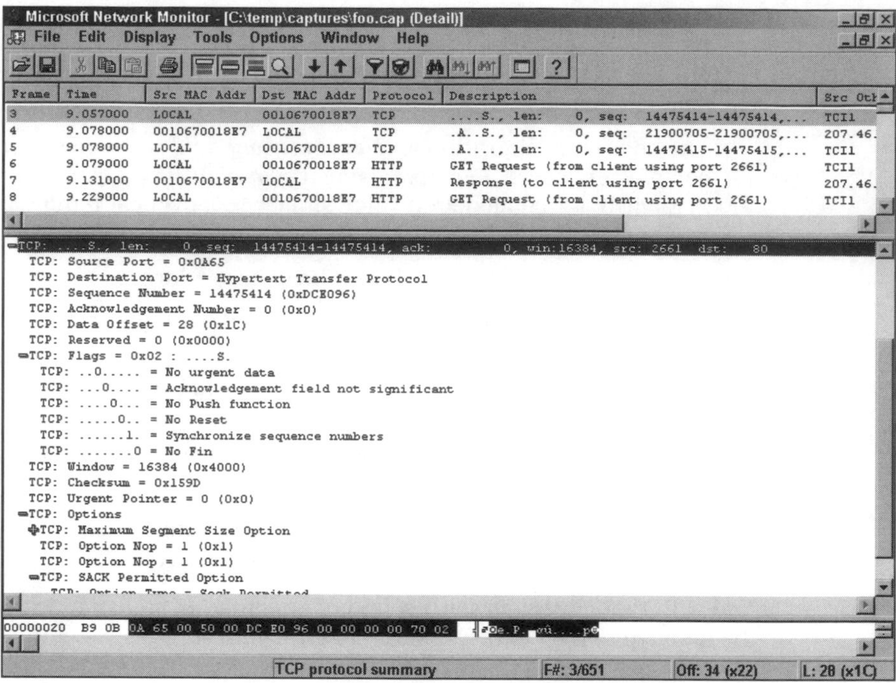

Figure 3-20: The TCP portion of our sample data frame

- **Data Offset: 4 bits.** This is the number of 32-bit words in the TCP header. This indicates where the data begins. The TCP header (even one including options) is an integral number 32 bits long.
- **Reserved: 6 bits.** Reserved for future use, this must be zero. This is exactly the type of field that a software developer, seeking an edge for its technology, might use to fundamentally modify TCP for its own purposes.
- **Flags: 6 bits (from left to right).** This is officially known as Control Bits in RFC 791. This list starts with the Urgent pointer field and ends with a No more data from sender setting:
  - URG: Urgent Pointer field significant
  - ACK: Acknowledgment field significant
  - PSH: Push function
  - RST: Reset the connection
  - SYN: Synchronize sequence numbers
  - FIN: No more data from sender

Our sample data packet in Figure 3-20 has these settings:

- No urgent data
- Acknowledgement field significant
- No Push function
- No Reset
- No Synchronize sequence numbers
- No Fin

- **Window: 16 bits.** This is the number of data octets beginning with the one indicated in the acknowledgment field that the sender of this segment is willing to accept.
- **Checksum: 16 bits.** The checksum field is the 16-bit ones complement of the ones complement sum of all 16-bit words in the header and text. If a segment contains an odd number of header and text octets to be checksummed, the last octet is padded on the right with zeros to form a 16-bit word for checksum purposes. The pad is not transmitted as part of the segment. While computing the checksum, the checksum field itself is replaced with zeros.

  The checksum also covers a 96-bit pseudoheader conceptually prefixed to the TCP header. This pseudoheader contains the Source Address, the Destination Address, the Protocol, and the TCP length. This gives the TCP protection against misrouted segments. This information is carried in the Internet Protocol and is transferred across the TCP/Network interface in arguments or results of calls by the TCP on the IP.
- **Urgent Pointer: 16 bits.** This field communicates the current value of the urgent pointer as a positive offset from the sequence number in this segment. The urgent pointer points to the sequence number of the octet following the urgent data. This field is only interpreted in segments with the URG (urgent) control bit set.
- **Options: variable.** Options may occupy space at the end of the TCP header and are a multiple of eight bits in length. All options are included in the checksum. An option may begin on any octet boundary. There are two cases for the format of an option:
  - **Case 1. A single octet of option-kind**
  - **Case 2. An octet of option-kind, an octet of option-length, and the actual option-data octets**

  The option-length counts the two octets of option-kind and option-length as well as the option-data octets. Note that the list of options may be shorter than the data offset field might imply. The content of the header beyond End of Option must be header padding (that is, zero).

  When adhering to strict RFC, TCP must implement all options. When not adhering to the RFC, software developers may elect not to implement all TCP options. Currently defined options are included in Table 3-4 (the Kind column is indicated in octal).

Table 3-4 TCP Options

Kind	*Length*	*Meaning*
0		End of Option List
1		No-Operation
2	4	Maximum Segment Size

Here are the specific option definitions for Table 3-4 to assist you in understanding each possible selection:

- Kind = 0 "End of Option List." This option code indicates the end of the option list. This might not coincide with the end of the TCP header according to the Data Offset field. This is used at the end of all options — not the end of each option — and need only be used if the end of the options will not otherwise coincide with the end of the TCP header.
- Kind = 1 "No-Operation." This option code may be used between options; for example, it may be used to align the beginning of a subsequent option on a word boundary. There is no guarantee that senders will use this option, so receivers must be prepared to process options even if they do not begin on a word boundary.
- Kind = 2 Length = 4 "Maximum Segment Size." Maximum Segment Size Option Data: 16 bits. If this option is present, then it communicates the maximum receive segment size at the TCP that sends this segment. This field must only be sent in the initial connection request (that is, in segments with the SYN control bit set). If this option is not used, any segment size is permitted.

- **Padding: variable.** The TCP header padding is used to ensure that the TCP header ends and data begins on a 32-bit boundary. The padding is composed of zeros.

Give yourself another round of applause. You've completed the detailed TCP discussion. Whew!

Internetworking with TCP/IP

TCP/IP is especially well suited to take advantage of the Windows 2000 Server paradigm — that is, that Windows 2000 Server is the digital nervous system for an enterprise. Because of its scalability, TCP/IP is an easily a solution for a peer-to-peer network or a global-wide area network for a Fortune 500 corporation.

Out of the box, Microsoft has released its TCP/IP stack for:

- Windows 2000 family (Server, Professional, et. al.)
- Windows NT Server family (3*x*, 4*x*)
- Windows NT Workstation family (3*x*, 4*x*)
- Microsoft TCP/IP-32 for Windows for Workgroups
- Microsoft LAN Manager

Breeder networks

One thing you can count on today in the networking profession is subnet proliferation once you deploy a networking solution in your organization. Inevitably, you will find your company opening a new branch office that must be connected to the central site. In many cases, you will eat or be eaten by a rival. Whatever the circumstance may be, you're bound to see your network group (or breed) once deployed. Plan for this in advance, even when it seems like the remotest of possibilities.

Heterogeneous networks

Perhaps the coolest thing about TCP/IP is its capability to communicate with foreign hosts in a way that no other protocol I'm aware of can. These foreign hosts include:

- Host systems on the Internet
- Unix-based host systems
- Macintoshes running TCP/IP protocol stacks such as MacTCP

Note that an Apple Macintosh can communicate and interact with a Windows 2000 server if Services for Macintosh are installed on an NTFS partition. In this scenario, the Macintosh and Windows 2000 server would be running AppleTalk as the common transport protocol.

- IBM-based mainframes
- Open VMS systems
- Printers with network adapters cards such as the HP JetDirect card

Although TCP/IP is obviously the preferred and recommended transport protocol, don't forget that other transport protocols are supported that allow Windows 2000 Server to be a good citizen on diverse and heterogeneous networks:

- IPX/SPX
- NetBEUI
- AppleTalk
- Third-party protocol stacks such as DECnet are supported

Windows Sockets

Just as Microsoft has selected TCP/IP as its default protocol to ensure wide support and acceptance in the networking community, the Windows Sockets applications programming interface (API) exists to provide a standard framework for developing applications. No doubt this API-based standard framework is provided to enable third-party developers to write network-based applications that will run well on Microsoft-based networks using Microsoft's TCP/IP protocol stack. And thank god for that. Could you imagine the state of affairs on Windows 2000 Server-based networks if such an API weren't provided for developers to hook into underlying services? It wouldn't be pleasant, to say the least.

So what exactly is WinSock, as the Windows Socket API is called? If you were on the proverbial 90-second elevator ride and had to explain it to a layperson, well... you couldn't. But this said, Microsoft refers to it as "... an interface and a communications infrastructure... not a protocol." Technically, it is an open specification derived from Berkeley Software Distribution (BSD) Unix 4.3 sockets API for TCP/IP. Starting with the original WinSock 1.1 specification, which was created in early 1993, WinSock has now matured to Version 2.0 and is now known as WinSock2. WinSock2 was originally introduced in late 1995 and shipped with Windows NT Server4.0. It is the version that ships with Windows 2000 Server. WinSock2 is completely backward compatible with applications developed under previous WinSock specifications.

Beyond providing robust backward compatibility, WinSock2 introduced:

- **Better performance capabilities. Underlying architectural changes to WinSock2 have taken the original WinSock subsystem and divided it into two layers. One layer is the DLLs providing the Windows Sockets APIs. The second layer is the service providers residing below the DLLs — these interact with upper-layer services via the Service Provider Interface (SPI).**
- **Name resolution. Basically, developers can write applications that access directory services such as Active Directory, DNS, NDS from Novell, and X.500.**
- **Concurrent access to multiple network transports. By writing to the SPI, developers can write once and use twice. That is, an application can use both TCP/IP and IPX/SPX under WinSock2.**

Third-party TCP/IP software support

Obviously, TCP/IP as an entity doesn't live in a static vacuum. In fact, just the opposite is the case. The design goals from the founding fathers of TCP/IP were to create an open and extensible protocol suite for use by the masses. That key tenet has not only resulted in the widespread acceptance of TCP/IP but has also spurred tremendous advances in TCP/IP tools, applications, and utilities. Developers, knowing that no one company explicitly owns TCP/IP, are emboldened to devote their best and brightest development resources on projects that extend the features, functionality, and manageability of TCP/IP.

In this section, I profile a few third-party solutions that extend TCP/IP beyond its native capabilities in Windows 2000 Server.

It's a fact: Even in Windows 2000 Server, Microsoft's TCP/IP protocol suite is incomplete and lacks certain connectivity utilities and server services (daemons) that are supplied by third-party software vendors, such as NetManage with its Chameleon TCP/IP protocol stack product line. One such service that is lacking is support for NFS or Network File System. In order to communicate with a Sun workstation and a computer running Windows 2000 (either Server or Professional), you must have NFS — Network File System — connectivity between the two dissimilar systems (otherwise you're doomed to ping or Telnet connectivity).

NetManage's Chameleon ViewNow NFS Client (see Figure 3-21) provides NFS-based connectivity between Unix systems and Windows 2000. NetManage is well known in particular for developing applications that are very robust and for fast NFS clients.

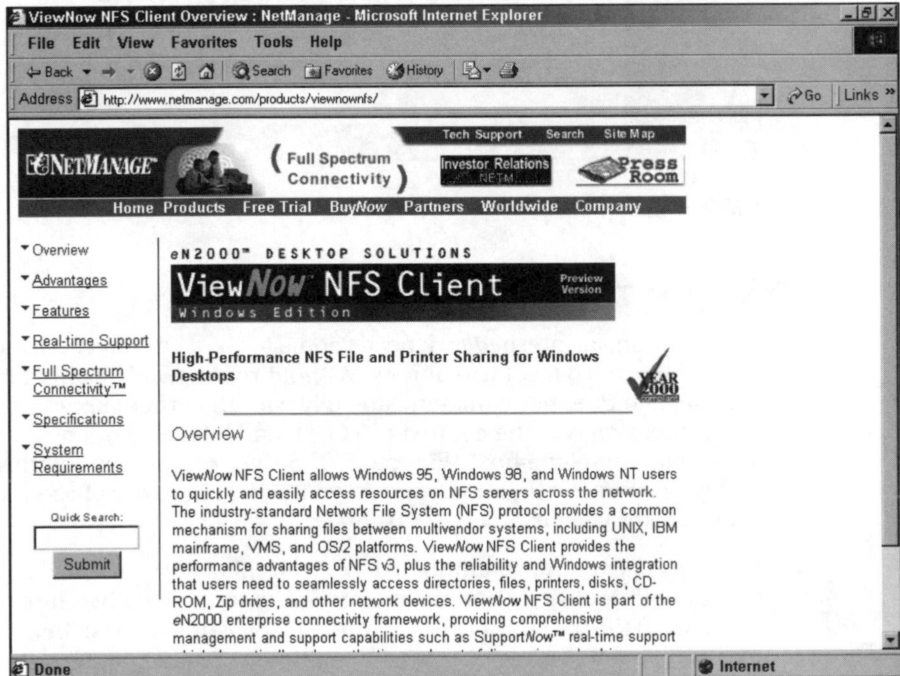

Figure 3-21: NetManage ViewNow NFS Client

The Seattle-based company, WRQ, supplements Microsoft's TCP/IP protocol stack with its connectivity solutions for connecting disparate systems. In particular, WRQ Reflection products are basically terminal emulation applications for HP, Digital, Unix, IBM, and X systems hosts and Windows-based clients. Reflection NFS Connection (see Figure 3-22) works with Windows 2000 Network Neighborhood and Windows Explorer.

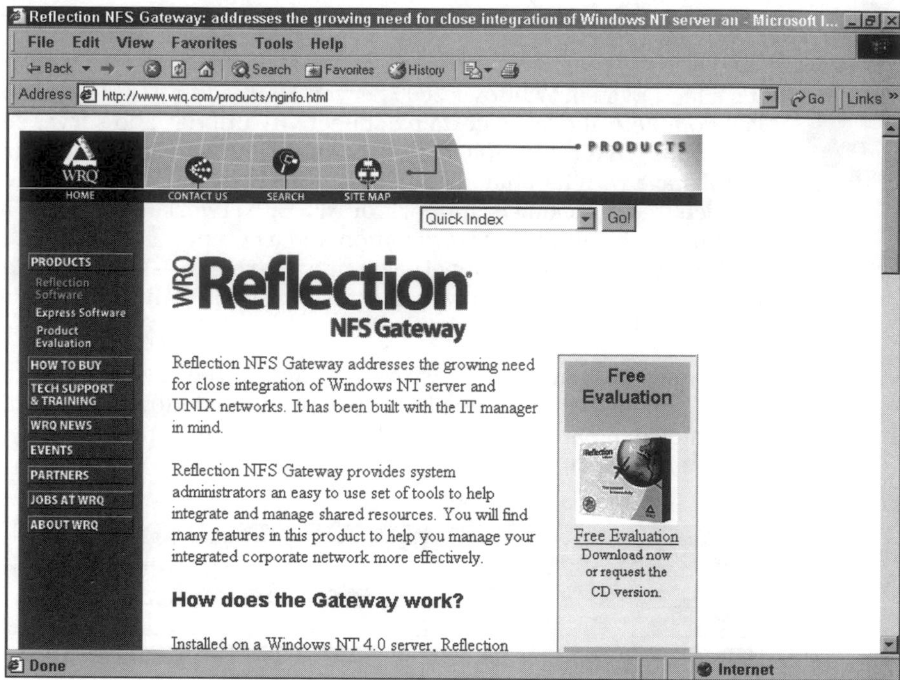

Figure 3-22: A WRQ Reflection NFS connection

Simple routing

By definition, an internetwork needs some form of OSI Layer 3 routing capabilities to connect its subnets. Without routing, each subnet lives in a vacuum and does not communicate fully with the other subnets. However, this discussion is in the context of TCP/IP and internetworking and thus is about the "out-of-the-box" Window 2000 Server routing capabilities. I would highly recommend that you educate yourself on hardware-based routing solutions for vendors such as Cisco.

When you hear term "multihomed," do you think of the well to do with homes both in the city and the country? The term actually refers to Microsoft TCP/IP's support for IP routing. You can use these built-in IP routing capabilities in systems with multiple network adapters attached to distinct and separate networks.

Implementing the multiple network adapter card-based routing capabilities of Windows 2000 Server is easy. The configuration is made via the Routing and Remote Access Microsoft Management Console (MMC) (see Figure 3-23).

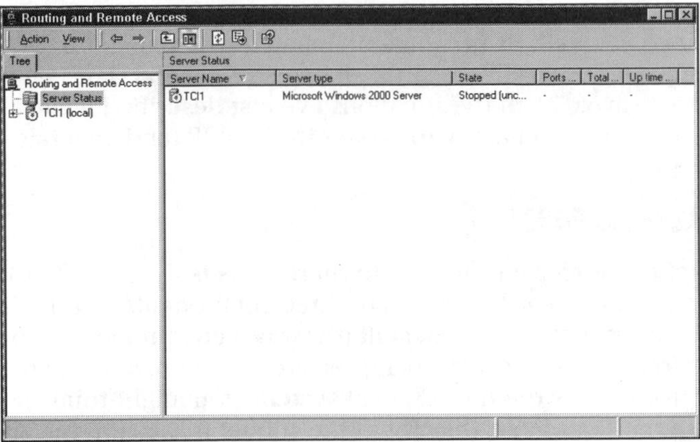

Figure 3-23: Routing and Remote Access

There are risks associated with native routing in Windows 2000 Server. For example, if your Windows 2000 server is connected directly to the Internet, then enabling this capability is akin to leaving the barn door open. Don't forget that IP routing is a two-way street; be aware that you are potentially inviting unwelcome guests to enjoy your network. This is even a problem in misconfigured implementations of Microsoft Proxy Server. Affectionately called the "poor man's firewall," Proxy Server uses a dual network adapter card to create the physical separation between your network and the Internet. However, if you accidentally and incorrectly implement Windows 2000 Server's routing capabilities, you have effectively defeated and overridden the firewall built by Proxy Server. Take this problem seriously; I've seen this mistake and unfortunately, the Proxy Server documentation assumes that you know this problem can occur.

Don't be fooled that Windows 2000 Server-based IP routing is the same as configuring and using a traditional hardware-based router such as a Cisco 4500. It is not. The IP routing capabilities found in Windows 2000 Server merely forward packets between physically separate subnets. No intelligent decisions are made with respect to IP filtering or cost-based path analysis.

Implementing TCP/IP

Now that you've seen TCP/IP, allow me to offer a second view. You have at least three reasons to be attentive to all of the basic TCP/IP issues and definitions presented in this chapter. First, there is the technical side. If you don't understand the basic components used to implement TCP/IP, you may very well create a network that doesn't work. An example of this is if you have the wrong subnet mask class associated with a specific range of IP addresses. If you do this, some of your older routers, being the unforgiving devices that they are, won't work properly. Second, if you lack the TCP/IP fundamentals, you are more likely to make a tactical error. Examples of these errors are endless and include humiliating yourself in front of other network professionals who know TCP/IP. Think of it as native English speakers finding humor in a non-native

English speaker's attempt to hold a fluent conversation. Third, you may make life harder on yourself. By not understanding the fundamentals of TCP/IP, you risk having to take the TCP/IP certification exam several times instead of only once. You can avoid all of the situations I've just described if you simply take the time, and use this chapter, to master the TCP/IP fundamentals.

Internet Addressing

The packet needs to get from here to there. This is the role of TCP/IP addressing. Remember that there are three components to a TCP/IP address: IP address, subnet mask, and default gateway. I encourage you to draw analogies from other "worlds" to appreciate the importance of these components. If this were the U.S. mail system, you might think of the street address as the IP address, the city as the subnet mask, and the zip code as the router. Take a moment to challenge yourself to think "outside" of the TCP/IP box and draw analogies to other parts of your life to better define the IP address, subnet mask, and default gateway (hint: try thinking out how telephone numbers are organized with area code, prefix, and telephone number).

IP addresses

The IP address is a 32-bit value that is used to correctly identify a source and destination address in packet-based network communications. An IP address typically reads something like 204.107.2.100. The address can be broken down into four positions of eight bits each and can also be represented in binary form. These positions are called *octet positions* and are each eight bits in length.

Make sure you commit to memory Table 3-5, which shows these octet positions. You will inevitably find yourself in a planning meeting or on a telephone call where others drop into what could be called TCP/IP shorthand. You'll hear terms such as "dot one hundred in the fourth octet position" thrown around freely, and you will be expected to keep up.

Table 3-5 IP Address Components for Sample Address 204.107.2.100

Value	*Octet Position*	*Standard Alpha Variable Notation**
204	First Octet	W
107	Second Octet	X
2	Third Octet	Y
100	Fourth Octet	Z

*This is how IP models typical refer to the octet position when referenced via alpha characters. This is conceptually similar to the study of algebra where discrete items are referred to as either A, B, C, or X, Y, Z.

To represent an address in binary format, let's revisit binary counting. Binary uses values of one and zero. In other words, it's the classic on-off mentality of digital computing that we've all grown up with and love. Table 3-6, a simple binary conversion table, helps you translate a dotted decimal value to its binary form.

Note: we are reading left to right, as with this sentence. So for the binary representation 11001100, which is the number 204, the first bit position of the octet is a one ("1"). While it may seem incredibly obvious to say that we read from left to right, it is necessary to communicate this point correctly because some areas in the TCP/IP and Internet worlds actually read right to left. For example, Internet domain names are technically read from right to left. Thus, the address is first evaluated as a commercial or "com" domain.

Table 3-6 Simple Binary to Decimal Conversion Table for Converting Octet Value 204 to Binary Value 11001100

Octet Position	*Decimal Notation*	*Binary Value*
1st Bit	128	1
2nd Bit	64	1
3rd Bit	32	0
4th Bit	16	0
5th Bit	8	1
6th Bit	4	1
7th Bit	2	0
8th Bit	1	0

Thus, the IP address of 204.107.2.100 would translate to the binary representation shown in Table 3-7.

Stated another way, 204.107.2.100 translates to zeros and ones, organized by octets in a column format, as shown in Table 3-8. This table helps you understand how a specific IP address appears when organized by octet.

Tip

Don't forget that an IP address should be thought of as a unique address on a TCP/IP network. Stated again, every node on a TCP/IP network must have a unique IP address. If two nodes on your TCP/IP network have the exact same IP addresses, you will experience unreliable network performance and receive error messages that identical IP addresses exist.

Table 3-7 Translation of IP Address to Binary Values

Octet Bit Position	*1st*	*2nd*	*3rd*	*4th*	*5th*	*6th*	*7th*	*8th*
Octet value/ dotted decimal notation	128	64	32	16	8	4	2	1
204 (first octet)	1	1	0	0	1	1	0	0
107 (second octet)	0	1	1	0	1	0	1	1
2 (third octet)	0	0	0	0	0	0	1	0
100 (fourth octet)	0	1	1	0	0	1	0	0

Figure 3-24 shows the error message that would be displayed by the Windows 2000 Server that was first to participate on the TCP/IP network before the second host appeared with a duplicate address. This first host will continue to operate without incident. In short, the first computer has obtained the specific IP address in question and doesn't have to give it up just because a second host wants it.

Table 3-8 Alternative View: Binary to IP Address Conversion

First Octet	*Second Octet*	*Third Octet*	*Fourth Octet*
11001100	01101011	00000010	01100100
204	107	2	100

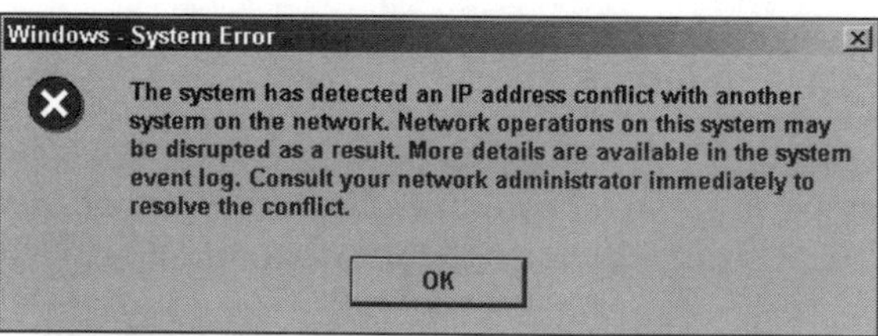

Figure 3-24: A Windows 2000 Server IP address conflict error message

The message shown in Figure 3-25 indicates that the computer operator has attempted to authenticate on the same network using an IP address that already exists. The resulting error message means that all networking functionality has been disabled because of the duplicate address conflict. In short, the second host simply can't have the same IP address that is being used by the first host.

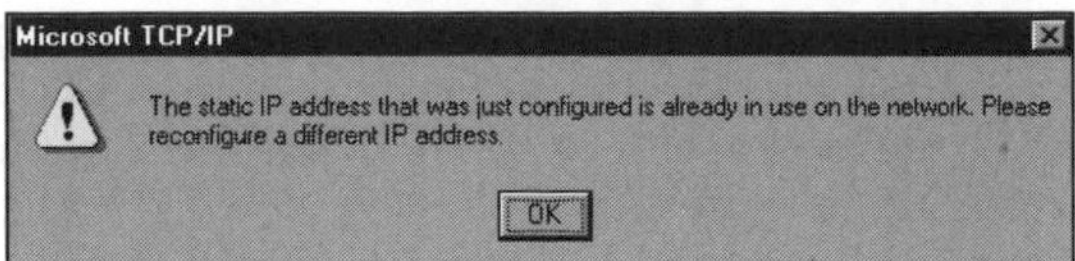

Figure 3-25: A second host IP address error message

Getting around a duplicate IP address scenario is actually quite easy. If you have a second transport protocol loaded and bound to your network adapter, you will be automatically authenticated as a network citizen using the second valid protocol. Of course, I'm assuming the Windows 2000 Server you are trying to attach to is also running this second protocol. Remember that in a nonrouted scenario, the NetBEUI protocol is a fine selection. In a routed scenario, however, you will need to consider using NWLink (IPX/SPX), which is routable.

The discussion so far relates to IP addressing issues on a LAN or a WAN that is not participating on the Internet via a full-time connection. When connected to the Internet, the rules may change, depending on your situation, but the basic rule still applies: any node on the Internet must have a unique address.

Remember, you must be especially careful that those computers directly connected to the Internet and not routed through a proxy server to use an authentic Internet IP address use the correct address — one that has been assigned by the Internet Network Information Center (InterNIC). Given the architecture of TCP/IP and how it is implemented on the Internet, it is essential there are unique IP addresses for nodes with direct Internet connections.

To receive a valid Internet address and connect to the Internet, contact: Network Solutions, InterNIC Registration Services, 505 Huntmar Park Drive, Herndon, VA 22070 (`www.internic.net`).

The IP green movement

Let's face it, TCP/IP addressing is not as easy as it looks; with a finite supply of IP addresses on the Internet, it is essential that you consider an alternate IP address strategy that enables your internal network nodes to have unique IP addresses while taking full advantage of the Internet. Think of this as the green strategy — you're doing your part to save IP addresses, as many good-hearted souls are trying to save the world's trees from harvest.

Although you can contact Network Solutions to get your unique Internet address (a.k.a. netid), I can offer a better idea.

There is one way to use both phony and real Internet IP Addresses on the same network. This situation requires the use of Microsoft Proxy Server, wherein the internal LAN may have "phony" IP addresses ranging from 131.107.2.100 to .200 and yet the organization may only have one real Internet

IP address, such as 204.222.104.2, for its "real" Internet connection. This is a perfectly legitimate way to connect to the Internet from the desktop and has the added benefit of helping save real Internet IP addresses (an endangered species). Proxy Server, with its routing and filtering capabilities, in effect converts the phony internal IP addresses to route to the Internet via the valid Internet IP address.

Mysteriously misappropriated Internet domain names

While writing this book, I twice observed situations in which domain names were "switched" to different Internet IP addresses (something that was unknown to all network parties that needed to be in the know), so I thought it was worth mentioning. Perhaps the mere telling of these stories will prevent you from suffering a similar situation. In each case, the clients noticed that their Internet e-mail service seemed to be failing. Both were running Windows NT Server as their network operating system and Microsoft Exchange 5.*x* as their e-mail application. **Note:** this same example applies to networks running Windows 2000 Server.

One day, client 1 (a small software developer) noticed that while the internal Exchange e-mail continued to operate as expected, the externally routed e-mail to the Internet, both internal and external, was failing. Of course, a round of network troubleshooting commenced: routers were tested, telephone company services were looped back, and Exchange services were analyzed. Many billable hours later this discovery was made: the marketing director had apparently taken advantage of, and been taken advantage of by, a discount Web-hosting firm that offered not only to develop your Web site but to host it as well. There was only one catch to this great deal. The Web hosting firm would take control of your domain name and the IP address assigned to your organization and repoint the domain name to the firm's server. Well, this caused fits with the Exchange-based Internet e-mail service. Once corrected — that is, once the domain name and IP address were pointed back to the client's original location — the Exchange-based Internet e-mail worked just fine. What is the moral here? Communication. This is a classic case where the marketing department did not communicate with the networking engineers. It sounds like the classic MBA lecture where marketing and engineering don't speak to each other by default; that is, many MBA case studies and far too many MBA lectures emphasize organizational conflict where departments are not on speaking terms. Perhaps you've experienced such political divisions in your own organization.

The second time I encountered a domain name and IP address reassignment was another situation where a management team member, the chief financial officer (CFO), contracted with a bargain Web-hosting firm to develop and host the firm's Web site. Here again, the sun rose one day and the Exchange-based Internet e-mail failed, although not completely — the performance was somewhat random at first; it would work for a few hours and then fail. After several hours of troubleshooting, including threatening to FDISK (use the format disk command) the Exchange Server machine and start from ground zero, the discovery was made that the Web-hosting firm had contacted InterNIC and pointed the client's domain name and corresponding IP address away from the client's original location. Once realized, the domain name and IP address were restored to their proper locations, and Exchange worked just fine.

So beware of low-cost Web-hosting solutions. More important, beware of other stakeholders in your organization accepting such offers on your behalf.

Just as there is a trend toward low-cost Web-hosting firms reassigning domain names and IP addresses inappropriately, be advised that there is a disturbing trend on the Internet that involves unethical bulk e-mailing organizations. Apparently these organizations have InterNIC reassign legitimate domain names to their illegitimate sites. Consequently, a flood of annoying bulk e-mailings are launched and the replies are gathered for several hours or days until the domain name assignment is discovered and cured.

Subnet masks

The subnet mask is used to distinguish the network portion of an address from the host or node portion of an address. It provides information about how an address should be read.

The subnet mask is extremely valuable for organizing IP address assignments on the Internet into classes. Ingeniously, we have Class A, Class B, and Class C. Important reasons exist for using address classes to manage all of the TCP/IP madness on the Internet. Although, as networking professionals, we are only concerned with Classes A, B, and C (shown in Table 3-9), there are two other classes. Class D is used for multicasting to a special group of nodes in a land where we mere mortals don't participate. Class E is reserved for future use and growth (thank goodness — we're going to need this class considering the incredible growth of Internet nodes).

Table 3-9 Internet Address Classes Using the 204.107.2.100 Sample IP Address

Class	*Network Address*	*Host Address*	*Bit Position That Separates Network and Host Address**	*Standard Subnet Mask Value*
A	204	107.2.100	8th	255.0.0.0
B	204.107	2.100	16th	255.255.0.0
C	204.107.2.	100	24th	255.255.255.0

*Remember that an IP address is expressed as a 32-bit value. The division points between octets occur at the 8th, 16th, and 24th bits.

The Microsoft Official Curriculum (MOC) for several Microsoft Certified Systems Engineer (MCSE) courses provides some damaging misinformation for the student who is new to TCP/IP implementations. Let's play, "What's wrong with this picture?" This is the actual configuration in the MOC instructor's manual I used for several of my MCSE courses, including these titles: Implementing and Supporting Windows 95, Supporting Windows NT Server 4.0 – Core Technologies, Supporting Windows NT Server 4.0 – Enterprise Technologies, Supporting Microsoft Internet Information Server, and Supporting Proxy Server:

```
IP Addresses: 131.107.2.100_–_.200
Subnet Mask: 255.255.255.0
```

So I ask you — what's wrong with this picture? Challenge yourself to find what is fundamentally flawed here. If you can do so immediately, my compliments to you. If you can't, read on; the following text might enlighten you further as to the fundamentals of TCP/IP and enable you to see what is wrong with this IP address and subnet mask combination.

In the example, the IP has an invalid beginning and ending private Internet network address range given the standard subnet mask value that is used. While this is not a problem on a single subnetted internal private network, it can wreak havoc when you work with "real" routers, such as the hardware-based Cisco offerings; they may or may not expect your addressing to conform exactly to the known valid private Internet network address ranges.

Although it is essential that you are able to identify the potential problems with this configuration, it's more important that you don't apply this misinformation to future TCP/IP implementations. Oh yes, it's also important that you don't incorrectly answer MCSE examination questions based on this misunderstanding. That, perhaps, is the worst consequence of this goof, given it was delivered in the context of an MCSE certification course!

Table 3-10 shows valid private Internet network address ranges, enabling you to arrive at the correct answer to the previous riddle. Remember that we are talking about the network portion of the IP address. As you shall see in a few moments, the subnet mask helps you distinguish which portion of the IP address is defined as the network address and which portion of the address is defined as the host address.

Table 3-10 Valid Private Internet Network Address Ranges

Class	*Start of Address Range in First Octet*	*End of Address Range in First Octet*
Class A	001	126
Class B	128	191
Class C	192	223

First octet values above 223 (starting with 224) are reserved and may not be used. Also don't forget the following:

- All network addresses must be unique. This statement holds true whether you are on the Internet or your own internetwork, and it is a good rule to adhere to.
- A network address cannot begin with 127 (the reserved address for internal loopback testing).
- You may not have all zeros in the first octet of a network address. If all bits are set to zero, that indicates a local address and prevents routing.
- You may not have 255 in the first octet of a network address. If all bits are set to one (which equals 255) the eight bits set to the value of one act as a broadcast.

Host addresses

Regarding the host portion of an IP address, you will find the following points vital in mastering the fundamentals of TCP/IP:

- Host addresses must be unique on a given network. This is a truism. Think about it. Each node on a network must have a unique address, and thus the host portion of the IP address must be unique. Table 3-11 shows valid host portion addresses within an IP address.

Tip

In the technical community, the word "host" is interchangeable with the term "node." That is, the two terms essentially have the same meaning, assuming correct usage.

- All "1" bits may not be used as the host address. If this is the case, the address is interpreted to be a broadcast address, not a host address.
- Likewise, all "0" bits may not be used as the host address. Doing so would communicate: this network only.

Table 3-11 Valid Host Portion Addresses

Class	*Start*	*End*
Class A	w.0.0.1	w.255.255.255
Class B	w.x.0.1	w.x.255.255
Class C	w.x.y.1	w.x.y.254

Caste system

Let's discuss Classes A, B, and C. Perhaps you'll agree that TCP/IP has such clear class distinctions that it might better be thought of as a caste society. Very important technical reasons exist for having classes. This separation enables you to better organize your network to achieve a best fit given the size of your network. If you are connected to the Internet, the class designation is even more important and is perhaps the most important way in which order is ultimately maintained on the wild and free wide-open world of the Internet.

Class A

Class A assignments are very rare and are for only the largest networks. Theoretically, only 127 Class A networks can exist on the Internet because the network portion of the 32-bit address is on seven of the first eight bits in the first octet. If all eight bits were used in this octet, the number of networks possible would be 128. The unused bit in the octet is referred to as the high-order bit and is reserved. But let's not stop there. Because the number 127 in the first octet is a reserved number, there can really only be 126 Class A networks.

The number 127 is reserved in the first octet position to facilitate such features as internal loopback testing. To perform an internal loopback test in TCP/IP using the ping command, type **Ping 127.0.0.1**.

The number of nodes possible on a Class A network is approximately 17 million (actually, it's 16,777,214 nodes). An example of a Class A network is the original Internet, which at first was called ARPANET and was managed by the Department of Defense.

Class B

Class B assignments are for medium-sized networks. This network address is 16 bits long and consumes the first two octet positions. Because two high-order bit positions are set to 1 and 0 respectively, there can only be 16,383 networks. But each network may have 65,534 nodes.

Class C

Class C allows for 2,097,151 networks and up to 254 nodes per network. Not surprisingly, this class is best suited for smaller networks. In fact, most of us work with Class C networks in the Internet. This class of license is by far the most popular address class. Three high-order bits have Class C addresses (set to 1-1-0 respectively).

Why only 254 nodes? Because 255 is a reserved number with TCP/IP addressing, typically employed for network- and internetwork-level broadcasting. Such a reservation is necessary for TCP/IP network management purposes.

Table 3-12 summarizes these network classes and nodes.

Table 3-12 Summary of Class A, B, and C Networks and Nodes

Class	*Actual Number of Networks Possible*	*Actual Number of Nodes Possible*
A	126	16,777,214
B	16,384	65534
C	2,097,151	254

Default gateways

Default gateways are important, and provide a place for IP hosts to seek help when trying to communicate with distant IP hosts on another IP network. In essence, the default gateway address points or instructs the host to use another node to handle its routing needs. The goal of default gateways is to make IP routing efficient. In fact, individual hosts (say workstations) use default gateways extensively to avoid being burdened with address resolution.

On a larger network with hardware-based routers, this entry field will typically be the IP address of your router. On smaller networks using the routing capabilities of Windows 2000 Server, this would be the address of the server. In either case, the default gateway maintains current and detailed knowledge of network IDs of other networks on an internetwork (that is, a network of networks).

Tip

If you are new to TCP/IP and don't know a lot about the network you are working with, just put the IP address of the Windows 2000 server in the default gateway field until you are able to better understand what the appropriate value for your network should be. (Of course this sage advice pertains to a smaller network; on a larger network, you should hire a Microsoft Certified Professional networking consultant to assist with your TCP/IP implementation.)

As shown in Figure 3-26, the default gateway is defined on the Internet Protocol (TCP/IP) Properties property sheet in Windows 2000 Server (under Network and Dial-up Connections in Control Panel, select Local Area Connection Properties).

Tip

On the Networking Essentials certification exam that you must pass to earn your MCSE designation, remember that the default gateway value is an optional entry in a TCP/IP scenario. The IP address and subnet mask are required.

This said, what are some situations where you might not enter a default gateway? One is with a small LAN where all nodes reside on one subnet. Before reading my second observation on not using a default gateway, take a moment to think about situations in your networking experience where you didn't use a default gateway entry.

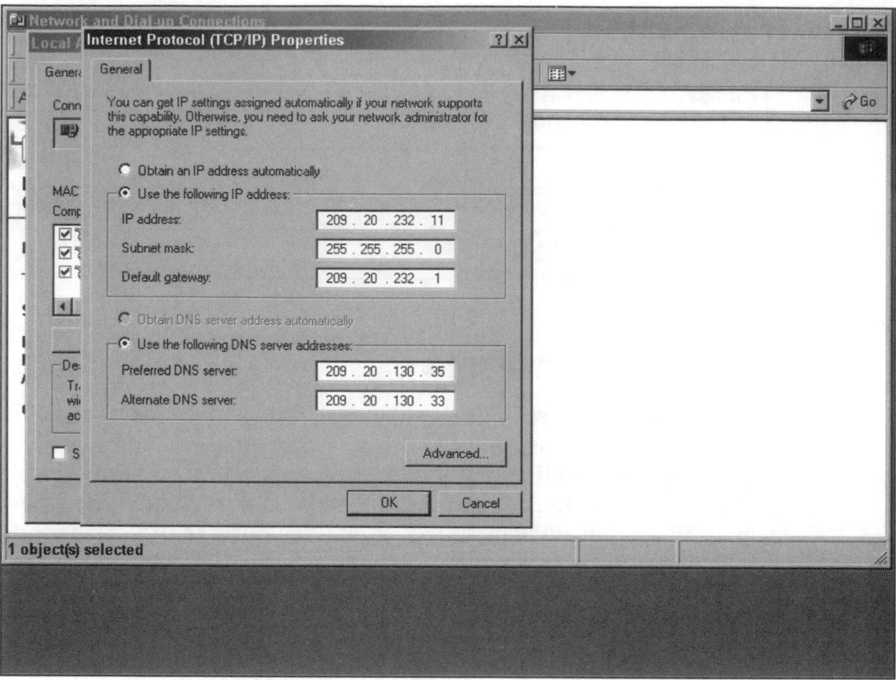

Figure 3-26: The default gateway

A second situation where you would be sans default gateway is with a network that, although it contains different segments, doesn't use a router to route packets. Perhaps such a network uses a switch. Remember that switches reside at Layer 2 of the OSI model (the Data-Link Layer) and don't require the kind of addressing information that packets do at OSI model Layer 3 (the Network Layer).

What are the mechanics of a default gateway and how is such a beast used on your Windows 2000 Server network? Suppose you have a network with a node called *Host 100* and a node called *Host 200.* Note that Host 100 is located on Network 1 and Host 200 is located on Network 2. Assume that Host 100 addresses and sends a packet to Host 200. After Host 100 checks its local routing tables and is unable to resolve the path to Host 200, it forwards the packet to the default gateway.

A Windows 2000 computer builds the local routing table automatically, making one entry per route. This is obviously important for routing and resolution purposes. The local routing table can be displayed via the ROUTE PRINT command:

```
C:> route print
Active Routes:
```

Network Address	Netmask	Gateway Address	Interface	Metric
0.0.0.0	0.0.0.0	131.076.120	131.107.6.120	1
127.0.0.0	255.0.0.0	127.0.0.1	127.0.0.1	1
131.107.6.0	255.255.255.0	131.107.6.120	131.107.6.120	1
131.107.6.120	255.255.255.255	127.0.0.1	127.0.0.1	1
131.107.255.255	255.255.255.255	131.107.6.120	131.107.6.120	1
224.0.0.0	224.0.0.0	131.107.6.120	131.107.6.120	1
255.255.255.255	255.255.255.255	131.107.6.120	131.107.6.120	1

The following sections describe the columns that are displayed above when we use the route print command. Such descriptions are necessary, as the output above, viewed alone, is both boring and somewhat difficult to interpret.

Network address

The first column is where the server searches for the network address. Possibilities include 0.0.0.0, a value that refers to "this network" (the current network that originated the packet). At the other end of the scale, you have 255.255.255.255, a value that includes all networks; this means all the hosts on all the networks that can receive limited broadcast traffic. Typically, the 255.255.255.255 address is implemented when the default gateway proves unresponsive; it initiates a broadcast to all hosts on all networks.

Netmask

The netmask is the second column. The entry found here represents the subnet mask that is associated with the network address.

A netmask of 255.255.255.255, which is all "ones" when displayed in binary format, tells us that this is the host entry; the network address and the IP address are exactly the same and so refer to one and the same machine (the local host).

Gateway address

The gateway address is the default IP address used by the local host to resolve network address (the address of the IP router used to forward IP packets to other IP networks).

Interface

The interface is the IP address of the local network adapter card on the machine. This network adapter card address will be used when forwarding IP packets to the network.

Metric

This is the number of hops required to travel to the IP destination. A hop count is conceptually similar to the hop count discussion you might have encountered when mastering Messaging Transfer Agents (MTA) in Microsoft Exchange or Microsoft Mail.

You can interpret the local routing table according to the entries in the Network Address column of Table 3-13. Note the information displayed in this example reflects a Windows 2000 Server that has its own IP address as the default gateway. As discussed earlier, it is common to put the Windows 2000 Server's IP address in the default gateway column on LANs that have no subnets or routers.

Table 3-13 Detailed "Route" Information

Network Address	*Description*
0.0.0.0	Default Gateway address line
127.0.0.0	Loopback address
131.107.6.0	Local network
131.107.6.120	Host IP address
131.107.255.255	Network-level broadcast
224.0.0.0	Multicast address
255.255.255.255	Internetwork-level broadcast

See the Gateway Address column (third column in the preceding list) for the correct default gateway address entry. In this case, that value is 131.107.6.120.Addresses are added to the local routing table via the ROUTE ADD command. This command once initiated IP-based WAN communications between two cities for a client when nothing else would. For example, imagine you have a situation in which you cannot successfully ping across a router. Now consider the following command:

```
C:>route add 204.107.3.0 mask 255.255.255.0 204.107.2.199 -p
```

So what's going on here? Challenge yourself to answer that simple question by considering this router command in the light of Figure 3-27. Hopefully you, like me, enjoy an occasional analytical exercise to solve. If you can quickly see the main point (hint: make a persistent route), I again applaud your understanding of TCP/IP fundamentals and encourage you to strongly consider taking the Microsoft TCP/IP certification exam if you haven't already done so.

The preceding route add command explicitly states that to get to the 204.107.3.0 subnet with a mask of 255.255.255.0, use gateway 204.107.2.199 and make this a static of persistent route by writing it to the Registry (-r).

This persistent route is written to `HKEY_LOCAL_MACHINE\SYSTEM\CurrentControl\Set\Services\Tcpip\Parameters\PersistentRoutes`. Shown in Figure 3-28, this is significant because it enables the persistent static route to survive the expiration of the current computing session. That is, when the Windows 2000 Server is rebooted, the persistent route is recreated on the basis of the Registry entries displayed in Figure 3-28. By analogy, think of a congressional bill that survives two different sessions of the U.S. Congress with the same number.

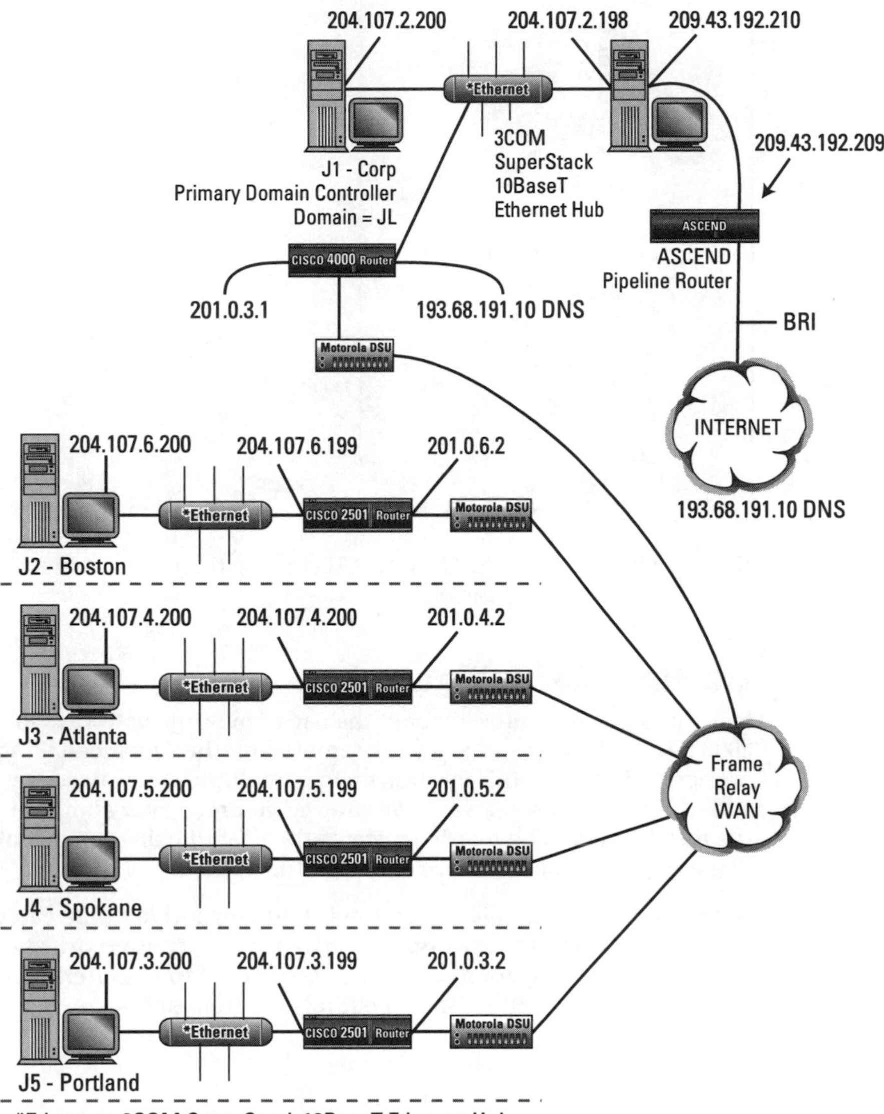

Figure 3-27: A network with routers

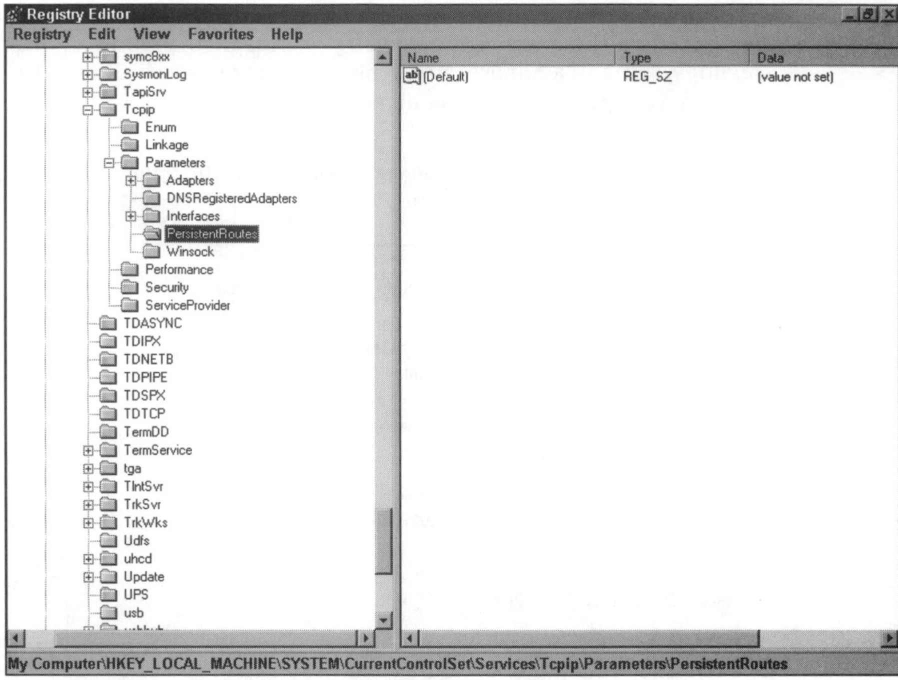

Figure 3-28: HKEY_LOCAL_MACHINE\SYSTEM\CurrentControlSet\Services\Tcpip\Parameters\PersistentRoutes

Multiple default gateways

Many people are confused about the use of multiple gateways in Windows 2000 Server. Multiple gateways are entered on the Advanced IP Addressing property sheet. Figure 3-29 shows where multiple gateway addresses are added. You may also elevate one gateway address over another by changing the metric value. The metric indicates the cost of using the default gateway. The lower the cost, the more desirable the path.

Note that a common misconception is that you add multiple gateway values to connect disparate networks. For instance, a corporate private WAN connected via Cisco routers could be connected to the Internet at some point via an ISDN router (and an entirely different subnet).

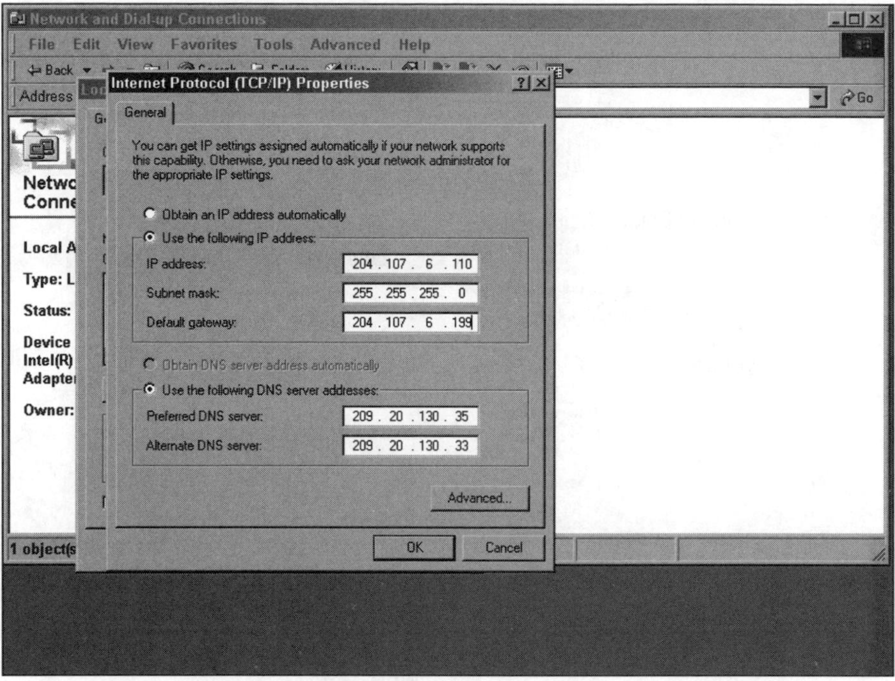

Figure 3-29: Preparing to add multiple gateway addresses

In Figure 3-30, notice the private WAN for this company is connected via Cisco routers. The Internet connection, via a 7×24 ISDN connection, is an entirely different network.

It would be a mistake to make the entry shown in the Gateways field in Figure 3-31 to account for both the Cisco and ISDN routers at the Corporate location. In the figure, notice that the Cisco router and ISDN router addresses have been entered as gateways on this Windows 2000 Server machine (located at Corporate in Figure 3-30). This is an incorrect way to try to connect two disparate networks that have multiple routers.

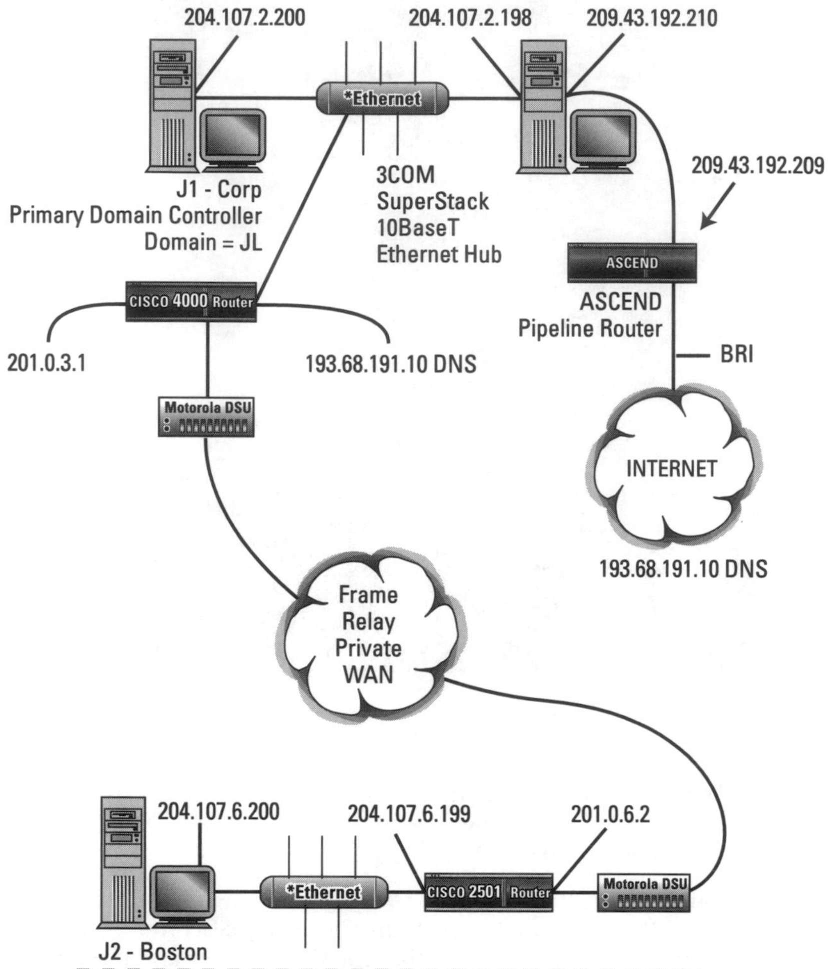

Figure 3-30: A private wide area network

The real purpose of the multiple gateway entries is not to account for the multiple routers at the corporate site in the preceding example, but to provide a backup route for WAN traffic routing should the "default" gateway fail or go down. Stated another way, only the default gateway is used. If it is down (by this, I mean it is physically unavailable and not just unable to resolve an address), the second gateway entry is employed to get the packet from Point A to Point B.

Here is a correct use of multiple gateway address. In this scenario, there is a backup WAN link between two sites via RAS. Should the regular WAN link, via the Cisco routers, fail, then we are rerouted and reconnected via the WAN connections. Note that this second gateway entry value would point to the dial-up adapter. As shown in Figure 3-32, the second gateway address relates to our second or backup WAN connection.

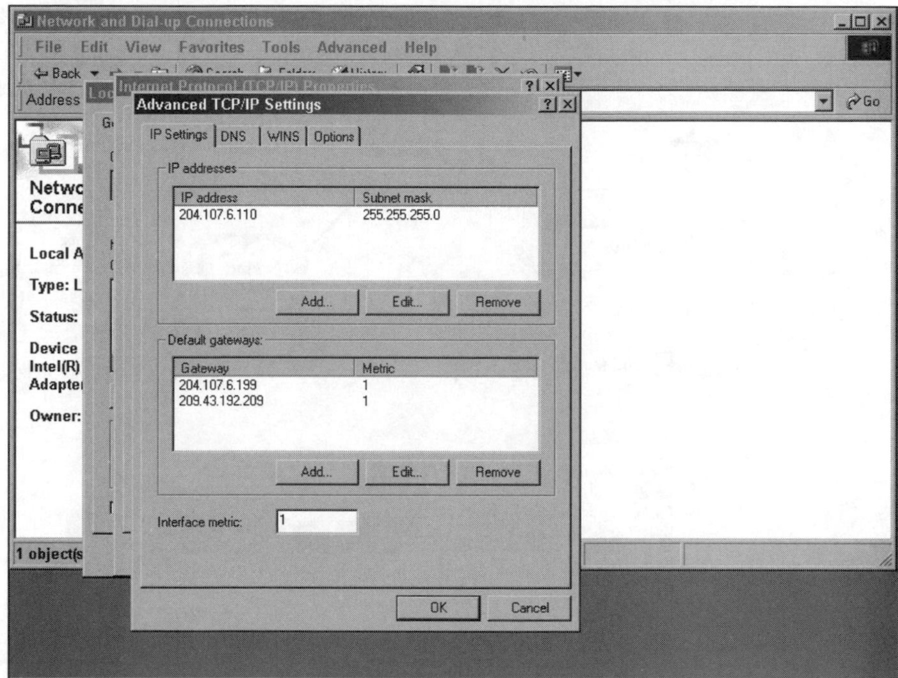

Figure 3-31: Router addresses on a Windows 2000 server

Understanding IP Routing

We technical types often remember our college days with both glee over the meaty technical courses we eagerly excelled in, and depression over the required liberal arts courses we suffered through. One such unmemorable course for many may well have been Communications 101. In this course, you learned about something called an *S/R model.* The basic S/R model, showing communications based on a sender and a receiver, appears in Figure 3-33.

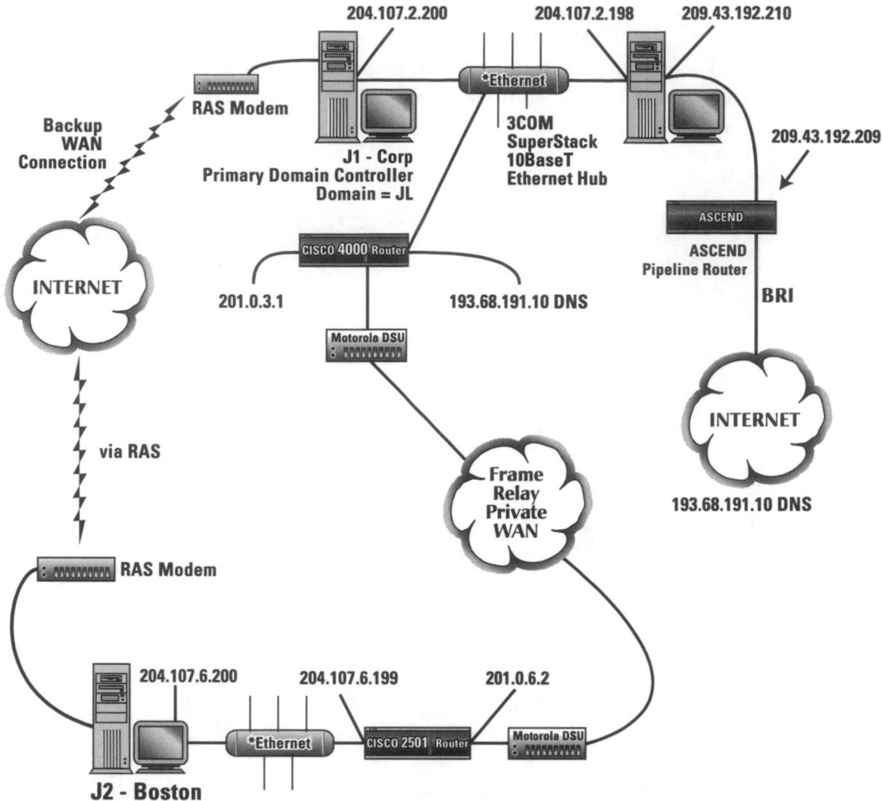

Figure 3-32: A second gateway address

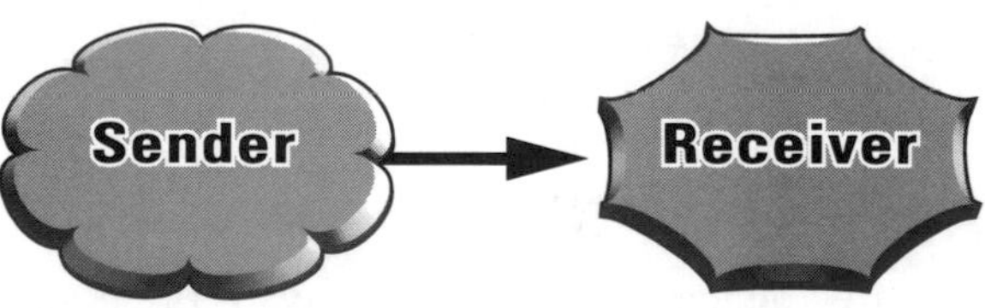

Figure 3-33: A basic S/R model

Likewise, the Communications 101 instructor probably told you that someday you would appreciate the lecture being delivered. Guess what?! The instructor was right. Not only is the S/R model the foundation of network communications, it is also the underlying theory behind routing. Think about it. Routing is nothing more then connecting two parties that want to communicate but need a helping hand because of some barrier, such as separate subnets. Thus routing is used to get the data packets — in this case, IP datagrams — from sender to receiver. In an IP routing scenario, you are basically concerned with two addresses, the destination address and the origination (or sender's) address.

Truth be told, routing is considered by many the primary function of IP. With IP routing, we're stationed at Layer three (the NetworkLayer) of the OSI model. Basically, the IP-related services evaluate each packet by examining the destination host address. The address is compared against the local routing table and evaluated to determine if any forwarding is necessary. If the destination address can be found on the local subnet, the packet is not forwarded. If the opposite is true — that is, the destination address is located on a distant and (for our purposes) physically separate network, then IP services undertake the appropriate forwarding steps. The steps include having the first router (which has evaluated the packet destined for a distant subnet) forward the packet to the other router (which is associated with that distant subnet).

Many of you know (but a surprisingly huge number of Windows 2000 Server professionals do not) that routers only forward information from router to router.

Officially, according to Microsoft, IP routers "use two or more network connection interfaces to attach and interconnect between each physically separate IP network for which they are enabled to forward packets between." And don't forget we use IP routing (and routing in general) to filter as much as we do to forward. In fact, IP routers, by default, do not forward broadcast packets beyond their native subnets. With respect to hardware-based routing solutions, it's best to think of these beasties as positive checkoff devices. You must elect to have certain packet types flow through the system. So out of the box, the average router is probably configured to do more filtering than forwarding.

Conversely, a negative checkoff is analogous to joining a mail-order CD-of-the-month club. That is, until you explicitly tell the company to stop sending you recordings, you receive monthly music in perpetuity. It's a negative checkoff because you are forced to explicitly stop a certain activity, and this is more akin to lower OSI-level devices such as switches. Typically, a switch forwards everything until told differently (that is, if you have a "smart" switch that can be instructed to perform limited filtering).

Now let's focus on common characteristics of IP routers. First, routers are *multihomed hosts*, meaning they have at least two network interfaces. The interfaces can be a Windows 2000 Server with two network adapter cards or a hardware-based router with an internal LAN network interface port and an external network adapter port. These interfaces provide the connection between the two separate networks, as shown in Figure 3-34.

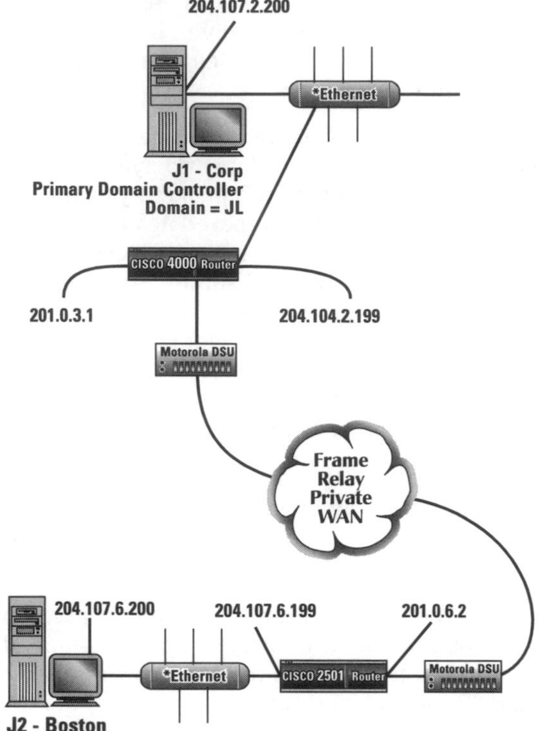

Figure 3-34: Separate networks connected by routers

Another function IP routers perform is forwarding packets for TCP/IP hosts. At a minimum, the IP router must be able to forward IP-based packets to other networks. And of course more often than not, it performs some level of filtering.

Finally, routers are both hardware based and out-of-the-box implementations, provided by such vendors as Cisco, Bay, and Hewlett-Packard. Software-based routing solutions included complex implementations of Windows 2000 Server's Routing and Remote Access.

Routing Tables

Routers depend on routing tables, which store addressing information about IP networks and hosts. Routing tables are called upon via a three-step approach (with an ultimate goal of getting the packet where it belongs):

1. The computer sends a packet. The computer then inserts its own source IP address and destination address into the IP header (see Figure 3-35).

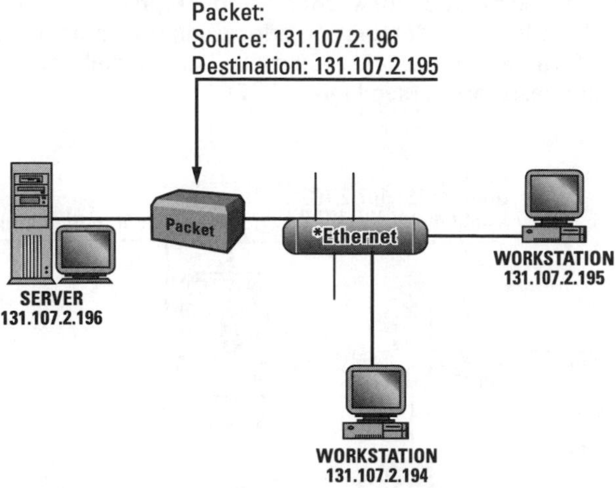

Figure 3-35: Step 1: The computer sends a packet.

2. The computer examines the destination address and compares it against the local routing table. Depending on what the computer finds in its local routing table, three possible course of action occur (see Figure 3-36).

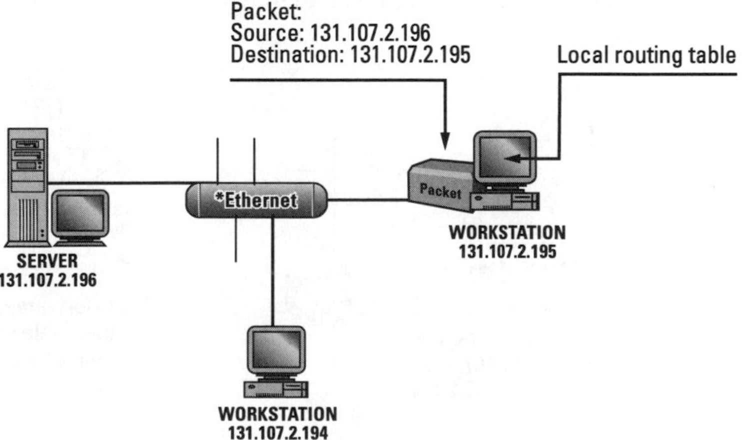

Figure 3-36: Step 2: The computer examines the destination address and compares it against the local routing table.

3. This step determines how the packet is routed. There are three possible choices:

a. The packet can be forwarded up to a higher protocol layer in the OSI model if the destination address is the same as the machine performing the packet evaluation. This packet has already arrived at its destination (see Figure 3-37).

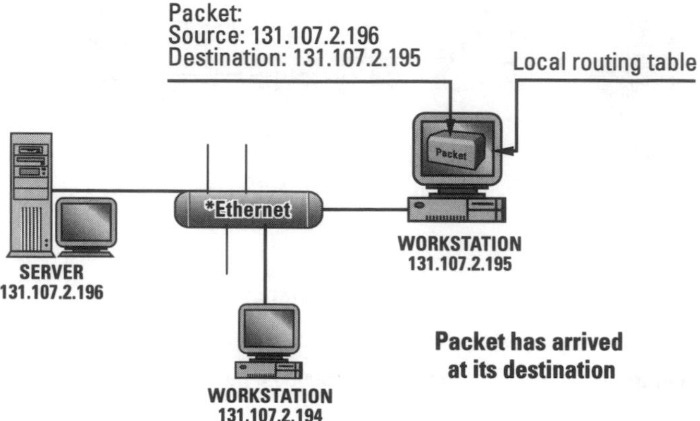

Figure 3-37: Step 3a: The packet can be forwarded up to a higher protocol layer.

b. The packet can be forwarded to another computer (or in the case of RAS, an attached dial-up adapter). See Figure 3-38.

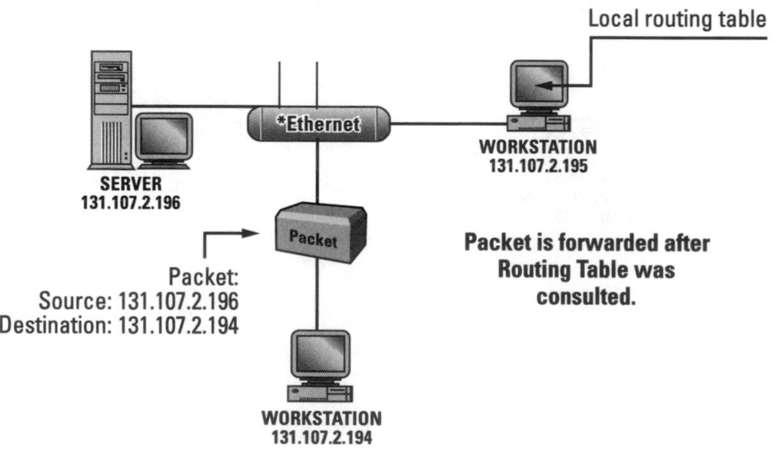

Figure 3-38: Step 3b: The packet can be forwarded to another computer.

c. If appropriate, the packet can be killed then and there (see Figure 3-39). This is referred to as *discarding*.

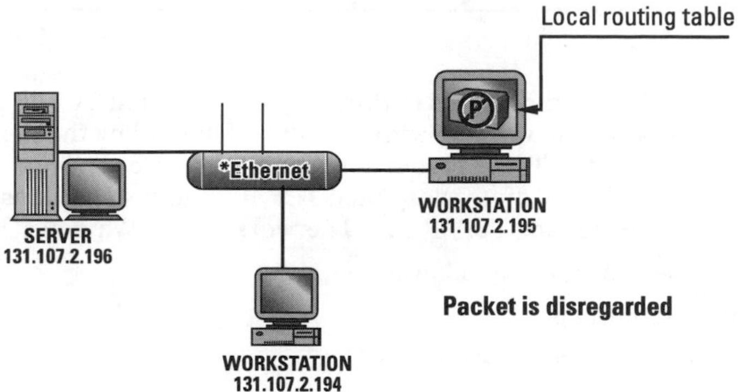

Figure 3-39: Step 3c: If appropriate, the packet can be killed.

In following these three steps, a packet on a routed network ultimately gets to where it belongs. This is in large part why many of us, as network professionals, are here: to make sure the packet gets from point A to point B. Do you remember the old saying about making the trains run on time?

A Word about Research

So we end this chapter on TCP/IP implementations. In the spirit of my next tip (research), I've placed a word about it at the end. That's because far too many of us either conduct our research too late in a project or implementation to save us, or, as is more likely the case, ultimately chalk up an implementation to research.

How often have you pursued a possible solution only to discover later that more research would have prevented mistakes? A fledgling ISP shared an experience that came about from inadequate research. After it was too late, this ISP discovered what has been already well-documented in the trade press and other published resources: Windows 2000 Server provides adequate or better solutions for those seeking an application server, file server, and Internet server all in one; NetWare is a stronger file server than either an application or an Internet server; and, UNIX is about as friendly as a junkyard dog. The lesson this ISP learned was: don't make your server into something that it is not. Only after investing many dollars did this ISP learn that Microsoft's networking solutions including Windows 2000 Server met its needs better than the UNIX system it had already purchased and deployed.

Tip

A final thought regarding TCP/IP: A simple system is the most trouble free. Start with a simple TCP/IP system and work your way up to the more complex one. If you are new to TCP/IP, it's critical that you start simple and progressively work your way into more complex TCP/IP implementations. If you break this rule, you will likely get in over your head.

Summary

The intense TCP/IP definitions in this chapter round out TCP/IP fundamentals that will assist you in working with TCP/IP and in reading the next several chapters devoted to TCP/IP. From here on out, you are ready to grow as both a Windows 2000 Server professional and TCP/IP practitioner. Godspeed to you as you start implementing TCP/IP-based networks using Windows 2000 Server.

This chapter covered the following:

- TCP/IP definitions
- Microsoft's implementation of TCP/IP
- A detailed analysis of TCP
- A detailed analysis of IP
- Windows Sockets — the definition and the application
- The three parts to Internet addressing: the IP address, the subnet mask, and the default gateway
- Windows 2000 Server basic routing

Chapter 4

Installing and Configuring TCP/IP

In This Chapter

- Installing TCP/IP
- Configuring TCP/IP
- Configuring additional TCP/IP services

This chapter provides all that you need to know to install and configure TCP/IP and its related services for Windows 2000. It is essential that you correctly install and configure the TCP/IP protocol if you intend to use it on your Windows 2000 Server network. Why? In Chapter 2, I discussed the initial setup of Windows 2000 Server as a foundational issue that will mark how your network performs forever. The same can be said about TCP/IP and its foundation-level role on your network. Simply stated, if you are not completely successful in installing and configuring TCP/IP, then TCP/IP misconfigurations will come back to haunt you for the life of your network. Got it?

TCP/IP Installation Preparations

The good news is that the previous TCP/IP chapter (Chapter 3) has prepared you for this moment: installing and configuring TCP/IP. And if that isn't good enough, feel free to peruse the next few TCP/IP chapters before performing the installation described in this chapter. Be advised that many problems on a network (including failed installations) can be traced to defective network protocol installations. That is, TCP/IP was installed (for example, during the Windows 2000 Server installation), but important TCP/IP-related information was incorrect or missing. And while these topics are touched on in other TCP/IP chapters, this is the chapter where the hands meet the keyboard.

A plain TCP/IP protocol installation in Windows 2000 requires a certain level of manual configuration. A few planning steps up front may dramatically lessen the chances of failure. To manually configure TCP/IP with Windows 2000 Server, you need to consider the following.

Will the computer function as a Dynamic Host Configuration Protocol (DHCP) server or will it act as a DHCP client (obtaining its TCP/IP configuration information from another DHCP server on the network)?

It has been my experience that you should manually configure TCP/IP on Windows 2000 Server and have true client workstations such as Windows 2000 Professional and Windows 95/98 act as DHCP clients, if for no other reason than that a clear demarcation line is drawn between server and client. Plus, it seems that you're always modifying the TCP/IP configuration on a server, but not necessarily the client workstation. And any such TCP/IP modifications that are made can be propagated very efficiently across your Windows 2000 network to DHCP clients when the DHCP lease is renewed. More on that nugget in a moment.

Determine whether you want this Windows 2000 Server to act as a Windows Internet Name Service (WINS) server. In a single-server environment, the answer is typically yes because WINS aids greatly in resolving NetBIOS names to TCP/IP addresses in mixed Windows NT and Windows 2000 network environments.

Windows 2000 Server supports WINS for backward compatibility reasons. Be advised the preferred method of name resolution in Windows 2000 Server is Dynamic DNS. Dynamic DNS is discussed in Chapter 6.

So assuming that you are going to manually configure TCP/IP on your Windows 2000 server and not receive your configuration from an existing DHCP server, let's revisit the "necessities" to configure TCP/IP. Of course, I'm assuming that you've read the earlier TCP/IP chapters and have a basic understanding of TCP/IP configurations. Map out the following information in advance of the TCP/IP installation process (see the sample as-built network diagram in Figure 4-1):

- The IP address and subnet mask for each network adapter card installed inside the machine.
- The IP address and subnet mask for any PPP connection you will make from the machine. This is typically modem-specific TCP/IP configuration information stored on a per-dialer basis under Dial-Up Networking (nested inside the Accessories menu selection from Programs). You will make this type of manual TCP/IP configuration when attempting to connect to the Internet via Dial-Up Networking from your machine.
- The IP address for the default gateway on the local subnet. Unless you are truly using routing (for instance, with a Cisco router), this value is typically one of the Windows 2000 servers on your subnet. It may even be the IP address of the Windows 2000 server on which you are configuring TCP/IP as part of this exercise.
- The IP address(es) and DNS domain name(s) of the DNS servers on your network/internetwork. Depending on whether you are connected to the Internet, these values will vary. I'll discuss this in more detail later on in this chapter.

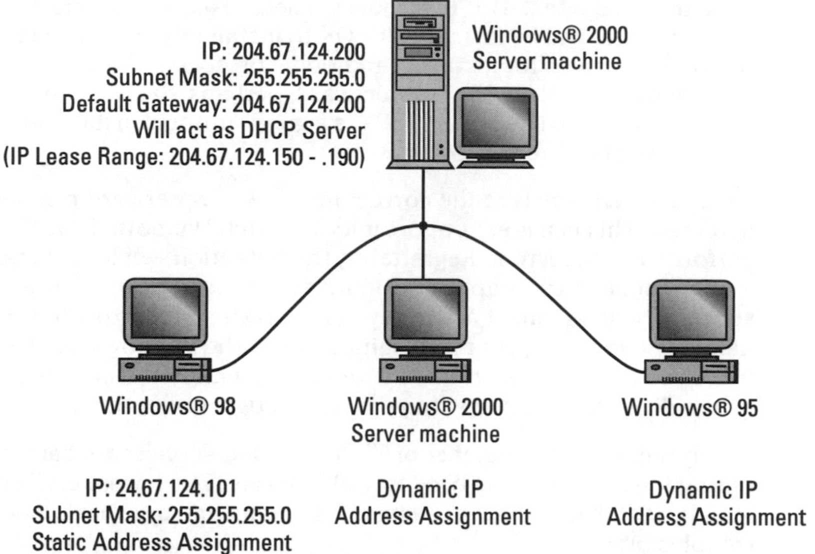

Figure 4-1: TCP/IP configuration on a small network

Tip

I strongly recommend that you consider creating a LAN/WAN plan as part of the as-built drawing process discussed in Chapter 1. There's nothing like a map to guide your TCP/IP configuration efforts.

Installing TCP/IP on Windows 2000 Server

The TCP/IP protocol is implemented by default when you are installing Windows 2000 Server. TCP/IP is thus known as the default protocol. Because Windows 2000 Server only allows the custom installation option during setup, you will have the opportunity to add other protocols and even remove TCP/IP. On that last point, I wouldn't recommend removing TCP/IP because it provides such great networking functionality in a Windows 2000 Server environment (such as supporting robust direct Internet connections!).

Secret

Did you know that the TCP/IP protocol became the default installation protocol commencing with Windows NT Server 3.51 and higher? Prior to that, the default protocol was NWLink IPX/SPX for Windows NT Server 3.50 and NetBEUI for Windows NT Advanced Server 3.1. Just a little trivia I thought you might enjoy.

At setup

Assuming you allow the installation of TCP/IP during the Windows 2000 Server setup, here are some issues to address.

First, make sure that TCP/IP is indeed selected as at least one of the protocols that will be installed. It's OK to install others, but always revisit the reasons for installing additional protocols. For example, if you are using an older HP JetDirect card, perhaps you will need to install the DLC protocol. NWLink IPX/SPX is a good protocol installation choice if you have NetWare servers present.

Second, make sure that the correct network adapter card has been detected. This is a great opportunity to watch Windows 2000 Server perform autodetection. Regrettably, the detection, while on target for known network adapters with drivers found in the `\i386` setup subdirectory, will most assuredly come up short (as expected) for newer network adapter cards shipped after the Windows 2000 Server build you are working with. Be sure to keep handy the network adapter driver disk that shipped with your new network adapter card.

Finally, minimize the number of TCP/IP-related services that are installed during the setup of your Windows 2000 server. The fewer services that are initially installed, the fewer suspects to detain and question when network troubles brew.

I've seen too many TCP/IP services installed at startup upset the apple cart. One example is the SNMP service, which is often installed only to enhance the number of object:counters available in Performance Monitor. Why else would SNMP be installed on a Windows 2000 Server when the network doesn't even use SNMP-aware devices or management applications? That said, under these scenarios, you can get startup event errors that not only populate the System Log in the Event Viewer, but can also cause other BackOffice applications to fail, such as Microsoft Exchange and Proxy Server. Be advised.

Even if you installed TCP/IP as part of the Windows 2000 Server setup, I recommend that you read the next section that discusses how to install TCP/IP. I call this my snow-day strategy. In my hometown of Seattle, Washington, whenever we receive snowfall, the city literally shuts down because of the hilly terrain. I've made a pact with myself that on these days, when I'm unable to get to work, I will trot down to my basement office and review my old BackOffice manuals, even though I probably have BackOffice (including Windows 2000 Server) running just the way I want it to. Well, given that we only receive snow once or twice a year, this forced review of BackOffice setups and administration always results in my remembering something simple I had forgotten, something I could be doing better, or perhaps something I should stop doing. So by reviewing the TCP/IP setup section next, perhaps you can benefit from my snow-day strategy.

On an existing Windows 2000 server

Perhaps you have valid reasons to install the TCP/IP protocol at a later date, or you need to reinstall the TCP/IP protocol when troubleshooting. Here is how you do it. It is important to understand that whether you install TCP/IP during the setup of your server machine or you add TCP/IP to an existing Windows 2000 Server, the desired end is still the same: a properly functioning TCP/IP protocol suite. Granted, the means for getting to this end are slightly different. For information on how to install TCP/IP during setup, review the discussion in Chapter 2. To install TCP/IP on an existing Windows 2000 Server, perform the steps that follow.

STEPS:

To install Microsoft TCP/IP

Step 1. Log on as an administrator or member of the Administrators group at the Windows 2000 Server machine on which you will be installing or reinstalling the TCP/IP protocol.

Step 2. Launch the Network and Dial-up Connections applet in one of two ways: from Control Panel or using the secondary menu from My Network Places (see Figure 4-2).

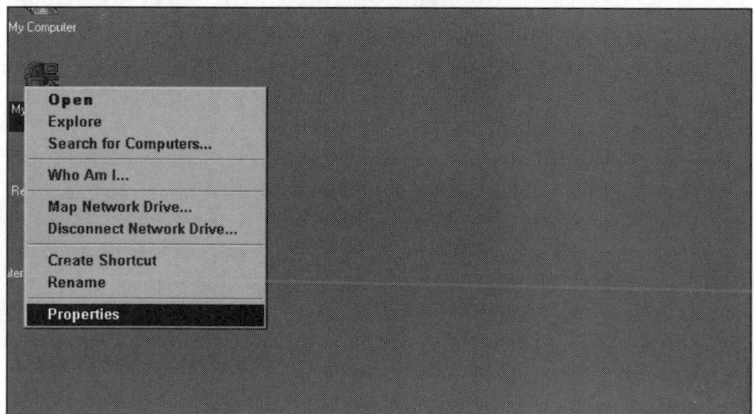

Figure 4-2: My Network Places secondary menu

Because the Network and Dial-up Connections applet is a commonly used tool, you might consider creating a desktop shortcut, as shown in Figure 4-3. To do this, simply right-click the Network and Dial-up Connections applet when Control Panel is displayed and select the Create Shortcut option. This selection will only allow you to place the shortcut on the desktop.

Continued

STEPS:

To install Microsoft TCP/IP *(continued)*

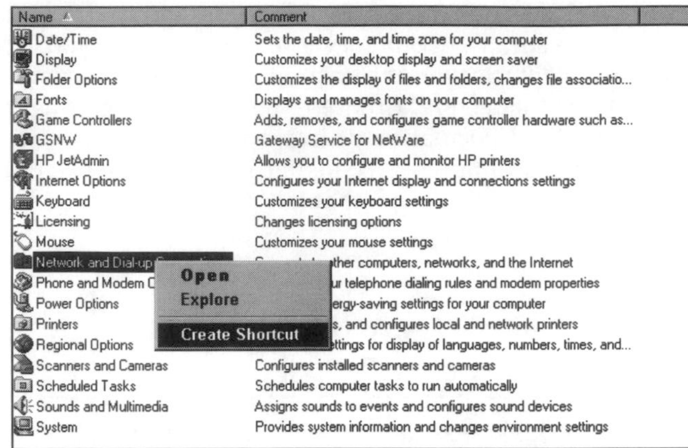

Figure 4-3: Creating a Network and Dial-up Connections shortcut

Step 3. Open, via a double-click, the Local Area Connection (in this example) or the appropriately named connection (which you would have created). The Local Area Connection Status dialog box will be displayed (see Figure 4-4).

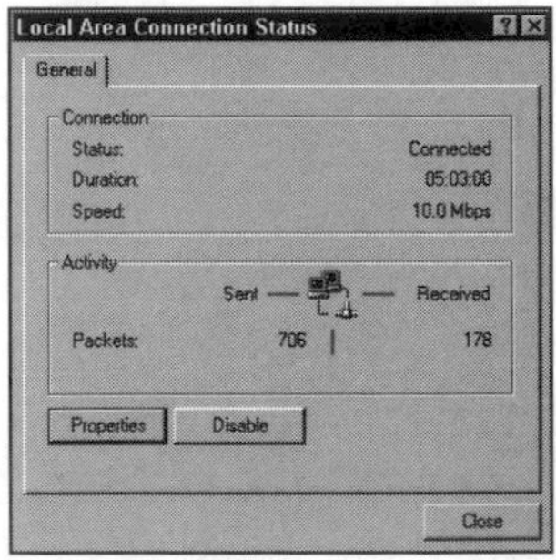

Figure 4-4: Local Area Connection Status dialog box

Step 4. Click Properties and the Local Area Connection Properties dialog box will appear (see Figure 4-5).

Step 5. Click Install and the Select Network Component Type dialog box will appear.

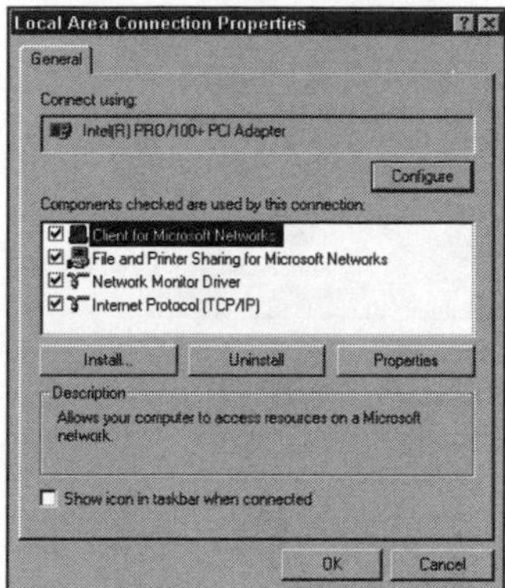

Figure 4-5: The Local Area Connection Properties dialog box

Step 6. Highlight the Protocol object and click Add. Select Internet Protocol (TCP/IP).

Step 7. The Internet Protocol (TCP/IP) installation will be automatically completed and you will be asked to specify whether the TCP/IP configuration information will be obtained from another DHCP server or whether you will manually configure the TCP/IP information, which is discussed in the next section.

Configuring TCP/IP

Remember that two cases arise in which you would configure TCP/IP manually on a Windows 2000 server. First, the server may be a DHCP server, requiring a static IP address. The second (you guessed it) is when you do not acquire your TCP/IP configuration information from a DHCP server. These points are fair game on the Windows 2000 MCSE exams.

Because you are now implementing manual TCP/IP configurations, be sure to revisit your network plan or as-built drawings so that you avoid duplicate IP addresses on the same network.

Duplicate addresses will result in the error message shown in Figure 4-6, and you will see unpredictable or downright weird behavior on your network. Typically, the host that had the IP address originally is unimpeded. However, the second host that attempts to assume the same IP address will have no network functionality. The rule regarding duplicate IP addresses? In general, the first host wins and all other hosts trying to use the same IP address lose.

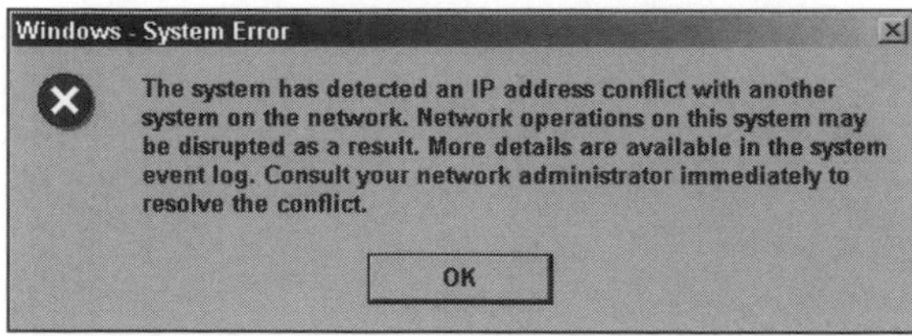

Figure 4-6: The duplicate IP address error message

STEPS:

To configure TCP/IP manually

Step 1. The Internet Protocol (TCP/IP) Properties dialog box (Figure 4-7) is the starting point for manually configuring TCP/IP. As shown previously, this dialog box will automatically appear in a manual configuration scenario when you are installing TCP/IP.

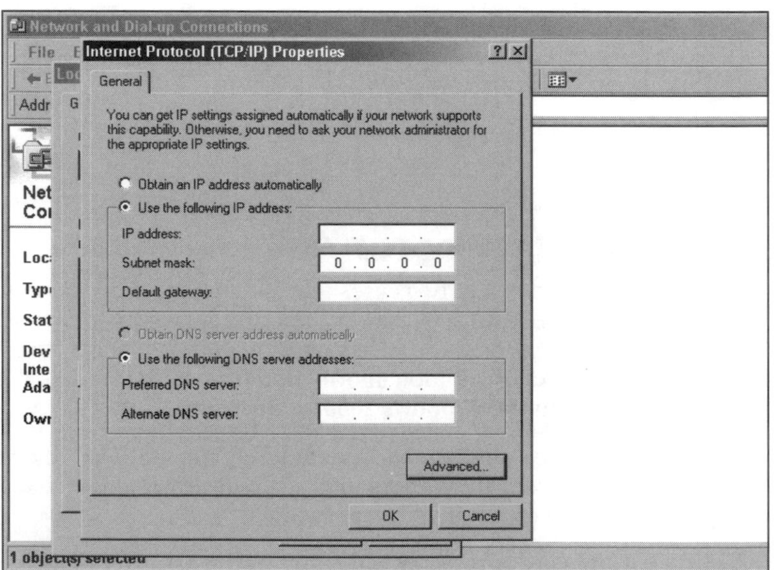

Figure 4-7: Internet Protocol (TCP/IP) properties

Note that if you attempt to close the Internet Protocol (TCP/IP) Properties dialog box without providing any TCP/IP configuration information, you will receive an error message communicating that the adapter needs at least one IP address (see Figure 4-8).

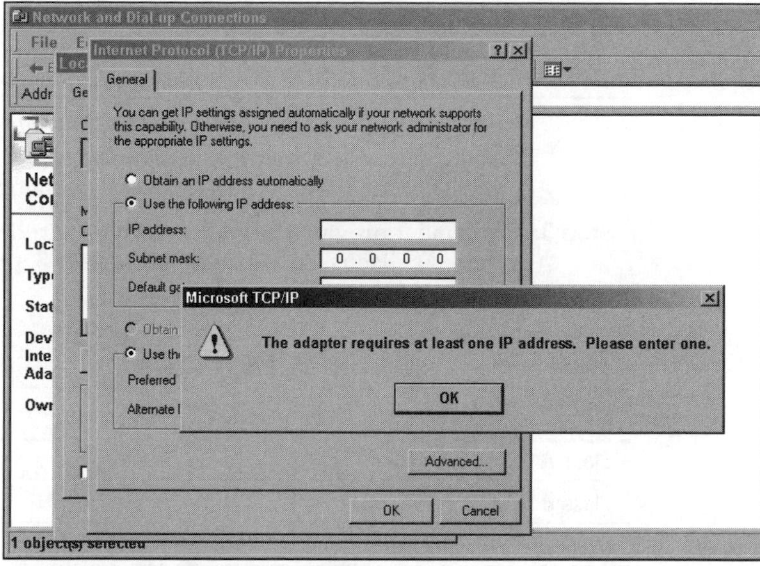

Figure 4-8: Configuration error message

Step 2. Complete the IP Address, Subnet Mask, Default Gateway and Preferred and Alternate DNS fields (see Figure 4-9). You must set unique IP address information for each bound adapter. Type that value in the IP Address field.

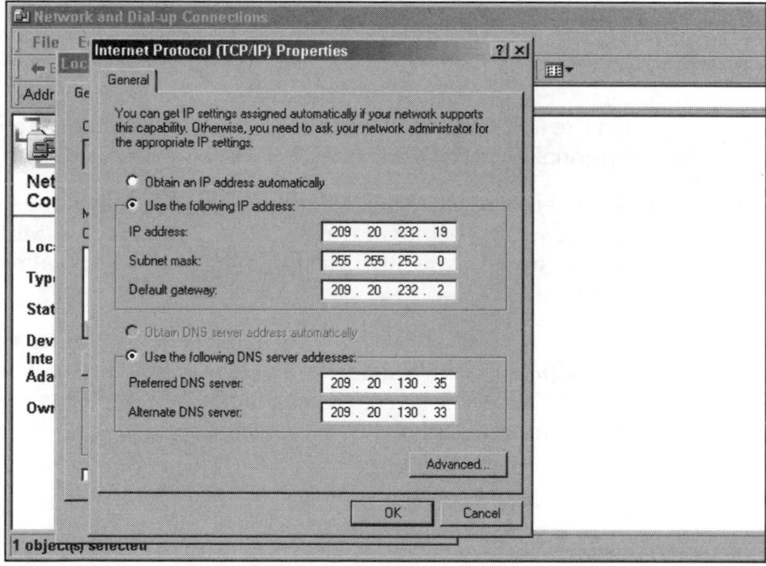

Figure 4-9: Completed Internet Protocol (TCP/IP) properties

Continued

STEPS:

To configure TCP/IP manually *(continued)*

Note that for automatic TCP/IP configuration via a DHCP server, you would select the Obtain an IP Address from a DHCP Server radio button in the TCP/IP Properties dialog box.

Step 3. You must provide the information required in the Subnet Mask field. As discussed at length in Chapter 3, this information may be any of the items in Table 4-1.

Table 4-1 Possible Subnet Mask Values

Class	*Value*
Class A	255.0.0.0
Class B	255.255.0.0
Class C	255.255.255.0
Other	Appropriate subnet mask based on your subnetting scenario (for example, 255.255.255.240)

Step 4. You may or may not provide an IP address value for the Default Gateway field depending on your situation. Here again, it's like tax law: everyone's situation is typically unique. If you are on a single subnet, this is not a required value.

On the MCSE exams, understand that the Default Gateway value is an optional entry on nonrouted networks.

Single subnet scenarios will typically leave this value blank or insert the IP address value of one of the Windows 2000 servers. Multiple subnet or routed scenarios will typically insert the value of the actual router (for instance, a Cisco router).

Leaving the Default Gateway value blank doesn't mean that your subnet doesn't participate in a routed network scenario. Routing may occur in other ways: Remote-Access Services (RAS), Microsoft Proxy Server, or the Windows 2000 Server routing table (via the route command).

Properly configured, RAS can act as a router to the other networks including the Internet. RAS can also do this while acting as a gateway that translates network-based communications between different types of protocols. RAS can even transport data from a fundamentally nonroutable network based on NetBEUI (a nonroutable protocol) to another network such as TCP/IP based on its capability to act as both a router and a gateway.

Another routing scenario on a Windows 2000 Server network when the Default Gateway field is left blank occurs when Microsoft Proxy Server is part of the picture. This occurs in one of two ways. First, when the WinSock Proxy (WSP) client is installed on a client, all Windows Sockets activity or calls are redirected to Microsoft Proxy Server. In English, that means you can leave your Default Gateway field blank on a client, yet have your Internet Explorer browser correctly find a resource on the Internet via Microsoft Proxy Server and a valid Internet connection. In essence, Microsoft Proxy Server is acting as the default gateway via the WSP client configuration and the Proxy Server declaration you make on the Connection tab sheet of Internet Explorer.

A second Microsoft Proxy Server routing scenario relates to the use of the IPX protocol for a client on your internal network and the TCP/IP protocol for your connection to the Internet. Properly configured (be darn sure to read the README and RELEASE NOTES files that ship with Microsoft Proxy Server to correctly implement an IPX client. Trust me!!!), the IPX-based client directs its Internet communications through Microsoft Proxy Server to the TCP/IP-based Internet. Bingo — routing and gateway functionality all in one.

The route command allows for routing when the Default Gateway field is left blank by enabling you to create static routes between networks. This was discussed in Chapter 3.

Static routes created by the route utility always override the default gateways.

Advanced TCP/IP configurations

Clicking the Advanced button on the Microsoft TCP/IP Properties dialog box will spawn the Advanced TCP/IP Settings dialog box (see Figure 4-10). Modify the settings on the IP Settings, DNS, WINS, and Options tabs as required. Don't panic, I'll be discussing these tabs in a moment! You will see that many of the IP address settings you've previously entered are shown again in the Advanced TCP/IP Settings dialog box.

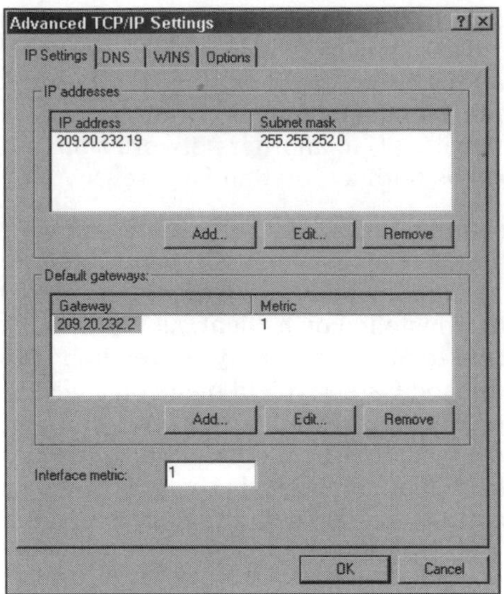

Figure 4-10: Advanced TCP/IP settings

Adding IP addresses

This is your opportunity to add multiple IP addresses to an adapter. Truth be told, I've learned the hard way that this is never more than an interim solution or workaround to a specific problem (such as the three I describe later). Regrettably, I've found that this feature exposes some of the fundamental weaknesses in the TCP/IP protocol stack in Windows 2000 Server. Adding multiple IP addresses to a single adapter "kinda" works, but never as well as adding multiple adapters, each with its own unique IP address, to the same Windows 2000 Server. Stated another way, I'd rather have three network adapter cards with three unique IP addresses than one network adapter with three IP addresses assigned to it. I've encountered different types of errors when assigning multiple IP addresses to a single adapter. One example was an intermittent network failure. Here, the inability of workstations to access a distributed database that relied heavily on TCP/IP-based communications, such as Windows network implementations of the Progress database application and their use of the good old HOSTS file, was ultimately traced back to having multiple IP addresses assigned to the network adapter in the server.

This is a known gotcha on the MCSE exams. Spend an extra few moments in this section understanding why you would or wouldn't assign multiple IP addresses to a single network adapter card.

Why would we ever assign multiple IP addresses to a single network adapter card? For several reasons, all based on TCP/IP encounters that I've had over the years:

- Scenario one: This is a case of a client being surprised by the rapid consumption of existing IP addresses.

  This scenario, from the Windows NT Server days, but with implications for the Windows 2000 Server era, involves a client that was underengineered and underserved by the previous Internet consultant. The consultant did not allow for growth, so the client received a small range of real IP addresses from the consultant. Later, the firm experienced growth and had a second but separate range of real Internet addresses assigned to the site. To enable all of the workstations to see and use the server, a second IP address from this new range of IP addresses was assigned and bound to the single adapter inside the server (see Figures 4-11 and 4-12).

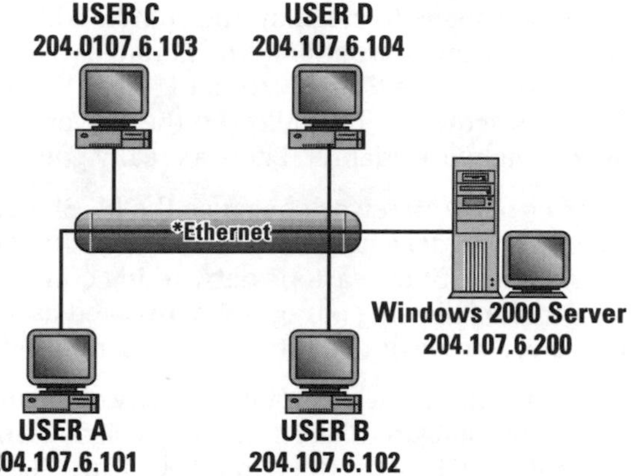

Figure 4-11: A small network with a single IP address assigned to the server network adapter card

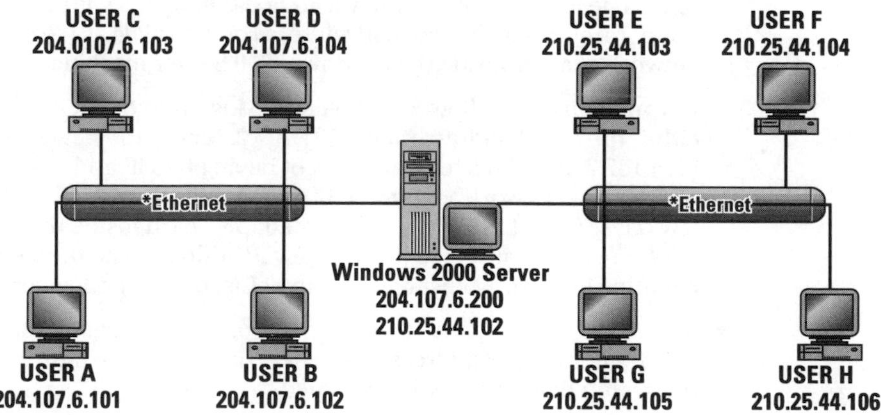

Figure 4-12: A small network with two IP addresses assigned to the server network adapter card

It didn't work. No sooner was this second address range implemented on the network than I (the newly hired consultant) started to receive service-related calls that User A couldn't browse the Internet, User B's Internet e-mail didn't work, and the point-of-sale machine (User H) couldn't write to the Progress database on the server machine. One $80 network adapter later (plus my labor, which of course exceeded the price of the network adapter), each subnet had a specific network adapter inside the server machine. And each of these network adapters had only one IP address. Life was good! (Note that I did turn on routing under the Routing tab sheet under TCP/IP Protocol properties. I will discuss this feature shortly.)

A follow-up comment to scenario one: Several months later, for a variety of reasons, an effort was made to clean up the split IP address layout. A new ISP was selected and an Internet IP address range that was more than sufficient to accommodate the present and future IP addressing needs for this firm was acquired. That allowed the server machine to operate with just one network adapter. Life was really good after that!

- Scenario two involves network rework because the MCSE textbook was followed too closely in designing the network, resulting in a TCP/IP design that wasn't the best fit for various networking components. The fix you will read of in the following paragraphs involved assigning two IP addresses to the server's network adapter for a short period of time.

  Here a client had a network that, while not incorrectly configured, wasn't (shall we say) optimally configured. This firm had designed a network right out of the Microsoft Official Curriculum (MOC) with "classroom" IP addresses of 131.107.2.2*xx* with a Class C subnet (255.255.255.0). It basically worked until the Cisco router engineer voiced objections to having a Class B range of host addresses associated with a Class C subnet mask. Fair enough. But because I couldn't get to each client machine instantaneously to change its IP address (even via lease assignments with DHCP), I had to temporarily assign a second IP address (perhaps 204.107.2.200) to the network adapter inside the Windows 2000 Server machine.

  It worked fine and allowed the clients to log on to the network under either the old IP address range (131.107.2.2*xx*) or the new IP address range (204.107.2.2*xx*). This temporary fix of having two IP addresses assigned to the same network adapter on the server was kept in place for just a few days. At that point, the network adapter card inside the Windows 2000 Server machine assumed just the new IP address. The problem was solved, resulting in a happy client and a happy Cisco router engineer.

- Scenario three is similar to scenario two. This is a case of "borrowing" private network IP addresses for a few days until the authentic Internet-registered IP addresses are obtained from the ISP.

  Often, a client will proceed with a TCP/IP-based network installation prior to receiving its real IP address assignment from the InterNIC. There are usually compelling business reasons to move ahead without regard for what IP addressing is being used. These reasons, of course, typically involve money, such as an expiring support agreement on an old AS-400 that the client (a) doesn't want to renew and (b) wants to convert to Windows 2000 Server and the BackOffice applications pronto! In these cases, I've used the dummy IP address range of 10.0.0.*x* while awaiting an IP address assignment (typically Class C) and domain registration from the InterNIC.

In the real life scenario involving my client, once my client received the Internet-registered IP address range from the Internet Service Provider, I briefly had to support the phony IP address range (10.0.0.*x*) and the real IP address range until each client machine could be properly reconfigured. Again, this example underscores the appropriate use of multiple IP addresses assigned to a single network adapter.

To add multiple IP addresses, simply click the Add button and enter the IP address on the screen shown in Figure 4-13.

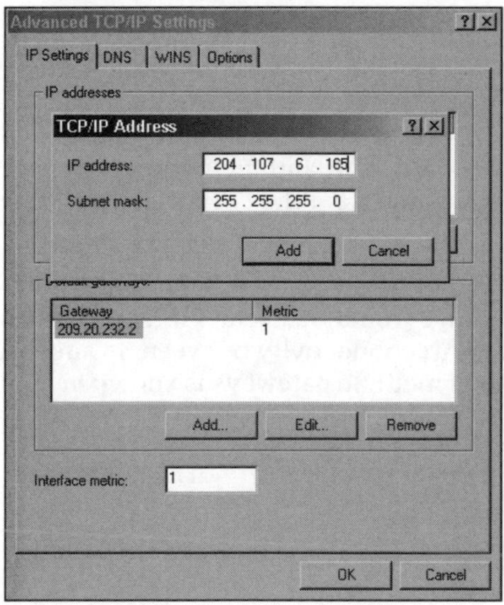

Figure 4-13: Adding TCP/IP addresses

Clicking anywhere on the Subnet Mask field will automatically populate this entry for you. Thus, you do not need to manually enter the required subnet mask value if you are conforming to the traditional Classes A, B, and C host range rules. For example, if you entered 204.107.6.165 as an additional IP address and clicked Add, the Subnet Mask column would already be populated with 255.255.255.0 (the Class C subnet mask value). Beware of using unusual combinations of IP address and subnet mask values and relying on the automatic Subnet Mask field populate feature. For example, if you were an ardent MCSE student and set up your network exactly like those found in classrooms using the MOC, you would be in trouble with the automatic Subnet Mask field populate feature. That's because the MOC setup of 131.107.6.*x* is a Class B host value, but the MOC uses a Class C subnet mask value. Bad news when using the automatic Subnet Mask field populate feature. In this example, you would need to overwrite the default subnet mask value of 255.255.0.0 and insert 255.255.255.0 to truly conform to the MOC class setup guidelines.

I successfully added one dozen TCP/IP values to one network adapter before tiring of the exercise. You can actually add up to 255 IP addresses to a single network adapter.

However, understand that Microsoft's official position with respect to assigning multiple IP addresses to a single network adapter is useful for a computer connected to one physical network that contains multiple logical IP networks. Enough said.

Multiple gateways

Hang on to your hat. This field isn't what you may think it is. Perhaps you thought this was the Holy Grail of having a Windows 2000 Server machine participate on two internetworks simultaneously. An increasingly common scenario, illustrated in Figure 4-14, is when the corporate LAN may be connected via a Frame Relay-based WAN and the Internet connection is via an ISDN or ADSL/DSL connection from the corporate headquarters.

However, the Gateways field isn't designed to accommodate this routing need. It is designed to create redundant routes on the same internetwork. Thus, defining multiple gateways would be useful for a corporate network that rightfully needs robust WAN connectivity between its sites and is willing to pay for it! The proper use of multiple gateways is shown in Figure 4-15.

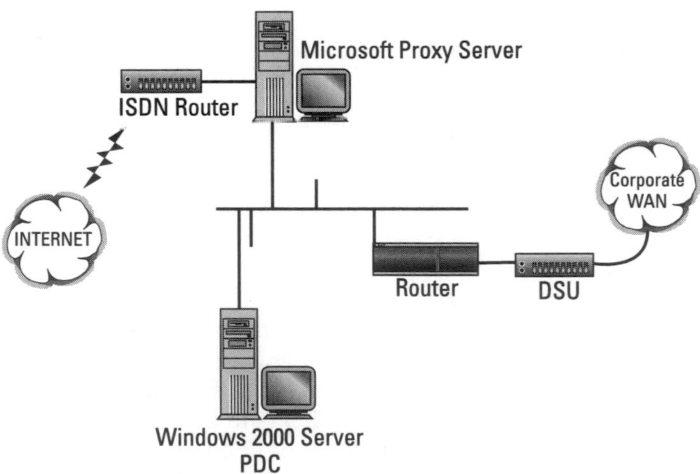

Figure 4-14: Corporate WAN and ISDN Internet connection

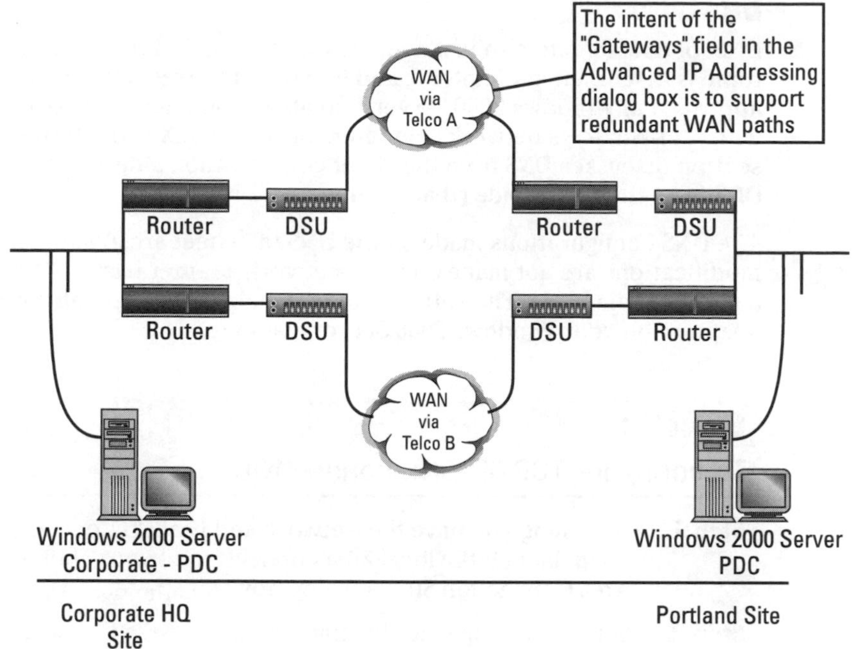

Figure 4-15: Windows 2000 Server on a corporate WAN

Tip

By the way, the solution for the multiple internetwork scenario presented in Figure 4-14 is to create multiple static routes via the route utility. And be sure to make those routes persistent with the –p command line switch, or else you will have to enter the static routes again when you reboot the Windows 2000 Server machine.

The bottom line on multiple gateways? Properly configured, internetworking communications capabilities are maintained even when transmission problems are occurring because the system will try other routers in the internetwork configuration to ensure success.

Secret

If you use multiple gateway entries, be sure to make wise use of the metric value. The lower the metric (a.k.a. cost), the higher the priority for that route. Stated another way, a metric of 1 has a lower cost than a metric of 2, and you should always be looking for ways to lower your costs. You may be interested to know the Metric field replaces the Up and Down buttons used for multiple gateways in the old Windows NT Server 4.0 days.

Other configuration issues

Several additional tab sheets on the Advanced TCP/IP Settings dialog box need configuring to fully implement the TCP/IP protocol stack. These tab sheets, beyond the IP settings discussed above, are DNS, WINS, and Options.

DNS

DNS, of course, offers robust name resolution for TCP/IP hosts. This lengthy topic is discussed in Chapter 6, and it is the preferred name resolution approach in Windows 2000 Server. You also should use DNS to interact better with non-Windows network computers such as UNIX and Internet hosts. This section discusses DNS from the client configuration side; Chapter 6 discusses DNS from the server side (that is, running a DNS server).

The DNS configurations made on the DNS tab sheet are global. These modifications are not made on a per-network adapter basis, but rather a per-machine basis. The entries that you make here affect all network adapters on your Windows 2000 Server machine.

STEPS:

To configure TCP/IP DNS connectivity

Step 1. Assuming you have the Network and Dial-Up Connections applet open, launch the local area connection of your choice. The Local Area Connection Status dialog box will appear.

Step 2. Select the Properties button. The Local Area Connection Properties dialog box will be displayed.

Step 3. Highlight the Internet Protocol (TCP/IP) component and select the Properties button. The Internet Protocol (TCP/IP) Properties dialog box will be displayed.

Step 4. On the General tab of the Internet Protocol (TCP/IP) Properties dialog box, select the Advanced button.

Step 5. Select the DNS tab. The DNS tab sheet will be displayed (see Figure 4-16).

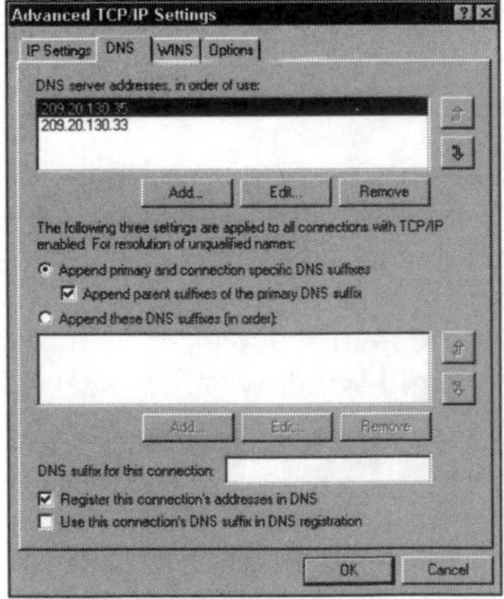

Figure 4-16: DNS tab sheet

Step 6. In the DNS address, in order to use the field, enter the values for your DNS servers. These are IP addresses, typically provided by your Internet Service Provider (ISP). Note that you most often enter a pair of DNS addresses so that you have multiple locations to seek name resolution.

If for some reason your ISP neglected to provide you with DNS addresses, you can typically find this information at the ISP's Web site as part of its support information or a Frequently Asked Question (FAQ). Why do I share this with you? Because on more than one occasion, in the wee hours of the morning, with the ISP staff safely in bed, I've found this critical DNS address information exactly this way.

You may also, via the up or down arrows, select the DNS site you want to visit first when attempting to resolve a host name.

You might also make a third entry, for your ISP's SMTP mail server, if you plan to use DNS resolution with the Microsoft Exchange IMS (Internet Mail Service) and the SMTP server is separate from the other DNS servers maintained by the ISP. Failing to make the correct entry in the DNS Service Search Order field and electing to use DNS with the IMS may result in message delivery failure to the Internet. In English, get it right and it will work.

Although Microsoft Exchange is a BackOffice application and Windows 2000 Server an operating system, this example does serve to demonstrate how BackOffice applications are integrated with the underlying Windows 2000 Server operating system. Figure 4-17 shows one form of such integration, with the selection of DNS being used by Microsoft Exchange's IMS.

Step 7. In the middle section of the DNS tab, there are three settings you may select. The Search primary DNS domain and DNS domain of each connection radio button allows you to limit third-level and other unqualified DNS domain name searches to the computer's parent DNS domain. Note that you can find a more robust definition of this radio button simply by right-clicking when your mouse is over the option (giving the radio button the focus) and selecting the What's This? secondary menu option.

The checkbox titled Search the parent domains of the primary DNS domain allows you to extend the search from the parent domain to the parents (for example, grandparents) of the parent domain. Again, the What's This? secondary menu option for this item provides an extensive explanation of this ability.

The Search these DNS domains (in order) radio button allows you to limit the DNS domain names that may be searched for, in so many words. Again, see the What's This? secondary menu option for a far more detailed and technical explanation (that is, if you really have time on your hands).

Continued

STEPS:

To configure TCP/IP DNS connectivity *(continued)*

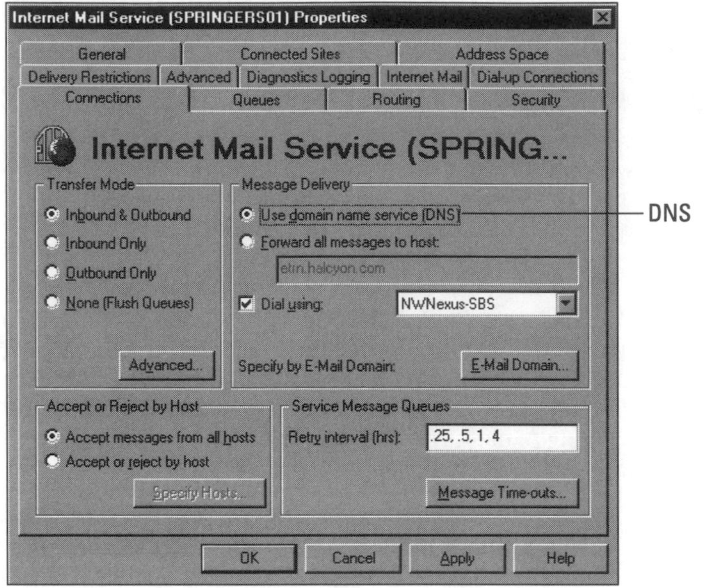

Figure 4-17: The Microsoft Exchange IMS configured to use DNS for message delivery

Step 8. Complete the DNS domain name field. This is the DNS domain name associated with this network connection. It's very important, as the next secret explains.

Failure to correctly complete the Domain field will cause the Internet Mail Service to fail upon startup in Microsoft Exchange 5.*x*.

Microsoft Exchange will write out Error #4067 to the Application log in Event Viewer (see Figure 4-18). But you'll probably learn of this misconfiguration another way, from the users who complain they don't have Internet-based e-mail. It seems that users are always your best error log.

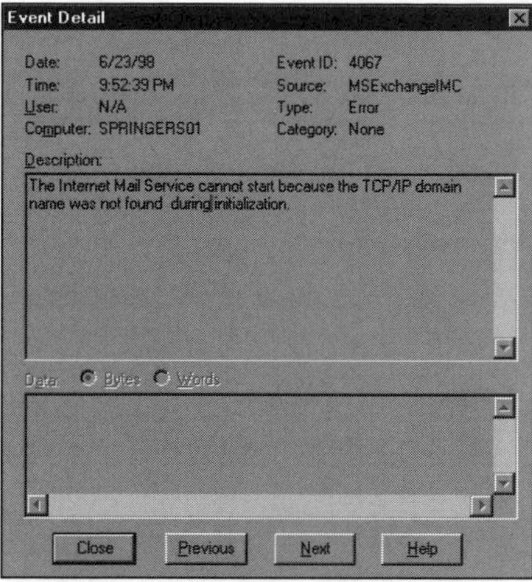

Figure 4-18: A missing TCP/IP domain name error generated by Microsoft Exchange

WINS addresses

The WINS Addresses tab sheet offers a client-side configuration to enable the machine you are configuring to point to one or more WINS servers. It is also where you may identify the machine you are setting up to be one of those machines you're pointing at as a WINS server (you can point to yourself, in short). You may make two selections that can have a dramatic impact on how names are resolved. The implicit assumption prior to performing the configurations on this tab sheet is that a WINS server exists on your network. More importantly, understand that WINS functionality is included to accommodate the older Windows NT networks, wherein WINS assumed a large name resolution role. As mentioned several times in this book, Dynamic DNS has largely replaced WINS as the name resolution method of choice.

STEPS:

To configure or reconfigure TCP/IP to use WINS

Step 1. Select the Advanced button from the Internet Protocol (TCP/IP) Properties. The Advanced TCP/IP Settings dialog box will be displayed.

Step 2. Select the WINS tab sheet (see Figure 4-19).

Continued

STEPS:

To configure or reconfigure TCP/IP to use WINS *(continued)*

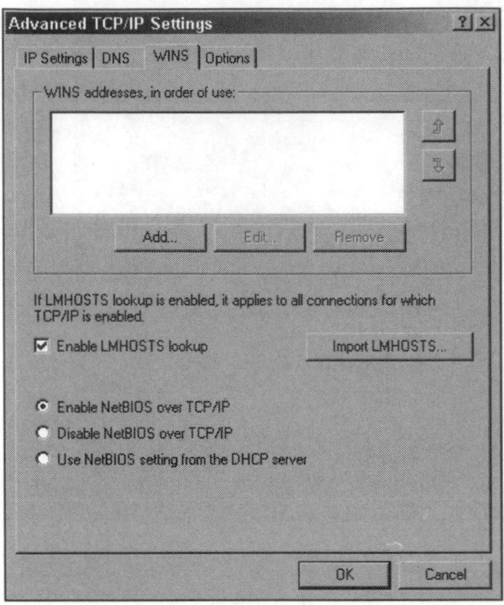

Figure 4-19: The WINS tab sheet

Step 3. Select the Add button and the TCP/IP WINS Server dialog box will appear. Enter the IP address of the WINS server and click Add (see Figure 4-20). Repeat this step as many times as necessary.

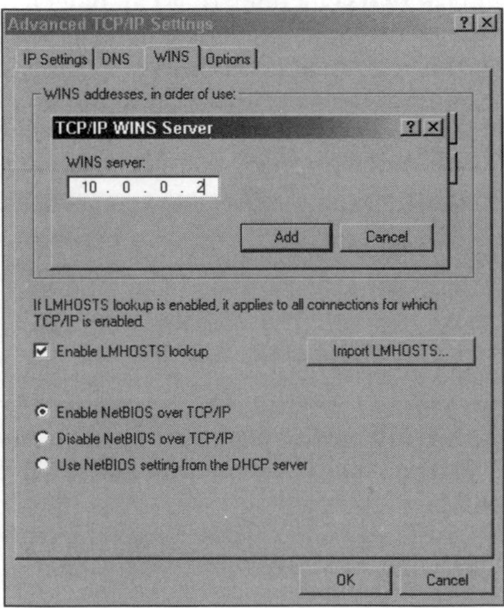

Figure 4-20: TCP/IP WINS Server dialog box

Step 4. To use the LMHOSTS file, select the Enable LMHOSTS Lookup checkbox. This is selected by default in Windows 2000 Server when the TCP/IP protocol stack is installed. By default, Windows 2000 Server uses the LMHOSTS file maintained in the `\WINNT\SYSTEM32\DRIVERS\ETC` subdirectory. The LMHOSTS file is discussed at length in Chapter 7. Alternate LMHOSTS file locations may be specified via the Import LMHOSTS button.

Note the Enable LMHOSTS lookup checkbox and Enable NetBIOS over TCP/IP radio button are selected by default. This causes several issues to surface:

- The names discovered via broadcasts are cached and can be displayed via the nbtstat command (discussed extensively in Chapter 7).
- Entries in the LMHOSTS file can be preloaded into the name resolution cache via the #PRE statement. This results in much faster name resolutions because this information is maintained in primary storage (cached in RAM memory) instead of requiring an access to secondary storage (the LMHOSTS file stored on the local hard disk). The LMHOSTS file is discussed extensively in Chapter 5.
- When in doubt about any name resolution dilemma, by all means feel free to reboot the Windows 2000 server to update the cached IP to name mappings. A reboot forces a refresh.
- WINS works great in Windows NT-based environments with an abundance of Microsoft-friendly clients (machines using NetBIOS names), but falls far short in its support for foreign client environments, such as Macintosh clients on a Windows 2000 Server-based network.
- WINS will be supported in Windows 2000 Server for backward compatibility purposes, but the future of IP-to-NetBIOS name resolution rests squarely with Dynamic DNS, one of the new features in Windows 2000 Server. Dynamic DNS is discussed more in Chapter 6.

Step 5. Not surprisingly, after you have completed configuring WINS, you should reboot your Windows 2000 Server machine for these changes to be properly implemented. What do I mean by properly implemented? Do I mean the time at the local hardware store when my East Texas accent provoked the sales clerk to remark that I was the first person that day to pass through who "spoke English properly"? Nope. I mean that, even though Windows 2000 Server won't require a reboot with these WINS changes, I feel better by performing a reboot. That's what I call implementing something "properly"—Windows 2000-style!

Options

Selecting the Options tab sheet (see Figure 4-21) allows you to implement IP security and TCP/IP filtering. IP Security (a.k.a. IPsec) is discussed in Chapter 13.

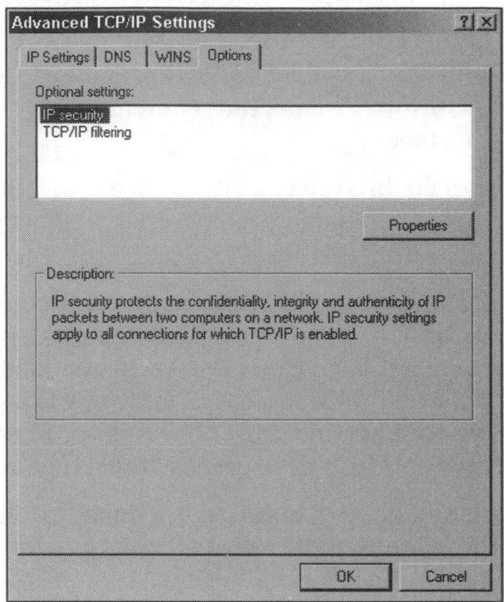

Figure 4-21: Options tab sheet

Selecting TCP/IP Filtering displays the TCP/IP Filtering dialog box (see Figure 4-22), which allows you to enable TCP/IP filtering for all adapters. Basically, with TCP/IP filtering, you may lock your network down further by specifying which ports are allowed to pass.

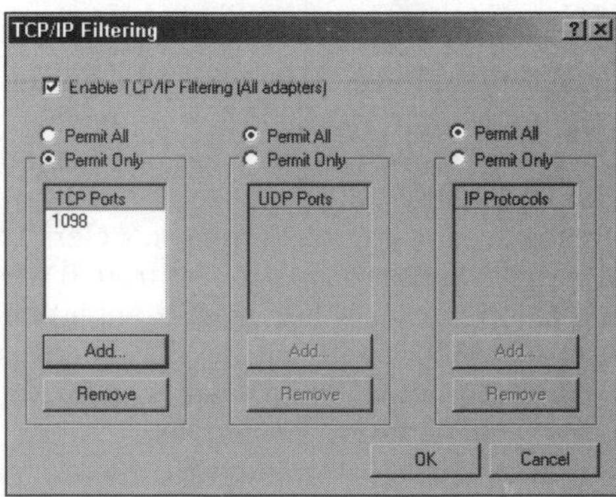

Figure 4-22: Enabling TCP/IP filtering

Remember that upper-range port values (between 1,024 and 65,536) are available to you for private use and in creating secure sessions. The problem, similar to a CB radio conversation between two truckers on upper CB channels, is that all parties using TCP/IP security and participating on your network must agree to the specific port values that will be allowed. Be careful here. Although TCP/IP security enables you to control the type of traffic (typically Internet) that actually reaches the network adapter card of your Windows 2000 server, your network can suffer greatly if these values are set incorrectly!

Supporting roving users with TCP/IP

A client showed me this problem that actually applies to the Windows 95 and Windows 98 Registry. He was faced with using real IP addresses at a half-dozen athletic clubs that he oversaw. Each athletic club had its own subnet. One problem was that, because of an older database, static IP addresses (referenced in a HOSTS file) made DHCP addressing impossible. And several managers carried laptops running Windows 95 between the clubs. These static IP addresses resulted in a "No Domain Server Available" message when a user traveled to a distant club with a different subnet and attempted to log on. The solution?

My client created a `*.reg` file for each of the six athletic clubs and placed these reg files on each user's Windows 95 (now Windows 98) desktop. The files had names that corresponded to club names, such as `ctc.reg` and `jbc.reg`. The contents of the `ctc.reg` file are:

```
[HKEY_LOCAL_MACHINE\System\CurrentControlSet\Services\Class\_NetTrans\
0001
"IPAddress" = "209.34.123.156"
"DefaultGateway" = "209.34.123.145"
"IPMask" = "255.255.255.240"
```

Each user, by double-clicking the appropriate `*.reg` file, changes the IP address information on the Windows 95 laptop and so is able to participate fully on the club's network. Again, the Registry entry, via the `*.reg` file approach, applies to Windows 95 and Windows 98. But in reality, it's an issue that you will confront when managing TCP/IP on your Windows 2000 Server network.

Installing and Configuring Simple Network Management Protocol (SNMP)

One of the reasons I so enjoy my interactions with businesspeople is that they, in the course of our conversations, help keep me grounded in reality. Though I'm most excited about some of the advanced and powerful features of Windows 2000 Server, my business brethren view technology simply as a tool to help them run their businesses better. If I can help them do so with my tool set, including Windows 2000 Server, so much the better.

For your part, you might view SNMP as a tool to help you run your network better. In fact, you might not be concerned about the finer points of SNMP, but more interested in its management-reporting capabilities. Most likely, you just want to know when something is wrong with your network. For you, SNMP is a great place to start.

In the real world, SNMP has become the accepted standard for managing network devices. HP Open View, CA-Unicenter TNG, and other management system tools rely on SNMP not only to gather network device information but also to manage and configure these devices. The bottom line on SNMP in general: it is a powerful and flexible tool to monitor and control networks. This is accomplished by its distributed architecture with basically two components, the management system (like the third-party products mentioned previously) and agents.

The bottom line on SNMP with Windows 2000 Server: loser. Natively, Windows 2000 Server doesn't use SNMP at any great level of depth. The only thing a Windows 2000 server may do running the SNMP service (without any enhancements) is to report its status to an SNMP management system on a TCP/IP network.

In other words, the Windows 2000 Server SNMP service is merely an SNMP agent. SNMP agents may only initiate trap operations. You may or may not know that a trap operation alerts management systems to events such as logon failure due to password violations. Microsoft's SNMP service is not natively an SNMP management system. To be one, it would have to be running SNMP management software, such as HP Open View.

This disappointment extends even to Microsoft System Management Server (SMS), a network management application that is included as part of Microsoft BackOffice. SMS is a popular management tool for Enterprise-level implementations of Windows 2000 Server. In fact, if you've taken the MCSE course on SMS, you will recall that SMS doesn't even use SNMP to gather network information. It is the one Microsoft application that you would expect to do so. Nope! SMS gathers network information via SMS agents that run on end-user workstations, including Macintosh, and other servers.

The only interaction between SMS and SNMP is at the Management Information Base (MIB) level. The configuration information from SNMP-compliant hosts running SNMP agents can be displayed via the "Event to Trap Translator" screen in SMS. That is, you may, in a read-only approach, view SNMP agent configuration information on your TCP/IP network. You may not actually manage the SNMP nodes from either SMS or Windows 2000 Server itself.

The only thing SNMP is really good for out of the box is to provide, as I've mentioned in passing, additional TCP/IP-related object:counters in Performance Monitor. Its value increases greatly when used in conjunction with third-party solutions such as HP Open View and CA-Unicenter. But SNMP on Windows 2000 Server — alone isn't much to write home about.

Architecturally speaking, the SNMP service runs at the application layer of the OSI model. Descending through Windows Sockets, the SNMP service uses UDP, not TCP, as its transport layer protocol. (You will recall that UDP is a connectionless, nonguaranteed connection mechanism).

Tip

If you are interested in developing for SNMP in Windows 2000 Server, you are best advised to contact the Microsoft Developer's Resource Group at `netman@microsoft.com`.

Planning for SNMP

Make sure that you've covered these three steps prior to installing the SNMP service:

- Have the IP addresses or host names for all hosts that will send SNMP traps.
- Be sure that the Windows 2000 Server name resolution methods you are using have the IP/host name mappings for all SNMP hosts on your network. For example, if you were using the LMHOSTS file, you would make name resolution mapping entries manually.
- Select an SNMP management system. To properly use the Microsoft SNMP service, you must have at least one SNMP management system (several choices, such as CA-Unicenter, were discussed earlier).

Installing SNMP service

Installing the Simple Network Management Protocol (SNMP) service is very simple. It is installed, as are many other services, via the Windows Components Wizard. To successfully install the SNMP service, you will need to be logged on as a member of the Administrators group.

STEPS:

To install SNMP

Step 1. Launch the Add/Remove Programs applet from Control Panel. The Add/Remove Programs dialog box will appear.

Step 2. Select the Add/Remove Windows Components button in the left pane of the Add/Remove Programs dialog box (see Figure 4-23).

Step 3. The Windows Components Wizard will be launched. Select the Management and Monitoring Tools component (see Figure 4-24).

Continued

STEPS:

To install SNMP *(continued)*

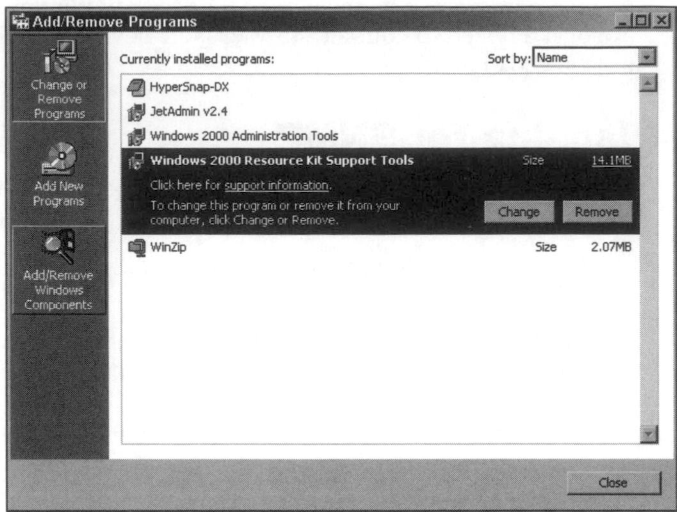

Figure 4-23: Add/Remove Programs dialog box

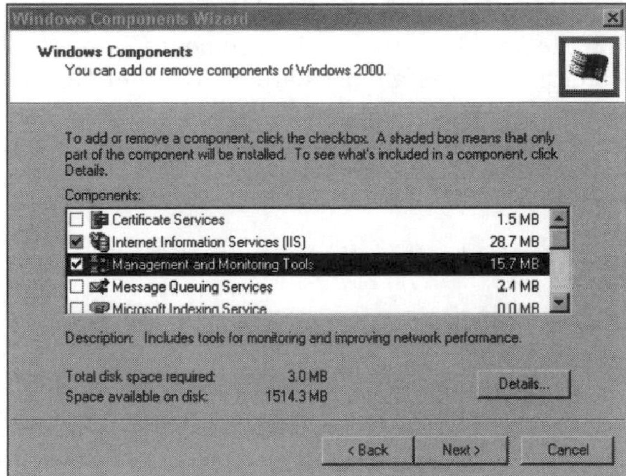

Figure 4-24: Windows Components Wizard

Step 4. The Management and Monitoring Tools dialog box will appear. Select the Simple Network Management Protocol subcomponent (see Figure 4-25).

Step 5. Click OK on the Management and Monitoring Tools dialog box.

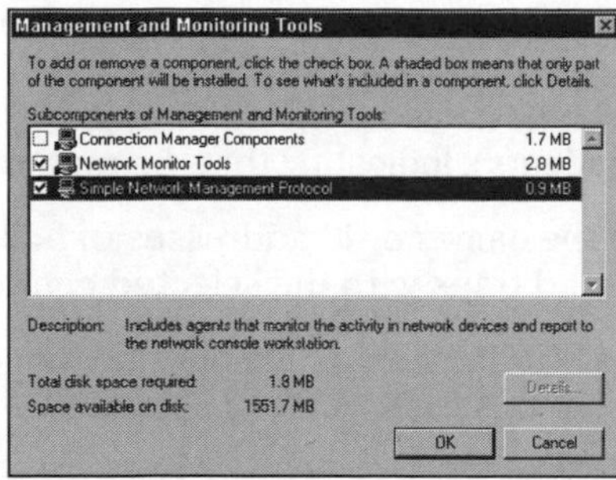

Figure 4-25: Management and Monitoring Tools

Step 6. Click Next on the Windows Component Wizard. The components that you selected (for example, SNMP agent) will be configured.

Step 7. Click Finish when the Completing the Windows Components Wizard screen appears. You have completed the SNMP agent installation.

Configuring the SNMP agent

First, you are asked to provide user contact and physical location information when presented with the default Agent tab sheet view of the Microsoft SNMP Properties dialog box. You will also elect what types of services may be reported based on the computer's SNMP agent configuration.

Remember that as you manage your Windows 2000 Server-based network, you will have plenty of opportunities to provide user and location information. Aside from the SNMP agent configuration, you will have the chance to provide similar information when creating a user in Microsoft Exchange and when Microsoft System Management Server performs a hardware inventory at a client machine (and creates an MIF file).

The reason I share this observation is that one of the underlying principles of database management is the creation and maintenance of a single table for certain data types. Just something to think about as you complete the SNMP agent configuration.

The SNMP configuration information identifies the following communities and trap destinations:

Community name. Much as the name implies, an SNMP community is a grouping of hosts running the SNMP service. Not surprisingly, communities are identified by a community name. An SNMP community is akin to a domain in Windows 2000 Server, an organization in Microsoft Exchange, or a site in Microsoft System Management Server. And like local security in SQL Server, an SNMP community name provides basic security and context checking for agents and management systems that receive requests/initiate traps and initiate requests/receive traps, respectively. The community name is embedded in the

SNMP packet when the trap is sent._When the SNMP service receives a request for information that does not contain the correct community name and does not match an accepted host name for the service, the SNMP service can send a trap to the trap destination(s), indicating that the request failed authentication.

Trap destinations are the names or IP addresses of hosts to which you want the SNMP service to send traps with the selected community name.

You might want to use SNMP for statistics but may not care about identifying communities or traps. In this case, you can specify the "Public" community name when you configure the SNMP service.

STEPS:

To configure SNMP agent information

Step 1. Assuming you are logged on as an Administrator, launch a Microsoft Management Console (by typing MMC in the Run dialog box accessed via the Start menu) and add the Services snap-in. Double-click the SNMP Service to display the SNMP Service Properties (Local Computer) dialog box. Choose the Agent tab (see Figure 4-26).

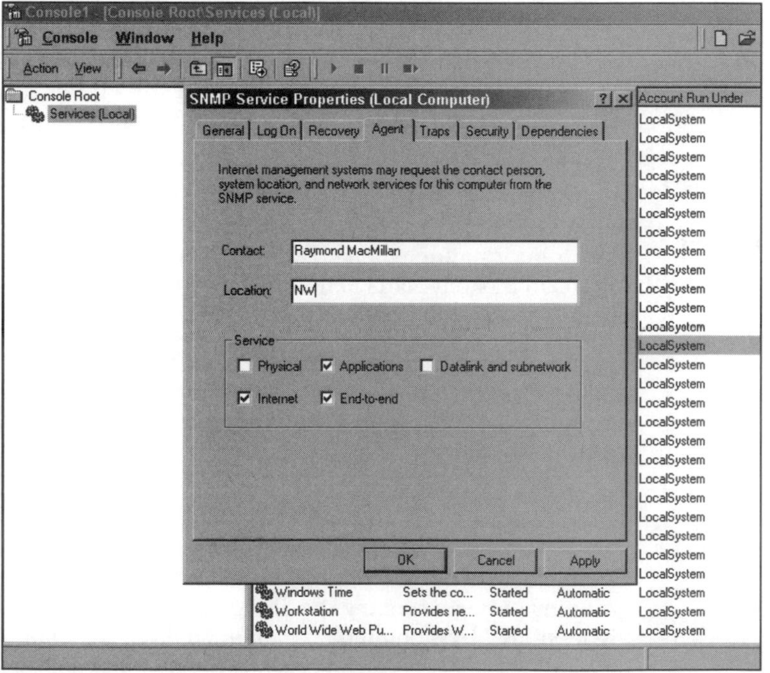

Figure 4-26: Agent tab

Step 2. Type the computer user's name in the Contact box and the computer's physical location in the Location box. These comments are treated as text and are optional.

Step 3. Set the Service options as described in Table 4-2. Check all the boxes that indicate network capabilities provided by your Windows 2000 computer. SNMP must have this information to manage enabled services.

If you have installed additional TCP/IP network devices, such as a switch or a router, you should consult RFC 1213 for additional information, as these configurations are beyond the scope of this book.

Step 4. Proceed to the next set of steps to configure SNMP Traps and Security. There are several SNMP-specific services to select, as seen in Table 4-2.

Table 4-2 SNMP Services

Option	*Description*
Physical	Select this option if this Windows 2000 computer manages any physical TCP/IP device, such as a repeater.
Applications	Select this option if this Windows 2000 computer includes any applications that use TCP/IP, such as e-mail. This option should be selected for all Windows 2000 installations.
Datalink/Subnetwork	Select this option if this Windows 2000 computer manages a TCP/IP subnetwork or datalink, such as a bridge.
Internet	Select this option if this Windows 2000 computer acts as an IP gateway.
End-to-end	Select this option if this Windows 2000 computer acts as an IP host. This option should be selected for all Windows 2000 installations.

Configuring SNMP communities and traps

Two necessary configurations for the SNMP service are community names and traps. Both of these configurations are set with the Traps tab sheet, as the next several steps will show you.

STEPS:

To configure SNMP traps

Step 1. In the SNMP Service Properties (Local Computer) dialog box, choose the Traps tab. The Traps dialog box appears, as shown in Figure 4-27.

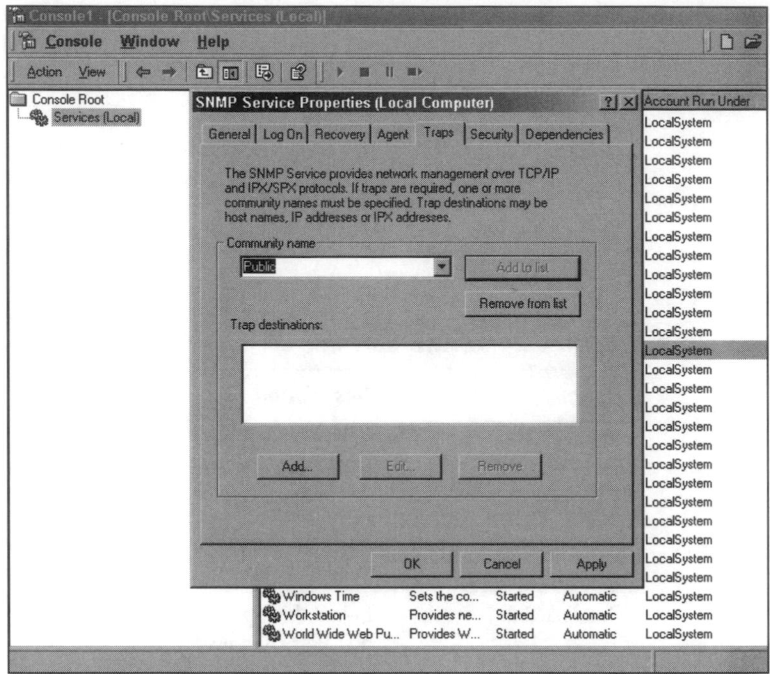

Figure 4-27: The Traps dialog box

Step 2. To identify each community to which you want this computer to send traps, enter the name in the Community Name box (for example, "Public"). After typing each name, choose the Add to list button.

Typically all hosts belong to Public, which is the common name of all hosts. To delete an entry in the list, select it and choose the Remove from list button.

Secret

An SNMP agent may be a member of multiple communities simultaneously allowing communications with SNMP managers from different communities. Note that community names are case sensitive.

Step 3. To specify hosts for each community to which you send traps, after you have added the community and while it is still highlighted, click Add under the Trap Destinations box. The SNMP Service Configuration dialog box appears (see Figure 4-28). Enter a host name, its IP address, or its IPX address in the Host Name, IP or IPX Address fields. Then choose the Add button to move the host name or IP address or IPX address to the Trap Destination for the Selected Community list.

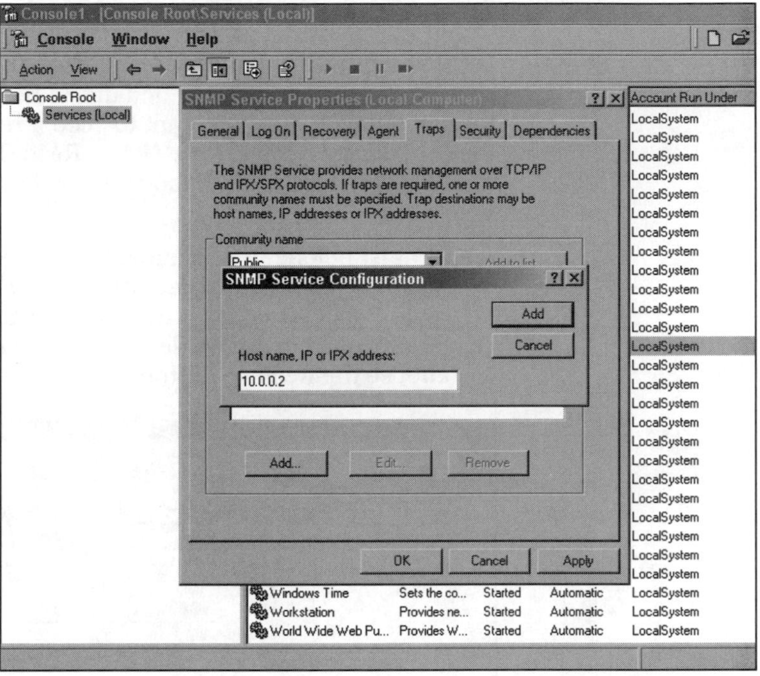

Figure 4-28: SNMP Service Configuration dialog box

Configuring SNMP security

SNMP security allows you to specify the communities and hosts from which a computer accepts requests and to specify whether to send an authentication trap when an unauthorized community or host requests information.

STEPS:

To configure SNMP security

Step 1. In the SNMP Services Properties (Local Computer) dialog box, choose the Security tab (see Figure 4-29).

Continued

STEPS:

To configure SNMP security *(continued)*

Step 2. If you want to send a trap for failed authentication, select the Send Authentication Trap checkbox.

Step 3. In the Accepted Community Names box, click the Add button. The SNMP Service Configuration dialog box appears. Type the community name you want to accept requests from and the community rights (None, Notify, Read Only, Read Write, Read Create). Click Add to move the name to the Accepted Community Names list.

A host must belong to a community that appears on this list for the SNMP service to accept its requests. Typically, all hosts belong to Public, which is the standard name for the common community of all hosts. To delete an entry in the list, select it and choose the Remove button.

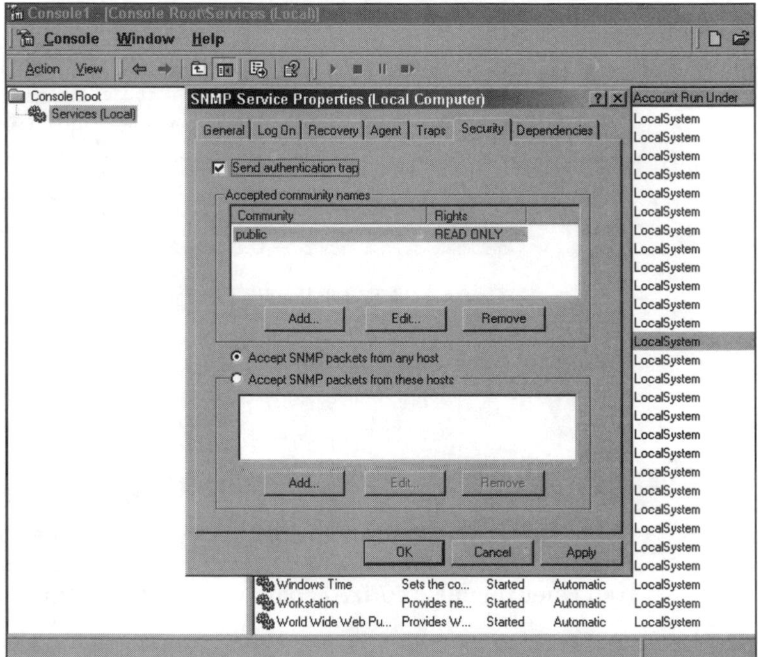

Figure 4-29: The Security tab

Step 4. Specify whether to accept SNMP packets from any host or from only specified hosts.

- If the Accept SNMP Packets from Any Host option is selected, no SNMP packets are rejected on the basis of source host ID. The list of hosts under Only Accept SNMP Packets from These Hosts has no effect.

- If the Only Accept SNMP Packets from These Hosts option is selected, SNMP packets are accepted only from the hosts listed. Click Add to display the IP Host or IPX Address dialog box. Then type the host names, IP addresses, or IPX addresses of the hosts from which you want to accept requests. Next, choose the Add button to move each host name or IP address to the list box. To delete an entry in the list, select it and choose the Remove button.

Step 5. Choose the OK button. You are returned to the Services (Local) MMC. The SNMP service and SNMP security are ready to start without rebooting the computer, but don't you believe that for a moment. When making such changes to the underlying network service, always reboot your Windows 2000 Server computer to ensure proper binding. As mentioned earlier in the chapter, it's part of implementing "properly."

TCP/IP-Related Services

This chapter ends with a quick review of TCP/IP-related services that may be installed via Windows Component Wizard. Having read this chapter and installed and worked with TCP/IP, you're now ready to add more services as needed.

Tip

Remember that you should never add more services than necessary. Not only do unnecessary services take up precious RAM, but it has been my personal experience that poorly implemented additional Windows 2000 Server services can lead to poor performance and even unexplained funky behavior, including blue screens. Use only what you need!

The way to extend and take advantage of all that TCP/IP has to offer isn't necessarily to type IP addresses into a dialog box all day. Rather, you extend TCP/IP on your Windows 2000 Server network by considering whether the services listed in Table 4-3 enable you to run your network better.

Table 4-3 TCP/IP-Related Services

Service	***Description***
Microsoft Internet	Microsoft Internet Information Server 5.0 is a BackOffice Information Server application that provides Web connectivity and Web page hosting, managing other features. This is considered a must-add, because the management of Internet and intranet Web sites is now standard operating procedure with Windows 2000 Server.
COM Internet Services Proxy	This allows DCOM to travel over HTTP-based sessions (via IIS).

Continued

Table 4-3 *(continued)*

Service	*Description*
Microsoft DHCP Server	Automatically configures TCP/IP on clients including Windows 2000, Windows 95/98, Windows for Workgroups, and Windows 3.11.
Windows Internet Service Name	Used for dynamically registering and querying NetBIOS (WINS) computer names on an internetwork.
Microsoft DNS domain Server	Domain Name Service (DNS) registers and queries DNS names on an internetwork.
Microsoft TCP/IP Printing	Implements the LPD printing service for accessing printers connected to UNIX-based computers. Note that this option must be installed if you want to use the Lpdsvr service so that UNIX computers can print to Windows 2000 printers. Note that discussion of this service has appeared on MCSE certification exams.
Internet Authentication Service	This allows verification of requests received via the RADIUS protocol.
QoS Admission Control here. Service	You may set the quality of network service by subnet
Site Server the LDAP Services	Monitors TCP/IP stacks and keeps directories up to date with most current user information.
Simple TCP/IP Daytime Services	Provides the client software for the Character Generator, Discard, Echo, and Quote of the Day services. Select this option to allow this computer to respond to requests from other systems that support these protocols.
SNMP Service	As discussed in this chapter, this service for the Simple Network Management Protocol installs SNMP agent software on the local Windows 2000 Server. SNMP Service also adds several robust TCP/IP object:counters visible under System Performance Monitor.

Summary

In this chapter, TCP/IP was installed and configured for use on a Windows 2000 Server network. The following topics were covered:

- Installing TCP/IP
- Configuring TCP/IP
- Configuring additional TCP/IP services

Chapter 5

Troubleshooting TCP/IP

In This Chapter

- Troubleshooting TCP/IP in Windows 2000 Server
- TCP/IP troubleshooting steps
- Defining which is the best TCP/IP troubleshooting tool to solve your problem
- Mastering basic TCP/IP utilities

Troubleshooting is, it seems, an exercise in matrix mathematics. That is, we use a variety of approaches and influences to successfully solve our problems, almost in a mental columns-and-rows format. These approaches may include structured methodologies, inductive and deductive reasoning, common sense, experience, and luck. And this is what troubleshooting is made of.

Troubleshooting TCP/IP problems is really no different from troubleshooting other Windows 2000 Server problems mentioned in this book, such as installation failures described in Chapter 2. Needless to say, Windows 2000 Server offers several TCP/IP-related tools and utilities to assist us, but more on the specifics in a moment.

TCP/IP Troubleshooting Basics

The goal in TCP/IP troubleshooting is very simple: fix the problem. Too often, it is easy to become overly concerned about why something happened instead of just fixing the problem. And by fixing the problem, I mean cost effectively.

1. **Be cost effective.** Don't forget that several hours' worth of MCSE-level consulting could more than pay for the additional bandwidth that may easily solve your TCP/IP WAN-related problem. Don't overlook such an easy fix when struggling to make a WAN connection between sites utilizing Windows 2000 Server. Too little bandwidth is typically the result of being penny wise and pound foolish. Oh, and it also causes nasty timeout conditions that can wreak havoc on your TCP/IP-based network. And if you want to make a complex database unhappy, just give it too little bandwidth on a TCP/IP-based WAN.

2. **Experience is the best teacher.** One of the more challenging corporate training assignments I frequently face is when I'm asked to deliver a custom TCP/IP and Windows 2000 Server troubleshooting session. The challenge is this: I'm not sure I can teach troubleshooting. It's really just something you do and you're ultimately skilled at it or not. TCP/IP troubleshooting ability is heavily based on experience. The good news is that the more time on the computer you put in ("stick time"), the better you will do.

3. **Use inductive reasoning.** Microsoft officially recommends pursuing a TCP/IP troubleshooting strategy of working from the bottom up, such as starting at the Physical Layer of the Open Standards Interconnections (OSI) model and proceeding to look at more broader influences such as the applications you are running. This enables you to isolate a problem. Such an approach is also known as induction or inductive reasoning, which *Webster's New World Dictionary* defines as "a bringing forward of separate facts or instances, esp. so as to prove a general statement." This mindset is largely the basis for this chapter, as individual tools and utilities that in reality would be used independently to solve a larger TCP/IP-related problem will be discussed. That is, you would start with a specific tool to solve a discrete problem and, as troubleshooting both goes and grows, resolve more global TCP/IP issues.

   In contrast, deductive reasoning is really better suited for the Windows 2000 Server developers in feature-set brainstorming sessions where the whole idea is to come up with great new features and then work down to the implementation specifics. *Webster's* defines deduction as "Logic — the act or process of deducing; reasoning from a known principle to an unknown, from a general to the specific."

4. **Use the in-house help.** Many wonderful tools are included in Windows 2000 Server for use in your TCP/IP troubleshooting efforts. These include native commands and utilities such as IPConfig and ping that will be reviewed in this chapter. And given that Windows 2000 Server is often bundled with the full version of BackOffice, don't forget the full-featured version of Network Monitor included in Microsoft Systems Management Server (SMS). You will recall that tools such as Network Monitor were discussed at length in Part VI of this book, "Optimizing and Troubleshooting Windows 2000 Server."

5. **Don't forget third-party tools.** Not surprisingly, a wide range of third-party TCP/IP troubleshooting tools is available to assist you. One favorite, which will be discussed in Chapter 9, is PingPlotter, a low-cost shareware application from Richard Ness at Nessoft (`www.nesssoft.com`). PingPlotter is included on the CD-ROM that accompanies this book. This application tests ping connectivity and measures ping performance across WAN hops.

6. **Always reboot.** Last, but certainly not least, you must always reboot when modifying anything related to the TCP/IP protocol stack in Windows 2000 Server. Even though the "stack" has improved dramatically, I still don't trust it completely. In my eyes, there is nothing like a complete reboot where you shut the computer down for 15 seconds after you've modified

any TCP/IP protocol settings. And it's an easy lesson to overlook! Here's why. Let's assume you switch your IP address from a dynamic DHCP-assigned address to a static IP address. So far, so good. But if at this moment, you run the IPConfig command that reports basic TCP/IP configuration information (discussed later in this chapter), you will note that the TCP/IP configuration information reports the new, updated IP address as if it were properly bound to the network adapter. Don't you believe it for a minute! Always reboot.

In fact, if you want my $59.95's worth, I'd highly recommend you follow Step Zero — that is to completely cold-reboot your Windows 2000 Server prior to concluding you have any problems with TCP/IP. Don't ask me why, but I've seen many Windows 2000 Server TCP/IP-related gremlins disappear this way. And that's something you won't read about in the official MCSE study guides. Trust me.

First Step: Ask the Basic Questions

So where do you go from here? Remember that troubleshooting any problem is a function of asking enough questions. Here is a short list of questions you can start your TCP/IP troubleshooting journey with. It is by no means inclusive.

- What's working?
- What's not working?
- What is the relationship between the things that work and the things that don't?
- Did the things that don't work now *ever* work on this computer or network?
- If the answer is yes, what has changed since they last worked?

You can ask more specific questions in your quest to resolve your TCP/IP problems. These questions are presented and answered at the end of the chapter.

Second Step: Define the Tools

Having completed this first step, you're ready to begin troubleshooting TCP/IP in Windows 2000 Server. Table 5-1 provides a list of TCP/IP diagnostic utilities and troubleshooting tools, many of which will be discussed further in this chapter.

Table 5-1 Windows 2000 Server TCP/IP Troubleshooting Tools and Utilities

Utility/Tool	*Description*
ARP	Address Resolution Protocol. Enables you to view local computer ARP table entries to detect invalid entries.
Hostname	Typing this at the command line returns the current host name of the local computer.
IPConfig	Current TCP/IP information is displayed. Command line switches enable you to release and/or renew your IP address.
Nbtstat	Connections using NetBIOS over TCP/IP and protocol statistics are displayed. The LMHOSTS cache is updated (purged and reloaded).
Netstat	Active TCP/IP connections are displayed in addition to TCP/IP statistics.
Nslookup	Internet domain name servers are queried and recorded; domain host aliases, domain host services, and operating system information is returned.
Ping	Packet Internet Gopher. Tests connections and verifies configurations.
Route	Displays, prints, or modifies a local routing table.
Tracert	Checks the route from the local to a remote system.
FTP	File Transfer Protocol. This tool is used for two-way file transfers between hosts.
TFTP	Trivial File Transfer Protocol. Provides another form of two-way file transfer between hosts. Typically used when one host demands TFTP. I've used this in conjunction with router configuration and troubleshooting scenarios.
Telnet	Basic terminal emulation program that establishes a session with another TCP/IP host running a Telnet host.
RCP	Remote Copy Protocol. Enables you to copy files between TCP/IP-based hosts.
RSH	Remote Shell. Enables you to be authenticated by and run UNIX commands on a remote UNIX host.
Rexec	Enables you to be authenticated by and run processes on a remote computer.
Finger	System information is retrieved from a remote computer running TCP/IP and supporting the Finger command.
Microsoft Internet Explorer	Browser used for locating information and retrieving resources from the Internet.

Two important TCP/IP-related "tools" that are missing in Windows 2000 Server are native NFS client support and the whois command. For NFS client support, as discussed in Part VI of this book, "Optimizing and Troubleshooting Windows 2000 Server," check with NetManage or WRQ, two independent software vendors that provide NFS client solutions for Windows 2000 Server.

Typing **whois** at the Windows 2000 Server command line results in the following error message:

```
'whois' is not recognized as an internal or external command, operable
program or batch file.
```

In a moment, in the Telnet discussion, I will share a secret for using the whois command with Windows 2000 Server.

Before going any further, it is important to establish your troubleshooting paradigm. Consider the following as you work with TCP/IP and read the remainder of this chapter. The following are considered TCP/IP diagnostic commands: ARP, hostname, IPConfig, nbtstat, netstat, ping, route, and tracert. These are considered connectivity commands: Finger, FTP, RCP, rexec, RSH, Telnet, and TFTP.

Did you know that FTP, rexec, and Telnet not only use but also rely on clear-text passwords in a Windows 2000 scenario? That's a huge departure from Windows 2000 Server's basic reliance on encrypted password-based security. Be sure to think about this little fact the next time you use these tools.

Third Step: Use the Tools

Now the details. Having read about the TCP/IP troubleshooting tools and utilities found in Windows 2000 Server, you're now ready to learn the finer points. This section includes an array of TCP/IP tools including:

- IPConfig
- Ping
- ARP
- Nbtstat
- Route
- Netstat
- Tracert
- Hostname
- FTP
- TFTP
- Telnet
- RCP
- RSH
- Rexec
- Finger
- Microsoft Internet Explorer

But before using the tools, I want to spend a moment discussing how to "learn" the variables, command line entries, and switches associated with each tool.

The next several pages detail each of the suggested TCP/IP tools and utilities you may use in your troubleshooting efforts. Don't forget that you may "capture" any command line details in Windows 2000 Server by redirecting the screen output to a text file. This is accomplished by appending your command line statement with the pipe or mathematical "greater than" sign (>). Observe:

```
C:\> dir >foo.txt
```

This command would direct the directory contents listing to the file `foo.txt`. That is a file that could easily be read in Notepad or another text editor. Be sure to use a filename without spaces when you redirect screen output to a text file. If you took the preceding example and directed the output to the filename "`foo one.txt`," it would be stored under Windows 2000 Server as "foo" with no additional attributes such as the ".txt" extension. That's problematic when you've created output with similar names such as "`foo.txt`" and "`foo one.txt`." Later, when you try to open your important output with Notepad or WordPad, the filenames look nearly identical.

Be careful when naming your output files from the command line. Be sure to use contiguous filenames such as "`fooone.txt`" to distinguish your filenames. Otherwise, as shown in Figure 5-1, the filenames are difficult to separate.

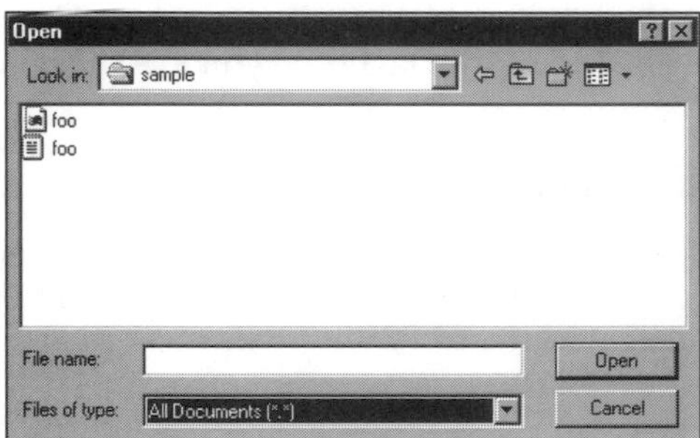

Figure 5-1: Incorrect naming of output files

IPConfig

The IPConfig command line utility provides a baseline view of where your system is with respect to TCP/IP. Host TCP/IP connection parameters are verified, and you may observe whether the TCP/IP configuration has properly initialized. It is a good first step to take because it enables us to check the TCP/IP configuration on the computer having the alleged problem.

There are several variations of the IPConfig command. These are implemented as command line switches:

```
Windows 2000 IP Configuration
USAGE:
   ipconfig [/? | /all | /release [adapter] | /renew [adapter] |
/flushdns | /registerdns]
| /flushdns | /registerdns
| /showclassid adapter
| /setclassid adapter [classidtoset] ]
   adapter    Full name or pattern with '*' and '?' to 'match',
            * matches any character, ? matches one character.
   Options
       /?           Display this help message.
       /all         Display full configuration information.
       /release     Release the IP address for the specified adapter.
       /renew       Renew the IP address for the specified adapter.
       /flushdns    Purges the DNS Resolver cache.
       /registerdns Refreshes all DHCP leases and re-registers DNS
                    names
       /displaydns  Display the contents of the DNS Resolver Cache.
/showclassid        Displays all the dhcp class IDs allowed for
                    adapter.
/setclassid         Modifies the dhcp class id.
```

The default is to display only the IP address, subnet mask and default gateway for each adapter bound to TCP/IP. For Release and Renew, if no adapter name is specified, then the IP address leases for all adapters bound to TCP/IP will be released or renewed.

For SetClassID, if no class id is specified, then the class id is removed.

```
Examples:
> ipconfig                              ... Show information.
    > ipconfig /all                         ... Show detailed information
    > ipconfig /renew                       ... renew all adapters
    > ipconfig /renew EL*                   ... renew adapters named EL....
    > ipconfig /release *ELINK?21*          ... release all matching
adapters,
                                                eg. ELINK-21,
                                                myELELINKi21adapter.
```

Tip

The most robust view of IPConfig is with the /all switch. Information for each physically bound network adapter card, modem connections, and even virtual bindings are displayed:

```
Windows 2000 IP Configuration
     Host Name . . . . . . . . . . : TCI1
     Primary Domain Name . . . . . : Main.local
     Node Type . . . . . . . . . . : Broadcast
     IP Routing Enabled. . . . . . : No
     WINS Proxy Enabled. . . . . . : No
     DNS Suffix Search List. . . . : Main.local
Ethernet adapter Local Area Connection:
     Adapter Domain Name . . . . . :
     DNS Servers . . . . . . . . . : 209.20.130.35
                                     209.20.130.33
```

```
Description . . . . . . . . : Intel(R) PRO/100+ PCI Adapter
Physical Address. . . . . . : 00-90-27-78-A9-CC
DHCP Enabled. . . . . . . . : No
IP Address. . . . . . . . . : 209.20.232.11
Subnet Mask . . . . . . . . : 255.255.255.0
Default Gateway . . . . . . : 209.20.232.1
Primary WINS Server . . . . : 10.0.0.2
```

When interpreting this IPConfig output, you can decipher whether a duplicate IP address has been configured. If the subnet mask appears as 0.0.0.0 for a particular IP address, that indicates that the said address is a duplicate IP address. Likewise, if you dynamically assign IP addresses to your network via DHCP, you can determine if your network adapter was unable to obtain an IP address. This is observed when the IP address appears as 0.0.0.0.

Take that last point to heart. Most TCP/IP problems I can recall having on a Windows 2000 network centered on duplicate or unobtainable IP addresses. Hopefully, you can avoid such a fate.

Don't forget to make use of "|more" when executing the IPConfig command at the Windows 2000 Server command line. Otherwise, the TCP/IP information will rapidly scroll past without stopping, causing you to mis-key TCP/IP configuration information. This command is especially critical when the /all switch is used with the IPConfig command and lots and lots of important TCP/IP configuration information is displayed.

If your system reports appropriate TCP/IP configuration and connection information, such as that displayed previously, proceed to use the ping command.

Remember that Windows 95/98 uses the winipcfg command in place of the IPConfig command. That distinction is important for both the MCSE certification exams and working with client and server operating systems in the field.

Ping

Assuming you've successfully executed and interpreted the preceding IPConfig command, you're ready to employ the ping command. Ping is my friend. It's a low-level command that anyone can execute, and thus it's a command that I ask clients to try while I'm performing over-the-telephone diagnosis. The answer to whether you have ping connectivity is either yes or no.

In layperson's terms, ping is used to diagnose connection-related failures. By executing the ping command, you can determine whether a particular TCP/IP-based host is available and responding in a non-dysfunctional manner.

Technically, the ping command is transmitting Internet Control Message Protocol (ICMP) packets between two TCP/IP-based hosts. Remember that ICMP relates to session management and special communications between hosts. With ICMP, messages and errors regarding packet delivery are reported. Great stuff!

The ping command has several command line switches that increase its functionality. These switches, listed here, may be observed by typing **ping /?** at the command line:

```
Usage: ping [-t] [-a] [-n count] [-l size] [-f] [-i TTL] [-v TOS]
            [-r count] [-s count] [[-j host-list] | [-k host-list]]
            [-w timeout] destination-list
Options:
    -t             Ping the specified host until stopped.
                   To see statistics and continue - type Control-
Break;
                   To stop - type Control-C.
    -a             Resolve addresses to hostnames.
    -n count       Number of echo requests to send.
    -l size        Send buffer size.
    -f             Set Don't Fragment flag in packet.
    -i TTL         Time To Live.
    -v TOS         Type Of Service.
    -r count       Record route for count hops.
    -s count       Timestamp for count hops.
    -j host-list   Loose source route along host-list.
    -k host-list   Strict source route along host-list.
    -w timeout     Timeout in milliseconds to wait for each reply.
```

Typing the basic ping command followed by a host IP address results in the following information, which indicates that basic, low-level TCP/IP connectivity has been established:

```
Pinging 209.20.232.10 with 32 bytes of data:
Reply from 209.20.232.10: bytes=32 time=15ms TTL=128
Reply from 209.20.232.10: bytes=32 time=16ms TTL=128
Reply from 209.20.232.10: bytes=32 time=16ms TTL=128
Reply from 209.20.232.10: bytes=32 time=16ms TTL=128

Ping statistics for 209.20.232.10:
    Packets: Sent = 4, Received = 4, Lost = 0 (0% loss),
Approximate round trip times in milli-seconds:
    Minimum = 15ms, Maximum =  16ms, Average =  15ms
```

If the host is unreachable, the ping command fails, as shown by

```
Pinging 10.0.0.5 with 32 bytes of data:
Request timed out.
Request timed out.
Request timed out.
```

```
Ping statistics for 10.0.0.5:
    Packets: Sent = 4, Received = 1, Lost = 3 (75% loss),
Approximate round trip times in milli-seconds:
    Minimum = 0ms, Maximum =  0ms, Average =  0ms
```

For the MCSE exam and other official purposes, follow the traditional six-step ping command food chain and its relationship to IPConfig (see Figure 5-2). I call this phenomenon of IPConfig and ping working together as being reunited!

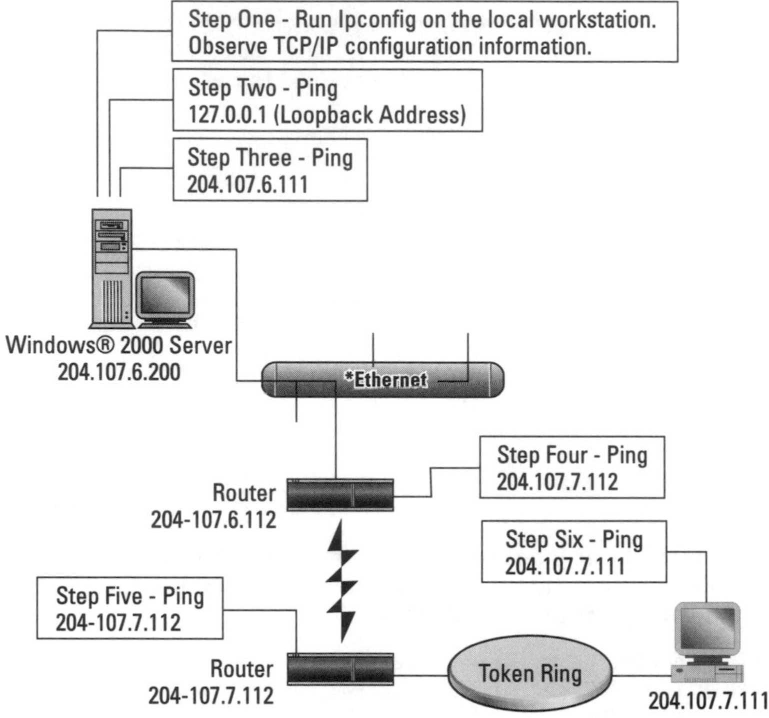

Figure 5-2: Six steps to success using the IPConfig and ping commands

STEPS:

To use the IPConfig and ping commands

Step 1. Run the IPConfig command on the local workstation and observe the TCP/IP configuration information.

Step 2. Ping the internal loopback address to verify that TCP/IP is installed and configured correctly on the local host computer. This address is 127.0.0.1, a reserved address that can't be used as a real IP address on a network. See Chapter 9 for more information.

Step 3. Ping the address of the local host computer to ensure that TCP/IP is working correctly. Here we are typically pinging the network adapter card(s).

Step 4. Ping the IP address of the router or default gateway so that you know and verify that the router or default gateway is functioning correctly. This also ensures that you have a functional infrastructure in place to communicate with a local host on the local network or subnet.

Step 5. Ping the distant router across a WAN link if appropriate. This is a step I've added to the traditional scenario that you may or may not see in the MCSE texts or exams. However, this is based on real-world experience. Often you can ping a remote router yet are unable to ping the desired remote host. That's because something as simple as a return route may not be programmed (see the route command discussion later in this chapter).

Step 6. Ping the IP address of the remote host. Success at this stage establishes that you can communicate through the remote router and that the remote host is functional.

Typically, I use the ping command in bankruptcy law fashion. What do I mean by that? I mean I work backward (remember that in U.S. bankruptcy law, one starts with Chapter 11 and moves backward to Chapter 7... get it?). So I first ping the remote host (Step 6) and work backward. This approach better typifies the real-world need to communicate with another workstation/server/host somewhere. If that doesn't work, I back up and ultimately try to find the source of failure.

The ping command is a great command for testing your implementation of IP security in Windows 2000 Server. If you've correctly implemented IP security, even the ping command will fail between two hosts that are not allowed to speak with each other. Further discussion on IP security can be found in Chapter 13 of this book.

For a really good time, use the ping command to test the Windows Sockets-based name resolution on your network. This is accomplished by pinging a host name. For example, on the Internet, I might ping the domain name of my ISP with the following command:

```
ping nwlink.com
```

If I enjoy successful replies, then I know there is no problem with address resolution or the network connection. However, if the ping command using a host name isn't successful but the ping command using the IP address is, then I know that I only have an address resolution problem, not a network connection problem.

A few general steps to consider when the ping command doesn't work include the following:

- Reboot the computer after TCP/IP was installed or modified (see my comments earlier under "Always reboot" in the "TCP/IP Troubleshooting Basics" section).
- Check that the local host's address is valid as displayed in the Internet Protocol (TCP/IP) Properties tab sheet under Local Area Connection Properties, found under Network and Dial-up Connections, if it is a static IP address (see Figure 5-3).
- If necessary, make sure Windows 2000 Server-based routing is operational and a link exists between routers. In other words, perhaps you're having a telephone company-related communications problem.

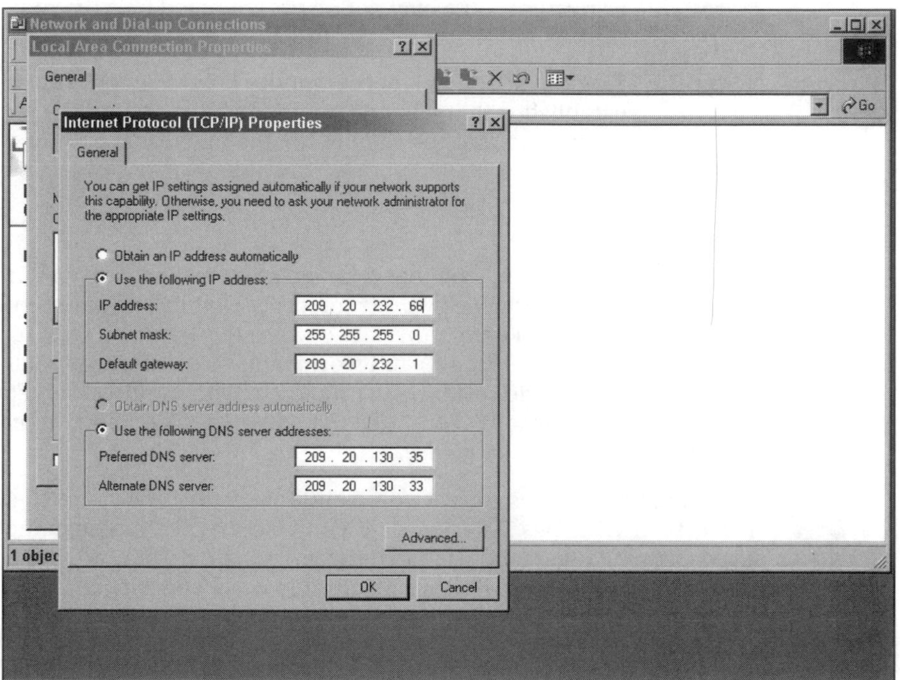

Figure 5-3: Verifying the host static IP address

ARP

The Address Resolution Protocol (ARP) cache is composed of both dynamic and static addresses. In reality, ARP is used several ways, but fundamentally, ARP maps an IP address to a hardware address. This role is defined in RFC 826. The hardware address is the Media Access Control (MAC), or physical address. This hardware address can best be obtained by viewing the "Physical Address" entry returned by the IPConfig command.

Tip

Other ways to obtain physical hardware addresses include using the install utility on the driver disk that comes with your network adapter card or trapping packets with Network Monitor. The former approach is good for workstations that might be running IPX/SPX or NetBEUI, and the latter is good for non-mainstream workstation implementations in a Windows 2000 Server environment such as Macintosh clients. See Chapters 19 and 21 for further discussions of these techniques.

The bottom line on network communications is that hosts must ultimately know each other's physical addresses to communicate on a network. Address resolution via ARP is the act of converting the host's IP address to its physical address. In that context, ARP is responsible for gathering the hardware addresses on broadcast-based networks. When operating in a dynamic discovery mode, this is accomplished by ARP issuing a local broadcast of the remote IP address to discover the physical address of the remote host. Having obtained the physical address, it adds it to the ARP cache. In fact, for a given host, both the IP address and the physical address are stored as one entry in the ARP table, for example:

```
Interface: 10.0.0.2 on Interface 0x2
  Internet Address      Physical Address      Type
  10.0.0.3              00-aa-62-c6-08-00     static
Interface: 131.107.6.171 on Interface 0x3
  Internet Address      Physical Address      Type
  131.107.6.88          00-60-97-ba-f1-25     static
```

The ARP cache is always read for an IP-physical address mapping before any ARP-related request broadcasts are initiated. Dynamic ARP table entries are maintained for ten minutes. This ensures the freshest ARP resolution information at all times. Static ARP table entries are maintained until the machine is rebooted. Remember that caching enables ARP to operate efficiently. If you did not have any ARP caching, your network would have far too many ARP-type broadcasts travelling to resolve IP addresses to physical addresses (as shown in Figure 5-4). Not a wise way to manage a network.

ARP broadcasts appear as shown in Figure 5-4 when viewed by Network Monitor.

Tip

Remember that Windows 2000 Server makes heavy use of address caching in its TCP/IP implementation. That's a helpful hint to keep in mind when things aren't going smoothly and you decided to reboot the server to refresh the address cache.

So how does ARP resolve an IP address? Before I discuss the steps that ARP undertakes, remember that the IP addresses for any two hosts must be "resolved" before a communications session may be established.

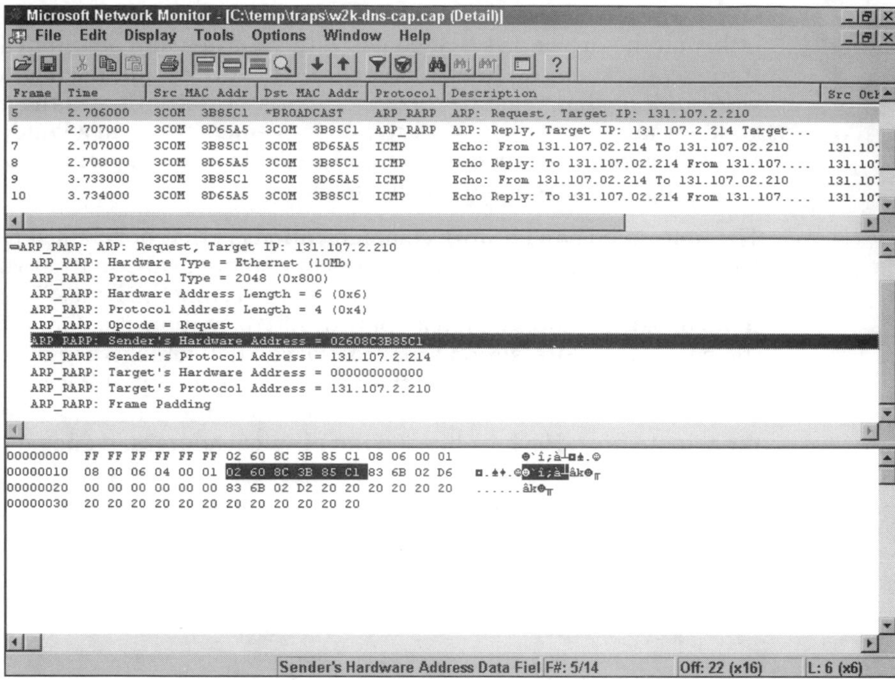

Figure 5-4: ARP broadcasting

1. Any time one host tries to communicate with another, an ARP request is initiated. An example of such a communication would be the ping command. If the IP address to physical address entry exists in the local table, then the address is resolved. End of story.
2. However, if no entry exists in the ARP table that resolves the IP address to a physical address, ARP starts asking questions in the form of a broadcast packet (such as the packet traffic displayed in Figure 5-4).
3. Every host on the local network evaluates the broadcast and determines whether the IP address in the ARP packet is the same as its IP address.
4. When a match is found, the destination host sends an ARP reply packet back to the source host. Again, this is akin to the traffic shown in Figure 5-4.
5. Routers in scenarios that span multiple subnets participate in ARP-related events in the following manner (also outlined in Figure 5-5): The ARP broadcast is forwarded to the default gateway for evaluation. The ARP broadcast packet is forwarded yet again to a remote router if necessary. Once a session is established with the remote router, the source host sends the ICMP-based request (such as a ping) to the remote router. The remote router resolves the request by sending the ping command to the destination host.

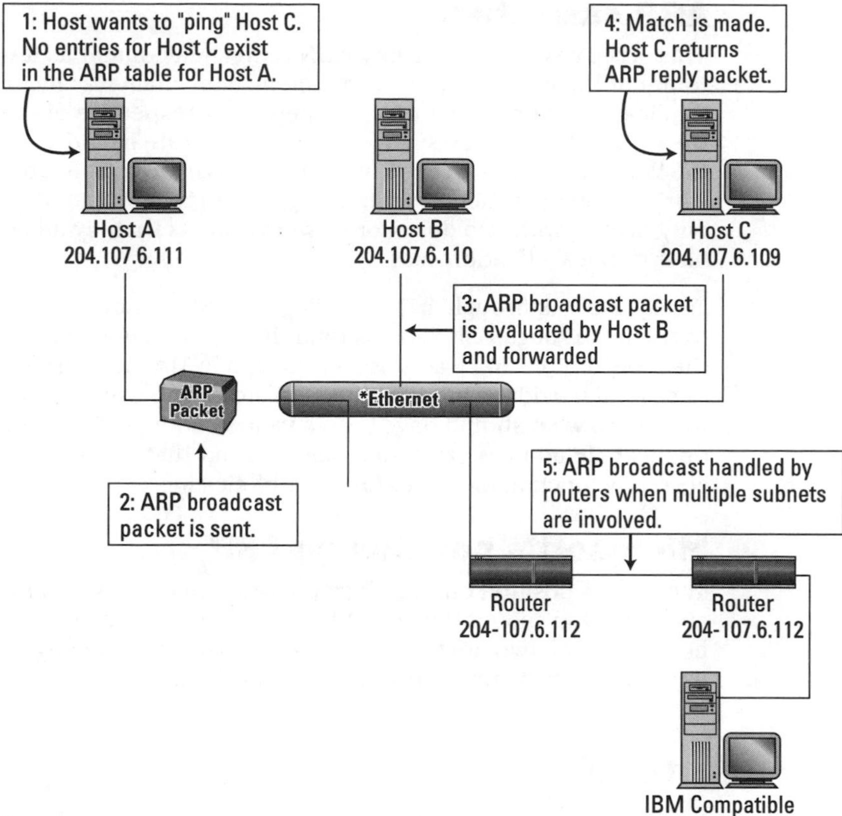

Figure 5-5: An ARP broadcasting scenario

Common ARP-related problems

Two common problem areas are associated with ARP. First is the problem of duplicate addresses. ARP operates on the FIFO principle. That means ARP table entries are made on a first-come, first-served basis. Thus it is possible that if duplicate IP addresses accidentally exist on the network, the wrong IP-based host may reply and cause an incorrect IP address-physical address entry to be added to the ARP table. The ARP case study that follows incorporates elements of this ARP problem.

Second, broadcast storms strike when subnet masks are invalid and countless ARP broadcasts looking for a host are sent in vain on the network. In essence, the numerous broadcast packets being sent are the storm. You and your users know the outcome as decreased network performance.

ARP case study

This is the case of the naughty ISDN router. Malcontent as it was, this ISDN router at the headquarters of an athletic club chain was incorrectly causing duplicate IP address errors on the network irrespective of the IP addresses we assigned to the hosts. We'd receive "duplicate IP address" errors at the Windows 95 workstation, whether we assigned the IP address to the workstation dynamically or statically. What gives, we pondered? We were only dealing with two dozen or so workstations that, by all accounts, didn't have duplicate IP addresses.

Finally, a breakthrough arrived. Using the ARP command, we were able to trace the "bogus" IP address (and there were a bunch of 'em) back to the ISDN router's MAC address. In short, one MAC address was mapped to several IP addresses. Whenever a Windows 95 workstation attempted to acquire what should have been a valid IP address, it of course got the duplicate IP address error. ARP bailed us out that day and got us a new, correctly functioning router for the athletic club.

Microsoft's position on ARP

Microsoft's position on TCP/IP troubleshooting is this: After running IPConfig and ping, you should then test IP-to-MAC address resolution using ARP. The bottom line? If two hosts can't ping each other, try running ARP commands to see if the host computers have the correct MAC addresses.

Nbtstat

One of the apparent dilemmas in a Microsoft Windows 2000 environment is the resolution of NetBIOS names to IP addresses. This is handled several ways, including Dynamic DNS, WINS server queries, local cache resolution, broadcasts, and LMHOSTS and HOSTS lookup. If you want to drop under the hood, you have the nbtstat command. In addition to acting as a name resolution troubleshooting tool, it enables you to correct or remove preloaded name entries.

Options for the nbtstat command are as follows:

```
NBTSTAT     [ [-a RemoteName] [-A IP address] [-c] [-n]
            [-r] [-R] [-RR] [-s] [-S] [interval] ]
  -a        (adapter status)     Lists the remote
                                 machine's name table given its name
  -A        (Adapter status)     Lists the remote machine's name table
                                 given its IP address.
  -c        (cache)              Lists NBT's cache of remote
                                 [machine]names and their IP addresses
  -n        (names)              Lists local NetBIOS names.  That is,
                                 names are displayed that were
                                 registered locally on the system by
                                 the server and redirector services.
  -r        (resolved)           Lists names resolved by broadcast and
                                 via WINS
  -R        (Reload)             Purges and reloads the remote cache
```

```
                                          name table (LMHOSTS)
  -S       (Sessions)                     Lists sessions table with the
                                          destination IP addresses
  -s       (sessions)                     Lists sessions table converting
                                          destination IP addresses to
                                          computer NETBIOS names.
  -RR      (ReleaseRefresh)               Sends Name Release packets to WINs
                                          and then, starts Refresh
RemoteName                                Remote host machine name.
  IP address                              Dotted decimal representation of the
                                          IP address.
  interval                                Redisplays selected statistics,
                                          pausing interval seconds
                                          between each display. Press Ctrl+C
                                          to stop redisplaying statistics.
```

In the following nbtstat example, I run the command with the -S switch to list the current NetBIOS sessions, complete with status and statistics:

```
Local Area Connection:
Node IpAddress: [10.0.0.2] Scope Id: []
                     NetBIOS Connection Table
Local Name           State    In/Out  Remote Host    Input    Output

SECRETS2    <03>     Listening
ADMINISTRATOR  <03>  Listening
```

A trick you may use to ensure that you're using a fresh local name cache is the nbtstat -r command. This command updates the local name cache immediately from such sources as the LMHOSTS file.

Route

The route command is discussed extensively in Chapter 5 in the context of IP gateways. However, a quick review is in order. Using the route command, you may view or modify the route table. The route table lists all current IP routes seen by the host. This includes routes that Windows 2000 Server creates automatically and routes learned by running the router information protocol (RIP). Common options for the route command are shown in Table 5-2.

Table 5-2 Common Options for the Route Command

Command	*Function*
Route print	Displays all current IP routes known by the host.
Route add	Used to add persistent and nonpersistent routes to the table. It is necessary to use the -p command line option with route add to create a persistent route. Otherwise, the route is lost when the machine is rebooted.
Route delete	Deletes routes from the table.

Netstat

This command displays the current TCP/IP connections and protocol statistics. Options for the netstat command include the following:

```
NETSTAT [-a] [-e] [-n] [-s] [-p proto] [-r] [interval]
  -a            Displays all connections and listening ports.
  -e            Displays Ethernet statistics. This may
be combined with the -s option.
  -n            Displays addresses and port numbers
                in numerical form.
  -p proto      Shows connections for the protocol
                specified by proto; proto
                may be TCP or UDP. If used with
                the -s option to display
                per-protocol statistics, proto may
                be TCP, UDP, or IP.
  -r            Displays the routing table.
  -s            Displays per-protocol statistics.
                By default, statistics are
                shown for TCP, UDP and IP; the -p option may
                be used to specify
                a subset of the default.
  interval      Redisplays selected statistics, pausing
                interval seconds between each display. Press
                CTRL+C to stop redisplaying
                statistics. If omitted, netstat will print
                the current configuration information once.
```

Here is sample output from the netstat command using both the -e (Ethernet statistics), -a (all connections and listening ports), -r (route table), and -s (per-protocol statistics) command line options:

netstat -e:

```
Interface Statistics
                           Received            Sent
Bytes                        291244          107280
Unicast packets                   0               0
Non-unicast packets            1509             758
Discards                          0               0
Errors                            0               0
Unknown protocols              1128
```

netstat -a:

```
Active Connections
  Proto  Local Address          Foreign Address         State
  TCP    SECRETS2:echo          SECRETS2:0              LISTENING
  TCP    SECRETS2:discard       SECRETS2:0              LISTENING
  TCP    SECRETS2:daytime       SECRETS2:0              LISTENING
  TCP    SECRETS2:qotd          SECRETS2:0              LISTENING
  TCP    SECRETS2:chargen       SECRETS2:0              LISTENING
```

```
  TCP    SECRETS2:ftp           SECRETS2:0             LISTENING
  TCP    SECRETS2:name          SECRETS2:0             LISTENING
  TCP    SECRETS2:domain        SECRETS2:0             LISTENING
  TCP    SECRETS2:80            SECRETS2:0             LISTENING
  TCP    SECRETS2:135           SECRETS2:0             LISTENING
  TCP    SECRETS2:443           SECRETS2:0             LISTENING
  TCP    SECRETS2:445           SECRETS2:0             LISTENING
  TCP    SECRETS2:printer       SECRETS2:0             LISTENING
  TCP    SECRETS2:548           SECRETS2:0             LISTENING
  TCP    SECRETS2:1025          SECRETS2:0             LISTENING
  TCP    SECRETS2:1026          SECRETS2:0             LISTENING
  TCP    SECRETS2:1028          SECRETS2:0             LISTENING
  TCP    SECRETS2:1031          SECRETS2:0             LISTENING
  TCP    SECRETS2:1034          SECRETS2:0             LISTENING
  TCP    SECRETS2:1035          SECRETS2:0             LISTENING
  TCP    SECRETS2:3389          SECRETS2:0             LISTENING
  TCP    SECRETS2:5162          SECRETS2:0             LISTENING
  TCP    SECRETS2:nbsession     SECRETS2:0             LISTENING
  TCP    SECRETS2:1027          SECRETS2:0             LISTENING
  TCP    SECRETS2:nbsession     SECRETS2:0             LISTENING
  UDP    SECRETS2:echo          *:*
  UDP    SECRETS2:discard       *:*
  UDP    SECRETS2:daytime       *:*
  UDP    SECRETS2:qotd          *:*
  UDP    SECRETS2:chargen       *:*
  UDP    SECRETS2:name          *:*
  UDP    SECRETS2:135           *:*
  UDP    SECRETS2:snmp          *:*
  UDP    SECRETS2:445           *:*
  UDP    SECRETS2:1030          *:*
  UDP    SECRETS2:1032          *:*
  UDP    SECRETS2:1033          *:*
  UDP    SECRETS2:9987          *:*
  UDP    SECRETS2:domain        *:*
  UDP    SECRETS2:bootp         *:*
  UDP    SECRETS2:68            *:*
  UDP    SECRETS2:nbname        *:*
  UDP    SECRETS2:nbdatagram    *:*
  UDP    SECRETS2:1029          *:*
  UDP    SECRETS2:domain        *:*
  UDP    SECRETS2:bootp         *:*
  UDP    SECRETS2:68            *:*
  UDP    SECRETS2:nbname        *:*
  UDP    SECRETS2:nbdatagram    *:*
```

netstat -r

```
===========================================================================
Interface List
0x1 ........................... MS TCP Loopback interface
0x2 ...00 60 08 3a 04 cb ...... 3Com 3C90x Ethernet Adapter
0x3 ...00 60 97 bf a1 23 ...... ELNK3 Ethernet Adapter
0x4 ...00 53 45 00 00 00 ...... WAN (PPP/SLIP) Interface
0x5 ...00 53 45 00 00 00 ...... WAN (PPP/SLIP) Interface
```

```
0x6 ...00 53 45 00 00 00 ...... WAN (PPP/SLIP) Interface
0x7 ...00 53 45 00 00 00 ...... WAN (PPP/SLIP) Interface
===========================================================================
===========================================================================
Active Routes:
Network Destination        Netmask          Gateway       Interface  Metric
         10.0.0.0        255.0.0.0         10.0.0.2        10.0.0.2  1
         10.0.0.2  255.255.255.255        127.0.0.1       127.0.0.1  1
   10.255.255.255  255.255.255.255         10.0.0.2        10.0.0.2  1
        127.0.0.0        255.0.0.0        127.0.0.1       127.0.0.1  1
      131.107.6.0    255.255.255.0    131.107.6.171 131.107.6.171  1
    131.107.6.171  255.255.255.255        127.0.0.1       127.0.0.1  1
  131.107.255.255  255.255.255.255    131.107.6.171 131.107.6.171  1
        224.0.0.0        224.0.0.0         10.0.0.2        10.0.0.2  1
        224.0.0.0        224.0.0.0    131.107.6.171 131.107.6.171  1
  255.255.255.255  255.255.255.255         10.0.0.2        10.0.0.2  1
===========================================================================
Route Table
Active Connections
  Proto  Local Address          Foreign Address        State
```

netstat -s:

```
IP Statistics
  Packets Received                   = 1646
  Received Header Errors             = 0
  Received Address Errors            = 685
  Datagrams Forwarded                = 0
  Unknown Protocols Received         = 0
  Received Packets Discarded         = 0
  Received Packets Delivered         = 997
  Output Requests                    = 748
  Routing Discards                   = 0
  Discarded Output Packets           = 0
  Output Packet No Route             = 0
  Reassembly Required                = 0
  Reassembly Successful              = 0
  Reassembly Failures                = 0
  Datagrams Successfully Fragmented  = 0
  Datagrams Failing Fragmentation    = 0
  Fragments Created                  = 0
ICMP Statistics
                            Received    Sent
  Messages                  12          6
  Errors                    0           0
  Destination Unreachable   0           0
  Time Exceeded             0           0
  Parameter Problems        0           0
  Source Quenchs            0           0
  Redirects                 0           0
  Echos                     0           0
  Echo Replies              0           0
  Timestamps                0           0
  Timestamp Replies         0           0
```

```
  Address Masks               0           0
  Address Mask Replies        0           0
TCP Statistics
  Active Opens                          = 0
  Passive Opens                         = 0
  Failed Connection Attempts            = 0
  Reset Connections                     = 0
  Current Connections                   = 0
  Segments Received                     = 0
  Segments Sent                         = 0
  Segments Retransmitted                = 0
UDP Statistics
  Datagrams Received      = 963
  No Ports                = 34
  Receive Errors          = 0
  Datagrams Sent          = 729
```

Tracert

A route tracing utility, tracert utilizes the IP TTL field and ICMP error messages to discover host-to-host routes through the network. Options for the tracert command include the following:

```
Usage: tracert [-d] [-h maximum_hops] [-j host-list] [-w timeout]
target_name
Options:
    -d                     Do not resolve addresses to hostnames.
    -h maximum_hops        Maximum number of hops to search for target.
    -j host-list           Loose source route along host-list.
    -w timeout             Wait timeout milliseconds for each reply.
```

Here is sample output from the tracert command:

```
Tracing route to SECRETS2 [131.107.6.171]
over a maximum of 30 hops:
  1   <10 ms   <10 ms   <10 ms   SECRETS2 [131.107.6.171]
Trace complete.
```

Hostname

This is a very simple but useful command. It returns the NetBIOS computer name for the machine on which the command was executed.

Tip

The hostname command is a quick and dirty way to find out (or remember!) which machine you are working on. This command line utility eliminates the need to find similar information via the MMC. It's a favorite command of mine in part because of its simplicity.

The hostname command and its output appear as

```
C:\>hostname
SECRETS2
```

where SECRETS2 is the actual host name.

You may not change the host name via the hostname command. The -s option is not supported in Windows 2000 Server. You must use the Network applet in Control Panel to change the host name, followed by a reboot.

FTP

This command remains very popular with Windows 2000 Server users. This is an important point because other TCP/IP processes from the same era (such as Gopher) have declined. Using Port 21, FTP is the basic command for transferring information from one Internet host to another. There are several "variations" of this command, two of which I will show you — the command line method and the Internet Explorer method. First, there is the command line version contained within Windows 2000 Server, which provides very basic, character-based two-way file transfer capabilities. Here is sample output with the FTP command using the fully qualified domain name:

```
C:\>ftp secrets2
Connect to SECRETS2.
220 SECRETS2 Microsoft FTP Service (Version 5.0)
User (SECRETS2:(none)): anonymous
331 Anonymous access allowed, send identity (e-mail name) as password.
Password:
230 Anonymous user logged in.
ftp>
```

Note that this session could have been initiated by using the IP address for SECRETS2 (for example, 10.0.0.2).

The return codes listed in the preceding FTP session, along with all of the other FTP return codes, may be found at `http://andrew2.andrew._cmu.edu/rfc/rfc640.html`.

Table 5-3 shows the commands that may be used during an FTP session such as the one just displayed. Note these commands are listed by typing "?" at the FTP prompt. You will note that most of these commands openly reveal their UNIX heritage.

Table 5-3 Commands for Use in an FTP Session

!	debug	ls	put	status
?	dir	mdelete	pwd	trace
append	disconnect	mdir	quit	type
ascii	get	mget	quote	user
bell	glob	mkdir	recv	verbose
bye	hash	mls	remotehelp	
cd	help	mput	rename	

close	lcd	open	rmdir
delete	literal	prompt	send

Table 5-4 provides explanations of the more common FTP commands.

Table 5-4 Common FTP Commands

Command	*Description*
!	Spawns an MS-DOS shell, but FTP remains active. Typing **exit** returns the user to the FTP prompt.
!command	Executes an MS-DOS command inside the FTP session on the local computer.
Bye	Terminates or ends the FTP session.
Delete	With appropriate permissions, files are deleted on the remote computer.
Dir	Lists the remote directory's files and subdirectories.
Get	Copies a file to the local computer from a remote computer.
Help	Displays FTP command descriptions.
Put	Copies files from the local computer to the remote computer.
Mkdir	With appropriate permissions, enables you to create a directory on a remote computer.

The key to using the command-line FTP command in Windows 2000 Server is that the host you are "FTP-ing" to will accept your request and initiate a session. FTP management is configured via the FTP service in Microsoft Internet Information Server (IIS), which is included with Windows 2000 Server. Note that changing the default TCP port value used by FTP is one way to create a more secure FTP server site. Both hosts must agree to use the same TCP port value to initiate a session. Using a non-default TCP port can thwart intruders.

Also, consider how you might really use this tool. Basically, I've used FTP for low-level file transfers when I don't have an NFS-based solution to communicate with true UNIX hosts and Windows 2000 Server. Specifically, I once used FTP to transfer files from Sun workstations to a Windows 2000 Server for storage and printing. The FTP service in Microsoft Internet Information Server (IIS) is shown in Figure 5-6.

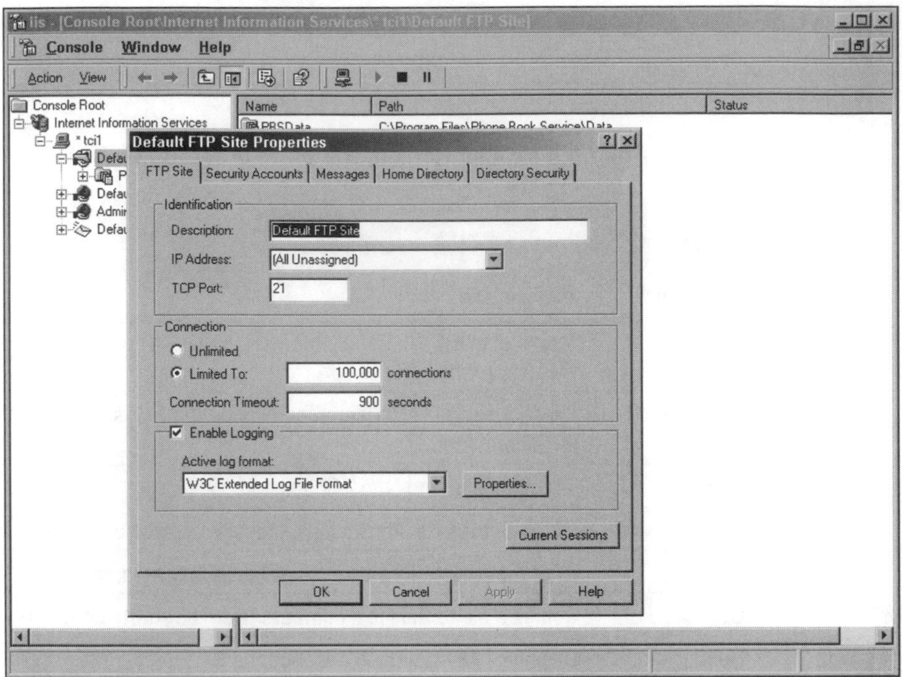

Figure 5-6: Managing the FTP service via the Internet Information Server application

TFTP

Operating on Port 69 by default, Trivial File Transfer Protocol is a variation of FTP that is used to transfer files to and from a remote computer. I've used TFTP to transfer files from a Windows 2000 Server machine to a Cisco router. Whatever works! Here are the TFTP commands available to you:

```
TFTP [-i] host [GET | PUT] source [destination]
  -i              Specifies binary image transfer mode (also called
octet). In binary image mode the file is moved
                  literally, byte by byte. Use this mode when
                  transferring binary files.
  host            Specifies the local or remote host.
  GET             Transfers the file destination on the remote host to
the file source on the local host.
  PUT             Transfers the file source on the local host to
                  the file destination on the remote host.
  source          Specifies the file to transfer.
  destination     Specifies where to transfer the file.
```

Telnet

Telnet is of course a basic terminal emulation feature that enables you to establish a terminal-mode session with another host. You might, for instance, use Telnet to establish a session with your Windows 2000 Server over the Internet. Another valid use is programming a router, either internally or externally, via the Internet.

When executing the Telnet command, you may save an extra step by appending the Telnet command with the IP address or host name of the server you intend to log on to. Such a command would appear as:

```
C:> telnet nwlink.com
```

Note that `nwlink.com` is the host name.

Telnet is used each and every day. Honest. When I'm at a remote site that is connected to the Internet, I like to Telnet back to my ISP to check my e-mail. Such a session involves issuing the Telnet command with the fully qualified domain name of my ISP and then launching pine, a character-based e-mail program that is hosted by my ISP (see Figures 5-7 and 5-8).

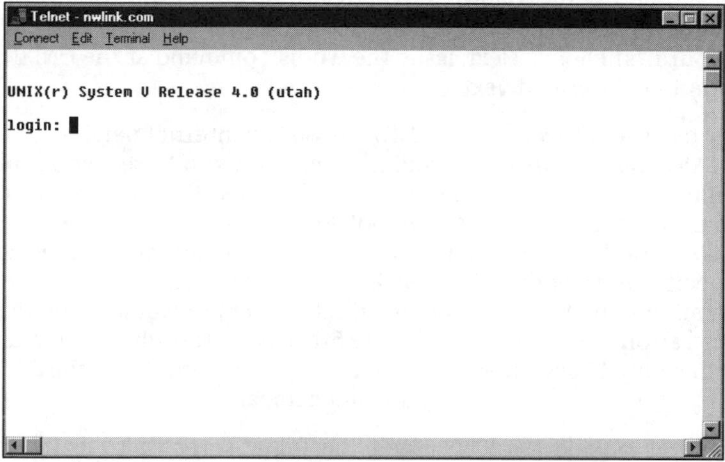

Figure 5-7: Using the Telnet utility to access an ISP from a remote location

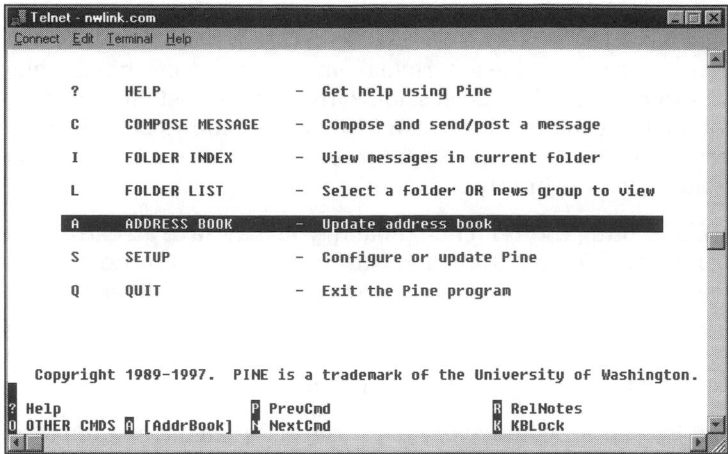

Figure 5-8: Remote access of e-mail via Telnet and other e-mail applications

Because Windows 2000 Server doesn't natively support the whois command, you should use the following trick to add this powerful command to your arsenal. Telnet to a bonafide UNIX server on the Internet. Your ISP should be your first choice. Next, issue the whois command at the UNIX command prompt as described next.

Why use the whois command? To spy on thy Internet neighbor, of course! Just kidding, but the whois command enables you to see who sent that junk mail by performing the whois command against the e-mail's Internet domain name to the right of the "@" symbol. More important, ISP customer service reps and perhaps you can use the whois command (see Figure 5-9) to see if a specific Internet domain name has been taken already (a.k.a. "registered"). At a minimum, the whois command returns important Internet domain registration information (see Figure 5-10). Note the whois command applies only to second-level (such as `idgbooks.com`), not third-level (`springers._nwnexus.com`) domain names.

Note that in Windows 2000 Server, the Telnet screen with its limited size requires two screens to display the full Internet domain name registration information.

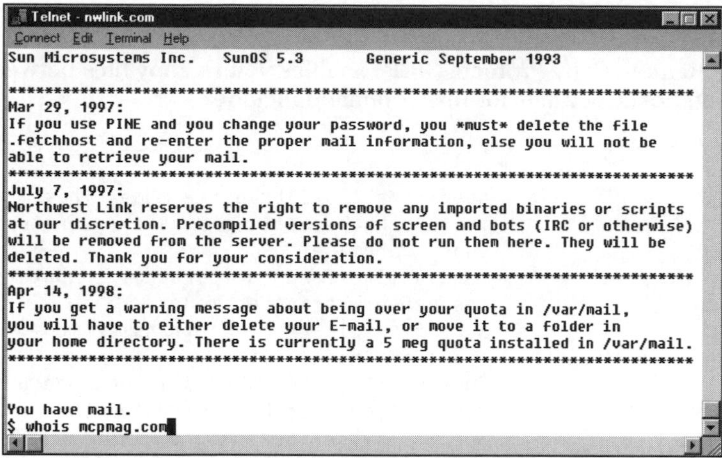

Figure 5-9: The whois command at the UNIX command prompt

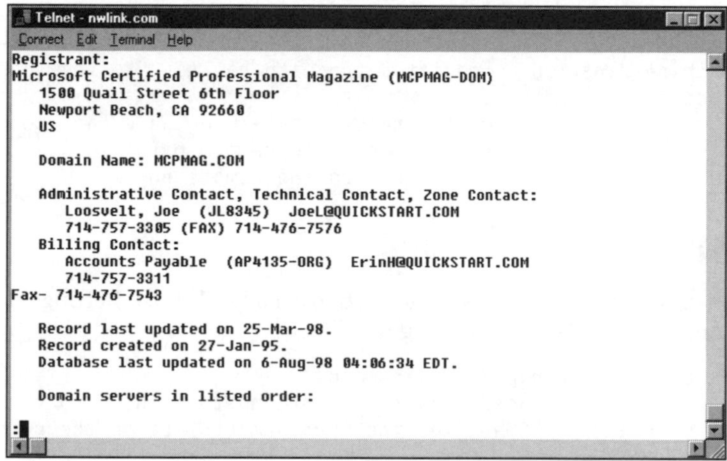

Figure 5-10: Valuable Internet domain name registration information

RCP

The Remote Copy Protocol (RCP) enables you to copy files between TCP/IP-based hosts. Settings for this command include

```
RCP [-a | -b] [-h] [-r] [host][.user:]source [host][.user:]
path\destination
  -a                  Specifies ASCII transfer mode. This mode converts
                      the EOL characters to a carriage return for UNIX
                      and a carriage
                      return/line feed for personal computers. This is
                      the default transfer mode.
  -b                  Specifies binary image transfer mode.
  -h                  Transfers hidden files.
  -r                  Copies the contents of all subdirectories;
                      destination must be a directory.
  host                Specifies the local or remote host. If host is
                      specified as an IP address OR if host name
contains
                      dots, you must specify the user.
  .user:              Specifies a user name to use, rather than the
                      current user name.
  source              Specifies the files to copy.
  path\destination    Specifies the path relative to the logon
directory
                      on the remote host. Use the escape characters
                      (\ , ", or ') in remote paths to use wildcard
                      characters on the remote host.
```

RSH

This command launches a remote shell on a UNIX host. Settings for this command include the following:

```
RSH host [-l username] [-n] command
  host              Specifies the remote host on which to run command.
  -l username       Specifies the user name to use on the remote host.
If
                    omitted, the logged on user name is used.
  -n                Redirects the input of RSH to NULL.
  command           Specifies the command to run.
```

Rexec

This command enables you to run commands on remote hosts running the rexec service. Rexec authenticates the user name on the remote host before executing the specified command. Settings for this command include the following:

```
REXEC host [-l username] [-n] command
  host              Specifies the remote host on which to run command.
```

```
-l username     Specifies the user name on the remote host.
-n              Redirects the input of REXEC to NULL.
command         Specifies the command to run.
```

Finger

This command displays information about a user on a specified system running the Finger service. Output varies based on the remote system. Settings for this command include the following:

```
FINGER [-l] [user]@host [...]
  -l        Displays information in long list format.
  user      Specifies the user you want information about. Omit the
            user
            parameter to display information about all users on the
            specified host.
  @host     Specifies the server on the remote system whose users you
            want information about.
```

Microsoft Internet Explorer

Even though I have touted the benefits of a robust Internet browser such as Internet Explorer (IE) several times in this book, it's worth repeating here. The "official" Microsoft party line is that IE is very much a troubleshooting tool for the TCP/IP protocol in Windows 2000 Server. That's because IE increasingly supports TCP/IP protocol suite utilities such as FTP. This is a capability beyond the original browser, which basically has Hypertext Transfer Protocol (HTTP) support. In reality, I use IE every day to go up on the Internet and download resources to optimize my Windows 2000 Server installations.

Other TCP/IP Troubleshooting Angles

Having reviewed the primary utilities that ship as part of the TCP/IP protocol suite in Windows 2000 Server, let's explore a few other time-tested TCP/IP troubleshooting tricks.

Troubleshooting TCP/IP database files

This section is written for the MCSE candidate in mind. In the real world, you and I rely on the GUI-interface presentation of TCP/IP information in Windows 2000 Server. However, whether you're an old-timer in the industry or you're trying to pass the demanding TCP/IP exams on the MCSE tracks, the files shown in Table 5-5 contain critical TCP/IP information. Everyone else can benefit by observing the file descriptions and contents.

Table 5-5 Windows 2000 Server UNIX-style Database Files

File Name	*Description*
HOSTS	Provides host name-to-IP address resolution for applications that are Windows Sockets-compliant.
LMHOSTS	Provides NetBIOS name-to-IP address resolution for Windows-based networking.
Networks	Provides network name-to-network ID resolution for TCP/IP management.
Protocol	Provides protocol name-to-protocol ID resolution for Windows Sockets applications.
Services	Provides service name-to-port ID resolution for Windows Sockets applications.

Sample output from the HOSTS file contained at `\%systemroot%\system32\drivers\etc` is as follows:

```
# Copyright (c) 1993-1999 Microsoft Corp.
#
# This is a sample HOSTS file used by Microsoft TCP/IP for Windows.
#
# This file contains the mappings of IP addresses to host names. Each
# entry should be kept on an individual line. The IP address should
# be placed in the first column followed by the corresponding host
name.
# The IP address and the host name should be separated by at least one
# space.
#
# Additionally, comments (such as these) may be inserted on individual
# lines or following the machine name denoted by a '#' symbol.
#
# For example:
#
#      102.54.94.97     rhino.acme.com          # source server
#       38.25.63.10     x.acme.com              # x client host

127.0.0.1       localhost
```

Sample output from the LMHOSTS (lmhosts.sam) file contained at `\%systemroot% \system32\drivers\etc` is as follows:

```
# Copyright (c) 1993-1999 Microsoft Corp.
#
# This is a sample LMHOSTS file used by the Microsoft TCP/IP for
Windows.
#
# This file contains the mappings of IP addresses to computernames
# (NetBIOS) names.  Each entry should be kept on an individual line.
# The IP address should be placed in the first column followed by the
# corresponding computername. The address and the computername
# should be separated by at least one space or tab. The "#" character
```

```
# is generally used to denote the start of a comment (see the
exceptions
# below).
#
# This file is compatible with Microsoft LAN Manager 2.x TCP/IP
lmhosts
# files and offers the following extensions:
#
#       #PRE
#       #DOM:<domain>
#       #INCLUDE <filename>
#       #BEGIN_ALTERNATE
#       #END_ALTERNATE
#       \0xnn (
non-printing character support)
#
# Following any entry in the file with the characters "#PRE" will
cause
# the entry to be preloaded into the name cache. By default, entries
are
# not preloaded, but are parsed only after dynamic name resolution
fails.
#
# Following an entry with the "#DOM:<domain>" tag will associate the
# entry with the domain specified by <domain>. This affects how the
# browser and logon services behave in TCP/IP environments. To preload
# the host name associated with #DOM entry, it is necessary to also
add a
# #PRE to the line. The <domain> is always preloaded although it will
not
# be shown when the name cache is viewed.
#
# Specifying "#INCLUDE <filename>" will force the RFC NetBIOS (NBT)
# software to seek the specified <filename> and parse it as if it were
# local. <filename> is generally a UNC-based name, allowing a
# centralized lmhosts file to be maintained on a server.
# It is ALWAYS necessary to provide a mapping for the IP address of
the
# server prior to the #INCLUDE. This mapping must use the #PRE
directive.
# In addition the share "public" in the example below must be in the
# LanManServer list of "NullSessionShares" in order for client
machines to
# be able to read the lmhosts file successfully. This key is under
#
\machine\system\currentcontrolset\services\lanmanserver\parameters\nul
lsessionshares
# in the registry. Simply add "public" to the list found there.
#
# The #BEGIN_ and #END_ALTERNATE keywords allow multiple #INCLUDE
# statements to be grouped together. Any single successful include
# will cause the group to succeed.
#
# Finally, non-printing characters can be embedded in mappings by
# first surrounding the NetBIOS name in quotations, then using the
# \0xnn notation to specify a hex value for a non-printing character.
```

```
#
# The following example illustrates all of these extensions:
#
# 102.54.94.97     rhino     #PRE #DOM:networking  #net group's DC
# 102.54.94.102    "appname  \0x14"          #special app server
# 102.54.94.123    popular             #PRE     #source server
# 102.54.94.117    localsrv            #PRE     #needed for the include
#
# #BEGIN_ALTERNATE
# #INCLUDE \\localsrv\public\lmhosts
# #INCLUDE \\rhino\public\lmhosts
# #END_ALTERNATE
#
# In the above example, the "appname" server contains a special
# character in its name, the "popular" and "localsrv"
# server names are
# preloaded, and the "rhino" server name is specified so
# it can be used
# to later #INCLUDE a centrally maintained lmhosts file
# if the "localsrv"
# system is unavailable.
#
# Note that the whole file is parsed including comments
# on each lookup,
# so keeping the number of comments to a minimum will
# improve performance.
# Therefore it is not advisable to simply add lmhosts file
# entries onto the
# end of this file.
```

I've highlighted in bold the two most valuable lines from this sample file. First, the line **102.54.94.97 rhino #PRE #DOM:networking** is an entry type that I've used to solve pesky resolution problems. Sometimes preloading the entry (the #PRE statement) and forcing a domain name for the host (#DOM) will solve nasty timeout conditions over slow WAN links. Been there, done that.

The other interesting entry is the **102.54.94.102 "appname \0x14"** line. What is occurring here, in English, is that the full 15 positions of the host name are being filled out or padded. This is necessary in some resolution scenarios. Most likely you will be working with Microsoft Technical Support when you get to the point at which this becomes necessary. As stated in the preceding sample file, the \0x14 represents nonprinting characters.

In fact, one time that I can recall where I worked extensively with the LMHOSTS file was when I was troubleshooting the dickens out of a Microsoft Exchange performance problem across two domains. Upon reflection years later, I now see that this was an exercise in using TPC/IP tools to troubleshoot an integration problem between a Microsoft BackOffice component and the underlying Windows NT Server operating system. Such lofty insights, garnered from bumps, bruises, and general maturity with Windows NT Server, have made me a more effective network professional. I'm sure you will enjoy the same positive results from ascending both the Windows 2000 Server and TCP/IP learning curves.

If you want to convert the `lmhosts.sam` file from being a sample file to acting as your real lmhosts file, you will need to remove the `.sam` file extension.

Sample output from the Networks file contained at `\%systemroot%\system32\drivers\etc` is as follows:

```
# Copyright (c) 1993-1999 Microsoft Corp.
#
# This file contains network name/network number mappings for
# local networks. Network numbers are recognized in dotted
# decimal form.
#
# Format:
#
# <network name>  <network number>     [aliases...]  [#<comment>]
#
# For example:
#
#    loopback     127
#    campus       284.122.107
#    london       284.122.108

loopback                 127
```

Sample output from the Protocol file contained at `\%systemroot%\system32\drivers\etc` is as follows:

```
# Copyright (c) 1993-1999 Microsoft Corp.
#
# This file contains the Internet protocols as defined by RFC 1700
# (Assigned Numbers).
#
# Format:
#
# <protocol name>  <assigned number>  [aliases...]   [#<comment>]

ip       0     IP       # Internet protocol
icmp     1     ICMP     # Internet control message protocol
ggp      3     GGP      # Gateway-gateway protocol
tcp      6     TCP      # Transmission control protocol
egp      8     EGP      # Exterior gateway protocol
pup      12    PUP      # PARC universal packet protocol
udp      17    UDP      # User datagram protocol
hmp      20    HMP      # Host monitoring protocol
xns-idp  22    XNS-IDP  # Xerox NS IDP
rdp      27    RDP      # "reliable datagram" protocol
rvd      66    RVD      # MIT remote virtual disk
```

Sample output from the Services file contained at `\%systemroot%\system32\drivers\etc` is as follows:

```
# Copyright (c) 1993-1999 Microsoft Corp.
#
# This file contains port numbers for well-known services
# as defined by
# RFC 1700 (Assigned Numbers).
```

```
#
# Format:
#
# <service name>  <port number>/<protocol>
# [aliases...]   [#<comment>]
#

echo               7/tcp
echo               7/udp
discard            9/tcp    sink null
discard            9/udp    sink null
systat            11/tcp    users                  #Active users
systat            11/tcp    users                  #Active users
daytime           13/tcp
daytime           13/udp
qotd              17/tcp    quote                  #Quote of the day
qotd              17/udp    quote                  #Quote of the day
chargen           19/tcp    ttytst source          #Character
generator
chargen           19/udp    ttytst source          #Character
                                                     generator
ftp-data          20/tcp                           #FTP, data
ftp               21/tcp                           #FTP. control
telnet            23/tcp
smtp              25/tcp    mail                   #Simple Mail
                                                     Transfer
                                                     Protocol
time              37/tcp    timserver
time              37/udp    timserver
rlp               39/udp    resource               #Resource
                                                     Location
                                                     Protocol
nameserver        42/tcp    name                   #Host Name Server
nameserver        42/udp    name                   #Host Name Server
nicname           43/tcp    whois
domain            53/tcp                           #Domain Name
                                                     Server
domain            53/udp                           #Domain Name
                                                     Server
bootps            67/udp    dhcps                  #Bootstrap
                                                     Protocol Server
bootpc            68/udp    dhcpc                  #Bootstrap
                                                     Protocol Client
tftp              69/udp                           #Trivial File
                                                     Transfer
gopher            70/tcp
finger            79/tcp
http              80/tcp    www www-http           #World Wide Web
kerberos-sec      88/tcp    krb5                   #Kerberos
kerberos-sec      88/udp    krb5                   #Kerberos
hostname         101/tcp    hostnames              #NIC Host
                                                     Name Server
iso-tsap         102/tcp                           #ISO-TSAP Class 0
rtelnet          107/tcp                           #Remote Telnet
                                                     Service
pop2             109/tcp    postoffice             #Post Office
```

```
                                                          Protocol -
                                                          Version 2
pop3              110/tcp                               #Post Office
                                                          Protocol -
                                                          Version 3
sunrpc            111/tcp     rpcbind portmap           #SUN Remote
                                                          Procedure Call
sunrpc            111/udp     rpcbind portmap           #SUN Remote
                                                          Procedure Call
auth              113/tcp     ident tap                 #Identification
                                                          Protocol
uucp-path         117/tcp
nntp              119/tcp     usenet                    #Network News
                                                          Transfer
                                                          Protocol
ntp               123/udp                               #Network Time
                                                          Protocol
epmap             135/tcp     loc-srv                   #DCE endpoint
                                                          resolution
epmap             135/udp     loc-srv                   #DCE endpoint
                                                          resolution
netbios-ns        137/tcp     nbname                    #NETBIOS Name
                                                          Service
netbios-ns        137/udp     nbname                    #NETBIOS Name
                                                          Service
netbios-dgm       138/udp     nbdatagram                #NETBIOS Datagram
                                                          Service
netbios-ssn       139/tcp     nbsession                 #NETBIOS Session
                                                          Service
imap              143/tcp     imap4                     #Internet Message
                                                          Access Protocol
pcmail-srv        158/tcp                               #PCMail Server
snmp              161/udp                               #SNMP
snmptrap          162/udp     snmp-trap                 #SNMP trap
print-srv         170/tcp                               #Network
                                                          PostScript
bgp               179/tcp                               #Border Gateway
                                                          Protocol
irc               194/tcp                               #Internet Relay
                                                          Chat Protocol
ipx               213/udp                               #IPX over IP
ldap              389/tcp                               #Lightweight
                                                          Directory Access
                                                          Protocol
https             443/tcp     MCom
https             443/udp     MCom
microsoft-ds      445/tcp
microsoft-ds      445/udp
#? kpasswd           464/tcp                            # Kerberos (v5)
#? kpasswd           464/udp                            # Kerberos (v5)
isakmp            500/udp     ike                       #Internet Key
                                                          Exchange
exec              512/tcp                               #Remote Process
                                                          Execution
biff              512/udp     comsat
login             513/tcp                               #Remote Login
```

```
who                513/udp    whod
cmd                514/tcp    shell
syslog             514/udp
printer            515/tcp    spooler
talk               517/udp
ntalk              518/udp
efs                520/tcp                          #Extended File
                                                      Name Server
router             520/udp    route routed
timed              525/udp    timeserver
tempo              526/tcp    newdate
courier            530/tcp    rpc
conference         531/tcp    chat
netnews            532/tcp    readnews
netwall            533/udp                          #For emergency
                                                      broadcasts
uucp               540/tcp    uucpd
klogin             543/tcp                          #Kerberos
kshell             544/tcp    krcmd                 #Kerberos remote
                                                      shell
new-rwho           550/udp    new-who
remotefs           556/tcp    rfs rfs_server
rmonitor           560/udp    rmonitord
monitor            561/udp
ldaps              636/tcp    sldap                 #LDAP over
                                                      TLS/SSL
doom               666/tcp                          #Doom Id Software
doom               666/udp                          #Doom Id Software
kerberos-adm       749/tcp                          #Kerberos
                                                      administration
kerberos-adm       749/udp                          #Kerberos
                                                      administration
kpop              1109/tcp                          #Kerberos POP
phone             1167/udp                          #Conference
                                                      calling
ms-sql-s          1433/tcp                          #Microsoft-SQL-
                                                      Server
ms-sql-s          1433/udp                          #Microsoft-SQL-
                                                      Server
ms-sql-m          1434/tcp                          #Microsoft-SQL-
                                                      Monitor
ms-sql-m          1434/udp                          #Microsoft-SQL-
                                                      Monitor
wins              1512/tcp                          #Microsoft
                                                      Windows Internet
                                                      Name Service
wins              1512/udp                          #Microsoft
                                                      Windows Internet
                                                      Name Service
ingreslock        1524/tcp    ingres
l2tp              1701/udp                          #Layer Two
                                                      Tunneling
                                                      Protocol
pptp              1723/tcp                          #Point-to-point
                                                      tunnelling
                                                      protocol
```

```
radius          1812/udp                    #RADIUS
                                              authentication
                                              protocol
radacct         1813/udp                    #RADIUS
                                              accounting
                                              protocol
nfsd            2049/udp    nfs             #NFS server
knetd           2053/tcp                    #Kerberos
                                              de-multiplexor
ttcp            5001/tcp                    #TTCP
ttcp            5001/udp                    #TTCP
man             9535/tcp                    #Remote Man
                                              Server
```

Reinstalling TCP/IP

Clearly one trick that is always available is to uninstall and reinstall the TCP/IP protocol suite in Windows 2000 Server. I mentioned previously that the Microsoft TCP/IP protocol stack is a weaker stack, and unfortunately this holds true in the heat of battle on occasion (and it always seems to be at the enterprise level, not at my home basement lab!).

So let's assume that you've tried just about every TCP/IP troubleshooting approach mentioned in this chapter and nothing, absolutely nothing, is solving your problem. Time for drastic action. Simply stated, remove and reinstall the TCP/IP protocol stack. Correctly done, this approach will work wonders.

But of course it isn't that simple. When reinstalling the TCP/IP protocol suite, it's entirely plausible that you will receive an error message that indicates "The Registry Subkey Already Exists." The fix is obvious. To fully remove TCP/IP, you must remove the "embedded" Registry entries the protocol suite made during installation.

Tip

Experienced Microsoft Exchange users will immediately recognize what's going on here. To completely remove Microsoft Exchange from a Windows 2000 server, you must manually remove its related Registry entries. The same can be said for TCP/IP.

The TCP/IP protocol suite and related services entries that should be removed from the Registry are as follows (note I'm assuming some services such as WINS have been installed, otherwise ignore the Registry references).

Connectivity utilities

Assuming you have removed the TCP/IP protocol "component," then you must remove

```
HKEY_LOCAL_MACHINE\Software\Microsoft\NetBT
HKEY_LOCAL_MACHINE\Software\Microsoft\Tcpip
HKEY_LOCAL_MACHINE\Software\Microsoft\TcpipCU
HKEY_LOCAL_MACHINE\SYSTEM\CCS\Services\DHCP
HKEY_LOCAL_MACHINE\SYSTEM\CCS\Services\LMHosts
HKEY_LOCAL_MACHINE\SYSTEM\CCS\Services\'NetDriver'\Parameters\Tcpip
HKEY_LOCAL_MACHINE\SYSTEM\CCS\Services\NetBT
```

SNMP service

Assuming you have removed the SNMP service, you must remove

```
HKEY_LOCAL_MACHINE\Software\Microsoft\RFC1156Agent
HKEY_LOCAL_MACHINE\Software\Microsoft\Snmp
HKEY_LOCAL_MACHINE\SYSTEM\CCS\Services\Snmp
```

TCP/IP network printing support

These entries relate to the LPDSVC line printer components. You must remove

```
HKEY_LOCAL_MACHINE\Software\Microsoft\Lpdsvc
HKEY_LOCAL_MACHINE\Software\Microsoft\TcpPrint
HKEY_LOCAL_MACHINE\SYSTEM\CCS\Services\LpdsvcSimple TCP\IP Services
```

The next two entries related to the simple TCP/IP service. You must remove

```
HKEY_LOCAL_MACHINE\Software\Microsoft\SimpTcp
HKEY_LOCAL_MACHINE\SYSTEM\CCS\Services\SimTcp
```

DHCP Server service

Assuming you have removed the HCP Server service, you must remove

```
HKEY_LOCAL_MACHINE\Software\Microsoft\DhcpMibAgent
HKEY_LOCAL_MACHINE\Software\Microsoft\DhcpServer
HKEY_LOCAL_MACHINE\SYSTEM\CCS\Services\DhcpServer
```

WINS Server service

Assuming you have removed the WINS Server service, you must remove

```
HKEY_LOCAL_MACHINE\Software\Microsoft\Wins
HKEY_LOCAL_MACHINE\Software\Microsoft\WinsMibAgent
HKEY_LOCAL_MACHINE\SYSTEM\CCS\Services\Wins
```

DNS Server service

Assuming you have removed the DNS Server service, you must remove

```
HKEY_LOCAL_MACHINE\Software\Microsoft\Dns
HKEY_LOCAL_MACHINE\Software\Microsoft\WinsMibAgent
HKEY_LOCAL_MACHINE\SYSTEM\CCS\Services\Wins
```

Tip

Few Windows 2000 Server professionals know about the required TCP/IP-related Registry housekeeping just detailed (removing Registry entries and so on). By following the preceding suggestions, you've set yourself apart from the 2000 pack!

TCP/IP Q & A

As promised, here are more specific TCP/IP troubleshooting-related questions and answers.

Is TCP/IP correctly installed on my Windows 2000 Server?

This question isn't as easy to answer as you might think, given the possibilities of corrupt TCP/IP protocol stack components that won't easily reveal themselves during the moment of need. However, you can always stick to a few basics. First, ping the loopback address of 127.0.0.1. Assuming this worked and a reply occurred, you're possibly home free. If it failed, however, observe the event logs and see what types of TCP/IP-related information were recorded in the system log. Second, ping another address (a host machine, another workstation, or such) and see if you receive a reply. If so, yet another TCP/IP-related hurdle has been passed.

I receive an Error 53 when connecting to a server. What is it?

Error 53 is returned when host name resolution fails. That's the bottom line. Possible resolution paths include confirming that the host name is spelled correctly (such as in the UNC format) when you attempt resolution (this assumes of course that the other computer is running TCP/IP). The preceding advice is valid for a remote host located on the same or a different subnet. However, if you are crossing to another subnet, the resolution scenario becomes more complex. For mixed Windows 2000 Server networks, you might also check that the WINS database contains the same type of name-to-IP address mappings. Heck, if you're really old fashioned, it wouldn't hurt to see if the LMHOSTS file contains the appropriate name-to-IP address mapping entries.

I'm relying on the LMHOSTS file for resolution. I've added a new name mapping, but I'm experiencing long connect times or timeout conditions. Why?

Supposing you have a large LMHOSTS file (of course this would only occur at the enterprise level), your new entries may be too far down the list for speedy name resolution. Therefore, it is better for you to preload the entry with the #PRE command. This and other LMHOST file goodies were discussed earlier in this chapter. You may also place your mapping higher in the LMHOSTS file.

I am having a difficult time connecting to a specific server. What gives?

Run the nbtstat -n to determine without doubt what names, including the server you are seeking, are registered on the network. See the nbtstat section earlier in the chapter for more information.

I cannot connect to a foreign host when using host names, but I can connect with IP addresses. Why?

Simply stated, you're having problems with DNS-related resolution. Check that the DNS Server setup for the TCP/IP protocol is correct. Make sure that the DNS addresses are correct and in the proper order. If you are using the HOSTS file, make sure that the remote computer name is spelled correctly with proper capitalization.

I'm communicating with a remote host, and the TCP/IP connection appears hung. I've confirmed this by observing TCP/IP-related errors in my error log. Why?

Using the netstat -a command, you can observe the port activity for TCP and UDP. A good TCP connection typically has 0 bytes in the send/receive queues. Blocked data will reveal itself as a connection problem. If this is not the case, then you're experiencing application delays or network problems. Don't overlook the possibilities of application delay. There's nothing like a client/server database suffering from contention problems that are disguised and appear as TCP/IP connection problems. If you're an experienced network professional, you probably have similar epic stories.

When using Telnet, the banner on the title bar isn't correct, but I'm sure I've specified the correct IP address. Why?

It's important to verify that the DNS name and HOSTS table are current. Also, verify that no two computers have the same IP addresses on the same network. Imposter problems such as this are among the most difficult to track down and resolve. Using the arp -g command, you will see mapping from the ARP cache. This will display the Ethernet (MAC) address for the particular remote computer, possibly enabling you to delete the import entry with arp -d if you know the erroneous MAC address. After undertaking these steps, try pinging the remote host address, an action that forces an ARP. Finally, check the ARP table again with arp -g.

I've received a message "Your default gateway does not belong to one of the configured interfaces." How can I solve this?

Basically, the default gateway doesn't appear to be on the same logical network as the computer's network adapter. This can be determined and resolved by comparing the network ID portion of the default gateway's IP address with the network ID(s) of any of the computer's network adapters.

I can't ping across a router when using TCP/IP as a RAS client. Why?

The RAS Phonebook is the culprit here. If you have selected "Use default gateway on remote network" under the TCP/IP settings in the RAS Phonebook, you will have this problem. The resolution is this: Using the route add command, add the route of the subnet you're attempting to connect to.

Additional TCP/IP Troubleshooting Resources

Just a short note to wrap up TCP/IP troubleshooting. Remember that the event logs such as System and Application will assist your troubleshooting efforts, as will Microsoft TechNet, the online Microsoft Knowledge Base found at `www.microsoft.com`; Microsoft Technical Support; and Performance Monitor. If you use Performance Monitor, make sure that you've installed the SNMP service on your Windows 2000 Server so that you have the full suite of TCP/IP-related object:counters.

Summary

This chapter explored all the important topics of troubleshooting TCP/IP:

- Learning how to troubleshoot TCP/IP
- Understanding TCP/IP troubleshooting steps
- Understanding TCP/IP utilities and tools used for troubleshooting
- Selecting the best tool to solve your TCP/IP-related problem

Chapter 6

DNS, DHCP, WINS

In This Chapter

- Learning DNS
- Learning DHCP
- Learning WINS
- Comparing and contrasting DNS, DHCP, and WINS
- Learning about Dynamic DNS

Three big topics and only one chapter available to cover them. Each topic, Domain Name System (or Domain Name Service, DNS), Dynamic Host Configuration Protocol (DHCP), and Windows Internet Name Service (WINS), is worthy of its own individual book. However, by studying these topics together, you may see how each has a different, yet integrated, role. In essence, Microsoft has implemented DNS, DHCP, and WINS so that they complement each other when used on the same network. Observe the following:

- **DNS.** Using DNS, clients can locate host resources via dynamic and static mappings maintained in the DNS database. In addition, any non-WINS-aware client that uses DNS to resolve names and has a static mapping to the DNS service can locate a WINS client, provided you configure the Microsoft DNS server to use a WINS server for additional names resolution. DNS and WINS typically are integrated for legacy support reasons.
- **DHCP.** The DHCP service enables you to allocate dynamic IP addresses automatically to DHCP clients that move among subnets.
- **WINS.** By using WINS, which typically is seen on legacy Windows NT Server networks, clients can register their computer name and IP address automatically, every time they start up their computer. If the computer moves among subnets, this information is updated automatically as well.

Be Resolved

First, a review of name resolution. And I'm not talking about the pop '90s "resolution" therapy where you deal with your resentments and make amends. This is network-based name resolution in which computer identifiers (typically hardware or IP addresses) are resolved to some form of name that is meaningful (computer name). "Names" on a computer network are really the following:

NetBIOS Name (for instance, TCI1)

TCP/IP Address (121.133.2.44)

Host Name (Abbey)

Media Access Control (MAC) — this is the network adapter hardware address

Note that these are four generally accepted naming conventions used on a Windows 2000 Server network. (I've omitted the names based on curses sometimes uttered by end users at misbehaving machines!) In the next few pages, I'll discuss the NetBIOS and Host name resolution process.

NetBIOS name resolution

As you know, these names must be resolved so that you can find someone or something on the network with which to interact. For NetBIOS names (such as those called from UNC commands), Microsoft uses a six-step resolution approach, as shown in Figure 6-1.

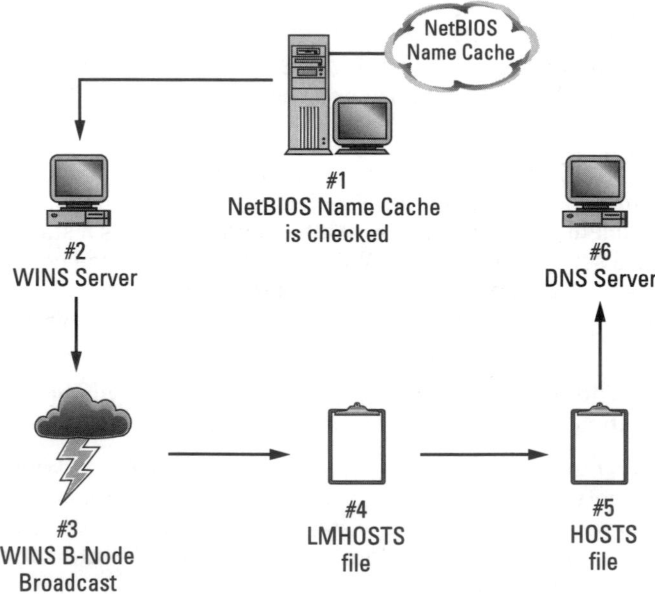

Figure 6-1: The Microsoft method for resolving NetBIOS names

STEPS:

To resolve NetBIOS names

Step 1. Check the cache. The NetBIOS name cache, built by the computer browser, is checked for the NetBIOS name/IP address mapping. If found, the resolution is complete.

Step 2. If the name isn't resolved from Step 1, the first of three attempts is made to contact the WINS server (if one is present). If the name is resolved, the IP address is returned to the source host. If the three attempts are unsuccessful, the resolution process continues.

Step 3. If the WINS server does not resolve the name, the client sends three b-node broadcasts on the local network. If the proper NetBIOS name is found on the local network, the resolution to the IP address is complete.

Step 4. Next, the LMHOSTS file is consulted. Here again, if resolution is reached, the name resolution process terminates.

Step 5. The HOSTS file is consulted, assuming none of the previous steps have worked.

Step 6. Finally, as a final name-resolution step, the source host sends a request to its respective domain name server, which resolves the host name to an IP address if successful.

Host name resolution

A similar, six-step name resolution approach is used for host name resolution in Windows 2000 Server (see Figure 6-2)

STEPS:

To resolve host names

Step 1. The host name typed by the user is compared to the local host name. If the two names match, resolution occurs without generating any network activity.

Step 2. Next, the HOSTS file is checked if the user-typed host name and the local name are not the same. Address resolution occurs if the user-typed host name is found in the HOSTS file. The host name is mapped to an IP address.

Continued

STEPS:

To resolve host names *(continued)*

Step 3. If the host name is still unresolved, the source host sends a request to the domain name server. If the host name is resolved by a DNS, an IP address is mapped to it. If resolution doesn't occur initially, more attempts are made on the DNS at 5, 10, 20, and 40-second intervals.

Step 4. Assuming name resolution hasn't occurred, the local NetBIOS name cache is checked next, followed by three attempts to contact and achieve resolution via configured WINS servers.

Step 5. The local host initiates three b-node broadcasts if name resolution still hasn't occurred.

Step 6. Last, the local LMHOSTS file is checked.

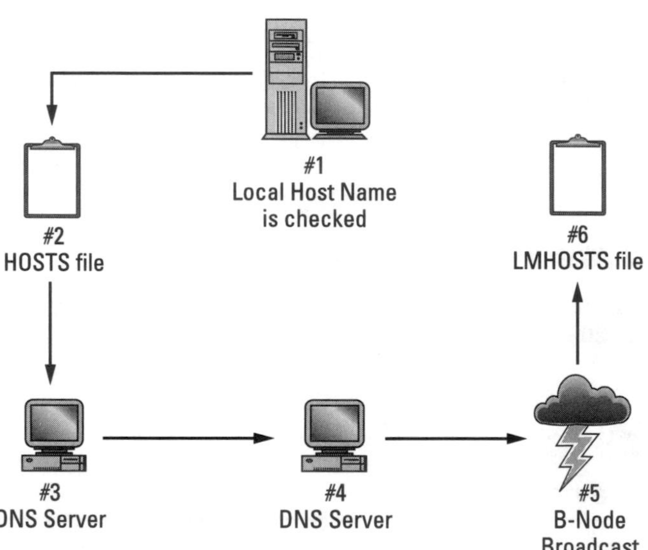

Figure 6-2: The Microsoft method for resolving host names

If all six steps fail and you are unable to resolve a host name to an IP address, then darn it, you're stuck with contacting the remote host via IP address (not host name). And most likely, a round of troubleshooting follows.

Tip

One sign that DNS is unsuccessful is when it has a timeout condition.

This typically results in some form of error message being returned to the user's terminal (see Figure 6-3). Resolution failure may be the result of hardware or software configuration errors. Determining what might be causing your resolution failure is the ongoing DNS challenge. My advice on DNS troubleshooting? First, read this entire chapter carefully. I share DNS administration insights along the way that will help facilitate your troubleshooting efforts. Second, simple as this may sound, start at one end of the equation, such as the DNS server located at your Internet Service Provider (ISP), and work backwards to your client workstation.

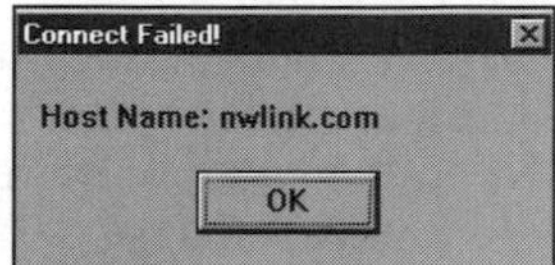

Figure 6-3: Host name resolution failure

Note

DNS tries to resolve names by making resolution attempts at 5-, 10-, 20-, and 40-second intervals.

DNS

At the most basic level, the *Domain Name System (DNS)* is a group of protocols and services widely used over the Internet and TCP/IP-based networks. Why? Because DNS provides name registration and name-to-address resolution capabilities. And DNS drastically lowers the need to remember numeric IP addresses when accessing hosts on the Internet or any other TCP/IP-based network. As an example, instead of typing **ping 131.107.6.200** to ping a specific host, you can type **ping harryb.com**, which is much easier (of course, my example assumes that 131.107.6.200 maps to the host name `harryb.com`). This user-friendly functionality of DNS can be employed on your private Windows 2000 Server network by running DNS locally (which is the default Windows 2000 network configuration). That, of course, is the purpose of this section and the DNS installation section in Chapter 4.

So hopefully, it is clear that DNS enables you to interact with your computer, its network, and the Internet using street or "friendly" names while, largely in the background, these friendly names are resolved to an address. Likewise, addresses may be reverse-engineered back to a friendly name. This reverse engineering is akin to this example involving cars. Suppose you're interested in a car driving alongside you. Perhaps you would like to purchase the car and it has a small "For Sale" sign with a telephone number to call. But at 70 miles per hour on the freeway, you only are able to safely write down the license number. Once home, you reverse-engineer the license number to its owner by scanning the Department of Motor Vehicles car registration lists. This is a real-world example of reverse engineering an address or numeric value back to a friendly name. Of course, in most states, motor vehicle records are confidential and unavailable. (But early in my computing career, I did have occasion to legally purchase a computer database of car owners in Alaska that was used for marketing purposes.)

DNS is well suited for the enterprise given its method of managing host names and other name resolution information via a distributed system of replicated and delegated name databases. Based on specifications RFC 1034 and RFC 1035, DNS is based on the hierarchical and logical tree structure known as the domain name space. The top of the tree is the Internet Network Information Center (InterNIC), which can be accessed at `www.ds.internic.net`. InterNIC truly can be thought of as the Internet god in its role of performing domain registration and administration tasks. Once entered into the master database at InterNIC, domain names are replicated and managed through the use of distributed databases. These databases reside on numerous name servers located across the Internet. Each name server maintains a zone file that contains pertinent database information for its use, given its position in the tree hierarchy.

Microsoft's DNS service is something that separates Windows 2000 Server from other popular networking alternatives such as Novell's NetWare, Artisoft's LANtastic, and Macintosh. Those other NOSes historically have not provided the same level of DNS support out of the box. And that's something to consider as networks become increasingly Internet-centric. Plus, Windows 2000 Server introduces Dynamic DNS — something that I discuss later in the chapter.

Before DNS, the practice of mapping friendly host or computer names to IP addresses was handled via host files. Host files are easy to understand. These are static ASCII text files that simply map a host name to an IP address in a table-like format. Windows 2000 Server ships with a HOSTS file in the `\winnt\system32\drivers\etc` subdirectory. I discuss the Windows 2000 Server HOSTS file at length in Chapter 5.

The fundamental problem with the host files was that these files were labor intensive. A host file is modified manually, and typically it is administrated centrally. What a pain as your network grows, especially if your network is the Internet! Much of that pain and agony has disappeared because DNS is a much more distributed and automated approach.

And before I go any further, mind if I speak about a little DNS expectation management? DNS isn't perfect, even in Windows 2000 Server. Why not? Because there still exists this gray area of uncontrollable variables, such as interacting with the Internet. Whereas you may deploy DNS on your Windows 2000 Server network in top form, in all likelihood, you're still subject to the comings and goings of the Internet: How long until your new domain name actually is registered? How long until a change to a MX record is propagated? And so on. It's not perfect yet.

WHOIS

When using the WHOIS command, which is not native tc Windows 2000 Server and is discussed in Chapter 5, you may note that every Internet domain registered with the InterNIC has at least two DNS servers associated with the domain name. Why? Believe it or not, this Internet-related feature is a much-appreciated U.S. Department of Defense design feature. According to my good friend, a highly placed source who has worked in government and academic computing communities since the Eisenhower era, this design paradigm stems from the Cold War. In the event of a thermonuclear war, the Internet as we know it would survive, in part due to its inherent redundancy. Having two separate DNS servers tied to each domain account is part of this redundancy.

Be sure that you verify that two DNS servers are associated with your Internet domain name (see Figure 6-4). The dual DNS server requirement is your responsibility and is in place to ensure that your Internet domain name is resolved properly on the Internet. Clearly, that is to your benefit. And if you're involved in electronic commerce, it is essential. Could you imagine customers not being able to find your storefront? Not having two DNS servers associated with your Internet domain name places you at risk of exactly this: lost sales because customers can't successfully find and use your Web site.

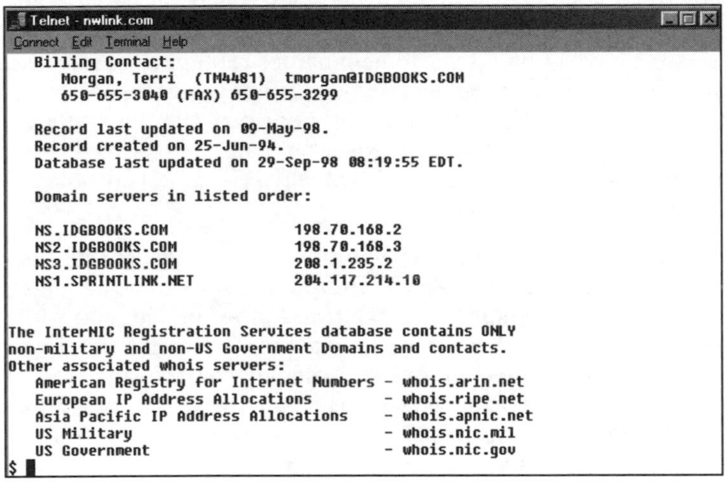

```
Telnet - nwlink.com
Connect  Edit  Terminal  Help
   Billing Contact:
      Morgan, Terri  (TM4481)  tmorgan@IDGBOOKS.COM
      650-655-3040 (FAX) 650-655-3299

   Record last updated on 09-May-98.
   Record created on 25-Jun-94.
   Database last updated on 29-Sep-98 08:19:55 EDT.

   Domain servers in listed order:

   NS.IDGBOOKS.COM              198.70.168.2
   NS2.IDGBOOKS.COM             198.70.168.3
   NS3.IDGBOOKS.COM             208.1.235.2
   NS1.SPRINTLINK.NET           204.117.214.10


The InterNIC Registration Services database contains ONLY
non-military and non-US Government Domains and contacts.
Other associated whois servers:
   American Registry for Internet Numbers - whois.arin.net
   European IP Address Allocations       - whois.ripe.net
   Asia Pacific IP Address Allocations    - whois.apnic.net
   US Military                            - whois.nic.mil
   US Government                          - whois.nic.gov
$
```

Figure 6-4: The DNS servers for idgbooks.com

As a network professional, you have the opportunity to work with a wide range of applications that, being TCP/IP-based, depend on DNS functioning properly. One example is from a small law firm that I advise. This law firm uses WestMate, an application from WestLaw, for its legal research. Older versions of this application used modem dial-up connections to a local telephone number or CompuServe. A later version, version 7.*x*, uses a Winsock-based connection to the law firm's existing Internet service to operate correctly. More specifically, the application uses FTP port 23 to communicate over the Internet. This application depends heavily on DNS operating properly because it connects to the site `westmate.westmate.com` when it launches and attempts to log on and authenticate the research-minded attorney. If DNS is somehow not working, the application fails, the lawyers are "researchless," and I receive a call to fix it.

As another example, observe how Internet Explorer — Microsoft's Web browser — works. When you type in the Uniform Resource Locator (URL), that name is resolved via DNS. So typing `www.idgbooks.com` triggers a series of events that connects you and your browser with the distant site on the Internet.

Finally, you may use DNS with your Microsoft Exchange application. A common configuration with the Internet Mail Service (IMS) in Microsoft Exchange is to have DNS perform the outgoing mail resolution. And even if you don't explicitly have DNS selected, providing a mail host name such as `smtp.nwnexus.com` when configuring the IMS assumes you have DNS capabilities that can resolve this street-friendly host name.

Exceptions to the rule of generally connecting to any Internet site you desire include little-known sites that literally are located in distant lands; these sites can be too many hops away. An example of this includes sites such as the far reaches of Alaska (if you are located in the 48 contiguous states). Perhaps these sites haven't had their domain names replicated across the DNS databases of the world. So, when you attempt to access this site, and the domain name can't be resolved easily, your browser may return a "host not found" error. In reality, the host exists but can't be resolved within the time window your browser supports. I typically refer to this problem as a host that is too many hops away.

The preceding problem has two solutions. First, request that the remote site mirror or publish its Web page to another server somewhere else in the world. This is what Microsoft, Novell, and other vendors do with their well-traveled Web pages. These large sites mirror their sites to other servers not for resolution purposes but for load balancing and reliability. When you have a popular Web site, you may need to use mirror servers just to keep up with the traffic demands. Just ask Microsoft and Novell. The second solution is my next secret, so read on.

One possible way to get around the problem of finding a site that is too many hops away and by all account appears unbrowsable is to use a search engine for your name resolution tasks and then click the hot link from the search engine hit list. Search engines to consider include Yahoo! (`www.yahoo.com`), Alta Vista (`www.altavista.com`), or Infoseek (`www.infoseek.com`). As you know, these search engines may be selected via the search button on the taskbar of your browser. Ideally, this would provide you another pathway to that faraway site. And the domain name resolution would have occurred differently, that is, via the search engine. By the way, do you want to know my favorite search engine? For a single search engine, I prefer Infoseek for reasons I fully explain (such as robust drill down) in Part VI, "Optimizing and Troubleshooting Windows 2000 Server." But here, where I want to find a little-known domain name or Web site, I want to cast as wide a net as possible so I typically perform these "domain-seeking" searches from a site that is a "clearinghouse" for search engines. This site is `www.dogpile.com`. Dogpile is a search engine of search engines. By executing your search here, you effectively search all the other engines.

How DNS really works

By now, you can appreciate that Windows 2000 Server administrators can (and should!) use DNS to manage domain names.

DNS uses a client/server model in which the DNS server maintains a static database of domain names mapped to IP addresses. The DNS client, known as the resolver, performs queries against the DNS servers. The bottom line? DNS resolves domain names to IP address using these steps (see Figure 6-5):

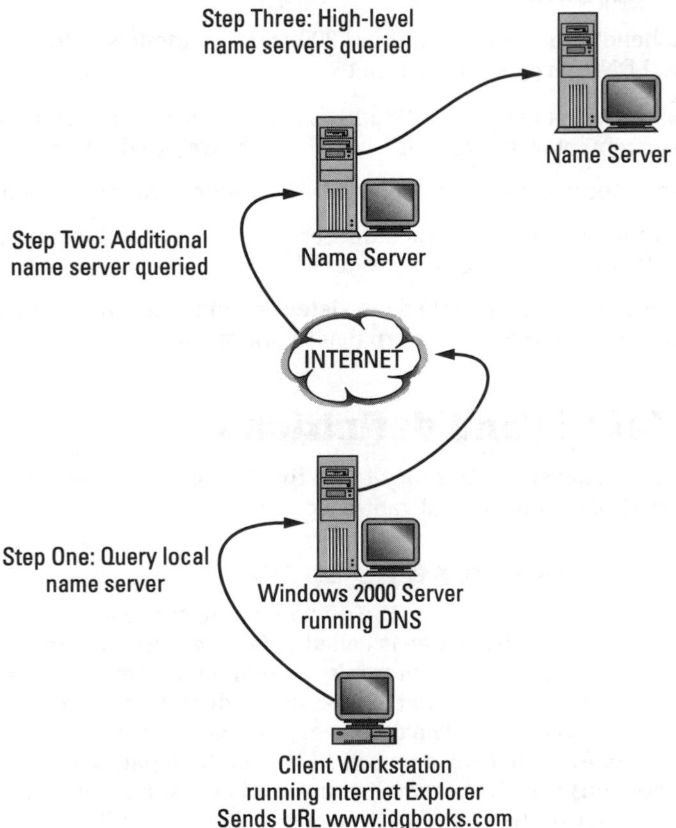

Figure 6-5: How DNS works

STEPS:

To resolve domain names to an IP address with DNS

Step 1. A client (or "resolver") passes its request to its local name server. For example, the URL term `www.idgbooks.com` typed into Internet Explorer is passed to the DNS server identified in the client TCP/IP configuration. This DNS server is known as the local name server.

Step 2. If, as often happens, the local name server is unable to resolve the request, other name servers are queried to satisfy the resolver.

Step 3. If all else fails, the request is passed to more and more higher-level name servers until the query resolution process starts with the far-right term (for instance, com) or at the top of the DNS tree with root name servers.

DNS benefits

Several benefits accrue to Windows 2000 Server administrators who have deployed DNS correctly in their networks:

- DNS provides the proper Windows 2000 Server name resolution management framework. It's just the right way to do it.
- Computer users may connect to UNIX systems via friendly names.
- Users may fully exploit the Internet via Internet naming conventions such as URLs (for instance, `www.idgbooks.com`).
- Enterprises can maintain a consistent naming structure for both external Internet resources and internal network resources.

DNS details and definitions

I use the next several pages to get into the details of DNS, now that you've considered DNS from several vantage points.

Defining domain name space

The DNS database is known as the domain name space and assumes a tree form. Each position in the tree is called a *domain*. Just as a tree can have branches shooting out from its trunk, a domain may have subdomains. The main thing to remember is that entries in the domain name space must adhere to the accepted DNS naming conventions. These conventions are quite simple. At each level, a period (.) is used to separate each child domain (or subdomain) from its parent. If you would like some more information on this topic, refer to the Windows 2000 Server Resource Kit.

Defining domains

Domains contain both hosts and other domains. A domain has five components, all of which may be present in any given domain name space, but not all five components (such as the subdomain name component) always are present in smaller domain name spaces.

The domain root

Considered to be the root node of the DNS tree, the domain root is known as the unnamed or null entry. You may see this referred to as the trailing period, which typically is not listed when displaying a domain name.

However, to display a fully qualified domain name (FQDN) requires this period (".") as the last term displayed on the far right of the domain name.

The top-level domain

In reality, the top-level domain is the far-right term in a typical Internet domain name as displayed. This domain level is managed specifically by InterNIC and is divided into three areas:

- **Organizational.** This is the three-character code any network professional or Internet surfer is familiar with. Table 6-1 lists these codes.
- **Geographical.** Based on ISO-3166 (a standard), these typically are country designations (such as `.nz` for New Zealand). Perhaps you've encountered these top-level domain designations in e-mail messages you've received from overseas.
- **In-addr.arpa.** This is the least known of the three top-level domains. It is a special, reserved domain used for IP-address-to-name mappings, also known as reverse lookups.

Did you know the United States has a geographic top-level domain of "us"? It does! Perhaps you haven't encountered this form, because it is seldom used.

Table 6-1 provides a list of top-level domain names in a DNS tree. The number of these names continues to grow, however.

Table 6-1 Top-Level DNS Domain Names

Domain Name	*Designation*
COM	Commercial (businesses, corporations)
EDU	Education (schools, universities)
GOV	Government (local, state, federal)
INT	International (such as the United Nations)
MIL	Military (such as the Navy and the Army)
NET	Internet service providers (for instance, `ibm.net`)
ORG	Nonprofit organizations (such as `mssociety.org`)

Second-level domains

Second-level domains are the names most familiar to network professionals, Internet surfers, and even the general audience. Such a name typically consists of a company name or a product name that is meaningful, useful, and memorable. For example, the publisher of this book, IDG Books Worldwide, has registered the second-level domain name `idgbooks.com` with the InterNIC. Not surprisingly, second-level domain names indeed are managed by the InterNIC in order to ensure that each name is unique.

Third-level domain names (subdomains)

The third-level domain name is an optional term in DNS. Typically, it is used to append or further subdivide the "regular" domain name. For example, perhaps you want to subdivide functional departments at the imaginary company Springers Unlimited. If the "regular" domain name known to all is `springers.com` and you want to further subdivide the domain name to better reflect your organization, you may have domain names such as `marketing.springers.com` and `legal.springers.com`. Another use of subdomains is to create distinctions by location. Following my example, if you further subdivide `springers.com` by locations, you may have a third-level domain titled `west.springers.com`. You get the picture.

Note that Microsoft makes extensive use of third-level domain names appended to its regular domain name of `microsoft.com` to distinguish different departments, programs, promotions, and such.

You, the network administrator, manage third-level domain names — not the InterNIC. You may, in theory, append as many third-level domain names to your regular or second-level domain name as you wish! In effect, all the employees in your organization can have their own domain names. Such names mean that name resolution occurs locally on your server designated to handle second-level domain name activity after the path is resolved correctly by DNS servers on the Internet that deliver the session communications. This process is shown in Figure 6-6, where traffic destined for `springers.com` from the Internet is further subdivided internally according to, in this example, departments.

In the preceding example, having the local Windows 2000 Server perform the third-level domain name resolution would require that the DNS service be installed and fully functional on the local Windows 2000 Server.

One instance when you might use third-level domain names is when you run the Internet Connection Wizard in Small Business Server (see Chapter 16). Here, the Internet Connection Wizard (ICW) offers the opportunity to create a third-level domain name when you open an account with an SBS-compliant Internet Service Provider (ISP). Note the ICW also enables you to create a second-level domain name as well with the new SBS 4.5 release. If I had registered Springers Unlimited with Northwest Nexus (a Pacific Northwest ISP), the third-level domain address that automatically would be created for me might be `springers.nwnexus-sbs.com`.

Second-level litigation

Second-level domains are causing lots of fun and litigation in the business community right now! Speculators are registering trademark names (with InterNIC) prior to the trademark holders doing so. Often, the company that holds the trademark then "purchases" the second-level domain registration from the speculator, who typically makes a handsome profit on his or her $50 InterNIC domain registration fee (although some trademark holders are suing, rather than paying, to recover trademark names being used as domain names). All in a day's work for some; but for others, the implicit message should be to register your second-level domain names as soon as possible before someone else does! By analogy, yesterday's mad rush to acquire 1-800 telephone numbers is today's rush to acquire the second-level domain name of your choice. And also be advised that the courts are casting a weary eye towards domain name speculators; more often than not, they now find for the trademark holder (for example, Pepsi) over the speculator who happens to register a domain name before the trademark holder does.

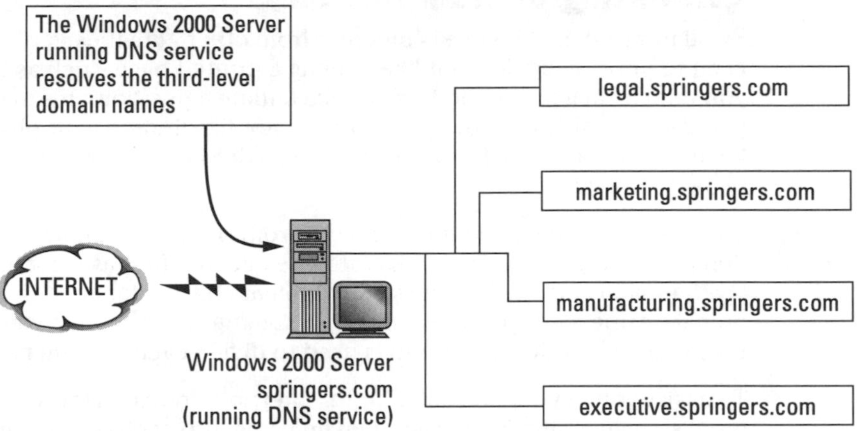

Figure 6-6: Using third-level domain names on your network

In reality, the use of third-level domain names is rare in the business community. Blame it on the marketing departments of companies across the land, but second-level domain names are in and third-level domain names look both cheap and kind of weird. The business community, which has no shortage of egos and public relations specialists, very much demands second-level domain names because image is everything. You are more likely to see a company use a second-level domain name and a virtual directory.

Make darn sure you understand the difference between a subdomain and a virtual directory. The key point is that subdomains are a way to divide your domain name space, and virtual directories point to storage areas on your server's hard drive. A virtual subdirectory typically is displayed as a forward slash after the top-level domain term (for instance, `/harryb`), and a subdomain name is displayed as a term to the left of the second-level domain name (as discussed previously).

It is not uncommon to see both a subdomain and a virtual directory displayed in a URL on the Internet. For example, `springers.nwnexus-sbs.com/~dawgs` shows the subdomain name `springers` and the virtual directory `~dawgs`. Virtual directories are discussed in Chapter 8.

Host names

Host names are, by default, the same as the computer name in Windows 2000 Server, but they need not be. In DNS, the host name appears to the left of the top-level and second-level domain names. This is similar to how third-level domain names appear.

As an example, the host name `harryb` in the domain `springers.com` would appear as: `harryb.springers.com`. Note that a Windows 2000 Server on your network would perform the host name resolution similar to the process discussed previously in relation to Figure 6-2.

Evaluating domain names

Evaluating a domain name is different from other activities you probably are used to performing. It is not like reading a printed page, such as this, where you read from left to right. It is not like finding a position on a map, where you use a column and row grid. And it is not like finding your physical location with a Global Positioning System (GPS) device, where you rely on high-altitude satellites.

Tip

You read a fully qualified domain name from right to left. A second-level domain name such as `idgbooks.com` is evaluated first as a commercial top-level domain, and then as the second domain term `idgbooks`. A third-level domain name may appear as `springers.nwnexus-sbs.com`. And once again, if you haven't noticed, a period is used to divide each domain name level.

To assist you in your efforts to better interpret domain names, Table 6-2 breaks down a sample Internet domain name into each domain level.

Table 6-2 Evaluating a Third-Level Domain Name

Domain Name Level	*Term*	*Comments*
Top-level domain name	com	Designates a commercial entity.
Second-level domain name	nwnexus-sbs	Registered with InterNIC (the Internet domain registration authority).
Third-level domain name	springers	Not registered with InterNIC. Typically, the holder of the second-level domain name creates as many third-level domain names as necessary. Third-level domain names are resolved by DNS running on a Windows 2000 Server on the local network (although this configuration isn't required).

Be advised that the term "domain" in the context of DNS relates to Internet domains, not Windows 2000 Server domains.

Take a moment to analyze your own Internet domain name if you have one. Does the preceding discussion help you to better understand how your domain name is structured? If not, take a few minutes to revisit the preceding discussion or consider my earlier suggestion that you peruse the Windows 2000 Server Resource Kit for a second take on the DNS discussion. No hard feelings! I just want you to get it.

DNS names that do not conclude with a trailing period (such as "`.com`") are not fully qualified domain names (FQDN).

Zones

In the MCSE certification course lectures that I deliver as an MCT, I often refer to Windows 2000 Server domains as administrative units. In the language of DNS, *zones* also can be thought of as administrative units. Database records relating to a particular portion of the domain name space, called a zone, are saved in a file known as a *zone file*.

Understand that a zone can consist of a single domain (DNS-style, not Windows 2000) or a domain with subdomains. A single DNS server can be configured to manage one or more zone files. A discrete domain node (known as a zone's *root domain*) anchors each zone.

Let's take a moment to make a distinction between a zone and a DNS-style domain. A domain refers to a single node and all of its child nodes. A zone is a full and complete set of resource records that is delegated to a specific name server. Another take on the matter is this: Domains represent a logical, hierarchical organization of name space. Zones represent the physical arrangement of how names and resource data are distributed or delegated to name servers.

Files used by DNS

Remember this as you master DNS with Windows 2000 Server: The underlying files in a DNS system are text files. The good news is that with Windows 2000 Server, you will enjoy using its graphical user interface, MMC-based DNS toolset, to edit and manage the DNS zone files.

Zone files

A database file or zone file is a file of resource records (RRs) for the portion of the domain for which the zone is granted responsibility. A *resource record* can be defined as an individual data entry containing a domain name and other information related to this named domain or host. Note that resource records may be either of the following:

- **Record type.** Type is used to indicate the type of data stored by each record. Type defines the format or individual field structures for each particular resource record. In other words, different types of records occur in zone files; you may elect to query for only one type of record.

- **Record class.** Class is used to indicate the class of network or type of software that this record supports. In most cases, the only class used for DNS data that is stored and used in most TCP/IP networks is the Internet Class (IC).

I define the important zone files that you need to know — ranging from Start of Authority (SOA) to Canonical Name (CNAME) — in Table 6-3, "Selected Zone Record Definitions" in the section "Configuring DNS."

Cache files

Cache files contain host names and addresses of root name servers. You can observe the default cache file (`cache.dns`) provided by DNS in Windows 2000 Server.

```
Cache file:
;
;  Root Name Server Hints File:
;
;     These entries enable the DNS server to locate the root name
servers
;     (the DNS servers authoritative for the root zone).
;     For historical reasons this is known often referred to as the
;     "Cache File"
;
@                        NS b.root-servers.net.
b.root-servers.net       A  128.9.0.107
@                        NS c.root-servers.net.
c.root-servers.net       A  192.33.4.12
@                        NS d.root-servers.net.
d.root-servers.net       A  128.8.10.90
@                        NS e.root-servers.net.
e.root-servers.net       A  192.203.230.10
@                        NS i.root-servers.net.
i.root-servers.net       A  192.36.148.17
@                        NS f.root-servers.net.
f.root-servers.net       A  192.5.5.241
@                        NS g.root-servers.net.
g.root-servers.net       A  192.112.36.4
@                        NS j.root-servers.net.
j.root-servers.net       A  198.41.0.10
@                        NS k.root-servers.net.
k.root-servers.net       A  193.0.14.129
@                        NS l.root-servers.net.
l.root-servers.net       A  198.32.64.12
@                        NS m.root-servers.net.
m.root-servers.net       A  202.12.27.33
@                        NS a.root-servers.net.
a.root-servers.net       A  198.41.0.4
@                        NS h.root-servers.net.
h.root-servers.net       A  128.63.2.53
```

For DNS installations not connected to the Internet, you may replace or modify this file. If you manage your own domain name space privately, you should include host records for root name servers within your private network that can be contacted to authoritatively resolve names not managed by the server's zone files.

To see the current Internet cache files for the worldwide Internet, go to `ftp://rs.internic.net/domain/named.cache` on the Internet.

Reverse lookup files

As the name implies, *reverse lookup files* are the files consulted when a reverse lookup is undertaken in the `in-addr.arpa` domain. A reverse lookup is performed when you supply the IP address and the computer, via a reverse lookup, returns the matching domain host name. The key point about reverse lookup files is that some applications depend on these types of reverse resolutions. One application area that takes advantage of them consists of NFS clients.

In Windows 2000 Server, a sample reverse lookup file titled 192.dns may be found at `c:\winnt\system32\dns\samples` and looks similar to the following:

```
;
;   192.dns
;
;   Reverse lookup file for 29.5.192.in-addr.arpa. domain.
;
;   This file provides address to name matching (reverse lookup)
;   for addresses 192.5.29.?.
;
;
;   Note that all domain names given in this file, which are not
;   terminated by a "." and hence fully qualified domain names (FQDN),
;   are implicitly appended with "29.5.192.in-addr.arpa."
;
;   Examples:
;       "6"  =>  6.29.5.192.in-addr.arpa.
;
;   If a name outside of "29.5.192.in-addr.arpa." is required, then it
;   must be explicitly terminated with a dot, to indicate that it is a
;   FQDN.
;
;   Example:
;       "7.30.5.192.in-addr.arpa."  =>  7.30.5.192.in-addr.arpa.
;
;
;   START OF AUTHORITY
;
;   The first record in any database file should be a "Start of
Authority"
;   (SOA) record.  The fields of this record are:
;
;   IN SOA <source machine> <contact email> <serial number> <refresh
time>
```

```
;    <retry time> <expiration time> <minimum time to live>
;
;    <source machine> is the machine on which this file was created.
;
;    <contact email> is the email address if the person responsible
;                    for this domain's database file.  Instead of
;                    writing an '@' in the email name, write a '.'
;
;    <serial number> The "version number" of this database file.
;                    Increase this number each time you edit a
;                    database file.
;
;    <refresh time>  A time, in seconds, that a secondary server
;                    will wait between checks to your server, when
;                    deciding if it is time to download a new copy
;                    of this domain's data.
;
;    <retry time>    A time, in seconds, that a secondary server
;                    will wait before retrying a failed zone download.
;
;    <expire time>   A time, in seconds, that a secondary server will
;                    keep trying to download a zone.  After this time
;                    limit expires, the old zone information will be
;                    discarded.
;
;    In order for a resource record to span a line in a database file,
;    parentheses must enclose the line breaks, as in the following
;    example.
;
;
;    YOU SHOULD CHANGE:
;        - "machine.place.dom." to the name of your name server.
;        - "postmaster.machine.place.dom." to your email name.
;

@    IN  SOA     nameserver.place.dom.
postmaster.nameserver.place.dom. (
                               1             ; serial number
                               36000         ; refresh   [1h]
                               600           ; retry     [10m]
                               86400         ; expire    [1d]
                               3600 )        ; min TTL   [1h]
;
;    NAME SERVERS
;
;    The following entries list the name servers for this domain.
;    This information allows other name servers to lookup names in
;    your domain.
;
;    YOU SHOULD CHANGE:
;        - The names of the DNS servers.
@        IN  NS      nameserver.place.dom.
@        IN  NS      nameserver2.place.dom.
```

```
;
;   WINS Reverse Record
;
;   The WINS-R RR is specific to WindowsNT and may be attached ONLY
;   to the zone root of a reverse lookup domain.
;
;   Presence of a WINS-R record at the zone root instructs the name
server
;   to use a netBIOS node status (nbstat) request for any reverse
lookup
;   requests for IP addresses which are NOT given in PTR records
below.
;
;   Examples:
;
;   1) A query for 135.29.5.192.in-addr.arpa. (192.5.29.135)
;       192.5.29.135 has a PTR record below, so DNS server responds
;       with the PTR record without nbstat lookup.
;
;   2) A query for 206.29.5.192.in-addr.arpa. (192.5.29.206)
;       192.5.29.206 is within the 29.5.192.in-addr.arpa zone, but
;       there is no PTR record for it in this zone file.
;       DNS will issue an nbstat query to 192.5.29.206.
;       If a response is received, the hostname in the response will
be
;       appended to the result domain in the NBSTAT record and used
;       as the hostname corresponding to 192.5.29.206.  The PTR
;       record will be cached and a response sent to the client.
;       If a response is NOT received, the DNS server responds to
;       the client with a name error.
;
;   3) A query for 29.5.192.in-addr.arpa. (192.5.29)
;       192.5.29 is within the 29.5.192.in-addr.arpa zone, but is NOT
;       an IP address.  Hence no nbstat lookup is done, and the server
;       responds with a name error.
;
;
;   WINS-R and zone transfer:
;
;   The MS DNS server, will configure WINS-R information as a resource
;   record to allow it to be transferred to MS DNS secondary servers.
;
;   If you have MS DNS secondaries, and want them to use exactly the
;   same WINS-R info as the primary server, then omit the LOCAL flag
;   in the WINS-R record.
;
;   If you have UNIX secondaries, or MS secondaries using different
;   WINS-R information, then use the "LOCAL" flag after the "WINS-R"
;   flag and the WINS-R information will NOT be considered part of the
;   zone's resource records and will NOT be sent in the zone transfer.
;
;
```

```
;   YOU SHOULD CHANGE:
;       - Change the resulting domain that should be appended to
;         names found with WINS-R lookup.
;       - Uncomment the line with LOCAL flag, if WINS-R information
should
;           not be transferred as part of the zone data.
;       - Uncomment the line without the LOCAL flag, if WINS-R
information
;           should be transferred to MS DNS secondaries.
;           OR
;       - Leave this line commented out, if WINS-R lookup not desired.
;@   IN  WINS-R          place.dom.
;@   IN  WINS-R  LOCAL   place.dom.

;
;   PTR RECORDS
;
;   The PTR record is used to map IP numbers to hostnames.  IP numbers
;   are written in backward order and prepended to "in-addr.arpa" for
;   this process.  As an example, looking up the name for "1.2.3.4"
;   requires a PTR query for the name "4.3.2.1.in-addr.arpa."
;
;   Since this is the domain file for 29.5.192.in-addr.arpa., this
file
;   provides lookup for IP addresses 192.5.29.?.
;
;   YOU SHOULD CHANGE:
;       - The final IP address digits.
;       - The corresponding host names.

2       IN  PTR     WINSsrv1.place.dom.
3       IN  PTR     WINSsrv2.place.dom.
7       IN  PTR     nameserver.place.dom.
8       IN  PTR     nameserver2.place.dom.
17      IN  PTR     mailserver.place.dom.
18      IN  PTR     mailserver2.place.dom.
112     IN  PTR     host.nt.place.dom.
;
;   Apparently, "host.place.dom." has two interfaces running TCP/IP,
;   and each of these interfaces' addresses needs to be listed in the
;   reverse-lookup files.
;
135     IN  PTR     host.place.dom.
82      IN  PTR     host.place.dom.
11      IN  PTR     other-host.place.dom.
21      IN  PTR     other-host.place.dom.
111     IN  PTR     other-host.place.dom.
```

Boot files

Boot files are used to configure the startup environment of DNS servers that use Berkeley Internet Name Domain (BIND). However, Microsoft DNS does not have complete BIND conformance, and thus boot files are present to support migrations from other BIND environments. The boot file contained at `c:\winnt\system32\dns\samples` appears as:

```
;
;   DNS boot file
;
;   NOTE:   It is NOT necessary to use a boot file to run the DNS
server.
;
;   The Microsoft DNS server is capable of reading configuration, zone
;   and cache information from a "boot" file or from the registry.
;
;   To take full advantage of the capabilities of the Microsoft DNS
;   server we suggest using the DNS Administration tool
(dnsadmin.exe).
;   If you are new to DNS or are setting up a new installation, then
we
;   strongly recommend using the Admin tool, in which case you need
not
;   setup a boot file.
;
;   However, if you are porting an existing BIND DNS installation,
then
;   the DNS server will be able to read your existing boot file.
Note,
;   that the file MUST be named "boot".
;
;
;   Boot file syntax:
;
;   Directives in this file instruct the DNS service when it is
starting.
;   Anything on a line following a semicolon ';' is a comment, and is
ignored.
;
;   This file and all files listed in this file must be in
;   %SystemRoot%\system32\dns directory.
;
;
;   CACHE FILE
;
;   The "cache" file is not really cache information.  Rather it
contains
;   name server and IP address information necessary to contact the
ROOT
;   domain name servers.
;
;   The syntax of this command is:
;
;       cache   .       <filename>
;
;   YOU SHOULD CHANGE:
;
;   =>  Nothing - do NOT change this line, if you are NOT a root
domain
;       server.
```

```
;       (Note:  if you are not connected to the Internet, be sure and
edit
;       the cache file to point at the root servers for your
intranet.)
;
;       OR
;
;   =>  Comment out this line, if this DNS server is the ROOT domain
;       server for a private intranet.
;
cache   .   cache.dns


;
;   PRIMARY DOMAINS
;
;   "Primary" domains are listed below.  The second column is the name
of the
;   domain for which this name server is authoritative.  The third
column is
;   the name if the database file which contains the authoritative
data.
;
;   The syntax of this command is:
;
;       primary <domain> <filename>
;
;   YOU SHOULD CHANGE:
;       - The names of the domains.
;       - The names of the database files.
;       - Comment out domains for which server will be secondary.
;
;primary   place.dom                 place.dns
;primary   29.5.192.in-addr.arpa     192.dns


;
;   SECONDARY DOMAINS
;
;   "Secondary" domains are listed below.
;
;   The syntax of this command is:
;
;       secondary <domain> <master DNS ip address> <filename>
;
;   YOU SHOULD CHANGE:
;       - The names of the domains.
;       - The names of the database files.
;       - The IP address of the primary DNS server (192.255.255.7).
;       - Uncomment domains for which server will be secondary, then
;         comment out the primary statement for that domain above.
;
;secondary   place.dom                 192.5.29.7   place.dns
;secondary   29.5.192.in-addr.arpa     192.5.29.7   192.dns
```

Name servers

Simply stated, a *name server* is any server that retains and stores information about the domain name space. Known on the network as DNS servers, these machines run vendor-specific DNS implementations such as DNS in Windows 2000 Server.

It is important that you understand that name servers have one or more zones for which they are responsible. To respond affirmatively to a name query, a name server must have the authority to do so for the zone in which the queried name resides. This authority is handled by the Start of Authority (SOA) record at the top of the zone file. SOA is discussed later, in Table 6-4 (see the section "Configuring DNS").

Three types of name servers

When building your DNS environment, you may implement three types of name servers. These servers are primary, secondary, and caching. Most of us working in smaller and medium-sized organizations use a primary domain server. However, if you work at the enterprise level (especially with geographical dispersed operations), you not only benefit from, but also seek to use, secondary and caching servers. The number and types of name servers you use directly correlate to the size of your network.

Primary servers

A primary server is a single server for each zone that contains the master database files (resource records for all subdomains, hostnames, and so on) for the zone it is permitted to service. This server retrieves its resolution information or zone data locally, and likewise, changes are made locally.

Secondary servers

If I were discussing Microsoft System Management Server (SMS), I would be referring to helper servers. That's what secondary servers are for DNS: helper servers. Secondary servers have a copy of the appropriate domain name space data from another name server on the network. The server that provides the copy has the authority to do so and is known as an authoritative server. The mechanism for copying the information to the secondary server? Replication. The replication process occurs via a regular zone transfer from the other name server.

Three important reasons exist for having secondary servers in the enterprise:

- **Load reduction.** Having secondary servers reduces the load on the primary name servers.
- **Distant locations.** Secondary servers, similar to BDCs in the context of Windows 2000 Server, should be placed at remote locations that have significant client activity. This avoids having clients suffer from slow WAN links when trying to query DNS.
- **Redundancy.** It is necessary to have at least two DNS servers for each zone. One server is the primary; the other(s) is/are secondary. Typically, these machines are placed on separate networks for sake of fault tolerance.

Caching-only servers

The caching-only type of name server doesn't contain any active database files and isn't associated with any specific DNS zone. It relies on other name servers for its knowledge of the DNS domain structure. Every time a caching-only server queries a name server, the information it receives back is stored in its name cache.

Keep this perspective when discussing caching. All DNS servers perform caching. That's because a name, once resolved, is stored for a discrete period of time.

Forwarders and slaves

Suppose the DNS server on your Windows 2000 Server network is unable to resolve the name query. In this case, additional DNS servers are consulted to satisfy the name query. Assuming you correctly configure your internal DNS servers to use forwarders, then other servers on the Internet typically are consulted, resulting in name resolution.

Remember that specific DNS servers, via the DNS Manager (discussed later in this chapter), are configured to use forwarders. Only forwarders may contact Internet-based DNS name servers.

Slaves are configured to use forwarders and return error messages if a request fails.

Resolvers

You can think of resolvers as client services that execute name queries against name servers. More specifically, resolvers typically are the parts of the client's operating system (such as the TCP/IP DNS configuration information in Windows 95/98) that:

- Oversee and manage communications between TCP/IP client programs using DNS and name servers
- Format the DNS query packets that are sent to name servers
- Cache previous DNS query replies to speed future name resolutions

Resolver programs perform the following three functions on behalf of the DNS client:

- **General lookup function.** Involves finding records with a specific name, type, or class.
- **Address-to-name translation.** This is reverse name resolution. When presented with a 32-bit IP address, the program returns a host name.
- **Name-to-address translation.** When given a host or domain name, the program locates the appropriate 32-bit IP address. This is the most common use of DNS.

Name resolution — how it works

By now, you certainly understand that the key point to DNS is name resolution. Users provide friendly names that are resolved to IP addresses. The IP addresses are necessary for many programs, such as your browser (for instance, Internet Explorer), to operate. In the next few sections, I discuss four types of name resolution: recursion, iteration, caching, and reverse lookup.

Recursion

First, your DNS name server must be configured to support recursive forwarding of name queries. In this scenario, your name server assumes responsibility for forwarding unresolved name queries until it receives either a positive or negative response. Stated another way, when a recursion-compliant DNS server is contacted, it contacts other name servers until a clear and definitive answer for the original name query is received.

The default condition for the DNS service in Windows 2000 Server allows for recursive requests.

Iteration

In the case of iteration, a name server responds to a resolver based on its most complete or best knowledge of the data being queried. That's it. A best effort. With iteration, the name server may provide the address of another name server for the resolver to use if the best efforts aren't good enough.

It is worth noting that clients typically are configured, via the client's TCP/IP setup, to use other DNS servers if the first DNS server can't resolve the name query.

Caching

The concept of caching is easily understood. As local name servers perform name queries for resolvers on a network, these servers build a name cache based on their findings. In effect, these local name servers learn along the way. Once name resolution information is stored in cache memory of the local name server, this information may be accessed again quickly when the local name server receives other name queries. Simply stated, the name cache — a very fast resolution approach — is consulted for the benefit of the resolvers.

Note that a Time to Live (TTL) value applies to records that are cached. That way, older records that may not be relevant or readily accessed again are deleted from cache memory. This benefits name server performance.

The contents of the `cache.dns` file found on Windows 2000 Server is loaded into cache memory when a Windows 2000 server running DNS is started. The file `cache.dns` is displayed earlier in the chapter.

Reverse lookup

Most lookups via DNS are forward lookups, where a "friendly" name is resolved to an IP address. But what about this scenario: Suppose you see the following graffiti at a road stop on the Information Superhighway, "For a good time visit 131.107.6.200." Being the curious Windows 2000 Server engineer that you are, you decide to see just who 131.107.6.200 is before finding out whether a good time can be had. A reverse lookup, presented to the special domain `in-addr.arpa`, reveals the identity of this address. It's as if you found a telephone number and wanted to know to whom it belonged. In fact, for a brief period in the 1980s when I was living in Alaska, a reverse telephone book was published before privacy concerns quashed it.

Zone transfer

Zone transfers are transmissions of name space information among DNS servers. Historically, this occurred when, periodically, the entire zone file from one name server was transferred to another name server. Now, this also is done by the incremental zone transfer method. Here, just the delta (or changed) information is transferred. Incremental zone transfer is discussed in RFC 1995.

Zone transfers among name servers are what we MCSE types in the real world view as propagation delays when implementing domain name transfers, starting new domain names, and such.

Configuring DNS

The DNS MMC, shown in Figure 6-7, has as its primary function the configuration of DNS objects. Each object has a discrete set of manageable properties. The DNS MMC is a visual interface or GUI-based tool used to configure the DNS objects. Windows 2000 Server's DNS is configured largely in a generic way during the installation. But let's face it. You've got some hours ahead of you if you really want to implement DNS properly. This section assists you with that journey.

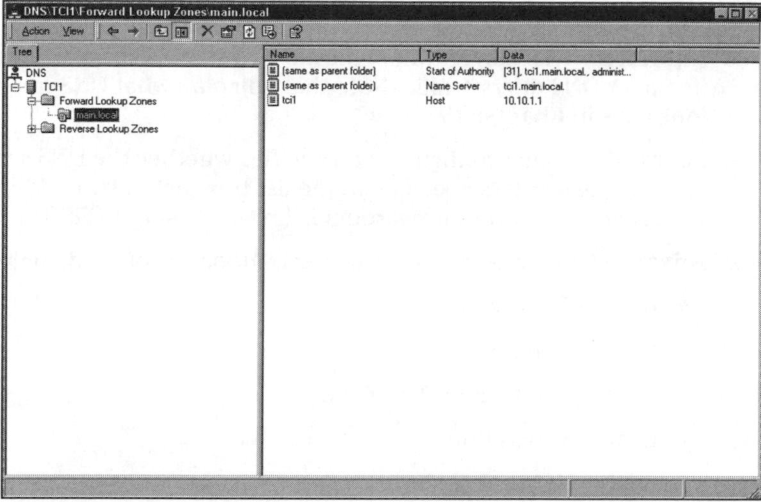

Figure 6-7: DNS MMC

Properties

There are numerous places that you make DNS configurations. The first is the property sheet of the host object and the second is the zone property sheet. Figure 6-8 shows the property sheet for the host object.

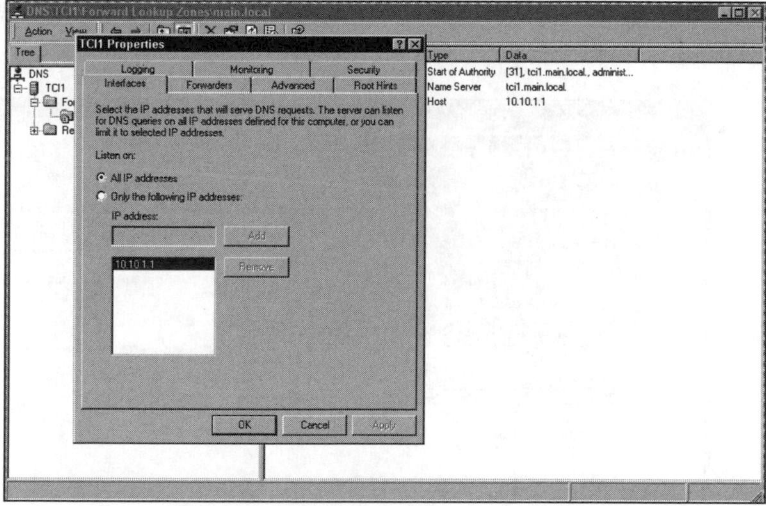

Figure 6-8: Host properties — interfaces

A brief explanation of each tab found on the Host properties follows:

- **Interfaces.** This configuration means that the DNS server (Host) should listen for DNS query traffic. Note that I display what DNS query traffic looks like in Chapter 19.
- **Forwarders.** This configuration specifies whether the DNS server first uses the forwarders specified in the list box (listed by IP address). Communications with forwarders is first-in, first-out (FIFO).
- **Advanced.** Several advanced server options are offered, including:
  - Disable Recursion
  - BIND Secondaries
  - Fail On Load if Bad Data Zone
  - Enable Round Robin
  - Enable Netmask Ordering
  - Secure Cache Against Pollution
- **Root Hints.** The contents of the available Name Server (NS) resource records are listed.
- **Logging.** This tab enables you to set numerous DNS debugging logging options. Use this when you are attempting to troubleshoot DNS.
- **Monitoring.** This is one of the cooler tabs in the DNS management area. It is here that you may configure and perform DNS-related tests. Test options include simple query and recursive query, as seen in Figure 6-9. You also may set the testing polling interval in seconds, minutes, and hours.

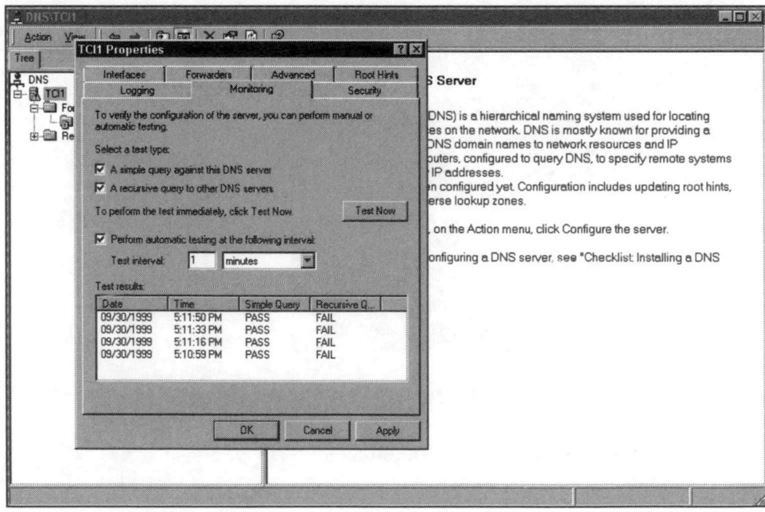

Figure 6-9: Monitoring tab

The shortest time interval that you may set with the polling interval is 30 seconds. It is not possible to set a shorter time interval.

- **Security.** This sets object permissions by user and group.

  You also may perform a variety of DNS configurations via the zone properties sheet (see Figure 6-10).

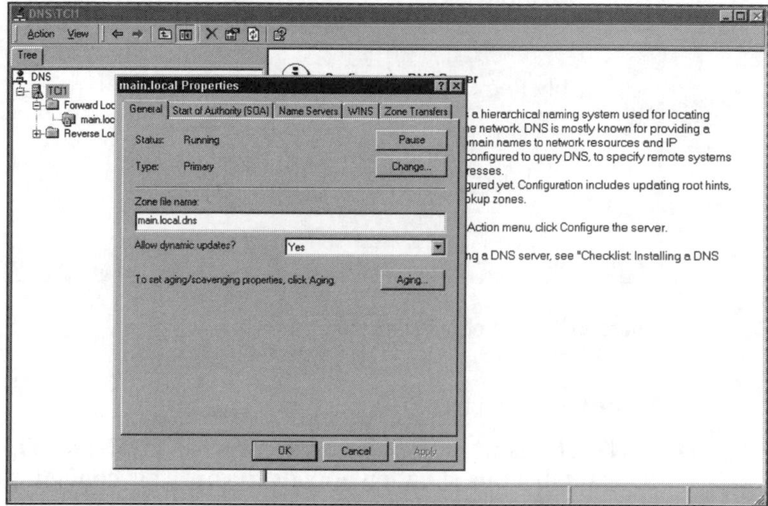

Figure 6-10: Domain properties

- **General.** This enables you to observe the status of the DNS service and the zone file name.

It is on the General tab that you invoke Dynamic DNS with the Dynamic update drop box. Dynamic DNS, one of the impressive new DNS features introduced in Windows 2000 Server, is discussed later in this chapter.

- **Start of Authority (SOA).** This relates to the Start of Authority record (see Figure 6-11). One of the settings that may be modified is the minimum default setting for Time to Live (TTL). Note that the TTL setting may be modified for seconds, minutes, hours, and days. Note that in Windows NT Server 4.0, this value also can accommodate weeks, months, and years.

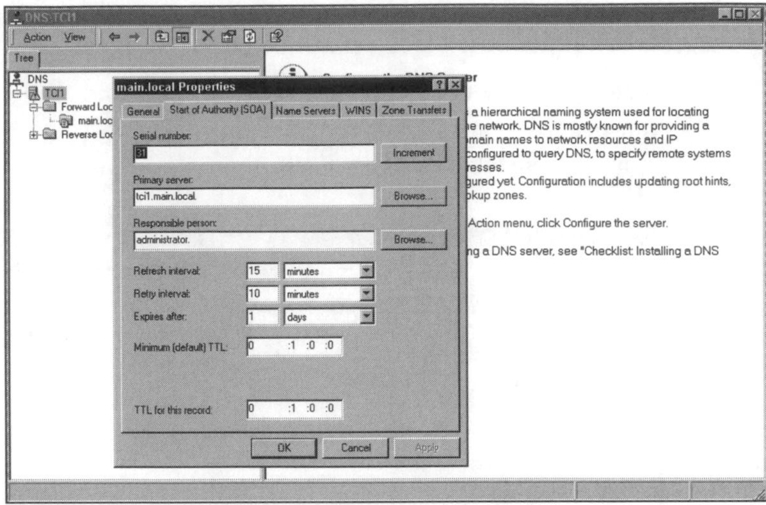

Figure 6-11: Start of Authority

- **Name Servers.** Lists the available name servers.
- **WINS.** This is where you integrate WINS and DNS (see Figure 6-12); it is a critical tab if this situation applies to you. This configuration is invoked to support older Windows NT Server machines on your Windows 2000 Server network. As far as I'm concerned, that's enough about WINS and DNS integration. Don't you agree?

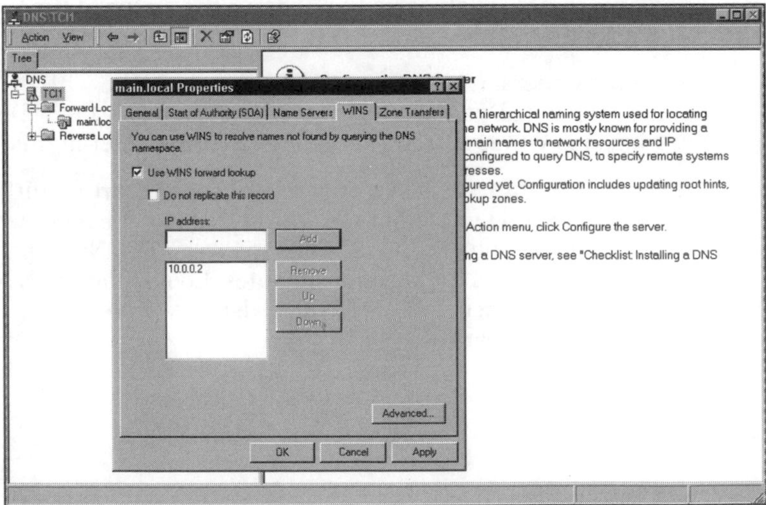

Figure 6-12: WINS tab

- **Zone Transfer.** Enables you to configure zone transfers from this server to other servers.

There are other ways to configure DNS in Windows 2000 Server. I review two of the ways here. First, there is the much appreciated Create New Zone Wizard. The other is a way to modify information at a more granular level (records types).

Create New Zone Wizard

Windows 2000 Server has introduced network professionals to an array of configuration wizards. One that you certainly will enjoy is the Create New Zone Wizard. This is launched from the secondary menu when you right-click the host in the left pane (see Figure 6-13). Select the Create a new Zone menu option to launch the Create New Zone Wizard (see Figure 6-14). The following steps help you to create a new zone.

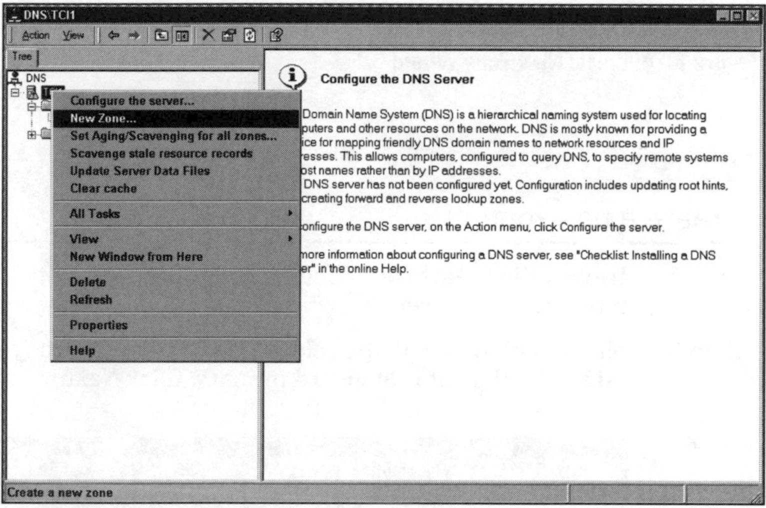

Figure 6-13: Secondary menu

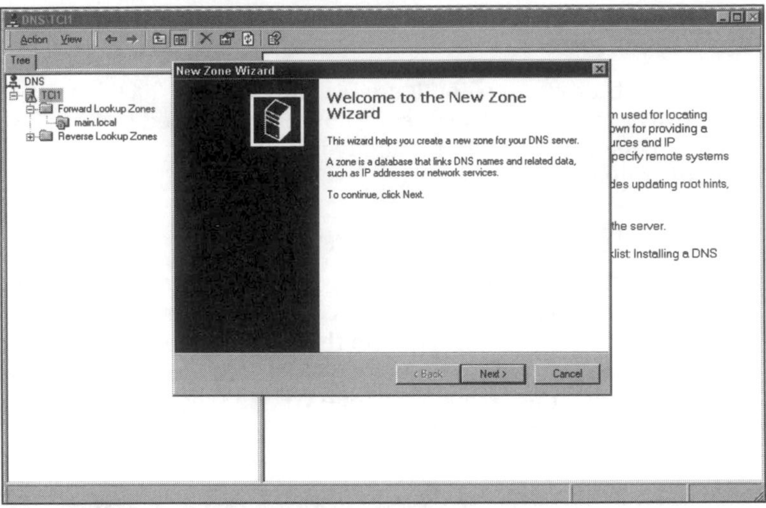

Figure 6-14: Create New Zone Wizard

STEPS:

Create a new zone

Step 1. Launch the Create New Zone Wizard. Click Next at the introductory screen.

Step 2. Make your choice on the Select a Zone Type screen (see Figure 6-15). The default is Standard primary. Click Next.

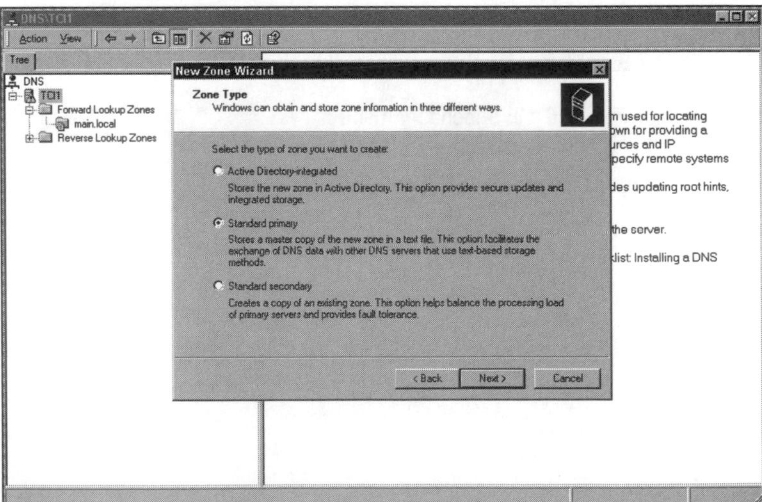

Figure 6-15: Select a Zone Type

Step 3. Make your choice on the Select the Zone Lookup Type (see Figure 6-16). The default is Forward lookup. Click Next.

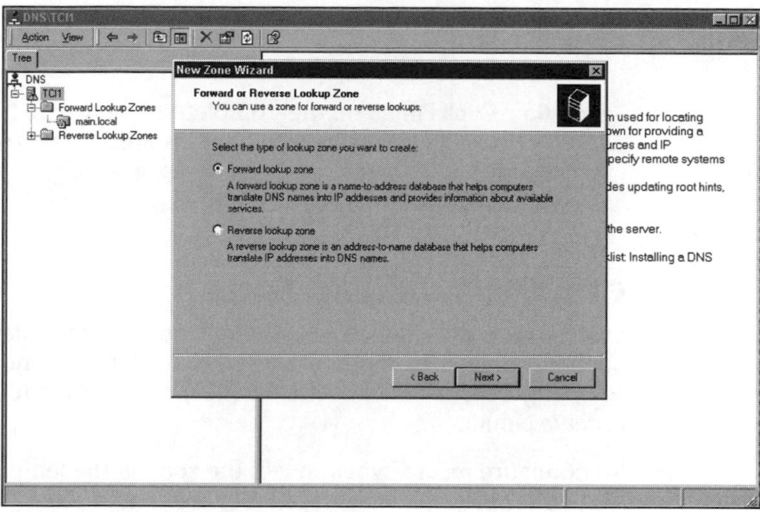

Figure 6-16: Select the Zone Lookup Type

Step 4. Provide a zone name (see Figure 6-17). Click Next.

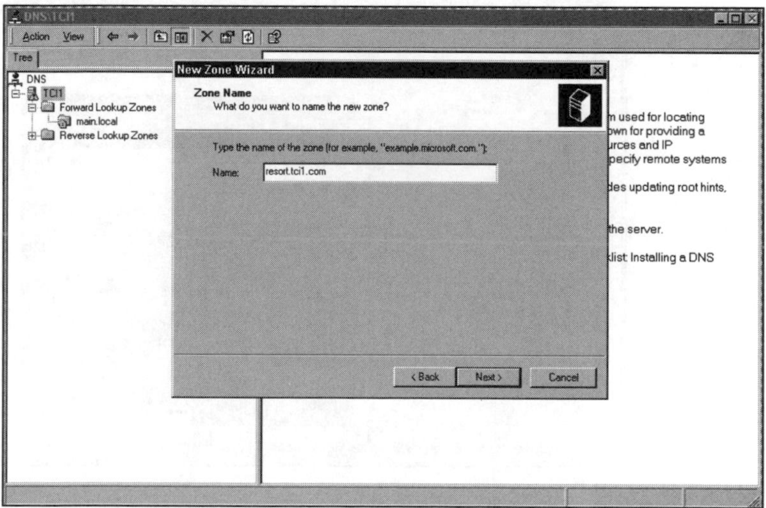

Figure 6-17: Zone Name

Continued

STEPS:

Create a new zone *(continued)*

Step 5. Provide a file name or accept the default file name on the File Name screen. Click Next.

Step 6. Click Finish on the Completing the Create New Zone Wizard. Congratulations. You have created a new zone.

Granular configurations

Once you create a new zone, you may perform granular-level configurations, such as configuring different record types for the zone. One popular record to configure is the Mail Exchange (MX) record so that you may send and receive e-mail.

To configure record types, select the zone in the left pane of the DNS MMC. Right-click to display the secondary menu and select New. You should see a submenu appear with several options to select from, including host, alias, mail exchanger, domain, delegation, as well as other records. If you select Other Record, the Record Type dialog box appears (see Figure 6-18).

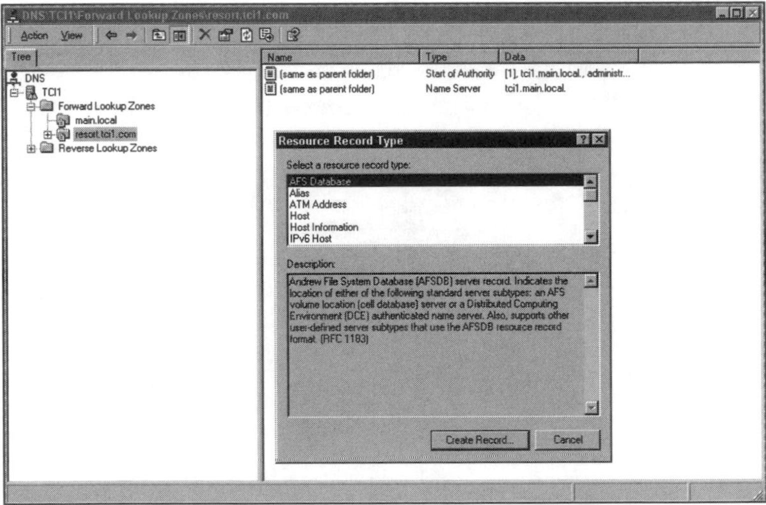

Figure 6-18: Record Type

Some of the record types you may select and configure are presented in Table 6-3.

Table 6-3 Selected Zone Record Definitions

Record Type	*Definition*
Host (A)	Maps host name to IP address in a DNS zone. Has three fields: Domain, Host Name, Host IP Address.
AAAA (IPNG)	Known as the address resource record, this maps a host name to an IPv6 address. This record will assume greater importance as the next generations of IP are implemented. Fields include: Domain, Host Name, IPv6 Address.
AFS Database (AFSDB)	Provides the location of either an AFS (Andrew File System) cell database server or a DCE (Distributed Computing Environment) cell's authenticated name server. Transac's AFS is a network file system, similar to NFS, but designed for WANs. The AFS system uses DNS to map a DNS domain name to the name of an AFS cell database server. The Open Software Foundation's DCE Naming Service uses DNS for a similar function, mapping the DNS domain name of a DCS cell to authenticated name servers for that cell. Fields include: Domain, Host Name (Optional), Server DNS Name, Server Type.
ATM (ATMA)	This is used to map a DNS domain name to an ATM address.
Aliases (CNAME)	Canonical name resource record that creates an alias for a host name. CNAME records typically are used to hide implementation details from clients. Fields include: Domain, Alias Name, For Host DNS Name.
Host Information (HINFO)	Identifies a host's hardware type and operating system. The CPU Type and Operating System identifiers should come from the MACHINE NAMES and SYSTEM NAMES listed in RFC 1700 (Assigned Numbers). Fields include: Domain, Host Name, CPU Type, Operating System.
Integrated Services Digital Network (ISDN)	This is used to map an ISDN telephone number to a DNS domain name.
Mailbox (MB)	This is used to map a specified domain mailbox name to a host address (A) record in the current zone that hosts this mailbox (RFC 1035).
Mail Group (MG)	This is used to add domain mailboxes via an individual MB record to the domain mailing group identified by name in this record (RFC 1035).
Name Servers (NS)	Identifies the DNS name servers in the DNS domain. NS records appear in all DNS zones and reverse zones. Fields include: Domain, Name Server DNS Name.

Continued

Table 6-3 *(continued)*

Pointer (PTR)	Maps IP address to host name in a DNS reverse zone. Fields include: IP Address, Host DNS Name.
Mail Exchange (MX)	Specifies a mail exchange server for a DNS domain name. Note that the term "exchange" does not refer to Microsoft Exchange, a BackOffice e-mail application. However, to connect Microsoft Exchange to the Internet via the Internet Mail Server (IMS), the MX record must be configured correctly by your ISP. A mail exchange server is a host that either processes or forwards mail for the DNS domain name. Processing the mail means either delivering it to the addressee or passing it to a different type of mail transport. Forwarding the mail means sending it to its final destination server via Simple Mail Transfer Protocol to another mail server that is closer to the final destination, or queuing it for a specified amount of time. Fields include: Domain, Host Name (Optional), Mail Exchange Server DNS Name, Preference Number.
Text (TXT)	Associates text with an item in the DNS database. A typical use might be to communicate a computer location such as Build 10, Room 1a. The Text string is limited to 256 characters. Fields include: Domain, Host Name (Optional), Text.
Well Known Services (WKS)	Describes the services provided by a particular protocol on a particular interface. Typically, this is the TCP or UDP protocol; but it can be any protocol listed in the PROTOCOLS file (located at `\winnt\system32\drivers\etc`). The services specifically are below Port 256 from the SERVICES file (located at `\winnt\system32\drivers\etc`). Fields include: Domain, Host Name, Host IP Address, Available Services, Available Protocol.
Responsible Person (RP)	This indicates who is responsible for the DNS domain or host. Multiple RP records may be specified for a single DNS domain. The record is divided into two parts: electronic mail address and a DNS domain name that points to additional information about the contact. Fields include: Domain, Host Name (Optional), Responsible Person Mailbox DNS Name, DNS Name for TXT Reference.
X.25 (X25)	A variation of the A record, the X25 record maps the host name to an X.121 address. Fields include: Domain, Host Name (Optional), X.121 PSDN Address.

DNS standards and revisions

I now end the DNS section with a return to the standards. Not surprisingly, additional DNS-related resources such as the RFC-type standards are available for you to continue your DNS education. Table 6-4 provides a list of DNS-related RFCs. If you want to learn more about this area, be my guest and feel free to tackle the RFCs.

Table 6-4 DNS RFC Standards

RFC	*Title*
1034	Domain Names — Concepts and Facilities
1035	Domain Names — Implementation and Specification
1101	DNS Encoding of Network Names and Other Types
1464	Using the Domain Name System to Store Arbitrary Strong Attributes
1536	Common DNS Implementation Errors and Suggested Fixes
1591	Domain Name System Structure and Delegation
1664	Using The Internet DNS to Distribute Mail Address Mapping Tables
1706	DNS NSAP Resource Records
1712	DNS Encoding of Geographical Location
1713	Tools for DNS Debugging
1794	DNS Support for Load Balancing
1886	DNS Extensions to Support IP version 6
1912	Common DNS Operational and Configuration Errors
1995	Incremental Zone Transfer in DNS
1996	A Mechanism for Prompt Notification of Zone Changes
2052	A DNS RR for Specifying the Location of Services
2065	Domain Name System Security Extensions
2136	Dynamic Updates in the Domain Name System (DNS UPDATE)
2137	Secure Domain Name System Dynamic Update

And finally, remember that DNS servers require static IP addresses. This fact is fair game on the MCSE exams.

DHCP

As you know, computers running TCP/IP must identify themselves via specific information that is unique to the network on which it resides. Such identification includes having a unique host name and a unique IP address. In this section of the book, you already have learned that the IP address for the computer may be assigned either manually (or statically) or dynamically via DHCP services in Windows 2000 Server. This part of Chapter 6 discusses configuring DHCP and using the DHCP MMC.

Benefits and overview of DHCP

Historically, TCP/IP environments have been difficult to configure. That is because you, as the network administrator and engineer, had to manage pesky TPC/IP configuration details that were easy to misconfigure. Have you ever transposed TCP/IP address values when fatigued late at night? Of course you have!

Enter the Dynamic Host Configuration Protocol (DHCP) approach that reduces, but does not eliminate, the configuration effort needed when using the TCP/IP protocol suite. DHCP is defined in RFCs 1533, 1534, 1541, and 1542. At the 50,000-foot level, you can view DHCP as centralizing TCP/IP configuration information and automatically assigning IP addresses to client systems configured to use DHCP.

Two types of systems use DHCP:

- **DHCP servers.** To use DHCP on your Windows 2000 Server-based network, you must have at least one Windows 2000 Server running the Microsoft DHCP service. This server needs to have a DHCP scope defined that specifies TCP/IP configurations and a pool of IP addresses that may be assigned to DHCP-compliant clients.

  The DHCP server accomplishes this by responding to a request from the DHCP client for an IP address lease. The DHCP server then selects from its address pool an unused address that it may lease out to the client. Typically, the DHCP server also provides additional TCP/IP configuration information for the client (which I discuss in more detail later in this section).

- **DHCP clients.** When installing TCP/IP on a DHCP client (such as Windows 2000 Professional or Windows 95/98), you can invoke the ability to have IP addresses assigned automatically by properly configuring the client. For example, in Windows 98 (see Figure 6-19), this is accomplished by selecting the Obtain an IP address automatically radio button from the IP Address tab sheet for TCP/IP Properties.

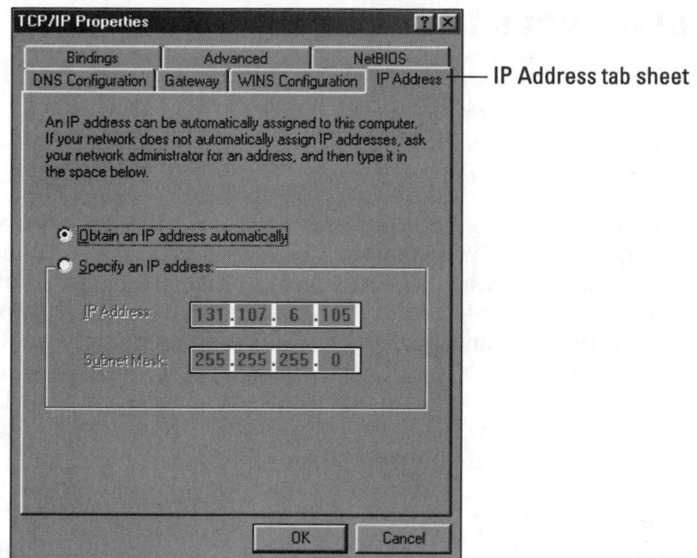

Figure 6-19: Enabling a DHCP client

Upon reboot of the Windows 98 client machine, you have created a DHCP client. Note that for Windows for Workgroups, this type of configuration requires that TCP/IP 32 be installed and that you configure several `*.INI` files manually.

As long as a DHCP server on the same network as the client responds with an IP address to lease, then the DHCP server fully loads the TCP/IP configuration information on the client and uses TCP/IP to communicate. Typically, the administrator or user supplies no additional configuration information, but there are exceptions. The biggest exception that I see involves people who don't take advantage of DHCP's rich configuration capabilities. For example, when the system is configured properly, you can supply DNS server information to the DHCP client automatically. But alas, I often see DHCP used only to assign IP addresses; rarely do I see it fully exploited with rich configuration information being supplied to the client.

So the benefits of using DHCP on your network are really twofold:

- The administrator can centrally define global and local subnet TCP/IP parameters for the entire internetwork or just the local LAN segment.
- Client computers do not require manual TCP/IP configuration. When a client computer crosses subnets, it can be reconfigured easily.

Whereas the DHCP server service may be started and stopped via the Services applet in the Control Panel, such is not the case with DHCP clients. To stop the DHCP client service in Windows 98, you must first disable the DHCP client capabilities by selecting the Specify an IP address radio button shown in Figure 6-19 and restart the computer.

Improvements to DHCP in Windows 2000 Server

Not surprisingly, the DHCP service has been improved in Windows 2000. The DHCP enhancements in Windows 2000 Server are primarily focused on additional tools, including the following:

- Detection of unauthorized DHCP server. This is an important addition long requested by MIS managers. Here's why. In a large company, there is often a need for testing LANs or small LANs in a training room that, while connected to the same cable runs as the larger corporate network, should indeed remain separate. Such is the case at my office. Our help desk often runs a small test LAN to resolve problems with applications. The server in is test scenario is typically configured with the DHCP service running. So when a bona fide worker bee logs on in the morning to the larger corporate network, they might receive an IP address dished out by the server on the test LAN if the test LAN was allowed to remain connected to the same cable run as the corporate LAN. Ouch! The user can't log on to the correct network, generating a user complaint.
- Integration with DNS. At different points in this chapter, I mention DNS and DHCP integration (see Figures 6-28 and 6-30 as examples). When an IP address is issued by DHCP in Windows 2000 Server, the IP address can also be registered with DNS name servers that support dynamic DNS. This feature has reduced both DHCP and DNS-related administration tasks.
- Support for superscopes and multicast scopes. Superscopes allow one DHCP server to issue IP addresses for multiple logical subnets. This wasn't possible in Windows NT Server 4.0. Multicast scopes are designed for multimedia clients that need to participate in collaborative application sessions.
- Option classes. Within a given scope, different clients may have different IP address configuration needs. Option classes allow you to place clients affected by the same scope into option classes so certain clients receive different types of configurations.
- Improved reporting. New DHCP-related reports have been created for monitoring and statistical purposes. In fact, some of the statistical data can now be displayed graphically!
- Ease of Administration. In the past, only Domain Admins could manage DHCP scopes. Now, with Active Directory, administrators at the organizational unit (OU) level can manage DHCP scopes for DHCP servers within their respective OU.

One little-known limitation with DHCP in Windows 2000 Server is that it's limited to participating in a single domain. Such a DHCP server may not issue IP addresses to clients housed in a separate domain. This limitation is greater than you might think because the Active Directory paradigm of sites, trees, and forests inherently emphasizes multiple domains.

How does DHCP really work?

In the beginning, there was the Bootstrap Protocol (BOOTP) that was based on RFC 951 and later modified to RFC 1542. In a layperson's terms, you may think of BOOTP as both the predecessor to DHCP as well as a sort of DHCP for UNIX systems. In fact, Microsoft had significant influence in the development of RFC 1542 (that incorporates DHCP). You aren't incorrect if you think of Microsoft as a founding father of DHCP.

The major advantage to having DHCP use the same message format as BOOTP is that an existing router may act as an RFC 1542 (BOOTP) relay agent to relay DHCP messages among subnets. But note that the operative term "may" is critical to understanding this concept. Not all routers support RFC 1542, and the older routers are the worst offenders. Newer router models released by Bay, Cisco, and others do not have this problem. So if you have a router that is 1542-compliant, it is possible to have a single DHCP server provide IP addresses and configuration information on both subnets in a two-subnet scenario.

This section also is familiar territory if you have taken the MCSE plunge and attended the MOC-687 or MOC-922 Microsoft Windows NT Server 4.0 Core Technologies course, where DHCP is covered in great detail. And as Windows 2000 Server courses are released, there will be considerable DHCP discussions in these new classes as well.

Leasing an IP address

To obtain an IP address from a DHCP server, DHCP clients pass through a series of states, as shown in Figure 6-20.

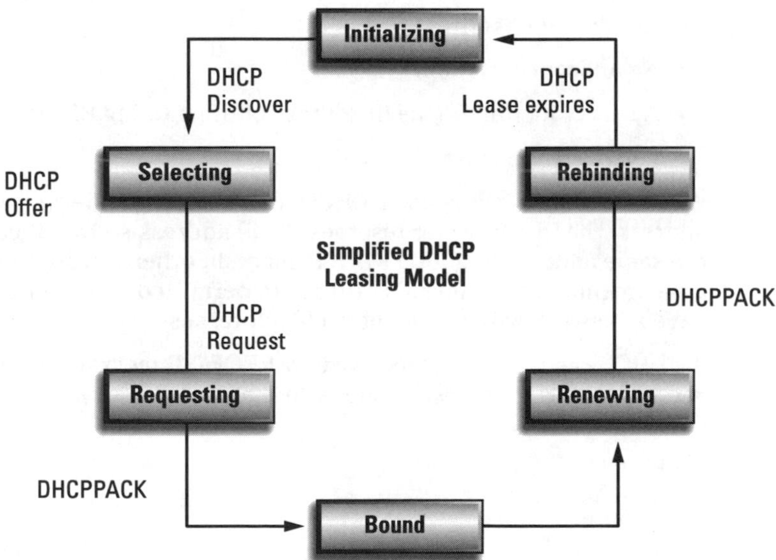

Figure 6-20: The DHCP client leasing model

- **Initializing state.** When a DHCP client boots, TCP/IP initially loads and initializes with a NULL IP address so that it can communicate with the DHCP server on the network via TCP/IP. The DHCP client then broadcasts a DHCPDISCOVER message to its subnet. The DHCPDISCOVER message contains the DHCP client's Media Access Control (MAC) address and computer name. This type of message, known as a packet, is discussed and displayed in Chapter 19. If the DHCP client has received an IP address successfully from a specific DHCP server before, the DHCP client includes the previous IP address in the DHCPDISCOVER message to try to lease the same IP address.

A Windows 2000-based DHCP client (such as Windows 2000 Professional) stores its leased IP address in the Registry. Each time the client system boots and sends out a DHCPDISCOVER message, it requests the IP address stored in the Registry.

Interestingly, the DHCP leased address list on the DHCP server is stored in a Microsoft Access-format (`*.mdb`) file.

  Because the DHCP client does not yet have an IP address and does not know the IP address of any DHCP servers, the source IP address for the DHCPDISCOVER broadcast is 0.0.0.0 and the destination address is 255.255.255.255.

- **Selecting state.** Any DHCP server that receives a DHCPDISCOVER message and has a valid configuration for the DHCP client responds with a DHCPOFFER message. The DHCP servers send their DHCPOFFER messages via broadcast because the DHCP client does not yet have an IP address. This message contains the following components:
  - The DHCP client's MAC address
  - An offered IP address
  - An appropriate subnet mask
  - A server identifier (the IP address of the offering DHCP server)
  - Length of the lease

  When a DHCP server sends a DHCPOFFER message offering an IP address, the DHCP server reserves the IP address so that it cannot offer the same address to another DHCP client. In other words, no double assignments of the same IP address are permitted. Otherwise, you would have a network with two identical IP addresses.

  If a DHCP client does not receive a DHCPOFFER message from a DHCP server on startup, it first notifies you that a DHCP server is unavailable (see Figure 6-21).

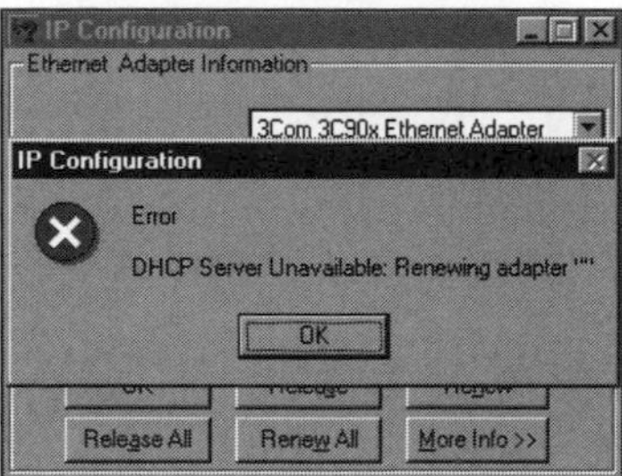

Figure 6-21: A client reporting no DHCP server located

Then, the DHCP client attempts its request for an IP address four more times every five minutes at four-, six-, eight-, and sixteen-second intervals.

The DHCP client accepts the DHCPOFFER under the following conditions:

- The client receives the requested IP address.
- The client is willing to accept any IP address.
- The client has tried unsuccessfully to accept an IP address two or more times.

- **Requesting state.** The DHCP client collects all of the DHCPOFFER messages, selects an offer — usually the first offer received — and sends a DHCPREQUEST message to the DHCP server. The DHPREQUEST message indicates that the DHCP client accepts the offered IP address. It includes, at a minimum, the server identifier from the accepted DHCPOFFER and also may include a request for any additional configuration information that the DHCP client requires, such as a default gateway and the IP address of a WINS server.

  Note that even at this stage, the TCP/IP protocol still is not fully initialized on the DHCP client, so the DHCPREQUEST message is sent via broadcast. Broadcasting the message ensures that the same DHCP servers that received the initial DHCPDISCOVER message also receive this message. Because the server identifier is included in the DHCPREQUEST, any other DHCP servers that offer the DHCP client an IP address basically withdraw the offer and return the offered IP address to their pool of available IP addresses.

- **Bound state.** The DHCP server responds to the DHCPREQUEST message with a DHCPACK (DHCP acknowledgment) message that contains a valid lease for the negotiated IP address as well as any configuration parameters. Here again, the DHCP server sends the DHCPACK message via broadcast because the DHCP client doesn't have an IP address yet. On receipt of the DHCPACK message, the DHCP client completes the TCP/IP binding and the client workstation can use TCP/IP to communicate over the network.

Renewing IP leases

As you know, DHCP clients lease their IP addresses from DHCP servers. When this lease expires, the DHCP client no longer can utilize that IP address. For that reason, DHCP clients periodically must renew their IP address leases, preferably before the lease has expired or is about to expire.

I also like to have DCHP clients renew their IP address leases frequently for other reasons. Often, when configuring a new network, I lease a phony set of IP address such as 10.0.0.x while I wait for final ID address configurations to be approved by both the client and the WAN engineer. Or, while waiting for the ISP to provide my sites real Internet IP addresses, I need to use phony IP addresses in the interim. Once I'm ready to implement a new IP addressing schema, it's nice that the DCHP clients automatically seek to renew their IP addresses and receive a "new" IP address from the properly configured DHCP server.

Referring to Figure 6-20, the DHCP client passes through the Renewing and Rebinding states to renew its IP address lease.

- **Renewing state.** The DHCP client first attempts to renew its lease when 50 percent of the lease time has expired. To renew its lease, the DHCP client sends a directed DHCPREQUEST message to the DHCP server that provided the original lease. If renewal is permitted, the DHCP server automatically renews the lease by responding with a DHCPACK message. This new IP address lease contains not only the original IP address, if still available (or another IP address otherwise), but also any TCP/IP client configuration information.
- **Rebinding state.** If, for whatever reason, the DHCP client is not able to communicate with the original DHCP server that executed its lease, it attempts another approach called *rebinding*. Here the DHCP client attempts to contact any available DHCP server when 87.5 percent of the lease time has expired. The leasing process is akin to that detailed over the last several pages.

Additional DHCP messages

You should be aware of a few additional DHCP messages that haven't been discussed yet:

- **DHCPDECLINE.** The DHCP client sends a DHCPDECLINE message to a DHCP server if the configuration parameter that the DHCP server sends is invalid.
- **DHCPNAK.** A DHCP server sends a DHCPNAK message to a DHCP client to notify the DHCP client that it has incorrect configuration information.
- **DHCPRELEASE.** A DHCP client sends a DHCPRELEASE message to a DHCP server to release its IP address and cancel its lease on the IP address.

Manually releasing and renewing the IP address in a DHCP client scenario is accomplished in one of two ways, depending on the workstation operation system that you use. For Windows 2000 (both Server and Professional), you enter **ipconfig/release** and **ipconfig/renew** at the command line. For Windows 98/95, you type **winipcfg** at the command line and select the Release and Renew buttons respectively that appear in the IP Configuration dialog box shown in Figure 6-22.

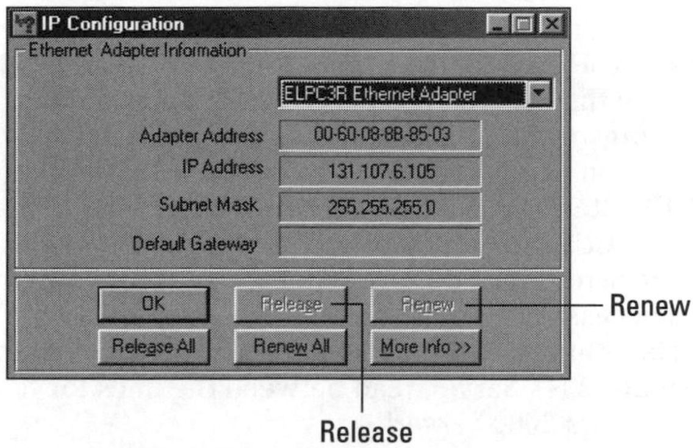

Figure 6-22: The IP Configuration dialog box

Planning for DHCP servers

The decision to deploy a Windows 2000 Server-based DHCP server on your network should not be taken lightly. You should honor several considerations prior to installing the DHCP Server service on Windows 2000 Server and configuring your workstations to act as DHCP clients.

On paper, having a DHCP server is a great idea. Who wouldn't welcome centralized network management at the protocol level? For Small Business Server (SBS) 4.5, the default network configuration is to have the Windows NT server act as a DHCP server. And it works reasonably well (be sure to read more on this in Chapter 16).

Another opportunity to effectively deploy a DHCP server is on a network that may be changing. Perhaps you are still learning Windows NT Server, or you haven't finalized the network design. When your network has a large delta factor (high propensity for change), having a DHCP server is great because you can change the TCP/IP configuration in a centralized manner at the Windows 2000 server without having to touch each workstation out on the floor.

But at times I notice that DHCP may not be the best choice. Understand that, like tax laws, these observations may or may not apply to your situation.

In enterprise-wide networks, it may go both ways. Many enterprises successfully use DHCP server and enjoy the great benefits of reduced IT-specific management of the TCP/IP configuration area. But I'd be remiss if I didn't share this observation about a North Seattle hospital. Administrators tried and tried to perfect the use of DHCP server in their legacy Windows NT Server environment, and regrettably they returned to using static IP addresses for workstations. The bottom line? Trying to make the DHCP

Server work flawlessly took more time than having the computer technicians just go out on the floor and touch each workstation. They concluded that, for whatever reason, DHCP just wasn't ready for prime time. I have every reason to believe that there are firms out there, just waiting to deploy Windows 2000 Server, that will suffer similar fates.

Other situations that didn't work for DHCP have included the athletic club that needed static IP addresses at workstations, defined on the legacy Windows NT server in the HOSTS file, so that its Progress database could work properly. And organizations that wanted to assign a permanent IP address to a workstation to facilitate an Internet videoconference (for instance, CUSEEME), often bypassing using DHCP server. That's because workstations that use CUSEEME or another videoconference solution need a fixed, real Internet-registered IP address. When using videoconferencing, such an address is necessary so that you may call the destination host using the IP address as something of a telephone number. Again, even though this story relates to Windows NT Server, read between the lines for how it may impact you with Windows 2000 Server!

Otherwise, you should honor the traditional planning steps of a network implementation when rolling out DHCP server and its services (design the network, run a pilot test, and so on).

Implementing DHCP servers in a small LAN

If you have a smaller LAN without routers and subnetting, a single DHCP server works just fine. Be sure to map out which computers immediately can become DHCP clients, which computers should retain static IP addresses, and what TCP/IP configurations you should create and invoke via DHCP server (see Figure 6-23).

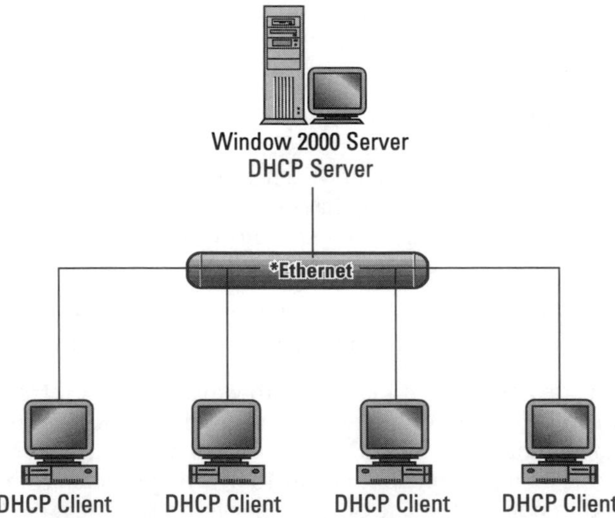

Figure 6-23: A small LAN with a single DHCP server

Implementing DHCP servers in a large LAN

Using DHCP servers on a large LAN elevates you to an entirely different league in the Windows 2000 Server community. It isn't as easy as it appears.

Large networks typically use routers and relay agents so DHCP Servers on one node of an internetwork may respond to TCP/IP configuration requests from distant remote nodes. The relay agent forwards requests from local DHCP clients to the DHCP Server and subsequently relays responses back to the DHCP clients. Besides the issues mentioned regarding a small LAN, additional planning issues for the large enterprise network include the following:

- **Compatibility with hardware and software routers with DHCP.** Routers must support RFCs 1532, 1533, and 1541. These RFCs speak toward the forwarding of packets required by the DHCP service. As mentioned earlier in this chapter, a correlation exists between the age of the router and support for these RFCs: newer routers tend to support these RFCs; older routers do not.
- **Physical subnetting of the network and relative placement of DHCP Servers.** This includes planning for the placement of DHCP (and WINS, which I discuss later in this chapter). Place servers on subnets in a way that reduces b-node broadcasts across routers. You should note that b-node resolves names using broadcast messages (see the name resolution discussion earlier in this chapter).
- **The DHCP option types and their values defined per scope for the DHCP clients.** This may include planning for separate scopes to meet the needs of specific user groups. An example is mobile users with laptops, who likely have different TCP/IP configuration requirements as they move from branch office to branch office. You also may have more advanced TCP/IP configuration needs on a large WAN with multiple subnets. You get the picture.
- **Multiple DHCP servers.** If you plan to implement multiple DHCP servers (which is a good way to distribute the load on a large network), each DHCP server must of course have a static IP address. Be sure to exclude these used IP addresses from your DHCP scope(s).
- **Static IP addresses.** Just as described in the preceding point, you must exclude static IP addresses that you need from the DHCP scope(s). These might include:
  - DHCP servers
  - Non-DHCP computers, such as workstations connected directly to the Internet via "real" static IP addresses
  - Routers
  - Non-Microsoft Remote Access Service (RAS) clients that use Point-to-Point Protocol (PPP) to connect to the network

  If you forget to make such exclusions, you can count on name/address conflicts occurring. Obviously, such conflicts can prevent your clients from communicating on the network and might even lead to network crashes (such as router failures).

- **DHCP server database backup.** Because the DHCP database contains all of the DHCP scopes for the DHCP server and the network's TCP/IP configuration parameters, it is a good idea to implement a backup policy. Typically, a well-designed, complete Windows 2000 server will back up the `*.mdb` files in the `SYSTEMROOT\SYSTEM32\DHCP` subdirectory. But as with any mission-critical backup scenario, you should consider manually backing up this subdirectory above and beyond the normal tape backups that you perform on your Windows 2000 Server.

Installing the DHCP server service

Installing the DHCP server service is very simple and typically not performed when you install Windows 2000 Server on your machine. However, it may be installed at a later date. To accomplish that, simply launch the Add/Remove Programs applet in the Control Panel. Then, select Add/Remove Windows Components. When the Welcome to Windows Components Wizard launches, select Dynamic Host Configuration Protocol (DHCP) from the Networking Services group (see Figure 6-24).

You must log on as a member of the Administrators group for the Windows 2000 Server that you install or administer as a DHCP server.

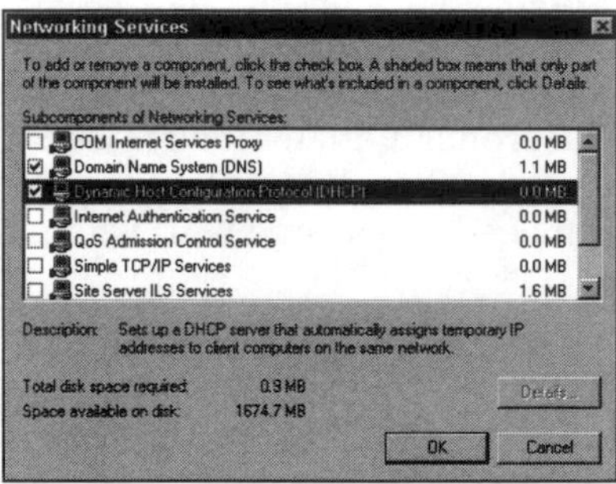

Figure 6-24: Networking Services

Also check that it is permissible to install the DHCP server service on your Windows 2000 Server. More than once, at my own job, nameless co-conspirators and I have inadvertently built "test" legacy Windows NT Servers and SBS servers running the DHCP server service to test-drive the latest BackOffice applications, Great Plains Accounting software releases, and so on. No sooner than we cross that line — that is, bring our test servers online — than our IS Director across the floor starts getting user complaints. Why? Our test servers dish out IP addresses to our firm's regular users as they log on. And guess what? Our test IP addressing layout is very different from that of our corporate network. Bottom line? Real users are unable to work because there are (inadvertently, of course) multiple DHCP servers, providing very different TCP/IP configurations, on the same network. Again, this Windows NT Server experience is completely applicable to your beloved Windows 2000 Server.

It is not possible for you to use DHCP "automatically" to configure a new DHCP server, because a computer cannot act as a DHCP client and DHCP server simultaneously. Configuring a DHCP server is still a manual process.

Creating DHCP scopes

A DHCP scope may be defined as an administrative unit or grouping of DHCP clients. Typically, you create a scope for each subnet on the network to facilitate TCP/IP configurations for that subnet.

These properties are common to all scopes:

- A subnet mask to determine the subnet related to a given IP address. Note that a scope may have the same subnet mask but different IP address ranges. The rule of thumb is to have one scope per subnet (the subnet mask provides this distinction).
- A scope name.
- Lease durations to be used by DHCP clients with dynamic addresses.

Larger networks will want to have two or more online DHCP servers so that a DHCP client may obtain valid TCP/IP configuration information. This is just another form of redundancy and load balancing that you should consider on your network.

Not only will DHCP clients fail if their IP address leases expire and cannot be renewed, but TCP/IP will not be configured and initialized properly by the DHCP client if there are no DHCP servers available. If TCP/IP is not configured and initialized properly on a DHCP client, that workstation cannot communicate on the network using TCP/IP (either another network protocol will need to be used, or network communications will fail).

One law regarding multiple DHCP servers on the network is to avoid overlapping scopes. The DHCP servers do not communicate with each other to adjudicate such issues. Duplicate IP addresses present a very real possibility.

Another consideration regarding DHCP servers is that each subnet must have its own DHCP server. This is a general rule that keeps you safe on the MCSE exams, but there are variations to this rule.

The first variation is one DHCP server per subnet with support for all subnets by any DHCP server. Here, each subnet has its own DHCP server, and a router supporting RFC 1542 (BOOTP) relay agents connects the subnets. An RFC

1542-compliant router modifies DHCP messages to indicate which subnet originated the broadcast. This action enables DHCP server to lease an IP address from the scope that applies to the DHCP client requesting the configuration.

The second variation is recognition that you do not need to have a DHCP server on each subnet. An RFC 1542-compliant router can forward DHCP requests across subnets.

If you already haven't done so, take a moment to sketch out how you use your existing DHCP scopes, or if you are just implementing a Windows 2000 Server-based network, how you might best use DHCP scopes. A few moments of planning now certainly yields tremendous dividends later.

Suppose you are on a true LAN with little need for a real router (such as Cisco) between subnets. You can, of course, configure a multihomed Windows 2000 Server to act as a router. Thus, a Windows 2000 Server running the DHCP server service with two or more network adapters (and the TCP/IP configuration "Enable IP Routing" enabled) enables, in this case, one DHCP server to serve multiple subnets. Be advised this isn't an ideal situation. It's the old "you get what you pay for." If you're serious about having one DHCP server for multiple subnets, purchase an RFC 5142-compliant router and do it right.

You must use DHCP MMC to create, manage, or remove scopes (see Figure 6-25). It is launched from the DHCP menu option in the Administrative Tools program group.

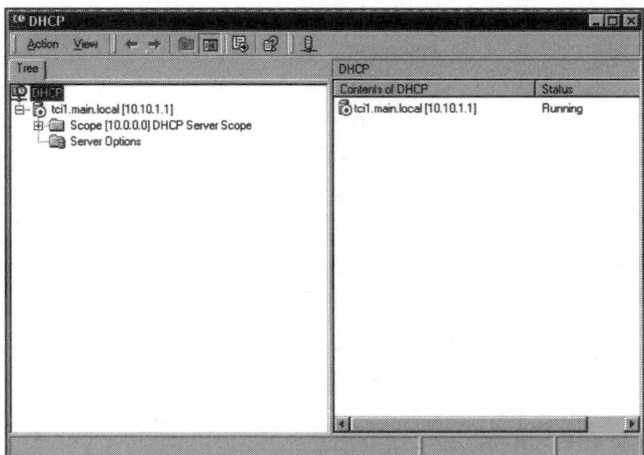

Figure 6-25: DHCP MMC

STEPS:

To create a new DHCP scope

Step 1. In the DHCP Servers list in the left pane of the DHCP MMC, select the server for which you intend to create a scope.

Step 2. Right-click to display the secondary menu for this server. Select New, Scope. This displays the Create Scope Wizard (see Figure 6-26). Click Next.

Figure 6-26: Create Scope Wizard

Step 3. Enter the name of the scope on the Scope Name screen. You also may add a comment. Click Next.

Step 4. Define the starting and ending IP addresses for this scope on the Address Range screen (see Figure 6-27). You also may modify the bit length of the subnet mask in addition to editing the subnet mask itself. Click Next.

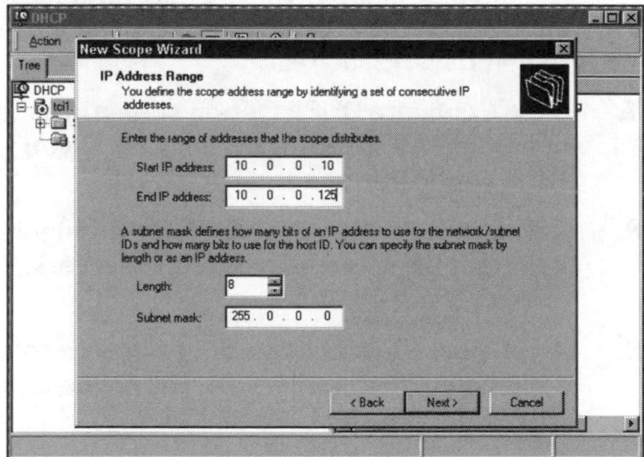

Figure 6-27: Address Range

Continued

STEPS:

To create a new DHCP scope *(continued)*

Step 5. Exclude IP addresses as necessary on the Add Exclusions screen. Type in the start and end of the IP address exclusion range. A single IP address that is being excluded has the same start and end IP address. Click Next.

I highly recommended that you always create at least a small IP address range that is excluded from the IP address pool that may be leased to DHCP clients. This exclusion range is useful in several situations, including badly behaved workstations that never successfully operate as DHCP clients. Another use for excluded IP addresses is for printers that are connected directly to the network, such as HP LaserJet printers and the HP JetDirect card. I've found that the many JetDirect card scenarios still consider dynamic IP address assignments to be via BOOTP, not Microsoft DHCP. Thus, I've encountered dynamic IP address assignment failures when it comes to JetDirect-based printer scenarios. When such is the case, I simply revert back to a static IP address, taken from the IP address exclusion range defined in my DHCP scope, to attach my HP LaserJet printer to the network.

Note that other uses for excluded IP addresses — beyond badly behaved workstations and HP JetDirect cards — include other DHCP servers that need a static IP address, non-DCHP clients on your network (such as Macintosh computers), diskless workstations, and RAS and PPP clients.

Step 6. Specify the lease duration to apply to the IP addresses in this scope on the Lease Duration screen. You may either select Unlimited or Limited To. You may limit leases to the days, hours, and minutes that you select. The default in Windows 2000 Server is eight days. Click Next.

Step 7. In the Configure DHCP Option screen, you may elect to configure numerous DHCP settings. Select Yes if you want to undertake such DHCP configurations and click Next.

Step 8. Screens appear that enable you to configure gateways, domain name and DNS servers, and WINS servers. You need to click Next after each screen.

Step 9. Select Yes on the Activate Scope screen to activate the scope you just created. If you select No, the scope is created but not activated. Click Next.

Step 10. The Completing the Scope Wizard appears. Click Finish to create the scope and exit the Create Scope Wizard.

Configuring DHCP options

The DHCP MMC is used to create rich TCP/IP configurations that a DHCP server assigns to a DHCP client. These configuration options are based largely on RFC 1542 (BOOTP) standard parameters. The DHCP Options are configured using the following steps.

STEPS:

To deploy DHCP configuration options

Step 1. Select and expand the scope that you want to configure in the left pane of the DHCP MMC window. This assumes that you have created scopes previously.

Step 2. Right-click the Scope Options folder for the scope that you selected. Select Configure Options from the secondary menu. The Configure DHCP Options: Scope Properties dialog box appears (see Figure 6-28).

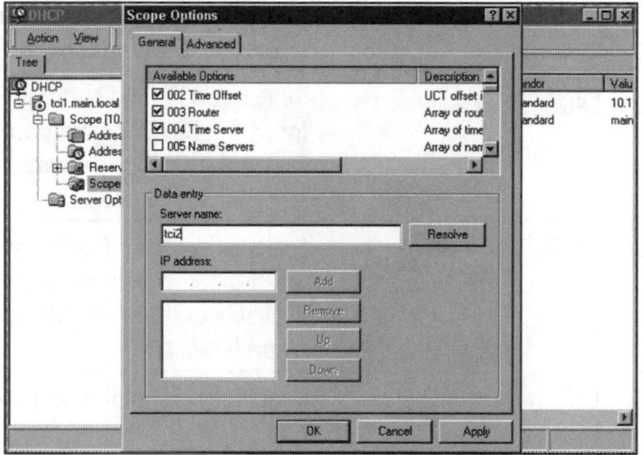

Figure 6-28: Configure DHCP Options: Scope Properties

Step 3. Select the option you want to configure in the Options list (left side). All of the available options are defined for you in Table 6-5.

Step 4. The Advanced tab enables you make more granular configurations based on vendor and user class.

Step 5. Select the OK button after you complete your DHCP-related changes.

DHCP server provides a robust list of DHCP client configuration options based on RFC 1533. Table 6-5 lists these predefined configuration options.

Table 6-5 DHCP Client Configuration Options

Code	*Option Name*	*Description*	*Configuration Category*
2	Time Offset	Specifies Universal Coordinated Time (UCT) offset in seconds.	Basic
3	Router	Specifies a list of IP addresses for routers on the client's subnet.	Basic
4	Time Servers	Specifies a list of IP addresses for time servers available to the client. Ordered by preference.	Basic
5	Name Servers	Specifies a list of IP addresses for name servers available to the client. Ordered by preference.	Basic
6	DNS Servers	Specifies a list of IP addresses for DNS name servers available to the client. Ordered by preference.	Basic
7	Log Servers	Specifies a list of IP addresses for MIT_LCS User Datagram Protocol (UDP) log servers available to the client.	Basic
8	Cookie Servers	Specifies a list of IP addresses for RFC 865 cookie servers available to the client. Ordered by preference.	Basic
9	LPR Servers	Specifies a list of IP addresses for RFC 1179 line printer servers available to the client. Ordered by preference.	Basic
10	Impress Servers	Specifies a list of IP addresses for Imagen Impress servers available to the client.	Basic
11	Resource Location Servers	Specifies a list of RFC 887 Resource Location servers available to the client.	Basic
12	Host Name	Specifies the hostname for a client adhering to the RFC 1035 character set. The name may be 63 characters long.	Basic

Code	*Option Name*	*Description*	*Configuration Category*
13	Boot File Size	Specifies the size of the default client boot image file in 512-octet blocks.	Basic
14	Merit Dump File	Specifies the path name for the crash dump file.	Basic
15	Domain Name	Specifies the DNS domain name that the client should use for DNS name resolution.	Basic
16	Swap Server	Specifies the IP address of the client's swap server.	Basic
17	Root Path	Specifies the path name for the client's root disk character set NVT ASCII.	Basic
18	Extensions Path	TTPT file for option extensions. Specifies a file that is retrievable via TFTP and contains information interpreted the same as the end or extension field in the BOOTP response, except the file length is unconstrained and references to Tag 18 in the file are ignored.	Basic
19	IP Layer Forwarding	Enables or disables IP packet forwarding on the client.	IP Layer Parameters per Host
20	Non-local Source Routing	Enables or disables nonlocal datagrams.	IP Layer Parameters per Host
21	Policy Filter Masks	Specifies policy filters that consist of a list of pairs of IP addresses and masks specifying destination/mask pairs for filtering nonlocal source routes. The client discards any source-routed datagram whose next hop address does not match a filter.	IP Layer Parameters per Host
22	Max DG Reassembly Size	Specifies a maximum size of datagram for reassembly by a client. Maximum size is 56 characters.	IP Layer Parameters per Host

Continued

Table 6-5 *(continued)*

Code	*Option Name*	*Description*	*Configuration Category*
23	Default Time-To-Live	The client uses the default Time-to-Live (TTL) on outgoing datagrams. Value may be between 1 and 255.	IP Layer Parameters per Host
24	Path MTU Aging Timeout	The timeout in seconds for aging Path MTU values. Based on RFC 1191.	IP Layer Parameters per Host
25	Path MTU Plateau	A table of MTU discovery sizes to use when performing Path MTU Discoveries as defined in RFC 1191. Table is sorted in size from the largest to the smallest. Minimum MTU size is 68.	IP Layer Parameters per Host
26	MTU Option	Sets the MTU discovery size for this interface. Minimum MTU value is 68.	IP Parameters per Interface
27	All subnets are local	Specifies whether the client assumes that all subnets of the client's internetwork use the same MTU as the local subnet where the client is connected. "1" indicates that all subnets share the same MTU. "0" indicates that the client should assume some subnets may have smaller MTUs.	IP Parameters per Interface
28	Broadcast Address	Specifies the broadcast IP address used on the client's subnet.	IP Parameters per Interface
29	Perform Mask Discovery	Specifies whether the client should use ICMP for subnet mask discovery "1" indicates the client should perform mask discovery. "0" indicates the client should not use it.	IP Parameters per Interface
30	Mask Supplier Option	Determines whether the client should respond to subnet mask requests via ICMP. "1" indicates the client should respond. "0" indicates the client should not use it.	IP Parameters per Interface

Code	***Option Name***	***Description***	***Configuration Category***
31	Perform Router Discovery	Determines whether the client should solicit routers using RFC 1256. "1" indicates the client should perform router discovery. "0" indicates the client should not use it.	IP Parameters per Interface
32	Router Solicitation Address	Specifies the IP address to which the client submits router solicitation requests.	IP Parameters per Interface
33	Static Route Option	Specifies a list of IP address pairs that indicate the static routes the client should install in its routing cache. Any multiple routes to the same destination are listed in descending order of priority. The routes are destination/router address pairs.	IP Parameters per Interface
34	Trailer Encapsulation	Specifies whether the client should negotiate use of trailers (RFC 983) when using the ARP protocol. "1" indicates the client should attempt to use trailers. "0" indicates the client should not use trailers.	Link Layer Parameters per Interface
35	ARP Cache Timeout	Specifies the timeout in seconds for ARP cache entries.	Link Layer Parameters per Interface
36	Ethernet Encapsulation	Specifies whether the client should use IEEE 802.3 (RFC 1042) or Ethernet v.2 (RFC 894) encapsulation if the interface is Ethernet. "1" indicates the client should use RFC 1042 encapsulation. "0" indicates the client should use RFC 894 encapsulation.	Link Layer Parameters per Interface
37	Default TTL Option	This is the default Time-to-Live option. Specifies the default TTL that the client should use when sending TCP segments. The minimum value of the octet is 1.	TCP Parameters

Continued

Table 6-5 *(continued)*

Code	***Option Name***	***Description***	***Configuration Category***
38	Keepalive Interval	The keepalive interval in seconds. A value of "0" indicates the client should not send keepalive messages on connections unless specifically requested by an application.	TCP Parameters
39	Keepalive Garbage	Specifies whether the client should send TCP keepalive messages with an octet of garbage data for compatibility with older implementations. "1" indicates a garbage octet should be sent. "0" indicates that it should not be sent.	TCP Parameters
40	NIS Domain Name	The name of the Network Information Service domain.	Application Layer Parameters
41	NIS Servers	Gives addresses of NIS servers on client's subnet.	Application Layer Parameters
42	NTP Servers	Gives addresses of Network Time Protocol servers.	Application Layer Parameters
43	Vendor Specific Info	Supplies binary information that clients and servers use to exchange vendor-specific information. Servers not equipped to interpret the information ignore it. Clients that don't receive the information attempt to operate without it.	Vendor-specific Information
44	WINS/NBNS Servers	Specifies a list of IP addresses for NetBIOS name servers (NBNS).	Vendor-specific Information
45	NetBIOS over TCP/IP NBDD	Specifies a list of IP addresses for NetBIOS datagram distribution servers (NBDD).	Vendor-specific Information
46	WINS/NBT node type	Enables configurable NetBIOS over TCP/IP clients to be configured as described in RFC 1001/1002, where "1" is b-node, "2" is p-node, "4" is m-node, and "8" is h-node.	Vendor-specific Information

Code	***Option Name***	***Description***	***Configuration Category***
47	NetBIOS Scope ID	Specifies a string that is the NetBIOS over TCP/IP scope ID for the client, as specified in RFC 1001/1002.	Vendor-specific Information
48	X Window System Font	Specifies a list of IP addresses for X Window font servers available to the client.	Vendor-specific Information
49	X Windows System Display	Specifies a list of IP addresses for X Window System Display Manager servers available to the client.	Vendor-specific Information
64	NIS+ Domain Name	The name of the client's NIS+ domain.	Vendor-specific Information
65	NIS+ Servers	A list of IP addresses indicating NIS+ servers.	Vendor-specific Information
66	Boot Server Host Name	The TFTP boot server host name.	Vendor-specific Information
67	Bootfile Name	Specifies the bootfile name.	Vendor-specific Information
68	Mobile IP Home	Gives mobile IP home agents in priority order.	Vendor-specific Information
69	Simple Mail Transport Protocol (SMTP) Servers	Gives a list of available SMTP servers available to client.	Vendor-specific Information
70	Post Office Protocol (POP3) Servers	Gives a list of POP3 servers available to client.	Vendor-specific Information
71	Network News Transport Protocol (NNTP) Servers	Gives a list of NNTP servers available to client.	Vendor-specific Information
72	World Wide Web (WWW) Servers	Gives a list of WWW servers available to client.	Vendor-specific Information
73	Finger Servers	Gives a list of Finger servers available to client.	Vendor-specific Information
74	Internet Relay Chat (IRC) Servers	Gives a list of IRC servers available to client.	Vendor-specific Information
75	StreetTalk Servers	Gives a list of StreetTalk Servers available to client.	Vendor-specific Information
76	StreetTalk Directory Assistance (STDA) Servers	Gives a list of STDA servers available to client.	Vendor-specific information

Configuration codes 69–76 are new to Windows 2000 Server.

The category configurations are defined as follows:

- **Basic.** Represents basic configuration options.
- **IP Layer Parameters per Host.** Specifies IP parameters on a per-host basis.
- **IP Parameters per Interface.** Represents IP parameters that affect the operation of the IP layer on a per-interface basis. Clients may issue multiple requests, one per interface, to configure interfaces with their specific parameters.
- **Link Layer Parameters per Interface.** Represents link-layer parameters per interface. These options affect the operation of the data-link layer on a per-interface basis.
- **TCP Parameters.** Represents TCP/IP parameters that affect the operation of the TCP layer, on a per-interface basis.
- **Application Layer Parameters.** Represents application-layer parameters that are used to configure applications and services.
- **Vendor-specific information.** Represents options for vendor-specific information.

If you use DHCP to configure WINS clients, be sure to set options 44, WINS Servers, and option 46, Node Type (from Table 6-5). These options enable DHCP clients to find and use a WINS server automatically.

Managing client leases

Managing client leases is accomplished via the Address Leases folder, which is found underneath the Scope you are managing.

Being able to determine what machine has what IP address often is important when you troubleshoot problems on your network.

Managing client reservations

Specific IP addresses may be reserved for a client. Managing client reservations is accomplished via the Reservations folder found underneath the Scope that you are managing. To create a reservation, simply right-click the Reservations folder and select New, Reservation.

Typically, this is undertaken for the following reasons:

- For domain controllers if the network also uses LMHOSTS files that define IP addresses for domain controllers
- For clients that use IP addresses that were assigned using another method for TCP/IP configurations
- For assignment by RAS to non-DHCP clients
- For DNS servers

It is important to note that if multiple DHCP servers provide the same scope addresses, each DHCP server must maintain the same client reservations (or else the DHCP-reserved client potentially receives different IP addresses).

The IP address and static name specified in WINS "wins" or takes precedence over the IP address assigned by the DHCP server. For such clients, create client reservations with the IP address that is defined in the WINS database.

DHCP and DNS

Here is a favorite interview question of mine when I'm interviewing a technical professional: "Given your choice, which would you use on a network, DNS or DHCP?" Of course, the answer is my favorite tax law response of "it depends." I then probe further into why my prospective employee might use only DNS on network, make use of DHCP, or more likely than not, use both DNS and DHCP on the network. Of course I am still speaking of a Windows 2000 Server-based network, because if I'm discussing a UNIX-based network and my candidate mentions DHCP, he or she is out the door. (Remember that the UNIX community uses BOOTP, not DHCP.)

Troubleshooting DHCP servers

Before leaving the DHCP discussion, here are several DHCP-related troubleshooting topics.

Routers used as RFC 1542 (BOOTP) relay agents

Many older routers do not function as RFC 1542 (BOOTP) relay agents with DHCP. That's because Microsoft DHCP contains new and modified fields with which these older routers simple can't deal. Thus, make sure that your routers support RFC 1541 and RFC 1542 before you assume that these routers can function properly as BOOTP relay agents.

DHCP server problems

These error conditions indicate that you are having problems with your DHCP server:

- **The RPC server is unavailable** or **Error 1753: The DHCP Server service is not running on the target systems.** When DHCP Manager attempts to connect to a DHCP server, the DHCP Manager application may return one of these error messages. Both of these errors indicate that the Microsoft DHCP server service isn't running on the system to which the DHCP Manager is attempting to connect.
- **The DHCP Client couldn't obtain an IP address** or **The DHCP Client couldn't renew the IP address lease.** A DHCP client may see one of these messages. Both error messages indicate that the DHCP client system can't communicate with a DHCP server. This may occur for a variety of

reasons, ranging from the DHCP server service not running on the target Windows NT Server to the DHCP client's connection to the network not functioning for some reason. The "DHCP Client couldn't obtain an IP address" error message also can be generated if the DHCP server has no more IP addresses available to lease.

If your network develops any of these problems, the first task is to make sure that the DHCP server service is running on your Windows NT server.

In reality, I find this message to reflect some fundamental weaknesses with Microsoft TCP/IP protocol stack. And given that time is of the essence when serving in my role as a network consultant, I have (regrettably) had to take some Windows NT Server sites back to static IP addresses (having never resolved — to my satisfaction — why the DHCP server-related process was acting up).

WINS

Successfully maintaining a Windows 2000 Server-based network means using every tool that you have on your shelf. Now add support for legacy Windows NT Servers and you've got even more fun awaiting you. Such interaction between the present (Windows 2000 Server) and the past (Windows NT Server 4) leads us to Windows Internet Naming Service (WINS). WINS is one of those tools we'll avail ourselves of to merge the present and past. Note that WINS has been displaced effectively by Dynamic DNS in Windows 2000 Server; so in reality, you can say that WINS is on its way out of favor and used only for legacy Windows NT Server support.

That said, this section provides you with a brief overview about WINS. It provides little more, given WINS' gentle exit from the Windows 2000 Server community. And although you certainly need to know WINS basics, be advised that your time is better spent mastering the first two topics of this chapter (DNS, DHCP).

The key point with WINS is its dynamic paradigm. Its database is updated dynamically or on the fly. By contrast, DNS maintains a static database of addresses that may be upgraded only by receiving a propagated delta DNS database periodically.

WINS is designed to eliminate broadcasts and maintain a dynamic database by providing computer name-to-IP address mappings. A WINS system has two components: servers and clients.

- **WINS servers.** WINS servers maintain the database that maps a WINS Client IP address to its NetBIOS computer name. Broadcasts for NetBIOS-type name resolutions are eliminated (or at least reduced) because the database on the WINS server may be consulted for immediate name resolution.

- **WINS clients.** A WINS client is a workstation that is configured with the WINS server(s) IP address(es). At system startup, the WINS client registers its name and IP address with the WINS server. When a WINS client needs a name resolved, the WINS server and its database are consulted. This results in fast and efficient name resolution.

At the enterprise level, a network typically has one or more WINS servers that a WINS client may contact for name resolution. In fact, WINS servers may be configured on a given network so that they replicate all computer names to IP address mappings to each other's respective databases.

Implementing WINS Server on your Windows NT Server network results in the following benefits:

- Reduced broadcast network traffic
- No need for a LMHOSTS file
- Dynamic name registration
- No duplicate computer names
- No specific need for a DNS server (although dispensing with one is not recommended!)

Improvements to WINS in Windows 2000 Server

Granted, WINS exists for underlying legacy support reasons. But WINS improvements have occurred in Windows 2000 Server. These improvements include the following:

- Persistent connections. Persistent connections between replication partners may now be maintained with WINS. This lessens the network traffic associated with creating and terminating replication partner connections.
- Manual tombstoning. When a record is marked for deletion, its tombstone state is replicated to all WINS servers.
- Improved management capabilities. WINS is now managed from the MMC and has stronger filtering and search capabilities. You may also export WINS databases to a comma-separated text file.
- Increased client-side fault tolerance. Windows 2000 clients, such as Windows 2000 Professional, may now look at up to 12 WINS servers for resolving NetBIOS names.
- Client-side dynamic re-registration. There is no need to restart your Windows 2000 client when it re-registers its NetBIOS name-to-IP address mapping.

How WINS works

Out of the box, when you configure a Windows NT Server-based network to use WINS for its name registration, it adheres to the h-node broadcasting methodology. Recall that the h-node refers to one of the NetBIOS over TCP/IP modes that defines how NBT identifies and accesses resources on a network.

During name resolution, the WINS client

- Checks to see if it is the local machine name
- Looks at its cache of remote names. Any name that is resolved is placed in a cache, where it remains for ten minutes
- Attempts to contact the WINS server
- Attempts broadcasting
- Checks the LMHOSTS file (if it is configured to use and check this file)
- Last, tries the HOSTS file and then DNS (if appropriately configured)

You may recall that I discussed this process early in the chapter in the "Be Resolved" section.

If a DHCP client has been configured to use m-node name resolution, the client first attempts to broadcast. The WINS server is consulted second.

When a WINS client boots, a Name Registration Request packet is sent to the WINS server so that the client computer name may be registered. The appropriate number of Name Registration Request packets are sent as necessary to register names. Not surprisingly, these packets contain the WINS client's IP address and name.

Final WINS musings

WINS is not installed on Windows 2000 Server by default. This fact underscores WINS' reduced role in the modern era of Microsoft-based networking environments such as Windows 2000 Server. To install WINS, you launch the Add/Remove Programs applet in the Control Panel. You then launch Add/Remove Windows Components. When the Windows Components Wizard launches, select Windows Internet Name Service (WINS) from the Networking Services group. This service consumes just less than 1MB of disk space once installed. You manage it from the WINS MMC.

And for a real good time, consult a Windows NT Server book, such as my *Microsoft Windows NT Secrets, Option Pack Edition* (IDG Books Worldwide) for rich WINS configuration discussion, similar to that found earlier in this chapter for DNS and DHCP.

Dynamic DNS

Imagine merging DNS and WINS together and using a best-of-breed name resolution tool. That is exactly what Windows 2000 Server has done with the introduction of Dynamic DNS. Dynamic DNS, based on RFC 2136, is a means for providing dynamic updates of zone data on a zone's primary server when an authorized server requests an update. In other words, the primary server can be configured to support host address information updates that are initiated by another server that supports Dynamic DNS. This update occurs in the form of an UPDATE message that includes a resource record (RR) or sets of resource records (RRsets) modifications. Note that it is OK to call Dynamic DNS by its other name, Dynamic Update.

There are really two places you interact with Dynamic DNS. And guess what, during the course of this chapter, you've already either seen these places or been very close. In the DNS MMC, you interact with Dynamic DNS via the Zone Properties sheet (see Figure 6-29). In the Dynamic update field, you may select these options:

- Allow Updates
- None

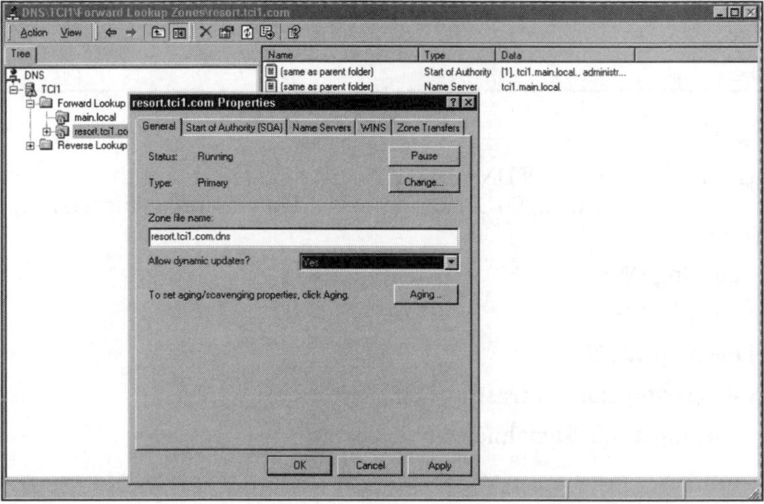

Figure 6-29: Dynamic update

With DHCP, you interact with Dynamic DNS via the Scope Properties sheet (see Figure 6-30). Select the Dynamic DNS tab and select the Enable dynamic update of DNS client information.

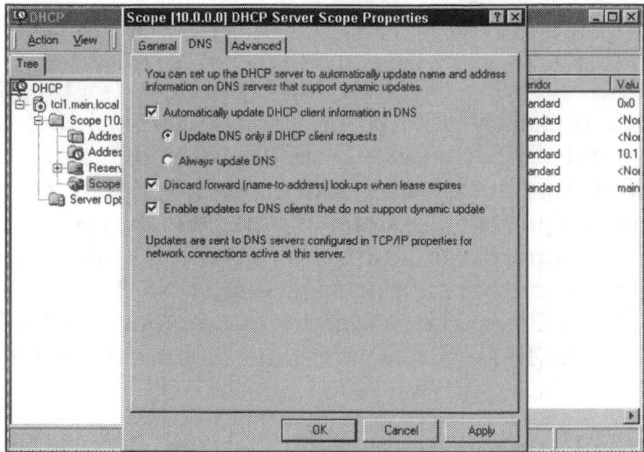

Figure 6-30: Dynamic DNS

Clearly, Dynamic DNS has several advantages over old-fashioned DNS. One such advantage is that updates are not limited to manual edits of a zone's resource records. A new message type for formatting DNS update requests handles this. My advice? Run, don't walk, to master DNS inside and out today (don't delay) so you can be in the best position to exploit Dynamic DNS in Windows 2000 Server!

Summary

This chapter describes DNS, DHCP, and WINS. These are three critical TCP/IP areas on a Windows 2000 Server network. This chapter emphasizes the following:

- Learning DNS
- Learning DHCP
- Learning WINS
- Comparing and contrasting DNS, DHCP, and WINS
- Learning about Dynamic DNS

Chapter 7

Subnetting via TCP/IP

In This Chapter

- Learn what subnetting is
- Learn what subnetting isn't
- Determine subnetting requirements
- Master subnet-related calculations

TCP/IP, of course, is a study into itself. Mastering the TCP/IP protocol suite in Windows 2000 Server is much more than understanding what IP addresses, subnet masks, and default gateways are. Mastering TCP/IP is akin to mastering mathematics. That is, while you might be hired as a Windows 2000 Server network administrator, having mastered TCP/IP enables you to be successful when troubleshooting and tackling those network issues that simply aren't covered in the books.

Learning the fine art of subnet masking is akin to learning how to operate a sailboat. What? How can that be? Here's how. Sailing has best been described as an endeavor that requires only common sense to be successful. That said, many of us who sail could improve our skills dramatically if we only sharpened our common-sense skills. Subnetting is very much the same as sailing: not terribly difficult, but making heavy use of our common-sense skills. So here we go!

What Subnetting Is

Subnetting is really the implementation of the divide-and-conquer strategy in the TCP/IP community. Routers are used to divide, or subnet, networks into multiple physical segments. So what comprises the conquering part? First on the list is simplification. Whenever confronted with a tough problem or a complex area, something that subnetting certainly is, a tried-and-true troubleshooting strategy is to divide the problem into smaller elements that you can manage, solve, and conquer, if you will. Thus, by subdividing a large network into smaller subnets, we conquer the network in our battles, not vice versa. So why would you do this? There are several benefits to subnetting including ease of administration, conservation of limited IP addresses, tighter and improved security, and more efficient use of networking resources via traffic management.

Easier administration

Administration potentially is made easier by subnetting because you can subdivide a large network logically and physically by routers. A clean network is a happy network. The use of subnetting, properly done, enables you to organize your networks. And don't overlook the harsh reality of corporate politics on your network. Subnetting allows you to divide your enterprise-wide network along political boundaries. How? Remember that the complete trust domain model typically was implemented when no one trusted each other and every little kingdom of users and resources had to be accommodated. With subnetting, we can create little LANs that reflect different groupings of users, resources and, in the language of the Windows 2000 Server, objects.

Less confining

Subnetting enables you to make network planning decisions without regard for the single LAN cable, if you so desire. Whereas many of us old-timers in the industry traditionally think of a network segment or subnet as a physical cable run, with subnetting you have the opportunity to think much more logically. Multiple TCP/IP subnets can exist with ease on a cable segment, allowing you to divide your network into small networks for reasons known only to you and God.

Likewise, you also may join unlike IEEE standards and media into a single subnet using subnetting, so users on a Token Ring network may communicate with users on an Ethernet network. These users are joined together on a single, logical IP network using subnetting.

IP address conservation

In other sections of this book, I tout Microsoft Proxy Server as a way to save precious IP addresses. Properly implemented, IP subnetting enables one real, or Internet-registered, address to be partitioned into numerous internal network addresses. Here, the router correctly routes packets between the external network or Internet and the internal or subnetted network. IP address conservation should be a fundamental guiding principle in your Windows 2000 Server network design and planning efforts.

Improved security

Properly implemented, subnetting can improve your network's security from external intruders. That's because, as implied above, the router routes between the visible external network and the invisible networks in your organization. And while we consider justice to be blind in America, in networking we know that peace is maintained the more that we make our internal networks invisible to external intruders. But don't get me wrong. This security discussion in no way substitutes for a real firewall. It only is meant to encourage you to think from a secure perspective when considering the design of your network.

Another name for switching?

What happens if ten WAN engineers get together to create a subnetting plan for a network? Inevitably, the discussion becomes one of routers versus switches. Properly implemented, we can direct traffic to its location efficiently without having to be evaluated by computers all across the network. In effect, we can use subnetting to create smaller networks that logically are designed to keep traffic within the neighborhood (see Figure 7-1). We also can use subnetting to reduce broadcasts in a similar manner.

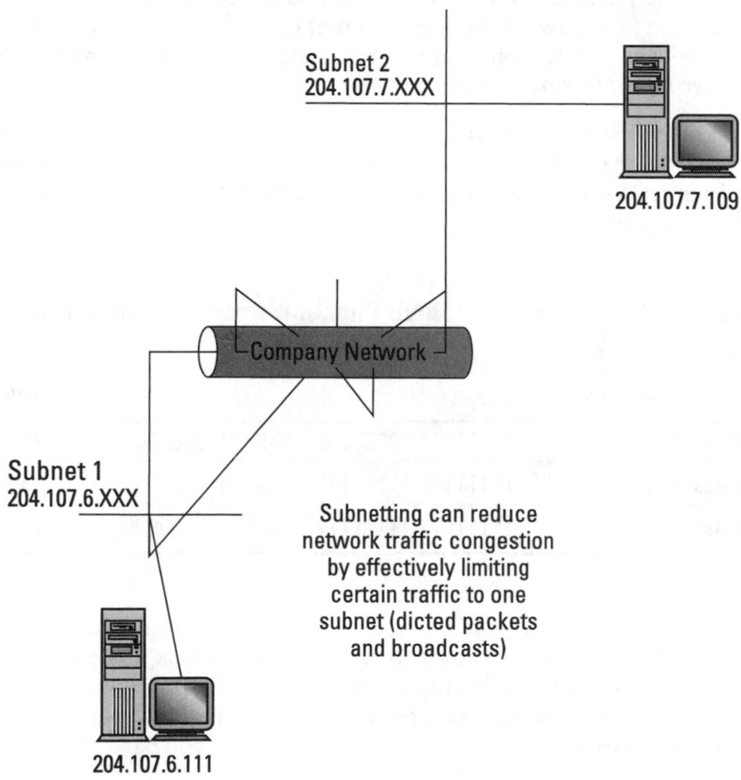

Figure 7-1: Subnetted or smaller networks within the larger network

Bottom line?

Know thy router when designing a network via subnetting. The router needs to be told how to distinguish between the host and network addresses. But more on that in a moment when we get into the details. Remember that subnetting provides planning and design flexibility and integration possibilities in ways you may or may not perceive today, but most likely will appreciate tomorrow.

What Subnetting Isn't

Subnetting is not some elixir that cures fundamental design errors in your network. In fact, the use of subnetting in a flawed network may compound problems, forcing you to return to the basics.

OK, so you subnet your network into several smaller networks. What's the downside to that? You've allocated a portion of the bit pattern to the network addresses, thus limiting the quantity of host addresses on each of the smaller networks. There are only so many bit positions, so if some of the bits are used to define network subnets, then of course fewer bits are available on each new subnet to define hosts. Surprisingly, this can be a real limitation on real-world, enterprise-wide networks.

First, it is essential that you be armed with this dotted decimal notation table for the different subnet mask classes. Why? You will see in a moment that you truly drop down to the bit level as you take and subnet an enterprise-wide network (see Table 7-1).

Table 7-1 Bit View of Default Subnet Masks for Standard IP Address Classes

Class of Address	*Bits*	*Subnet Mask*
Class A	11111111 00000000 00000000 00000000	255.0.0.0
Class B	11111111 11111111 00000000 00000000	255.255.0.0
Class C	11111111 11111111 11111111 00000000	255.255.255.0

Leave it to the router guys and gals to teach me a thing or two in life. These three classes really are known as the following: Class A is called an eight-bit mask in the router community, Class B is called a 16-bit mask, and Class C is called a 24-bit mask. So if you're speaking with internetworking or router gurus, be sure to speak the correct form of geek speak!

Code Breaking 101

So here we go, lower and lower to the bit level. Another view of subnetting is that of code breaking in the military. When breaking a communication code, we look for the pattern. Once the pattern is discovered, we can break the code successfully and decode the communication. As we work through the low-level details of subnetting, I encourage you to keep this perspective.

First, let's look at the simple patterns relating to basic subnets. From Table 7-1, you can see that subnet mask values in each octet position determine whether the network is operating with a Class A, B, or C license. The subnet mask thus becomes a decoder for the network to use in separating an IP address into the Network ID and the Host ID. For example, a Class C subnet mask of 255.255.255.0 and an IP address of 204.107.7.109 suggest a network ID of 204.107.7 and a host ID of 109. This is known as subnet along a byte boundary. It is what most people think of when they hear the term subnet or subnetting. In reality, no "subnetting" is being used.

So far, so good. But what if we want to take our Class C license and further divide it; that is, engage in "subnetting" along a non-byte boundary? Then, the exercise becomes more complex.

When subnetting is employed with a Class C scenario, we take advantage of the fourth octet position of the subnet mask value to communicate some additional information on the network. As you know, an octet is made up of eight bits, or one byte, as shown in Figure 7-2.

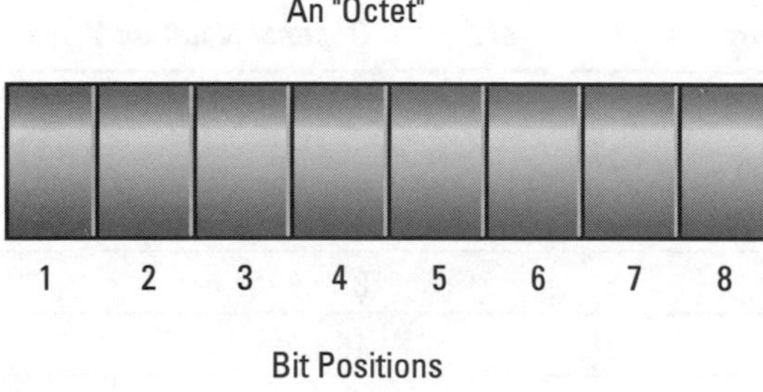

Figure 7-2: An octet position has eight bits.

Now before I go any further, allow me to share Table 7-2. Based on subnet "size", this table provides all-important decimal to binary bit conversion information. This information is invaluable as we create complex subnetting scenarios.

Table 7-2 Subnet Size, Binary Bit Values, Decimal Values

Subnet Size Measured in Bits	*Binary Bit Values*	*Value in Decimal*
1	10000000	128
2	11000000	192
3	11100000	224
4	11110000	240
5	11111000	248
6	11111100	252
7	11111110	254

Let's quickly revisit how binary bit values are converted to decimal. Remember that with binary, we use a base two counting system (versus a base 10 counting system used in the "real world"). You may recall with the binary system, any value up to 255 can be represented as either a one ("1") or zero ("0") within a byte or eight-bit positions. This phenomenon can be displayed two ways: as a "Power of 2" table (see Table 7-3) or as a simple chart showing the value of each bit position in a byte (see Table 7-4).

Table 7-3 Powers of 2

Bit Position Within Byte	*Power of 2*	*Decimal Notation Value*
00000001	2^0	1
00000010	2^1	2
00000100	2^2	4
00001000	2^3	8
00010000	2^4	16
00100000	2^5	32
01000000	2^6	64
10000000	2^7	128

Table 7-4 Value of Each Bit Position in a Byte

Bit Position	***1***	***2***	***3***	***4***	***5***	***6***	***7***	***8***
Decimal Value	128	64	32	16	8	4	2	1

Any questions? Great! Let's move on. Referring back to Table 7-2, notice that you can place the decimal value (found in the far-right column) in the fourth octet position of the Class C subnet mask value to further subnet my network. Here is what I mean. Remember that the subnet mask communicates to the network which portion of the IP address to mask as the subnet number, and thus be default; the host number value is the balance. So if I present the following subnet mask to the network, the network knows that the first four bits of the fourth octet are "masked" to communicate subnet number information. This is perhaps better explained in the following table, wherein we show the details for the subnet mask 255.255.255.240. Note the table only shows the details for the fourth octet position. Octet positions one, two, and three would be populated fully with ones ("1s") to achieve the value 255.

Table 7-5 communicates that the first four bit positions are masked out as part of the subnet number, as these bit positions are occupied with a binary one value and, most importantly, this information is conveyed in the context of the subnet mask value (where it is meaningful).

Table 7-5 Subnetting Via "240" in the Fourth Octet Position of Subnet Mask 255.255.255.240

Bit Position	***1***	***2***	***3***	***4***	***5***	***6***	***7***	***8***
Decimal Value	128	64	32	16	8	4	2	1
Actual Bit Flags	1	1	1	1	0	0	0	0

Which leads us to an exercise based on the information presented thus far in the chapter: With the following information, please determine what the subnet number and the host number are:

Subnet mask: 255.255.255.240

IP address: 204.131.7.109

Subnet number: ________

Host number: ________

The solution set is as follows:

1. Understand that subnetting is being used.
2. The fourth octet of the subnet mask has a value of 240. Based on Table 7-5, this can be interpreted to mean that the first four bit positions on the fourth octet position in the IP address relate to the subnet number; the final four bit positions relate to the host number.
3. As the IP address has a fourth octet position of 109, we need to break the code and determine what explicitly relates to the subnet number. This is accomplished as shown in Table 7-6.

Table 7-6 Bit Breakdown of 109 Value

Bit Position	***1***	***2***	***3***	***4***	***5***	***6***	***7***	***8***
Decimal Value	128	64	32	16	8	4	2	1
Actual Bit Flags	**0**	**1**	**1**	**0**	1	1	0	1

   To assist our efforts, I boldfaced the four bit positions of this fourth octet in the IP address so that it's easy to determine that the bit positions in boldface relate to the subnet number. Now, let's add the boldfaced value to determine the rest of the subnet number. This is accomplished in Table 7-7.

   Therefore, based on this information, the subnet number is 96.

4. Now the host number is calculated. It is the balance of the bit positions in the fourth octet position of the IP address 204.131.7.96. This is shown in Table 7-8.

Table 7-7 Calculating the Subnet Number (First Four Bit Positions) of the Fourth Octet Position of IP Address 204.131.7.109

Bit Position	***1***	***2***	***3***	***4***	***Subnet Number***
Decimal Value	128	64	32	16	
Actual Bit Flags	**0**	**1**	**1**	**0**	**96**

Table 7-8 Calculating the Host Number (First Four Bit Positions) of the Fourth Octet Position of IP Address 204.131.7.109

Bit Position	***5***	***6***	***7***	***8***	***Host Number***
Decimal Value	8	4	2	1	
Actual Bit Flags	1	1	0	1	13

The solution set is:

- Subnet number = 96
- Host number = 13

You can depict this network graphically, as shown in Figure 7-3:

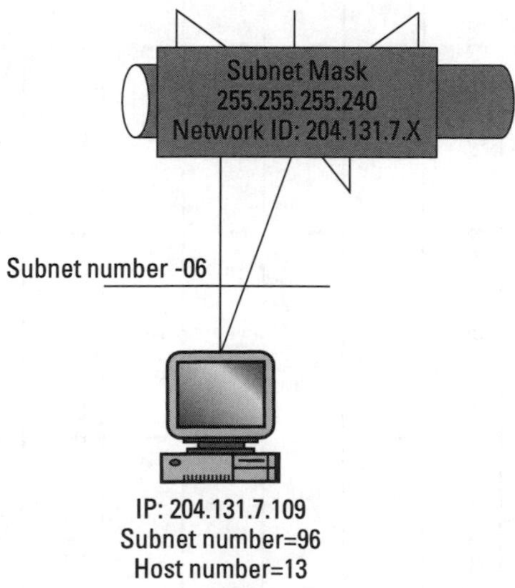

Figure 7-3: A network with a subnet mask of 255.255.255.240

So if we have a basic understanding of the preceding example, we easily can interpret the next table, Table 7-9, where the actual bit flags are displayed for each of the possible subnetting bit values available for a Class C (255.255.255.*x*) network. Again, referring to Table 7-2 assists our efforts to better understand subnetting. The bit portion of the fourth octet position that relates to the subnet number is in boldface to help in our comprehension.

Table 7-9 Possible Class C Subnetting Values and Impact on Sample IP Address 204.131.7.109

Description	*Bit1*	*Bit 2*	*Bit 3*	*Bit 4*	*Bit 5*	*Bit 6*	*Bit 7*	*Bit 8*	*Evaluation of sample IP address 204.131.7.109 for each subnetting example*
Subnet mask: 255.255.255.128	**1**	0	0	0	0	0	0	0	Subnet number = 0 (INVALID! We can't have zero subnets or a subnet with a value of zero. Host number = 109
Subnet mask: 255.255.255.192	**1**	**1**	0	0	0	0	0	0	Subnet number = 64 Host number = 45
Subnet mask: 255.255.255.224	**1**	**1**	**1**	0	0	0	0	0	Subnet number = 96 Host number = 13
Subnet mask: 255.255.255.240	**1**	**1**	**1**	**1**	0	0	0	0	Subnet number = 96 Host number = 13
Subnet mask: 255.255.255.248	**1**	**1**	**1**	**1**	**1**	0	0	0	Subnet number = 104 Host number = 5
Subnet mask: 255.255.255.252	**1**	**1**	**1**	**1**	**1**	**1**	0	0	Subnet number = 108 Host number = 1
Subnet mask: 255.255.255.254	**1**	**1**	**1**	**1**	**1**	**1**	**1**	0	Subnet number = INVALID Host number = INVALID
Decimal values by bit position	128	64	32	16	8	4	2	1	This row is presented to assist in interpreting this table.
Binary bit representation of 109	0	1	1	0	1	1	0	1	This row is presented to assist in interpreting this table.

By the way, you may use another technique to convert a decimal value to its binary bit cousin. This method involves a simple use of division and the number two. Because the binary counting system is based on a counting system of "base 2," it is plausible that you can take any number and divide by 2 several times to arrive at the binary equivalent. Isn't it?

Let's see how a base 2 scenario works. Take the number 109 again — our sample number.

STEPS:

To convert a decimal value to its binary bit cousin

Step 1. Divide 109 by 2.

109/2 = 54 with a remainder of 1.

Take the remainder as our first bit value, starting with the far right of our bit listing. Stick with it; you will see the pattern in a moment.

The cumulative bit order is 1.

Step 2. Divide 54 by 2.

54/2 = 27 with a remainder of 0.

Thus, the bit value is 0.

The cumulative bit order is 01.

Step 3. Divide 27 by 2.

27/2 = 13 with a remainder of 1.

Not surprisingly, the bit value is 1.

The cumulative bit order is 101.

Step 4. Divide 13 by 2.

13/2 = 6 with a remainder of 1.

The bit value is 1.

The cumulative bit order is 1101.

Step 5. Divide 6 by 2.

6/2 = 3 with a remainder of 0.

The bit value is 0.

The cumulative bit order is 01101.

Continued

STEPS:

To convert a decimal value to its binary bit cousin *(continued)*

Step 6. Divide 3 by 2.

3/2 = 1 with a remainder of 1.

The bit value is 1.

The cumulative bit order is 101101.

Step 7. Divide 1 by 2.

1/2 = 0 with a remainder of 1.

The bit value is 1.

The cumulative bit order is 1101101.

Step 8. As the division is complete, we add a zero to the final bit position to "close" the exercise. The resulting bit order is: 01101101.

Congratulations! You just successfully used another tool for converting a base 10 number to a base 2 number.

Secret

You also may use the built-in calculator in Windows 2000 Server for decimal and binary bit conversions (and as a tool for subnetting).

The built-in calculator is found under the Accessories area from the Start button (via Programs). After starting the Calculator, perform the following steps.

STEPS:

Using the built-in calculator for decimal and binary bit conversions

Step 1. Launch the Calculator applet. Convert the calculator from Standard view to Scientific view (see Figure 7-4). You accomplish this via the View menu on the Calculator menu bar.

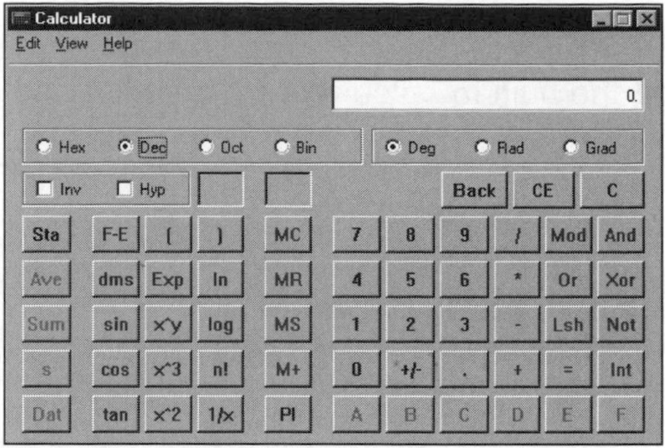

Figure 7-4: The Scientific view

Step 2. Type in the decimal value. Use 109 for continuity. Make sure the "Dec," or decimal notation radio button, is selected, as shown in Figure 7-5.

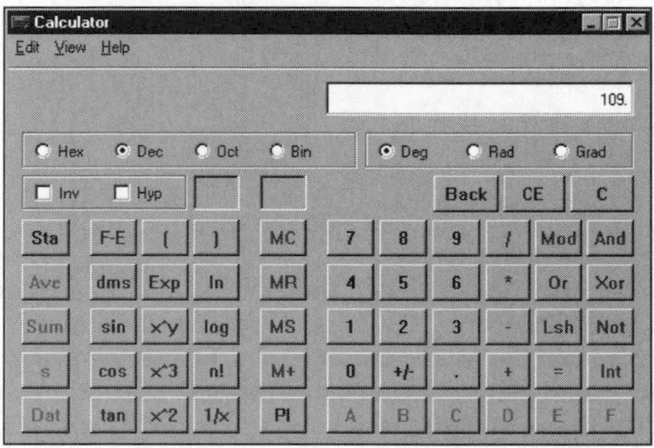

Figure 7-5: Decimal value 109 keyed into the Calculator entry field

Step 3. Select the "Bin," or binary notation button, to convert the decimal value to the binary value of 1101101 (see Figure 7-6). Don't forget to add the preceding zero(s) ("0") when only a partial binary value is presented.

Continued

STEPS:

Using the built-in calculator for decimal and binary bit conversions *(continued)*

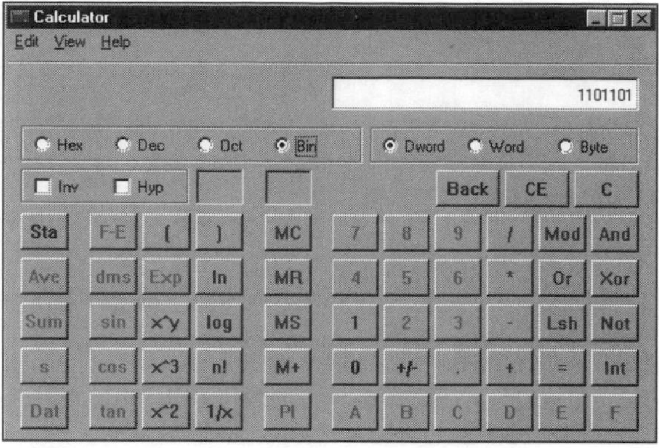

Figure 7-6: The Bin radio button

The Calculator contained within the confines of Windows 2000 Server is truly a time-saving tool as you implement TCP/IP subnetting on your networks.

And one more take on subnetting so that you are armed completely for your Windows 2000 Server TCP/IP-related battles. A different tack on subnetting is to view it from the MCSE perspective. That is, exam cram! A peer from the industry, John Lambert, shared with readers in *Microsoft Certified Professional Magazine* the following points about mastering subnetting from the practical perspective of just passing the darn TCP/IP certification exam.

Arguably, the TCP/IP elective exam in the MCSE track is the most difficult of all. This is the exam wherein certification candidates emerge from the testing room looking like ghosts (or at least with a catatonic gaze). Likewise, I can say with some degree of certainty that you will encounter the advanced areas of TCP/IP during your tenure as a Windows 2000 Server professional.

But fear not. It's really as simple as 1-2-3. That is, the following two charts serve as your guide to quickly assessing

- What class a TCP/IP address falls into (refer to Table 7-10)
- The possible number of subnet numbers and host numbers per subnetting scenario (see Table 7-11)

Table 7-10 IP Class Chart

Class	*1st Binary Digits*	*Decimal Range of 1st Octet*
A	0	1–126
B	10	128–191
C	110	192–223

Two quick questions to test your understanding of advanced TCP/IP concepts. The answers follow.

Questions:

1. Why is the decimal value 127 not included in the third column of the preceding table (Table 7-10)?
2. For the Class C row, why are the first binary digits 110 instead of 11?

Answers:

1. The decimal value 127 can't be used for network/host IDs, as it is the IP address area used for loopback testing.
2. IT makes the Class C range end at 223. Remember that initial octet values ranging between 224–255 are reserved for multicasting, research, and so on, and may not be used for network/host IDs.

The next table (Table 7-11) is perhaps the most useful of all. At its core, the table displays the number of subnets and hosts for each subnetting scenario and IP address. More importantly, it draws out specific relationships that make you a crack codebreaker... er... subnetter in no time.

Table 7-11 Subnet Mask Chart

Bit Split	*Subnet Mask*	*Max. Usable Subnets*	*# C IPs/ Subnet*	*# B IPs/ Subnet*	*#A IPs/ Subnet*
2/6	192	2	62	16382	4096K
3/5	224	6	30	8190	2048K
4/4	240	14	14	4094	1024K
5/3	248	30	6	2046	512K
6/2	252	62	2	1022	256K
7/1	254	126	0	510	128K
8 / 0	255	254	0	254	64K

Here is how you can interpret this chart. First, the bit split is simply the division of bits between the subnet and the host. This is similar to the presentation of such a split in Table 7-9, wherein I used boldface to distinguish among the subnet and host positions.

The subnet mask column shows all possible masks. Remember that zero appears in some masks, but a zero octet doesn't mask any bits. As its name implies, the third column refers to the maximum useable subnets for a given scenario. Columns four, five, and six speak to the number of usable IP addresses for each subnet, given an IP address class.

One of the patterns that is important to see is the trade-off between the number of subnets and hosts as the subnet-related value in the fourth octet position of the subnet mask increases. Seeing this relationship enables you to be both a great codebreaker and subnetter!

Summary

This chapter has armed you with the fundamentals of TCP/IP subnetting. Because Windows 2000 Server relies so much on the TCP/IP protocol suite for basic local area and wide area network connectivity, it is essential that you carry forward a deep understanding of the subnetting discussion presented in this chapter.

- Defined TCP/IP subnetting
- Performed TCP/IP subnetting calculations
- Mastered both the theory and mechanics of TCP/IP subnetting

Chapter 8

Internet Secrets

In This Chapter

- Learning how to connect to the Internet
- Understanding Virtual Private Networks (VPN)
- Understanding Point-to-Point Tunneling Protocol (PPTP)
- Configuring Internet Explorer for Proxy Server and HTTPS (Secure)

This chapter could easily be an entire book. In fact, there are many books on the Internet (you can see many of these books listed at `www.idgbooks.com`). More important, let me set the tone for this chapter so that you will know what to expect. The Internet is necessarily discussed in almost every chapter of this book. So I am using this chapter to answer a few questions about the Internet, ones that I frequently encounter as a practicing Windows 2000 Server consultant.

Obviously the history of the Internet has been covered in more texts than you or I care to count, so I'll leave that topic alone. But it is interesting to note that the Internet is creating its own history each day. Its short life to date suggests that there are untold opportunities for you to capitalize on the Internet. But for you to do that, you first need to successfully attach your Windows 2000 server to the Internet. You have several ways to do this. In this chapter, after installing Remote Access Service, I'll proceed with the dial-up approach and work toward more complex Internet configurations.

Configuring Remote Access Service

Hail to Windows 2000 Server, for it has simplified many tasks from its NT predecessors, including the installation and configuration of Remote Access Service (RAS). But first, a quick history lesson. You will recall that Remote Access Server (RAS) has been part of the remote networking solution set in Microsoft's networking family since the earliest days of Windows NT Server (at which time it would only interact with the NetBEUI protocol).

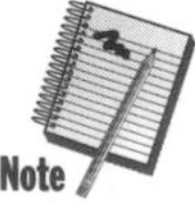

RAS has made something of a political comeback in the networking community. For years, RAS enjoyed mixed reviews at best for its unreliable support for modem-based dial-in and dial-out activity. However, with the advent of Virtual Private Networks (VPNs), RAS is back. It actually manages the VPN function very well in Windows 2000 Server, and I will discuss this later in this chapter.

Well, RAS has come a long way in Windows 2000 Server. The RAS installation is much more intuitive, starting with the Windows 2000 Configure Your Server screen (see Figure 8-1). Following are the steps to configure Remote Access Service for inbound Internet-based traffic. This sets the foundation for the Virtual Private Networking (VPN) discussion later.

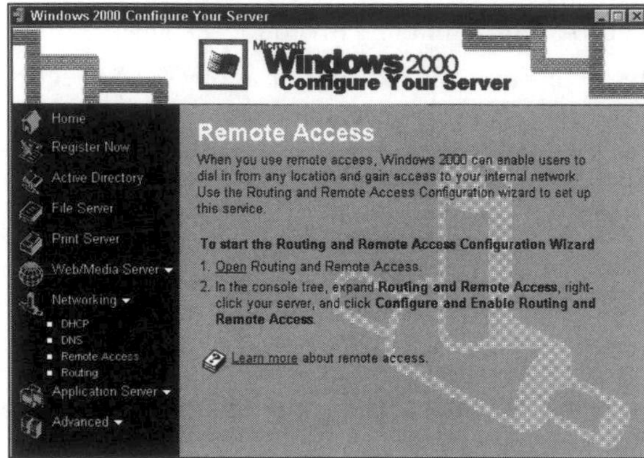

Figure 8-1: Windows 2000 Configure Your Server

STEPS:

Configure Remote Access Service

Step 1. From the Windows 2000 Configure Your Server screen, select the Networking link in the left pane and then select Remote Access. Select the "Open" link to launch the Routing and Remote Access MMC.

Right-click the server object in the left pane (for example, TCI1) and select Configure and Enable Routing and Remote Access from the secondary menu (see Figure 8-2).

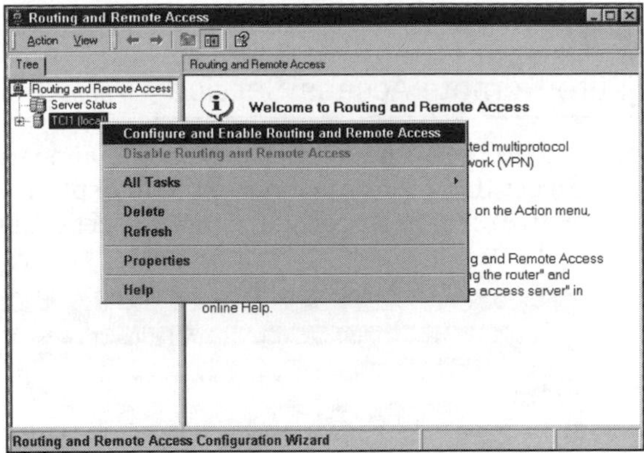

Figure 8-2: Configure and Enable Routing and Remote Access selection

Step 2. The Welcome screen of the Routing and Remote Access Server Setup Wizard appears. Click Next.

Step 3. The Common Configurations screen appears (see Figure 8-3). Select Remote Access Server. Click Next.

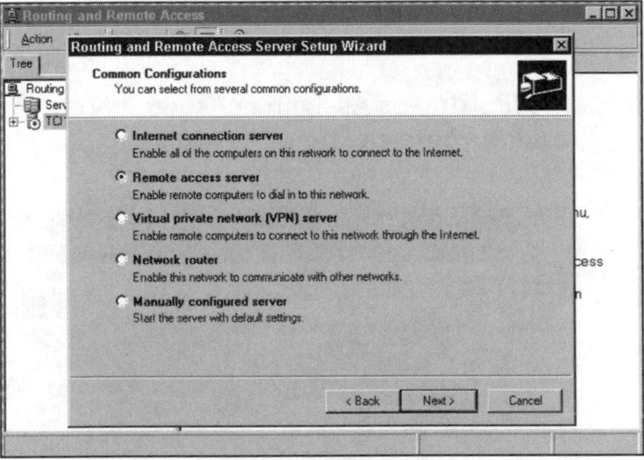

Figure 8-3: Remote Access Server

Be very careful about selecting the Network router option. First of all, there are many compelling reasons, such as advanced configuration management, to use true routers (such as Cisco) on your Windows 2000 network. Second, it enables two-way routing of network traffic to and from the Internet (if you're connected directly to the Internet) and overrides the safeguards imposed by Microsoft Proxy Server's local address table (LAT).

Continued

STEPS:

Configure Remote Access Service *(continued)*

Step 4. The Remote Client Protocols screen appears (see Figure 8-4). Select the appropriate button to accept or elect to add more networking protocols for remote access. Click Next.

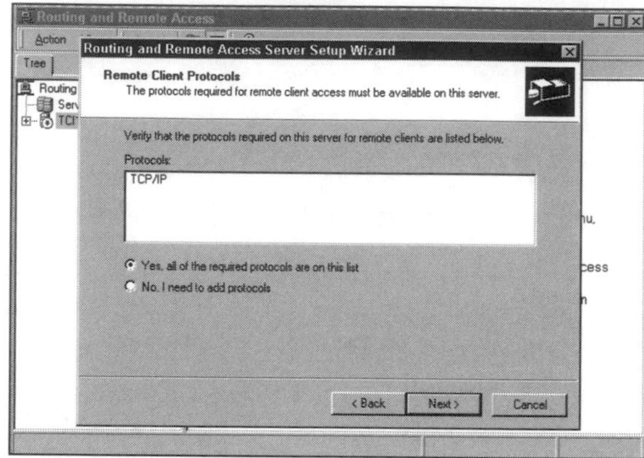

Figure 8-4: Remote Client Protocols screen

Step 5. The IP Address Assignment screen appears (see Figure 8-5). After making your selection, click Next.

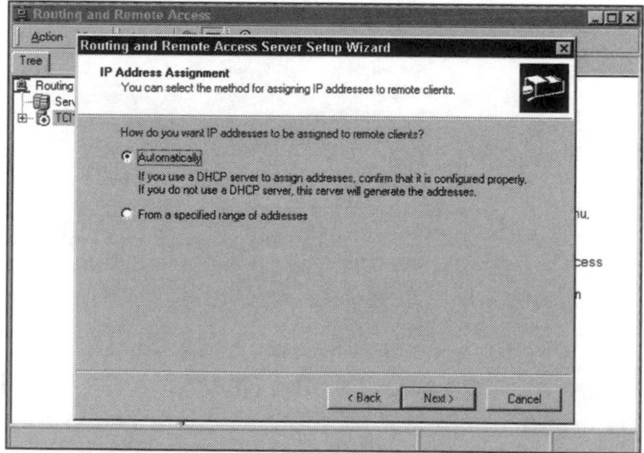

Figure 8-5: IP Address Assignment screen

Step 6. The Managing Multiple Remote Access Servers screen appears (see Figure 8-6). The screen allows you to elect to manage all RAS servers from a central point. This election clearly depends on whether you are managing a smaller LAN with only one RAS server (in which case the answer would be "No") or managing a RAS server farm (in which case the answer would be "Yes"). Make a selection and click Next.

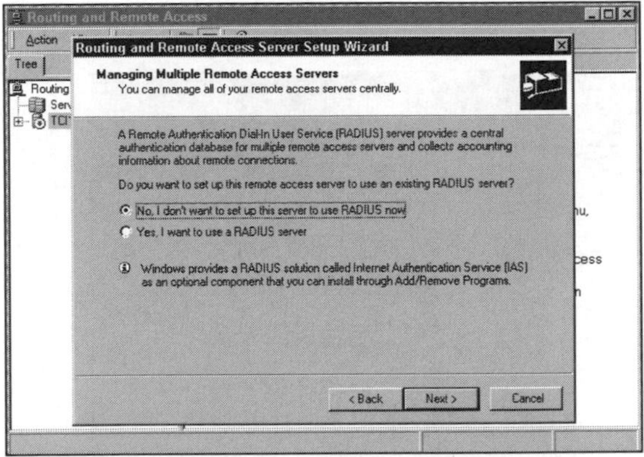

Figure 8-6: Managing Multiple Remote Access Servers screen

Step 7. Click Finish on the Completing the Routing and Remote Access Server Setup Wizard to complete the RAS configuration (see Figure 8-7). You will be returned to the Routing and Remote Access MMC. Select the WAN Miniport and click the Configure button. Select the Remote access (inbound) checkbox and enter the number of Maximum ports you want to allow (see Figure 8-7). The default is five for Maximum ports, which means you've configured five virtual circuits for your Virtual Private Network (VPN). That means up to five VPN connections can exist at one time.

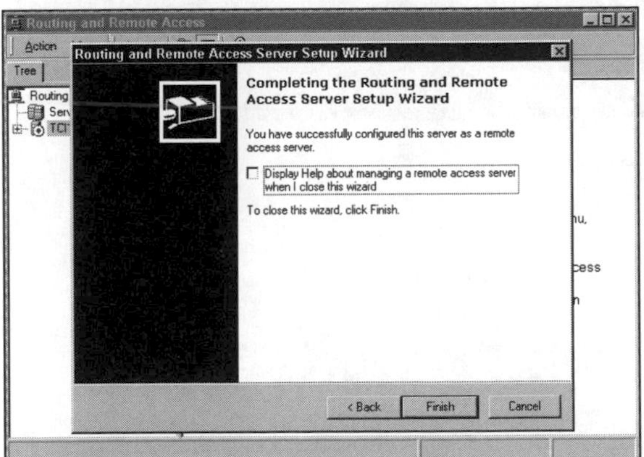

Figure 8-7: Finishing the RAS configuration

Take a moment to look over the RAS configuration you have created by expanding the objects in the left pane of the Routing and Remote Access MMC. For example, if you select the Ports object in the left pane (below the server object), you will see the WAN Miniports that have been created with VPN support in the right pane (see Figure 8-8).

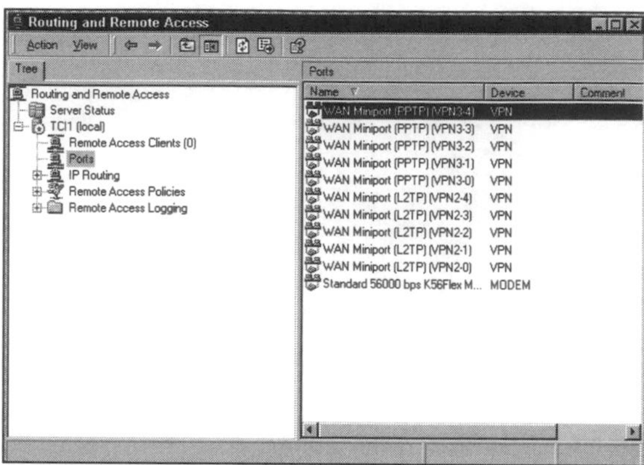

Figure 8-8: Ports

The L2TP ports relate to having the Remote Access Server use Internet Protocol security (IPSEC), a topic I cover in Chapter 13.

If you right-click on the Ports object in the left pane and select Properties from the secondary menu, a Port Properties dialog box will be displayed that provides detailed information on the ports and allows you to modify the configurations (see Figure 8-9).

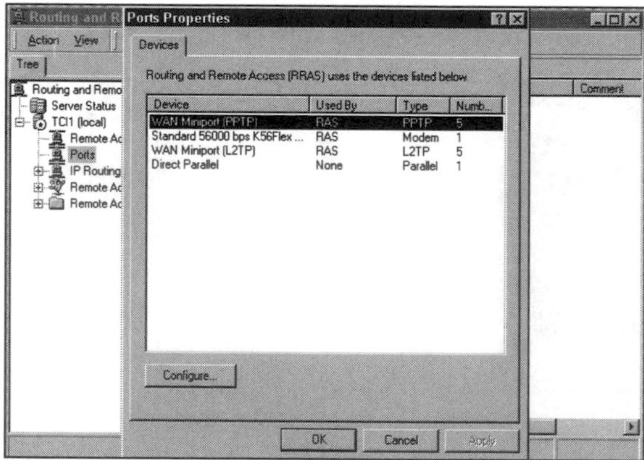

Figure 8-9: Ports Properties

The number of maximum ports you configure will create the denominator for the multiplexing algorithm used in Windows 2000 Server VPN scenarios. Huh? Simply stated, if you configure five ports, and you have five VPN sessions occurring simultaneously, the five sessions collectively divide the WAN bandwidth you have. For example, if your WAN link were a 256Kbps connection, this bandwidth would be divided amongst the active VPN sessions. Be sure to consider that fact when you decide on the maximum ports to configure. Perhaps you only want a few (say two) ports configured to protect your WAN-related bandwidth!

To modify the configuration, select the Configure button while one of the devices is selected. The Configure Device screen will appear. Note in Figure 8-10, the PPTP WAN Miniport is configured for inbound connections only. This occurs because the Remote access connections (inbound only) checkbox is selected.

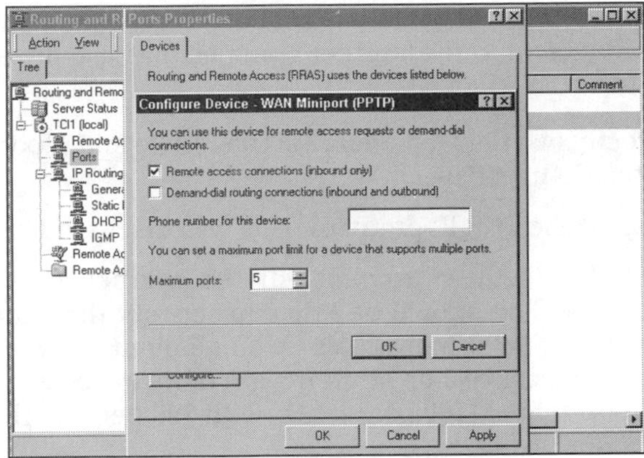

Figure 8-10: Port configuration

With a right-click on the Remote Access Policies object, and by selecting New, Remote Access Policy from the secondary menu, you can create a RAS policy that meets your needs. For example, you can establish day and time restrictions that a user can or cannot access your network via a VPN connection (see Figure 8-11).

Dial-Up Connection

Historically, RAS has been presented in the context of dial-in users. But did you know that RAS is used to expedite connections to the Internet as well? I'll explore RAS's role in Windows 2000 Server starting with a simple dial-up scenario.

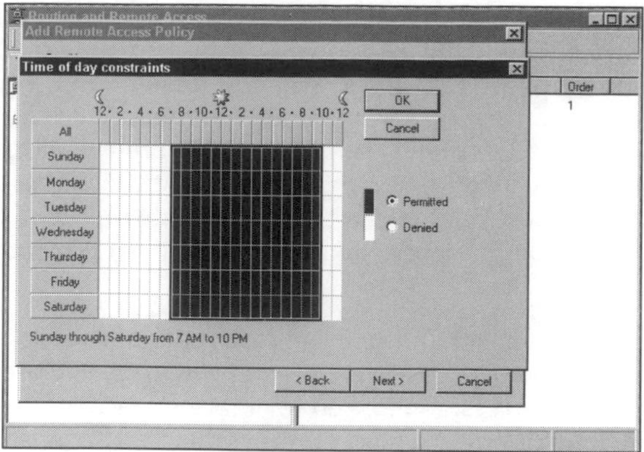

Figure 8-11: Time of day constraints

A simple dial-up connection to the Internet assumes that you have performed several tasks:

- You have correctly installed a modem via the Phone and Modem Options applet under the Control Panel.
- You have installed the TCP/IP protocol. This was discussed in Chapter 4.
- You have a valid Internet user account with the Internet service provider (ISP) of your choice. This should be a dial-up account that supports PPP, not SLIP. Such accounts for individuals with unlimited use average $20 to $25 per month. Business dial-up accounts are more expensive, but can easily be found for under $100 per month, with $50 per month being the average.
- You have installed and configured RAS using the preceding steps (in the Configuring Remote Access Service section).
- It is also important that the dial-out RAS capabilities be configured to use the TCP/IP protocol for an Internet connection scenario (again, see the preceding discussion in the Configuring Remote Access Service section).
- You have configured a network and dial-up connection. These steps are explained in the text that follows.

Creating and configuring a dial-up connection to the Internet can be dramatically easier if you request the setup configuration information from your ISP. By working closely with your ISP, you can save time when configuring your dial-up Internet connection.

Every ISP that I've worked with will provide setup instructions on their Web page to assist you (see Figure 8-12). What information isn't provided on their Web page can usually be obtained with a quick telephone call to the ISP's technical support group. In fact, the ease with which you obtain the configuration information that you need is a leading indicator of how strong your relationship with the ISP will be.

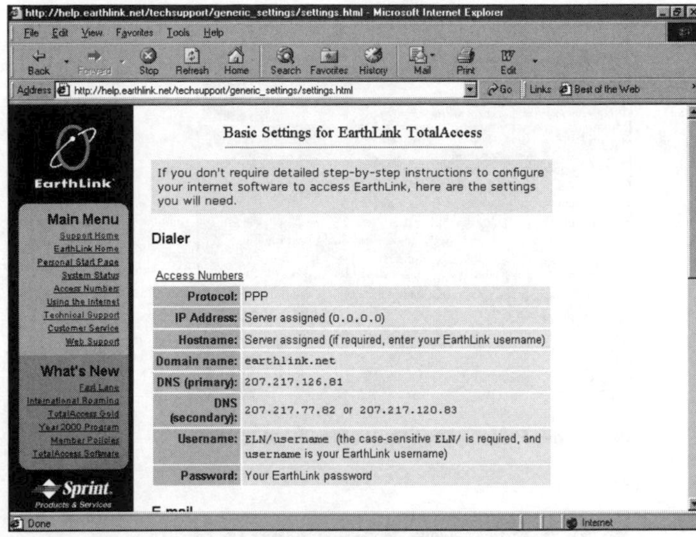

Figure 8-12: An ISP dial-up configuration FAQ

Configuring a network and dial-up connection

Assuming that you've addressed each of the prerequisite points just described, it is now time to configure a dial-up connection.

STEPS:

To configure a dial-up connection

Step 1. Launch the Network and Dial-up Connections applet in Control Panel. The Network and Dial-up Connections screen will appear.

Step 2. Double-click the Make New Connection button. The Welcome to the Network Connection Wizard appears. Click Next.

Step 3. The Network Connection Type screen appears (see Figure 8-13). Select the Dial-up to the Internet radio button. Click Next. The Internet Connection Wizard appears (see Figure 8-14).

Continued

STEPS:

To configure a dial-up connection *(continued)*

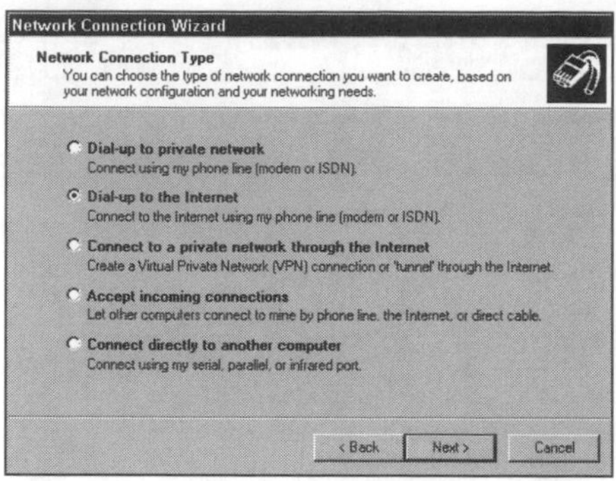

Figure 8-13: Network Connection Type screen

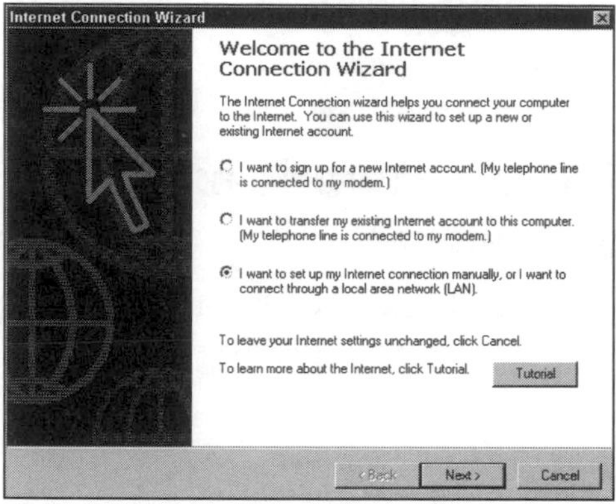

Figure 8-14: Internet Connection Wizard

The Internet Connection Wizard (ICW) first made its appearance in Small Business Server (SBS) and, having proved popular, was imported to Windows 2000 Server. I discuss SBS in Chapter 16.

Step 4. The Setting up your Internet connection screen appears. You will select between connecting to the Internet with a phone and modem or from a local area network (LAN). After making your selection, click Next.

Step 5. The Step 1 of 3: Internet account connection information screen appears (see Figure 8-15). Enter the telephone number for your Internet Service Provider (ISP).

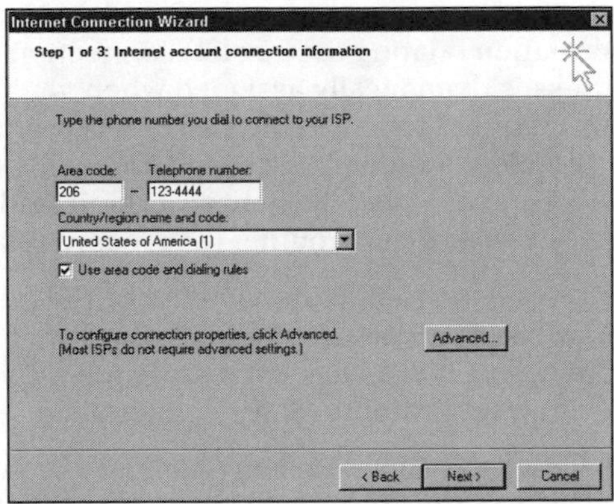

Figure 8-15: Internet account connection information

Microsoft claims "Most ISPs do not require advanced settings" on the Internet account connection information screen. This is not true. In fact, more often than not, you will need to click the Advanced button to provide DNS server information.

Step 6. Click the Advanced button. The Advanced Connection Properties dialog box will be displayed. Select the Addresses tab (see Figure 8-16). Complete the address information as required and click OK.

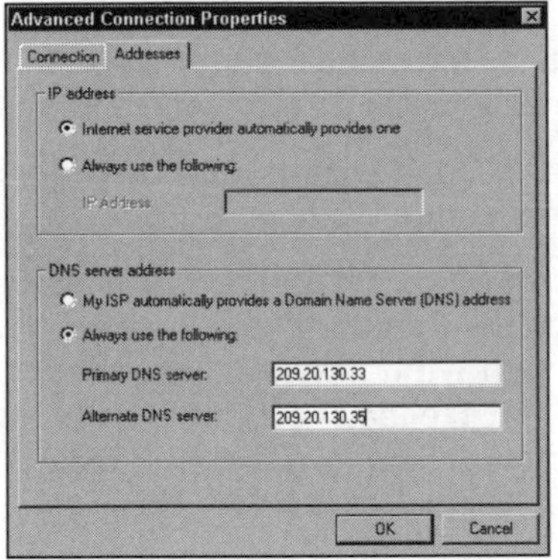

Figure 8-16: Advanced Connection Properties — Addresses

Continued

STEPS:

To configure a dial-up connection *(continued)*

It is here that you will provide IP address information and DNS information relating to your ISP connection. In most cases, your IP address is dynamically assigned when you're just a good old end user; if you're using a dedicated dial-up connection for your server and it's running Microsoft Exchange (and the Internet Mail Service), you'll most likely have a dedicated IP address to facilitate your e-mail routing (MX record-related).

Also note on the Connection tab of the Advanced Connection Properties that Point to Point Protocol (PPP) is selected by default. This is typically correct, as few ISPs now support Serial Line Internet Protocol (SLIP) connections.

Step 7. Assuming you completed any advanced configurations, you are now back at the Step 1 of 3: Internet account connection information screen. Click Next.

One final word on telephone numbers. Be advised that you may need to enter the full ten-digit telephone number for additional telephone numbers supported by your ISP within the same general geographic area. With the advent of area code redistricting, ten-digit telephone numbers may be needed to place a call within your city (or even the same neighborhood!). For example, in Seattle, the metropolitan area now has several area codes, including 206, 425, 360, and 253. You only need to dial the area code and the telephone number to place a call locally; you do not need to precede the area code with a "1" when calling these area codes within the Seattle area.

Step 8. The Step 2 of 3: Internet account logon information screen appears. Enter your ISP logon name and password. Click Next.

Step 9. The Step 3 of 3: Configuring your computer screen appears. Provide a connection name and click Next.

Step 10. The Set Up Your Internet Mail Account screen appears. It is here you would configure your POP e-mail account. To be honest, in most cases with Windows 2000 Server it is unlikely you would be configuring a POP e-mail account at the server. You are more likely to use a Microsoft Exchange-based e-mail account (let's be serious here!). Select Yes or No and click Next.

Step 11. Assuming you selected No in Step 10, the Complete Configuration screen will appear. Click Finish to complete dial-up configuration via the ICW.

The preceding steps to configure an Internet dial-up connection will automatically modify your Internet Explorer (IE) configuration to use the new default dial-up connection that you have created. If you are on a network and using a full-time Internet connection, this will come as a big surprise to you. To fix this undocumented misconfiguration, simply launch IE and select Internet Options from the Tools menu. Select the Connections tab. Note the Always dial my default connection radio button was automatically selected for you as a result of the steps you just performed. I recommend that you select the Dial whenever a network connection is not present radio button.

Dialing the Internet

It is now time to call your ISP, successfully connect, and start using the Internet. There is no greater test in the eyes of your users than the ability to connect to and use the Internet. In fact, it's unlikely users have much interest in the settings covered in this chapter; they just want to use the Internet. My advice on connecting to the Internet? Be sure to test this feature several times under different conditions and times of day before announcing your new Internet connection. There is nothing more disconcerting than to implement many of the Internet dial-up settings displayed in this chapter only to have your users call and say, "I can't get my Internet e-mail." Proper and extensive testing of the Internet dialing capability will prevent such calls.

Assuming that you have successfully configured your network and dial-up connection (the steps earlier in this chapter), you are now ready to connect to the Internet.

STEPS:

To connect to the Internet via Network and Dial-Up Connections

Step 1. Launch the Network and Dial-Up Connection applet from Control Panel.

Step 2. Double-click the connection you want to use (for example, NWLink).

Step 3. The Connect dialog box appears (see Figure 8-17). Confirm the user name and password you will use to connect to the Internet. Click the Dial button.

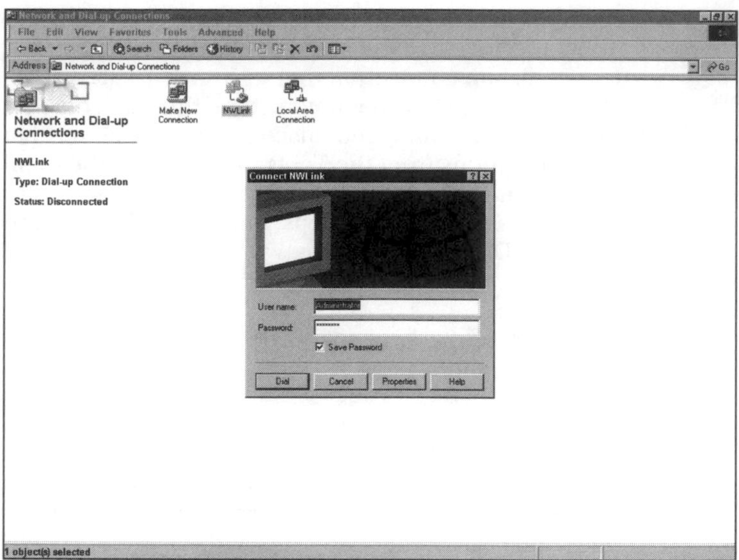

Figure 8-17: Connect dialog box

Step 4. After a few moments, you should be successfully connected to the Internet via your ISP.

You are now ready to browse with your Web browser.

If you have any troubles with your Internet dial-up connection, click the Properties button on the Connect dialog box. You may then double-check you settings on the General, Options, Security, Networking, and Sharing tabs.

Dial-up connection status

Often, it is desirable to know whether or not you are still connected to the Internet or to know the speed at which you are connected. Just observing the dancing activity light on an external modem is not helpful.

You can monitor your Internet connection activity via the Routing and Remote Access MMC. Simply expand the server object in the left pane (for example, TCI1) and click Ports so that all of the ports are listed in the right pane (see Figure 8-18).

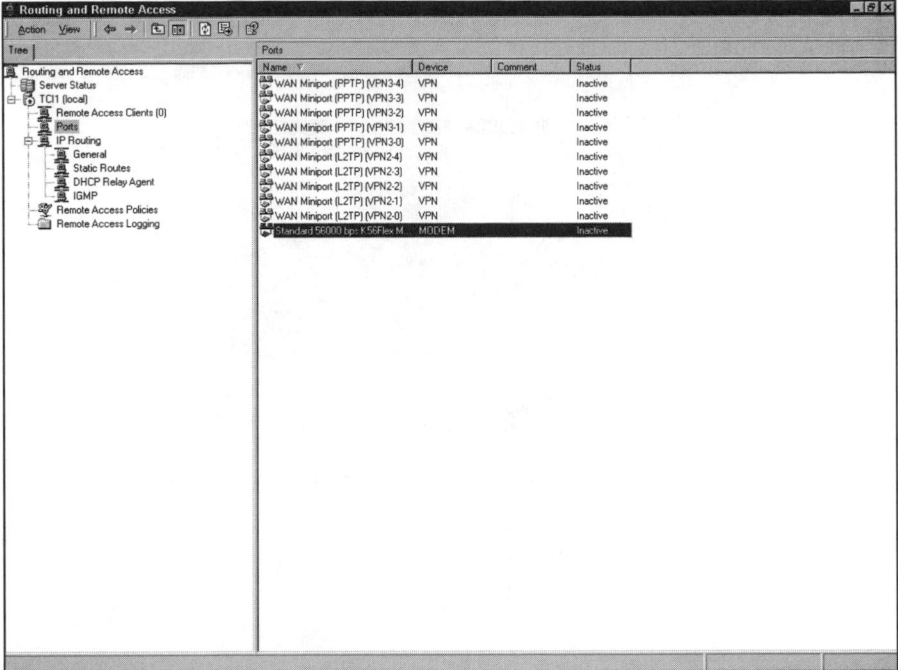

Figure 8-18: Routing and Remote Access MMC

Then double-click the port which is responsible for your Internet connection (for example, Sportster 28800...Modem). The Port Status dialog box will be displayed (see Figure 8-19). I have found the Port Status dialog box to be useful for more than just confirming my connection, connection speed, and call duration. It has been invaluable when working with technical support from the ISP to troubleshoot connection problems.

The Port Status dialog box replaces Dial-Up Networking Monitor from Windows NT Server's Control Panel. You might recall Port Status was a tab sheet in Dial-Up Networking Monitor (the other two tab sheets were Summary and Preferences).

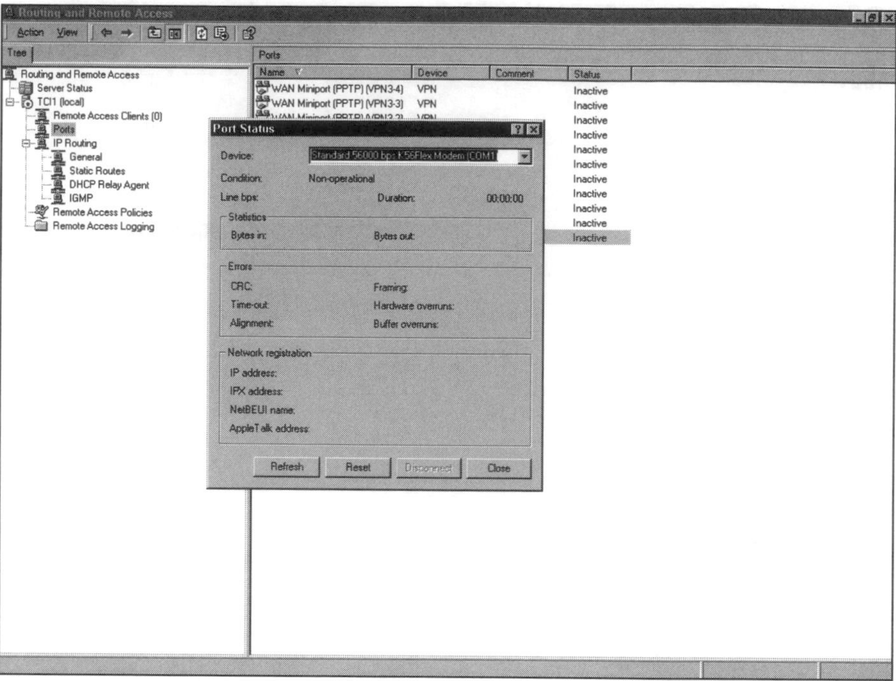

Figure 8-19: Port Status dialog box

Port Status does not update dynamically, so you don't have to press F5 or open and close it repeatedly for screen refreshes. You may recall that the Status tab sheet in Windows NT Server 4.0's Dial-Up Networking Monitor did update dynamically.

Dial-up networking with ISDN modems

Connecting to the Internet via Network and Dial-up Connections with an ISDN modem is not very different from connecting via an analog modem. Two items must be addressed. First, make sure you have ordered and worked closely with your local telephone company to ensure that you have a fully functional and tested ISDN line at your location. Second, be sure to correctly install your ISDN modem on your Windows 2000 server. It will most likely be necessary to use the Windows 2000 Server drivers on the driver disk that ships with your ISDN modem.

Note that the preceding discussion applies to ISDN modems, not ISDN routers. ISDN routers are discussed in the text that follows.

Digital and Wide Area Network Internet Connections

Certainly one of the most popular, reliable, and robust ways for Windows 2000 servers to connect to the Internet is directly via a digital network connection. But the term "directly" can mean a lot of different things. I will discuss five Internet/network connection scenarios, but understand that depending on how you design your Windows 2000 Server network, there are many different ways to connect to the Internet.

Scenario 1: ISDN router

An ISDN router (see Figure 8-20) is a low-cost solution for many businesses that enables a robust connection using either one (64Kbps) or two (128Kbps) ISDN channels to connect to your ISP. Typically, ISPs offer an ISDN connection solution that may act as dial-on-demand where the ISDN router calls the ISP and establishes a connection every time Internet-bound activity is detected by the ISDN router. These ISDN dial-on-demand arrangements usually have a monthly connect hour limit (say 200 hours), after which the business pays something like $10 per hour for each additional connection hour. Such dial-on-demand arrangements can often cost under $200 per month. Another ISDN router-based solution is a full-time connection to the ISP, which by definition assures unlimited connection hours. This type of arrangement typically starts at $300 per month, but the charges may vary widely between ISPs.

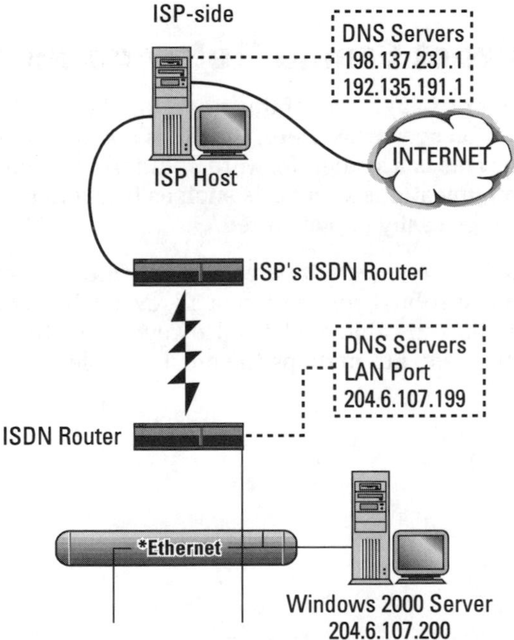

Figure 8-20: An ISDN router connection path to the Internet

This router-based Internet connection solution requires that you make two entries on your Windows 2000 server for the connection to be fully functional. It also requires that your ISDN router be properly programmed to accommodate LAN and real Internet IP addresses and dial the ISP. First, you will need to make sure that the default gateway value for the TCP/IP configuration is populated with the address of the router's LAN port. Second, you will need to complete the DNS fields on the DNS tab sheet with the DNS IP address values provided by your ISP.

Note that in the remaining four Internet/network connection scenarios, it will be necessary to populate the default gateway and DNS fields in a similar manner. The key point to remember is that the default gateway field is typically the LAN port of the router (unless you are instructed otherwise, such as in a firewall scenario) and the DNS IP address values are the DNS servers used by the ISP. And in each of these scenarios, significant programming of the routers is required. Don't kid yourself otherwise.

Scenario 2: ISDN and WAN combination

An ISDN connection may be combined with a WAN (see Figure 8-21) by small companies that may have an existing corporate WAN and want the Internet connection to be separate. I've seen this type of implementation in older business firms where old-guard CEOs and the like believe a separate Internet connection is the safest connection. And who is to say that they are wrong? Such a scenario also centralizes all Internet traffic through a single point, typically the home office of the company.

Scenario 3: Direct Frame Relay connection

Direct Frame Relay (Figure 8-22) is one of the most popular Windows 2000 Server Internet connection scenarios. Here, the ISP is connected via a frame relay WAN connection. This is a straightforward solution that enables different types of communications standards such as fractional T1, full T1, or even faster solutions to be easily implemented.

Many old timers in the WAN connectivity area still consider a frame relay connection to be the most robust connection of all, even when compared to such new offerings as DSL and cable modems. However, note that I didn't say frame relay was the cheapest, but perhaps the most reliable.

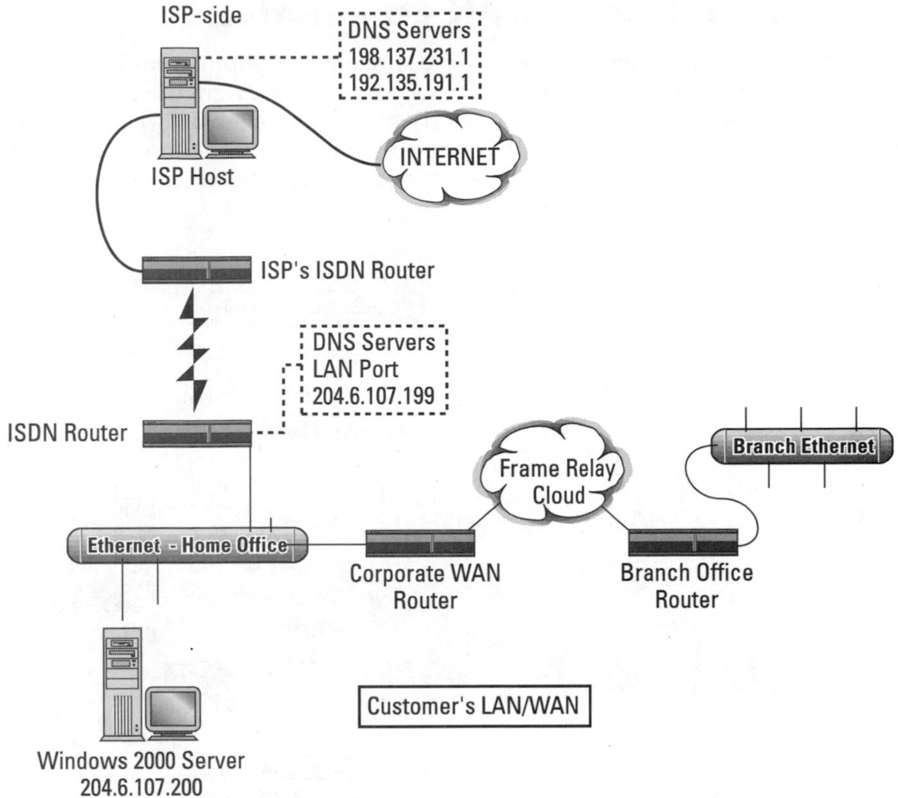

Figure 8-21: An ISDN and WAN connection to the Internet

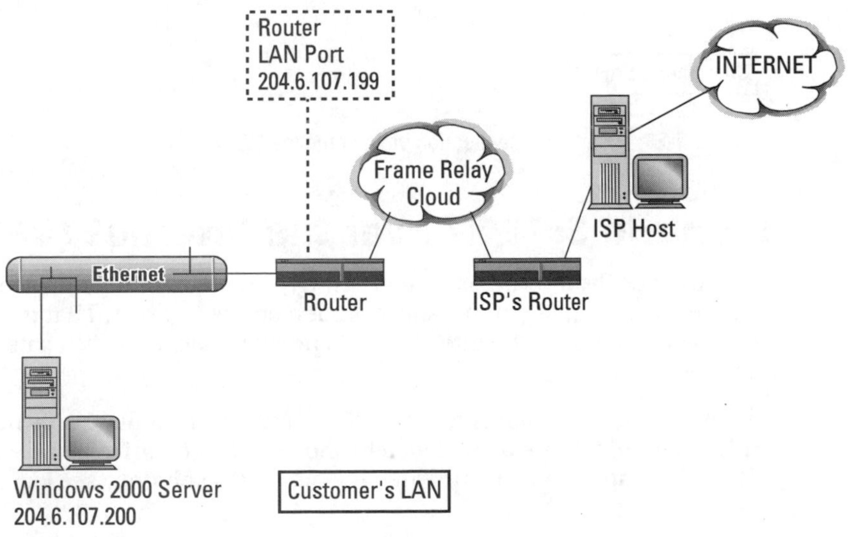

Figure 8-22: A frame relay connection between customer and ISP

Scenario 4: WAN connection

A WAN connection (Figure 8-23) is another popular Internet connection scenario for Windows 2000 Server networks. Here the ISP is a node on the company WAN. Simply stated, other nodes such as branch offices connect directly to the ISP without having to route Internet-bound traffic through the home office. With sufficient firewall protection in place, this is a both a viable and desirable solution.

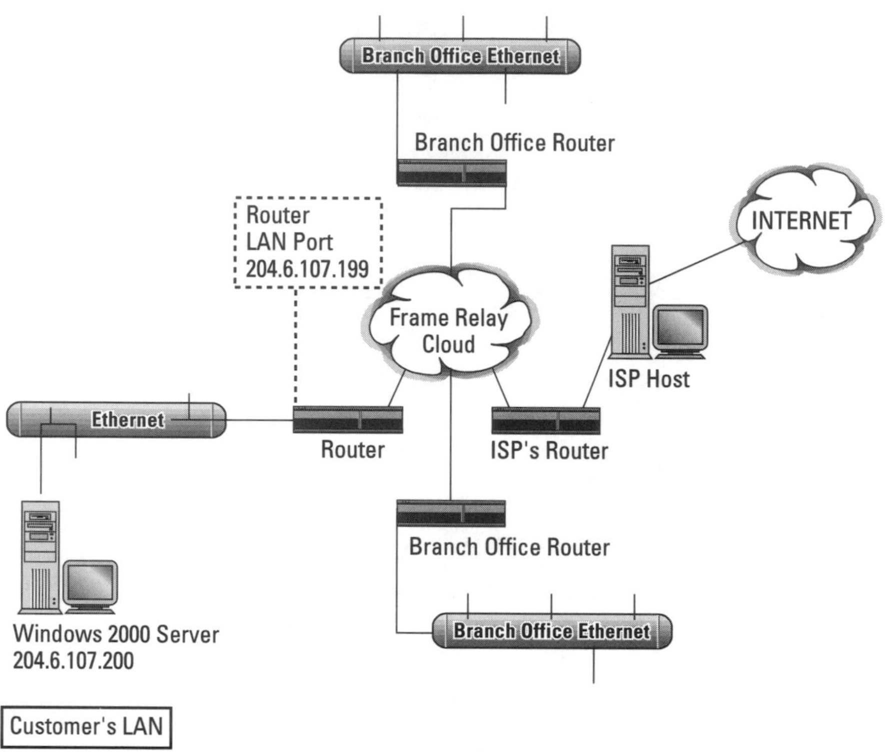

Figure 8-23: An Internet connection via a company WAN

Scenario 5: WAN over the Internet (VPN)

A WAN over the Internet is an increasingly popular connection scenario where each company node is also a node on the Internet. That is, the company WAN uses the Internet as its network backbone in a safe and secure manner.

Such a scenario demands that the ISP be reliable, as it plays a central role in this solution. It is not a good idea to shop for ISPs by price alone when looking at implementing a virtual private network (VPN) solution (see Figure 8-24).

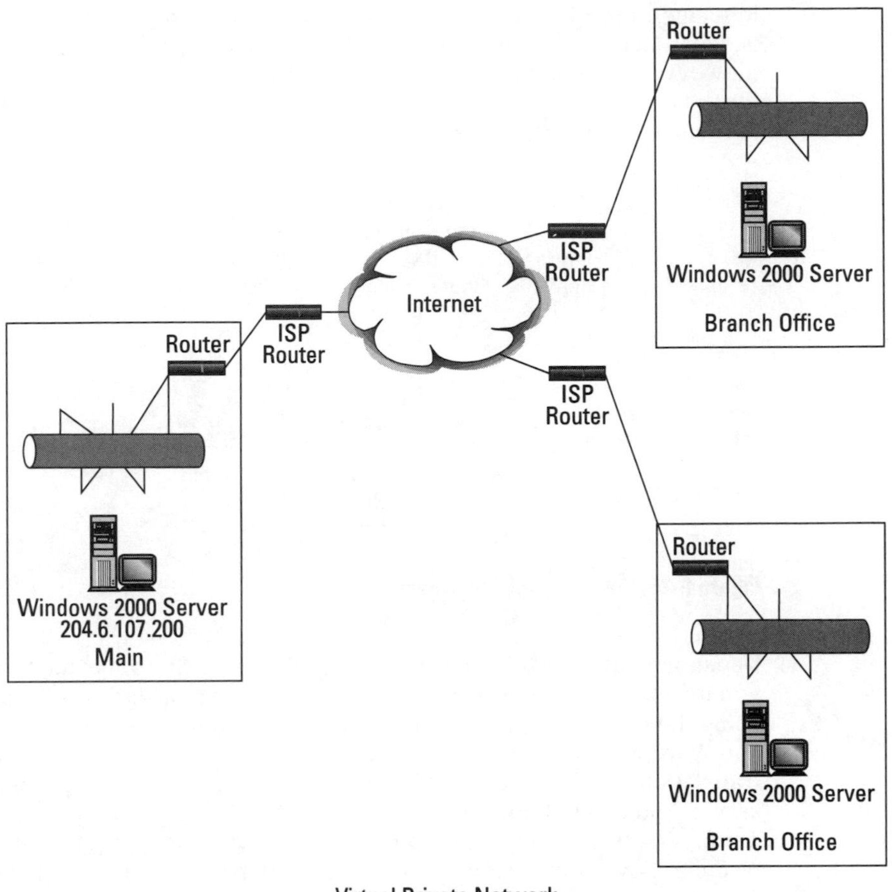

Figure 8-24: A company VPN over the Internet

The good news is that everyone enjoys a robust connection to the ISP and thus the Internet. That will keep the Web surfers happy.

VPNs are further discussed in the next section on Virtual Private Networks.

Scenario 6: DSL connections

Another popular broadband connection to the Internet today is Digital Subscriber Lines (DSL). Using telephone lines (copper wire), you can make a high speed, full-time connection to the Internet for a surprisingly low cost (as low as $30 per month for full-time connection to the Internet).

Implementing a DSL solution is easy. It's the old two NIC-a-roo trick. That is, you place two network adapters in your Windows 2000 server. The first network adapter is for the internal LAN (say 10.0.0.x). The second NIC card is for the direct connection, using a crossover cable to the DSL router (a.k.a. modem, bridge). Figure 8-25 shows the most common DSL implementation.

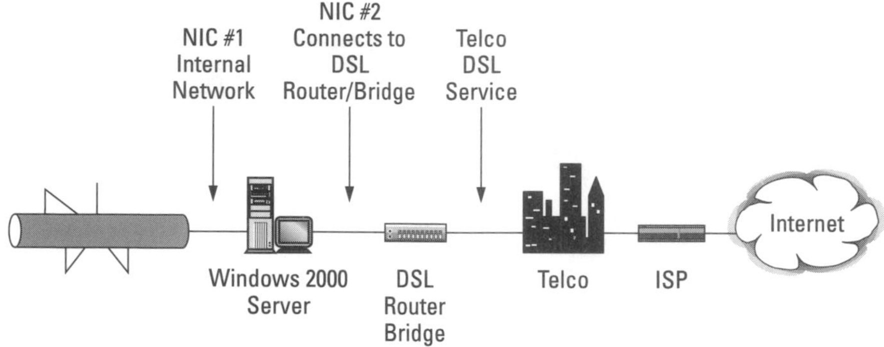

Figure 8-25: Common DSL implementation

Depending on your telephone company, ISP and DSL router manufacturer, you may be using the DSL router as a modem or a bridge. You'll know you're using the DSL router as a router when you explicitly program the LAN and WAN ports with IP addresses and perhaps enable network address translation (NAT) so your SMTP-based e-mail can flow through to your mail server. You can tell you're using your DSL router as a modem or bridge if you perform virtually no configuration tasks and you just plug it in, enabling traffic to flow through it without any activity performed against the traffic (for example, routing).

Many telephone companies are in the business of providing DSL services (see Figure 8-26). In fact, I can say that it's most likely the fastest growing segment of telephone company services today. Why? You're already wired for it in your business and home if you have a telephone line connected and are located near one of the telephone company's central offices.

You typically must be within 15,000 linear cable feet of a telephone company's central office to qualify for DSL service. This isn't a good old "as-the-crow-flies" measurement. Rather, it's within 15,000 feet of cable, and given the odd twists and turns cable runs can snake themselves into, 15,000 feet for the purposes of measuring DSL eligibility is going to be significantly less than you would imagine if you were to get into your car, drive to the neighborhood central office (CO), and determine your drive was less than three miles or approximately 15,000 feet.

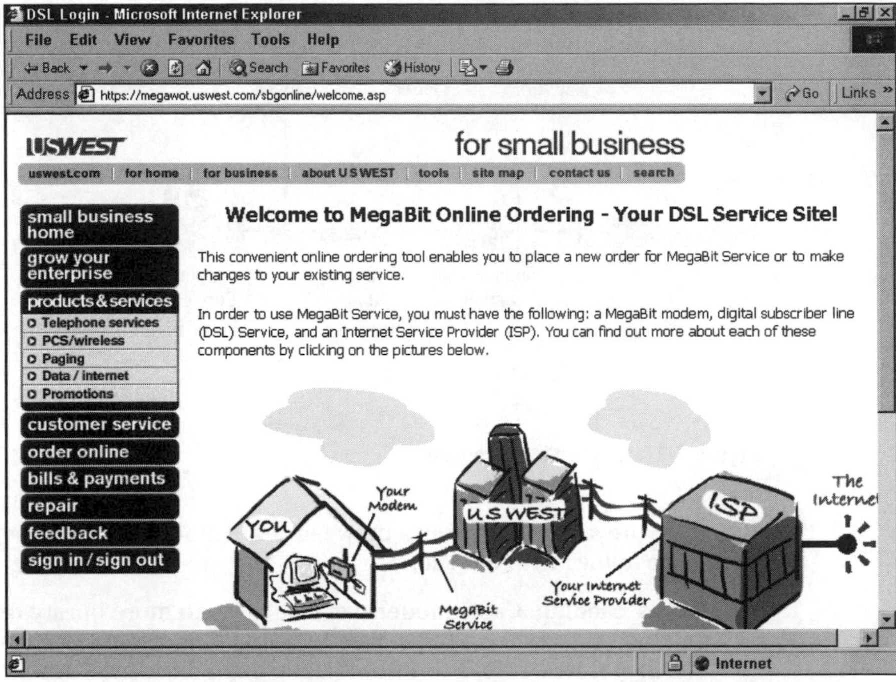

Figure 8-26: US West DSL Service

The 15,000-foot CO-related DSL eligibility limitation mentioned previously is subject to change as telephone companies perfect the delivery of DSL services, develop better communication algorithms and, best of all, place repeaters between you and the CO to regenerate the DSL signal! In other words, the 15,000-foot value is likely to increase to 20,000 feet or more in the near future.

Scenario 7: Cable modems

A viable alternative to DSL service when seeking a high-speed and low-cost connection to the Internet is the use of cable modems. Cable modems, as the name implies, are network communication devices that connect your computer to the coaxial TV cable you've probably become addicted to (not the cable, but the cable service!). Dollar for dollar, cable modem-based Internet connections compare with DSL services when it comes to speed, cost, and reliability (not that all three components can't be improved). And in many ways, the cable modem infrastructure is similar to DSL (two network adapters, communications intermediary), as seen in Figure 8-27.

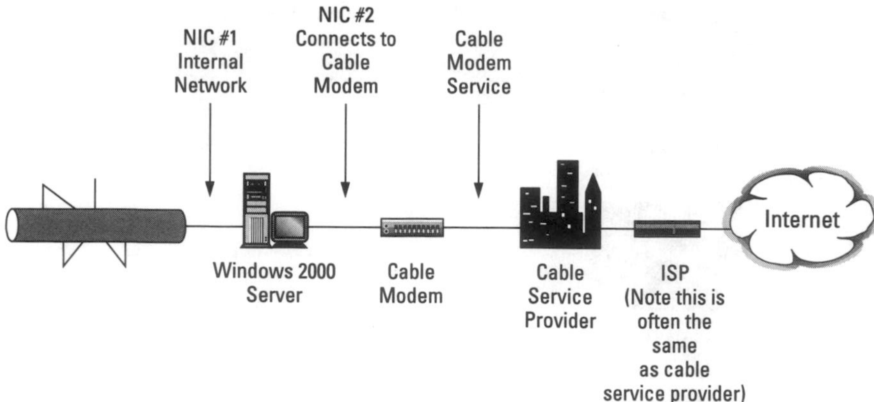

Figure 8-27: Cable modem service

But there are subtle differences between cable modem and DSL service. I've found the following to be true:

- **Bursty caching.** Cable modem service is much more bursty than DSL. I found this out when a DSL-based VPN could accommodate entries into the corporate database without falling behind the keystrokes. The same scenario with cable modem service found the users getting ahead of the keyboard (that is, the character typed didn't appear on the screen for several seconds).
- **Multiplexed situation.** You are one with your neighbors in a cable modem scenario. Why? Because you are dividing that coaxial cable with your teenage kids watching MTV-2, your neighbor's cable modem session, and that sports nut down the block watching ESPN. Simply stated, with cable modem service, you split the available bandwidth with everyone using the cable service on your block. That means, of course, that you will suffer poor performance via the cable modem connection as more and more neighbors log on to the Internet using the same approach.

With cable modems, if possible, attempt to do your Internet computing session during non-peak hours such as midday when fewer neighbors are watching cable TV. It makes a dramatic difference in the performance you will enjoy with your cable modem service.

- **Primarily home use.** The cable service providers have positioned cable modem services for use by homes, not businesses. One workaround for this is to run a small business from home, which won't raise the suspicions of the cable company.
- **No Internet hosting.** Because cable modem services are multiplexed solutions and are oriented to home use, the cable companies are very strict that you should not run a bona fide Internet server on the host

computer you've attached to the cable modem service. In other words, don't be runnin' a WWW or FTP server from your Windows 2000 Server at your home office when you have a cable modem service.

It's another case of necessity being the mother of invention. Consider the following the next time you're in the middle of the boonies and you don't qualify for DSL service: try cable modem service! That's exactly what I did for a branch office of a not-for-profit that was literally located miles down a country road. It quickly became apparent that DSL wouldn't work, but TCI provided cable modem service in the area. The service was ordered and implemented, enabling the end result, creating a VPN back to the home office, to be successfully achieved at a relatively low cost compared to frame relay. My point is that you should consider cable modem service when nothing else works.

Several cable companies, including TCI (see Figure 8-28), are now providing cable modem services. To be brutally honest, the rollout of cable modem service is lagging significantly behind that of DSL services. Part of the reason is that cable companies must make significant infrastructure upgrades to accommodate cable modem service (such as making the flow of information two-way instead of one-way).

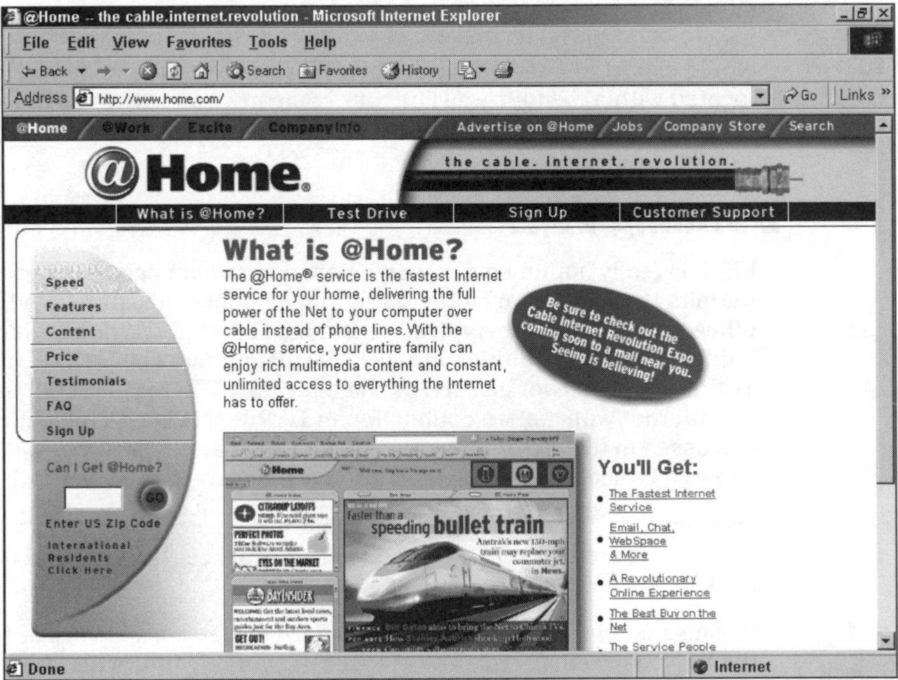

Figure 8-28: TCI cable modem service

Virtual Private Networks

I'll never forget that day. There I was, sitting in the IS Director's office at a leading water cutting tool manufacturer. I was being quizzed relentlessly over the pluses and minuses of Windows NT Server 4.0, which at that time had just been released. The question posed was to name the top new features in Windows NT Server 4.0. After striking out with the obvious answers such as the new Windows 95-like GUI desktop, I gave up. The correct answer, in the eyes of the IS Director, was that Point-to-Point Tunneling Protocol (PPTP) was the top new feature in Windows NT Server 4.0.

My experience that day spawned a lingering curiosity to learn more about PPTP and VPNs and to visit sites that have successfully deployed this solution. Whereas in the Windows NT days, finding successfully deployed VPNs were a challenge, I can report with great excitement that in the era of Windows 2000 Server, VPNs are now commonplace.

Defining Virtual Private Networking

It is now possible to feel connected to your company's network while working from home or traveling on the road via a virtual private network (VPN). More importantly, network administrators appreciate the security provided by the point-to-point tunneling protocol (discussed next). As you would expect, the virtual nature of a VPN means that you do not have to be located within the four walls of your company. You can be outside, connecting to the company network via the Internet. Read on.

Defining PPTP

PPTP is really nothing more than a network communications protocol that permits the secure transfer of data from a remote site, such as a branch office, to a host server (typically the main server at the home office). Implementing this solution creates a virtual private network running over TCP/IP-based networks, such as the Internet. PPTP may be implemented over the Internet with dial-up connection or LAN/WAN digital connections as discussed in the previous section. In fact, Scenario 5 depicted a VPN that shows a typical PPTP implementation (see Figure 8-24).

Security is implemented via encryption. The encryption occurs when the data is prepared for transmission over the Internet "tunnel" and the data packets are encapsulated by PPTP.

Because of this encapsulation, the underlying LAN or network at the ends of the VPN may actually use any of three networking protocols: TCP/IP, NetBEUI, or IXP/SPX. Contrary to popular belief, the VPN clients do not need to use TCP/IP on their internal LANs.

It is also important to understand that your ISP must support PPTP. The list of ISPs that provide such support is growing. When Windows NT Server 4.0 was first released, there was only one ISP in the Seattle area (Microsoft's hometown) that provided such support. Now it is an exception to find an ISP that doesn't support PPTP. Even the granddaddy of them all, CompuServe, supports PPTP (believe it or not!).

The PPTP server must be Windows 2000 Server or Windows NT Server 4.0. PPTP clients may be Windows 2000 Server, Windows 2000 Professional, Windows NT Server 4.0, Windows NT Workstation 4.0, or Windows 98/95. Many resources are available for learning about how to implement PPTP over the Internet. Your ISP will provide you with specific PPTP configuration parameters, such as IP addresses, use of PPTP filtering, and so on. Searching Microsoft support area on its Web site (`www.microsoft.com`) will yield several pages on PPTP configurations.

PPTP was installed on a Windows 2000 Server in the first part of this chapter in the Configuring Remote Access Service section. You will also need to install PPTP and VPN functionality on the client machine that will "VPN" into the corporate network. Here are the steps for implementing PPTP on a Windows 98 workstation.

STEPS:

To install PPTP on a Windows 98 client

Step 1. Launch the Network applet in Control Panel.

Step 2. Select the Add button.

Step 3. Select Adapters. Select Microsoft as the manufacturer and then select the Microsoft Virtual Private Networking Adapter as shown in Figure 8-29. Click OK and, if necessary, provide the path to the Windows 98 source files.

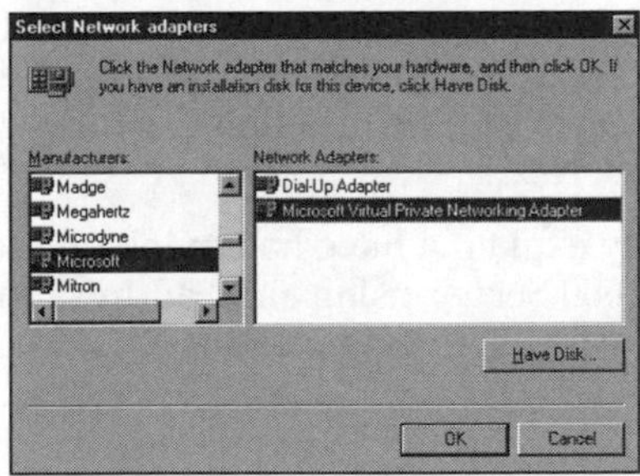

Figure 8-29: The Microsoft Virtual Private Networking Adapter

Continued

STEPS:

To install PPTP on a Windows 98 client *(continued)*

Step 4. If you have already installed TCP/IP, click OK at the Network dialog box and reboot your Windows 98 machine. If necessary, install the TCP/IP protocol.

Step 5. Log on to your Windows 98 workstations and launch Dial-up Networking from My Computer.

Step 6. Double-click Make New Connection. The Make New Connection dialog box will appear.

Step 7. Complete the name and device fields in manner similar to Figure 8-30. It is important you select Microsoft VPN Adapter in the Select a device field. Click Next.

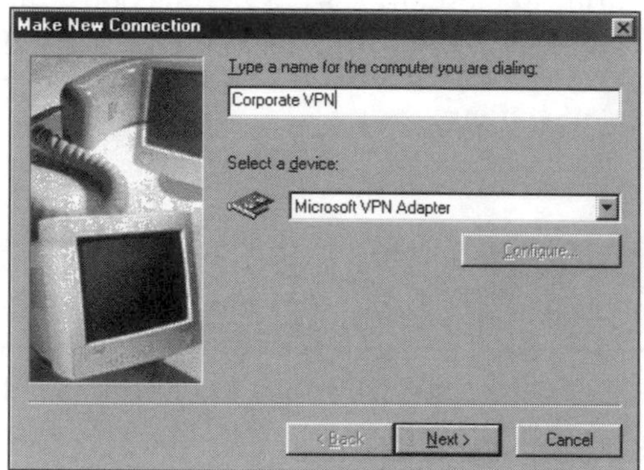

Figure 8-30: Make New Connection dialog box

Step 8. On the next screen, type in the host name or IP address (see Figure 8-31). This is the Internet-side IP address of the Windows 2000 Server network adapter card. This address is akin to dialing a telephone number to reach the VPN-capable Windows 2000 Server. It is also the address that is configured as an RAS-capable device. Click Next.

For reasons I can't fully explain, I have had much greater success trying to VPN into a Windows 2000 Server using an IP address than the host name. Somewhere, somehow the name resolution is going south on the ether.

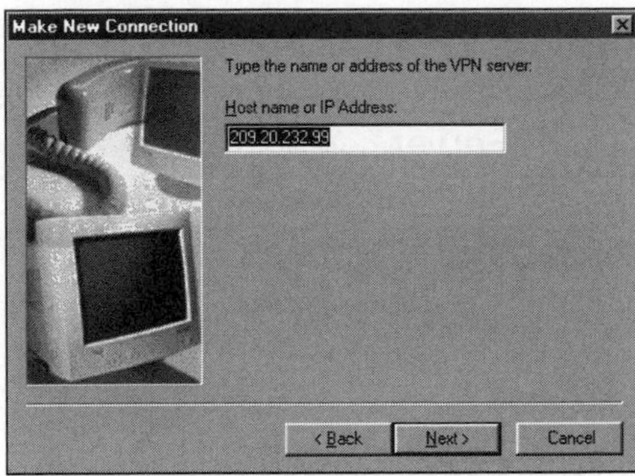

Figure 8-31: Host name or IP address

Step 9. Click Finish. You have completed the Windows 98 client-side VPN configuration.

You are now ready to implement a VPN between a PPTP server and a client. Here is how you would accomplish that. First, confirm the Windows 2000 Server and the workstation you intend to use have been properly set up. You are then ready to initiate a VPN session between remote host and Windows 2000 Server.

STEPS:

To create a VPN session between a Windows 98 client and Windows 2000 Server

Step 1. From Dial-up Networking on the Windows 98 client, launch the VPN dialer you just created (for example, Corporate VPN). The Connect To dialog box will appear.

Step 2. Enter your Windows 2000 domain user name and password (see Figure 8-32). Confirm the IP address or host name of the VPN-enabled Windows 2000 Server you will contact.

Continued

STEPS:

To create a VPN session between a Windows 98 client and Windows 2000 Server *(continued)*

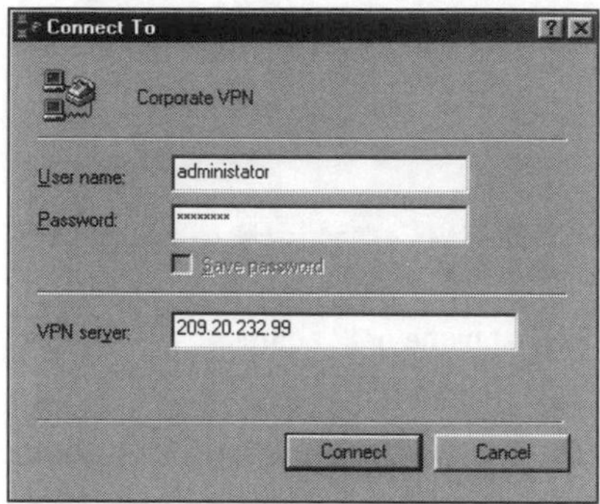

Figure 8-32: Connect To dialog box

Step 3. Click Connect. An attempt to connect to your Windows 2000 Server will be made. If successful, you will be logged on to the domain. You have now established an RAS-based VPN session with a Windows 2000 Server.

Another way to tell that you have successfully connected via a VPN session to a Windows 2000 Server is to look for the tell-tale network connection icon on the right side of your Windows 98 task bar. You know what I'm talking about — those little green dual computers!

Step 4. Many sites that use VPN solutions further extend the VPN session by having the remote client (for example, the Windows 98 client) attach to and make use of a Terminal Server (a.k.a. Microsoft Windows Terminal Server) on the company network. Assuming you plan to do this and have installed the Windows Terminal Server client on your Windows 98 client, it is now time to launch the Terminal Server Client (see Figure 8-33) found in the Terminal Server Client program group.

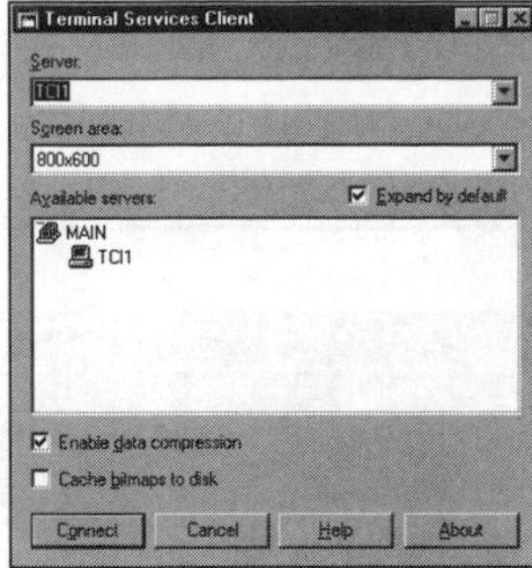

Figure 8-33: Terminal Server Client

Step 5. Enter the Terminal Server name or IP address (for example, 10.0.0.4) in the Server field and click Connect. A Terminal Server session will be launched and the logon screen will appear (see Figure 8-34). Note that I've had more luck trying to connect to a Terminal Server via its IP address than its NetBIOS name (go figure!).

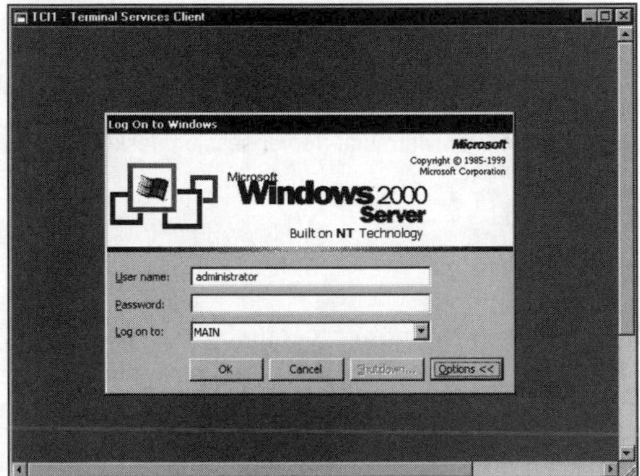

Figure 8-34: Terminal Server session logon

Step 6. Logon with your domain user name and password. Once authenticated, you will be presented with a bona fide Terminal Server session desktop (see Figure 8-35). You are now ready to accomplish your work.

Continued

STEPS:

To create a VPN session between a Windows 98 client and Windows 2000 Server *(continued)*

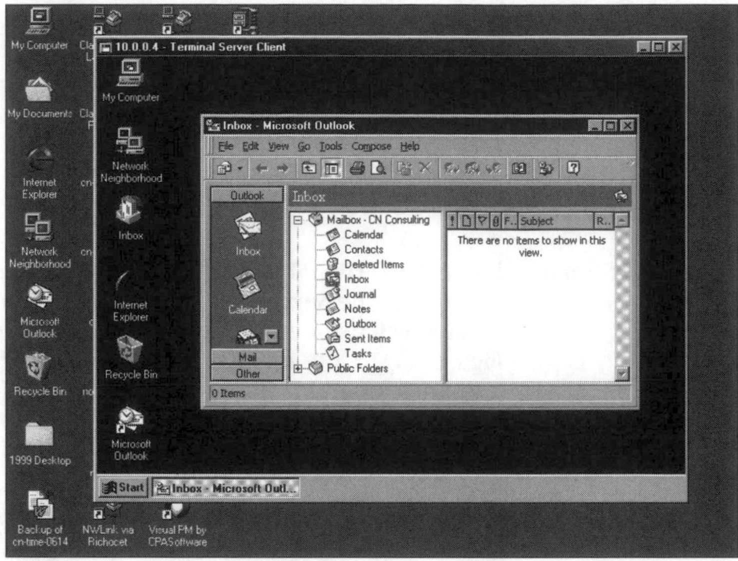

Figure 8-35: Terminal Server session desktop

Want a final look at "VPNing," as I like to call the verb form of this activity? In Figure 8-36, you can see the packet capture, via Network Monitor, of a VPN session between two Windows 2000 servers over the Internet.

You will note the first several packets in the capture related to TCP and SMB session establishment. Once the VPN session is established, the data is encrypted and can't be read with Network Monitor. I cover packet analysis and Network Monitor in Chapter 19.

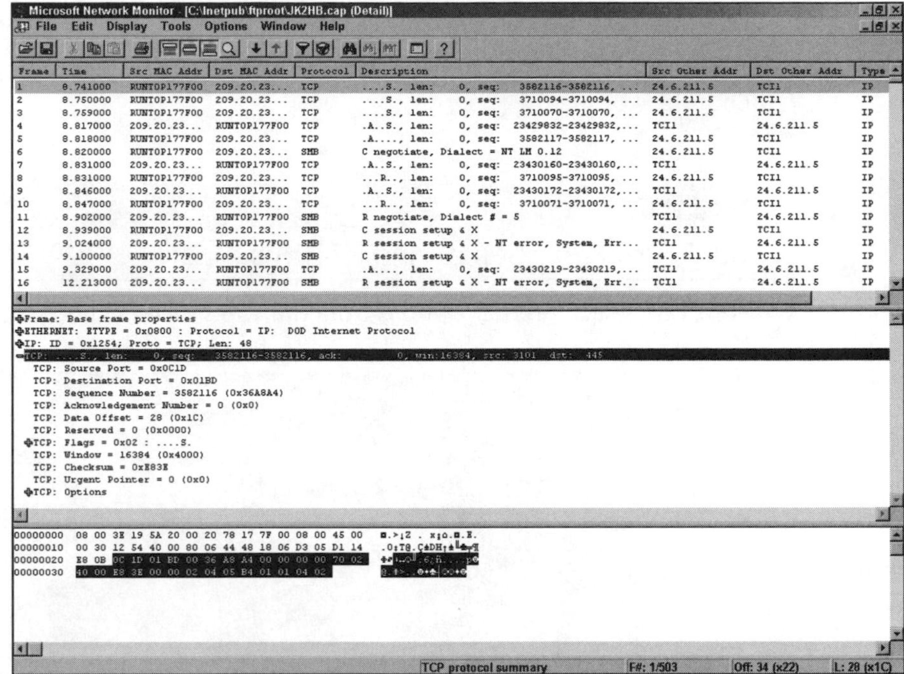

Figure 8-36: Packet capture of Windows 2000 Server-based VPN session

Internet Explorer Secrets

I would be remiss if the Web browser topic wasn't at least addressed in this chapter. On the other hand, it is important not to repeat the work of others that will teach you how to use a browser. Such browser basic books are listed at IDG Book's Web site (www.idgbooks.com).

I assume that you know how to use a browser to access information on the Internet. This assumption includes the ability to type an address, or URL, in the address field of Internet Explorer (IE) to get to a Web site on the Internet.

Secret

Here's an important secret that's worth sharing. It's an actual experience that I've had at client sites involving IE. The situation was this: A law firm administrator was responsible for managing the firm's money market account at one of the online stock brokerages (such as e*trade). Like many networks that are connected to the Internet, this firm used a proxy server to protect itself from intruders. But not only did the law firm need the firewall protection of Proxy Server, but as I learned, an IS configuration modification was required to permit the client to access the firm's confidential trading account information (which was an HTTPS secure session).

When implementing an Internet connection via a proxy server, it is necessary to configure the proxy settings in IE so that browsing activity is directed through the proxy server and HTTPS is permitted. To do this, complete the following steps.

STEPS:

Configure Proxy Server and HTTPS support

Step 1. Select Internet Options from the Tools menu in IE (Figure 8-37).

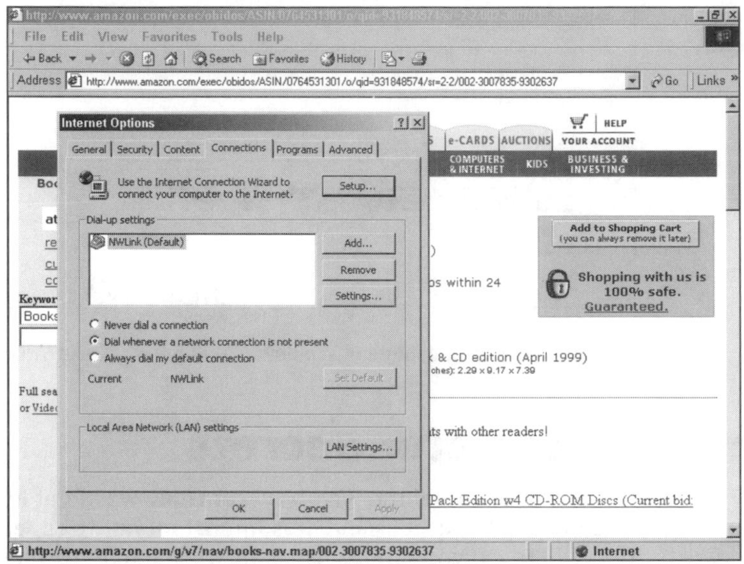

Figure 8-37: Internet Options — Connections

Step 2. Select the LAN Settings button.

Step 3. Select the Use a proxy server checkbox.

Step 4. Select the Advanced button. The Proxy Settings dialog box will appear.

Step 5. Complete all of the fields with the appropriate Proxy Server IP address (or host name) and Port value (see Figure 8-38). You may also select the Use the same proxy server for all protocols checkbox after populating the HTTP field to auto-populate each of the remaining fields except the Socks field. Click OK. You will be returned to the Local Area Network (LAN) Settings dialog box.

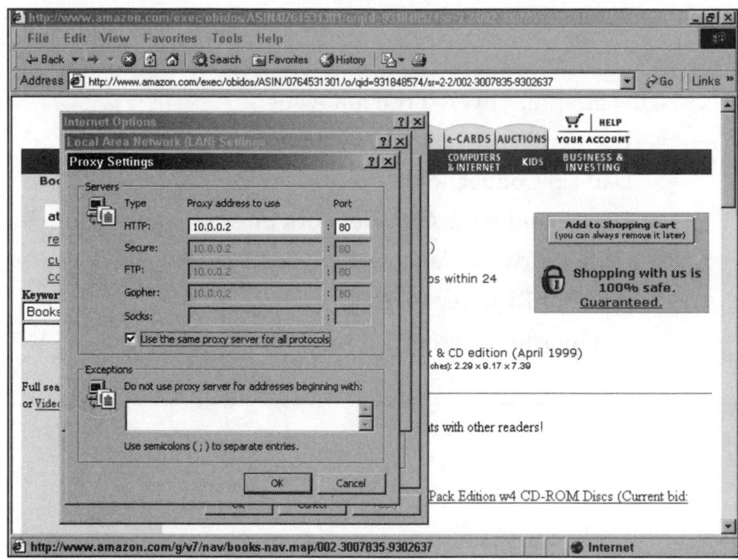

Figure 8-38: Proxy Settings dialog box

Step 6. Click OK. You will be returned to the Internet Options dialog box.

Step 7. Click OK. You will be returned to IE. You must close and open IE for the new changes to take effect.

It is common to only configure the HTTP setting in the Proxy Settings dialog box when using a proxy server on a network with IE. But many sites use HTTPS, which is the Secure field on the Proxy Settings dialog box. If the Secure field is left blank, you cannot access sites such as online stock brokerages. And that was exactly the problem at the law firm. Once I "fixed" the Secure field in IE's Proxy Settings, the legal administrator was once again able to manage the law firm's money. That was an important victory for me, the Windows NT Server consultant.

The Proxy client configuration in Microsoft Small Business Server (SBS) leaves the Secure field blank (even though it populates the remaining Type fields in the Proxy Settings dialog box). So if you want to access HTTPS sites on an SBS client, you will need to manually configure the Secure setting on your IE browsers. SBS is discussed in Chapter 16 of this book.

Summary

This chapter covered the following:

- Configuring Remote Access Service
- Dial-Up Connection
- Digital and Wide Area Network Internet connections
- Virtual Private Networks
- Internet Explorer secrets
- Configuring Internet Explorer for Proxy Server and HTTPS (Secure)

Part III

Windows 2000 Server Administration

Chapter 9

The Daily Dozen

In This Chapter

- Verifying your Windows 2000 Server network is protected from viruses
- Performing tape backups and verifying backups via test restores
- Observing Windows 2000 Server system health
- Managing users, groups, and computers
- Verifying day-to-day security needs are met
- Creating drive mappings to allow access to server-based resources
- Monitoring user logon and logoff status
- Verifying network, Internet, and Web site connectivity
- Performing necessary software and hardware additions
- Providing end-to-end support for end users
- Using the Windows 2000 Server/MCSE Toolkit
- Documenting your network via the network notebook

Let's face it. As a Windows 2000 Server professional, in whatever role you serve (be it IS manager, network engineer, administrator, consultant, candlestick maker, butcher, or baker), you're only as good as your last completed task. That's show biz and life with Windows 2000 Server. Many times, you'll be eaten up and spat out, as it were. But this chapter can help mitigate the harsh realities of Windows 2000 Server infrastructure deployment and management.

At this point, I assume you have a functional Windows 2000 Server. The approach I take to save both your skin and sanity with Windows 2000 Server is to narrow down to a one-page checklist the top items you likely will encounter on a daily basis as you manage Windows 2000 Server. Now granted, not every day you will see each and every item listed in Table 9-1, but on any given day, you may be subject to at least half of the items on the Daily Dozen Checklist. In all likelihood, you'll be subject to the remaining items the next day or the day after. You get the point.

Table 9-1 The Daily Dozen Checklist

Item	*Description*	*Comments*	*Completed*
1	Virus Detection		
2	Tape Backup/Restore		
3	System Health		
4	Adding Users/Groups/Computers		
5	Security (Sharing, NTFS)		
6	Mapping Drives		
7	Logon/Logoff Status		
8	Verifying Connectivity		
9	Add/Remove Software and Hardware		
10	End User Support		
11	Using Windows 2000 Server/MCSE Toolkit		
12	Updating Network Notebook		

Before jumping into the details where I describe, at length, each item on the Daily Dozen Checklist, I'd like to share with you how I created this list. In large part, this list is based on my prior Secrets title (*Microsoft Windows NT Secrets, Option Pack Edition,* IDG Books Worldwide, ISBN 0-7645-3130-1). And based on your feedback and changing world conditions, I reordered several Daily Dozen list items, such as placing virus detection first. Next, I took an in-depth and critical look at Windows 2000 Server to better understand what should be emphasized each day and which areas demand less frequent attention. Those areas of lesser need or lower frequency constitute the following chapter (Chapter 10). Finally, I realize as well as you that many of our best and worst experiences with Windows 2000 Server still await us. It's a young product with its own strengths, weaknesses, opportunities, and threats. And who knows, perhaps this list will grow to become the Daily Two Dozen in the next edition!

And for those advanced Windows 2000 professionals among us, there's something in this chapter for them, too. On the surface, the dozen points seem simple and so obvious. But if such is the case, why do so few of us actually perform these tasks on a regular and consistent basis? Let me put it another way: If you don't consider standardizing your Windows 2000 Server administration, your competitor will.

Step 1: Virus Detection

My, how the world has changed. It wasn't long ago when virus detection, while always important, was considered something of a monthly task. That was until early 1999, by my estimates, when a combination of foreign hostilities and anti-Microsoft sentiments seemed to converge, resulting in an almost daily outbreak of computer network viruses. And it is for that reason that I have placed virus detection as my new number one on the Daily Dozen Checklist.

It is in the virus detection area that Windows 2000 Server is most vulnerable. Namely, a lot of evil people have the motive to hurt Microsoft products (many people simply don't like Microsoft). And any security expert will tell you that motive reigns supreme when it comes to committing a crime. Second, Windows 2000 Server provides virus detection capabilities.

To protect your Windows 2000 Server from computer viruses, please consider the following steps that include acquiring and deploying a third-party virus protection solution; closing virus entry points; deploying virus protection at the server, workstation, and application levels; and performing ad-hoc virus detection application data file updates.

Third-party virus protection applications

Because Windows 2000 Server doesn't provide virus protection out of the box, you need to purchase a virus protection solution. There are numerous virus protection products on the market today and you can find these by searching on the Internet using a search engine such as Infoseek and searching on keywords such as "virus protection."

I've used the following virus protection products and can attest that each provides at least basic virus protection.

- **Computer Associates InoculateIT:** InoculateIT is an old favorite from an enterprise-savvy vendor, Computer Associates (see Figure 9-1). You may not know that Computer Associates made its name in the big iron world and more recently has started to provide solutions for the client/server community. That paradigm typically is evident in their products and pricing. The pluses include that InoculateIT is an established virus protection product. The negatives that I've seen include that the telephone support is on a callback basis, and I average 72-hour callback times. I also have noticed that the virus detection data files (DAT) for InoculateIT aren't updated as quickly as they are with the next two vendors that I mention. Call it a pet peeve, but it's becoming a more critical concern with the increasingly rapid deployment of viruses in our world.

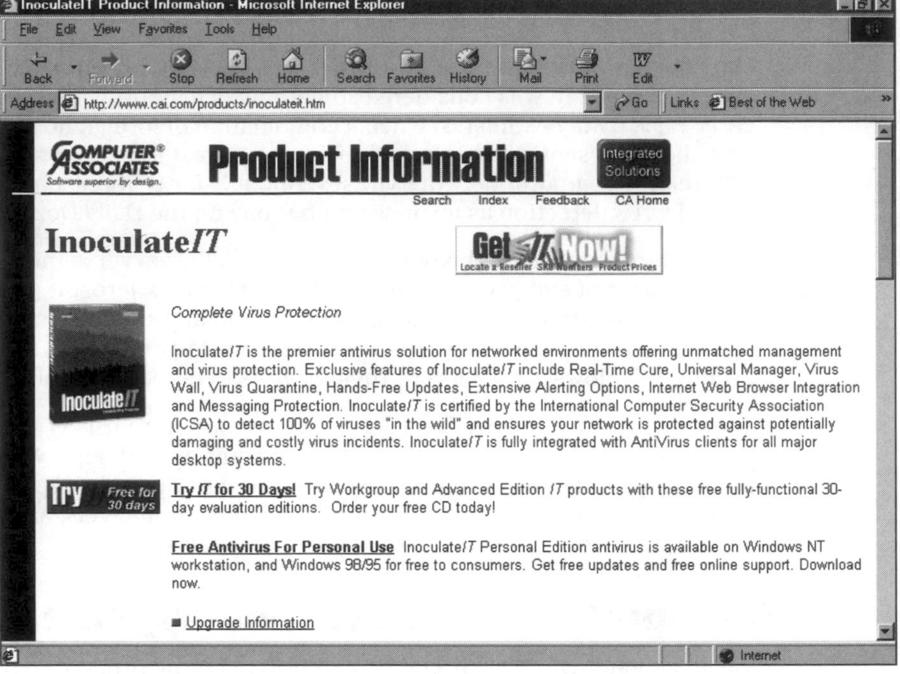

Figure 9-1: InoculateIT

- **Symantec Norton AntiVirus:** A product of the personal computer generation, Norton (see Figure 9-2) is especially strong at the desktop. High marks, in my humble opinion, to Norton for its rapid DAT file updates and ongoing research on viruses. I have used Norton's virus protection application with great results.
- Network Associates' **McAfee VirusScan:** This well-known virus protection application is perhaps best known for being a free application loaded on your new Dell workstation (see Figure 9-3). In fact, it has been my experience that many people who are pleased with the free desktop McAfee application purchase the McAfee server version. I've been pleased especially with McAfee's ability to find and cure Word macro-based viruses when other virus protection applications haven't.

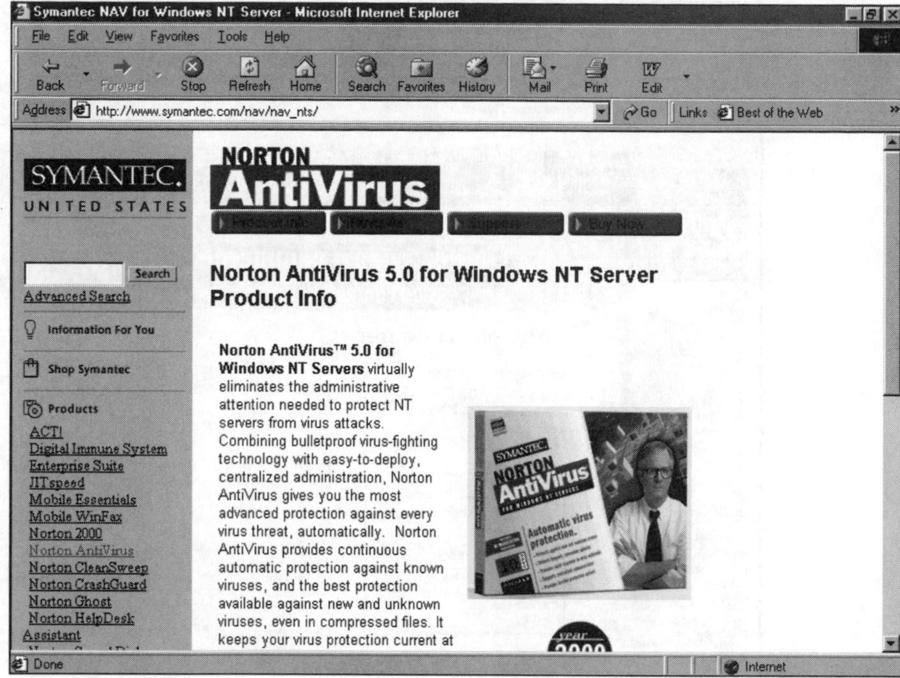

Figure 9-2: Norton AntiVirus

Want to save your job? Then follow this sage advice. At some of my most paranoid sites, I've implemented redundant virus detection approaches with great success. These approaches include running two major virus detection applications at the server level or running one brand of virus detection application at the server and one brand at the workstations. The results have been wonderful. One brand of virus detector detects and cures a certain virus and then, days later, it's vice-versa. Strange but true, and such extra effort undoubtedly will come back to benefit you — like saving your job because you prevented a massive virus attack on your Windows 2000 Server network.

More on the dual virus protection strategy: If you had to stare eye to eye with a CEO and defend your virus protection practices, wouldn't you want to demonstrate that you went beyond what was reasonable and beyond the call of duty? You bet! The downside of this strategy is that it is taxing to your Windows 2000 Server and desktops.

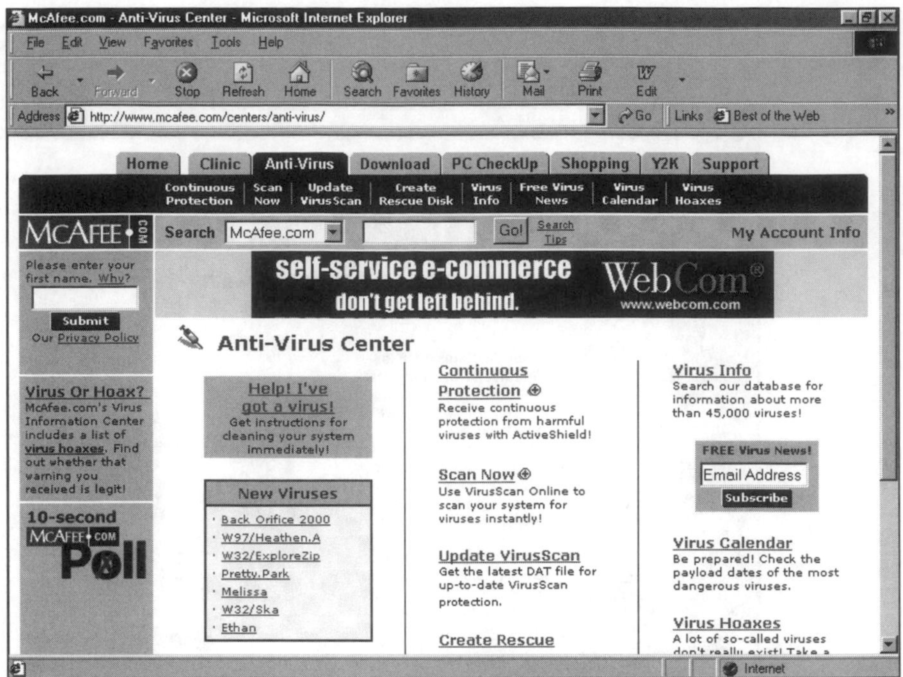

Figure 9-3: McAfee

Many end users may complain when you run a single virus protection application on their workstations. Factor in the uproar if you run two virus protection applications.

Another dual virus detection approach is to run one brand on the server and another brand on the desktop. This has been successful for some of the same reasons already presented. That is, one vendor can detect a virus that the other can't. Also, on occasion, it has been a money saver. Buy the server side and get the client side for free when you purchase a major brand name desktop computer, such as Dell.

One more point about dual virus detection strategies. Each vendor releases its respective DAT files on different days, depending on world events, the position of the moon, whether the chief developer had a fight at home, and so on. In short, the release dates for DAT files are random. Yet, you depend on updated DAT files to protect you from any one of 500 new viruses plaguing the world daily. Since an outdated DAT file renders your virus protection application worthless and the DAT file release dates are random, you truly need to consider a multivendor approach when deploying your virus protection so as to remove some of the randomness associated with virus protection today. Essentially, you attempt to close the window of virus vulnerability.

Closing virus entry points

It's a known fact that viruses enter organizations via one of a few entry points. Viruses rarely are created and released within an organization. The three main virus entry points are Internet activity, floppy disks, and disgruntled employees.

- **Internet:** Over the Internet, the common transport for virus is e-mail attachments. Downloads from suspect sites are a problem as well. To combat this, make sure your virus protection applications scans incoming and outgoing e-mails (including attachments) for virus infections.
- **Floppy Disks:** Floppy disks, while not the primary cause of computer infections today, still (unwittingly) play a role. More often than not, a floppy disk virus carrier is the result of an employee seeking to work at home. Said employee uses floppy disks to carry documents and spreadsheets to and from work. At home, the employee's PC has virus, perhaps because a teenager has been engaging in some unsafe computing. When these conditions exist, bingo, you now have a virus on your computer network.

Three factors help to minimize floppy disk-based virus infections. First, Windows 2000 networks have robust support for virtual private networks, so a home-based employee can attach to the company network via the Internet and take advantage of Windows 2000 Server and its Terminal Server implementation. Second, more and more companies use thin clients (Net PCs) to attach to Windows 2000 Server's Terminal Server application. As you may know, a thin client doesn't have a floppy drive locally. Finally, some companies, concerned about viruses as much as floppy diskette-based data theft, deploy workstations without local floppy drives. All of these methods are effective deterrents in stymieing floppy disk-based viruses.

- **Disgruntled Employees:** The deliberate act of sending a virus is always a threat when dealing with disgruntled employees. Such employees can get very creative, such as disabling virus protection on their machines, thereby allowing the introduction of a virus onto your network. This is perhaps your greatest virus protection challenge.

Three levels of virus protection

In the political circles of Washington D.C., it's called triangulation. In horse racing, it's a trifecta. In baseball, it's a triple. Call it what you like, but when it comes to virus protection on your Windows 2000 Server network, each and every day you should make sure you have at least three levels of virus protection: server, workstation, and application.

Server

I've discussed server-based virus protection products. Your daily challenge is to make sure such protection is up and running. Are infected files being cured, or are you simply being notified of infected files? Remember that notification demands your attention. You must read and respond accordingly to the virus-detection notices. Are infected files being quarantined? Are all files being checked, not just program files? It's critical that you check all files in order to detect Word macro viruses. Each server product I mention has some form of realtime monitoring, such as the Realtime Manager in InoculateIT (see Figure 9-4).

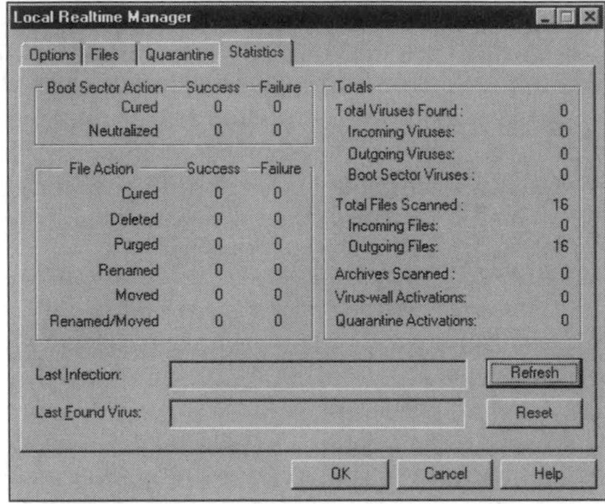

Figure 9-4: Realtime Manager

Workstation

Again, as previously mentioned, McAfee ships on many popular workstation brands such as Dell. So far, so good. But it's been my experience that many people don't manage their desktop virus protection very well. There are four major concerns here. First, is the virus protection even running (both at startup and in realtime)? With McAfee, you can easily tell if it's working realtime by observing the red "V" character on the left side of your desktop taskbar. Second, is your desktop virus protection application scanning for all files? By default, programs such as McAfee only scan for program files, but should be set to scan for all files (see Figure 9-5). Scanning only program files does nothing to fight Word macro viruses or other cleverly disguised viruses.

Third, is the desktop virus protection application receiving current DAT file updates from the Mother Ship? I've observed many sites that diligently keep the server virus protection application DAT files current at the expense of letting the workstation DAT files age. This renders the workstation's virus protection application worthless in short order.

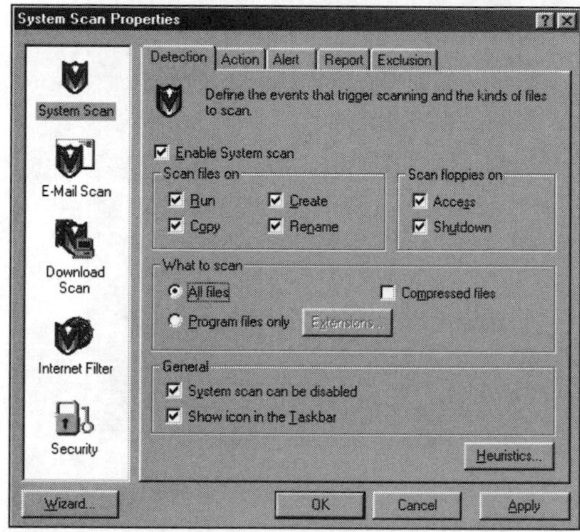

Figure 9-5: Scan for all files

Fourth, have you turned on the desktop virus protection application's bells and whistles? Notice in Figure 9-5 that there are options for e-mail and Internet download scanning. Take a few moments both to learn and effectively deploy these advanced features. Who knows? Your future employment may depend on it.

Applications

I end the virus protection discussion by returning to the Open Systems Interconnection (OSI) Layer 7 — Applications. Huh? Did you know that many of your applications offer limited forms of virus protection? One such application is Microsoft Word, which enables you to detect macro viruses (see Figure 9-6). Another application is Microsoft Excel, which also enables you to detect macro-related viruses (see Figure 9-7).

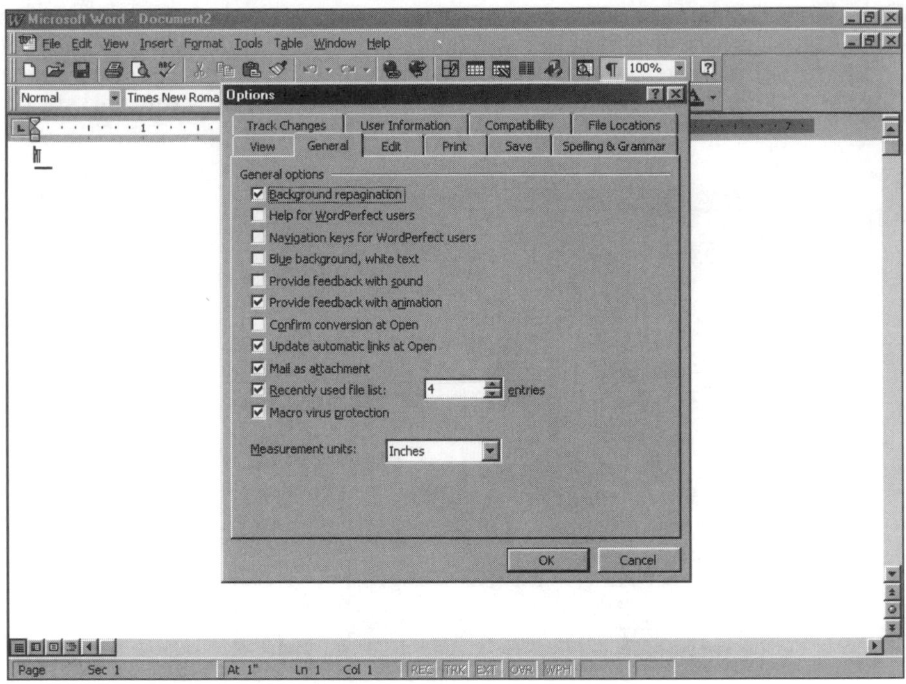

Figure 9-6: Microsoft Word macro virus detection

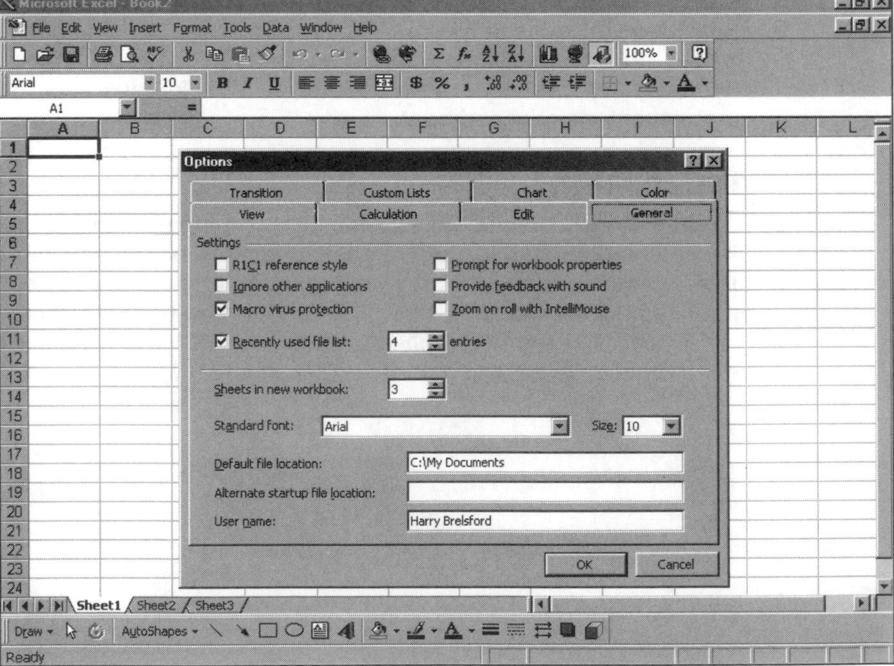

Figure 9-7: Microsoft Excel macro virus detection

Ad-hoc DAT file updates

Perhaps you're reading *USA Today* on the road while staying at a hotel. Maybe you're listening to National Public Radio's "All Things Considered" on the way to work. Or possibly your harmless surfing to `www.cnn.com` for the latest news has allowed you to find out that a new computer virus has descended upon the world. However you find out, your immediate response must be to go manually to your virus protection application vendor's Web site and see if they've released a new DAT file with an appropriate fix. Once the new DAT file is downloaded, it must be deployed at the server and workstation levels. You know the drill. More importantly, it's your job to be alert to such matters. So start reading the paper and listening to news radio! In the future, you may find yourself performing DAT file downloads daily.

Step 2: Tape Backup/Restore

A close second to virus protection is the tape backup and restore function. In fact, you could argue that tape backup and restore is the most important daily task, but that's for another cup of espresso.

You must perform, without fail, a daily backup of your data. That statement goes unchallenged. But first things first. What is data? Where does it get backed up to? What backup application actually backs up the data?

Defining data

Data isn't just the information contained on the proverbial C: drive of your Windows 2000 Server machine. Data is defined more completely as:

- Files and folders stored on the server's hard disks. This typically includes the information stored on your Windows 2000 Server's hard disks.
- E-mail information. This typically includes the Microsoft Exchange Information Store (IS) and Directory Services (DS). If you use another e-mail application, make sure you understand what needs to be backed up.
- Database devices, databases, tables and records. You may be surprised to know that real corporate-strength databases need to perform their own backups, separate from the tape backup program you use.
- Registry. It's critical that you back up the Windows 2000 Server Registry. This is separate from just backing up the `\%systemroot%\WINNT\repair` directory.
- Open file conditions. How are open files backed up? Are user-created open file conditions treated differently than open files conditions created by the Windows 2000 Server operating system?

In short, each of the above data forms need to be honored as part of your Windows 2000 Server daily backup strategy.

Backup media

Now it's time to answer the question of where to back up to. Today, there is an array of supported backup devices that simply didn't exist with Windows NT Server 4.0. These backup devices include tape devices (of course), hard disks, CD drives with write capabilities, optical backup devices, ZIP drives, JAZ drives, and even floppy disks (yeah, right). Tape backups are still preferred over other backup devices, but that may change as the CD media is engineered to handle more and more GBs of stored data.

Backup applications

There are several backup applications to select from for protecting your Windows 2000 Server network. These range from the much improved built-in backup program to tried-and-true favorites such as Backup Exec and ARCserveIT to a surprising favorite: Legato NetWorker.

Built-in backup

Talk about an improved application! Backup, also known as the built-in backup application found in the System Tools program group, is a fully functional tape backup program (see Figure 9-8).

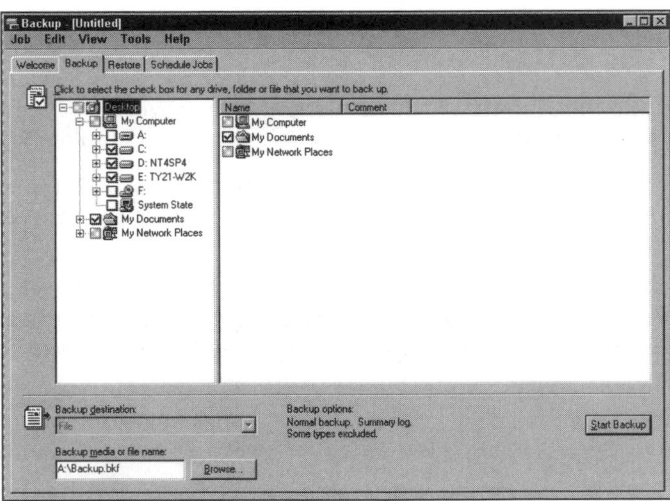

Figure 9-8: Backup

Backup's main improvement is its ability to schedule backups without using the dreaded AT command-line approach. Backup now uses a Calendar, which is real world, with a 30-day view. Very nice.

Another reason that Backup is so improved over the version contained in Windows NT Server 4.0 is that Seagate developed Backup. Don't believe me? Simply select the About Backup menu option from Backup's Help menu and see for yourself.

Using Backup is very intuitive. You simply complete the Backup Wizard on the Welcome tab sheet or use the Backup tab sheet to select the drives and other resources to back up. These other resources include Microsoft Exchange resources. Once you complete your backup selection, you start the backup either immediately or on a schedule. And don't forget to perform a test restore on a weekly basis — at least. It's funny how test restores, the one thing you never seem to have time for, are indeed that one thing that can save your job.

Backup has one fatal flaw that forces you to purchase one of the following third-party backup products. That flaw is the inability to back up Microsoft SQL Server databases. And SQL-based databases are very important resources to back up, right?

Backup Exec

A moment ago, I shared with you that Seagate developed the built-in Backup program found in Windows 2000 Server. It's fair to characterize the built-in backup program as "Backup Exec Lite." Thus, it also is a fair characterization to define Backup Exec (retail version) as "heavy duty" (see Figure 9-9). Without going into the step by step on how to use Backup Exec, I can attest that it is sufficient for any Windows 2000 Server site up to the true enterprise level. The SOHO and medium-sized Windows 2000 Server sites can benefit greatly from considering Backup Exec. Enough said.

Figure 9-9: Backup Exec

In mid-1999, Seagate sold its storage software division (including Backup Exec) to Veritas.

ARCserveIT

A latecomer to the Windows NT party, and ergo, the Windows 2000 Server party, ARCserveIT is best known for its dominating position in the NetWare community. I have just as many sites running ARCserveIT as Backup Exec (literally) with the same level of success. ARCserveIT is a product of Computer Associates (see Figure 9-10).

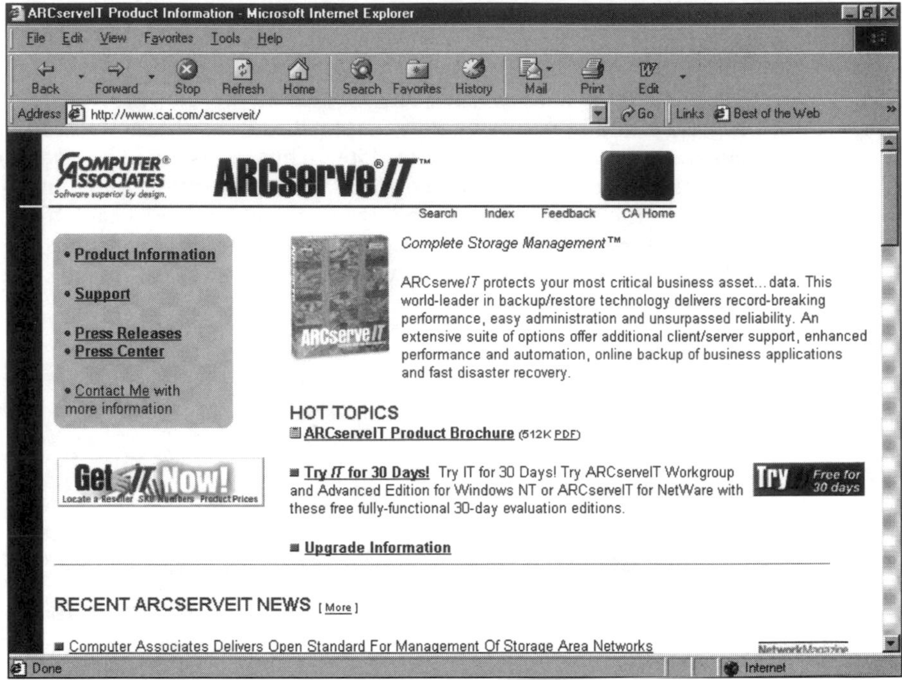

Figure 9-10: ARCserveIT

Legato NetWorker

Ever seen the magazine called *DuPont Registry*? It's a magazine dedicated to the lifestyles of the rich and famous. The underlying theme is that if you have to ask, you can't afford it. Now let me put a slight twist on the paradigm as I introduce Legato NetWorker. Here is a case of if you have to ask, you probably don't need it! That's because Legato NetWorker is oriented toward enterprise-level backup needs. You won't find it on the shelves at CompUSA. Rather, if you work with Windows 2000 Server at the true enterprise level, you probably already know that pedestrian products such as Backup Exec and ARCserveIT probably can't meet your mission-critical needs. In that case, it's likely you've already bumped into the Legato family of products, Legato NetWorker in particular (see Figure 9-11).

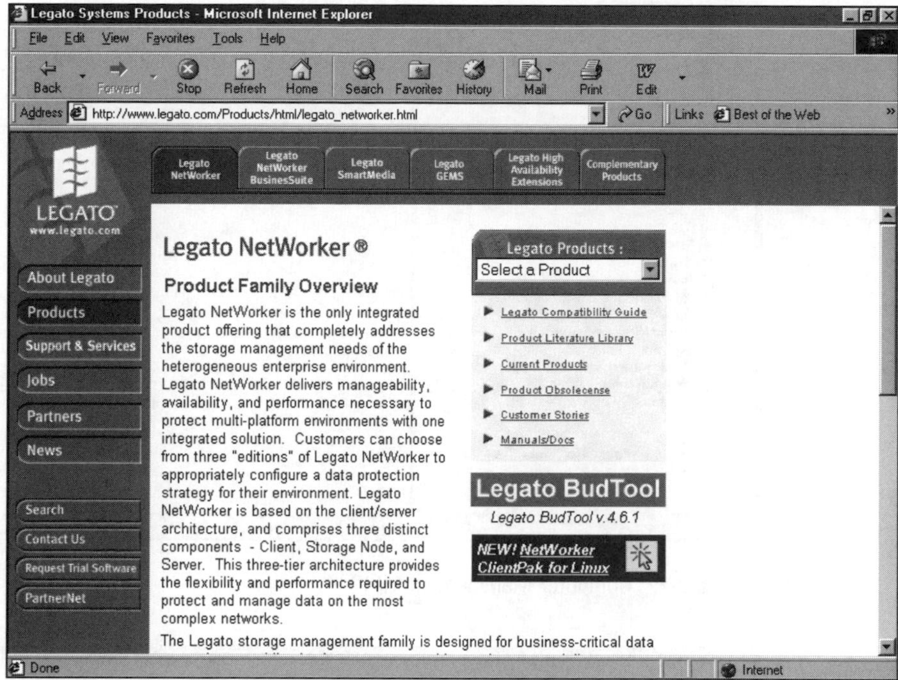

Figure 9-11: Legato NetWorker

Step 3: System Health

I'm happy to report massive system health improvements with Windows 2000 Server. Instead of a widely dispersed set of operating system-related reporting tools from the Windows NT Server 4.0 days, Windows 2000 Server got it right with the Computer Management MMC (see Figure 9-12).

The Computer Management MMC is found via the Administrative Tools program group. Once launched, you have a centralized repository of basic system information, which is extremely valuable at a glance. For your reading pleasure, I've selected the following as my top views from the Computer Management MMC.

- **System Information/System Summary:** At a glance, this view provides basic system information including physical and virtual memory measurements (see Figure 9-13).

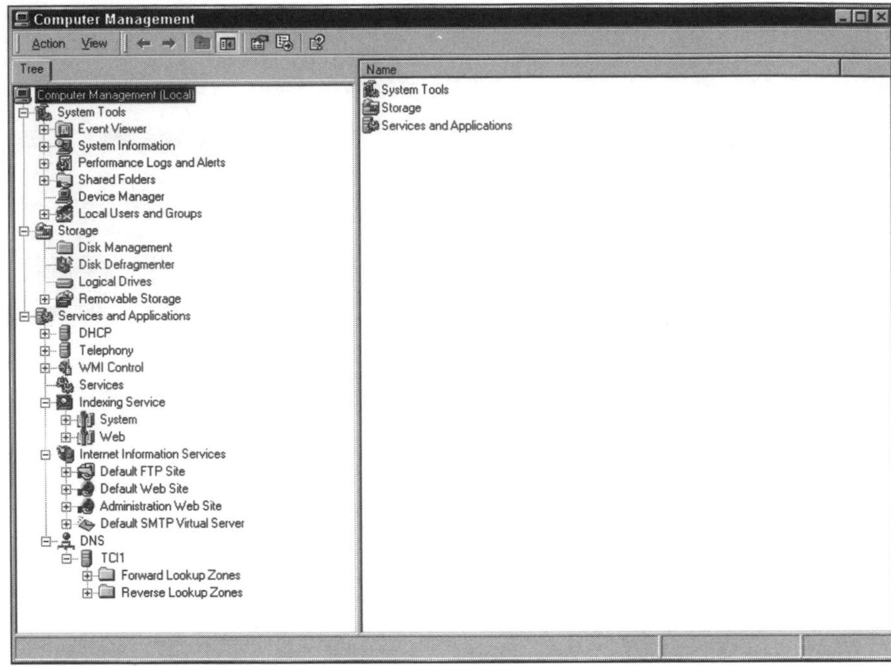

Figure 9-12: Computer Management MMC

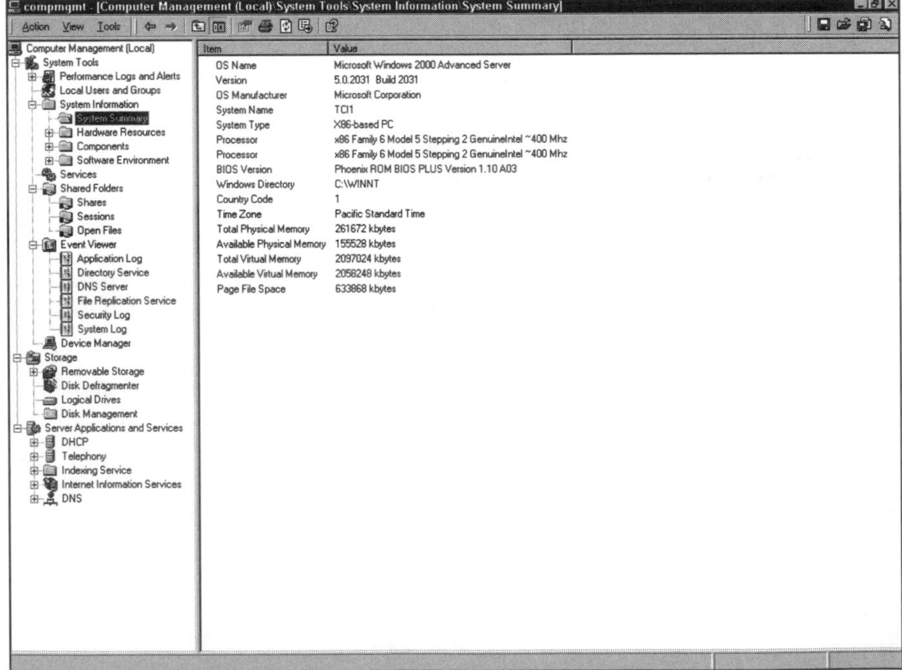

Figure 9-13: System Information/System Summary

- **Services:** This view provides an accounting of which services are running or not, as well as the description of each service is a new and much appreciated feature in Windows 2000 Server (see Figure 9-14).

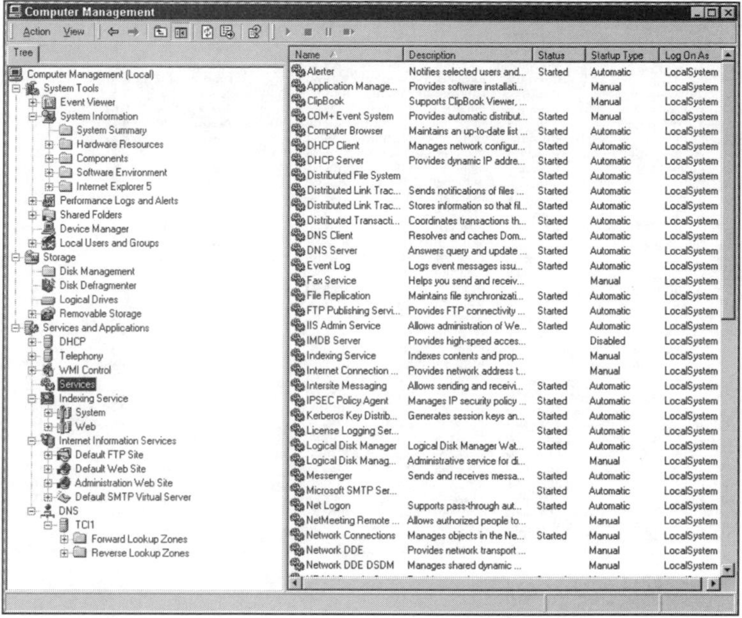

Figure 9-14: Services

You can reorganize the column order when viewing services simply by dragging one column heading to another part of the screen. This is extremely useful when you want to view the service information in the proper order of importance. Here is what I mean. By default, the Description column is to the immediate right of the Name column. But if you want to expand the Description column so that you can read the description (a good idea), then you can't observe the service's Status or Start Up settings. To get the best of all worlds, simply grab the column heading titled Description via your mouse cursor and move it two columns to the right (just to the right of Start Up). Your column order should now read Name, Status, Start Up, and Description. You may display as much of the Description information as you deem meaningful, yet immediately see the Status and Start Up information on the left, closest to the service Name.

- **Event Viewer:** This ole friend from the Windows NT Server days has been greatly improved. Three additional logs have been added: Directory Service (see Figure 9-15), DNS Server, and File Replication Service. For the experienced network professional, it goes without saying how valuable the different logs in Event Viewer are for maintaining your server.

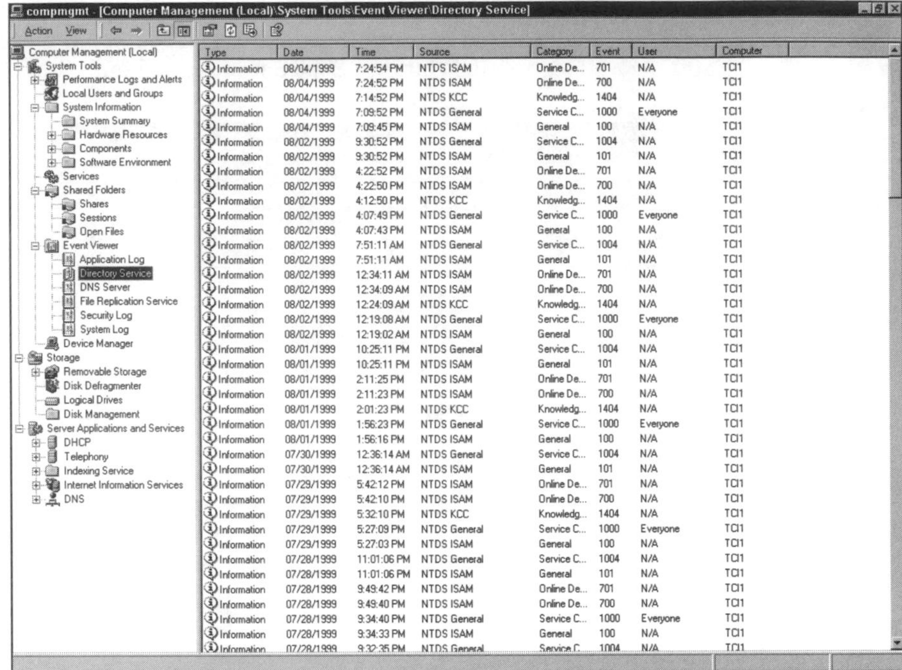

Figure 9-15: Event Viewer

Event Viewer can be configured to open saved logs from other servers, or in my case, other servers at different client sites. First, understand that Event Viewer logs are saved with the `.evt` extension. You can see this by right-clicking any Event Viewer log (for example, Application) and selecting Properties from the secondary menu. Second, right-click the Event Viewer object in the left pane of the Computer Management MMC and select New, Log View. The Add Another Log View dialog box appears. Select the Save radio button and provide the path information to the Event Viewer log you want to open. Click OK and the log opens.

- **Storage/Disk Management:** This is one of my favorite views because I can assess quickly how much free secondary storage space I have, plus the health of the volume (see Figure 9-16).

My goal was to move the Status column next to the Volume column in Disk Management. You cannot do this. The Status column width may be adjusted, but it must remain in the fifth column position.

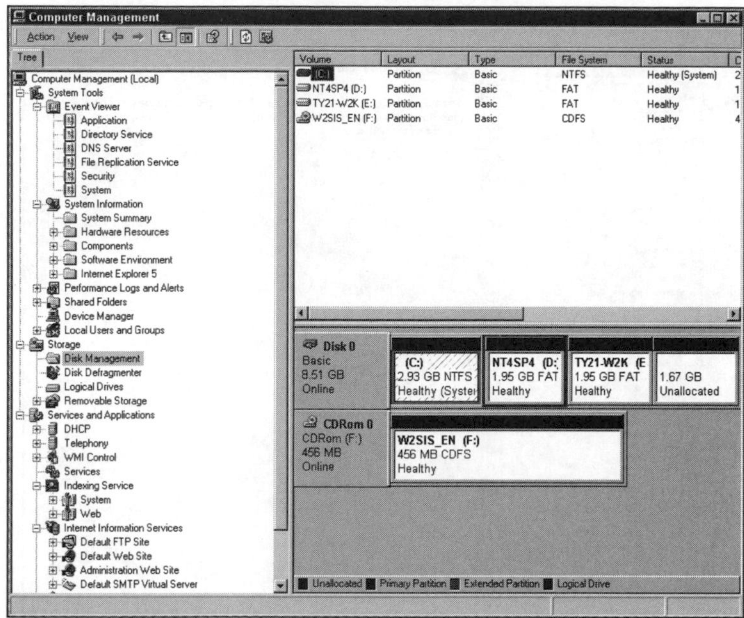

Figure 9-16: Storage/Disk Management

Third-party issues

Windows 2000 Server doesn't live in a vacuum. There are third-party issues related to system health, such as your uninterruptible power supply (UPS). Most UPS manufacturers include PowerChute, a popular UPS monitoring program, with their UPS batteries. Assuming you've installed PowerChute, it's a good idea to look at the PowerChute UPS Monitoring application each day to make sure the battery is charged and your site is receiving clean power. You may notice that Windows 2000 Server has no native UPS monitoring application. Such an application was present in Windows NT Server 4.0 but was dropped with Windows 2000 Server.

Step 4: Adding Users, Groups, and Computers

Talk about a paradigm shift. The management of users and groups has changed dramatically in Windows 2000 Server. First, it's up, up, and away with User Manager for Domains from the Windows NT Server days. Second, if your computer is a domain controller, the Local Users and Groups option doesn't work for you either (see Figure 9-17). So, that leaves you with Active Directory as the only portal for managing users and groups.

Active Directory is discussed at length in Chapters 11 and 12 of this book.

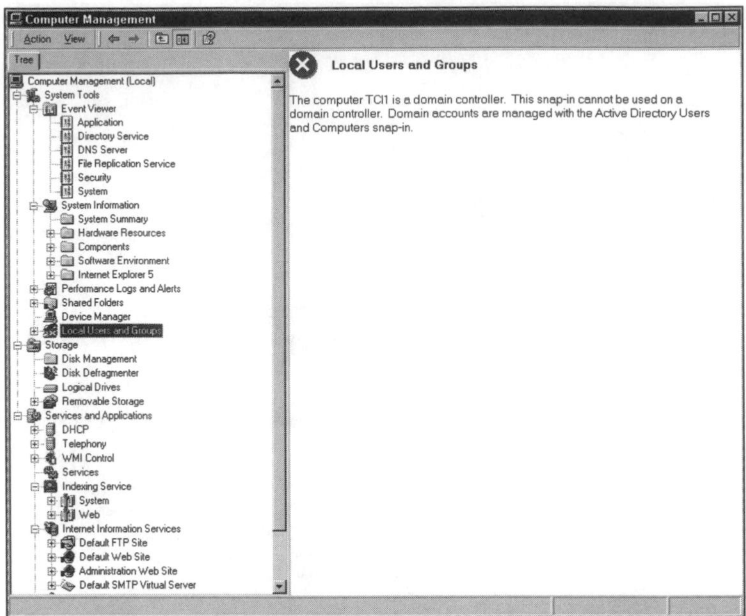

Figure 9-17: Local Users and Groups error message

Adding users

Adding users in Windows 2000 Server is very easy. Follow these steps:

STEPS:

Adding a user

Step 1. Select the Active Directory Users and Computers menu option from the Administrative Tools program group.

Step 2. Observe the domain listed in the left pane (for example, `main.local`). Right-click the domain object and select New ⇨ User from the secondary menu (see Figure 9-18).

Step 3. The New Object - User dialog box appears (see Figure 9-19). On the first screen, you provide the basic First, Last, and User logon names. Click Next.

The Downlevel or pre-Windows 2000 logon name is the user's logon name associated with computers running pre-Windows 2000 operating systems, such as Windows NT Server 4.0 or earlier. This file is populated automatically for you.

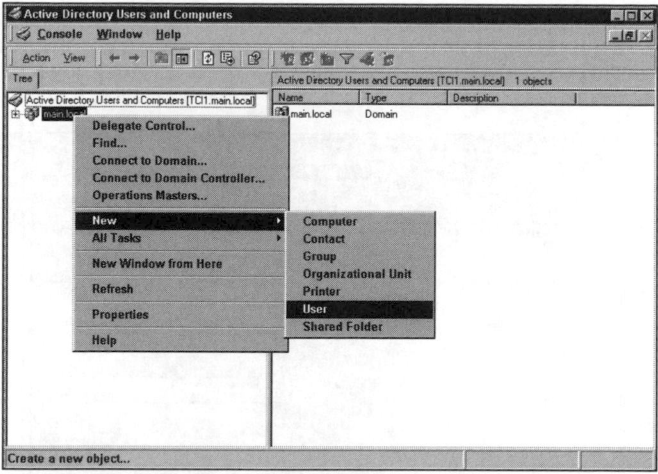

Figure 9-18: New ➪ User secondary menu option

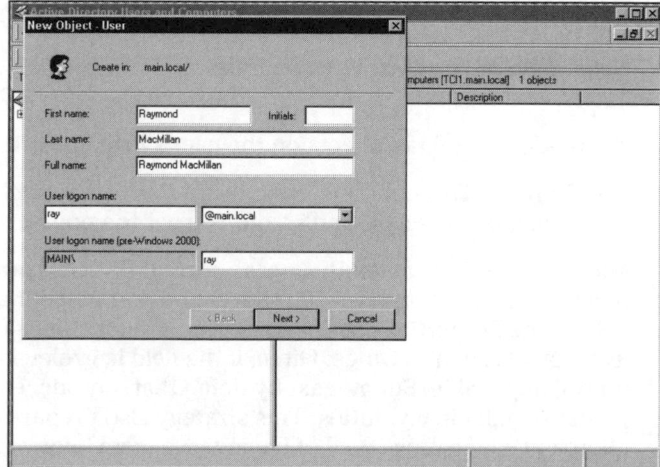

Figure 9-19: New Object - User

Step 4. The next screen asks you for a password and basic password settings. Complete and click Next.

Always have a password with mixed case (at least one capitalized letter) and mixed alphanumeric (at least one number).

Step 5. The next screen allows you to review your user setting before actually creating the user. Click Finish. You now have an added user to your Windows 2000 Server environment.

Once a user is created, you actually manage the users by selecting Properties from the user secondary menu (found when you right-click a user name). This displays the Properties for the user (see Figure 9-20).

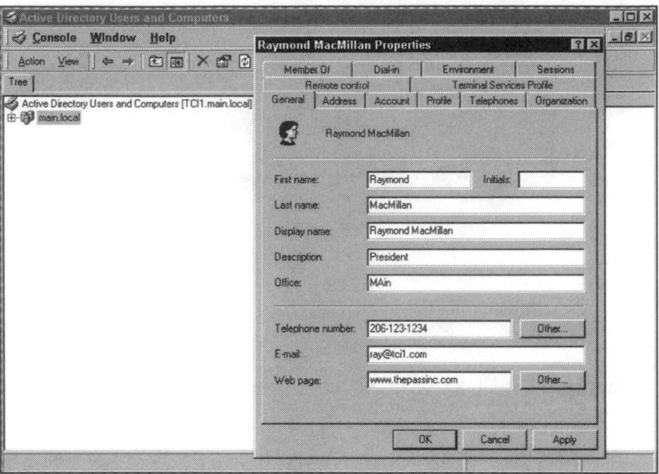

Figure 9-20: Raymond MacMillan Properties

There are several tab sheets on the user's Properties dialog box.

- **General:** This contains basic user information such as First Name, Last Name, Department, and so on. You get the point.

Mind if I steal from Small Business Server (SBS) best practices for a moment? I recommend as a Windows 2000 Server best practice that you populate each field in the Properties box for each user. That includes field you normally may leave blank, such as Office. Often, if the field is irrelevant, I simply type "N/A" for not applicable. But at least by doing that, my successors know that I wasn't derelict in my duties. This strategy also prepares your site for Microsoft's long-range goal of having true meta-information. The basic user information you enter here is used across the full BackOffice family and by other vendors' software applications.

- **Address:** You enter basic address information on this screen.
- **Account:** You may modify the account name, account options, logon hours, and account expiration, as well as which computers to allow logons from.
- **Profile:** Enter user profile, home directory, and shared documents folder. The shared documents folder — network path is a new feature in Windows 2000 Server that allows you to point to the user's shared data storage location.

- **Dial-In**: You set the rights to allow either dial-in or VPN access here. The default denies access.
- **Member Of:** This displays the groups of which the user is a member.
- **Organization:** This allows you to enter internal organizational information, such as manager name and direct reporting relationships.
- **Terminal Services Profile:** This is used to configure the user's Terminal Services profile. Items include allow logon to terminal server and setting the local path.
- **Remote Control:** This allows you to configure Terminal Server remote control settings.
- **Environment:** This allows you to configure the Terminal Services startup environment. Settings include startup programs and file and printer redirection.

The ability to redirect local activity such as client-side file management and printing is new to Terminal Services in Windows 2000 Server. In the past, you had to purchase Citrix Metaframe to take advantage of such features. Metaframe accomplished this via its ICA protocol. The cost savings are tremendous. Metaframe often matched or exceeded the cost of Windows NT – Terminal Server in the pre-Windows 2000 Server days.

- **Sessions:** This allows you to configure Terminal Services timeout and reconnection settings. This is critical when using Terminal Services. For example, if you are running database software that end users access via a Terminal Services session, and that database performs posting operations such month-end postings, then you would want the Terminal Services session to continue even if you experienced a disconnect. My company uses this feature for tax accountants preparing tax returns from home. The reason? If a disconnect occurs during the tax preparation session, all of that tax data isn't lost. The tax account simply reconnects and is taken back to the exact spot when the disconnection occurred.
- **Telephones**: You can enter standard telephone contact information here (home, work fax), as well as enter an IP Phone value.

So just where is much of the extra contact information described here used in Windows 2000 Server? Well, unfortunately, it's not where you'd like it to be. The need for the information, in my humble opinion, is in the form of a Contact record in Microsoft Outlook connected to Microsoft Exchange. Such is not the case. Rather, the information is retained as you see it on the property sheet and also as part of the user properties in the Microsoft Exchange Global Address list. Thus, the information isn't as meaningful as it could be.

Adding groups

Not surprisingly, adding groups is very similar to adding users. As with the steps for adding a user, simply select New ➪ Group from the secondary menu for the domain object. Once the New Object - Group dialog box is displayed, complete the fields and click OK (see Figure 9-21).

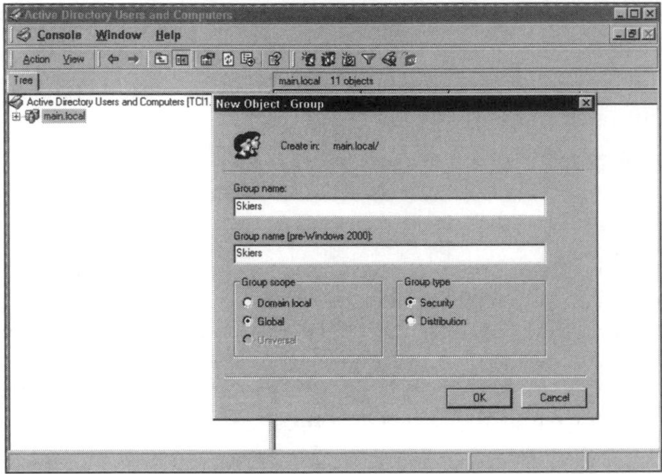

Figure 9-21: Creating a group

The main reasoning behind groups is to manage your network, shall it be said, properly. Remember that it is far easier to assign rights to groups than to try and assign (and manage) rights at the individual user level. It's that simple. Drilling down into the group discussion, you need to distinguish between security and distribution groups.

- **Security:** A security group is used to manage network security. Note that e-mails can be sent, in a broadcast fashion, to security groups.
- **Distribution:** This typically is a group of internal users that are organized under one group title for purposes of sending e-mail. You may not apply security rights to a distribution group.

Under the Windows 2000 Server environment, a distribution group can contain only users that participate in the Windows 2000 security model (have a logon name and password). This type of distribution group cannot contain custom recipients that are outside of the networks (such as those you might place in a Microsoft Exchange Global Address List). You may recall that in Microsoft Exchange, you easily can add external e-mail recipients to a distribution list, such as the Global Address List, by first creating a custom recipient.

A group may be changed from distribution to security and vice-versa in Windows 2000 Server native mode. Such changes are not possible when Windows 2000 Server is in mixed mode.

You are able to select from three group scopes: universal, global, and domain local.

- **Universal:** This is the broadest type of group. It may contain user accounts, global groups, and even other universal groups from any Windows 2000 domain in the forest.

A domain must be configured for native mode to allow the creation of security groups with universal scopes.

- **Global:** May contain user accounts and other global groups within the domain. From other domains, the global group may contain only user accounts. Global groups may be granted permissions to all domains in a forest irrespective of the location of the global group.
- **Domain Local:** This is similar to local groups in the Windows NT Server days. In native mode, this group may contain user accounts, global groups, and universal groups from any domain in the forest. Interestingly, you also may include local groups from the same domain. Call it embedded local groups. In mixed mode, domain local groups may contain global groups and user accounts from any domain.

Remember the old MCSE trick on the Windows NT Server Enterprise exam of "Users go into Global groups, which are placed in Local groups, which are assigned the Rights"? This was memorized as a simple mnemonic phrase: UGLR. Well, it's back in a varied form in Windows 2000 Server. The group planning strategy in Windows 2000 Server is that you assign users to global groups that are placed in domain local groups, which are assigned permissions. UGLR has become A-G-DL-P.

What about changing groups from something other than their respective universal, global, or domain local status? The bottom line is any group can be changed to universal when Windows 2000 Server is in native mode.

Adding computers

To create a computer account, select New ⇨ Computer from the domain's secondary menu. The New Object - Computer dialog box is displayed (see Figure 9-22). Type in a computer name and click OK.

Once you create a computer account, Active Directory replicates it to all other domain controllers within the domain.

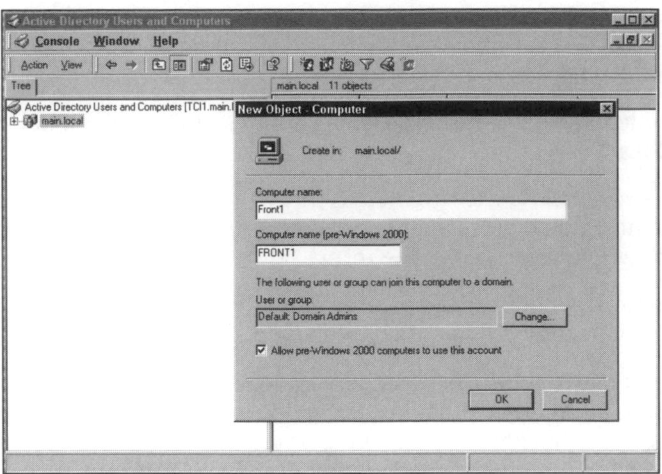

Figure 9-22: Creating a computer

Group policy

To effectively manage your users, groups, and computers on a day-to-day basis, you need to master group policy in Windows 2000 Server. Touted as a way to lower your total cost of ownership (TCO), group policies are an enhanced version of the policies and profiles used in Windows NT Server. In short, group policies allow Windows 2000 administrators to engage in change and configuration management for both users and computers.

Group policies may be set for the following areas:

- **Security:** This includes network, domain, and local security settings.
- **Software Installation:** Group policies are the foundation for IntelliMirror and remote operating system installations. This is a centralized way to manage software updates and removal.
- **Scripts:** User logon and logoff scripts. Machine startup and shutdown scripts. Scripts typically are created in conjunction with the Windows Scripting Host (WSH), another new feature in Windows 2000 Server.
- **Administrative Templates:** This is similar to the Security Configuration Editor (SCE) in the Windows NT Server 4.0 Option Pack. The Group Policy MMC has templates for Windows Components, Start Menu and Taskbar, Desktop, Control Panel, Network, and System (see Figure 9-23).
- **Folder Redirection:** This is the ability to store user data on a network for protection and preservation purposes.
- **Anytime, Anywhere:** If a user moves, the data, settings, and applications follow. This typically is known as *user settings management.*

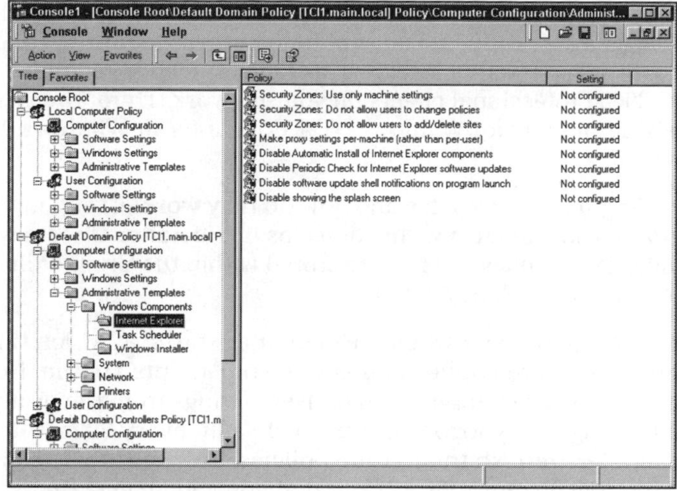

Figure 9-23: Group Policy MMC

STEPS:

To use Group Policy MMC

Step 1. From the Run dialog box (via the Start Menu), type **MMC** and click OK. The MMC launches.

Step 2. Select Console ➪ Add/Remove Snap-in. The Add/Remove Snap-in dialog box appears.

Step 3. Select the Add button. The Add Standalone Snap-in dialog box appears.

Step 4. Select Group Policy in the Snap-in list. Click Add. The Select Group Policy Object dialog box appears.

Step 5. The Local Computer Group Policy Object is selected by default. By clicking Browse, you also may select the Default Domain Policy and Default Domain Controllers Policy. Make your selections and click Finish.

Step 6. Select Close at the Add Standalone Snap-in dialog box. You now have configured the Group Policy MMC for use.

You may not be aware that using Windows 2000 Server's group policy capabilities is tricky stuff. You must adhere to these following conditions. First, you must have Active Directory installed. Second, you must have Windows 2000 Professional clients on your network. Third, there is absolutely no support for Windows NT 4.*x* or earlier or Windows 9*x* clients. Ouch!

So where do group policies live and how do they work? Group policies live within group policy objects within domains in the Active Directory. More specifically, group policy objects are stored within the Group Policy Container and Group Policy Template.

Group policies go to work when the computer starts, at which time the computer settings are applied and any startup scripts are run. Next, the user logon triggers the application of user settings from the group policy plus the running of any logon scripts. By default, every 90 minutes the client computers refresh their group policies. This refresh rate is five minutes for domain controllers. Note that you can change these refresh times by modifying settings in the Administrative Templates.

So how do you apply group policies? Follow these steps (I assume that you've created a Group Policy MMC as outlined earlier) that start with group policy object creation and end with a test logon.

STEPS:

Group Policy Object (GPO) creation

Step 1. From the Administrative Tools program group, launch Active Directory Users and Computers.

Step 2. In the left pane, right-click the Active Directory container where you want to create a GPO. This object can be the domain or an organizational unit (OU).

Step 3. Select Properties from the secondary menu.

Step 4. Select the Group Policy tab sheet.

Step 5. Click New and provide a name (for example, General TCI Policy) for the GPO (see Figure 9-24).

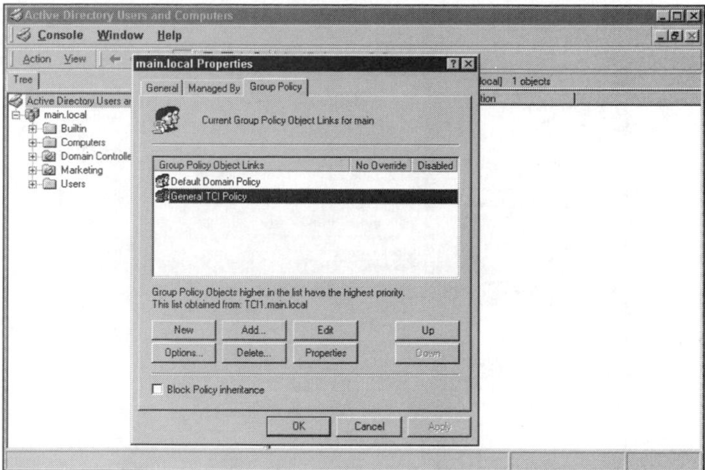

Figure 9-24: GPO creation

Step 6. Press Enter and then Close. The GPO is created.

You must be a member of the Enterprise Admins group in order to create a GPO.

Now, edit the group policy for this GPO by selecting Edit. An MMC will launch that displays the GPO object and the GPO's explicit Computer Configuration and User Configuration selections. (This is the same view as seen earlier when you created a Group Policy MMC.) Modify the group policy as you see fit. For example, you might modify the Disable Task Manager policy under User Configuration, Administrative Templates, System, and Logon/Logoff (see Figure 9-25). Now, a user to whom this group policy applies is still able to use the Task Manager if the Disable Task Manager policy is disabled.

Did you catch the double-negative speak going on with group policy configuration? Remember from your boarding-school mathematics courses that two negatives multiplied equal a positive value. Such is the case with many group policy settings. If you disable a group policy that indeed was designed to disable something, you effectively have allowed the behavior to occur. Get it?

To save the modifications to the group policy, simply close the Group Policy MMC.

You now must apply the GPO as you see fit. This is accomplished by selecting Properties when the GPO (for example, General TCI Policy) is selected. When the Properties dialog box appears, select the Security tab sheet (see Figure 9-26).

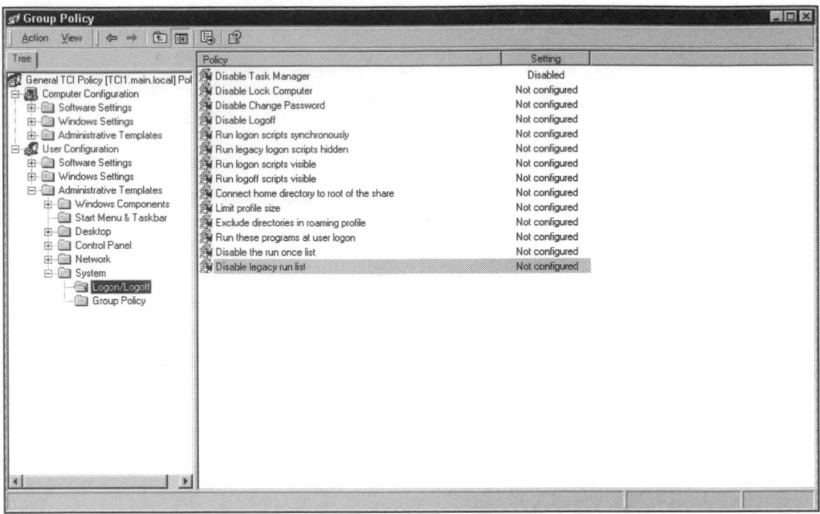

Figure 9-25: Modifying group policy

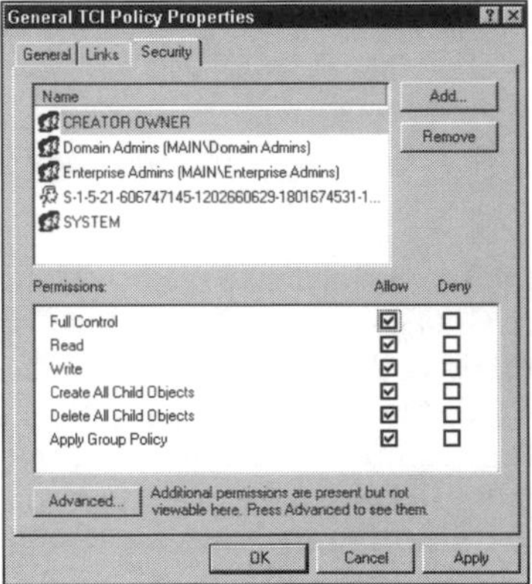

Figure 9-26: Security tab sheet

Notice that Authenticated Users is highlighted by default and that Apply Group Policy in the Permissions section is selected. In English, this communicates that the GPO's group policy settings are applied to every authenticated user in the domain. For giggles, select other names such as Creator Owner and System. Do you notice that the group policy isn't applied? In fact, group policy is only applied to authenticated users by default.

If you want to apply the group policy on a more selective basis than every single authenticated user, follow these steps.

STEPS:

Applying group policy selectively

Step 1. Click Add on the Security tab sheet. The Select Users, Computers, or Groups dialog box appears.

Step 2. Select the specific user or group that you want to apply the group policy to and click Add. The users and groups you select appear in the list of selected names (see Figure 9-27).

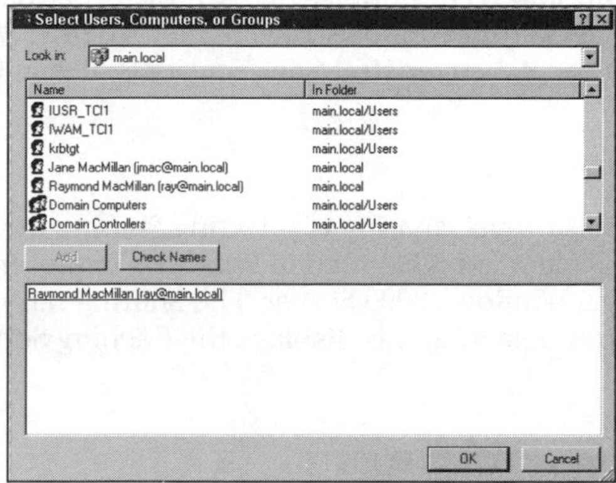

Figure 9-27: Selected names

Step 3. Click OK. Notice that the Names list is updated on the Security tab sheet.

Three final thoughts on group policies for now (although I revisit group policies at other points in the chapter when applicable). First, another way to modify to which individuals group policies apply is to use the Remove button on the Security tab sheet. For example, you can remove Authenticated Users from the mix and then have the policy applied selectively to specific users and groups.

Second, there exists the opportunity to create a pretty intense group policy management matrix here. You can have different GPOs applying radically different group policies to selected users in the same domain by simply creating multiple GPOs that are configured to your liking.

Third, there is the issue of group policy inheritance. Here, you can have multiple GPOs apply to the same group of users (say, Authenticated Users), but the order of operations is determined by the GPO's position in the list of all GPOs (see Figure 9-24). The higher the GPO in the list, the higher its priority.

Be sure to log on as the affected user to test these group policies before you apply them widely to your Windows 2000 Server network. The extra few minutes you spend testing your group policy configuration can not only save you hours later but also allow you to manage your public relations with management and the end users.

Step 5: Security

The good news is, on a day-to-day basis not much has changed in managing security on your Windows 2000 Server network. For all practical purposes, it's still sharing and NTFS permissions. On the other hand, security has changed greatly within Windows 2000 Server when viewed from the strategic or 50,000-foot level. I cover strategic security issues in Chapter 13.

Sharing

At the most basic level, sharing is selecting Sharing from the secondary menu when a folder is highlighted in Windows Explorer. But there is a twist with sharing in Windows 2000 Server. The Sharing tab sheet now contains a Caching button. Selecting this displays the Caching Settings dialog box (see Figure 9-28).

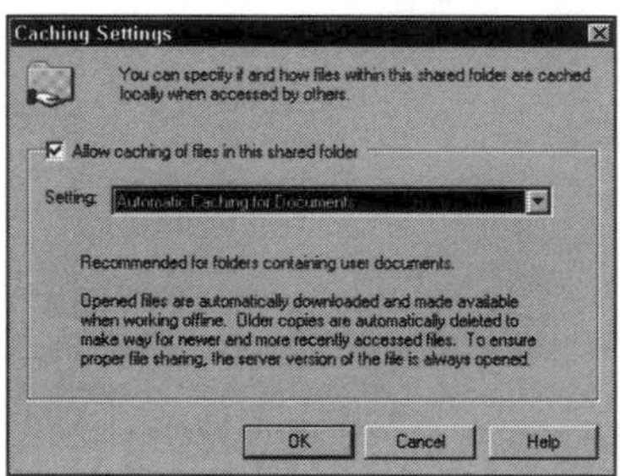

Figure 9-28: Caching

Caching allows you to make files available at the local workstation when the share point on the server is unavailable. This is similar to caching and active caching in Microsoft Proxy Server, where Web pages are returned to the user from a local cache, not the original Internet site. In the case of Microsoft Proxy Server, Web page caching is performed to significantly increase the perception of download times. But it's also done to allow access to Web pages if the host Web server is, for some reason, unavailable. It's the same story with caching network shares and files. There are three caching settings:

- **Manual Caching for Documents:** Users must elect which files they want to be available when they work offline.

- **Automatic Caching for Documents:** Opened files are downloaded from the server automatically and are available when working offline.
- **Automatic Caching for Programs:** This is the least reliable caching method as file availability is promised. Typically used for read-only files.

Doggone it! You still have to create your own hidden shares in Windows 2000 Server. I, like you, had the highest hopes that a hidden share attribute would be available in Windows 2000 Server. It's not. You need to terminate your share name with the dollar sign ($) in order for it to remain hidden from view. Remember that hidden shares often are used as a security measure: out of sight means out of mind.

NTFS security

Same old, same old at the day-to-day level. Using the Security tab sheet, found on the Properties dialog box for either a folder or file on an NTFS partition (see Figure 9-29), you can manage security down to a deep, granular level. Basic NTFS permissions include:

- Full Control
- Modify
- Read & Execute
- List Folder Contents
- Read
- Write

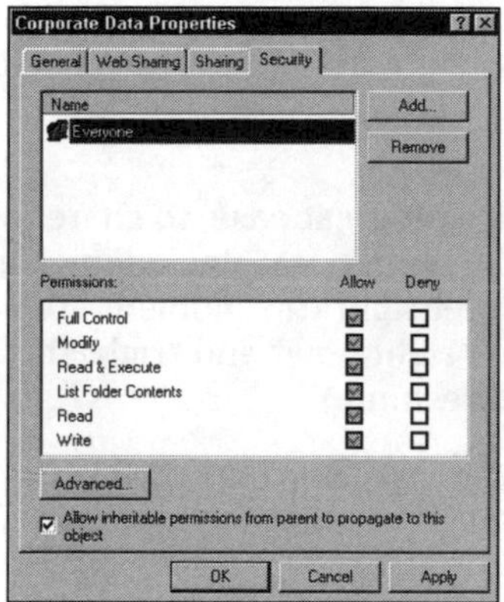

Figure 9-29: Security

The List Folder Contents and the List Folder/Read Data permissions are similar to the Hidden attribute in NetWare. It is here you may allow access to a resource, but keep it invisible to the naked eye.

You also may select special NTFS permissions. These include:

- Traverse Folder/Execute File
- List Folder/Read Data
- Read Attributes
- Read Extended Attributes
- Create Files/Write Data
- Create Folders/Append Data
- Write Attributes
- Write Extended Attributes
- Delete Subfolders and Files
- Delete
- Read Permissions
- Change Permissions
- Take Ownership

You will note that No Access is missing. I discuss that issue in the context of share-level security in this section. As you know, the mechanics for applying specific NTFS permissions are to select a folder or file and apply the permission arrangement you seek. This is the same process as with Windows NT Server 4.0.

Web sharing

This feature is very cool. It allows you, with great ease, to share folders (not files) as Web virtual directories. In other words, imagine telling a user that you'll post a project folder on the intranet right this moment. Remember that end users love to hear phrases such as "right now" and "right this moment." (They somehow find that to be very refreshing.)

To invoke Web sharing, simply select the Web Sharing tab sheet from the property sheet of a folder located on an NTFS volume (see Figure 9-30). Select the Web site on which to share the folder and select the Share this folder radio button. You need to provide an alias name, which by default is the same as the folder name. That's it! A very handy tool indeed.

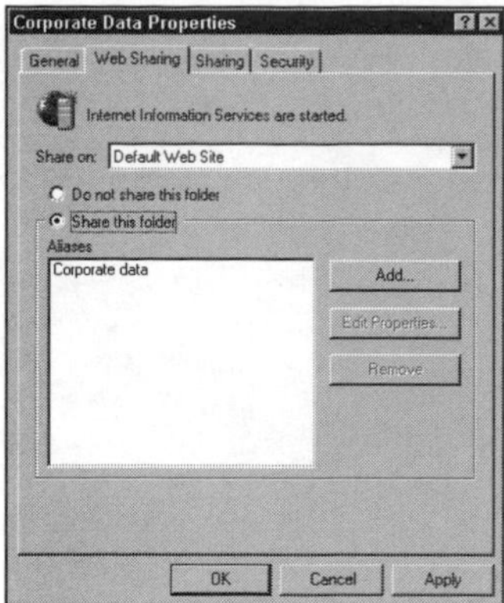

Figure 9-30: Web Sharing

Relationship between NTFS and sharing security

Possibly you are bewildered by the explicit relationship between NTFS security and share-level security. Kindly allow me a few moments to draw out these two security models via compare and contrast.

Partition format

NTFS security may be used only on an NTFS partition. Sharing-level security may be applied to both NTFS and FAT partitions.

First things first

First, you must share a resource for a network user to access it. Simply granting someone NTFS-level permissions to a folder or file without it being shared at some level does not allow access over the network.

If you are logged on locally to the server machine, you do not need to have a resource on the server's local hard disk shared in order to access them. Only the NTFS permissions on an NTFS partition applies. And if you have a FAT partition on the local server machine, a locally logged-on user has complete access to that partition. Ouch!

Masking

The real relationship between NTFS security on an NTFS-formatted partition and sharing permissions can best be seen when you use both. First, you share a resource on a server partition for use by network users.

The share-level permission granted by default in Windows 2000 Server is Full Control for Everyone. These are the same, very generous permissions that also were granted back in the Windows NT Sever 4.0 era.

Aside from Full Control, other share-level permissions include Change and Read (see Figure 9-31).

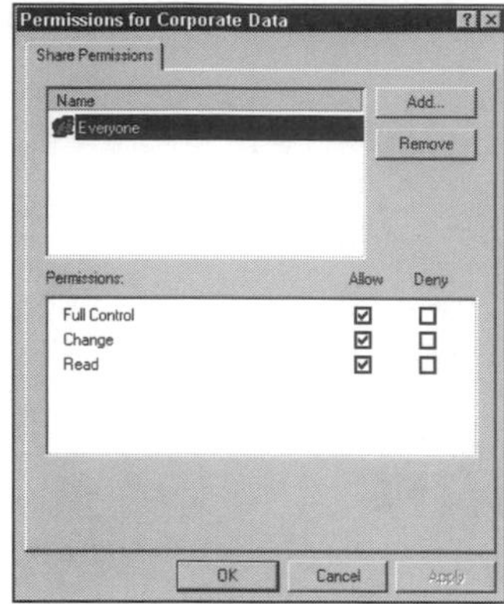

Figure 9-31: Share Permissions

Did you notice that sharing permissions in Windows 2000 Server is missing something from both NTFS and sharing permissions in Windows NT Server 4.0? It's the No Access attribute. However, with sharing, you can create the No Access attribute manually by selecting Deny for Full Control, Change, and Read. Using the Deny filed with NTFS permissions also can achieve the No Access outcome.

The share-level permission that you set acts as a mask. That is, if you allow Raymond MacMillan to have the share-level permission of Change on the folder FOO, then this becomes the lowest common denominator for his security relating to this resource. Suppose that inside the folder FOO there are two other folders: DATA and MARKETING. Each folder has a document. And of course, this all resides on an NTFS partition.

The Change share-level permission at the share level (FOO) sets that mask through which all lower-level resources are affected. So, as you can see in Figure 9-32, the Change mask allows the effects of the more restrictive NTFS security to be applied to the MARKETING folder, but doesn't allow the effects of the more liberal Full Control permissions to be applied to the DATA folder (as far as our user Raymond MacMillan is concerned).

Bottom line? In this scenario, based on Raymond MacMillan's across-the-network access of a shared resource titled FOO, he is subject to the Change mask. Get it?

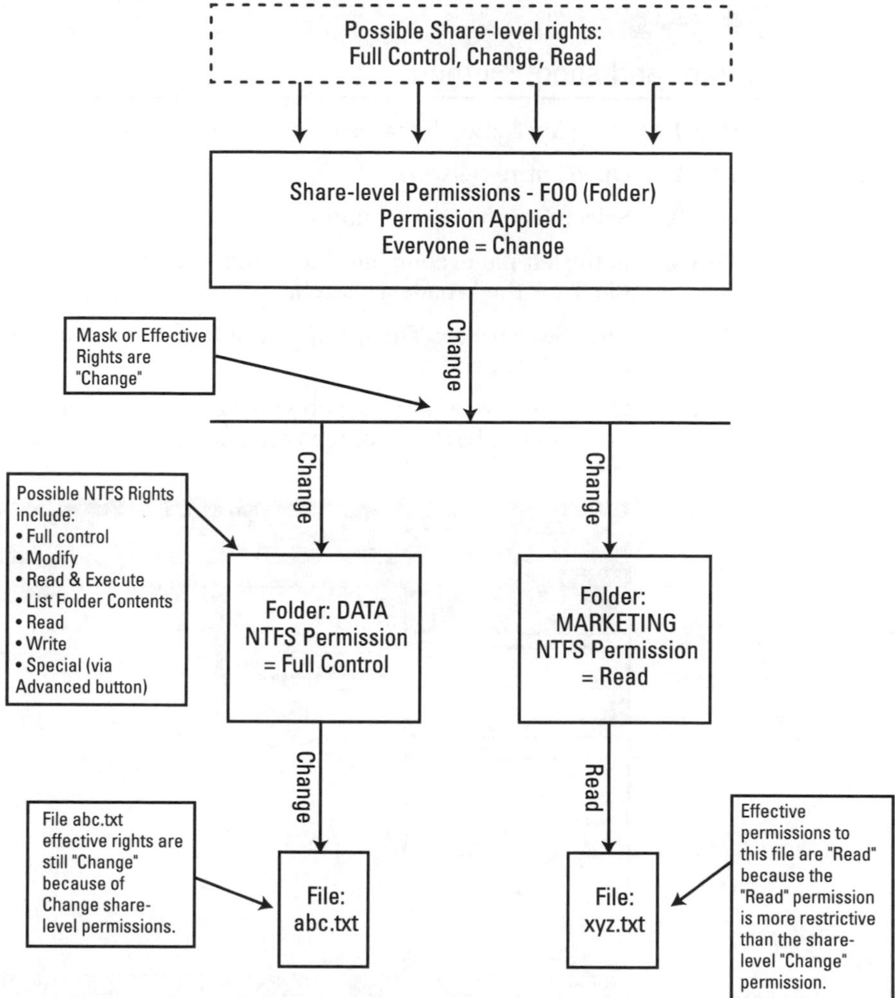

Figure 9-32: NTFS and Sharing Security Relationship

Step 6: Mapping Drives

On any given day, you likely will map a drive to provide a resource to some user somewhere in your organization. This is normal and to be expected. Note that mapping drives hasn't changed all that much from Windows NT Server 4.0. There are still three basic methods for making it happen: the point and shoot method, the GUI method, and the geek method.

Point and shoot method

This is perhaps the simplest and most intuitive way in which to map a network drive. Go find it and map a drive to it.

STEPS:

Point and shoot method

Step 1. Open My Network Places from your desktop.

Step 2. Open Entire Network.

Step 3. Select Search for computers.

Step 4. In the left pane, complete the Computer Name field or leave it blank for the broadest search.

Step 5. Click Search Now. The list of computers on your network appears in the right pane.

Step 6. Open the computer to which you want to map a drive. The computer's shared resources are displayed (see Figure 9-33).

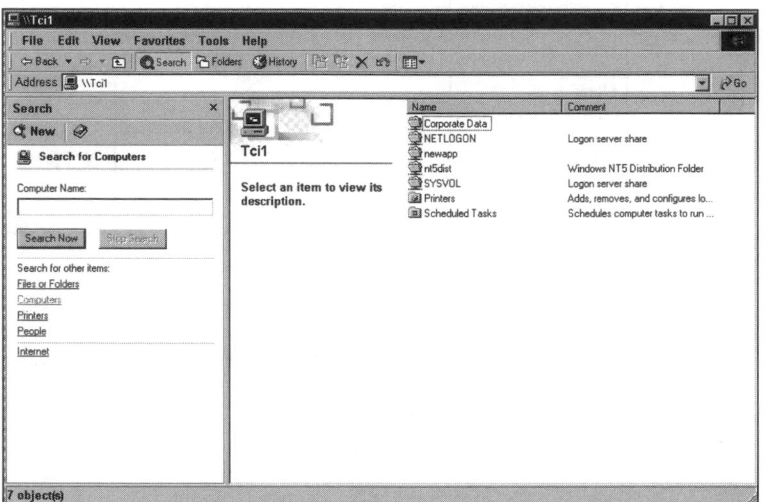

Figure 9-33:: Shared resources on TCi1

Step 7. Right-click the shared resource you want to map a drive to and select Map Network Drive from the secondary menu.

Step 8. The Map Network Drive dialog box appears with the folder path already populated for you with the shared resource to which you pointed. Select a drive letter in the Drive field (for example, G:) and click Finish.

GUI method

The GUI method actually is very similar to the final few steps of the point and shoot method. It's faster, but alas, not as friendly.

STEPS:

GUI method

Step 1. Secondary click My Network Places on your desktop.

Step 2. Select Map Network Drive from the secondary menu. The Map Network Drive dialog box appears.

Step 3. Complete the Drive and Folder fields and click Finish (see Figure 9-34).

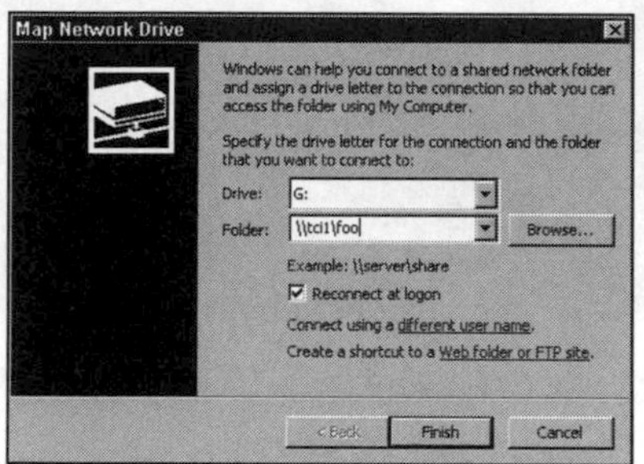

Figure 9-34: Map Network Drive

Windows 2000 Server has modified the Map Network Drive to allow you to log on as a different user and create a shortcut to a Web folder or an FTP site. Very nice touches. Thank you, Microsoft.

Geek method

And then there's the die-hard crowd. These are the oldtimers who either started in the MS-DOS days, or reluctantly have migrated over from the UNIX community. These are the command-line commandos! Mapping a network drive from the command line requires you to use the NET USE command.

STEPS:

Geek method

Step 1. Open a Command Prompt window by selecting Command Prompt from the Accessories program group.

Step 2. At the command prompt (for example, C:>), type **NET USE drive letter:** `\\server name\shared resource` in the traditional UNC naming format (explained more in a minute). For example, to map drive G: to the FOO share point on the server TCi1, you type `NET USE G: \\tci1\foo` at the command prompt (see Figure 9-35).

Step 3. Hit Enter. You have mapped a drive via the geek method.

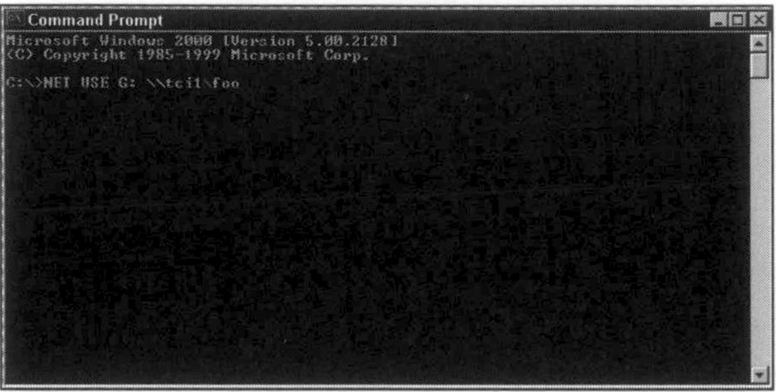

Figure 9-35: NET USE command

Uniform Naming Convention

Windows 2000 Server uses the Uniform Naming Convention (UNC) method to map drives and/or otherwise access network resources, as do other Microsoft networking environments dating back to when Bill Gates was a pre-billionaire. If you carefully deconstruct the UNC mapping method, you find that it really has three terms. The first term immediately follows the two \\ symbols is the NetBIOS name of the computer. The second term, which follows the \ symbol (which immediately follows the computer's NetBIOS name), is the share name you assign (see "Security" earlier in this chapter). The final term is the lower-level folders and files contained within a shared folder. You can't explicitly map a drive to an embedded folder or file inside a shared folder; you must navigate to these resources. This discussion is condensed into Figure 9-36.

In fact, the inability to map, via the UNC approach, a drive to a lower-level folder or file inside a shared folder is something that confuses Red Heads (NetWare users) who are new to Windows 2000 Server. I summarize the Windows 2000 Server UNC and NetWare drive mapping differences in Table 9-2.

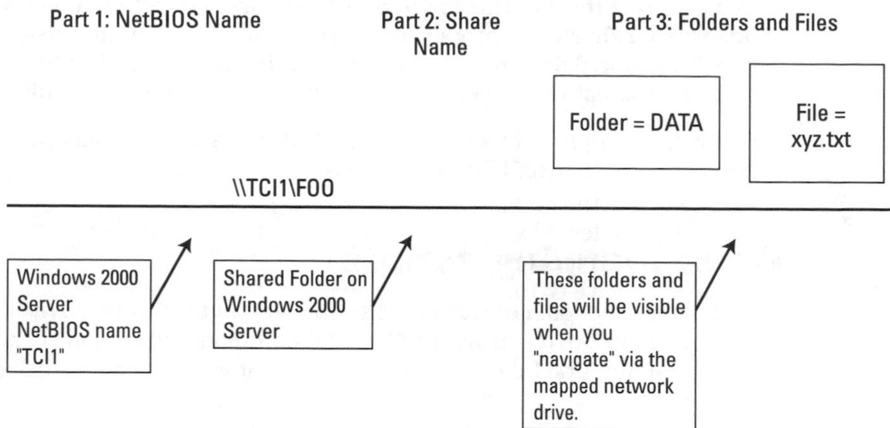

Figure 9-36: Deconstructing the UNC command

Table 9-2 Windows 2000 Server versus NetWare Drive Mappings

Windows 2000 Server	***NetWare***	***Comments***
`\\TCI1\FOO`	`F:=TCI1\FOO:`	Comparable.
NetBIOS machine name = TCI	Machine name = TCI	Comparable.
Share Name = FOO	Volume Name = FOO	Windows 2000 Server uses share names. NetWare uses volume names.
No directory mapping. Must navigate to directory "DATA"	Directory mapping allowed: F:= TCI1\FOO:DATA	Big differences between Windows 2000 Server and NetWare.
No search drives	Search drives S1–S16	Big differences between Windows 2000 Server and NetWare.

Mapping sans drive letters

Lastly, don't forget you can map to a shared Windows 2000 Server resource without drive letters. This is something I've found of great comfort and familiarity to Macintosh users attempting to use Windows 2000 Server. If you don't know, Macintosh users have been mapping without drive letters forever.

You can best think of this method as the shortcut method. If you've ever observed a shortcut's properties on your client workstation desktop, you may have noted that many shortcuts simply have the UNC path in the Target field. This is entirely acceptable and works well with many applications.

Many older applications require drive letter-based mappings (for example, F:) and cannot use strict UNC mappings.

Drive mapping scripts

In the next section, I discuss long scripts at length. But be advised that you also can map drives, using the NET USE command, via logon scripts. This is a very common practice and a very convenient way to manage drive mappings.

Step 7: Logon and Logoff Status

I can guarantee that each and every day you'll confront the logon and logoff issue. It reveals itself in many ways. You may ask end users, "Are you logged on?" when they complain that they can't print. A user may call and whine, "I can't log on!" Or my favorite, as a Windows 2000 Server consultant, "Ever since you left yesterday, no one can log on to the network!"

There are a few quick ways to check a user's logon status. In Windows 2000 Server, this is best accomplished by launching Computer Management from the Administrative Tools program group and looking at Session (found via System Tools ⇨ Shared Folders). You also may use the NET SESSIONS command at the Windows 2000 Server command prompt.

On the workstation side, remember that in Windows 98 you quickly can tell the logon/logoff status of a user by glancing at the Logoff (user name) Start menu entry (lower part of the Windows 98 Start Menu). If the Logoff (user name) option is present on the Windows 98 Start Menu, then indeed the user is logged on. From Windows 2000 Professional, the process is much easier. Simply press **Ctrl-Alt-Del** and read the information in the Logon Information portion of the Windows Security dialog box.

Windows Script Host

Windows 2000 Server supports a tool, Windows Script Host (WSH), and it scripts very nicely (thank you!). Essentially, WSH allows you to execute VBScript and JScript-based tools. It represents nothing short than the demise of the traditional (and limited) MS-DOS batch file era. WSH, with its underlying ActiveX scripting architecture, is both a server and a scripting tool. Scripts can be run directly from the desktop by launching a script shortcut as a logon script or as a logoff script.

WSH has two flavors: GUI-based and command prompt-based. To launch the GUI-based version, simply type **wscript** at the command prompt. The result is the Windows Scripting Host Settings dialog box (see Figure 9-37). The command prompt-based WSH is launched by typing **cscript** at the command prompt.

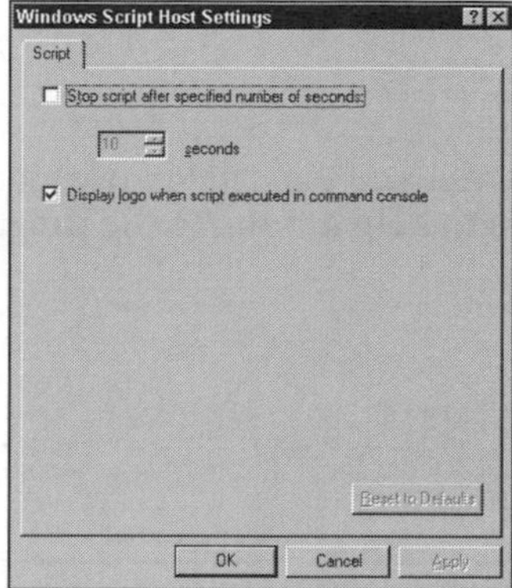

Figure 9-37: Windows Scripting Host Settings

But let's get practical for a moment. How do you actually create the scripts you might use to set environmental variable and map drives at logon? Having a VB buddy is perhaps the best way. The online help discussion for WSH is another. But the absolute best way to implement meaningful scripting in your organization, bar none, is to download and modify the script samples at `http://msdn.microsoft.com/scripting`. And tell them Harry sent ya!

Step 8: Verifying Connectivity

Another daily task is to quickly verify that your server is connected to both your internal network and the external Internet. That is, you want to make sure everybody on the network is talking. You may be surprised how basic LAN/WAN connectivity issues can affect your entire day! I guess it's another way of addressing what I call the Fairbanks, Alaska radio DJ dilemma. It was a dark (really dark) and cold (really cold) winter night when the DJ at a Fairbanks, Alaska radio station, sensing that absolutely no one was listening to him, asked if any caller would call in and let him know that someone was out there. Seconds passed. Minutes passed. An hour passed. No one ever called. Let's just say this lonely DJ had a lack of connectivity.

But all good humor aside, what was the DJ really doing? Wasn't he testing connectivity with his listeners? And the reply he received was a time-out condition, right? You bet. This can be accomplished in a couple of ways, depending on the size of your network and the tools at your disposal. If you use an SNMP network management system, such as HP OpenView, Tivoli NetView, or Computer Associates Unicenter TNG, your SNMP console tells you in an instant whether network links are up or down. However, if you're in a smaller organization that doesn't budget for these rather expensive tools, you easily can verify whether your network is intact each day.

I use the same method for verifying connectivity. I have three approaches: once a day, ongoing, and Web-based.

Once a day

Follow these steps to ping both an Internet and external IP host manually. Afterwards, I also show you a batch file to help automate the process and save the results to a text file.

STEPS:

Manually verifying connectivity

Step 1. Ping an external Internet site such as `winfiles.com`. You should quickly receive a reply from this site. If so, proceed to Step 3.

Step 2. If you don't receive a reply from pinging the name of an Internet site, trying pinging its IP address. In the case of `winfiles.com`, that IP address is 207.159.129.100. You should receive a reply. If you do with this approach but not at Step 1, you have established external connectivity, but you may have an Internet name resolution problem.

Step 3. Ping an internal network number, such as a running Windows 2000 Professional workstation. For example, ping 10.10.1.5, if this is the IP address of an active host on your Windows 2000 network. If this ping exercise works, you have internal network connectivity; proceed to Step 7.

Step 4. If Step 3 fails, ping the IP address of your network adapter card (for example, 10.10.1.1) so that you can verify the TCP/IP protocol is bound properly to the network adapter card and the card itself is actually working. If this works, proceed to Step 7.

Step 5. If Step 4 fails, ping the loopback address of the TCP/IP protocol stack (127.0.0.1) to verify that the TCP/IP protocol stack is in good working order and hasn't become corrupted. If this works, proceed to Step 7.

Step 6. Consider reinstalling the TCP/IP protocol stack if the above exercises fail.

Step 7. You have completed the connectivity test.

You easily can write a batch file that uses the TCP/IP ping utility to attempt to reach all servers and network devices on your LAN and WAN. This batch file then can write its results to a text file that's available for your inspection or sent by e-mail to your home office for analysis. If you use IPX exclusively and do not have TCP/IP running on your networks, you can write a routine that connects to remote machines via RPC calls, such as attempting to map a drive on the remote machine.

A TCP/IP ping batch file might look something like this:

```
REM Testing network connectivity on LAN and WAN
ping server1 > conntest.txt
ping server2 > conntest.txt
ping server3 > conntest.txt
ping wan1server2 > conntest.txt
ping wan2server1 > conntest.txt
end
```

Once you have your text file available, you can inspect it and look for ping timeouts and excessive turnaround times that might indicate a problem with your network. In fact, it's a good idea to automate this process with Windows 2000 Server's Scheduler (found via My Computer from the desktop) so that you can schedule the connectivity test batch file to run a few minutes before you get into the office. That way, the results are available when you arrive, and you can take action if necessary.

We use this method to monitor connectivity at my office. While it's not as fancy as some of the network management tools, it is effective, it gives us what we need, and it enables us to make sure our users in faraway branch offices stay as connected as the folks in the home office.

Ongoing

What if you're really good at your job and you want to test connectivity continuously during the day? Read on.

If you need a slightly more sophisticated approach than the homegrown variety displayed previously, you should consider Ping Plotter, a low-cost shareware application from Richard Ness at Nessoft (`www.nessoft.com`). Ping Plotter, shown in Figure 9-38, also may be found on the CD-ROM that ships with this book. Not only does this application testtests ping connectivity, but it also enables you to observe ping performance across several WAN hops. The hop path is even mapped for you! MCSE consultant-types typically use this tool for testing telco/WAN performance. That is to say that Ping Plotter enables you to test the links down the food chain on your WAN. This ultimately enables you to answer your questions regarding the subscribed bandwidth the telco sold you and the performance that you actually are enjoying. Important questions indeed to get answers to, might I say, on a daily basis.

Tools such as Ping Plotter are also great for keeping a green machine awake. Here is what I mean. Perhaps you've installed Windows 2000 Server on a truly low-cost workstation. But try as you might, you can't disable the sleep function at the workstation's BIOS level (it's happened to me). To keep the workstation from sleeping and crashing Windows 2000 Server, you can use Ping Plotter to maintain a constant activity level that prevents, shall I say, napping. Problem solved.

Whatever your preferred pinging method, the bottom line is that you are trying to verify connectivity. On your bad Windows days, that becomes an end in itself. Otherwise, this step should just be second nature. And you always can count on your end users to be your connectivity eyes and ears. If they can't connect, you'll know.

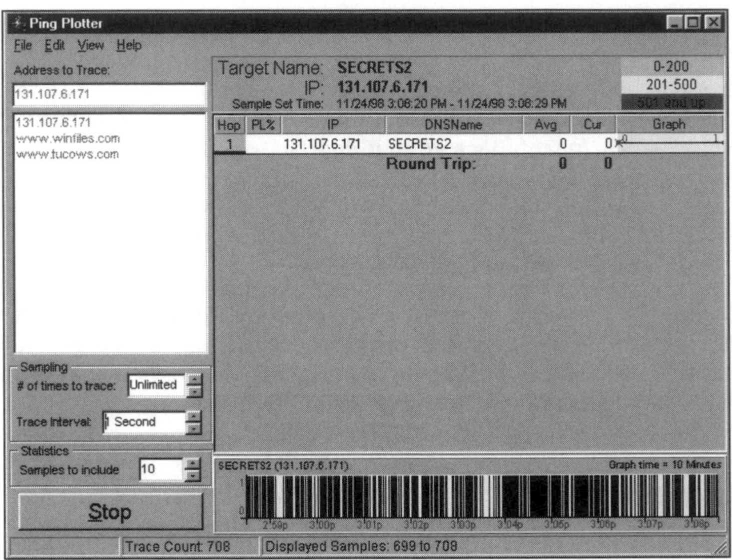

Figure 9-38: Ping Plotter

You should also introduce yourself to the Monitoring tab sheet found on the domain property sheet in the DNS MMC. Monitoring allows you to perform simple and recursive queries against your Windows 2000 Server running DNS and other DNS servers. The testing interval may be set to recur automatically, say every minute. This is an excellent LAN and WAN testing tool which is new with Windows 2000 Server (it wasn't available in Windows NT Server 4.0). DNS-based monitoring is discussed in Chapter 6.

Web

I don't know if Windows 2000 Server can take all of the credit or if it's just a case of good timing. But as you and I sit here at the beginning of the new world order of e-commerce and the new millennium, Microsoft's Windows 2000 Server and BackOffice solutions are especially well positioned for life out on the wild, wild Web. So if Microsoft has made the requisite paradigm shift from strict client/server, our daily habits must follow. This new view can be applied to testing connectivity. No longer is it sufficient to test network connectivity. You also must test your Web connectivity. And I don't mean those in-house employees trying to day trade from their desks. Nope. I'm talking about your customers trying to do business with you via your e-commerce Web site.

As you read this, do you know whether or not your Web site, and ergo, your company, are really open for business? Or is your Web site down, effectively displaying a "We're Closed" sign? How do you really know? I've found an answer to these questions. A firm called WebPartner (`www.webpartner.com`), as of this writing, has a free service for testing your Web storefront (see Figure 9-39).

Figure 9-39: WebPartner

If, for some reason, the results of this service—which runs every 15 minutes on average and attempts to contact your Web site—come back negative, you receive an e-mail notifying you. There are other immediate contact options as well. The e-mail that you receive from WebPartner is similar to the following:

```
ALERT FROM WebPartner:
======================================================================

WebPartner has detected an error on
     URL: http://www.versuslaw.com/
     At: Sat Aug 07 15:15:56 PDT 1999
     Rechecked: Sat Aug 07 15:21:59 PDT 1999
     HTTP service not responding to browser requests
======================================================================

Suggested Action:
Please contact your web site host provider or provide this information
to the person responsible for supporting your web site. This type of
problem usually indicates an issue with the web server running your
web site, your web hosting service provider's network or the
Internet infrastructure itself.

======================================================================
======================================================================
==                Detailed Error Event Information                  ==
======================================================================


                        ===                   ===
                        === Site Information ===
                        ===                   ===

             Site URL: http://www.versuslaw.com/
              Site IP: 206.129.142.6
        Site Hostname: versuslaw.com
Last successful check: Sat Aug 07 15:00:38 PDT 1999

                        ===                    ===
                        === Event Information ===
                        ===                    ===

            WP Event ID: 1622-12424352
Error event triggered at: Sat Aug 07 15:15:56 PDT 1999
      Error confirmed at: Sat Aug 07 15:21:59 PDT 1999

                        ===                    ===
                        === Error Description ===
                        ===                    ===

     HTTP service not responding to browser requests

                      ===                        ===
                      === Analysis Information ===
                      ===                        ===
```

```
Site's IP address Pinged at: 07-Aug-99 3:25:04 PM
                     Result: Success
         Host response time: 31.0 ms.

Name server (DNS) Lookup of: www.versuslaw.com
                         at: 07-Aug-99 3:25:04 PM
                Resolved to: 206.129.142.6
```

The information provided by WebPartner is more than a simple "ping"-style test. It also offers competitive analysis with respect to response time. You also may log on to the WebPartner site and view historical trend information for your Web site. Very good stuff — and in some ways more important than good old internal ping testing!

Step 9: Add/Remove Software and Hardware

Hardly a day passes where you don't add a software application to your network or a new piece of hardware. That's life as a network warrior. You will be delighted to know that the installation of new software and hardware has improved with Windows 2000 Server.

Software

There are no less than three distinct ways to install software on a Windows 2000 Server network. I start with the new and preferred group policy approach available in Windows 2000 Server.

Group policies

The official policy is group policies when it comes to installing software with Windows 2000 Server. This software application deployment approach is very System Management Server (SMS)-like, with you having the ability to publish software packages. This approach is called: Windows 2000 Software Installation and Maintenance Technology. You basically create GPOs to install applications, upgrade applications, or remove applications. More importantly, here's how you do it.

Like other group policy features, Software Installation and Maintenance Technology only works on pure Windows 2000 clients, such as Windows 2000 Professional.

STEPS:

Deploying a new software application

Step 1. Place the software package and related installation files in a shared folder. Note that the software package must be a Windows Installer package file. A Windows Installer package file replaces the traditional `setup.exe` with a `*.msi` file (a new file format) and contains specific installation instructions.

Step 2. Launch the Active Directory Users and Computers MMC from the Administrative Tools program group.

Step 3. Right-click the organizational unit (OU) of your choice and select Properties from the secondary menu.

Step 4. Select the Group Policy tab, select the Group Policy Object Links of your choice (for example, Default Domain Policy), and click Edit.

Step 5. Select and expand the Computer Configuration if you want to assign the software to a computer. Select and expand User Configuration if you want to assign the software to a user.

Step 6. Double-click Software Settings and right click Software Installation to display its secondary menu. Select New ⇨ Package.

Step 7. The Open dialog box appears. Navigate to the shared folder containing the application you want to install and select the `.msi` file (see Figure 9-40).

Figure 9-40: Selecting an `.msi` file

If you try to deploy a non-compliant `.msi` file from a non-shared folder, you receive an error message saying the network path cannot be verified, but do you still want to deploy this package using this path? You need to answer Yes or No.

Step 8. The Deploy Software dialog box appears that allows you to select the deployment method. You may select from Published, Assigned, or Advanced published or assigned package properties (see Figure 9-41). Configure package properties allows further installation customization.

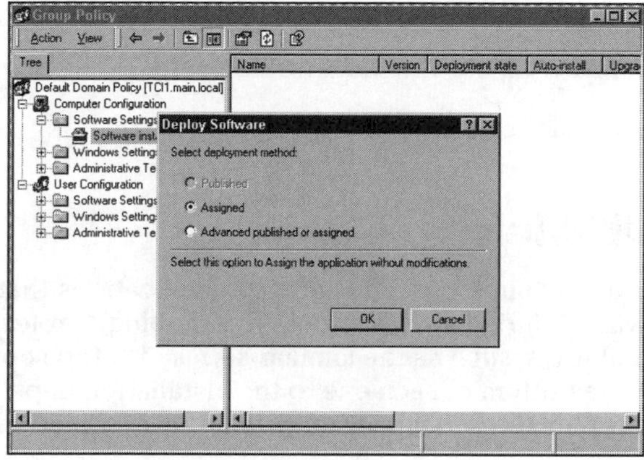

Figure 9-41: Deploy Software

Step 9. The software application to be deployed appears in the right pane of the Group Policy MMC when the Software installation object is highlighted. It is now ready to run.

Add/Remove Programs

Some good things never really change, like the Add/Remove Programs applet in Control Panel (see Figure 9-42). Its appearance has been improved, and it's still your spot for installing software locally on the actual Windows 2000 Server machine.

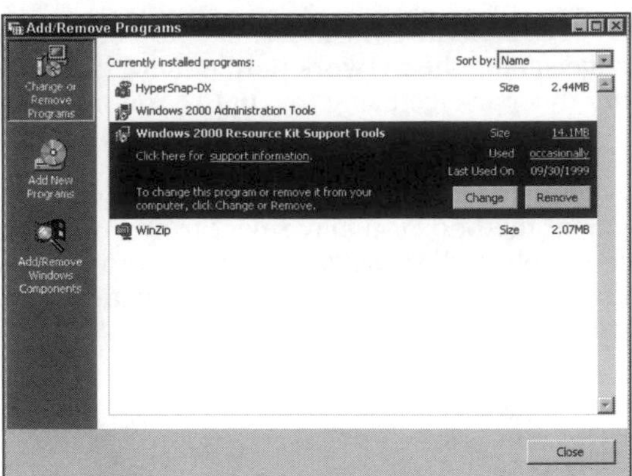

Figure 9-42: Add/Remove Programs

InstallShield

You have, no doubt, installed software applications that used InstallShield's setup wizard during your tenure as a technology professional. You know this in several ways, such as the familiar series of setup screens where you click Next at the bottom of each one to the installation in-progress thermometer (which shows the percentage of installation completion).

And you might even know a close cousin of InstallShield called Uninstall. Uninstall is used to remove an application from the computer — warts, DLLs, and all.

I usually tell Uninstall to retain the DLL files for an application when I'm asked. You never know when one application's DLL file is actually used by other applications.

Setup.exe

It goes almost without saying that developers still use good old `setup.exe` to install programs. You know the drill. Insert a CD-ROM disc or a floppy disk in your computer. Double-click `setup.exe`. Answer any relevant questions, and the application is installed. Perform a reboot if necessary. Enough said.

Hardware

First things first. Windows 2000 Server supports Plug and Play (PNP) devices. That's a welcome change from the old Windows NT Server 4.0 days. However, you still need to install Industry Standard Architecture (ISA) devices manually with the driver diskettes provided by the manufacturers.

And speaking of hardware drivers, consider the following. You always should attempt to use the latest hardware driver available for your hardware device. While Windows 2000 Server has been tested and shipped with countless hardware drivers, time marches on. That means the hardware drivers that shipped with Windows 2000 Server will become outdated fairly quickly. You typically need to download the latest Windows 2000 Server driver from the vendor's Web site or use the one from the CD-ROM or floppy disk that accompanies your hardware device. With a new operating system such as Windows 2000 Server, it's predictable that vendors will revise hardware drivers frequently to fix bugs and run more optimally. Bottom line? Always use the latest hardware driver.

To add hardware to a Windows 2000 Server machine, first physically install the hardware device. If the hardware is PNP, the hardware will be detected on startup of the Windows 2000 Server machine. If the hardware is ISA, use the Add/Remove Hardware applet in Control Panel, which launches the Add/Remove Hardware Wizard (see Figure 9-43).

Figure 9-43: Add/Remove Hardware Wizard

Once hardware is installed on your Windows 2000 Server machine, you use Device Manager to manage it (see Figure 9-44). Device Manager is similar to that found in Windows 98, so you should be comfortable with it from day one. Device Manager is found via the System Properties applet in Control Panel. Select the Hardware tab sheet.

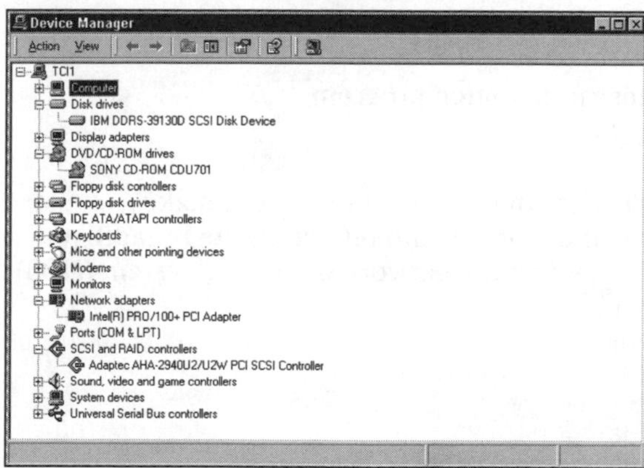

Figure 9-44: Device Manager

Device Manager also may be accessed by right-clicking My Computer, selecting Properties, and selecting the Hardware tab sheet.

Step 10: End User Support

Now for the real reason we have networks and a lot of the work associated with networks. I'm speaking of the end users. Many in the networking profession will tell you end users are the reason to get up in the morning and go do your job. As a billable-hour consultant, I concur, but only to a point. If not for the end users, I would truly have fewer billable hours in my chosen profession. This section explores end user support from several aspects, including the physical network, applications, and even the politics of end user support.

Physical

"I can't print" is a cry heard frequently on Windows 2000 networks. No matter how hard you try, how fast you run, you can never get away from it. Networks are, by definition, part physical: printers, workstations, hubs, and cabling. So don't fight the "I can't print." Just prepare and arm yourself accordingly (see Step 11: Using the Windows 2000/MCSE Toolkit).

Layer seven: applications

Ya gotta love 'em. While many Windows 2000 professionals, present company included, like to hang out in the lower and middle OSI layers, our jobs also include layer seven: applications. In my tenure as an MCSE, working with Microsoft BackOffice solutions including Windows 2000 Server, these are just a few of the applications I've learned and mastered to satisfy my customers.

- West Law
- BNA Employment Law
- BenchTop (a SQL Server application)
- Office 2000
- Microsoft Outlook
- Corbel document preparation program
- and many more

The point is this: I'm sure that if you sit down and make a similar list, it might cause you to pause for a moment and reflect on the breadth and scope of your job. It's clearly not just the network operating system (NOS).

Geopolitical

Every seasoned network administrator has experienced this one: You're at your desk, on the verge of solving that server performance problem that's been nagging you for weeks, when the VP of Finance walks up and rather testily informs you that she is unable to print. Read: Hold everything! It's a fire! Next thing you know, you've spent an hour removing and reinstalling the VP's print drivers, undoing the damage her free online service software did to the PC's network setup, and you can't even remember your fantastic server performance solution.

These fires are frustrating sometimes, but it's key for Windows 2000 Server administrators and engineers to remember that the end users are our raison d'etre. They are our customers: why we do what we do. Many of them also approve our budget. Even if you're lucky enough to be insulated from the end users by a first-tier help desk, chances are that you'll be called upon to provide escalation support at least once a day.

Here are some techniques I've learned that help me dispatch fires as they come up — and hopefully prevent new ones.

Make a note

When a support issue comes up, whether it's bad print drivers or users unable to connect to the network because of a server crash, always jot down a little note to yourself before jumping up from your desk to fight the fire. Five times out of six, before I started doing this, I'd forget what I was working on when I got back to my desk after correcting the problem.

Remember your manners

Even if you're interrupted in the middle of a major breakthrough by what you may consider a minor problem, remember that your minor problem may be a major one for the user. Think back to the days when you were an end user, and how you felt if technical support people blew you off because they considered your problems inconsequential. Nobody wants to be Dogbert the mean network administrator, and in the real world, brushing off end users' problems can be severely career limiting. Keep your role as doctor in mind, and solve the problem quickly and professionally. You can get back to your breakthrough soon enough.

Educate the user

If possible, explain to the users the steps you take to solve their problems. An educated user is a happy user. Obviously, some users are not interested in this level of detail, preferring to be notified "when the darn thing works." But many users do appreciate this extra information. The same goes for first-level tech support people: If they learn how to solve this specific end-user problem, chances are the same end users won't be escalating the same problem to your attention next time. Also, many help desk staffers are grateful for the chance to observe more senior administrators. I started my IT career on a help desk, and every chance I got, I went into the server room and watched as the network administrators solved a problem. This exposure proved very valuable in later years.

Document your solutions

After fighting a fire, it's always a good policy to write an e-mail message or note to yourself explaining the problem and the solution, so you have that knowledge available in case the problem crops up again. I can't count the times I've been trying to solve a nagging support issue when I've gotten the feeling that I've dealt with the same thing several months before. Had I documented the problem and resolution, I wouldn't have had to reinvent the wheel. If your company has a help-desk application or a homegrown solutions database, enter the situation so that the information is available next time. If the solution is particularly interesting, or you think the issue will come up again, share the information with other members of your group, so they are "in the know" if they're tapped to solve the problem later.

Like it or not, end-user support is a big aspect of any Windows 2000 Server administration career. If you have the right attitude and follow the proper procedures, you can learn a lot from those day-to-day fires.

Planning ahead

As a Windows NT professional, it is imperative that you keep the needs of your users in the front of your mind at all times. After all, they are your customers, and despite what your org chart might say, you work for them. After you break out of the front-line support game and earn a position back in the server room, it's sometimes easy to put these thoughts aside, crucial as they may be. I've worked in shops that cover both ends of the spectrum — from a place that drops the Exchange server midday if deemed necessary, to another employer where one of the IT department's primary goals is to remain invisible so the users don't even know we're there. I prefer the latter, even if it means quite a bit of after-hours and weekend work. The users' main impression of the company's network is that it just *works*. Your users should feel the same way. To that end, here are some helpful tips I've picked up over the years.

Protect the users

If you have a choice, choose the action that impacts the users least. For example, a few months back we noticed that one of our servers was starting to go downhill. Unexplained Server service-warning events were showing up in the event logs, response times were increasing slightly, and it was evident that something was wrong. At this point, it was a judgment call for my group. Do we leave the server up in the expectation that it will make it to the end of the day; or do we reboot it now, in the middle of the afternoon? As we evaluated the situation, we noted that the problem likely would not cause any data loss and we took into account that this was one of the busiest days of the month. We decided to gamble and leave the server up until the end of the business day, and it coasted along fine. Decisions like these are tough, because you obviously don't want the server to come crashing down if you can help it — but we decided that the minimum user impact would be to leave the server up. It was a decision between 10 minutes of *guaranteed* downtime for a reboot, or 10 minutes of *possible* downtime if the server crashed later and had to be rebooted. We did, however, take steps to notify all affected groups about the situation, which brings me to my next point.

Keep the users informed

In my experience, users have an easier time accepting a service interruption if they know it's coming. In the preceding example, my group sent out a company-wide e-mail message advising the users that the server was having problems and might crash, and telling the users to save often. We got positive feedback about this approach; even though the users weren't happy that the server might die in the middle of the day, they appreciated the warning. Had the machine crashed, they would have lost a lot less work than if they hadn't had any warning.

End users do like to know the basic reasons for downtime, but it's also a good practice to keep technical jargon out of end-user communications. While you may think it's neato to explain the intricacies of ESEUTIL in an e-mail message informing users that the Exchange server will be down for the weekend, the fact is that most people just don't care. Keep your communications straightforward and to the point, and your message will come across loud and clear. If an end user really is interested in what you're doing with the Exchange box, he or she can reply and ask for more information. For everyone else, a simple note saying, "The Exchange e-mail server will be down this weekend for database maintenance" suffices.

Keep the help desk informed

When I worked on an enterprise help desk, it always seemed as if we were the last to know about vital information that would affect the users. Half the time, we gathered this information from the users themselves as they called, which was terribly frustrating and embarrassing. Like every other tech support veteran I know, I swore up and down that once I got to the back of the shop, I'd make help desk communications a priority so that my first-level support would never be without the proper information. Have I made good on this promise? Mostly, although I'm still not as communicative to our help desk as I'd like. It's a good goal to have, though; the better informed your first-level support people are, the better the users' impression are of your department as a cohesive unit where groups communicate with one another.

Strive for 100 percent uptime

Continuous uptime may seem like an obvious goal for anyone who runs a computer system, but keeping it in your mind at all times is a real challenge. Now, everyone who's worked with networks for any length of time knows that servers need reboots every so often, but a really good administrator should try to minimize this need. Keep your servers simple, assign them only the tasks you need them to perform, and don't clog up the system with additional services or applications unless they're absolutely essential. There's a saying that a person's body is his or her temple; make temples out of your production boxes. Have fun with your test servers; but when you have a spare moment, spend it working to make your Windows 2000 servers as fault tolerant as possible. As I mentioned earlier, many administrators don't have a problem spending hundreds or thousands of dollars to make their hardware bulletproof. Put in the hours necessary to make your operating systems and software just as bulletproof.

Oh, and what about you? Challenge yourself to work smarter each and every day. This might include reading trade journals such as *InfoWorld, PC Week,* and the like. You might read another chapter in this book just for the heck of it. Consider taking an in-classroom or online course. But each and every day, be sure to make a capital investment in yourself so that you work smarter tomorrow than you did today!

Step 11: The Windows 2000 Server/MCSE Toolkit

I now share my Windows 2000 Server/MCSE toolkit with you. That is, these are the resources I have found you most likely will be called upon to use in performing your duties as both an MCSE and a Windows 2000 Server network administrator.

So what's in my toolkit? My virtual toolkit consists of many of the tools I described earlier in "Step 3: System Health," and the Windows 2000 Configure Your Server Wizard (discussed in Chapter 2). My physical toolkit ranges from bona fide tools such as a screwdriver to a list of peers' telephone numbers to a parts catalog. In short, my experience base is reflected in what I carry on my person and in my auto as a day-to-day practicing MCSE. If you haven't already done so, take a moment to look at what you carry or have easy access to as your tools of the trade. Such a self-assessment speaks volumes about how you leverage your time and knowledge as a Windows 2000 Server professional and/or certified professional (such as an MCSE).

Real hardware tools

I carry a limited set of real tools including two Phillips screwdrivers, two flathead screwdrivers, a "Compaq" (Torx) screwdriver that has a star pattern on the end to open older Compaq servers, a chip extractor, and a static energy discharger wristband. This is the type of kit that may be purchased from national resellers such as PCZone (`www.pczone.com`, 1-800-258-2088) or MicroWarehouse (`www.warehouse.com`, 1-800-328-2261) for under $50. It's safe to say that this type of toolkit is a necessary and required fixture for any MCSE. I mean, any MCSE has to at least be able to connect a cable or open a workstation! If you're gonna earn the lofty salaries paid to MCSEs, you gotta at least have the basics down.

Because the leather pouch that contains my "real" toolkit has extra room, I carry other invaluable items. These include a modern network adapter such as the 3COM 3C9*xx* series with drivers and an old-fashioned true NE2000 network adapter. The modern network adapter allows me to fix a common point of failure on a workstation or server: layer one of the OSI model (better known as the network adapter). Hey, anyone with the MCSE title should be able to replace this component at the very least. The NE2000 network adapter shows my age. In the old days when knights were bold and kings owned all the gold, the NE2000 network adapter was fashionable. Today, I carry my remaining NE2000 because it always works. There are some late nights at clients' sites when I've had it up to my neck with PNP and I'm saved by my good old ISA-based NE2000 card! It's a trick worth remembering and adding to your MCSE toolkit.

Oh, two extra items that I added to my toolkit based on my own errors and omissions are a small dental mirror that extends several inches, and a pen-sized flashlight. With these tools working in tandem, I easily can see the back side of components and motherboards during surgery. Makes a heck of a difference when you're trying to insert RAM chips into tight slots.

A CD-ROM library

If you were a physical laborer, you would enjoy increasing returns and perform your work better if you went to the gym and lifted weights. That activity might enable you to work longer or faster than your peers. As knowledge workers, you and I need to undertake a different type of workout. That work is to increase both our active knowledge base (the information we retain in our heads) and our available knowledge resources. For me, that means carrying a meaningful CD-ROM library that contains, within minutes, most of the knowledge I need as an MCSE to complete my work. So here's what I carry in my soft-sided CD-ROM carrier. These selections represent CDs that I frequently need to access and that are current. It is important to make regular additions and subtractions to your CD-ROM library so that it remains germane. Truth be told, not too long ago I had the opportunity to purge my CD-ROM library of oldies but goodies, such as the complete CPM operating system reference.

- Microsoft TechNet (the full edition of six CDs, including the Technical Information Network, Client Utilities, Microsoft BackOffice Products Evaluation, Service Packs, Server Utilities, Supplemental Drivers, and Patches). It goes without saying how valuable this collection of CDs is each and every day. Using the term "near" when performing Boolean-type searches in TechNet typically works best. "Near" finds matches within 15 words; it's kind of a fuzzy logic search that works well for us humanoids.
- Compaq Systems Reference Library version 2.*x*. This resource is, of course, invaluable when you work with Compaq servers and workstations.
- HP JetAdmin Software for JetDirect Print Servers. You may be surprised how often you need to implement a new JetDirect card and don't have the correct software. The CD version I carry has the drivers for every network known (from AppleTalk to UNIX).
- Business Resources Kit and Sales Training Interactive CD. Microsoft provided these CDs as part of our firm's participation in the Microsoft Certified Solution Provider program. Although these CDs are used to fortify my sales efforts, remember that we MCSE consultants must hunt before we can eat.
- *Windows 2000 Server Secrets* CD-ROM. This is included at the back of this book. Packed with meaningful utilities, this CD-ROM isn't just a marketing ploy to ship a compact disc. Far from it. To create this CD-ROM, I sought and received the contributions of network professionals from the enterprise level down to the workgroup level.
- Windows Support Source CD. This is a CD-ROM subscription service from Cobb, the renowned newsletter publisher, which has an archive of articles that may interest the practicing MCSE.
- Internet service provider (ISP) CD. I carry the CD that my ISP issues, which contains ISP-specific signup information, drivers, and FAQs. This CD is extremely helpful in the field as I implement Internet service on behalf of my clients.
- Microsoft Evaluation & Migration Planning Kit CD (Part #098-63878). This CD contains blank templates for creating your BackOffice migration proposal, project schedule, budget, and the like. It saves a lot of time during the management of your project.
- Novell Support Connection CD (monthly). The rumors aren't true. Big Red isn't dead.
- Microsoft BackOffice CDs #1 – #4. How many times are you asked to insert a specific CD to complete the installation of a driver? How many times do you need the BackOffice CD library to install SQL Server Books Online after the fact? How many times have you tried to install client management tools for SMS only to find that you don't have your BackOffice CD library handy?

- Windows 2000, Windows NT, Windows 95, and Windows 98. Here again, how many times have you been asked to insert a CD so that a driver can finish installing? Don't forget that you need to carry at least two versions of these CDs: the original retail version and the upgrade version. Windows 95/98 has a nasty way of knowing whether an operating system was installed previously on the machine; thus, it asks for one "type" of CD instead of the other.
- Microsoft Project: BackOffice Deployment Templates CD (Part #098-634461). More project management templates for your BackOffice engagements. I've found that a few extra minutes with this CD can save hours of planning time!
- Windows 2000 and Windows NT Workstation and Server Resource Kit CDs. Yes, you need both CDs. The Server edition contains several more utilities than the Workstation version. These CDs are no substitute for having the hardcopy resource kits, as I discuss in a moment.
- Windows NT 4.0 Service Pack 3 (or higher) CD. How many times do you go to a site, including perhaps your own, and discover that the legacy Windows NT machines (servers and workstations) don't have the latest service packs installed? Just try getting official Microsoft technical support if that's the unfortunate case. This same reasoning will apply as service packs are released for Windows 2000 Server.
- Office 97 (or higher) CD. Ever been caught flat-footed, needing the Microsoft Exchange Server resource driver for Outlook 97? I'll bet you discovered that it wasn't on your operating system CD. One of the places it's magically kept is on the Office 97 CD. Just try setting up an Exchange-based mailbox, not personal folders, without this resource. I'm sure you'll carry this CD after that experience.
- Network Professional Association Technical Resource CD. This goodie contains cross-platform utilities, product demos, and an article archive. I've found this CD to be of value when I'm working in heterogeneous networking environments (like every day). Check out the NPA at `www.npa.org`.
- McAfee VirusScan CD-ROM for Windows 95, 98, NT. Be careful to honor the licensing agreement (installed on only one machine at a time). But, I typically install, run, and deinstall the virus detection program contained on this CD prior to performing surgery on a machine. The reasons are obvious.

More MCSE toolkit items

Finally, my toolkit includes an alphabet soup patchwork of resources I've gathered over the years and of which I still make active use. It is here that upon close reflection, I think you may find that you, too, have gathered goods that you use almost unconsciously in your role as a network professional. I like to think of the following as my network tackle box, where I have a special lure for every occasion.

- Floppies. Still very much alive, here are a few floppies that I carry in my MCSE toolkit. A good old-fashioned bootable MS-DOS 6.22 disk with EDIT, XCOPY, and a few other invaluables. How many times, for reasons you can't quite explain, do you need to boot from A:> into a real DOS environment to get something done? This need always seems to rear its ugly head on Saturday night at 10 p.m. Wonder why that is? Because applications such as INSTALL.EXE program contained on 3COM's EtherDisk disk (yes, this is another mandatory floppy to carry) still *only* run under a true MS-DOS environment. And in many cases, this is the *only* way that you accurately can test your 3COM network adapter for failure, configuration settings, and such. It's also not a bad idea to make and carry a copy of the emergency repair disk (ERD) for your favorite Windows NT servers. You never know when you'll need them.
- Resource kits and other well-tattered books. Nothing like having a resource kit or two, along with your favorite books, spread in front of you when you're performing server surgery.
- PC Zone catalog, Data Comm Warehouse catalog, and so on. Like you, I receive the monthly catalog mailings from the national hardware/ software resellers. Surprisingly, these catalogs are invaluable when discussing technology solutions with clients (when you literally need to draw a few prices out of thin air).
- Computer User monthly newspaper. In Seattle, the January issue of the *Puget Sound Computer User* lists a potpourri of local reseller, consulting, labor, and publishing resources for the technology community to patronize (the "Business Directory" issue). This type of publication, by KFH Publications, Inc., is available in many other North American areas including Colorado (*Rocky Mountain Computer User*). The January issue allows me to refer my clients to competent professionals in technical areas that I don't serve, such as UNIX.
- A handheld tape recorder to record observations. Nothing like creating a journal of the steps undertaken to troubleshoot a problem or build a server. An invaluable addition to carry.
- Laptop computer with ability to connect to the Internet and download drivers, and search the knowledge base at `www.microsoft.com`. If you live in Seattle, the San Francisco Bay Area, or Washington D.C., you can use the Ricochet modem (`www.ricochet.net`) to establish a high-speed connection to the Internet without tying up a fax or voice line.
- An external modem with modem cable (serial 9 to 25 pinout). Sometimes the client's modem just doesn't work correctly and work needs to get done. Because of my experience with SBS, I now carry an external US Robotics 33.6 Sportster modem. It's for "just in case," and it always works!

- A really long telephone line and an analog telephone. The really long telephone line is for reaching the telco wall jack that is always across the room. The analog telephone is for plugging into that wall jack to test the telephone service thoroughly.
- Telephone numbers of peers to call for advice. There's nothing like calling a BackOffice buddy to help you out of a jam.
- A portable file cabinet to maintain working client files that contains office layout drawings, field notes, and billable hour charge sheets. A well-organized MCSE is a happy MCSE. Trust me.
- A portable tape deck/radio. When the cat's away (client or boss), why shouldn't the mice have just a little play?
- Kneepads. No, these aren't to wear so that you can kneel down and take client or supervisor abuse. I carry them to protect my old skier's knees when I'm fishing cable around a crowded server room.
- Working suit, pullovers, and tennis shoes. Many MCSEs face today's formal/casual clothing challenge. One moment you're selling your MCSE services in a glass tower. The next hour, you're implementing SBS in a dusty warehouse. Better carry a change of clothes and be prepared to change in the water closet.
- Peanut butter chocolate chip cookies and granola bars! Funny how an elevated blood-sugar level allows you to accomplish amazing feats.

Step 12: Updating Network Notebook

One of the first things to ask when a new server problem crops up is whether anything changed on the server just before the problem began. Any NOS can be a fickle system, and even the most innocuous change has the potential to send it into a tailspin, sometimes for unexplained reasons. Keeping a detailed log of any and all changes to each server on your network can save you countless hours of troubleshooting. In my office, we have an Excel spreadsheet with separate sheets for each server. We record the date, time, and nature of each change to the server, from installing new software to scheduled or unscheduled reboots, adding new drives or other hardware, and so on. These logs have proved very valuable in the past, when a change we made one week caused problems the next. Unfortunately, this technique hasn't helped us with the current challenge, so we moved on to the process of elimination.

While it's not as active a task as other tasks mentioned in this chapter, documentation is very important for the success of any network. There is absolutely no sense in one person being proficient at a network administration or process while his or her coworkers are in the dark. In my mind, this is actually a dangerous situation, especially if the task in question is vital to the health of the network. What if that person was hit by a truck? What would the rest of you do?

Documentation is one thing that's a high priority at my workplace; we are encouraged, in fact required, to document new processes as they are developed and perfected. This isn't just for others' sakes, either. Ever get a process down perfectly, only to forget it after a couple of months? Find yourself wishing you had written it down before? I sure have — many times over the years.

In my office, we have a procedures directory that contains more than 100 documents on the network. Some are out of date now, but we keep them around anyway. Some of the tasks detailed could crop up again, or the techniques could be adapted for our current network. In addition, we train each other on new procedures as they are written and do "beta testing." When one of us creates a new procedure, such as installing a new application or restoring a Microsoft Exchange mailbox from backups, that person documents it thoroughly. The next step is to have another administrator do the "monkey test," where someone just follows the procedure step by step, making sure to leave any outside knowledge at the computer room door. When all we have to go on is the procedure before us, it's easy to identify holes or assumptions and correct them. Some of our procedures are so good that any end user could come into the server room and perform the task by following the step-by-step procedure document. Yikes: That's not very good for job security!

If you ever have a bit of downtime between fighting fires and the endless upgrades, think a moment about procedures you use that may not be documented as well as they should be, and address those issues. Good documentation initially makes a Windows NT professional's job *much* easier later on.

If you are a consultant, performing the documentation task is a great way to find and bill additional hours. Such additional work is great for three reasons. First, it requires virtually no marketing to get. It's easier to sell your existing clients on additional work than it is to sell work to new clients. Second, the work is easy to perform. Third, it helps you toward reaching your annual billable hour goal. Be sure to use Visio or some other networking diagramming tool as part of your network documentation approach.

Summary

This chapter outlines the 12 most important day-to-day Windows 2000 administration tasks. On any given day, you are likely to perform most, if not all, of these tasks discussed in this chapter.

- Windows 2000 Server network virus protection
- Windows 2000 Server tape backups and restores
- Windows 2000 Server system health observations
- User, group, and computer management
- Security verification
- Use of drive mappings to access resources
- Determining logon and logoff status
- Network, Internet, and Web connectivity verification
- Implementing new software and hardware on your Windows 2000 Server network
- End user support
- Using the Windows 2000 Server/MCSE Toolkit
- Network documentation.

Chapter 10

Monthly and Annual Windows 2000 Activities

In This Chapter

- Auditing your network
- Reviewing security
- Performance benchmarking and monitoring
- The monthly reboot
- Managing disk space on servers
- Disaster recovery simulation
- Implementing operating system service packs and hotfixes
- Implementing network application upgrades
- Creating month-end or quarterly archives
- Annual budgeting for your network
- Setting up an active technology committee
- Evaluating systems on the horizon
- The annual planning retreat

You're proud of your Windows 2000 Server network. You spent a lot of time during planning and setup, configuring every aspect of your systems to your specifications, conducting stress testing, developing foolproof daily and weekly maintenance plans, and migrating the users onto the new system. Your network runs smoothly, and the users are happy with its performance. However, even in a network as trouble-free as yours (which most of us can only wish for), certain administrative tasks require attention each month and every year. This chapter will introduce you to many of the tasks I've seen during my time as a network administrator. These tasks are conveniently shown in Table 10-1 as a checklist. Hopefully this baker's dozen checklist will enable you to integrate some of these tasks into your own network management approach. You won't see step-by-step instructions on how to delete users; instead, I'll talk about some good habits to get into that will make your day-to-day job easier and also enable you to more easily train new network administrators as they come on board. After all, you'd like to be sitting in the CIO's leather chair someday, wouldn't you?

Table 10-1 The Monthly/Annual Checklist

Item	*Description*	*Comments*	*Completed*
1	Auditing your network		
2	Reviewing security		
3	Baselining and monitoring performance		
4	The monthly reboot		
5	Managing disk space on servers		
6	Disaster recovery simulation		
7	Implementing service packs and hotfixes		
8	Upgrading and removing applications		
9	Creating month-end or quarterly archives		
10	Annual budgeting		
11	Technology committee formation and meetings		
12	Evaluating new systems		
13	Annual planning retreat		

Auditing Your Network

In a working day-to-day Windows 2000 network, new users, directories, and shares are created daily; in a large, growing enterprise, administrators in various locations may create hundreds of these objects in a busy week. Much of that discussion was covered in Chapter 9. How in the world does a Windows 2000 Server professional keep track of all this, and more important, how can you ensure that users, shares, and such are deleted properly when someone leaves the business? A well thought out checklist for adding and deleting users is a very good start, but some auditing will always be necessary because steps will be missed and some tasks might fall through the cracks.

Here are the steps I use when deleting a user account:

1. Require an account deletion form. This is useful for two reasons; first, it assures that you have the CYA factor, and second, you can file these forms away for review at the end of the month. Without these forms, it's difficult to remember whom you've deleted during the month, especially in a large organization.
2. On the date specified on the deletion form, change the account password and disable the account. Do not delete the account at this point, in case the user's replacement is coming on board soon (in which case you can just rename the original user account to the new account name) or if the

user comes back to the organization for some reason. At the same time, inform your end user support group of your action, so they will not accidentally re-enable the account if the former employee calls in.

3. Determine if the user's manager needs access to the user's old e-mail. If not, go ahead and delete the e-mail account if it is not likely that the user will return soon, as some temporary employees do, for example.
4. If necessary, give the manager permission to access the user's home directory, so he or she may get to documents as needed. Give the managers a set amount of time (usually until the end of the current month) to move any documents they might need before deleting the directory itself.
5. At the end of the month, go through all accounts that have been disabled during the month. If they are still not needed, delete the accounts from the Windows 2000 Server Active Directory, and also delete the user's home directory and any network shares specific to that user. If your system logon scripts have references for individual users (and they shouldn't, if you can avoid it) check to see if the deleted accounts were referenced in those scripts. If so, modify the scripts as necessary.

In addition to reviewing user deletions, you also will want to take a look at how your network has changed over the month. For example, let's say a specific application on your network required the creation of several network shares on your main server. During the last month, that application was replaced with another vendor's product. As part of your end-of-month audit, you'll want to make sure that the shares created for the old application are deleted; not only will this clean up your users' views in My Network Places, it might improve your network performance.

Reviewing Security

Documenting your network's security is an essential part of maintaining your Windows 2000 Server network. During daily operations, NT File System (NTFS) and network share security settings will be changed, added, and deleted. Without proper monitoring and auditing each month, these settings can get out of control and you won't know which folders and shares have the proper security.

Consider two alternate ways to test your security, ways that will expose your greatest weaknesses. First, download the SATAN tool from any of the numerous shareware sites (`www.winfiles.com`, `www.shareware.com`). SATAN is a tool that you may configure to test the security of your system against outside intruders. It does have a learning curve, so allow yourself a few weeks to master it and achieve the end results you seek — a more secure Windows 2000 Server!

Second, hire the enemy. Have you ever noticed that successful hackers are often offered jobs by the very firms that they hacked into? It is true and probably happens more often than the media reports. In your case, I'd recommend that you consider hiring a high school or college kid and let the kid take a "controlled" run at your system to test your security. Many hackers come from this socioeconomic group, so why not hire the enemy and get 'em on your side?

Establishing and maintaining security settings on your Windows 2000 Server network isn't difficult, provided you stay on top of changes as they happen each day, week, or month. Here are three steps that will help you keep your network secure:

1. **Set up and implement a plan.** Implementing an initial security plan is the first step toward a well-maintained network security setup. Every responsible Windows 2000 Server professional should create a spreadsheet, database, or other document outlining their network's security setup when the network is installed. This type of document should be maintained in your network notebook. Before you turn users loose onto the network, make sure that the actual security on shares, files, and directories is as you intended it, and as you documented it.
2. **Document changes as they occur.** Any security document is a "living document" and must be updated and changed to reflect changes made to the network each day, week, month, or whenever. A security document, be it a database, spreadsheet, or text, must be your security template and reflect the network as it should be.
3. **Audit security regularly.** Once a month, or more often if your environment requires it, compare the security settings in the template with actual security on the network. Are they different? Do you know why they're different? If so, update the security template to reflect the changes, and scold yourself or the administrator responsible for not updating the template when the settings were changed.

If you find inconsistencies or mistakes in your network security, change the permissions back to their intended settings. Make sure that you are satisfied with your audit before moving on to other monthly tasks; security maintenance is one of the most important parts of a Windows 2000 Server professional's job. If you doubt this, just wait until the CEO's personal documents are e-mailed throughout the company.

Baselining and Monitoring Performance

Windows 2000 Server's Performance Monitor tool is extremely useful in helping you tune your Windows 2000 network. However, for any monitoring data to be useful, you must first generate benchmark measurements so that you have a baseline to compare against. This matter is discussed at length in Part V, "Optimizing Windows 2000 Server," but it's worth mentioning here. And it should certainly be on your monthly/annual list of activities!

In a growing network, Windows 2000 Server's performance baseline may change significantly each month or every few months, as new users, services, and applications are added to the system. Because of this, that Performance Monitor baseline you recorded back in February may be far from accurate in August.

In my current network, I usually do a performance benchmark every three months or so, and more frequently if there is a major user conversion going on. My coworkers and I save these files for future use and refer to them for comparison when trying to troubleshoot a server problem using Performance Monitor.

Performance baselining and monitoring will be discussed in detail later in the book, but I wanted to mention it in this chapter because accurate baselines are a crucial part of understanding whether your Windows 2000 Server network is humming along happily or whether it's headed for a screeching halt.

The Monthly Reboot

All operating systems use and release primary memory, or RAM, as needed. This is normal and occurs constantly. In fact, one way to monitor the RAM usage on your Windows 2000 Server is to run Task Manager (selected from the taskbar properties on your Windows 2000 Server desktop). Task Manager is discussed at length in Chapter 20. The Performance tab on Task Manager enables you to see, on the lower right of the screen, the memory consumed over the memory available on you system (see "Mem Usage:"), as seen in Figure 10-1. Another good memory indicator is the memory chart in the middle of the Performance tab that shows a memory consumption histogram view on the left and a memory consumption time line or time series at the middle right.

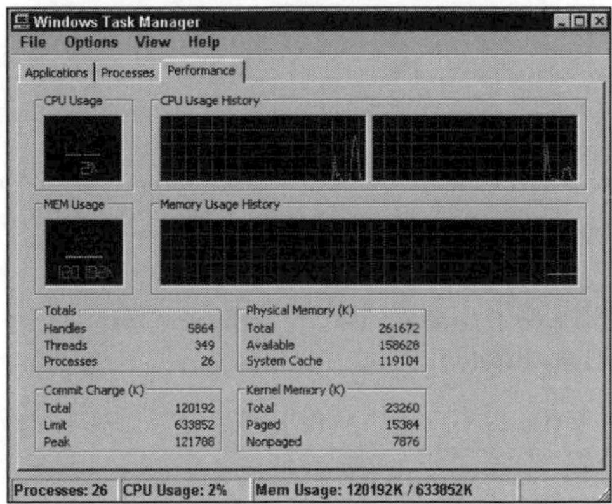

Figure 10-1: The Task Manager Performance tab

Under the best of circumstances, the memory consumption information displayed in Figure 10-1 would increase over the course of a month because Windows 2000 Server, in the process of using and releasing RAM, will slightly fragment this primary memory. That is, not all of the RAM used will be returned properly and counted again as unused. In English, Windows 2000 Server doesn't give back all of the RAM it uses when it is done with it. And I haven't even started to discuss how applications affect RAM. It has been my experience that Microsoft Exchange Server can be a poor server citizen when it comes to releasing unused RAM. Microsoft SQL Server can be trained to be a good server citizen because you can specify how much and in what ways SQL Server will use RAM (this is done via the server property sheet in SQL Server's Enterprise Manager).

Third-party applications are what may just cause your Windows 2000 Server machine fits when it comes to releasing RAM. I've already seen offenders (including the backup engine service of a well-known third-party backup application) that not only fail to release all of the RAM used when the application was open but sometimes, in a badly behaved way, cause the Windows 2000 Server to consume all available memory. That is, some poorly written applications will cause the memory histogram and time line shown in Figure 10-1 to "max" at the top of the chart. Perhaps you've experienced this, and would know that your server slows down so much that it is difficult to launch another application at the server or sometimes even move the mouse on the server machine.

Enter the monthly reboot to "reset" and form contiguous RAM space. By rebooting your Windows 2000 Server, you flush and defragment RAM and get a fresh start. This will certainly solve the slow buildup of memory consumption from the operating system and applications not returning all consumed RAM. To see for yourself, consider the following experiment.

STEPS:

To monitor RAM consumption and defragmentation

Step 1. Launch Task Manager from the taskbar properties of Windows 2000 Server.

Step 2. Observe and record the Mem Usage value on the lower right of the Performance Tab sheet.

Step 3. Launch one or two server-based applications such as Microsoft Exchange Server or Oracle.

Step 4. Observe and record the Mem Usage value again (as in Step 2) after launching the server-based applications.

Step 5. Let both Task Manager and the applications launched previously (Step 3) run for several days. Continue to use your network as usual.

Step 6. Several days later, observe and record the Mem Usage value again and terminate the applications you launched in Step 3.

Step 7. Now observe and record the Mem Usage value with the applications successfully terminated.

Step 8. You will now compare the different Mem Usage values over the past few days. Ideally, if there were no RAM leaks, the Mem Usage values in Step 2 and Step 7 would be the same. But most likely these values are not the same, reflecting the fact that not all RAM was returned to available memory once the applications were terminated. Indeed, the Mem Usage value in Step 7 should be larger than the Mem Usage value in Step 2, all other things being equal.

You can also perform the preceding experiment where you simply run Task Manager for several days or weeks without explicitly launching and terminating server-based applications just to observe what level of RAM fragmentation may be attributed to the underlying Windows 2000 Server operating system. And above all, perform that monthly reboot to flush and reset your RAM to battle this form of memory fragmentation. You might also be interested to know that I like to use the monthly reboot to test the bulletproof nature of my Windows 2000 Server machine. It is my goal to have networks in place that I can reboot with confidence each month. If I'm afraid to reboot a Windows 2000 Server machine each month because I'm afraid it won't restart and come back up, I probably have larger, more serious underlying problems with my network than simple RAM fragmentation.

I'm very comfortable providing the preceding advice regarding the monthly reboot to those of you working on small- and medium-sized Windows 2000 Server networks. However, I am reluctant to advise you to override strict and necessary system management policies at the enterprise level. Be sure to check with your Windows 2000 Server network stakeholders (including your boss) before rebooting your Windows 2000 Server each month. At the enterprise level, accept my advice as something to consider.

Managing Disk Space on Servers

In Chapter 9, I mentioned disk space monitoring as an important task that Windows 2000 Server professionals should do at least weekly. On a monthly basis, I recommend going one step further and monitoring the growth of individual directories on your servers and running a disk defragmentation utility. A weekly look at total free disk space is fine, but once a month, a more detailed look is called for. While this seems like (and is) a lot of work, it's also essential; if you don't know which directories are growing out of control, you can't stop a problem before the server runs out of disk space.

Disk quotas

The manual method for managing disk space on Windows 2000 Server networks is to impose storage quotas on a per-user basis. This is a great new feature in Windows 2000 Server, one that was clearly long overdue. Implementing disk quotas is very easy. Simply configure the Quota tab sheet from any hard disk's Properties sheet. Disk quota entries may be made on a default, group, or individual user basis.

Automatic management

A blast from the past. This Windows NT Server story applies equally well to Windows 2000 Server today. After spending a few months manually recording each folder's size on our NT server, my fellow administrators at work and I decided there must be a better way to determine which directories are growing the fastest. We started looking into third-party utilities and settled on Storage Resource Manager from Highground Systems (`www.highground.com`). While this tool was written as a user space quota utility, it works very well for our needs; we can generate database reports indicating which directories on our servers are biggest, and which are growing at alarming rates. Using this information, we can stop any out-of-control growth before it takes out our server's free disk space.

A real-world war story

One of my clients, an online research firm, found that it didn't know exactly where its mission-critical data was located on the network. Of course this discovery was made during a hard disk failure when it was time to perform data restoration. From that experience, a table such as the one shown in Table 10-2 was devised to better map out how the disk space on the network was being utilized. I've created one example for your benefit. The intent is to have you fill in the blanks with your own information as part of the data location exercise.

Table 10-2 Data Location

Data	*Size*	*Physical Location*	*Drive Letter Based Location*	*UNC Location*	*ARC Path Location*	*Comments*
Alaska	12MB	Server1	c:\data\ak	\\server 1\ak	multi(0) disk(0)rdisk (1)partition(2)	Is backed up nightly.

Closely related to disk space calculations is the topic of disk fragmentation. Contrary to popular belief, NTFS partitions do indeed suffer fragmentation from the ins and outs of daily Windows 2000 Server activity. This of course isn't news at the desktop level with FAT and FAT32 in the traditional end user Windows environment. Windows 98 performs disk maintenance activities for you with ease.

Windows 2000 Server provides defragmentation support right out of the box. This is a big improvement on Windows NT Server 4.0, where you had to purchase third-party utilities. To defragment your disks in Windows 2000 Server, simply select the Defragment Now button on the Tools tab sheet of any volume's Properties sheet.

Before running a disk utility to "recombine" your fragmented secondary storage space, make sure that you've made bona fide and verified tape backups of your data. Just in case!

Dynamic disks

Be advised that Windows 2000 Server emphasizes the concept of dynamic disks as the primary storage type. Contrast that with the old paradigm of basic disks. What's the difference? The basic file system has the partition view, whereby you could have either four primary partitions or three primary partitions and one extended partition. But the dynamic disk view essentially does away with those partition limitations and just defines everything as volumes.

You can only convert disks from basic to dynamic using the Disk Management MMC. You cannot convert disks from dynamic to basic. Likewise, you can only create volumes on dynamic disks in Windows 2000.

The dynamic disk volume types include the following:

- Simple volume. This is disk space on a single disk.
- Spanned volume. This is disk space combined from two or more disks.
- Mirrored volume. This is an identical copy of a simple volume.
- Striped volume. Similar to stripe sets in Windows NT Server 4.0.
- RAID-5 volumes. This is comparable to the stripe steps with parity RAID-5 volumes in Windows NT Server 4.0.

I recommend you implement RAID-5 at the hardware level, not the Windows 2000 Server software level. This is because hardware-based RAID-5 implementations use the processing capability of the RAID controller card and don't significantly add operational overhead to your Windows 2000 Server machine.

Another way to understand the concept of dynamic disks is to look at it from a logical viewpoint. Dynamic disks de-emphasize the physical view of partitions and emphasize the logical view of volumes.

Distributed file systems (Dfs)

Extending the logical view of storage is distributed file systems (Dfs). Dfs is a view of storage across the entire enterprise network whereby disparate storage media and geographically diverse locations may be viewed as a single storage resource. You may also create a hierarchical tree of storage resources in the enterprise with Dfs. This is accomplished by selecting Distributed File System from the Administrative Tools program group. This will launch the Distributed File System MMC, which will allow you to create a Dfs storage structure.

The first time you run the Distributed File System MMC, you will need to run the Create New Dfs Root Wizard to create a "root" container. This is accomplished by selecting the New Dfs Root Volume menu option from the Action menu.

Recovering from Disaster

First and foremost, update your Emergency Repair Disk (ERD) each and every month, even if you don't believe significant system activity has occurred that might warrant such action. Never underestimate the passing of time and its effects on a Windows 2000 Server. Sure, you may not have added any users in the past month, but with a default password change duration of 42 days in Windows Server, it's likely that user accounts have been updated in the past month, with or without your knowledge. This immediate example is only one of several "background" system update possibilities that warrant the monthly ERD creation process. The ERD is discussed in more detail in Chapter 21.

Because the ERD resides on a floppy disk, I suggest that each month you create a new ERD and save the old one. I'd hate to see you get in the habit of overwriting the ERD each month and ultimately suffer a floppy disk media failure. Also, note the ERD isn't created with the RDISK command any more. In Windows 2000 Server, the ERD is created via the Backup tool in the Accessories, System Tools program group.

You and I both can learn a lot from the mainframers of yesteryear, specifically, in the area of disaster recovery. The client/server networking community has done a very poor job of addressing disaster recovery. Novell took the lead years ago with its NetWare SFT III specifications, wherein hot "mirrored" servers were kept online some distance away from the main production NetWare servers. Microsoft is, to be quite candid, just arriving at the disaster recovery party with its Windows 2000 Server clustering solution (see the online help system under clustering for a more detailed discussion).

So how can you address the disaster recovery issue in Windows 2000 Server today? There are several ways.

Native clustering

Clustering in Windows 2000 Server is managed and implemented via the Cluster Administrator. This tool is part of Windows 2000 Administration Tools. Windows Clustering provides three clustering technologies:

- Network load balancing clusters
- Server clusters
- Component load balancing clusters

These clustering technologies, used alone or together, provide scalability and high networking availability, never before seen in a Microsoft-based networking solution. They provide a total clustering and load balancing solution for all application architectures. You may also manage remote clusters via the Cluster Administrator.

Third-party solutions

Larger Windows 2000 Server sites will initially look at third-party solutions ranging from robust optical-based backup systems to clustering applications until viable and tested Microsoft solutions, such as native clustering, are deployed. One notable third-party clustering solution in the Windows 2000 Server environment is Vinci (which was recently acquired by Legato).

Identical spare servers

Consider implementing this approach from the old Windows NT Server 4.0 days. Here, two of my Windows NT Server clients purchased identical servers (down to the network adapter card). One acts as the production server, the other is a spare (see Figure 10-2). The idea is that if the production server crashes or fails, the hard disks can be moved to the identical spare server and the organization will have its network up and running again within one business day. An alternative approach is to restore from backup tape to the spare server.

Believe it or not, this spare server approach will actually work in a Windows 2000 Server environment. I have only performed this in a medium-sized environment, and clearly, at the enterprise level a more robust solution such as clustering would be used instead.

One lesson I learned from using the spare server approach was how long it took to get back online. Early on I thought I could have an organization back online within one or two hours. Wrong! For whatever reasons (glitches, unexpected issues), the spare server approach takes a full business day to implement. With this fact in mind, I can now manage everyone's expectations appropriately.

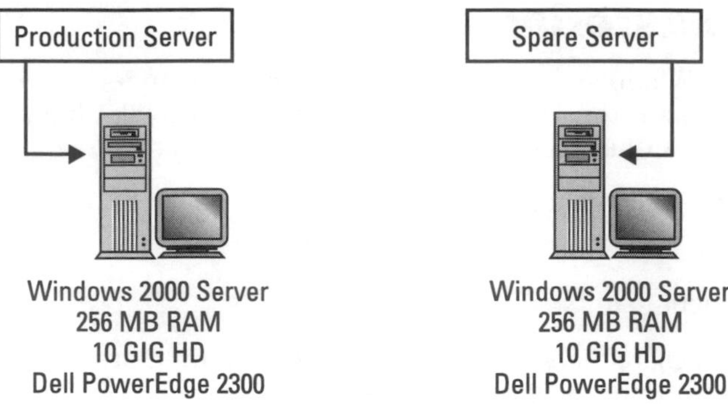

Figure 10-2: Using a spare server

If you haven't already done so, take a few minutes to assess how you are managing the downtime expectations for the stakeholders on your Windows 2000 Server network. Have you communicated that server-related downtime might be measured in hours, if not days (but rarely minutes)? If necessary, take a moment to jot down a few ideas on how you might better manage expectations (perhaps an e-mail message to everyone in the office advising people to have alternative work processes ready in case the server is down for a day).

Although the spare server solution will work, you must plan for how you will handle the "different" SID value on the backup server, assuming you use the same server and domain naming conventions. If you are using Windows 95/98, this is not a serious problem, as these desktop operating systems don't bind the SID to their logon process. But if you are using Windows 2000 Professional or Windows NT Workstation at the desktop, you've got major problems. That is because the spare server's SID numbers (machine and domain) will be different from the original networked environment. In all likelihood, you will need to use a SID changer, an application found at popular shareware sites (`www.winfiles.com`, `www.shareware.com`).

Reciprocity agreements/hot sites

Our firm occasionally offers its spare training PCs as potential "rescue" computers for our smaller clients in a crisis. By that I mean that if the property management firm calls with a crashed server, we can trot over with a bare-bones spare Windows 2000 Server and have the ten users printing from Microsoft Word by lunch. Not a perfect solution, but one that works in a crisis.

Larger enterprises contract with hot sites to address possible failures. These are the airlines, hospitals, and large corporations of the Windows 2000 Server community. Although this approach is expensive, when properly configured, the enterprise customer's network can limit downtime to minutes, not hours or days.

Why bother?

Wouldn't it just be easier to do nothing and wait for the problems at your site to work themselves out instead of following all of the preceding approaches to disaster recovery? Well, you know what the answer is: Of course not, for at least one reason — the cost of downtime. Even small organizations can calculate the cost of downtime in the range of several thousands of dollars per hour. Such high costs make a spare server or third-party disaster recovery solution seem cheap.

Annual drill

Regrettably, too many of us in the networking community don't perform an annual disaster recovery exercise. The customers I have that do this typically perform this activity in response to some form of EDP audit or at the request of government regulators (if they are in a regulated business).

The annual disaster recovery drill can take many formats. It can be as simple as the CIO pulling a drive out of a RAID array chassis unannounced (after making sure the evening backup tapes were successful — wink wink). A client of mine that runs an online research service performed that exercise, and it was an eye-opener, to say the least.

Another disaster recovery exercise is to have your IT consulting firm arrive unannounced, grab last evening's backup tape and several IT staff members, and have said staff perform a complete and successful system restore — within one business day. Again, such an exercise is a real eye-opener.

Implementing Service Packs and Hotfixes

In every operating system, bugs and shortcomings are bound to appear. Because of this, operating system vendors periodically release bug fixes for system administrators to apply to their servers. Microsoft's method for large-scale updates of Windows 2000 Server systems involves groups of enhancements and bug fixes they call service packs. No surprise here. This is what Microsoft did back in the NT days too! While service packs are generally safe, many problems have cropped up as a result of applying them, so it's extremely important for administrators to know exactly what they're doing before attempting to update a production system.

In my experience, it's very important to have the following questions answered before applying any service pack:

1. **Why is this necessary?** Do you have a compelling reason for installing the service pack, or are you just trying to keep your servers up to date? This phenomenon of riding the latest versions or upgrades is often called the "bleeding edge," and with good reason. No matter how much Microsoft or other vendors test their products, some instabilities or incompatibilities will always come up. Remember; if it ain't broke, don't fix it. If the server crashes and you have to restore it from backups, you'd better have a good explanation when the CIO asks you why you were messing with the production environment.
2. **Do you have a back out plan?** What if something does go wrong? While Murphy's Law does not always apply in the world of Windows 2000 Server networks, you'd better be ready for anything when doing any sort of operating system upgrade. In all cases, update your servers' Emergency Repair Disks and use the "Create an Uninstall Directory" option when applying a service pack. Also spend some time planning what you would do if the server refused to boot after the upgrade; do you have a reliable method for restoring it from "bare metal" if you have to format the drives to correct the problem?
3. **Have you tested the service pack in your environment?** Do you really know how the new files will interact with your production systems? On occasion, third-party or homegrown applications do not respond well to changes made by a service pack and may either refuse to run or behave strangely. Make sure you thoroughly test how the service pack will affect your production environment.
4. **Have you properly researched the upgrade and its possible side effects?** When you're thinking about applying a service pack or performing an application upgrade, Windows 2000 Server user groups on the Internet can be invaluable. Before we applied Service Pack 2 to our Microsoft Exchange 5.0 server, I spent a few days on the Net, gathering information from the MS Exchange support forum (`www.msexchange.org`) and other sources. It's well worth your time to take advantage of these resources and enlighten yourself about the possible consequences of the upgrade.
5. **Have you scheduled an appropriate time window for the work?** Because service pack installations require a server reboot and may require additional downtime, they obviously should not be performed during production hours. In a smaller shop where users work from 8 to 5, this is fairly easy; you can schedule the work for any weeknight after everyone has gone home. In a 24/7 shop, scheduling downtime is not quite as easy. Choose a period of time when the system will be under minimal use, such as the middle of the night. These "O' Dark Thirty" projects may not be fun for you, but this scheduling is necessary to minimize user impact. Also, make sure you give yourself some "cushion" time, in case something goes wrong. Estimate your downtime as accurately as possible, and schedule an hour and a half of downtime, even if you think the work will only take an hour. If you have the system back up and running early, you'll be a hero. If it's late, you'll have some explaining to do the next day.

Hotfixes

While service packs replace many files and sometimes add new features, hotfixes are "quick-fix" solutions to urgent problems that come up. Hotfixes replace only a few files at a time and are not as thoroughly tested as service packs are. As with service packs, caution is advised when applying hotfixes; if you are not experiencing the specific problem described in a hotfix Readme file, then don't apply the fix.

Hotfixes are also tricky in that they often must be installed (and removed!) in a specific order, or they won't work properly. As such, it's important that administrators take advantage of all information available about the hotfix they're thinking of installing. Hotfixes also usually require a server reboot, so be sure to schedule some downtime.

Be conservative

The recommendations in this section may sound overly conservative, and this type of caution is definitely not necessary for all environments. However, it is absolutely required in larger enterprises and is a very good idea even in the smallest of shops. If you run your small 25-node, single-server network as you would run that of a huge conglomerate, your colleagues and users will respect your professionalism and concern for their interests, and this will pay off later on, believe me.

Upgrading and Removing Applications

Be sure to honor the upgrade cycle of your software vendors. With certainty, you can anticipate upgrading your mission-critical applications every 18 months if not sooner. And many software vendors will release interim upgrades monthly and quarterly. Your challenge as a Windows 2000 Server professional is to implement these application upgrades in a noninvasive manner. That's a kind of way of saying you'll first test each application upgrade on a test server to make sure it works. Then you'll install the application upgrade on the production servers on the weekends when no one is around. Heck, you didn't want to use those weekends for skiing or fishing anyway. Regarding the "how" of installing an application upgrade, you will recall this was discussed in Chapter 9.

Creating Backup Archives

In many businesses, it's necessary to create special archives that can be shipped to an offsite storage facility for long-term safekeeping. Some companies are required to do this by governmental regulations, and others keep data as a safety net in case of litigation or other unforeseen circumstances. Many offices are governed by state regulations and must keep all business data for seven years. At the end of each month, these sites do a special data export from their backup system and ship them to an offsite storage area. You may not be required to perform this action for your network, but if so, make sure you develop a consistent plan and schedule, and stick to it. It's easy to miss an archive window, especially if it is supposed to happen during a busy time, such as the holiday season.

Budgeting for Your Network

Like it or not, a lot of what you accomplish as a Windows 2000 Server professional centers on the budget you have to work with. Part of your monthly and annual activities include paying attention to the financial side of Windows 2000 Server networking. Here are several approaches to addressing the budget issues, including zero-based budgeting, linear percent growth, percent of revenue, and Windows 2000 Server on $5 a day.

Zero-based budgeting

This is my favorite. Here, as part of the budgeting exercise, you start with a blank spreadsheet. Each and every expenditure category is critically reviewed. By that I mean each item, down to the network adapter cards you keep on hand, is evaluated for usefulness. Questions to ask are as follows:

- Why do you have so many computer parts in inventory?
- Do you need to add staff? How can you justify such an addition?
- If you're planning to add two more servers, what else would be needed? Here the idea is that adding a server results in other additions, such as a printer or a modem. Each of these additions would be listed as a line item under the new server, as shown in Figure 10-3.

Zero-based budgeting is similar to designing a bill of materials (BOM) system in manufacturing. You build up the budget from the lowest levels.

Tip

If you want to learn more about zero-based budgeting, consider learning it the way I did: from a management consultant. If you have consulting funds available, hire a nontechnical management consultant who specializes in business practices such as zero-based budgeting. After you work closely with such an individual once, in all likelihood you will be able to create your own zero-based budget in later years.

Linear percent growth

This is the simplest and most popular way to create your IT budget. Here, you simply apply a growth factor to last year's budget. For example, you might say that you'll increase this year's IT budget by five percent across the board. This means that each expense category will simply grow by five percent. Call it overly simplistic, but it works, and this method is used extensively.

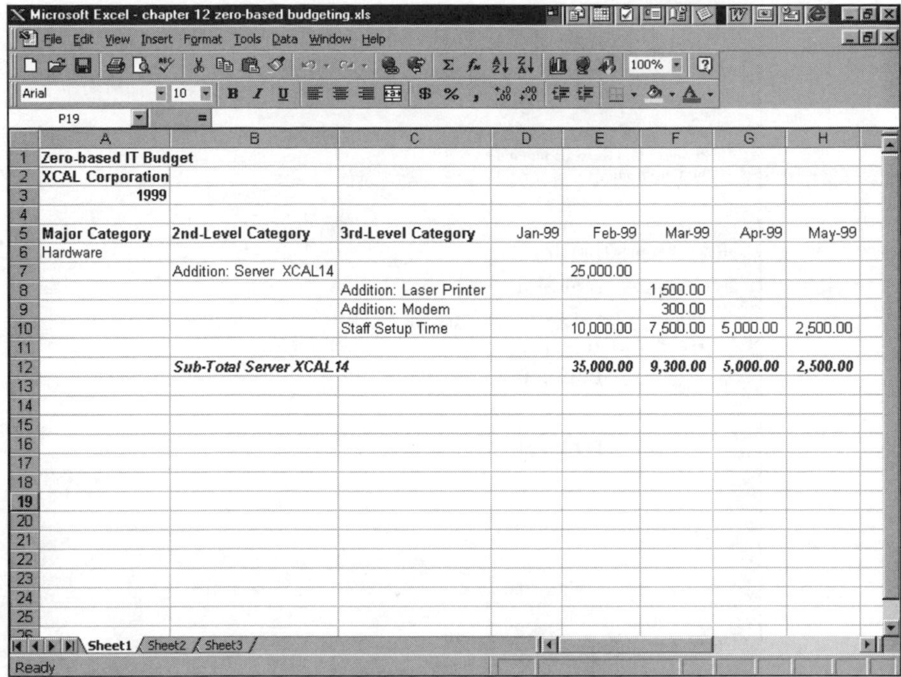

	A	B	C	D	E	F	G	H
1	**Zero-based IT Budget**							
2	**XCAL Corporation**							
3	**1999**							
4								
5	**Major Category**	**2nd-Level Category**	**3rd-Level Category**	Jan-99	Feb-99	Mar-99	Apr-99	May-99
6	Hardware							
7		Addition: Server XCAL14			25,000.00			
8			Addition: Laser Printer			1,500.00		
9			Addition: Modem			300.00		
10			Staff Setup Time		10,000.00	7,500.00	5,000.00	2,500.00
11								
12		***Sub-Total Server XCAL14***			***35,000.00***	***9,300.00***	***5,000.00***	***2,500.00***

Figure 10-3: A zero-based budgeting example

Percent of revenue

This is how the accountants in your organization think. That is because industry ratios comparing IT expenses as a percentage of total revenues are widely published. For example, many believe that IT as a whole shouldn't exceed two percent of the firm's total revenue.

To use this method, first you would agree on a percent-of-revenue value. This consensus might be arrived at via the technology committee (I speak of technology committees in the next section) or the board of directors. Once that value is selected, simply create a spreadsheet similar to Figure 10-4 and enter the Percent of Revenue.

Tip

Industry ratios that may be useful for your budgeting purposes are indeed widely reported. One of the best sources for this information is *Computerworld*, a weekly trade newspaper. Another great source is *CIO* magazine.

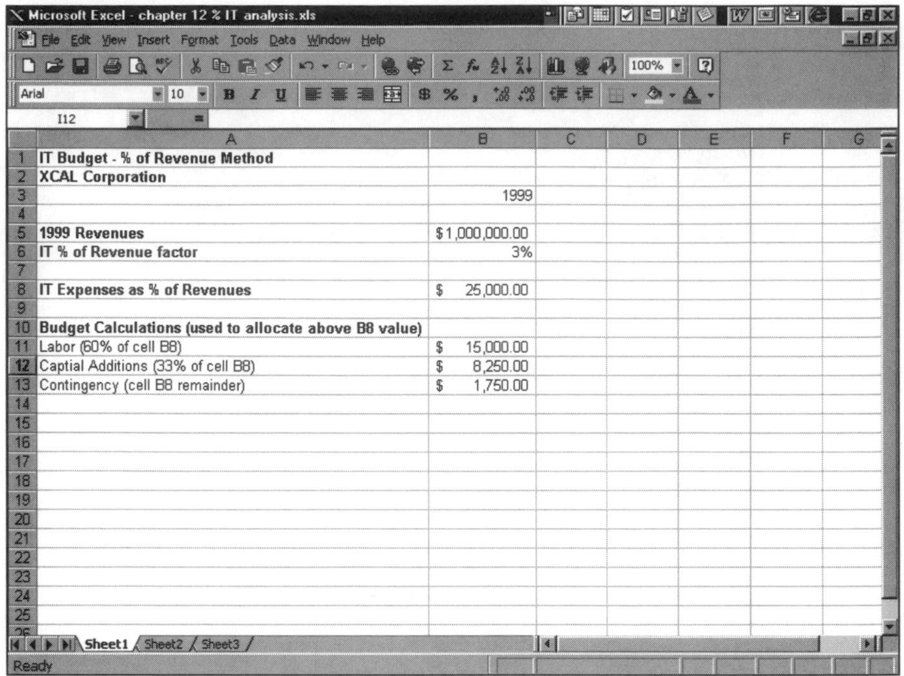

	A	B
1	**IT Budget - % of Revenue Method**	
2	**XCAL Corporation**	
3		1999
4		
5	**1999 Revenues**	$1,000,000.00
6	**IT % of Revenue factor**	3%
7		
8	**IT Expenses as % of Revenues**	$ 25,000.00
9		
10	**Budget Calculations (used to allocate above B8 value)**	
11	Labor (60% of cell B8)	$ 15,000.00
12	Captial Additions (33% of cell B8)	$ 8,250.00
13	Contingency (cell B8 remainder)	$ 1,750.00

Figure 10-4: Budgeting via Percent of Revenue

Windows 2000 Server on $5 a day

Closely related to the Windows 2000 Server network budgeting process is the "Windows 2000 Server on $5 a day," or marginal budgeting approach. Believe it or not, it is highly likely that you already understand this approach well. Remember the last time you purchased the car you drive? Did the salesperson attempt to "up-sell" you into getting a better car stereo or seat warmers? Was the argument made that these extra features would only cost an additional $1.00 per day over the life of the car? (And wouldn't you enjoy that high-end stereo much more in traffic jams, all for just a $1/day?) The good news is you can apply the same reasoning to your Windows 2000 Server network!

Let's assume that you plan to amortize, or recover the cost, of your network software and hardware over 36 months, a reasonable recovery period. This is approximately 1,095 days. Now suppose you are considering the purchase of a Dell PowerEdge server that is dual-processor-capable. You are currently unsure if you should add a second processor to the server now or purchase one a few years down the road. You do realize that a second processor would provide immediate and significant benefits to the overall performance of your network. Consider the following.

A second server-class processor is approximately $1,000. And you expect to keep the server for three years (or approximately 1,095 days). This second processor effectively will cost you $1,000/1095 days = $0.92 per day (rounded up). That's 92 cents a day to keep everyone happier on your network! Seems like a good investment. And imagine how much more performance and reliability you could add to your network if you were willing to spend an additional (or marginal) $5.00 per day. Depending on your situation, perhaps that extra $5 a day would enable you to have a mirrored RAID array, something that is highly desirable in a production SQL Server environment.

Creating a Technology Committee

Early on in the life of your Windows 2000 Server network, it is essential that you create a technology committee, populated with key network stakeholders, that meets on a regular basis. I've enjoyed assisting many firms with the process, and establish a monthly meeting rather than a quarterly one (this area moves too quickly for a quarterly meeting). Stakeholders that sit on your technology committee include

- **Executives.** This group, at the C-level (CEO, CIO, CFO, COO), has the ability to make valuable contributions about how technology fits into the mission of the overall organization. They also control the IT budget (something that shouldn't be lost on you).
- **Line managers.** This group is critical. It is from this group that your applications needs will be best identified, including new features that would make the organization run more efficiently. Line managers are typically experts in their processes, knowing more than you or I do about what they need out of the computer system.
- **End users.** Another critical group. These technology committee members can offer you insights on how the network is performing on a day-to-day basis. Can they print when they need to? Do they receive prompt attention from you or the help desk when problems occur? Do they trust the network? A great group of people with lots of important feedback for you.
- **Outside IT consultant.** An outside presence is a very meaningful addition to the technology committee. An outsider is typically innocent of the political shenanigans that occur internally in an organization. Outsiders offer that distant view so appreciated by senior management, plus expertise gathered at other sites that can benefit you.
- **You.** Don't forget the role you have as the firm's Windows 2000 Server professional. Welcome to the table!

Consider having the outside IT consultant serve as the coordinator for the technology committee. When I've seen this process managed by in-house staff, it tends to fade and fall off the radar screen after several months. However, an outside IT consultant brings both the freshness and the motivation to keep the committee alive. The "motivation" I speak of means the hours that the outside IT consultant will bill to coordinate and serve on the technology committee. For an IT consultant, there is perhaps no greater motivation than the prospect of billable hours.

Because a picture is worth a thousand words, perhaps Figure 10-5 will enable you to understand the technology committee better. Our roles as Windows 2000 Server professionals don't just encompass hardware and software issues, but also communication with our stakeholders every step of the way.

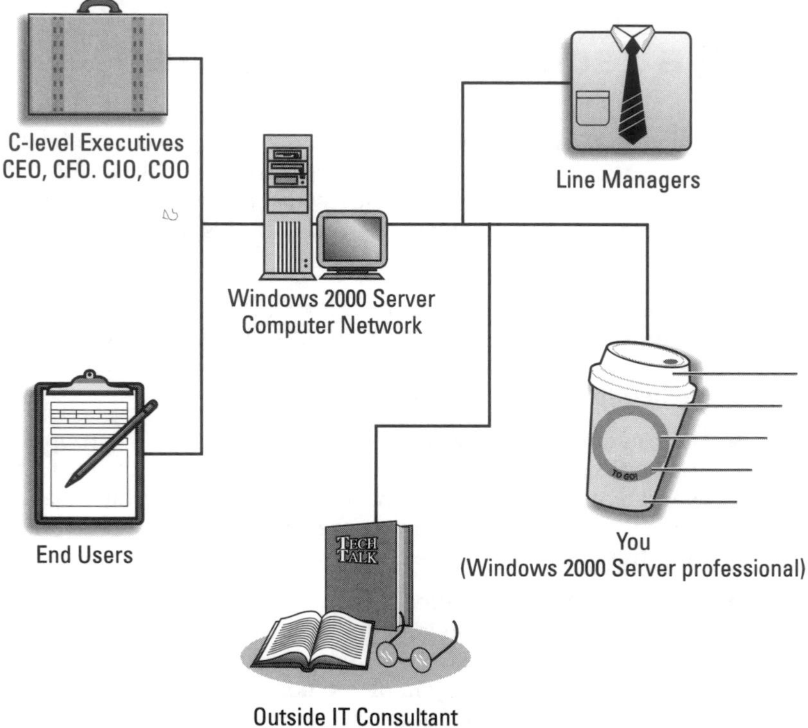

Figure 10-5: Technology committee membership

Issues addressed by the technology committee include, but are not limited to, the following:

- Budget versus actual expenditures
- Implementation schedules
- IT hiring decisions (in-house staff, consultants)
- Vendor selection (services, products, presentations)
- Network performance review (end user satisfaction surveys, network uptime reports, performance monitoring charts and analysis)

Evaluating Systems on the Horizon

One of the biggest frustrations of working with modern information technology is the constant barrage of upgrades and enhancements that seem to come down the pike. Talk to anybody at a Windows 2000 Server conference, and they'll all say the same thing: Once you finally have that new office suite or e-mail system rolled out to your 10,000-user environment, there's no time to rest before you have to start working on integrating the product's next version. If you let it get to you, this frantic upgrade schedule can cause untold stress and grief. So what's a frazzled administrator to do?

The answer is simple: Exercise moderation. The reasons software vendors hit us with endless upgrades is the incredible competition they face and the perceived huge demand for these new versions. Who generates this perceived demand? Us! So stand up to them; go to your 2000 conference hotel room window, lean out, and shout, "We're mad as hell and we're not going to take it any more!" Seriously, the upgrade frenzy won't stop until the IT world in general learns to relax a bit and capitalize on their current systems. This phenomenon has already started taking root, thankfully, and should continue through the next couple of years.

Two real-world examples

Mind an old war story? Some time ago, at my office, we completed migration from Microsoft Mail to an Exchange Server based e-mail and groupware system. Our primary reason for doing this was that the text-based and decentralized nature of MS Mail post offices created an administrative nightmare for us, and our users were clamoring for the new features available in Exchange Server. When we began the project, the current version of Exchange Server was 5.0, so that's the system we went with. Now that all the users are on the system and things are running smoothly, we are beginning to evaluate the move to version 5.5. At this point, we haven't seen anything that would really push us over the edge as far as undertaking (and paying for!) an upgrade. Sure, there are many new and useful features in 5.5, plus a better back-end database, but at this point we haven't found any "gotta have it" features that would apply to our network. We also want to see what's coming down the pike in Exchange Server 6; we don't want to be upgrading our e-mail system more than once every couple of years. So we're going to play it cool for a while, keeping our existing Exchange Server 5.0 system on the latest service pack, and enjoying the calm between the migration storms.

At the same time that we were doing the Exchange migration, our three-person network administration group was moving our 175 users from nine NetWare 3.12 servers to one central Windows NT 4.0 server. When that migration was completed, users worked along every day, basically oblivious to the system that manages all of their files and printers. After a year of client and server conversions, we enjoyed the lull, believe me. We were also very conservative about messing with our production systems; we didn't put Service Pack 4 on a single production box right away, but waited and watched the Internet forums carefully to see what kinds of problems might await us. We didn't have an urgent need to move to SP4, so we were being rather conservative about it and waited for the first round of hotfixes to come out before proceeding. Consideration should be given to learning Windows 2000 Server and what effects it will have on your network before deploying it on production servers. In other words, deploy Windows 2000 Server on test servers as soon as you can, but also think about a reasonable delay (for learning and testing) before deploying Windows 2000 Server on your production servers.

What do these examples have to do with your network? I'm hoping to convey that you don't have to jump on the latest operating system or application upgrade in order to have a successful, well-maintained system. Be aware of what's coming and start thinking about how to integrate it, but don't rush it. Unless the new system is ripe with features your users absolutely can't live without, they won't care what version they're on, as long as they can log on and work each day. Life on the bleeding edge can be fun and exciting, but it can also be painful for you and your users. So be open to the possibility of delaying upgrades for a while. Take a few months, optimize your current systems so that they hum along perfectly, and enjoy the silence.

Looking inward

Don't forget to look inward at Windows 2000 Server when you've got your forward-thinking strategic planning hat on. By that I mean you may consider implementing additional features in Windows 2000 Server that may not have made the most sense in year one (the first year you implemented Windows 2000 Server in your organization). One such feature that many firms can take advantage of is the built-in Terminal Services. In the past Windows NT Server 4.0 era, terminal-like functionality was provided by a separate Windows NT product called Terminal Server. In Windows 2000 Server, terminal functionality is provided out-of-the-box as Terminal Services.

You implement Terminal Services just like Terminal Server by installing the Terminal Services client component on the workstations, after Terminal Services has been loaded on your Windows 2000 Server. These workstations can then launch a session to connect to the Terminal Services running on the Windows 2000 Server. You may recall this session is typically a large session window on the monitor of the existing workstation. You may also attach "thin clients," which are similar to dumb terminals, to your network. You will find the greatest use of Terminal Services for remote users who dial in or VPN (virtual private network) into the corporate network, users who regularly destroy their local desktops and benefit from the "roving" profile nature of Terminal Services, and strategically deployed thin-clients.

Remembering the Annual Planning Retreat

My favorite! But seriously folks, there are valid reasons for getting away each year for an annual planning retreat. It is critical that this be held off-site so that participants aren't distracted by the telephone, e-mail, pagers, and the like. It is here that budgets are made and better friendships between the business staff and the IT department are cultivated. It is here that the strategic vision for technology is cast.

Tip

Use the annual planning retreat to hear from your main technology vendors. Vendors such as Microsoft, Cisco, Oracle, Novell, and others will be happy to send a sales engineer to your retreat, for free, to educate you on their existing and forthcoming solutions. To arrange for such presentations, just call your account representative at the vendor of your choice.

And don't forget that the annual retreat is a chance for you to both show off your successes and receive accolades for a job well done as a Windows 2000 Server professional.

Summary

In addition to daily administration, Windows 2000 networks require monthly and annual attention to continue running smoothly and to keep up with the technology that users demand. In this chapter, I covered some of these monthly and yearly tasks:

- Auditing your network
- Reviewing security
- Performance benchmarking and monitoring
- The monthly reboot
- Managing disk space on servers
- Disaster recovery simulation
- Implementing operating system service packs and hotfixes
- Creating monthly or quarterly archives
- Implementing network application upgrades
- Annual budgeting for your network
- Setting up an active technology committee
- Evaluating systems on the horizon
- The annual planning retreat

Part IV

Active Directory and Security

Chapter 11

Active Directory, Part I

In This Chapter

- Managing Active Directory expectations
- Defining Active Directory
- Taking a logical view of Active Directory
- Taking a physical view of Active Directory
- Comparing and contrasting Active Directory and Domain Name System (DNS)
- Learning the 4 P's of Active Directory planning

Mind if I spend a few minutes engaging in Windows 2000 Server expectation management? No Windows 2000 Server feature I can think of has received more publicity and advanced buildup than Active Directory. While you will enjoy Active Directory very much, the power of which I will unleash over the next two chapters, you must also manage your expectations. With such hype, many are looking to Active Directory to solve world population problems and the like. You and I are bound to be disappointed at some point with Active Directory while working with Windows 2000 Server. Why? For several reasons:

- **Learning Curve.** First, the more time you spend with Active Directory, the more you will be able to see for yourself its relative strengths and weaknesses. Early on in your Windows 2000 Server experience, you're not qualified or experienced enough with Active Directory to make that decision.
- **Red Head Revenge.** Get ready for this barrage. NetWare prophets will dance madly, celebrating the fact the NDS is more mature, more stable, more everything than first-generation Active Directory. As a former Novell NetWare practitioner (a.k.a. Red Head) and current Certified NetWare Engineer (CNE), I see both sides. NDS is now over five years old; this is not the case with Active Directory. And because no operating system is immune to the necessary and lengthy process of debugging (er...perfecting), it is true NDS has aged very nicely and shows the signs of maturity that Active Directory doesn't. Throw this into the expectation management stew.

- **Growing Pains.** Many of us MCSE types are also forming families at home when we're not designing Active Directory trees. Just as your child first turns over, then crab walks around the house, takes baby steps, and ultimately walks, the same forces of nature apply to Active Directory. It's safe to say that Active Directory is in its infancy, and will have some growing pains. Some will be humorous, others painful.
- **Great Expectations.** The one thing you can count on is that Active Directory will improve. To attain these improvements, it will necessarily undergo changes via additions and deletions to its core feature set. In short, the Active Directory you work with today won't be the same Active Directory that your children will work with.

But enough about Active Directory expectation management. What are these two Active Directory chapters really about? This chapter, Active Directory Part I, is about planning. The next chapter, Active Directory Part II, is practical and pragmatic with an emphasis on implementations, rollouts, and even keystrokes you will perform. So, in the next few pages, I speak to the solution architects amongst us. Next chapter, I honor the in-the-trenches gang, the hands-on MCSE-types. Enjoy!

What is Active Directory?

Because Active Directory is new on the Windows 2000 scene, I am right there with you in defining what Active Directory is. Two reference points that I'm using to better understand Active Directory are based on my life experiences in technology. A reference point is data structures in C programming. For the uninitiated, data structures are where you define what data and information are at a very foundational and object level. Another more pragmatic reference point for relating to Active Directory is NetWare's NDS; this is Novell's directory services offering that I discussed in the introduction of this chapter. What parallels to Active Directory might you draw from your own technology background? I'd encourage you to engage in this intellectual exercise for a few minutes so that you're better prepared to learn the new terminology and constructs associated with Active Directory. Remember that learning is often a function of having reference points that relate well to something new and unfamiliar.

Technically speaking, Active Directory is based on the Lightweight Directory Access Protocol (LDAP). LDAP is actually a heavyweight component in the whole directory services arena, so its name is somewhat misleading. It is the industry standard protocol used to access Active Directory and integrates Active Directory with the Internet. LDAP performs several functions. First, LDAP facilitates the descriptive entries in the directory database. Second, LDAP is the hierarchical tree that facilitates each object's unique pathway in Active Directory. Next, LDAP provides the query mechanism for retrieving information. Last, and certainly not least, LDAP accommodates authentication protocols, meaning only authenticated users can access information.

The "official" party line from the Big M (Microsoft) is that Active Directory is the directory service in Windows 2000 Server that identifies and manages all network resources. Active Directory can be considered from two viewpoints: size and capabilities.

S – M – L – XL

To be honest, my smaller clients won't initially benefit from Active Directory. These are typically the Small Business Server (SBS) sites that will continue to function just fine under Windows NT Server 4.0's single domain model (something I discuss at length in Chapter 16). Enough said. Contrast that with the large electronics manufacturing firm mentioned in Chapter 15. Without naming names, this firm and its 140,000 users span the entire reach of the globe. Active Directory was designed with this firm in mind.

Capabilities

Back to basics for a minute. Active Directory essentially provides basic directory management capabilities or "services, hence the term *directory services*. Active Directory provides a way to organize, manage and enable access to resources on the network. Much like a real-world directory, such as an Internet white pages (for example, `www.whowhere.com`), users may use Active Directory, whether they really know it or not, to locate and use network resources.

Active Directory is designed to make your life as a Windows 2000 Server professional easier. This is accomplished by its capability to query objects in the Active Directory tree, replicate itself to prevent damage from system failures, lay down the law so that unauthorized access is prohibited, and integrate with other operating systems and directory services.

Limitations

In this first iteration of Active Directory, there are some glaring omissions. But hey—who's to say that Microsoft won't get it right for the third generation of Active Directory? If you think back to just a few years ago, it's not like NDS was code-complete with the first release of NetWare 4.*x* either.

The two most obvious limitations in Active Directory today are its continued reliance on multiple layers of groups (especially local and global) and its non meta-information orientation. Using multiple group layers is offensive to those of us who come from the NetWare community. Active Directory retains the global and local groups of Windows NT Server and even adds universal groups. But I for one can live with the groups. Less easy to live with is Active Directory's myopic view of the directory as an operating system thing. What I had hoped for and don't see is true meta-information management. Meta-information is best described as uniform information. That is, when you add a user to a computer system, the user accounts in the e-mail, database, human resource, and accounting systems are automatically created. You see hints of it when you add a user and the user is automatically added as a Microsoft Exchange recipient, but what I really needed to see is that the basic user information you enter for a user automatically populates a Contact form in a Public Folder-based Contacts file in Microsoft Outlook. That's an example of something that's practical and you and your users would really use. It's simply not present in Active Directory at this time.

Logical Structure

Time for a virtual visit to Active Directory. Before getting physical, let's first define Active Directory logically. The components include

- Objects
- Domains
- Organizational units (OU)
- Trees
- Forests

I will now define each of the components.

Objects

Objects are relative to exactly what you're speaking about. That is, objects mean different things to different people and at different times. For example, objects can be viewed from a very granular level. You might say that a user is an object.

There is something in Active Directory called a *container object.* Strictly speaking, container objects house other objects. An example of this is the organizational unit (OU), which I will define later in this chapter. In the NetWare community, these (Windows 2000 Server's container objects) are akin to containers.

And then there is the issue of the object food chain (see Figure 11-1). Objects have characteristics that are called attributes. Attributes have values. An attribute might be the zip code field and a value for that might be 99005.

Objects may be represented by a variety of shapes, including machines, people, and folders (see Figure 11-2).

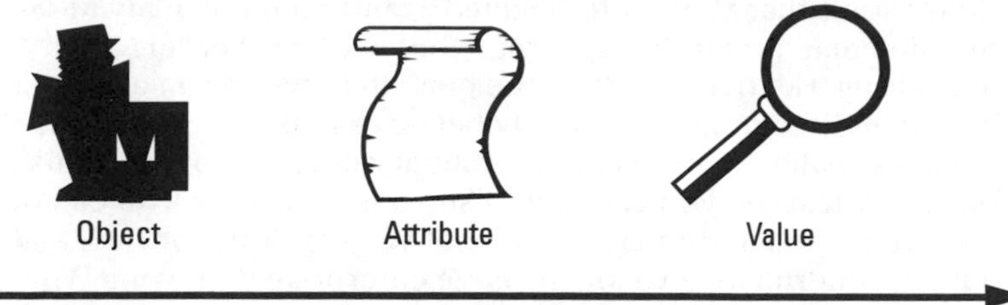

Figure 11-1: Object food chain

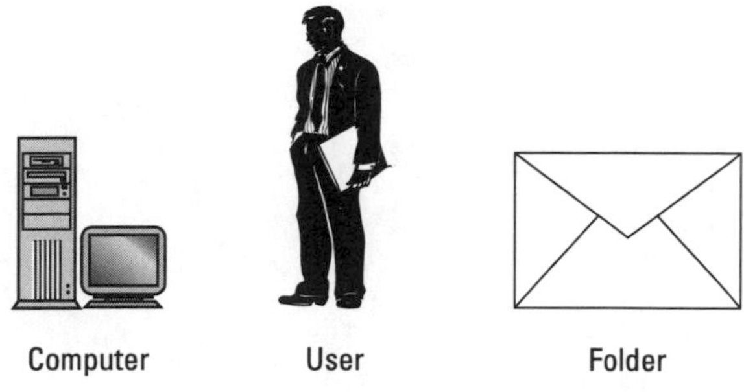

Figure 11-2: Objects

Schema

In the context of objects, a schema is akin to a data dictionary. A schema consists of the definitions and rules for all objects in the Active Directory.

Global catalog

Plainly speaking, a global catalog stores information that contains a subset of all objects' attributes in an Active Directory. Via the global catalog, the location of an object in the directory can be determined quickly. I'll discuss global catalog servers later in this chapter.

Domains

A quick quiz for the legacy MCSEs reading this book. If you were taking the Windows NT Server 4.0 Enterprise exam on the TV show "Jeopardy," where you have to try to guess the answer with a question, what would the question be for the following? "The answer is, core administrative unit"? Well, you guessed it. The question would be, "What is a domain?" Fast forward to Windows 2000 Server and both the question and the answer are still the same.

Huh? Didn't that Microsoft Certified Trainer tell me in my MCSE classes that domains would disappear in Windows 2000 Server? Well, that MCT was wrong. Get over it. While the domain serves as an administrative unit in Active Directory, it's probably better cast as a security unit. That is, domains really define security boundary lines. Because of this Active Directory feature, you can have a sub-administrator who can only manage his or her explicit domain. Again, not very exciting for the small company, but a wonderful feature for the large enterprise deploying Windows 2000 Server. And just what is the importance of security boundaries? For that answer, be sure to catch my lead-in to Chapter 19, where I discuss the power of corruption in both political and networking circles.

Domains are typically represented by a triangle shape (see Figure 11-3).

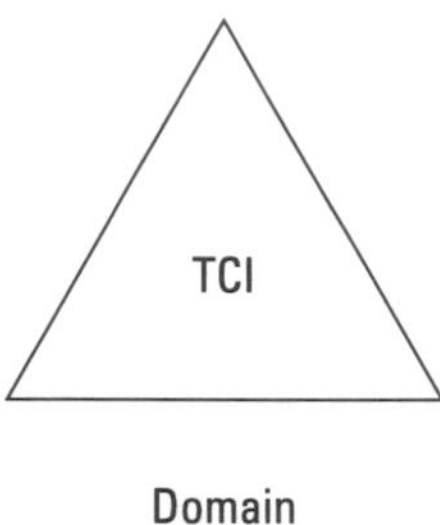

Figure 11-3: Domain

Organizational units (OU)

Those from the NetWare community will now find common ground with Windows 2000 Server's Active Directory. Even MBAs from the business side of the organization get it when it comes to organizational units. Just as the name implies, *organizational units* typically reflect a grouping of users, groups, other OUs, and so on. The point is that, more often than not, organizational units reflect the alleged structure of the organization (that is, how it officially perceives itself, the grapevine and gossip aside).

It is with OUs that the touchy-feely management consultants will reap the rewards of Windows 2000 Server deployments. It is here that they can interpret the departmental and geographical boundary banter to create OUs that reflect the organizational structure of the firm.

MCSEs, on the other hand, will initially view OUs from the perspective of administrative responsibilities. One example might be creating an OU for printers to simplify the management of printers in the enterprise.

OUs are typically depicted as circles (see Figure 11-4).

Figure 11-4: Organizational unit (OU)

Trees

You would think you've stumbled into the wrong classroom. Perhaps you were on your way to attend an MCSE course on Windows 2000 Server at a local college, but mistakenly in your confused state you find yourself in an MBA class, listening to a lecture about seeing the forest for the trees. It might take you more than a few minutes to realize you're attending the wrong class. That's because Active Directory not only uses the forest-and-trees terminology, but uses these metaphors in a manner similar to the MBA community.

An Active Directory *tree* is a top-down configuration of one or more Windows 2000 domains. A simple Active Directory tree is displayed in Figure 11-5.

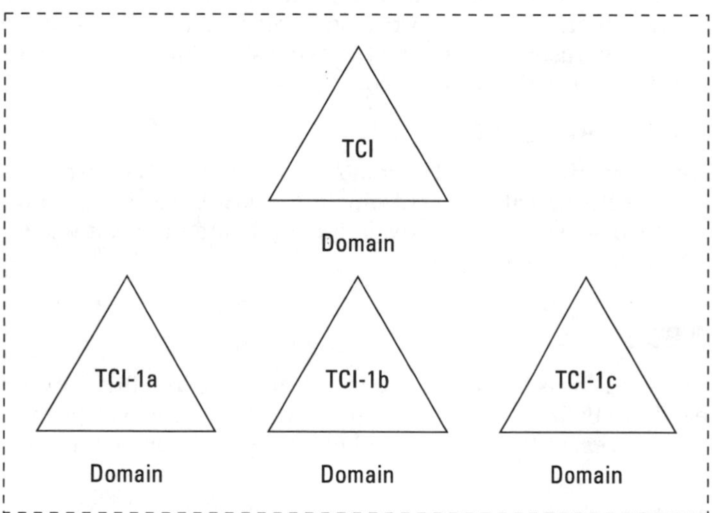

Figure 11-5: Active Directory tree

A tree in Active Directory is conceptually similar to a tree in NetWare's NDS.

Child care

A domain that is added to an existing tree becomes by definition a child domain of an existing parent domain. This is conceptually similar to sites in Microsoft System Management Server (SMS), where the parent/child relationship is also employed.

Trust me

Maybe you thought life was getting better and you left trusts back with Windows NT Server 4.0. Not so. Trusts are back, albeit they have gotten mysteriously more palatable. Active Directory supports two types of trusts: two-way transitive trusts and one-way transitive trusts.

Two-way, transitive

Hallelujah! Transitive trusts, the ultimate trick question on the Windows NT Server 4.0 Enterprise exam, now exist in Windows 2000 Server. Transitive trusts are easily understood. Borrowing from Figure 11-5, if Domain TCI-1a trusts TCI-1b and TCI-1b trusts TCI-1c, then by strict definition, TCI-1a trusts TCI-1c.

A two-way trust is the same as it was in Windows NT Server 4.0. Here, Domain TCI-1a would trust TCI-1b and vice versa.

Even though the Windows 2000 Server exams haven't been created as of this writing, be aware that a common trick question regarding trusts focuses on the wording. Here is what I mean: It is common to say "two-way trust" when that is the situation that you are describing. But it is also permissible to say "two one-way trusts" to describe the same situation. The MCSE exams have been known to use the play-on-words ploy.

One-way, non-transitive

Simply stated, the fact that Domain A trusts Domain B doesn't mean that Domain B automatically trusts Domain A. It's a one-way trust, not the two-way trusts discussed previously. In the legal community, it would be stated as reciprocity not being a given.

Forests

The small business folks can skip to the next section. But the enterprise folks will easily visualize an Active Directory *forest*. A forest is a grouping of Active Directory trees, as the name would imply. Very simple metaphor, eh?

Physical Structure

There are several physical planning considerations with Active Directory, including *sites, domain controllers,* and *global catalog servers.*

Sites

If you're a brazen BackOffice warrior, you've bumped into sites already. But you might recall that a site in Exchange is a different site or boundary from a site in SMS. And a domain, a type of site, is a different type of site from an IP subnet, which is the underlying definition of a site in Active Directory. Officially speaking, an Active Directory site is one or more IP subnets that are connected via high-speed links. These links can be LAN or WAN in nature, but are assumed to be over 128Kbps (that's two-channel ISDN speed). Note that subnets are discussed extensively in Chapter 7 as well as other chapters in Part II. The basic modus operandi behind sites is to speed Active Directory replication traffic and facilitate reliable user logons to domains.

Here's a braintwister for you. A single site may have multiple domains, yet a single domain may span multiple sites.

Domain controllers

This should be a fairly easy definition for you. The Windows 2000 Server that stores a replica of the directory is a *domain controller*. This makes a lot of sense if you think about it. From your Windows NT days, you may recall that a domain controller contained a copy of the security accounts manager (SAM), permitting local logons to the bigger domain. If you accept the basic premise that Active Directory is a newer and more improved SAM, then the notion that a domain controller contains a directory replica makes perfect sense.

Active Directory behaves like the old SAM model in that it acts as the security subsystems and manages access authentication, data storage, security model, and trust information.

But there's a slight twisted end to my tale. Active Directory borrows a page out of the NetWare NDS book and uses multi-master replication. Here, come hell or high water, no single domain controller is the master domain controller. Instead, all domain controllers maintain directory copies.

At any given moment, one domain controller may contain some information in its directory copy that hasn't been replicated to the other domain controllers yet. Thus, the purpose of replication is to distribute such delta changes as often as is practicable. If you haven't had a course in statistics, you might need to know that delta represents only the changed values. So only the changes to the database are distributed, not the entire database. Two design issues you will encounter are concerns about where to place domain controllers (for example, across slow WAN links) and how often domains replicate their directory changes.

Global catalog servers

Simply stated, a global catalog server stores and processes a global catalog. Global catalogs were discussed earlier in this chapter (they are used to enhance performance when searching through Active Directory forests).

Active Directory and DNS

Time for a little compare and contrast. Exactly what is the relationship between Active Directory and DNS? Certainly the underlying common relationship relates to name space. DNS provides name resolution and Active Directory names things.

Whereas Active Directory may consist of one or more domains, DNS identifies domains. The domain names compare straight across very well: DNS and Active Directory share the same domain names. However, by contrast, DNS creates and manages zone records and Active Directory creates and manages domain objects. Note that DNS is discussed extensively in Chapter 6.

Each Active Directory domain requires a unique DNS domain.

Tying it all together, understand that LDAP is the "glue" between Active Directory and DNS. It is the protocol that enables the two distinct bodies to communicate and interact.

4 P's of Active Directory Planning

The goal of this chapter, as stated earlier, is to provide a planning platform for your implementation of Active Directory. It's critical to revisit that underlying theme as I continue to manage your Active Directory expectations and conclude this chapter.

Early on with Active Directory, you will encounter the four P's of Active Directory planning: politics, physical issues, perspectives, and practical considerations.

Political

Many solutions architects will make good money just operating in the political realm as they design and introduce Active Directory into the organization. That's because Active Directory, with its boundary orientation, calls into question what resources belong where in the organization and who controls them. Thank goodness for the capability to have administrators at the single domain-level so the political considerations relating to empowerment and decentralization may be easily accommodated. And you always wanted to work on a political campaign, right?

Physical

On the one hand, the physical location of resources really doesn't matter under Active Directory. This is similar to the strict domain concepts in Windows NT Server. It doesn't matter if a machine is located in Building 42 or Building 55 on the campus. Here, when talking about locations, the logical groupings of physical things win every time. In other words, you might group everyone in the marketing area into an OU called Marketing, even thought these people are physically located, shall we say, across state lines.

And as far as Active Directory is concerned, I've already defined its physical attributes via the discussion on objects, sites and the like. However, there is one physical concern mentioned in passing to which you should pay careful attention. The concern relating to replication is paramount. A poorly designed WAN, at the true enterprise level, could suffer poor Active Directory performance due to slow logons, replication traffic choking the links, and so on. Be advised.

Perspective

This chapter and this book were written to convey a broad array of secrets, tips and tricks relating to Windows 2000 Server. It's a tall order because almost any chapter could easily be a book in itself. In fact, there are many good books on Active Directory (and they're thick, too!). The point is this. You need to keep a proper perspective on Active Directory. It's not an area sufficiently covered in one or two chapters of any book. Rather, your next step as you embark on the study of Active Directory is to take the foundational Active Directory knowledge garnered from this and the next chapter and leverage upon that as you acquire and use a specialized Active Directory book. In such a specialized book, you will gain insights into advanced directory issues such as:

- Multidomain directories
- Replication
- Naming strategies
- Administrative authority
- Active Directory data recovery
- Active Directory maintenance
- Schema modifications
- Integration with Microsoft Exchange
- Windows NT Server domain upgrades to Active Directory

I would also encourage you to avail yourself of some or all of the following Microsoft certification courses. It will be essential for MCSEs to heed this advice in order to remain competitive.

- Course 1560: Updating Support Skills from Microsoft Windows NT 4.0 to Microsoft Windows 2000
- Course 1561: Designing a Microsoft Windows 2000 Directory Services Infrastructure
- Course 1562: Designing a Microsoft Windows 2000 Networking Infrastructure
- Course 1563: Designing a Change and Configuration Management Infrastructure for Microsoft Windows 2000 Professional

The preceding course titles and numbers are subject to change by Microsoft (and frequently are!).

Practical

Above all, keep your wits about this Active Directory stuff. It's easy, much like the aspiring MCSE in the old Windows NT Server days, to over-design an Active Directory. Stay practical and justify each and every layer of complexity you introduce into your Active Directory. Let's face it, most of us work for firms that are not in the Fortune 1000. Statistics show that more people (namely, end users) are employed by small- and medium-sized organizations than by enterprises. So in Microsoft's justifiable enthusiasm to conquer the enterprise, understand that its written works and that of many authors speak towards organizations that are global in scale.

The best advice I was ever given by a peer relating to NetWare's NDS also applies equally well to Active Directory. Over lunch at a Tex-Mex restaurant, this NetWare guru told me to just keep it simple and "throw everything into one OU." He was basically communicating, in NetWare terms, to start from the bindery perspective. In Windows NT Server terms, that would translate into throwing everything into a single domain. In Active Directory terms, the translation is straight across: Start by throwing everything into a single OU.

Now, of course my lunch buddy was advising me on a medium-sized network that had been over-engineered and super-sized by the last network engineer, but you get the point. Start simple. If you're a smaller organization, truly put everything in one OU and then "discover" why you would need and can justify increasing levels of complexity in your Active Directory. Call it the Zen of Active Directory.

Summary

This ends the high-level view of Active Directory planning topics. In the next chapter, a more pragmatic Active Directory approach is presented. In this chapter, the following topics were discussed.

- Managing Active Directory expectations
- Defining Active Directory
- Taking a logical view of Active Directory
- Taking a physical view of Active Directory
- Comparing and contrasting Active Directory and Domain Name System (DNS)
- Learning the 4 P's of Active Directory planning

Chapter 12

Active Directory, Part II

In This Chapter

- Actively managing the Active Directory
- Understanding the difference between Active Directory planning and practical uses of Active Directory
- Optimizing organizational units in Active Directory
- Configuring and delegating OU permissions in Active Directory
- Adding and moving common Active Directory objects including users, groups, and computers
- Understanding Active Directory site and domain management

Believe it or not, you've already been working with Active Directory! If you've followed many of my examples and steps since the beginning of the book, you've installed a domain controller, and thus you have installed Active Directory (see Chapter 2). If you've added users, as discussed in Chapter 9, then you have used Active Directory to accomplish a task. I share this with you so that you can minimize if not eliminate any Active Directory anxiety you've built up.

This chapter is the "yang" to the "yin" of the last chapter. Whereas the last chapter was planning-centric, this chapter focuses on the practical and pragmatic aspects of Active Directory. It's hands-on, so let's get going.

Optimizing Organizational Units

I've come to believe the organizational units (OUs) are where the MCSEs and MBAs can find common ground. I talked about this coming together of business and technical perspectives in the last chapter. In this chapter, we make it happen. Ideally, your Active Directory will be, first and foremost, pragmatic. I believe that the OUs can be designed with the underlying organization in mind, be it corporations, not-for-profit organizations, or government agencies. That is, OUs can be created for different functional areas of responsibility, such as marketing, manufacturing, and legal. Another possibility that works for many firms is to create OUs by geographic location: corporate headquarters, branch offices, project sites, and even vendor sites.

Of course, if you feel the world should be run by MCSEs, you might build a complex Active Directory based on subnets, hardware locations, and other technology-based dimensions. The choice is yours. You can create an Active Directory with a focus on business functions, technology resources, or a combination of the two.

Remember that OUs may contain users, groups, and computer accounts. OUs are typically used to delegate administrative control.

OUs are best deployed if they define administrative boundaries in your domain.

To create an OU, follow these steps.

STEPS:

Creating an OU

Step 1. Select Administrative Tools, Active Directory Users and Computers on the Start menu. The Active Directory Users and Computers MMC will appear.

Step 2. Right-click the domain icon in the left pane. The secondary menu will be displayed.

Step 3. Select New, Organizational Unit from the secondary menu.

Step 4. The Create New Object - (Organizational Unit) dialog box will appear (see Figure 12-1). Name the OU.

Step 5. Click OK. The OU will appear in the left pane of the Active Directory Users and Computers MMC (see Figure 12-2).

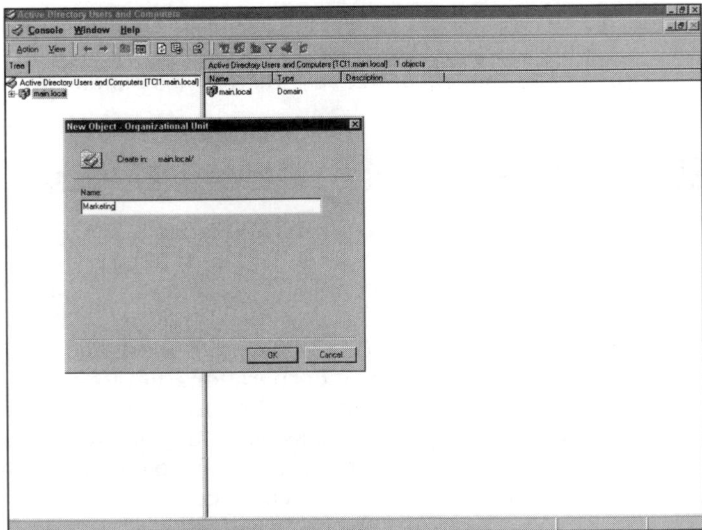

Figure 12-1: Creating an OU

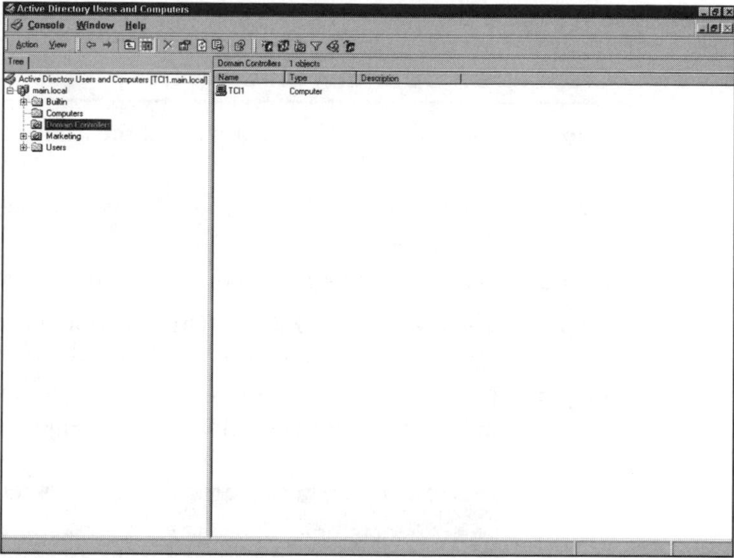

Figure 12-2: OU displayed in Active Directory Users and Computers MMC

You may recall a secret near the end of Chapter 11 where I suggested you consider creating just one OU and putting everything in it, at least to start with. You would then critically evaluate the need for additional OUs on a case-by-case basis. But be advised that while this advice is valid, it clearly applies to small and medium-sized organizations, not full-scale enterprises.

You want to be master of your own destiny with your Active Directory and create at least one OU right away. That's because the built-in default containers shown in Active Directory Users and Computers are not very useful or practical. First, these containers are not true OUs. Second, you cannot create OUs within these default containers. Finally, you can't apply group policy to these default containers. Take my advice and create your own OU or OUs as soon as possible.

An OU inside an OU

There are very important reasons to consider creating an OU within an OU. For example, this might make the best sense if you work in a decentralized or matrix organization. Another reason to have OUs within OUs would be a project management organization, where the embedded OU might be named after a project of limited scope and duration. To create an OU within an OU, follow these steps.

STEPS:

Creating an OU within an OU

Step 1. Select the OU in the left pane of the Active Directory Users and Computers MMC.

Step 2. Right-click the OU that you selected. The secondary menu will appear.

Step 3. Select New ⇨ Organizational Unit from the secondary menu.

Step 4. The Create New Object - (Organizational Unit) dialog box will appear. Enter the name of the OU in the Name field.

Step 5. Click OK and observe that the new, embedded OU appears indented under the original OU (see Figure 12-3).

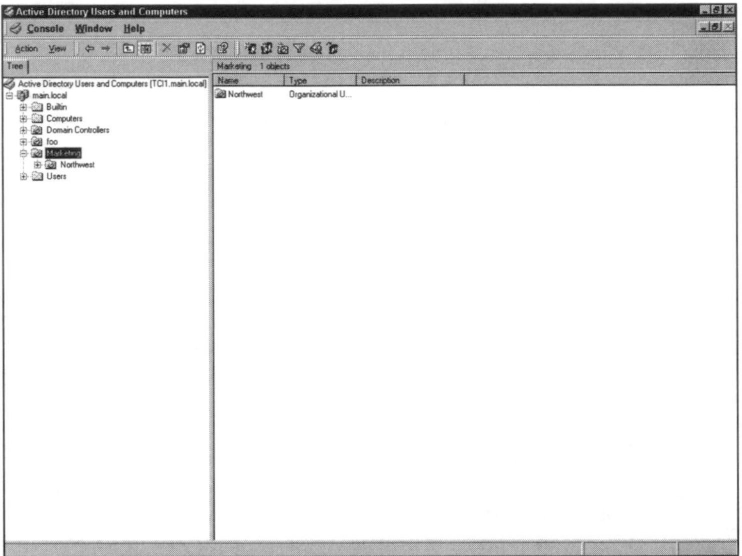

Figure 12-3: OU within an OU

OU permissions

In order to create an OU within an OU (as you did when creating Northwest inside of Marketing in the previous example), you must have the following permissions in the parent container (for example, Marketing):

- Create Organizational Unit Objects
- List Contents
- Read

The List Contents right isn't truly necessary when creating an OU within an OU. However, if you don't provide the List Contents correctly, you would not be able to see the embedded OU you just created. Not only is out of sight the same as out of mind, it's also out of management (can't be managed).

To assign and modify Active Directory permissions, follow these steps.

STEPS:

Managing Active Directory permissions

Step 1. In the Active Directory Users and Computers MMC, select View ⇨ Advanced Features.

Step 2. Right click an object (for example, the Marketing OU). Select Properties from the secondary menu.

Step 3. Select the Security tab on the OU's Properties sheet.

Step 4. You may now grant or deny the Full Control, Read, Write, Create All Child Objects, and Delete All Child Objects permissions.

Step 5. If you select the Advanced button, the Access Control Settings appear. You may set advanced permissions such as Special.

The Access Control Settings dialog box displays permissions entries in the column-and-row format that many of us have been searching for. Many times, I have wanted to know who has access to what, and wanted the information presented in a columnar report-type format. The Access Control Settings dialog box does exactly that.

Step 6. Click OK to return to the Active Directory Users and Computers MMC. You have now modified the permissions for an Active Directory object.

On the Security tab of an OU's properties sheet, you may select the Allow inheritable permissions from the parent to propagate to this object checkbox. Simply stated, this allows this OU to inherit rights from its parent.

Likewise, on the Access Control Settings dialog box, selected via the Advanced button from the Security tab of an OU's properties sheet, you can have the existing OU's permissions propagate to any existing or future children. This is the last-will-and-testament option. To invoke this option, select the Allow inheritable permissions from the parent to propagate to this object checkbox.

And in all cases, there is no usurious inheritance tax.

Delegating control

Another cool Active Directory feature, viewed from the OU perspective, is that it allows you to delegate control of an OU to someone else. This is how you can create mini-administrator, a highly desirable new feature in Windows 2000 Server. The basic reason for delegating control is to make your life easier by having someone help you manage an OU. It is also easier to track permissions at the OU level. Follow these steps to delegate control.

STEPS:

Delegating control

Step 1. Select an OU, right click and select Delegate Control from the secondary menu. The Delegation of Control Wizard will appear (see Figure 12-4).

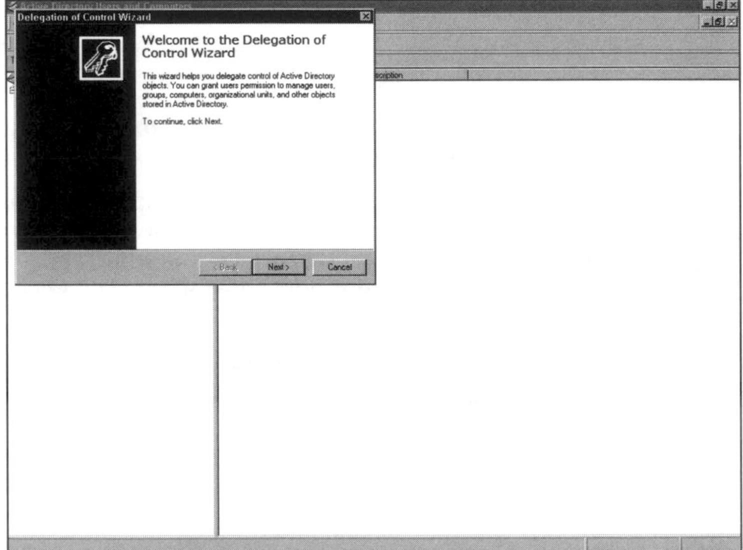

Figure 12-4: Delegation of Control Wizard

Step 2. Click Next. The Users or Groups screen appears (see Figure 12-5). Select the group or user that you want to delegate control to via the Add button. Click Next.

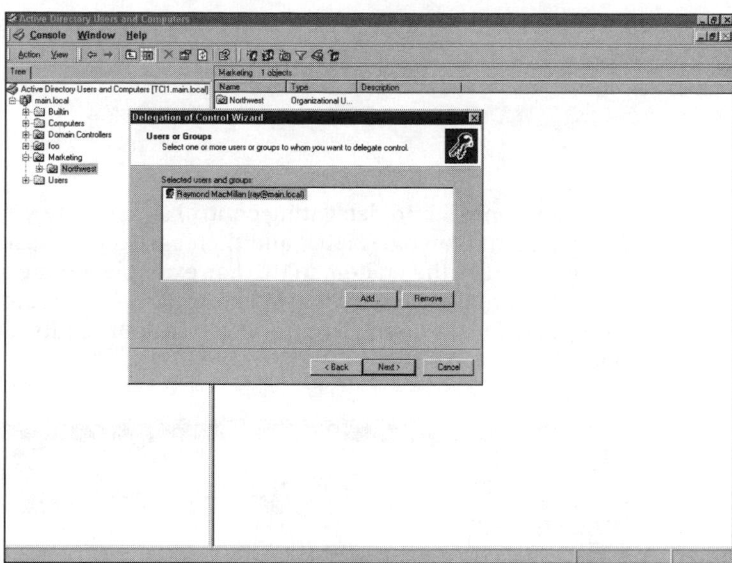

Figure 12-5: Users or Groups Selection screen

Step 3. Select the Tasks to Delegate from the list of common tasks or create a custom task to delegate (see Figure 12-6). Click Next.

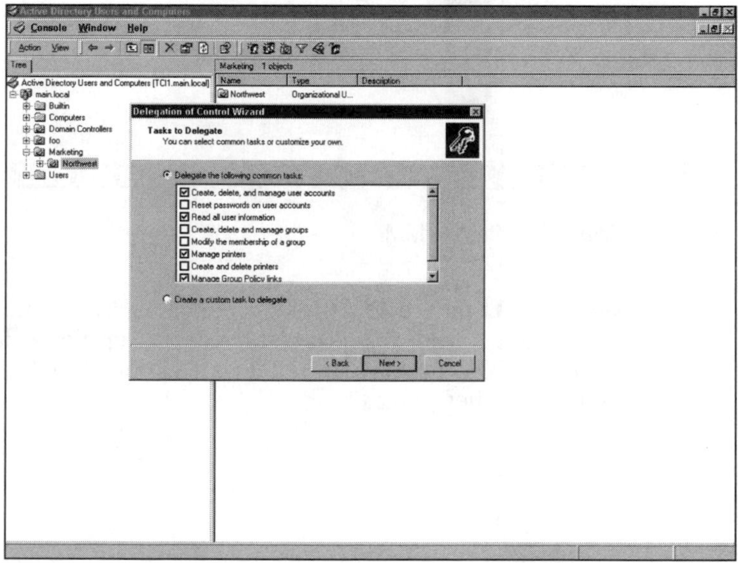

Figure 12-6: Tasks to delegate

Step 4. Click Finish at the Completing the Delegation of Control Wizard screen. You have now delegated the OU control you elected to delegate to a user or group.

Another approach to delegating control is to create your own Microsoft Management Console (MMC) and then assign permissions that permit a delegate to use the custom MMC. For example, create an MMC with three or four of your favorite snap-ins. In Figure 12-7, I've created an MMC with the Computer Management, Event Viewer, Resource Kits, and Performance Logs and Alerts snap-ins.

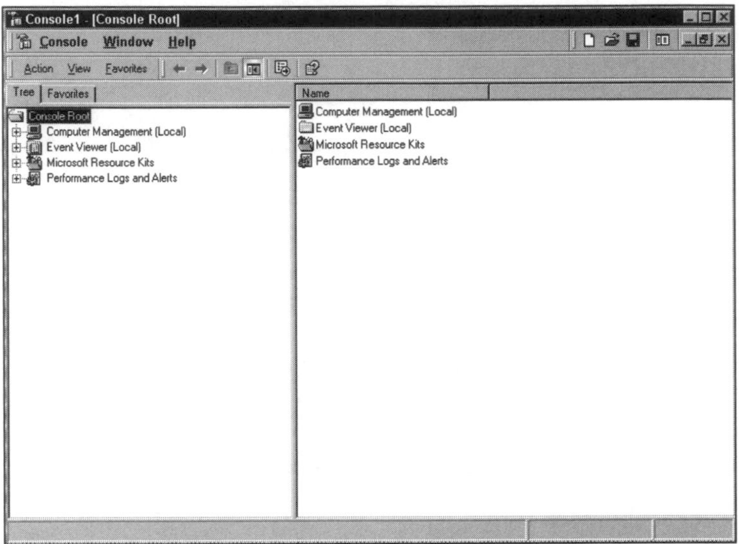

Figure 12-7: Custom MMC

Next, select options from the Console menu. The Options dialog box will appear. Select the Console tab and select User mode - full access (see Figure 12-8). Click OK. You have now delegated control to this MMC. Be sure to save your MMC when you exit.

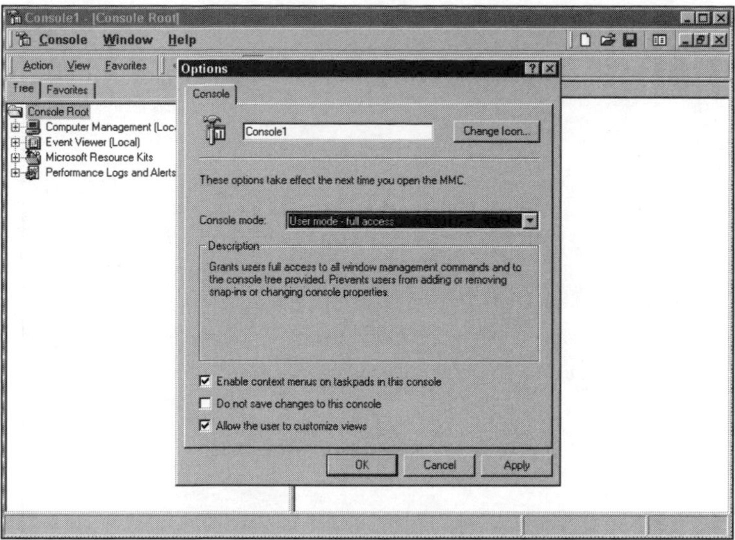

Figure 12-8: Console mode

You may now distribute this MMC to other users. By setting the MMC console to User mode, the other users may not modify this custom MMC, but rather they may use it to complete system management tasks. You may have noticed that the Console mode field had several selections:

- **Author mode:** Allows access to all MMC functionality including adding, creating, and modifying the MMC. You may also navigate the entire MMC tree.
- **User mode - full access:** Users have access to all MMC management functionality and the MMC tree. However, users cannot add or remove snap-ins or change console file options. The Save commands are disabled.
- **User mode - limited access, multiple window:** This is a more restrictive setting. Users cannot modify the MMC, open new Windows, or see areas of the console tree that weren't visible when the MMC was last saved. Multiple windows are allowed.
- **User mode: limited access, single window:** Same as the multiple window option except that only a single window is displayed.

Advanced features

A little known secondary menu option, displayed when you right-click the domain object, is View ⇨ Advanced Features. When selected, Advanced Features displays several more Active Directory components in the MMC, as seen in Figure 12-9.

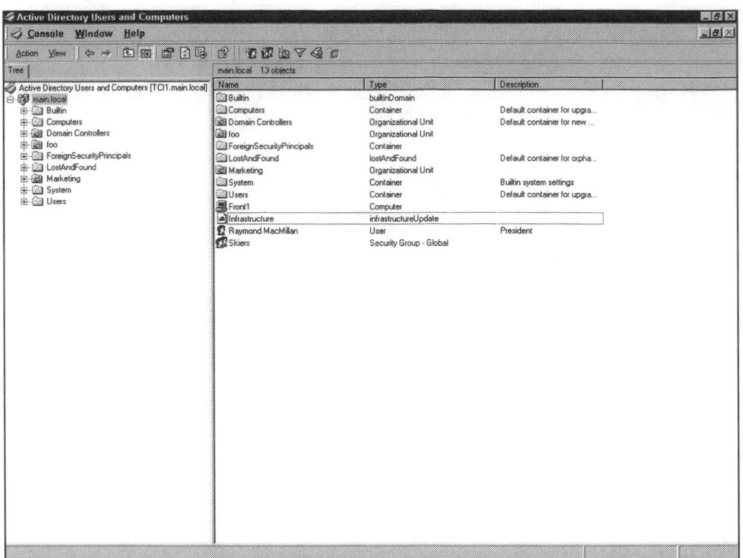

Figure 12-9: Advanced Features

For example, one of the objects displayed is LostAndFound. This object is the default container for orphaned objects. Orphaned objects are created when the relationship that ties these objects to other objects is somehow lost or broken. And to be brutally honest, orphaned objects can be created with no mistake on your part. Sometimes computers just hiccup or act in inexplicable ways.

Creating Users, Groups, and Computers

This section is actually a review for those of you who diligently read Chapter 9. Because of that, I'll quickly review how you add users, groups, and computers.

The first steps are the same. To create a user, group, or computer, simply right-click the domain or OU in the left pane of the Active Directory Users and Computers MMC. From the secondary menu, select New. You would then select User, Group, or Computer depending on the task you want to complete.

If you select User, the Create New Object - (User) Wizard will be displayed (see Figure 12-10). Complete each screen to create the user.

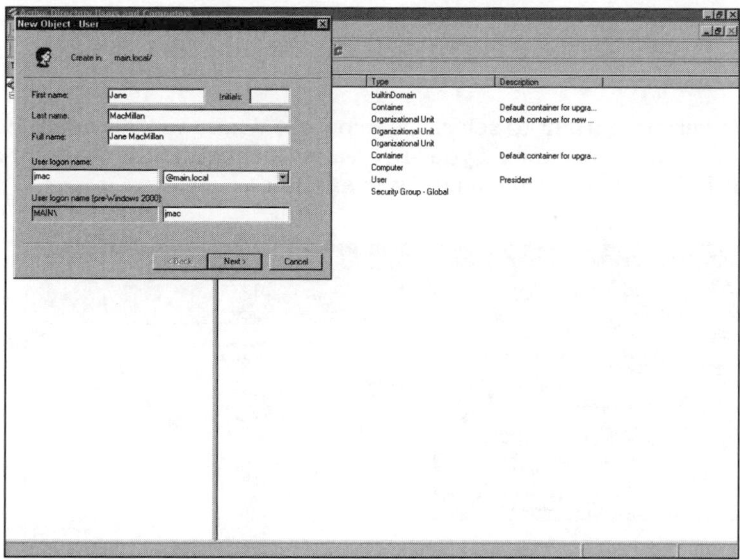

Figure 12-10: Creating a user

If you select Group, the Create New Object - (Group) Wizard appears (see Figure 12-11). Complete each field and click OK to create the group.

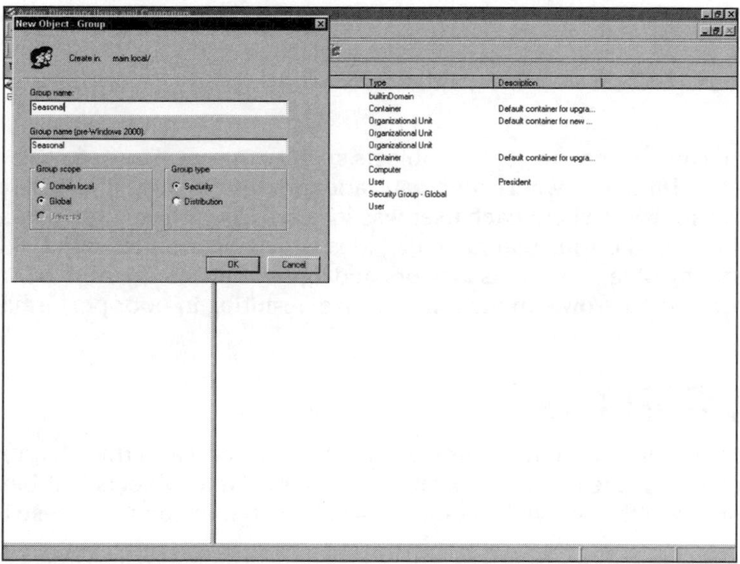

Figure 12-11: Creating a group

If you select Computer, the Create New Object - (Computer) Wizard will be displayed (see Figure 12-12). Name the computer and click OK to create the computer.

It is very important to select the Allow pre-Windows 2000 computers to use this account checkbox if you are creating a computer account for a Windows NT 4.0 Workstation machine (as an example).

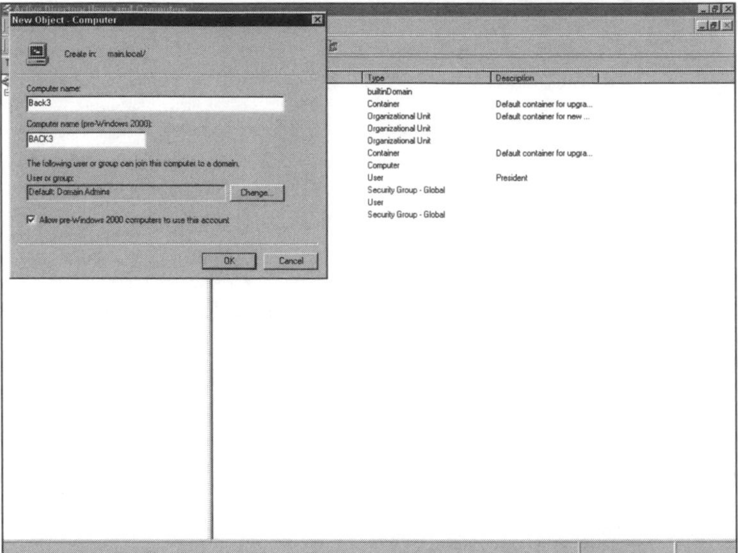

Figure 12-12: Creating a computer account

You can also create custom objects such as figures. I've seen this done in Active Directory where an organization wanted to have a picture of a floor plan showing where each user was located. Good idea when conceived on the whiteboard during planning. Bad idea when fully implemented. Why? Because creating objects such as artwork and figures causes the Active Directory database to grow exponentially in size, resulting in poor performance.

Moving Objects

If you've followed the examples in both Chapter 9 and this chapter, you will notice that the user, group, and computer exist as objects just below the domain in the Active Directory. It would be better to move these to an OU.

Be advised about the basic guidelines concerning moving objects such as users, groups, and computers. Object permissions move with the object, but inherited permissions do not move.

Follow these steps to move a user, group, and computer to the Marketing OU (again, assuming you've created that).

STEPS:

Moving a user, group and computer

Step 1. Select the object you want to move. Right-click the object to display the secondary menu. In this example, I've selected Raymond MacMillan, a user.

Step 2. Select Move. The Move dialog box appears.

Step 3. Select the container that you want to move the object to. In this example, I've selected Marketing (see Figure 12-13).

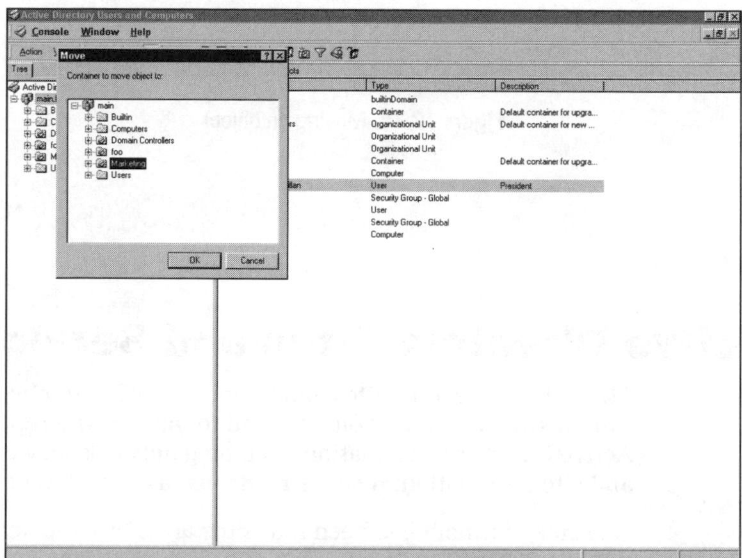

Figure 12-13: Move dialog box

Step 4. Click OK.

Step 5. The object, Raymond MacMillan, has moved to the Marketing OU (see Figure 12-14). Repeat steps 1 to 4 to move a computer or group.

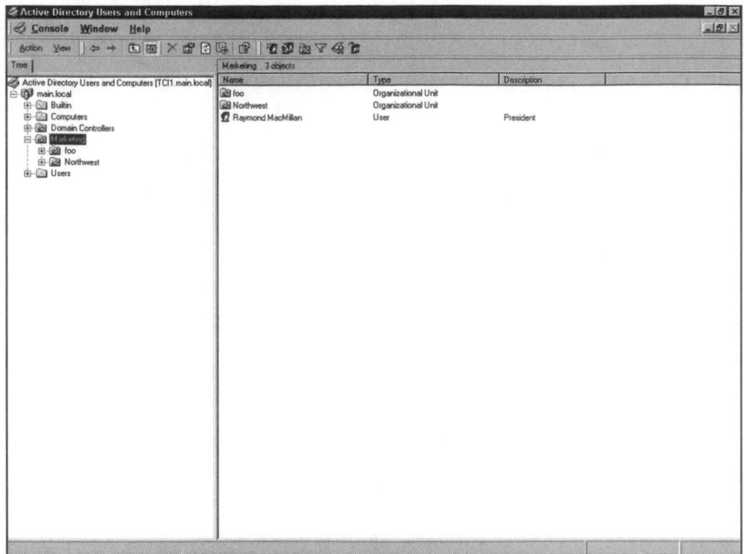

Figure 12-14: Moving an object

Active Directory Sites and Services

The Active Directory Sites and Services MMC, launched from the Administrative Tools group, is used to manage the replication of critical Active Directory information, including network services, domain controller, and site information. A site is really just a collection of subnets.

Tip

One rule of thumb has been that sites are LANs and separate sites represent a WAN.

The replication process is managed via the Active Directory Sites and Services MMC (see Figure 12-15). A few facts about replication might be of interest to you. First, configuring replication often means you must choose between accurate data and high performance. If replications are performed frequently, the data contained at each domain controller will be as accurate as possible. That is a good thing. But this data accuracy comes at a price. This frequent replication pattern consumes network bandwidth. The trade-off is this: accurate data versus network traffic issues.

When discussing one site, the originating domain controller with a delta change to its Active Directory database is responsible for notifying the replication partners about such changes. This occurs via a communication known as change notification. The replication partner, typically within five minutes of receiving this message, pulls down the delta Active Directory changes. When discussing multiple sites, replication is scheduled manually.

Once exception to this change notification process is that security-sensitive updates, defined as security-related attributes, are pulled down by the replication partner immediately.

Replication pathways within a single site are created via the Knowledge Consistency Checker (KCC). KCC creates pathways that are feasible within three hops. New domain controllers, when added to the network, are automatically added to the replication pathway by KCC.

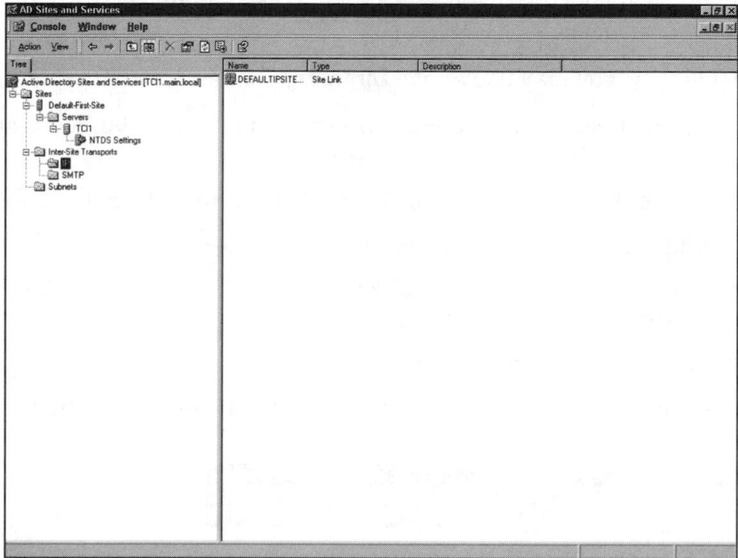

Figure 12-15: Active Directory Sites and Services MMC

All replication traffic, whether within one site or across multiple sites, use Remote Procedure Calls (RPC) as the underlying transport mechanism. With multiple site communications, Simple Mail Transport Protocol (SMTP) may also be used. The RPC communication process is shown in Figure 12-16.

Figure 12-16: The RPC communication process

Because you are using RPCs in your site replication, you will need to use the RPING utility from Microsoft Exchange to assist in troubleshooting replication problems. RPING is discussed in Chapter 20.

Active Directory Domains and Trusts

The Active Directory Domains and Trusts MMC (see Figure 12-17) is launched from the Administrative Tools program groups. Its main function is to manage domain trusts and user principal name suffixes and change the domain mode. Domains are administrative units typically created to assist you in organizing and managing your network resources. Trusts create secure pathways between domains.

Specifically, you may use Active Directory Domains and Trusts to

- Support mixed mode domain operations in mixed Windows 2000 and Windows NT domain environments
- Configure operations to run in strict Windows 2000 native mode
- Add/remove domain names
- Change the domain controller that holds the domain naming operations master role
- Create and modify domain trusts
- Gather and observe information about domain management

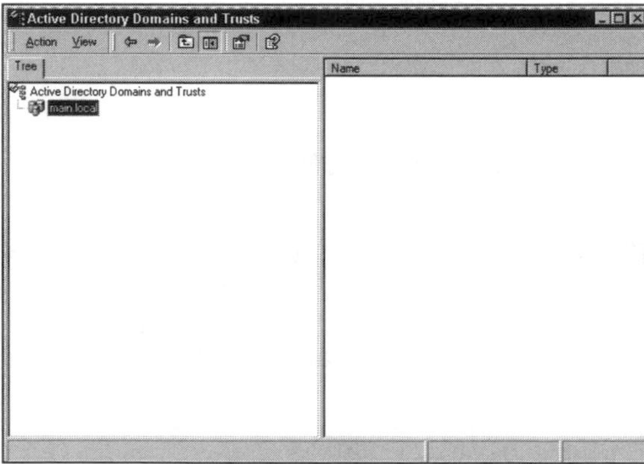

Figure 12-17: Active Directory Domains and Trusts

Summary

This chapter brought a discussed the practical aspects of Active Directory.

- Implementing Active Directory in your organization
- Creating and moving objects in Active Directory
- Understanding which Active Directory MMC to use under what circumstances
- Delegating OU permissions in Active Directory
- Understanding Active Directory site and domain management

Chapter 13

Windows 2000 Server Security

In This Chapter

- Implementing IPsec (Internet Protocol security)
- Discovering Kerberos V5
- Learning about Smart card support
- Implementing Encrypted File System (EFS)

If you feel you already know everything you need to know about Windows 2000 Server security, please proceed to the next chapter. If not, welcome to Chapter 13. Perhaps you've always assumed your security needs ended after you physically secured the server, forced users to log on with passwords, and applied sharing and NTFS-level permissions (see Figure 13-1). Think again. In the four years since NT 4 was released, security has become a major concern for corporations and individual users deploying Microsoft networking technology. From network attacks to disgruntled employees, network systems (including Microsoft's Windows 2000 Server) have come under continual assault:

- Password-cracking tools are readily available for downloading on the Internet.
- The cost of network monitoring (sniffing) equipment has declined considerably.
- Web sites from Microsoft to the White House have undergone service interruptions and altered content from outside attacks.
- A 21-year-old hacker obtained over 1,700 user IDs and passwords via a sniffer running inside TRW Credit in the mid-90s.
- A United States Senate subcommittee found that as of the mid-1990s, 58% of major US corporations have had break-ins; 18% suffered losses greater than $1 million, and 20% of break-ins were linked to competitors.

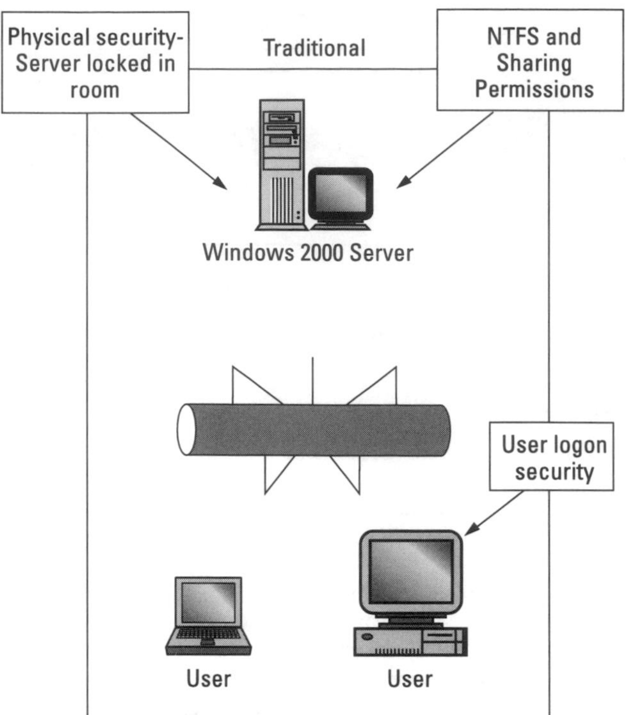

Figure 13-1: Traditional network security model

Of course, to a great degree, security is a function of common sense. And just like the sport of sailing, which is also based largely on common sense, many of us need to sharpen our common sense skills, right? How many of your users store their passwords in their top desk drawer? Are you checking logs to see who is RASing in at night? Can your firewall alert you to potential attacks in progress? Akin to sailing, this security-oriented behavior is similar to completing the boat's logbook.

Although the integrity of any system is primarily the result of intelligent planning and vigilant management, some technological advances that can help you improve security have been included in Windows 2000 Server. The security paradigm shift that has occurred between Windows NT Server 4.0 and Windows 2000 Server is two-fold: Internet and Enterprise. To make that point abundantly clear, observe Figure 13-2, in which the traditional network security model is upgraded for Windows 2000 Server.

In this chapter, I will deal with four additions to Windows 2000 Server that improve security: IPsec (Internet Protocol security), Kerberos V5, Smart Card support, and Encrypted File System (EFS). Note these are high-level security issues. In other words, these are security issues that are typically addressed at the 50,000-foot-deep level of strategic planning. Back at sea level, your day-to-day security issues are discussed in Chapters 9 and 10.

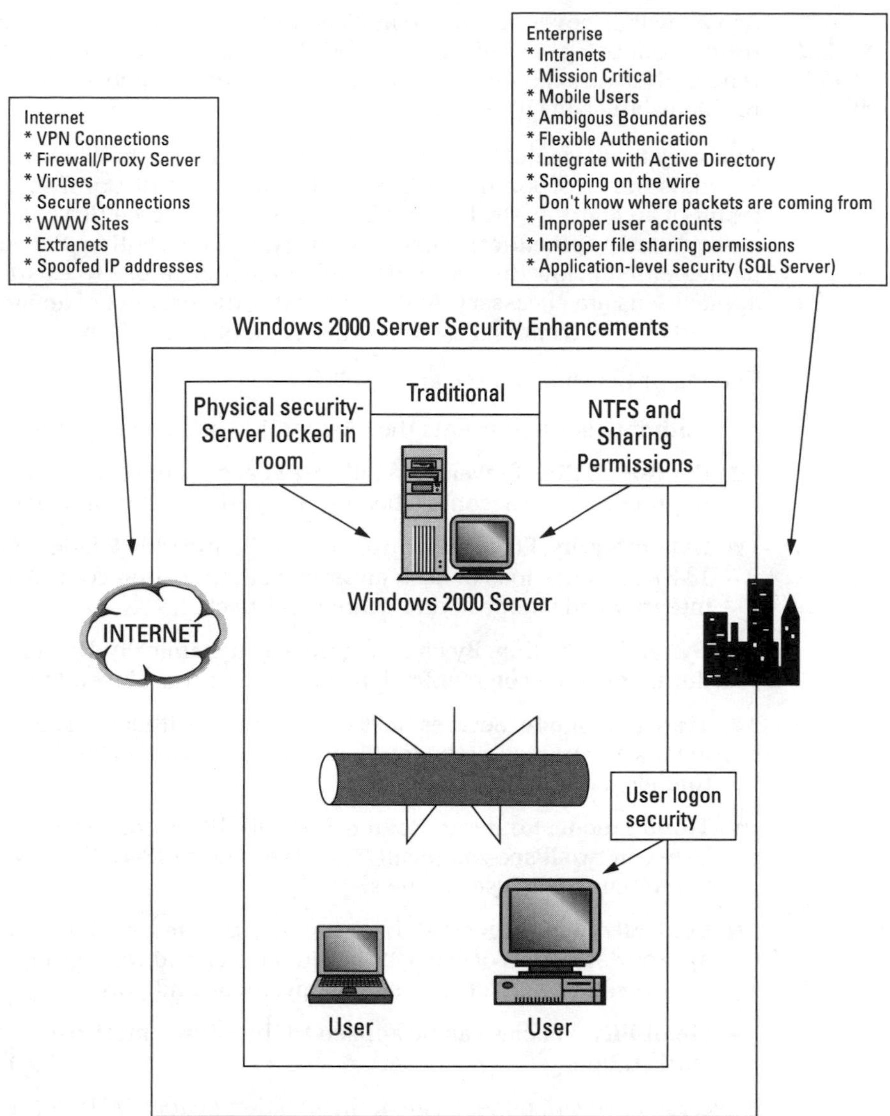

Figure 13-2: Enhanced network security model, Windows 2000 Server-style

IPsec

It goes without saying, but I'll say it anyway. Network security is a major issue these days. Some of the most dreaded attacks occur at the physical level, where sniffers and network monitors are capable of capturing and interpreting network packets. Note that I discuss Network Monitor, warts and all, in Chapter 19. Often these intrusions come from within an organization. With the tools currently available, data can be viewed, copied, or modified without a trace.

As you will discover in a moment, IPsec will indeed protect your network traffic from being viewed with Network Monitor. The bad news is that it renders Network Monitor useless in trying to resolve network traffic problems involving IPsec. Ouch!

At a very fundamental level, one of the major changes in Windows 2000 Server is the incorporation of Internet Protocol Security, or IPsec. IPsec is the result of an effort by the Internet Engineering Task Force (IETF) to provide network-level authentication, data security, and encryption. Because it is implemented below the transport level, no modifications to existing applications are necessary. And because it is the product of an industry-wide consortium, interoperability with other computing platforms is assured.

The major benefits of IPsec are as follows:

- **Authentication.** Prevents the interception of data via impersonation.
- **Confidentiality.** Prevents unauthorized access to sensitive data when required. This is accomplished by encryption of IP traffic per packet.
- **Data integrity.** Ensures the use of IP authentication headers (see Figure 13-3) and variations of hash message authentication code. Also known as integrity and source authentication per packet.
- **Dynamic rekeying.** By changing the key dynamically, Dynamic rekeying during ongoing communications helps protect against attacks.
- **Transport mode.** Secures links end to end — within the same domain or across any trusted path (see Figure 13-4). Windows 2000 Server L2TP tunnels use IPsec transport mode.
- **Tunnel mode.** Router to Router. Basically, IPsec creates a secure tunnel between two IPsec-compliant hosts (see Figure 13-4). Windows 2000 Server supports IPsec tunnels.
- **Centralized management.** Uses security policies and filters to provide appropriate levels of security, based on user and work group. Filtering is also available per address, subnet, protocol, and port.
- **Flexibility.** Policies can be applied to the entire enterprise or a single workstation.

IPsec uses two components: an authentication header (AH) to provide source authentication and integrity, and an encapsulated security payload (ESP) to provide confidentiality. By using both public keys and shared secret keys, IPsec provides a high degree of security to data communications, both within and between organizations.

One example of IPsec's defense against common attacks is how the sequence number is handled. You my recall from the Windows NT Server Enterprise MCSE course, where you were probably introduced to Network Monitor for the first time, that sequence numbers are very important in reconstructing the order of arriving packets by the receiving hosts. It's as if packets had sequence numbers of 1, 2, 3, 4, and 5 and maybe arrived out of order as 2, 3, 4, 1, and 5. The receiving host uses the sequence number to put the packets back in order as 1, 2, 3, 4, and 5. IPsec encrypts the sequence numbers via cryptohash to foil would-be hackers.

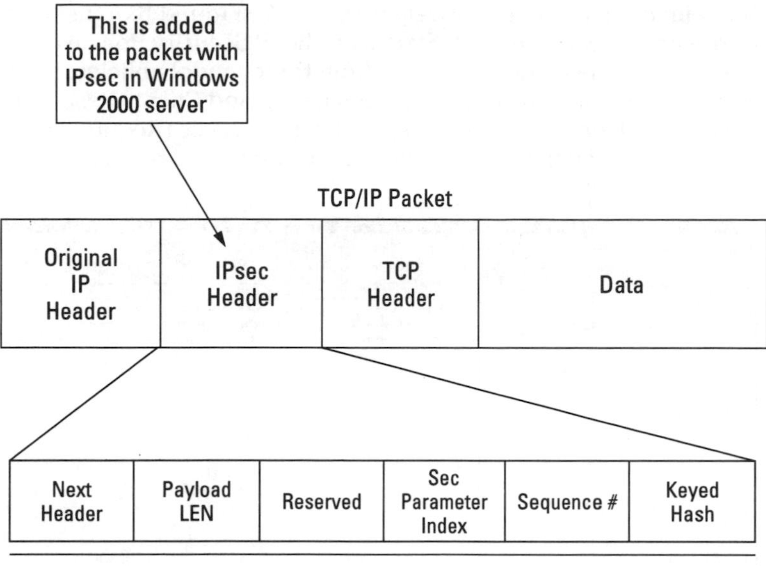

Figure 13-3: IPsec header

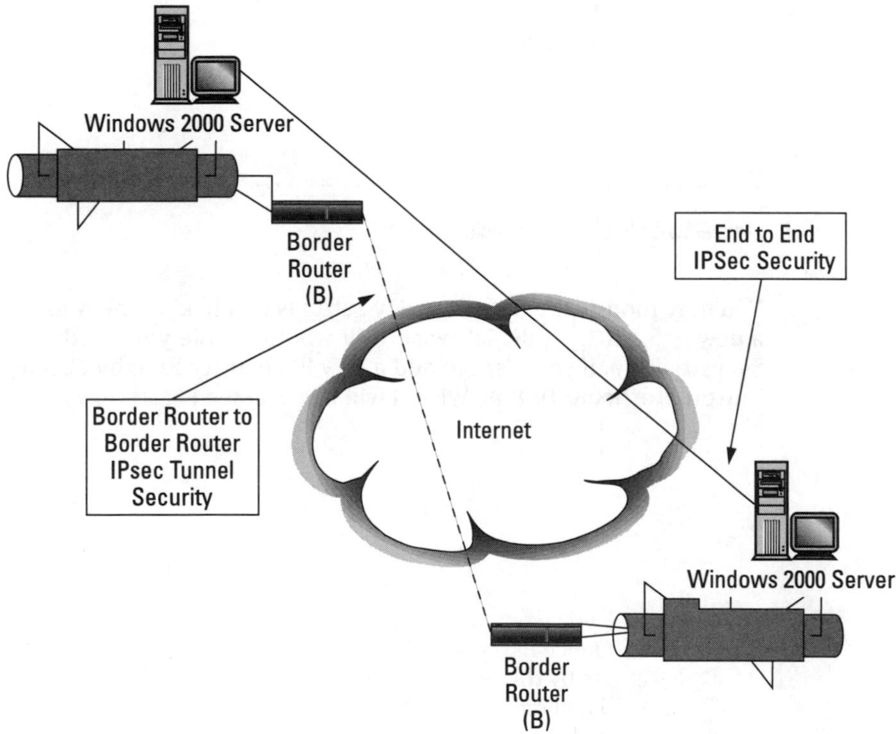

Figure 13-4: IPsec end-to-end versus tunnel

Implementing IPsec is relatively easy, and I've found that just doing it is one of the best ways to learn it. Start with the IP Security Policies MMC (see Figure 13-5). Here you may select from three model policies: Server (Request Security), Secure Server (Require Security), and Client (Respond Only). Double-click one of the policies, say Secure Server (Require Security), to display the properties sheet (see Figure 13-6).

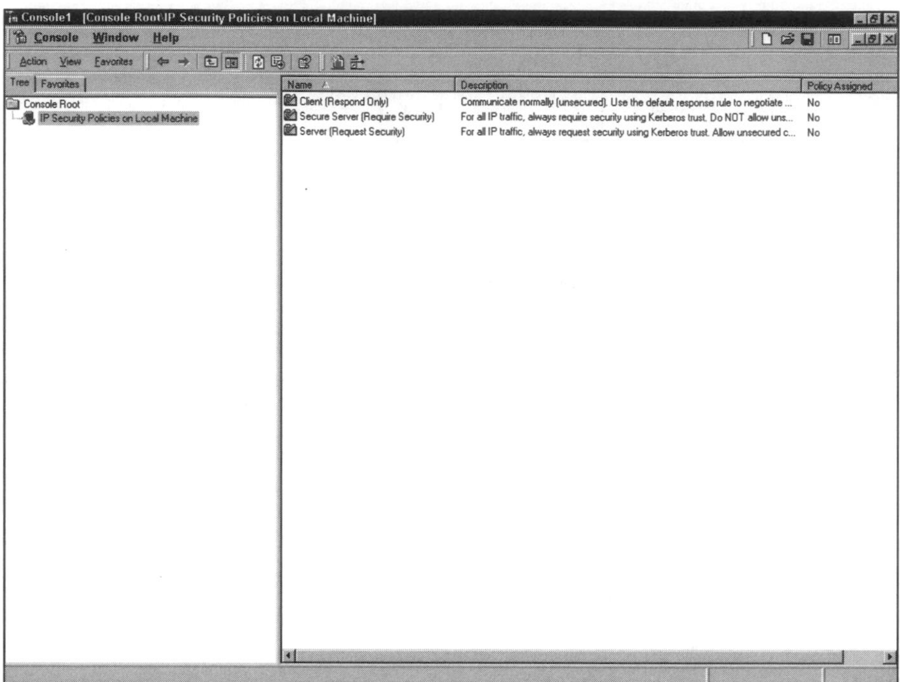

Figure 13-5: IP Security Policies MMC

You may modify the default policy settings by clicking the Add button to add a new IP Security Rule. Likewise, Edit would enable you to edit an existing IP Security Rule. If you elect to add a new IP Security Rule by clicking the Add button, the Security Rule Wizard will launch (see Figure 13-7).

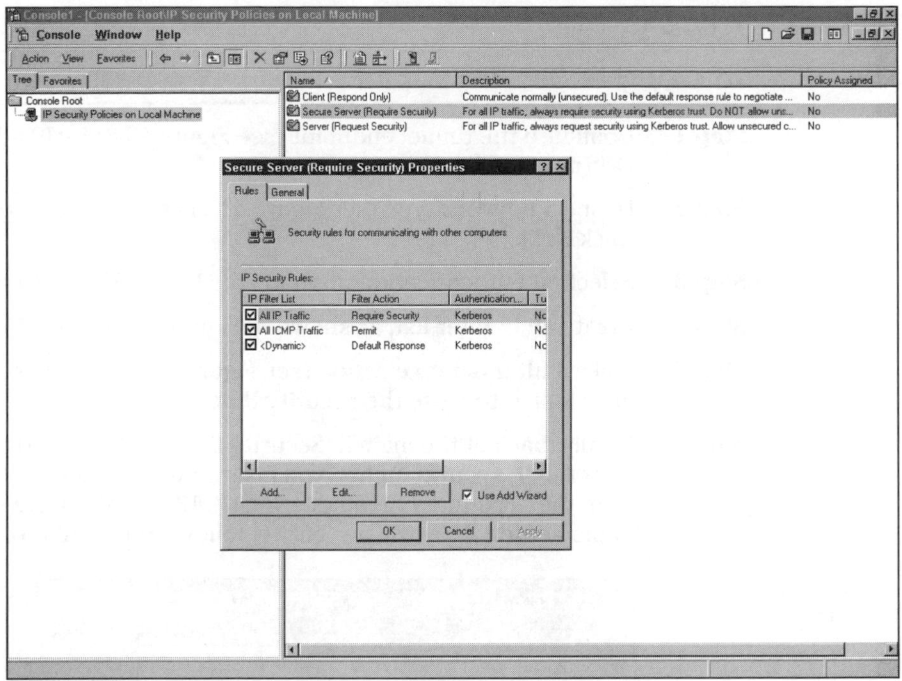

Figure 13-6: Secure Server (Require Security) properties

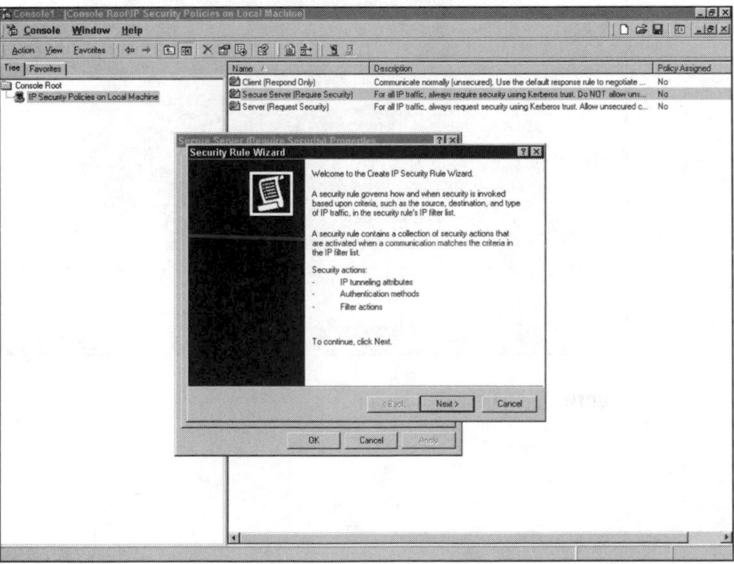

Figure 13-7: Security Rule Wizard

STEPS:

To configure Security Wizard

Step 1. Configure the tunnel endpoint (see Figure 13-8) by IP address or DNS name. Click Next.

Step 2. Define a network type (see Figure 13-9) as either local or remote. Click Next.

Step 3. Select an authentication method (see Figure 13-10). Click Next.

Step 4. Create an IP filter list, as shown in Figure 13-11. Click Next.

Step 5. Make a filter action election (see Figure 13-12). Click Next. You will click Finish to close the Security Rule Wizard.

Step 6. Finally, back at the main IP Security Policies MMC screen, right-click the IP security policy you just modified and select Assign from the secondary menu (see Figure 13-13). You have now implemented IPsec via a security policy. Congratulations.

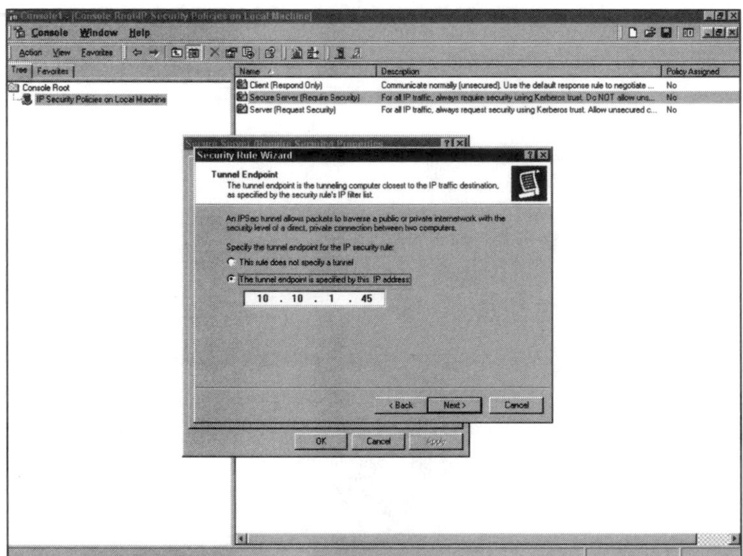

Figure 13-8: Tunnel endpoint

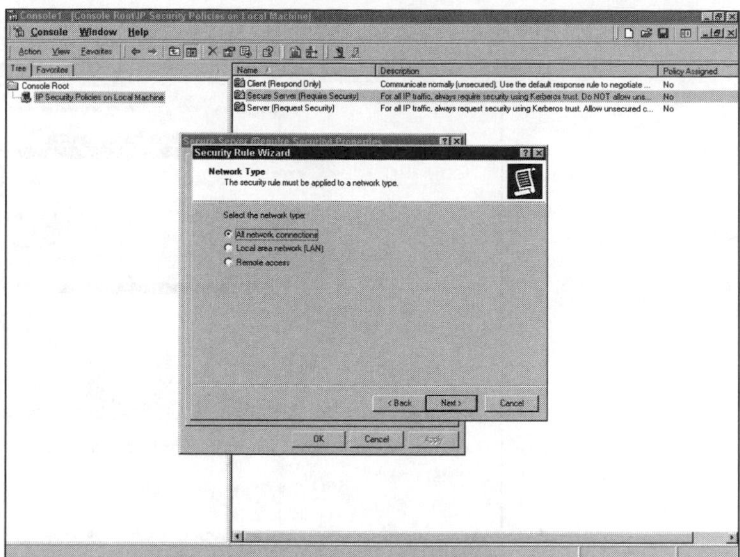

Figure 13-9: Network type

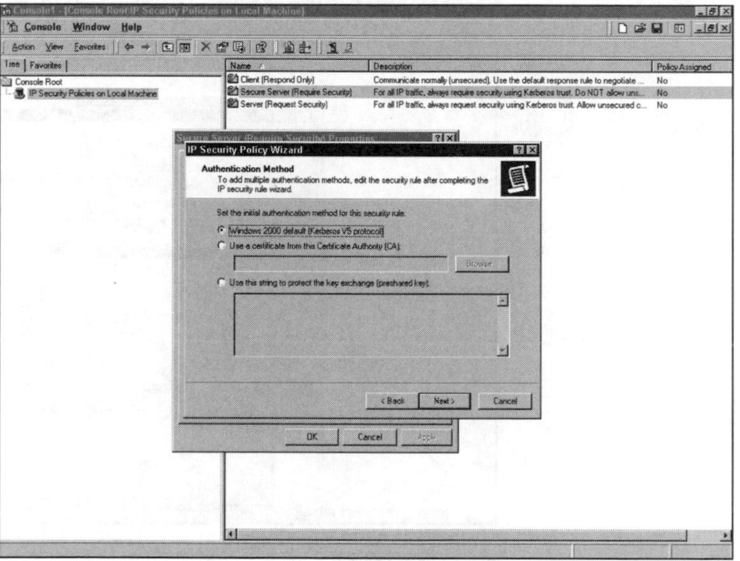

Figure 13-10: Authentication method

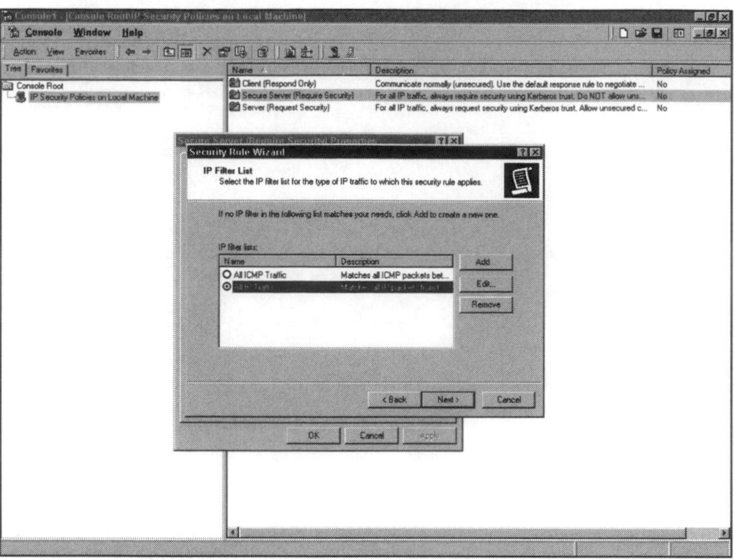

Figure 13-11: IP filter list

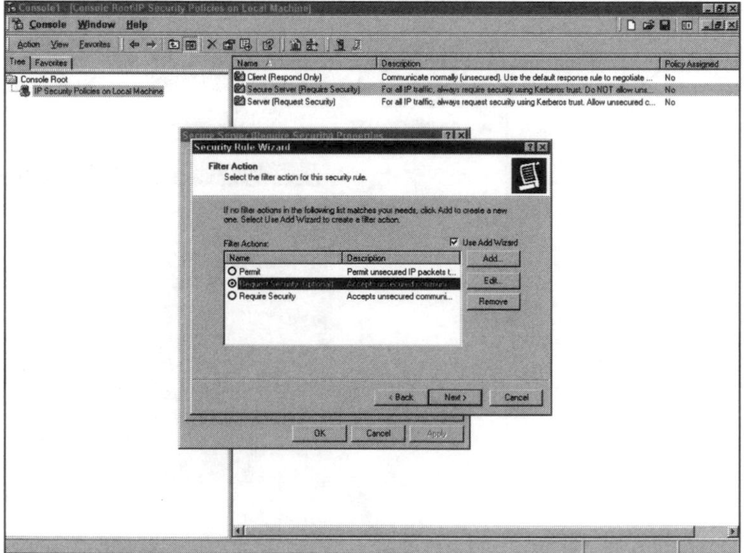

Figure 13-12: Filter action

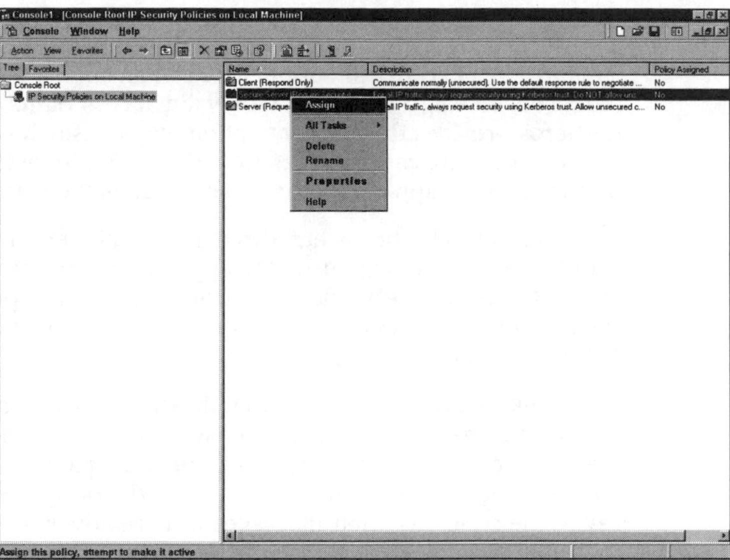

Figure 13-13: Assigning policies

Be careful now that you've created an IP security policy. If implemented, it will really work at this point. You might be surprised that you can accomplish nothing more than you've allowed. In short, you might find yourself uttering, "I think I've created a monster." Beware.

Kerberos V5

Ah, you and I have finally reached Windows 2000 Server security Mecca. Time to take in the Zen of Kerberos! It's a key (get it?) component of the Windows 2000 Server security model. That's because the root of the security authentication for Windows 2000 Server has moved from the LAN Manager model (NTLM) to the Kerberos model. And while Kerberos is receiving a lot of press with respect to the Windows 2000 Server security architecture, I think you'll be surprised to see that it really functions in the background.

What is Kerberos?

First, let's answer the question: What *was* Kerberos? This makes a wonderful technical trivia question. In Greek mythology, Kerberos (or Cerberus) was the three-headed dog that guarded the gates of Hades, or Hell. What better example for a mechanism that provides access security for your resources?

Kerberos was developed as part of Project Athena (more Greek mythology) at the Massachusetts Institute of Technology in the 1980s. It is primarily a method of verifying that a user is who they say they are. For example, we all know how easy it is to send e-mail purporting to be from someone else. Similarly, in a network situation, how can an application be sure that the request is coming from a user with valid access rights and not an imposter? Kerberos provides this authentication mechanism. It is also bilateral; not only can the application be assured of the identity of the user, the user can be sure that the application being accessed is the authentic one.

As the mythical Kerberos had three heads, the Kerberos security protocol uses three entities — the user, the application or server, and a "trusted third party." In the case of Windows 2000 Server, the third party is the Key Distribution Center (KDC) using information contained in the Active Directory.

Let's walk through an example that illustrates how Kerberos functions. As kids, Samantha and Molly used to pass notes back and forth in school. After they were embarrassed by having a note read aloud in class by the teacher, they devised a simple code. As they were the only ones who knew what the key to the code was, their messages were relatively secure — by applying the shared key to decode the message, Molly could be sure that the message actually came from Samantha. Later, however, they wanted to include Cassandra in their note-passing scheme. They had two choices — either each one of them could share a key with one of the others and a different key with the other one, or they could all use the same shared private key. As the circle of friends widened, these choices had obvious limitations: either too many keys to keep track of, or the likelihood that one of them would expose the single key.

Now let's transpose this situation to a network. Samantha (a client) can't meet with Molly (a server) in a secure area to tell Molly what the key is — anyone with a sniffer on the network would discover the key. What the network needs is a trusted repository of keys, a secure system that shares keys with each entity on the network that needs authentication. In very simple terms, this is how it works: when a user requests to communicate with a server, the trusted repository, or Key Distribution Center (KDC), sends back to the client two data structures: a session key, encrypted with the client's key; and a session ticket, which contains the server's session key and information about the client. The session ticket is encrypted with the server's key. When the client requests information from the server, it sends the session ticket (still encrypted with the server's key) to the server, along with an authenticator encrypted with the session key. The server decrypts the ticket, extracts the session key, decrypts the authenticator, matches it with the client information contained in the ticket, and proceeds with the transaction, assured that the client really is who they say they are. If the client has requested authentication of the server, the server then uses the session key to encrypt a part of the client's authenticator and returns it to the client, who then can trust the server.

Session tickets have a defined lifetime, typically around eight hours, and are thus reusable. This means that the KDC does not have to be contacted for every interaction between the client and the server as long as the session ticket is still valid. As the session keys are only kept in volatile memory on the client and the server, not on disk, the credentials memory cache is flushed and no record exists of the session when the user logs off.

When the user logs first logs on, the Kerberos client on the user's machine encrypts the password entered by the user and sends it on to the KDC, along with the user name. This encrypted password is referred to as the user's *long-term key*. The KDC looks up the user name in its database, compares the encrypted password it received with the long-term key, and creates a session key/session ticket as described above. This ticket, because it is used to communicate between the user and the KDC, is referred to as a *ticket-granting ticket*, or TGT. Likewise, the session key between the user and the KDC is called a *logon session key*, valid for as long as the user is logged on.

So, to clarify the interaction described above, when a client wants to connect to a server, it searches its cache for a session ticket for that server. If it finds one, it communicates directly with the server. If there is none, the client uses the logon session key and TGT to request a session ticket from the KDC.

Reasons for the move

Kerberos Version 5 is now the default authentication protocol for Windows 2000 Server. The previous default, Windows NT LAN Manager protocol (NTLM), will continue to be used to authenticate NT 4.0 clients.

There were five primary reasons why Kerberos was selected as the authentication protocol:

- **Network efficiency:** Because each client-server or server-server transaction does not need to be authenticated by a domain controller, network bandwidth is conserved.
- **Bilateral authentication:** With NTLM, the server could be sure of the client's identity, but the server was never authenticated to the client. With Kerberos, if the client requests, the server can be easily authenticated.
- **Three-tier authentication:** In both NTLM and Kerberos, the client is impersonated on the server to determine resource access rights. In a three-tier architecture, NTLM had no way of letting the intermediate server authenticate the client to the other server. Kerberos uses a proxy mechanism that allows servers to impersonate a client on another server.
- **Simplified trust relationships:** By default, trust relationships under Kerberos are bilateral and transitive. This means that once credentials for each security authority in an organization are mutually authenticated, two-way trust relationships automatically exist. If Domain A trusts Domain B, Domain B automatically trusts Domain A. In addition, if Domain B trusts Domain C, the transitive nature of Kerberos authentication means that Domain A also trusts Domain C, and vice versa.

- **Interoperability:** As Kerberos Version 5 is a standard incorporated into other operating systems, it is conceivable to have trust relationships between Windows 2000 Server domains and Unix Kerberos realms, for example. Also, individual users with Kerberos clients on other operating systems can be validated and mapped to Windows 2000 Server domain accounts.

Want another take on Kerberos? Take a moment to adhere to the old maxim that a picture is worth a thousand words (or at least a run-on bulleted list). In Figure 13-14, the Kerberos logon flow is displayed as an example of how Kerberos "fits" in the Windows 2000 Server security model.

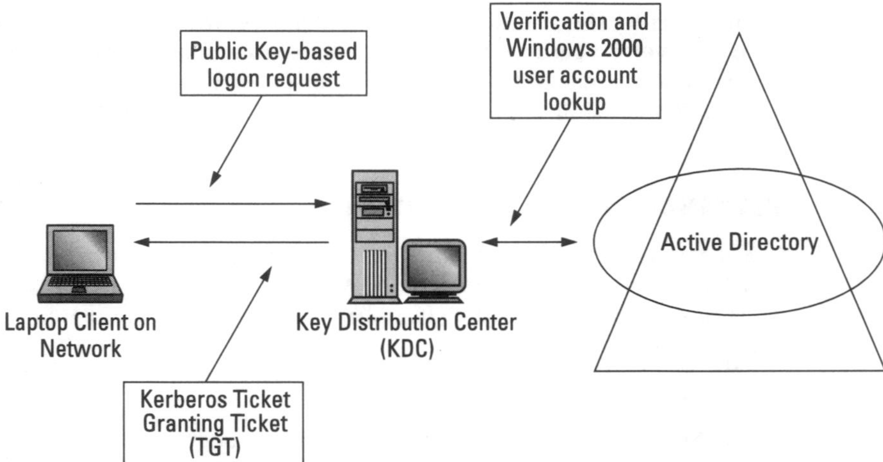

Figure 13-14: Kerberos logon flow

How is it implemented in Windows 2000 Server?

In Windows 2000 Server, the KDC is implemented as a domain service, using the Active Directory as its account database. There is a KDC located on every domain controller, along with the Active Directory. Both services start automatically and cannot be stopped. Each runs in the process space of the Local Security Authority (LSA). Any domain controller can authenticate and issue tickets.

Policies for Kerberos implementation are determined at the domain level and contained in the Active Directory as part of the domain security policy. Settings for Kerberos policy include:

- Maximum user ticket lifetime. This setting determines the life, in hours, of the TGT.
- Maximum lifetime that a user ticket can be renewed, in days.
- Maximum service ticket lifetime. This setting determines the life of a session ticket, in minutes, between 10 and the value of *Maximum user ticket lifetime*.
- Maximum tolerance for synchronization of computer clocks. As timestamps are part of session keys and session tickets, there must be some accommodation for variations in clocks on the various systems. Settings are in minutes.
- Enforced user logon restrictions. This setting determines whether the KDC will validate each request for a session ticket by examining whether the user has the right either to Log On Locally or Access This Computer from the Network. This is an option because the extra lookup involved can slow down the network.

In all likelihood, you are going to bump into Kerberos while undertaking some security task that uses it. For example, in the IP Security Policy Wizard, the Authentication Method screen allows you to select the Kerberos V5 protocol (see Figure 13-15). This type of encounter is most likely going to create your best memories of Kerberos in Windows 2000 Server.

Kerberos extensions in Windows 2000 Server

As I mentioned, Kerberos is a shared secret technology. Many of the other advances in cryptography are based upon public key implementations, where the certifying authority (CA) is an external third party. And within Windows 2000 Server, you have already seen Kerberos in action under the guise of IPsec.

Kerberos also rears its head in other ways within Windows 2000 Server. In particular, smart cards use public key encryption for authentication. In order to support smart cards for logon access, some interaction between public keys and Kerberos is required. Microsoft, in conjunction with IETF, has developed extensions to the Kerberos protocol to substitute the public/private key pair on a smart card for the shared secret key derived from the user's password. The KDC encrypts the logon session key using the user's public key; the client uses the private key to decrypt the logon session key.

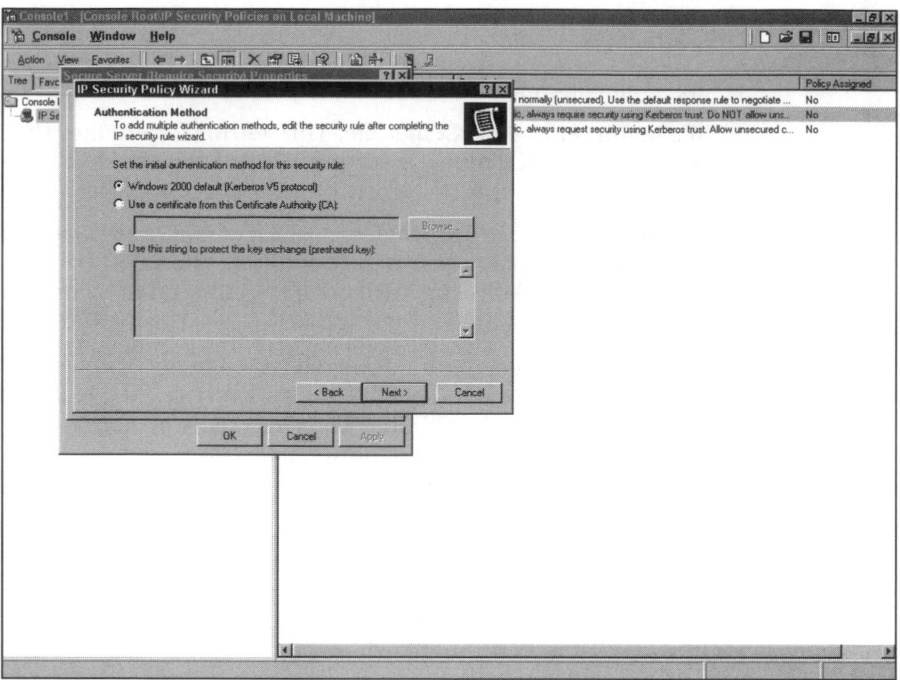

Figure 13-15: Kerberos in action!

Smart Card Support

When you play Monopoly, what is the most valuable card you can get? The Get Out of Jail Free card, of course! Well, in the real world, there is another valuable card you can have — a Get Onto the Network Easily card, or *smart card*. Smart cards have been developed for all sorts of purposes, but in the context of this chapter, smart cards are used to authenticate the identity of the owner to log on.

Smart cards have a number of advantages:

- Making the storage medium for private keys and other personal information tamper-resistant
- Offloading security computations from the rest of the system
- Providing a portable authentication mechanism that insures accurate logon information for many systems

Smart cards use microchip technology to hold the information needed for public key encryption. Earlier in this chapter, I noted that Windows 2000 Server uses the Kerberos protocol, based on shared secret keys, to authenticate users. In order to bridge the differences between public key and shared secret key technologies, Microsoft has, in conjunction with the IETF, developed extensions for Kerberos which enable the logon process to use the public/private key information on the smart card as a substitute for the shared secret key information derived from the user's password. The smart card architecture in Windows 2000 Server is shown in Figure 13-16. Note that Server Cache Synchronization Protocol (SCSP) refers to a general approach to solving cache synchronization/cache replication problems in distributed protocol entities. Crypto API/SSCP refers to an encryption application program interface, and common dialog refers to the smart card's interface.

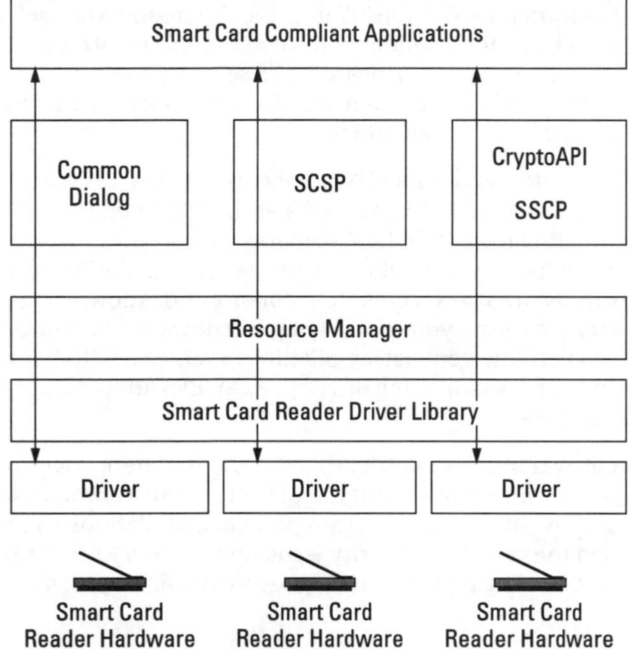

Figure 13-16: Smart card architecture

Smart cards can also be used for client authorizations using the Secure Sockets Layer (SSL). This is an application level authorization, requiring the holder of the smart card to identify itself before processing. This technology using SSL provides for mutual authentication, meaning that the user is authenticated to the application as well as the application being authenticated to the user.

Finally, smart cards are also useful for remote access. Using third party authentication modules, smart cards can be used to provide credentials for authentication via RAS.

If you would like more information on smart cards, go to the `www.smartcardsys.com` Web site.

EFS Encryption

One of the security features touted when Windows NT was first launched in 1993 was a new file system, the NT File System or NTFS, which would provide a high degree of security for disk-based data. NTFS uses access control lists for all objects, meaning that permissions could be granted to individual users down to the file level. As the file system could be accessed only from NT, not from DOS, it was thought to be a very secure method to store data.

The Titanic was thought to be unsinkable, too. Microsoft set itself up again to the target of attacks against whatever it said couldn't be attacked. Soon, tools that enabled a user to bypass intricate NTFS security when an NT system was booted using a DOS diskette, became readily available to the public. Files were thus laid wide open for an attack.

Previously, you could bypass local NTFS security, at least before EFS, by simply installing Windows NT Server 4.0 a second time on the same NTFS partition and booting from it. In that scenario, new Security Accounts Manager (SAM) in hand, you could browse the NTFS partition to your heart's delight! Historically, this was a common workaround, known as a parallel installation, for recovering your underlying Windows NT Server operating system when something went astray big time (such as a failed upgrade from a single to multiple processor using `uptomp.exe`). EFS addresses the parallel installation weakness.

But don't forget, war stories such as those presented here suggest you should always have physical security in place for your server, first and foremost, thus preventing unauthorized parallel installations to begin with! Easy to do when the physical security issue applies to a locked-up server. But what about the traveling laptop? There goes the basic physical security premise, eh?

So, given this immediate discussion regarding NTFS security weaknesses, the answer is to encrypt the file. This has been possible in the past with third-party utilities, but there are several drawbacks: the encryption/decryption is manual, not automatic; temporary files may not be encrypted; and the encryption is usually password-based, which third-party password crackers can decrypt.

In Windows 2000 Server, the Encrypting File System (EFS) is available as an integrated file system. EFS can use any symmetric encrypting algorithm, although only DESX is supported in the first release.

EFS generates a public/private key pair and registers it with a certificate authority (CA) if one is configured, or handles the registration itself if no CA is available. Individual files or entire directories can be encrypted, both locally and on remote volumes. Encryption and decryption are automatic and transparent to the user as the bytes are read from or written to disk.

EFS also supports data recovery using a master recovery key. This is helpful, for example, in examining a former employee's files or when the specific encryption keys are lost.

It is easy to use EFS in Windows 2000 Server. EFS is turned on or off for files or directories using the Advanced button on the General tab of the properties for that entity (see Figure 13-17). After making the encryption selection, you will receive an encryption warning (see Figure 13-18) that warns you if you are encrypting a file in an unencrypted folder. You are offered the opportunity to encrypt the folder at this time.

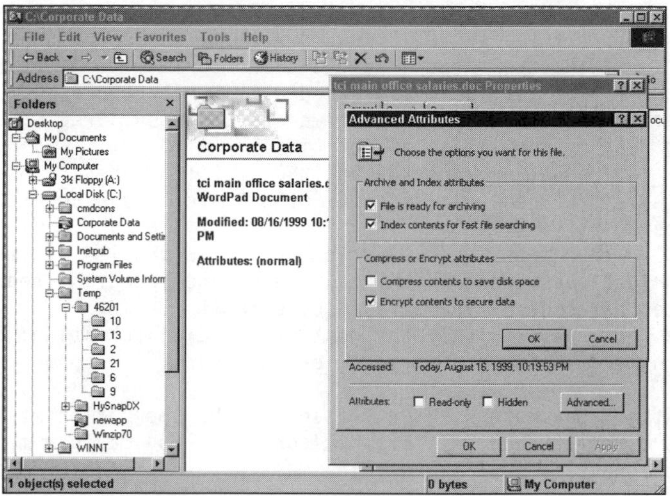

Figure 13-17: File encryption settings

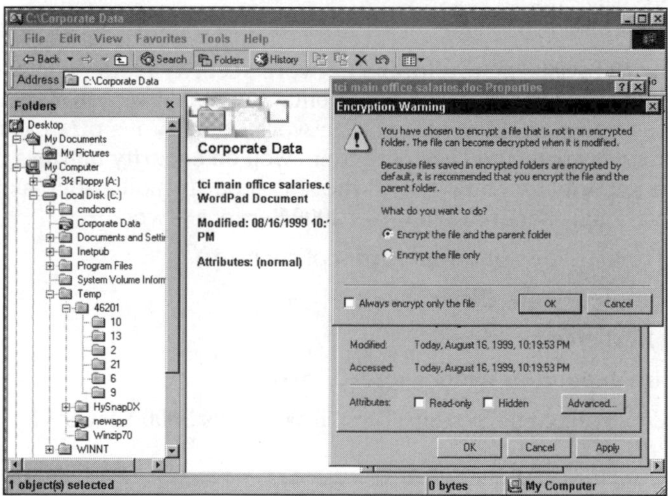

Figure 13-18: Encryption warning

Alternatively, a command line utility, **cipher**, can be used to encrypt or decrypt files or directories. The cipher command contains the following options.

```
Displays or alters the encryption of directories [files] on NTFS
partitions.
  CIPHER [/E | /D] [/S:dir] [/I] [/F] [/Q] [dirname [...]]

    /E       Encrypts the specified directories. Directories will be
marked so that files added afterward will be encrypted.
    /D       Decrypts the specified directories. Directories will be
marked so that files added afterward will not be encrypted.
    /S       Performs the specified operation on directories in the
given directory and all subdirectories.
    /I       Continues performing the specified operation even after
errors have occurred.  By default, CIPHER stops when an error is
encountered.
    /F       Forces the encryption operation on all specified
directories, even those which are already encrypted.  Already-
encrypted directories are skipped by default.
    /Q       Reports only the most essential information.
    dirname  Specifies a pattern, or directory.

Used without parameters, CIPHER displays the encryption state of the
current directory and any files it contains. You may use multiple
directory names and wildcards. You must put spaces between multiple
parameters.
```

Summary

It's one thing to revisit the traditional network security model and then learn about the significant security enhancements (such as IPsec) in Windows 2000 Server. But as final parting wisdom on network security, it's often as important to recruit honest people and educate them well on security matters. In short, it's both the security technology and the soft security skills, such as training, that make for a fully secured Windows 2000 Server network.

- Reasons to use IPsec (Internet Protocol security)
- Steps to implementing IPsec
- Defining Kerberos
- Smart card support in Windows 2000 Server
- Role of Encrypting File System (EFS) in Windows 2000 Server

Part V

All In the Family

Chapter 14

Windows 2000 Professional

In This Chapter

- Defining Windows 2000 Professional
- Windows 2000 Professional features
- Windows 2000 Professional strengths

This chapter is the first of three that explore the family members of Microsoft networking-related solutions. After learning about Windows 2000 Professional in this chapter, you will learn about Windows 2000 Advanced Server and Datacenter in Chapter 15. Finally, in Chapter 16, I spend a few minutes with you on Small Business Server 4.5, which is the best darn solution for small sites even today.

When it comes to networks, if there is a server, there needs to be at least one workstation. Together, the server and workstation form the basic network. Windows 2000 Professional constitutes the workstation side of the basic network equation. Before diving into the Windows 2000 Professional depths, allow me to set your expectations for a moment. This chapter is part of the "all in the family" paradigm that considers each Microsoft Windows 2000 and network-related offering. This chapter is also limited in scope with respect to Windows 2000 Professional.

One final note regarding the presentation of Windows 2000 Professional in this chapter. I have hand picked the best and brightest features and secrets to present to you. Undoubtedly you have additional Windows 2000 Professional features that you like. Great!

Where the Work Gets Done

You could argue that the workstation side via Windows 2000 Professional is where the work really gets done on the network. It's where the users perform their tasks. Let's take a moment to find out exactly how their work can be accomplished with Windows 2000 Professional. That is, what capabilities in Windows 2000 Professional enable the workers to be productive?

Improved ease of use

One of Windows 2000 Professional's shticks is its improved usability. As you would expect, operating systems are evolutionary. Call it OS Darwinism.

Mobile computing support

My favorite improvement in Windows 2000 Professional is the Synchronization Manager (see Figure 14-1). This tool globally updates the network copy of information that you worked with offline. This addresses the age-old issue of having your company's information stored centrally, yet enabling mobile workers to work offline.

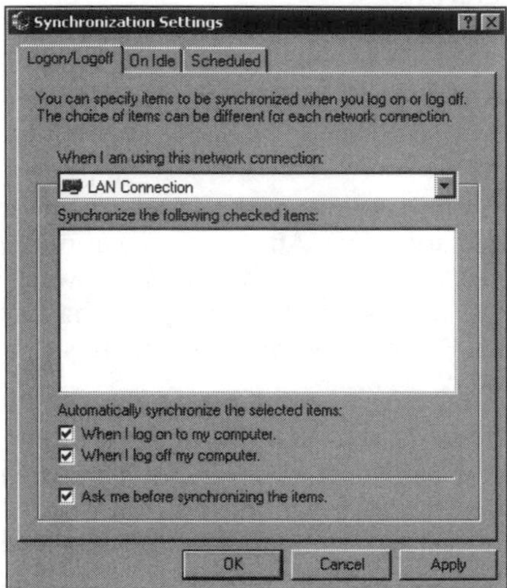

Figure 14-1: Synchronization Manager

Synchronization Manager, the latest incarnation of Briefcase, is found in the Accessories program group. It will synchronize documents, calendars, and e-mail messages.

Synchronization Manager will not synchronize database information at the table or field level. That's a task usually managed from within a sophisticated database application.

Another access favorite is Windows 2000 Professional's commitment to Virtual Private Networking (VPN). Windows 2000 Professional is, not surprisingly, the most VPN-compliant desktop OS I've worked with from Microsoft. I cover the VPN topic extensively in Chapter 8.

Looks better

My favorite improvement here is the Start menu management capabilities. With past Microsoft desktop operating systems, you were basically limited to adding or deleting Start menu items. That has changed with Windows 2000 Professional. Now, via the Taskbar Properties (see Figure 14-2), you can customize menu display options, a great improvement.

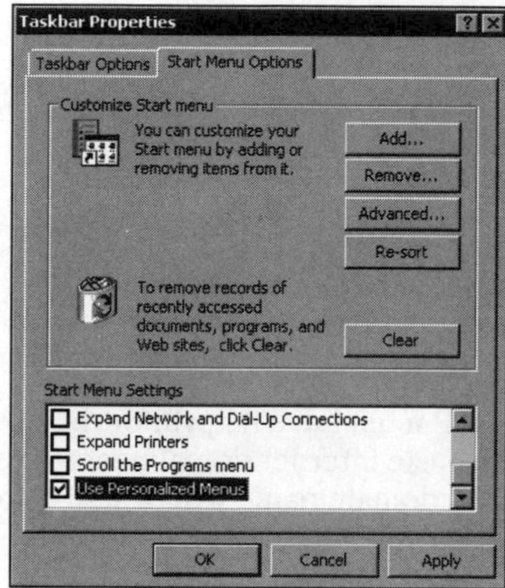

Figure 14-2: Taskbar Properties

Another cool menu management feature is the Use Personalized Menus option. It's touted by Microsoft as a housecleaning feature that causes only the most recently selected menu options to be available. To display all of the menu items, you simply click the double-down arrows (which will fully extend a menu).

I call the Use Personalized Menus option the "shelf space" algorithm. Like a bookstore or the local grocery, the most popular items, in this case Start menu options, get the most space.

Prints better

Printing is printing, right? Well, Windows 2000 Professional has shifted that paradigm slightly by adding Internet printing support, known as the Internet Printing Protocol (IPP). With this feature, you can print to an Internet address (for example, `www.springers.com/hp4000`). The Internet print capability is configured on the Locate Your Printer screen of the Add Printer Wizard (see Figure 14-3). Note that you can also print to an intranet site as well.

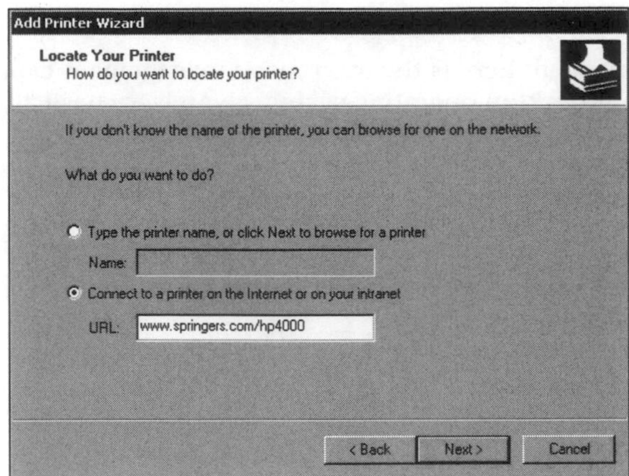

Figure 14-3: Internet printing configuration

The URL you are printing to using IPP must have its printer defined as a virtual directory to the right of the basic Internet domain name. You cannot configure IPP to print to a third-level domain name where said third-level domain name represents the printer.

Improved management

It can be said, and justifiably so, that the user experience is a function of management. That is, while just about everyone can use computers now, the user's ultimate computing experience will be a function of his or her ability to manage the computer. Such reasoning wasn't lost on the wonderkids from Redmond as Windows 2000 Professional was developed. Two management improvements in Windows 2000 Professional stand out.

Improved Add/Remove Programs

Good old Add/Remove Programs has aged well and turned out to be a good kid. In addition to a new look and feel, Add/Remove Programs (see Figure 14-4) now allows you to automatically receive Windows 2000 Professional-related updates over the Internet with the push of a button called Windows Update. Such updates include device drivers, patches, fixes, and operating system enhancements.

The Windows Update functionality is very similar to a popular desktop application called Oil Change. Perhaps Microsoft should have called it the Oil Change Killer!

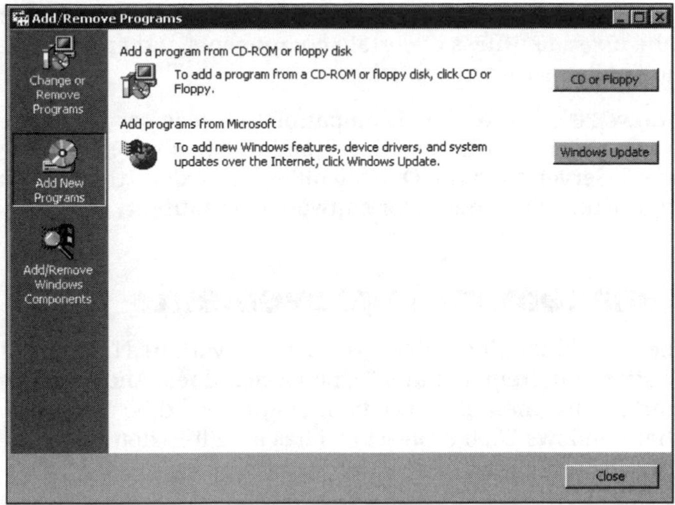

Figure 14-4: Add/Remove Programs

Improved setup tools

One new Windows 2000 Professional feature stands out here. Windows 2000 Professional server has disk-duplication capabilities, which are found in the System Preparation Tool. Here, you can create an image of your computer's hard disk. Then, using a third-party disk-duplication tool such as Ghost, you can duplicate your hard disk to other like-configured machines.

Secret

I call the capability to create an image of your Windows 2000 Professional hard disk the "manual mirroring secret." Why? Because Windows 2000 Professional doesn't implicitly support RAID 1 mirroring. But you can fool the system into mirroring, albeit with significant time lags, via the System Preparation Tool's disk imaging capabilities.

Troubleshooting

The primary improvement here is Automated System Recovery (ASR). This tool is the ultimate undo, as far as I'm concerned. Via Backup, you can configure ASR to make a backup copy of your system files. This is conceptually very similar to the role of the Emergency Repair Disk (ERD), but ASR saves more information, such as ARC naming paths to your disks. Note that ASR doesn't save application-level information, such as that contained in Microsoft SQL Server (master table, indexes, and so on) or Microsoft Exchange (global address list objects, and so on).

The compatibility tool, as it's generically known, runs when you upgrade to Windows 2000 Professional from supported operating systems such as

Windows 95, Windows 98, or Windows NT 4.0 Workstation. Basically, it will test for the upgrade fitness of certain components and applications. You will be notified of items that might fail.

The Windows 2000 Professional compatibility tool is very similar to the NT Hardware Qualifier (NTHQ) tool that I (and perhaps you) used back in the old Windows NT Server 4.0 days. One big difference exists, though: this compatibility tool also checks for software compatibility.

File management improvements

And whoever said Windows 2000 Professional, with its NTFS partitions, doesn't suffer from fragmentation? Of course it does. And while I recommend a third-party defragmentation utility in Chapter 9, I'd be remiss if I didn't report that Windows 2000 Professional has a built-in defragmentation tool (see Figure 14-5).

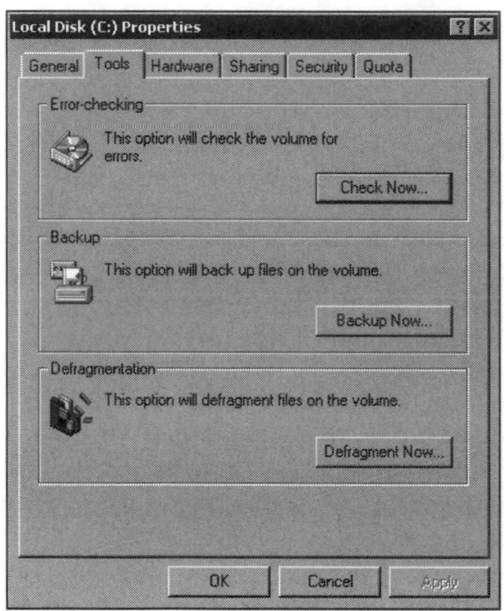

Figure 14-5: Defragmentation tool

The defragmentation tool in Windows 2000 Professional has similar defragmentation capabilities to those found in Windows 98 and Windows 95.

Hardware Support

Of course hardware support has improved in Windows 2000 Professional when compared to past desktop operating systems from Microsoft. However, it has already been my experience that although Windows 2000 Professional brought forward and even improved hardware Plug and Play support, those of us who work at older sites will find our ISA devices go undetected. Bummer. That means you'll need to keep those ISA component device driver diskettes handy and use the Add/Remove Hardware wizard for those oldies but goodies (ISA devices, not music).

I highly recommend that you install Windows 2000 Professional on nothing less than a dual-processor machine. Yes, you read correctly. Dual processor power at the desktop. A nice option if you can afford it. Otherwise be prepared to suffer the wrath of a single processor's poor performance.

Security

Big hugs here for Microsoft. Windows 2000 Professional incorporates the following:

- Internet Protocol security (IPsec). Supports encrypted traffic over an intranet or VPN connection.
- Encryption File System (EFS). Provides local file encryption that requires a password to penetrate.
- Kerberos Version 5. Hail to the king, for Kerberos is here. It is a fast and well-accepted Internet security standard.
- Smart card support. Smart card devices enable authentication away from the physical location of the network, therefore increasing portability.

Windows 2000-related security matters are discussed in more detail in Chapter 13.

Summary

A Windows 2000 Server-based network is made of up both servers and workstations. This chapter introduced Windows 2000 Professional, which is the workstation offering from Microsoft in the Windows 2000 family.

- Defined the role of Windows 2000 Professional
- Defined Windows 2000 Professional features
- Discussed the strengths and weaknesses of Windows 2000 Professional

Chapter 15

Windows 2000 Advanced Server and Datacenter Server

In This Chapter

- Defining Windows 2000 Advanced Server
- Understanding the enterprise challenge
- Analysis and information gathering required for Windows 2000 Advanced Server
- Issues surrounding Windows 2000 Advanced Server installations and upgrades
- Understanding processing threads
- Understanding load balancing
- Avoiding rolling upgrade problems
- Defining Datacenter Server

I can tell you for a fact that being part of an enterprise-level IT group is never boring. In fact, you can always expect the unpredictable, and I'm not just talking corporate politics here. While I have many on-the-job case studies to date, I will share with you a handful of them that relate specifically to the environments for which Windows 2000 Advanced Server and Datacenter Server are best positioned.

My plan in this chapter is to present some interesting enterprise-level situations, all of which are based on actual events, and how I resolved them. At each turn, I'll incorporate how I will be using the new Windows 2000 Advanced Server product as the potential solution. It is my hope that by applying this advanced extrapolative analysis, you will see a little of yourself in these case studies and be better off when you actually deploy these products at the enterprise level. I will also provide you with some details on the Advanced Server and Datacenter Server products. Without further ado, welcome to the tales of enterprise networks...

Case Study: The Great Mac Attack

In one of my many consulting ventures, I stumbled across a large international firm with over 100,000 employees that had many years ago adopted the Macintosh as its chosen business machine. The fans loved the GUI, the ease of use, and by gosh, you could even run Microsoft applications such as Microsoft Office on it. What more could you ask for?

AppleShare servers were bountiful. They cropped up in all locations. At one point, I was administering six AppleShare servers — one MS Mail server, one SMTP gateway, and four file servers. The Macintosh population was so predominant, it was rumored there were more zones at this firm than at Apple. We had conquered the creator!

A few of the business managers ventured into the unknown, setting up a PC here, a PC there because they needed the platform for connectivity issues, for testing purposes. Some of them had PC-specific applications they had to work with. Products were being designed on Windows, as most of the world out there was using Windows. Very soon, the slow and painful transition to PCs invaded this international firm like a virus. More and more departments migrated to Windows 95, to Windows 98. The infrastructure began changing. AppleShare servers transformed themselves into Windows NT 4.0 servers, Exchange servers blossomed from the wreckage of MS Mail servers. The future was upon us, and there was no going back.

Do you see any problems developing yet? Remember the zone count? As each department and local area of this international firm moved away from the Macintosh and started welcoming Windows NT technology, the demand for a domain model evolved. Domains and trusts popped up like popcorn, some one-way, some two-way. "Who's trusting whom" became the motto. NT 4.0 workstations pushed out the old Macintosh systems. Domains replaced zones. Over-used NT 4.0 servers gathered in server rooms across the globe. From this short tale, it's plain to see the difficulty with any enterprise-level migration.

Deconstructing Windows 2000 Advanced Server

To be brutally honest, Microsoft Windows 2000 Advanced Server is the new release of Windows NT 4.0 Enterprise Edition. It provides the same features as Windows 2000 Standard Server, but with some significant differences and reasons to consider this operating system in your enterprise environment. The key differences are additional features and scalability, as you shall see.

In addition to the new Windows 2000 features, such as Kerberos, Public Key Infrastructure (PKI), Terminal Services, COM+, and others, Advanced Server provides a more powerful server operating system, offering an enhanced clustering infrastructure and memory support to 8GB. Advanced Server also supports new systems with up to eight-way symmetric multiprocessing (SMP). Because of its high availability and scalability, Advanced Server is a good solution for a database-intensive environment and network-focused load balancing. High-performance sorting is another new feature in Windows 2000 Advanced Server. I will touch on all these features in greater detail later in this chapter.

Here are the system requirements for Microsoft's enterprise candidate, Advanced Server:

- 166MHz Pentium or higher processor
- 64MB RAM (128MB recommended), 8GB maximum
- 2GB hard disk with 850MB minimum for the setup process. To calculate the space needed, start with 850MB and add 2MB for each MB of memory on your computer. More space may be needed, depending on the following:
  - The components being installed. Additional components will require more disk space.
  - The file system to be installed. FAT requires 100–200MB additional free disk space.
  - The installation method. For network installations, allow 100–200MB additional space, as additional driver files need to be available during installation across the network, as compared to installing from a CD.
  - In addition, an upgrade may require much more space than a new installation, because the existing user accounts database may expand by as much as a factor of ten during the upgrade as Active Directory functionality is added.

See all the good news? If you are already running a decent Windows NT Server 4.0 domain, you are probably already meeting these requirements. You may only need to consider an upgrade.

On the other hand, let's be realistic. In the LAN of the enterprise, with its large six- and seven-figure IT budgets, such hardware minimums are laughable. The performance minimums (processors, memory, storage), in most cases, should be tripled.

Another interesting Windows 2000 Advanced Server factoid: It looks very similar, on the surface, to Windows 2000 Server. This is shown in Figure 15-1 with the Configure Your Server screen.

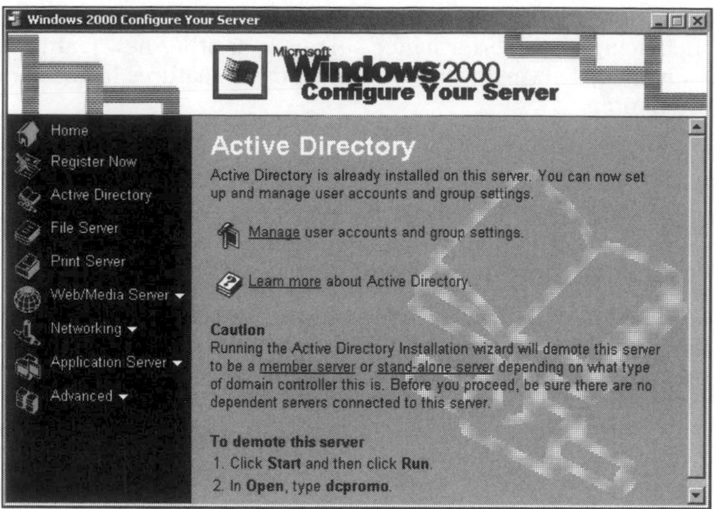

Figure 15-1: Configure Your Server screen

Planning Your Upgrade

Before installing your server, make sure your hardware supports Windows 2000 Advanced Server by referring to the Hardware Compatibility List (HCL). Refer to the `HCL.TXT` in the `\SUPPORT` directory on the Windows 2000 Advanced Server CD. If your hardware is not listed, you may not achieve a successful installation. (Note that one type of hardware no longer supported is the Micro Channel bus.) If you have Internet access, you can view the latest HCL on the World Wide Web at `www.microsoft.com/hwtest/hcl`.

Also, make sure you have the latest drivers for your devices as well as the latest system BIOS. Typically, you can find these files on the vendors' Web sites. Also, before installing Windows 2000 Advanced Server, consider taking a device inventory of the hardware devices in your computer.

Windows 2000 features Plug and Play technology so devices such as video and network cards or adapters are automatically recognized by the operating system. As a result, configuration conflicts are avoided, and you do not have to manually configure each device's settings. However, you may have devices that are not Plug and Play, or that are not implemented exactly to the standards. In this case, you will want to take measures to avoid device configuration conflicts, such as obtaining IRQ numbers and settings prior to installing Windows 2000 Advanced Server. You may also want to view system BIOS information.

Case Study: Not Working on the Workstation

Although the names have been changed to protect the guilty, this story comes to us from the conversion channels of yet another international firm looking to migrate from Windows 95 to Windows NT Workstation 4.0, the latest powerhouse enterprise operating system. Sure, there are hardware requirements and the computers meet them just fine. And upgrading should be a breeze, especially because most of the software is Microsoft's anyway (Office, FrontPage, Access). So when Susie and Paul want to upgrade their machines, they do just that. Paul is considerably computer-adept and knows how to double click the Setup icon that pops up on his Windows NT Workstation 4.0 CD. Smiles all round, this is easier than imagined. The installation goes fine although Paul does not recall seeing the upgrade option. He configures the drive for FAT and everything should be fine, right?

OK, so it's a little stretched. The truth is that you couldn't upgrade to Windows NT Workstation. You needed to back up all your files and restore later, as well as reinstall all applications (that is, if they worked on the new NT platform). To top this story off, one of the legacy sound cards was inoperable under NT.

So it's always best to research where you're headed. In terms of Windows 2000 Advanced Server, you have several things to investigate before making Paul's mistake.

Even though Windows 2000 Advanced Server automatically takes a device inventory during setup, taking your own inventory helps prevent some difficulties such as

- Two or more adapters sharing IRQ settings or memory addresses. Windows 2000 Advanced Server may not be able to resolve the conflict. To prevent this, take one of two approaches. First, remove one of the adapters before running Setup, and then reinstall it afterward. A second approach is to modify one adapter's IRQ settings and memory addresses before running Setup, so that each adapter's settings are unique.
- Adapters do not respond in a standard way to the attempts by Windows 2000 Advanced Server to detect or enumerate them. In this instance, Windows 2000 Advanced Server may receive indecipherable or inaccurate information. Here, you may need to remove these devices before running Setup, and reinstall and configure them afterward.

Table 15-1 is a guide to help you decide what information to gather before installing Windows 2000 Advanced Server.

Table 15-1 Windows 2000 Advanced Server Information Gathering

Adapter	*Information*
Video	Adapter or chipset type and how many video adapters
Network	IRQ, I/O address, DMA (if used) connector type (for example, BNC or twisted pair), and bus type
SCSI Controller	Adapter model or chipset, IRQ, and bus type
Mouse	Mouse type and port (COM1, COM2, bus, or PS/2) or USB
I/O Port	IRQ, I/O address, and DMA (if used) for each I/O port
Sound Adapter	IRQ, I/O address, and DMA
Universal Serial Bus (USB)	Devices and hubs attached
PCMCIA	What adapters are inserted and in which slots
Plug and Play (PnP)	Whether enabled or disabled in BIOS
BIOS Settings	BIOS revision and date
External Modem	Com port connections (COM1, COM2, and so on)
Internal Modem	Com port connections; for non-standard configurations, IRQ and I/O address
Advanced Configuration and Power Interface (ACPI); Power Management	Enabled or disabled; current setting
PCI	What PCI adapters are inserted and in which slots

Windows 2000 Advanced Server supports up to eight multiprocessors. If you are upgrading a computer running Windows NT Server or Windows NT Server Enterprise Edition (that supported more than four processors), this processor support will be preserved when you upgrade to Windows 2000 Advanced Server.

The setup process requires the free disk space described in the section, "Deconstructing Windows 2000 Advanced Server" in this chapter. After installation, actual hard disk space used for the operating system (excluding user accounts) is usually less than the free space required for setup, depending on the system components installed.

Case Study: Upgrade or New Grade

Following up on Susie and Paul from the last case study, not only did they need to look at their workstation requirements, they needed to examine the server situation. You see, Susie and Paul and the rest of their sales department have a server they share with the payroll department. The machine has plenty of RAM (they think), it has the latest processor (it can support two), and it has a smoking RAID array with more than enough space. (I know — they're probably further on than most of you reading this, right?) Sounds promising.

But there's more. The machine is the acting Exchange Server, IIS server, and SQL server, as well as performing regular tasks such as file and print services. Needless to say, the machine has a few hiccups every now and then. There is the option of upgrading, but yours truly feels this may be a processor-intensive situation. Sure, we could all use a little more RAM, and if we add a processor, we will naturally add more RAM.

In this situation, I suggest upgrading to Microsoft Windows 2000 Advanced Server to better handle the SMP tasks.

Upgrading

Before running Windows 2000 Advanced Server Setup, you need to consider whether you want to upgrade or perform a new installation. Upgrading entails installing Windows 2000 Advanced Server over an existing version of Windows NT. Installing involves deleting the previous operating system, or installing Windows 2000 Advanced Server on a drive or partition with no previous operating system.

Make sure you do not install Windows 2000 or upgrade to Windows 2000 on a compressed drive unless the drive was compressed with the NTFS file system compression utility. You must uncompress a DriveSpace or DoubleSpace volume before running Windows 2000 Setup.

If you are upgrading and you have an existing domain, be sure you understand the new features of Windows 2000 Advanced Server mixed and native domains. Make sure you have planned a tested and thorough process to upgrade to Windows 2000 Advanced Server in your workgroup or domain.

In addition, if you are upgrading, you also need to consider converting the file system to NTFS if you have any existing FAT or FAT32 partitions.

When upgrading, Windows 2000 Advanced Server is installed in a disk partition that already contains certain versions of Windows NT. An upgrade automatically installs Windows 2000 Advanced Server into the *same* folder as the currently installed operating system.

Upgrade paths

The versions of Windows NT from which you can upgrade to Windows 2000 Advanced Server are shown in Table 15-2.

Table 15-2 Windows 2000 Advanced Server Upgrade Paths

Advanced Server Product	*Products from Which You Can Upgrade*
Windows 2000 Advanced Server upgrade	Windows NT version 4.0 Enterprise Edition
Windows 2000 Advanced Server, full product	Windows NT 3.51 Server Windows NT 4.0 Server Windows NT 4.0 Terminal Server Edition Windows NT 4.0 Enterprise Edition

If you have a version of Windows NT Server earlier than 3.51, you *cannot* upgrade directly to Windows 2000 Advanced Server from it; you must first upgrade to Windows NT Server 3.51 or 4.0. Bummer.

There are several reasons for you to choose to upgrade, assuming you can update from your current operating system. Configuration is much easier; and your existing users, settings, groups, rights, and permissions are retained. Also, files and applications do not need to be recopied to the disk after installation. However, if you plan any major changes to the hard disk, you should plan on backing up the disk before installation. If you want to upgrade and then use the same applications as before, be sure to read the Applications section of the Release Notes (`Relnotes.doc` located on the Windows 2000 Advanced Server CD).

Upgrade preparation

Follow these six basic steps when preparing your system for upgrading to Windows 2000 Advanced Server:

1. **Back up your files.** Before upgrading, you should back up your current files. You can back up files to a disk, a tape drive, or another computer on your network.
2. **Uncompress the drive.** If necessary, uncompress any DriveSpace or DoubleSpace volumes before upgrading to Windows 2000 Advanced Server. You should not upgrade to Windows 2000 Advanced Server on a compressed drive unless the drive was compressed with the NTFS file system compression utility.

3. **Disable disk mirroring.** If you have disk mirroring installed on your target computer, disable it before running Setup. You can re-enable disk mirroring after completing the installation.

4. **Disconnect UPS devices.** If you have an uninterruptible power supply (UPS) connected to your target computer, disconnect the connecting serial cable before running Setup. Windows 2000 Advanced Server Setup attempts to automatically detect devices connected to serial ports; UPS equipment can cause problems with the detection process.

5. **Review applications.** Before starting the Windows 2000 Advanced Server Setup program, be sure to read the Applications section of the Release Notes (`Relnotes.doc` located on the Windows 2000 Advanced Server CD) and look for information regarding applications that need to be disabled or removed before running Setup.

6. **Mixed Mode or Native Mode.** There is a real simple rule of thumb here for picking Active Directory domain support. For pure Windows 2000 Server networks without any Windows NT Server machines, select native mode. Native mode only supports Windows 2000-based servers in the Active Directory domain architecture. The default selection (see Figure 15-2) is mixed mode, which supports both Windows 2000-based server and Windows NT-based servers.

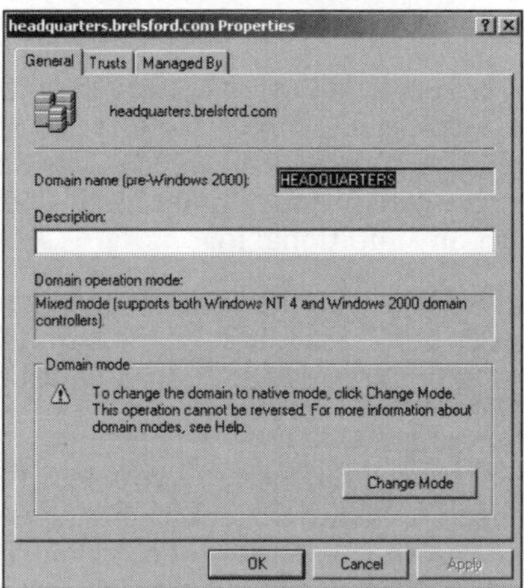

Figure 15-2: Default mixed mode selection

First looks

Whew, did you get all that? Now lean back and take a deep breath, because we're going to take a first look at what it takes to perform a fresh or new installation of Advanced Server.

If you are installing Windows 2000 Advanced Server on a disk partition that contains applications you want to keep, you will need to back them up and reinstall them after installing Windows 2000 Advanced Server.

There are many features to Advanced Server. Prior to a new installation, you need to consider some technical areas. The following sections present these areas with some details.

What licensing mode to use

Windows 2000 Advanced Server supports two licensing modes: per-seat and per-server. If you choose the per-seat mode, each computer that accesses Windows 2000 Advanced Server requires a separate Client Access License (CAL). With one CAL, a particular client computer can connect to any number of servers running Windows 2000 Advanced Server. This licensing method is most commonly used for companies with more than one Windows 2000 Advanced Server.

Per-server licensing means that each concurrent connection to this server requires a separate CAL. This means that at any one time, this Windows 2000 Advanced Server may support a fixed number of connections. For example, if you selected the per-server client licensing mode and selected five concurrent connections, this Windows 2000 Advanced Server could have five computers (clients) connected at any one time. No additional licenses would be necessary for those computers.

Small companies favor the per-server licensing approach with only one Windows 2000 Advanced Server. It is also useful for Internet or remote access servers where the client computers may not be licensed as Windows 2000 Server network clients. You can specify a maximum number of concurrent server connections and reject any additional logons.

If you are unsure which mode to use, choose per server, because you can change once from per server to per seat at no cost. Be careful, however; you cannot change from per seat to per server, and you will not be able to revert after you convert to per seat.

If you plan to use Terminal Services, I recommend you select per-seat licensing, and you will also need to install the components used by Terminal Services. With Terminal Services, the generally accepted licensing mode is per seat, except with the Terminal Services Internet Connector license, where the mode would always be per server. If you use Terminal Services, you will also need to install two components: Terminal Services and Terminal Services Licensing.

Whether the computer will use a dual-boot configuration

If you need to use different operating systems, a dual-boot configuration will let you choose from different operating systems at startup or reboot.

What file system to use

The file systems to choose from are NTFS, FAT, and, FAT32 (FAT32 for larger disks). NTFS is recommended for many reasons — it supports security and is the only file system that supports Active Directory. Active Directory includes important features such as domain-based security. However, it may be necessary to have a FAT or FAT32 partition in certain dual-boot situations, such as testing or research and development.

What partition you will install on, or creating a new partition to install

If you are performing a new installation, you will need to review your disk partitions before installing. As upgrades use existing partitions, this is only necessary for new installations. A partition divides a disk into one or more areas that can be formatted for use by one file system. After installation, you can modify the partitioning of the disk if necessary.

What components to install

There are a variety of optional components to choose from when installing Windows 2000 Advanced Server. Your choices depend on how you will use your server. See the Advanced Server component list later in this chapter, under the section “Advanced Server Components.”

How to handle networking, IP addresses, TCP/IP name resolution, and other protocols

Most networked computers currently use TCP/IP as the network protocol because it is the Internet standard. If you use different protocols, be sure you document current configurations and settings before installing Windows 2000 Advanced Server. With TCP/IP, you will need to make decisions about how to handle IP addresses and how they will be resolved into names that users recognize (DNS, DDNS, and so on).

Whether to create domains or workgroups for your servers

If you haven’t addressed this with your IT/MIS team, you need to plan this out thoroughly before installing Windows 2000 Advanced Server, as it is a very complex operating system that demands strategic considerations. If you are considering Advanced Server, odds are you are set up in a domain already. Consult with your team for necessary domain specifications. You should also review the two Active Directory chapters in this book (Chapters 11 and 12).

Case Study: Dueling Swords (a.k.a. Dualing Swords)

Yet another tale from the enterprise involves the not-so-humble, but ever-so-common power user. He or she knows more about the facets and features of Microsoft products than the administrators do, and more about how to run the enterprise than its many vice presidents and chairpeople do. In our little tale of intrigue, the power user has assumed the identity of Rusty. Now Rusty has been running Windows 98 for years now, and ran Windows 95 for years before that. Now he's forced to run Windows NT Workstation 4.0, but he needs Windows 98 for his research and development software. Hmmm... sounds like a good old dual-boot story to me.

On the server side, it is not customary to suggest dual-boot configurations. There are situations similar to Rusty's story, and also horror stories of restricting enterprise budgets that force us into "dualing" swords, that is, competing interests.

Dual-Booting

A consideration when installing Windows 2000 Advanced Server is whether to configure dual booting. It is possible to install Windows 2000 Advanced Server and also enable the computer to sometimes run another operating system by setting up a dual-boot system. However, this situation presents complexities because of file system issues.

For example, if you had a server that needed Windows 2000 Advanced Server most of the time but would occasionally need to run an older application requiring Windows NT Server version 4.0, you could set the server up with dual booting. In this situation, you would need to make specific file-system choices and would probably need the latest service pack.

If you use dual booting between Windows 2000 Server and any other operating system, you *must* place Windows 2000 in a separate partition on the computer to ensure that Windows 2000 will not overwrite critical files used by the other operating system.

Before deciding whether to use dual booting, you should be aware of the following:

- For a dual-boot configuration with Windows 95 or Windows 98, compressed DriveSpace or DoubleSpace volumes won't be available while you are running Windows 2000. However, if you access these volumes only with Windows 95 or Windows 98, it is not necessary to uncompress the volumes.
- To set up a dual-boot configuration between MS-DOS or Windows 95 and Windows 2000, you should install Windows 2000 last. Otherwise, important files needed for starting Windows 2000 could be overwritten. However, if you configure a dual-boot using Windows 98 and Windows 2000, there is no need to install the operating systems in any particular order.

- For a dual-boot configuration of Windows 2000 with Windows 95 or MS-DOS, the primary partition must be formatted as FAT. For a dual-boot configuration with Microsoft Windows 95 OSR2 or Windows 98, the primary partition must be formatted as FAT or FAT32, *not* NTFS.

The reason for choosing dual booting with Windows 2000 and another operating system is that you can use applications that only run with a particular operating system (by restarting with that system). However, there are definite drawbacks to dual booting. With dual booting, valuable disk space is taken up by each operating system, and compatibility issues, including file system compatibility and application functionality, may arise.

Tip

Be your toughest critic. Challenge yourself to justify why you would ever dual-boot an enterprise-level server. Is it really an enterprise-level server or just a server located in an enterprise?

If you are considering using dual booting to ensure that you will always have a way to boot the computer (in case of driver or disk problems), you should be aware of the variety of disaster-recovery features available in Windows 2000. One of these features is Safe Mode, which restarts Windows 2000 with default settings and the minimum number of drivers, ensuring the capability to start even if a new driver is causing a problem.

Dual booting between Windows NT 4.0 and Windows 2000 Advanced Server

If you plan a dual-boot configuration with Windows NT 4.0 and Windows 2000 Advanced Server, review the following precautions:

- Dual booting is not necessary if your only concern is ensuring that you can always boot the computer.
- Using NTFS as the only file system on a computer that dual-boots between Windows 2000 and Windows NT is not recommended. You should consider a FAT partition.
- Make sure that Windows NT 4.0 has been updated with the latest service pack.
- Install each operating system onto a separate drive or disk partition. When you perform a new installation of Windows 2000 Advanced Server, the installation is placed by default on a partition on which no other operating system is located. You can specify a different partition during installation.
- Don't install Windows 2000 on a compressed drive unless the drive was compressed with the NTFS file system compression utility.
- On any partition where you perform a new installation of Windows 2000, you will need to reinstall any programs after installation is complete.

- Install the programs used by each operating system on the partition with that system.
- If the dual-boot computer is in a Windows NT or Windows 2000 domain, each installation of Windows NT 4.0 Server or Windows 2000 Advanced Server must have a different computer name.

If you need more information on dual booting, please consult the Windows 2000 Resource Kit (which may be purchased at your favorite bookstore).

Dual booting between multiple Windows 2000 partitions

You can set up a server so that it dual-boots between multiple Windows 2000 partitions (Windows 2000 Professional and/or Server). Remember that you must use a different computer name for each installation if the computer participates in a Windows 2000 domain. Because a unique security identifier (SID) is used for each installation of Windows 2000 on a domain, you cannot boot between multiple installations of Windows 2000 and use the same computer name for each installation.

Dual booting and file system compatibility

Compatibility becomes more complex with dual booting when you consider what file system(s) to use. The file systems to choose from are NTFS, FAT, and FAT32. (For more information, see the "Choosing the File System" section later in this chapter.)

NTFS is normally the recommended file system because it offers important features, as I mentioned earlier. You need to consider compatibility questions with dual booting and NTFS, because the version of NTFS in Windows 2000 Advanced Server has additional new features. Files that use any new features will be completely usable or readable *only* when the computer is started with Windows 2000 Advanced Server. For example, a file that uses the new NTFS encryption feature obviously won't be readable when the computer is started with Windows NT Server 4.0. This could lead to many problems, so be aware when configuring your dual-boot setup.

If you want to have a dual-boot computer that boots between Windows NT and Windows 2000, and you want to have an NTFS partition, the only appropriate version of Windows NT is version 4.0 with the latest service pack. Using the latest service pack maximizes compatibility between Windows NT 4.0 and the updated NTFS file system used with Windows 2000 Advanced Server (Service Pack 4 and later). Still, this does *not* provide file access to files using the new features in NTFS.

It is not recommended to use NTFS as the only file system on a computer that dual-boots between Windows 2000 and Windows NT. In that situation, a FAT or FAT32 partition containing the Windows NT 4.0 operating system ensures that when booted into Windows NT 4.0, the computer will have local access to needed files.

If you set up a computer to dual-boot Windows NT 3.51 or earlier on a FAT partition, and Windows 2000 Advanced Server on an NTFS partition, the NTFS partition will not be visible when that computer boots with Windows NT 3.51.

Choosing the File System

You can choose between three file systems for disk partitions on a computer running Windows 2000 Advanced Server: NTFS, FAT, and FAT32. NTFS is the recommended system. FAT and FAT32 are similar to each other, except that FAT32 is designed for larger disks than FAT. NTFS works most easily with large disks, and has always been a more powerful file system than FAT or FAT32. Windows 2000 Advanced Server includes a new version of NTFS, with features such as Active Directory that add to the flexibility of its existing security features, such as domains and the user accounts database. You can easily convert your partition to the new version of NTFS during installation, even if it has used FAT before. You can also convert a FAT or FAT32 partition to the new version of NTFS after installation by using `convert.exe`. Whether carried out during or after installation, this kind of conversion does not corrupt or damage your files. For more details about features in NTFS, see the section entitled "NTFS" later in this chapter.

You can only use such important features as Active Directory and domain-based security by choosing NTFS as your file system.

There is one situation where you might want to choose FAT or FAT32 as your file system. If it is necessary to have a dual-boot computer that you sometimes run with an earlier operating system and at other times with Windows 2000 Advanced Server, you will need to have a FAT or FAT32 partition as the boot partition on the hard disk. Because most earlier operating systems can't access the local partition if it uses the latest version of NTFS, which is NTFS 5.0 in Windows 2000 (all versions), you need to set the boot or primary partition to FAT or FAT32. The one exception is Windows NT version 4.0 with Service Pack 4 or greater, which has limited access to a NTFS 5.0 partition. Windows NT cannot access local files that have been stored using NTFS 5.0.

Table 15-3 describes the compatibility of each file system with various operating systems.

Table 15-3 File System Compatibility

File System	*Description*
NTFS	A computer running Windows 2000 can access files on the local hard disk. A computer running Windows NT 4.0 with SP4 or greater might be able to access some files locally. Other operating systems will not be allowed to access local files. Minimum size is about 10MB. Recommended maximum is 2 terabytes (TB). Cannot be used on floppies. File size is limited only by size of volume.
FAT	Local access available through MS-DOS, all versions of Windows, Windows NT, Windows 2000, and OS/2. Volume size ranges from floppy disk size (1.4 MB) to 4GB maximum. Does not support domains. Maximum file size is 2GB.
FAT32	Local access available through Windows 95 OSR2, Windows 98, and Windows 2000. Volume size ranges from 512MB to 2TB. In Windows 2000, you can format a FAT32 volume only up to 32GB. Does not support domains. Maximum file size is 4GB.

NTFS

The Setup program makes it easy to convert your partition to the new version of NTFS, even if it has used FAT or FAT32 before. Setup begins by checking the existing file system. If it is NTFS, conversion happens automatically, and if it is FAT or FAT32, you are given the choice of converting to NTFS. You can also convert a FAT or FAT32 partition to the new version of NTFS after installing Windows 2000 Advanced Server by using `convert.exe`. Whether carried out during or after installation, this kind of conversion keeps your files intact.

If you're setting up a dual-boot configuration of Windows 2000, you must install Windows 2000 on its own partition. This ensures that Windows 2000 will not overwrite crucial files needed by the other operating system.

FAT and FAT32

FAT and FAT32 are alternative file-system options. You will need to use them if you must have a dual-boot computer that you sometimes run with an older operating system and sometimes with Windows 2000.

The basic criterion for choosing between FAT and FAT32 is the size of the installation partition; use FAT32 rather than FAT on partitions that are 2GB or larger.

Windows 2000 supports FAT32 volumes of any size created by Windows 95 or Windows 98. However, Windows 2000 formats FAT32 volumes only up to 32GB. If you choose to format a partition as FAT during Setup and the partition is larger than 2GB, Setup will automatically format it as FAT32. For volumes larger than 32GB, Microsoft recommends using NTFS rather than FAT32.

Disk partition planning for new installations

You will need to plan your disk partitions before running Setup only if you are performing a new installation, not an upgrade. Remember, if you plan to delete or create partitions on a hard disk, be sure to back up the disk contents beforehand, because these actions will destroy any existing data. Also, do not install Windows 2000 on a compressed drive unless the partition was compressed with the NTFS file system compression utility. You must uncompress a DriveSpace or DoubleSpace drive before running Setup on it.

Before running Setup to perform a new installation, you will need to determine the size of the partition on which to install Windows 2000 Server. There is no set formula for figuring a partition size; the basic principle is to allow plenty of room for the operating system, applications, and other files that you will group together on the installation partition. The files for setting up Windows 2000 Server require between 850 and 1250MB of free space on the disk, as described in the section titled "Deconstructing Windows 2000 Advanced Server" at the beginning of this chapter. However, I recommend that you allow considerably more disk space than the minimum amount. Allowing 2–4GB on the partition is not unreasonable, and for larger installations, it is good to allow 10GB. This allows space for a variety of items, including optional components, user accounts, Active Directory information, logs, future service packs, the pagefile used by the operating system, and other items.

If you plan to use Remote Installation Services on this server so that you can install operating systems onto other computers, you will need a separate partition for use by Remote Installation Services. If you need to create a new partition for this, you should plan on doing it after setup, and leave enough unpartitioned disk space so that you can create it. Alternatively, you can plan to use dynamic disk format, which allows more flexibility in the use of the disk space than basic format.

Case Study: The Case of the Missing Ingredient

Once a coworker of mine, I'll call him Mitch, set up a Windows NT Server 4.0 server, but it could have just as easily been Windows 2000 Advanced Server. He had done some research into the various features of the operating system, perused the endless save-the-world hype packaged by Microsoft, and dug in. Now because Mitch has installed a working server, there was a certain amount of braggadocio that accompanied that achievement. He felt invigorated, to say the least, by the variety of features and programming tasks he learned in the process. However, one day his manager, following an involved discussion on the features of NT with a Microsoft technician, asked if a particular service was running, Mitch could only respond with a glazed look. He didn't even recognize the name.

The key here is to understand what's in the soup. Know what makes it tick. In Windows 2000, you really have to sit down and wrestle through the documentation. I strongly recommend setting up a test network, if possible, to install Windows 2000 Advanced Server and try out its features before considering it for production.

Advanced Server Components

Windows 2000 Advanced Server includes a wide variety of core components, including a number of administrative tools that are installed automatically. In addition, you can choose from a number of additional components that extend the functionality of Windows 2000 Advanced Server. These components can be installed at setup or added afterward through the Add/Remove Programs option in Control Panel. Choosing more of these components means providing more possibilities on the server; however, you should choose only the components you need, as each component requires additional disk space. The following list will help you choose the components you need in your installation.

- **Certificate Services** provides authentication support, including secure e-mail, Web-based authentication, and smart card authentication.
- **Cluster Service** provides support for clustering, where several servers or *nodes* work together to provide users with constant access to server-based resources. If one of the nodes in the cluster fails, another node begins to provide service. This process is known as *failover.*
- **Internet Information Services (IIS)** provides support for Web site creation, configuration, and management, along with Network News Transfer Protocol (NNTP), File Transfer Protocol (FTP), and Simple Mail Transfer Protocol (SMTP).
- **Management and Monitoring Tools** provides network management and monitoring tools, along with services that support client dialing and the updating of client phone books, and a tool for migrating from Novell Directory Services to Windows 2000 Active Directory. Also includes the Simple Network Management Protocol (SNMP).

- **Message Queuing Services** provides services that support the messaging needed by distributed applications, allowing these applications to function reliably in heterogeneous networks or when a computer is temporarily offline.
- **Microsoft Indexing Service** provides indexing functions for documents stored on disk, allowing users to search for specific document text or properties.
- **Microsoft Script Debugger** provides script development support.
- **Networking Services** provides important support for networking, including the items in the following list. For information about network monitoring, see "Management and Monitoring Tools" earlier in this list.
    - Dynamic Host Configuration Protocol (DHCP). Gives a server the capability of providing IP addresses dynamically to other servers on the network. With DHCP, you do not need to set and maintain static IP addresses on any intranet servers except for those providing DHCP, DNS, and/or WINS.
    - Domain Name System (DNS). Provides name resolution for clients running Windows 2000. With name resolution, users can access servers by name, instead of having to use IP addresses that are difficult to recognize and remember.
    - Windows Internet Name Service. Provides name resolution for clients running Windows NT and earlier versions of Microsoft operating systems. With name resolution, users can access servers by name, instead of having to use IP addresses that are difficult to recognize and remember.
    - COM Internet Services Proxy. Supports distributed applications that use HTTP to communicate through Internet Information Services.
    - Internet Authentication Service. Provides authentication for dial-in users.
    - QoS Admission Control Service. Allows you to control how applications are allotted network bandwidth. Important applications can be given more bandwidth, less important applications less bandwidth.
    - Simple TCP/IP services. Supports Character Generator, Daytime Discard, Echo, and Quote of the Day.
    - Site Server LDAP Services. Supports telephony applications, which help users access features such as caller ID, conference calls, video conferencing, and faxing. This support depends on Internet Information Services (IIS).
- **Other Network File and Print Services** provides file and print services for Macintosh and print services for UNIX.

Case Study: Choking on Threads

For all of you database and Web server enthusiasts out there, I bet you've never seen this one before. The database server starts running a little slow. Of course, the software is designed to accommodate more connections than are currently established, and you should have enough RAM, so why is this thing clunking along? Your new administrator (who's not yet ready to handle the perfmon and netmon thing yet) issues a direct order to purchase additional RAM. "Double the RAM!" is his battle cry. And the little town of Accounting buys into his remedy with tears of joy as the newly purchased RAM is inserted into the database server. Unfortunately, nothing changes. Now it's a bandwidth issue. Surely the 10BaseT, non-switched network must be experiencing problems. Oh, that poor little processor. What are we going to do? Well, let me introduce one of the enhanced features of Advanced Server — good old SMP.

- **Remote Installation Services** provides services that enable you to set up new client computers remotely, without the need to visit each client. The target clients *must* support remote booting. On your Windows 2000 Advanced Server, you will need to configure a separate partition for Remote Installation Services.
- **Remote Storage** provides an extension to your disk space by making removable media, such as tapes, more accessible. Infrequently used data can automatically be transferred to tape and retrieved when needed.
- **Terminal Services** provides the capability to run client applications on the server, so client computers can function as terminals rather than independent systems. The server provides a multisession environment and runs the Windows-based programs normally used on the client computers. You must also install Terminal Services Licensing (see next item).

I can think of few better uses for Windows 2000 Advanced Server than Terminal Services. Talk about a demanding application, running simultaneous user sessions. It is here that Windows 2000 Advanced Server really shines, bringing its capability to scale to a large number of multiprocessors and address huge amounts of primary memory.

- **Terminal Services Licensing** provides the capability to register and track licenses for Terminal Services clients. If you install Terminal Services, you must also install Terminal Services Licensing (to license Terminal Services clients). However, temporary licenses can be issued which permit clients to use Terminal Servers for up to 90 days.
- **Windows Media Services** provides multimedia support, allowing you to deliver content using Advanced Streaming Format over an Internet, or the Internet.

Hungry yet? I hope so; I've got a few more stories for you.

Symmetric Multiprocessing (SMP)

As I mentioned earlier in the chapter, Windows 2000 Advanced Server provides some additional features over the Standard Server version. Advanced Server upgrade provides a more powerful server operating system, offering memory support to 8GB, and up to eight-way symmetric multiprocessing (SMP). Windows 2000 Advanced Server retail supports up to four-way SMP in the retail kit, and up to eight-way SMP under the OEM terms and conditions of sale. Improved performance is expected to be most pronounced on systems with eight-way or more than eight-way designs. While this level of CPU support is unchanged from Windows NT 4.0, considerable improvements in the implementation of the SMP code allow for enhanced linearity of scaling on high performance systems.

Basically, with symmetric multiprocessing, the operating system runs threads on any available processor. As a result, SMP makes it possible for applications to use multiple processors when additional processing power is required to increase the throughput capability of a system. This is key to distributing CPU resources. Note that three additional functions: (1) hardware interrupts, (2) deferred procedure calls (DPCs), and (3) software interrupts at a low Interrupt Request Level (IRQL) may also run on any available processor determined by the hardware abstraction layer (HAL).

Although most SMP systems running Windows 2000 dynamically distribute threads and hardware interrupts equally among all available processors, you may sometimes want to restrict threads and interrupts to one or more processors rather than distribute them in order to improve processor cache locality and overall system throughput. I will talk about thread partitioning and others later in the chapter.

Analyzing performance on SMP systems

You can monitor your SMP system activity by using Performance Monitor. To evaluate your system's performance, look at the following factors:

- Processor utilization and queue length. You may need to partition the workload so that a particular processor handles a particular workload in order to achieve better performance.
- Processor performance data, such as context switches, interrupts, threads, and processes. Activity rates and usage levels for these types of data that are higher than expected for a particular throughput can reveal inefficiencies in how your processors handle their workload. As a result, you may need to partition these types of activity.
- Overall resource utilization on your system. Scaling to multiple processors can increase the load on resources such as disk, memory, and network components, and it might be necessary to increase the capacity of these components.

Application developers are the design keys to controlling how processes behave in an SMP environment.

SMP impact on system resources

The increased processing power and throughput on SMP systems could possibly cause other system resources such as memory, system bus, disks, and network to experience heavier loads. Heavy use among shared resources will increase memory latency. This is because code running on SMP systems needs to lock shared data to ensure data integrity, and locking shared data may result in contention for shared data structures. Also, the synchronization mechanisms used to lock shared data structures will increase the processor code path. As a result, when the number of processors on a system is scaled up, it is generally necessary to increase other resources on the system, such as memory, disks, and network components. Consider the analysis in the following sections.

Processors

A large processor cache delivers the best performance. In multiprocessor configurations, the cache can reduce memory latency on the shared system bus and can reduce resource access.

Memory

Your SMP system should have more than 64MB of memory, as it most likely bears a heavier workload than a single-processor system. It also runs more processes and threads. In general, you should scale memory with processors.

If you add a second processor to a machine running with 64MB of memory, you should increase your memory to 128MB.

Scaling

Scaling is the process of adding processors to your system to achieve higher throughput. Applications that benefit from multiprocessor configurations are typically those that are processor-intensive, such as database servers, Web servers, and active file and print servers. Servers that perform heavy computations, including detailed calculation for scientific or financial applications, complex graphic rendering, computer-aided design (CAD)-based modeling, or electrical-engineering design may also demand multiprocessor systems.

I won't go into too much detail on monitoring activity on multiprocessor systems, but I do want to share some of the concepts and methods. Don't fall asleep on me yet! When examining a multiprocessor system, you should monitor Thread\Context Switches/sec and Thread\% Processor Time to observe which threads are running on what processors, and to find out how frequently the threads switch between processors to do the work of a particular process. This is important for you to know because there can be occasions when the switching of threads impedes optimal performance. For more reading on Performance Monitor, please see Chapter 18.

Soft affinity

Windows 2000 uses a soft affinity algorithm that favors running a thread either on the last processor that serviced it or its ideal processor, which is a processor specified by the program developer in the application code. This is why I mentioned earlier that application developers are key in designing how a process behaves in SMP. Affinity is the mechanism for associating a process with a processor. With soft affinity, the association can vary between processors, as opposed to hard affinity, where the association is fixed to a specific processor. In general, soft affinity is an optimal design that takes advantage of cache locality. However, when threads migrate from one processor to another processor, they may no longer have access to previously cached data and must re-read data from memory. At worst, thread migration may cause false sharing because, to the cache coherency hardware of the CPU, it may appear that multiple processors are sharing a cache line.

As a result, monitoring context-switching activity and thread processor usage is useful to application developers in understanding thread behavior.

Maximizing performance

There are a couple ways to maximize performance from your system. They involve partitioning your workload so that a specific processor is servicing all threads, interrupts, and deferred procedure calls (DPCs) associated with that work.

Thread partitioning

The first method is called *thread partitioning*. Partitioning threads to specific processors is called setting a *processor affinity mask*. The affinity mask contains bits for each processor on the system, defining which processors a particular process or thread can use. When you set affinity for a process to a particular processor, all threads of the process inherit the affinity to the same processor.

Interrupt partitioning

A second consideration is *hardware interrupt partitioning*. Some processor platforms can distribute interrupts across available processors; this capability is called *symmetric interrupt distribution*. These platforms typically include Pentium Pro and later processors; however, some Pentium processors also have this capability. Although symmetric interrupt distribution is designed as a way to balance interrupt activity, it can sometimes result in poor processor-cache performance. Partitioning interrupts to a specific processor is a strategy for addressing this problem. The IntBind tool on the Windows 2000 Resource Kit companion CD enables you to set the affinity for interrupts generated from disks or network adapters to a particular processor. This improves efficiency by taking advantage of cache locality, which can be lost when interrupts are serviced by any available processor rather than the one on which they were queued.

Sometimes your hardware may limit your ability to make use of this tool. Support for partitioning interrupts depends on the characteristics of the processor and the interrupt assignment mechanism, such as the Advanced Programmable Interrupt Controller (APIC) on systems based on the Intel Pentium, Pentium Pro, Pentium II, and Xeon processors. Consult your processor vendor for details about the interrupt-distribution capabilities of your hardware. In addition, see Windows 2000 Resource Kit tools for information about the requirements for using IntBind.

If you find that your hardware does not support the use of IntBind, you may want to consider upgrading to a processor that provides this support. If you choose to add a new processor, select one with a large secondary (L2) cache. File server applications, Web servers, and databases are a few examples of the many workloads that benefit from a large processor cache. A large processor cache, ranging from 512K to 4MB or larger, is recommended to improve performance.

Clustering and Fault Tolerance

As enterprises begin focusing on system availability, the concept of clustering develops. Many enterprise companies are tracking their server uptime metrics and comparing them to others in the industry. Believe me, you don't want to be at the bottom of this list. Clustering is quickly becoming an accepted fault-tolerance method. Once viewed as expensive and overboard, studies show that server downtime and loss of employee productivity far outweigh the cost of clustering.

As ever more critical enterprise deployments are made, there is a growing need for the failover high availability and load balancing power that comes from joining multiple computers into clusters. *Clustering* refers to linking individual servers and coordinating communication between them so they can perform as a single integrated unit. Should one server stop functioning, it automatically fails over to the next server to provide continuous service. One particular (and popular) use of clustering is to provide two servers with access to the same application or database, with one server active and the other waiting for a message to begin operations should the first server fail. But servers can also be clustered so that both are active, each able to take on the workload of the other, and to provide for load balancing and application scalability.

The objective of clustering is to provide very high levels of application and data availability. Clustering addresses both planned sources of downtime (like hardware and software upgrades) and unplanned, failure-driven outages. New in Windows 2000 Advanced Server and Datacenter Server is support for rolling upgrades of both OS releases (versions, service packs, hotfixes) and of layered products. Clustering is improved in many other ways in Windows 2000 Advanced Server and Datacenter Server, including improved setup, integration with the management architecture, and a broader list of cluster-aware system services.

Windows 2000 Server Clustering Services, available in Windows 2000 Advanced Server, can provide fully redundant, fault-tolerant DHCP services. Clustering Services, when used with DHCP, can provide for significantly higher availability, easier manageability, and greater scalability than would otherwise be available. The DHCP server service can now be run natively as an application on top of Clustering Services. The DHCP configuration database is stored on the cluster's shared disk array. If a failure occurs on the first machine in the cluster, the name space and all services are transparently reconstituted to the second machine. There will be no changes for the client, which will see the same IP address for the clustered DHCP server. Consequently, unlike Windows NT Server 4.0 or NetWare 5.0 implementations, DHCP services will remain totally uninterrupted in the event of a system failure.

Microsoft Cluster Service (MSCS) for Windows 2000 Advanced Server can automatically recover mission-critical data and applications from many common types of failure — usually in under a minute. In addition, using the Plug and Play technology, the Clustering Service detects the addition and removal of network adapters, TCP/IP network stacks, and shared physical disks.

Built-in clustering services in Windows 2000 Advanced Server and Datacenter Server enable two servers to be connected into a cluster of up to 64 CPUs for higher availability and easier manageability of server resources. The two servers do not have to be the same size or configuration.

New enhancements in Windows 2000 Advanced Server and Datacenter Server include Active Directory support, support for high-availability dial-in network connections and additional cluster-aware system services (DHCP, WINS, Dfs), and rolling upgrade support. In a rolling upgrade, one machine in the cluster is brought down while the other is upgraded. Upon completion of the upgrade, the machine is brought back online in the cluster, then the next is brought offline and upgraded.

Caution! Rolling upgrades

Rolling upgrades, those that accommodate legacy predecessors, are fully supported for the following services:

- Core resources
- Printing
- Web services — Internet Information Services (IIS) 5.0
- Transaction services (Distributed Transaction Coordinator)
- Message queuing services (Microsoft Message Queue Server)

Obviously, a rolling upgrade from previous builds of Windows 2000 Cluster service is not supported if a DHCP service or WINS resource has been already created.

The following services do not support rolling upgrades:

- MSMQ; Primary Enterprise, Primary Site, and Backup Site services
- Internet Information Service 3.0
- Distributed Transaction Coordinator
- Print spooler that is not on an LPR port

Before performing a rolling upgrade, consult with the vendor of any third-party software used for a cluster resource.

Easier Clustering Service setup and configuration

The latest version of Clustering Service contains changes to the user interface that make the setup and administration of a cluster easier. The checklist for setting up clustering is your first step in the configuration process (see Figure 15-3). Cluster Administrator contains a new Cluster Application wizard that makes it easier to configure a new application to run on a cluster. The Application Setup wizard leads you through all of the steps required, including creating a virtual server to host the application, creating resource types for all associated resources, creating dependencies between resources, and setting failover and failback policies. The Cluster Administrator now uses the Windows 2000 standard security dialog boxes to control the security settings for the cluster and for file share resources.

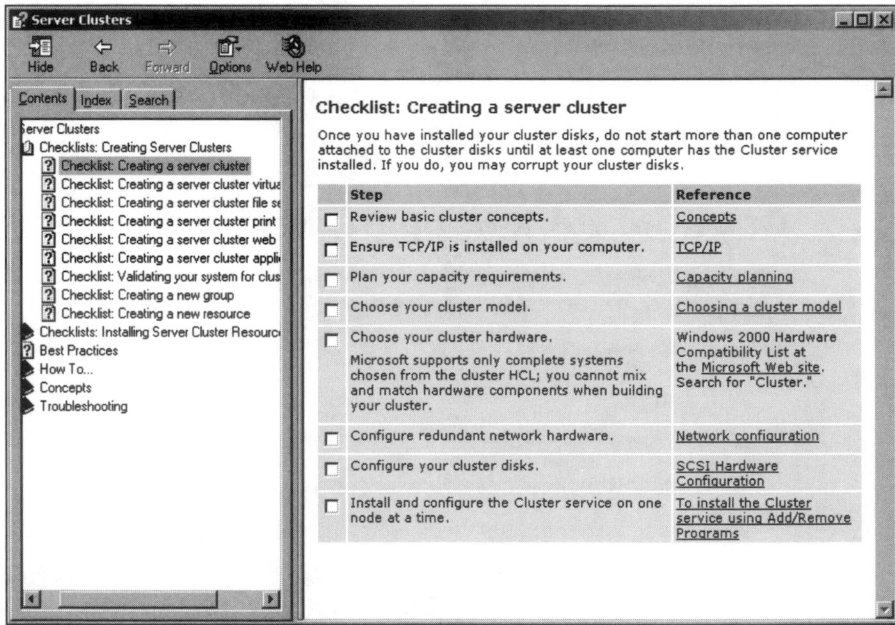

Figure 15-3: Cluster server checklist

The Microsoft Cluster Server application found in Windows NT Server 4.0, Enterprise Edition and the Windows Load Balancing Service has been enhanced and made standard features as part of the Windows 2000 Advanced Server package. Improvements can be summarized as follows:

- Rolling upgrades. Administrators can easily take a server that is a cluster member offline for maintenance, permitting rolling upgrades of system and application software. There are two major advantages to a rolling upgrade. First, service outages are very short during the upgrade process. Second, the cluster configuration does not have to be recreated — the configuration will remain intact during the upgrade process.
- Active Directory and MMC Integration has been added to the Clustering Service for Windows 2000 Advanced Server. Active Directory is automatically utilized to publish information about clusters. All management is now accomplished with the Microsoft Management Console, making setup easier and allowing administrators greater control in visually monitoring the status of all resources in the cluster.
- Recovery from Network Failure support has also been added to the Clustering Service in Windows 2000 Advanced Server. A sophisticated algorithm has been included to detect and isolate network failures and improve failure recovery actions. It can detect a number of different states for network failures and then utilize the appropriate failover policy to determine whether or not to failover the resource group.
- Plug and Play Support can now be utilized by the Clustering Service to automatically detect the addition and removal of network adapters, TCP/IP network stacks, and shared physical disks to help expedite configuration.
- WINS, Dfs, and DHCP Support have been added to the Clustering Service for automatic failover and recovery. A file share resource can now serve as a Distributed File System (Dfs) root or it can share its folder subdirectories for efficient management of large numbers of related file shares. This provides a higher level of availability for mission-critical network services than prior versions of Windows NT.
- COM Support for the Cluster API has been added, providing a standard, cross-platform API set for developing and supporting cluster-aware applications. This API can be used to create scalable, cluster-capable applications that can automatically balance loads across multiple servers within the cluster. Additionally, the Windows Scripting Host (WSH) can also be utilized to control cluster behavior and to automate many cluster administration tasks. You will manage COM from either the COM+ Event System services tab (see Figure 15-4) or the COM+ Applications MMC (see Figure 15-5).

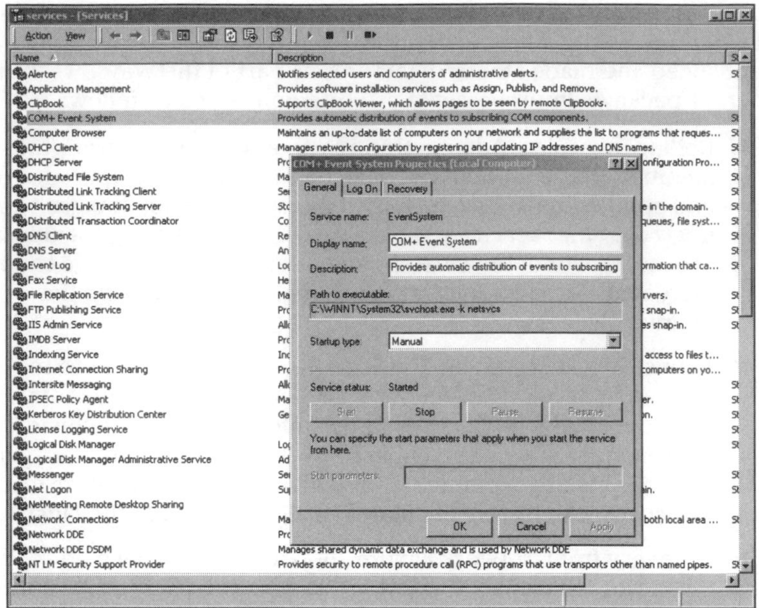

Figure 15-4: COM+ Event System services tab

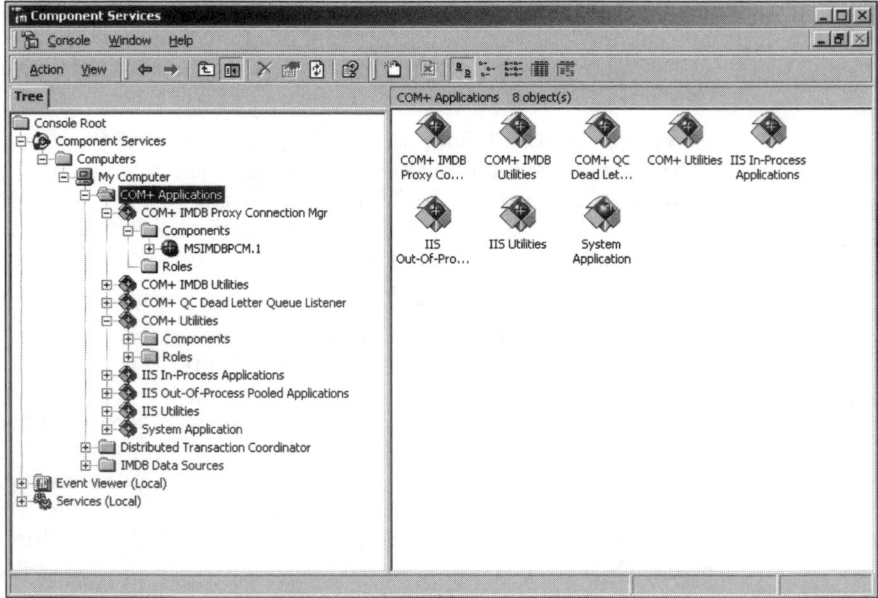

Figure 15-5: COM+ Applications MMC

Case Study: The Balancing Act

One of my enterprise clients had a PDC that functioned as a Web server and an Exchange server, as well as providing file and print services. While this may not sound like overwhelming tasks for a server with adequate RAM, processing, and disk resources, there were times when it peaked network activity. At the time we were not aware of such concepts as network load balancing, where two or more computers are combined to provide availability and scalability benefits to mission-critical applications, such as IIS, databases, or e-mail. Network load balancing balances incoming TCP/IP traffic between servers and is most commonly used for running Web server programs.

Network Load Balancing

Network load balancing (NLB) manages TCP/IP traffic to maintain high availability for IP-based services. When a host fails or goes offline, NLB automatically reconfigures the cluster to direct client requests to the remaining computers. This redirection of tasks usually takes less than ten seconds. While connections to the failed server are lost, the offline computer can transparently rejoin the cluster and reclaim its tasks. NLB also handles inadvertent subnetting and rejoining of the cluster network. This fault tolerance is enabled by a unique distributed architecture, which avoids the single points of failure or performance bottlenecks of other load-balancing solutions.

Load balancing is not a new concept to Enterprise Server. However, in Windows 2000 Advanced Server, it provides the following enhanced features:

- It balances and distributes client connections (TCP/IP connections) over multiple servers scaling the performance of TCP/IP services, such as Web, Proxy, or FTP servers.
- It supports up to 32 computers in a single cluster.
- It optionally load-balances multiple server requests from a single client.
- It automatically detects and recovers from a failed or offline computer.
- It is easy to tailor the workload for each computer using port management rules and to block undesired network access to certain IP ports.
- It remotely starts, stops, and controls network load balancing actions from any networked Windows 2000 computer using console commands or scripts.
- It installs as a standard Windows 2000 networking driver component and requires no hardware changes to install and run.
- Server applications don't need to be modified to run in a network load balancing cluster and all operations require no human intervention.

You can automatically upgrade Windows Load Balancing Service (WLBS) for Windows NT 4.0 Server or Windows NT 4.0 Server, Enterprise Edition to Network Load Balancing for Windows 2000 Advanced Server. You cannot upgrade WLBS to Windows 2000 Professional or Windows 2000 Server. Your first step in implementing network load balancing is to complete the network load-balancing checklist (see Figure 15-6).

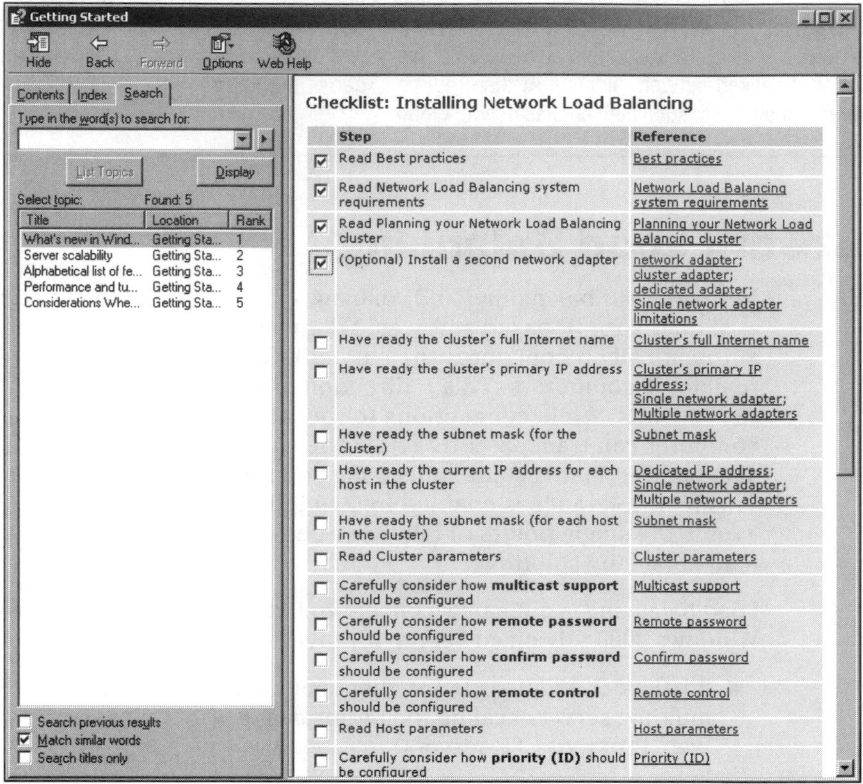

Figure 15-6: Network load-balancing checklist

Other Enterprise Improvements

Here are some final improvements to Windows 2000 Advanced Server that will make life better at the enterprise level. These improvements include better memory management and high-performance sorting capabilities.

Memory management improvements

The memory management infrastructure of Windows 2000 Server has been greatly improved with the introduction of the Enterprise Memory Architecture (EMA). EMA allows Windows 2000 Advanced Server systems to take advantage of physical memories larger than 4GB. Applications that are "large memory aware" can use addresses above 4GB to cache data in memory, resulting in extremely high performance.

The Compaq Alpha and Intel Pentium II Xeon microprocessors feature their own standards to take advantage of large physical memory arrays. Windows 2000 Server supports both the Compaq Alpha Very Large Memory (VLM) and Intel Page Size Extension (PSE36), allowing Windows 2000 Advanced Server machines to address as much as 64GB of physical memory.

High performance sorting

High performance sorting support has been introduced in Windows 2000 Advanced Server. This basically applies to commercial sorting performance of large data sets, which has been optimized. This improves the performance of common tasks such as preparing to load data in batch for data warehouse/datamart operations and preparing large sort-sensitive print and batch operations.

Datacenter Server

Simply stated, Datacenter Server builds on Advanced Server. Two key points that separate Datacenter Server from Advanced Server are SMP scalability and physical memory.

- SMP Scalability. Datacenter Server supports up to 32 multiprocessors.
- Physical memory. Datacenter Server supports up to 64GB of RAM memory.

Similar to Windows 2000 Advanced Server, the Datacenter Server offering supports cluster and load balancing right out of the box. You're likely to see Datacenter server positioned in the "dot com" community because, with its horsepower, it is especially well suited for e-commerce implementations.

Summary

This chapter addressed the needs of the enterprise and Microsoft's Windows 2000 offerings for this segment: Windows 2000 Advanced Server and Datacenter Server.

- Defining Windows 2000 Advanced Server
- Understanding the enterprise challenge
- Windows 2000 Advanced Server needs analysis and information gathering
- Issues surrounding Windows 2000 Advanced Server installations and upgrades
- Understanding processing threads
- Understanding load balancing
- Avoiding rolling upgrade problems
- Defining Datacenter Server

Chapter 16

Small Business Server 4.5

In This Chapter

- Defining Small Business Server (SBS)
- Understanding the small business environment
- Identifying Small Business Server design goals and philosophy
- Planning for your Small Business Server implementation
- Installing the Small Business Server — Client components
- Using the Small Business Server To Do List
- Troubleshooting Small Business Server
- Planning for future releases of Small Business Server

One of the most wonderful things to happen to Windows NT Server 4.0 was the introduction of Small Business Server (SBS) in late 1997. The second best thing was the upgrade to SBS 4.5 in late spring 1999. Why? Because Microsoft, by releasing and updating SBS, addressed and continues to address the underserved small business market. Firms under 50 users, the connection limit for SBS, have historically tried to make regular Windows NT Server and regular Microsoft BackOffice applications fit. And it was a tight fit because small businesses are very different from larger businesses, as I will explain.

The arrival of SBS heralded an era of right-sizing a Microsoft solution to meet very different, small business-specific needs. Now, one piece of software provides a viable and respected networking solution for the long-neglected small business, and the upgrade to SBS 4.5 dramatically increases performance and functionality.

So now the question is, "Why an SBS chapter in a book on Windows 2000 Server?" It's a legitimate question for which there are several answers. First, SBS 4.5 networks will interact with Windows 2000 clients (such as Windows 2000 Professional) as part of Microsoft's all-in-the-family strategy. Second, speaking of all in the family (which is the overriding theme for this section), note that in this era of Windows 2000, SBS 4.5, with its Windows NT Server 4.0 foundation, is still the best solution today for small businesses if for no other reason than its simplicity. Third, the future of SBS (tentatively known as SBS 5.0) will clearly incorporate Windows 2000 Server as its underlying operating system, so an appreciation and understanding of SBS 4.5 today affords you the opportunity to pay your SBS dues today and reap your SBS dividends tomorrow. Fourth, some of the best features in SBS, such as its ease of administration paradigm (via the SBS Console), will likely be incorporated into larger business computing environments that have deployed Windows 2000 Server. Need an example? Just think about the enterprise that has branch offices. It's not lost on the developers at Microsoft or you or me that branch offices have many of the same characteristics as small businesses.

This chapter intends to go beyond just introducing SBS and show you how it is set up and operates. At every turn, I intend to compare and contrast SBS with Windows 2000 Server and good old Windows NT Server 4.0. It has been my experience that many Windows 2000 Server gurus are bewildered by SBS because, starting with its initial setup and continuing through the ongoing administration phase, SBS is very different from Windows 2000 Server. This chapter will explain those differences, which range from the SBS Console to the single primary domain controller limit.

Defining Small Business Server

If you were on an elevator and only had 90 seconds to explain SBS 4.5 to a fellow elevator rider (this is the proverbial 90-second test in life), where might you start? You could of course say that SBS is an alphabet soup mix from Active Server Pages to Windows NT Server 4.0. You might say that it is the Windows NT Server 4.0 operating system, several Microsoft BackOffice components, plus a few additional features thrown in, including faxing and modem-sharing. Or you might take the approach in Table 16-1, which uses a client/server model. On the SBS server side are the operating system and server-based applications. On the SBS client side are client applications such as Internet Explorer; Microsoft Outlook; and SBS redirectors for modems, faxing, and Proxy Server. Have I used up my 90 seconds yet?

First, a short list (Table 16-1) of all SBS components. This is followed by detailed explanations of the SBS server-side components that comprise SBS 4.5. In the table, I've divided the information between server and client components to help you view SBS from a client/server perspective.

Table 16-1 SBS 4.5 Components

Component	*Description*	*Server or Client Component*
Windows NT Server 4.0 with Service Pack 4	32-bit network operating system	Server
Microsoft Exchange Server 5.5	E-mail application	Server
Microsoft SQL Server 7.0	Database application	Server
Microsoft Proxy Server 2.0	Internet security and firewall gateway application	Server

Component	***Description***	***Server or Client Component***
Microsoft Internet Information Server 4.0	Internet/intranet development and management application	Server
Microsoft Fax Service 4.5	Fax pooling and management application	Server
Microsoft Modem Sharing Service 4.5	Modem pooling and management application	Server
Microsoft Index Server 2.0	Search engine application	Server
Microsoft Active Server Pages Server 1.0b	Internet development environment for `*.asp` files	Server
SBS Console	GUI-based management console	Server
Server-based wizards	SBS Server Setup Wizard, Internet Connection Wizard, device and peripheral management	Server
To Do List	Step-by-step to-do list	Server
Online Guide	Robust online help manual for SBS Administrators	Server
Default Intranet Page	Provides extensive SBS information for administrators/users	Client/Server
Internet Explorer 5.0	Internet browser for navigating both the Internet and intranets. Installed on both the SBS server machine and SBS clients	Client/Server
Setup Computer Wizard	Step one creates and registers workstations on the SBS server machine. Step two, via the client installation disk, configures and attaches a network-ready workstation to the SBS network	Client/Server
Client Installation Diskette	A disk that is formatted and created on the SBS server machine. At the client workstation, the setup phase configures the client (TCP/IP protocol, NetBIOS name, user name assigned to machine, and so on). Affectionately known as the "magic disk"	Client/Server
Microsoft Outlook 2000	Client-based e-mail, scheduling, and contact management application	Client
Microsoft FrontPage 98	Web site creation application	Client

Continued

Table 16-1 *(continued)*

Component	*Description*	*Server or Client Component*
SBS Fax Client	Faxing functionality and capabilities	Client
SBS Modem Pool Client	Modem pooling functionality (port redirector)	Client
SBS Proxy Client	Client-side Microsoft Proxy Server functionality (WinSock Proxy redirector)	Client
Office 2000	An optional configuration that includes Word 2000, Excel 2000, Access 2000, PowerPoint 2000, and Publisher 2000	Client
SBS Client	Basic SBS workstation client application (assists in modifying client configuration)	Client

Before launching you directly into SBS, let's take a few moments to define in painful detail what the SBS product is. As you know, SBS consists of the components that I listed in Table 16-1. But leaving that high-level hooey behind, it's now time to get into the details.

Small Business Server 4.5

I assume that you are using SBS 4.5, which started shipping in May 1999. If you purchased SBS prior to that, it was most likely version 4.0 or 4.0a. Upgrading to SBS 4.5 from prior editions of SBS is typically an uneventful upgrade and warrants limited discussion in this chapter.

But allow me a moment to discuss the Zen of SBS 4.5. It's been my experience that you either get it or you don't when it comes to SBS 4.5. This product demands a delicate touch if you're an enterprise-level Windows 2000 Server expert. Big iron attitudes don't fit in the SBS paradigm. Another group that struggles with SBS 4.5 is the MCSE crowd. MCSEs, in my experience, have displayed little patience and desire to work within SBS's framework. SBS 4.5, while a member of the Microsoft networking family, is very different from Windows 2000 Server.

I will use the next several pages to discuss the major components of SBS 4.5. This detailed discussion builds upon the component list in Table 16-1.

Windows NT Server 4.0

Briefly, Windows NT Server 4.0 is the operating system that supports file and printer sharing, acts as an applications server, supports native remote access capabilities (RAS), manages user accounts and security, and has network protocol support (including TCP/IP).

But now for an SBS perspective. This is and isn't your father's Windows NT Server.

This is your father's NT server

By this I mean it is, at a very basic level, the same Windows NT Server 4.0 that you've by now come to love and leave (see Figure 16-1). The Windows NT Server 4.0 that forms the foundation for SBS 4.5 is good old build 1381 with Service Pack 4 installed. This is what I affectionately refer to as "normal" or "regular" Windows NT Server 4.0.

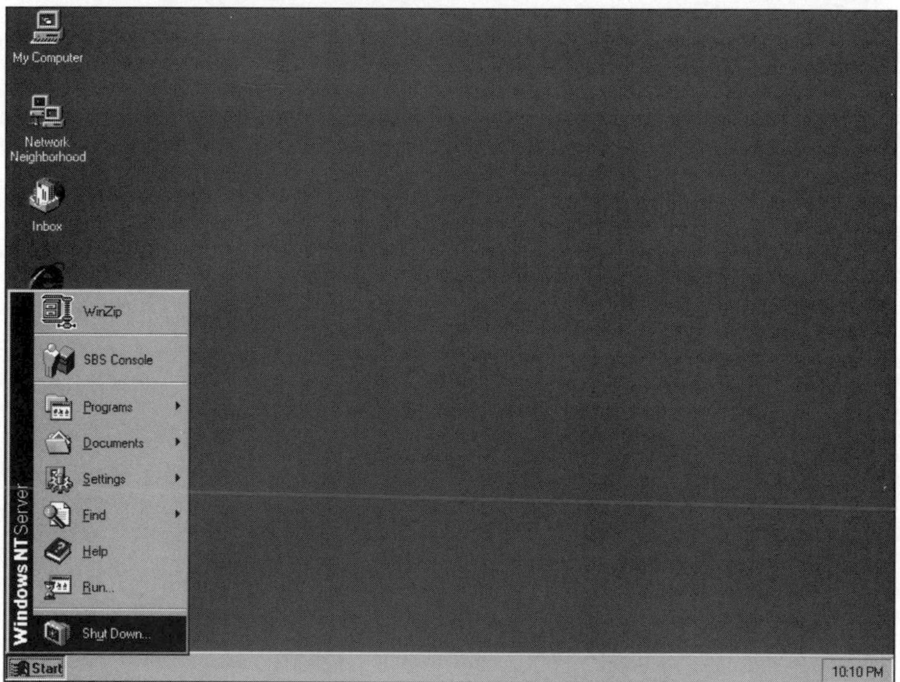

Figure 16-1: "Normal" Windows NT Server 4.0

It is important to understand that SBS indeed ships with "regular" Windows NT Server from a customer's point of view. Given that Windows NT Server 4.0 was entirely acceptable in terms of stability circa Service Pack 4, I've found that customers have a need to know both that SBS ships with Windows NT Server and that said Windows NT Server isn't some type of skinny or light version. I guess that insecurity reflects how many people have felt short-changed by "bundles" where the underlying applications are the "sample" or "skinny" versions. This is not the case with SBS. It's the real thing.

Based on the discussion contained in this section and Table 16-1, it is critical that you understand that SBS includes Windows NT Server. Don't embarrass yourself, and worse yet, lose an attractive SBS engagement, because you incorrectly bid an SBS job like my good friends at national consulting firm X (I've changed names to protect the innocent). Here, the SBS bid included SBS, Windows NT Server 4.0, and Proxy Server. Of course the last two items are automatically included with SBS. The two redundant items, Windows NT Server 4.0 and Proxy Server, were quickly exposed. Needless to say, the representatives did not get the job.

For details on "regular" Windows NT Server 4.0, may I suggest you consider your past life as an Windows NT practitioner and one of my previous books, *Microsoft Windows NT Secrets, Option Pack Edition* (IDG Books Worldwide).

This isn't your father's NT server

Suffice it to say, the Windows NT Server 4.0 operating system contained in SBS is slightly modified from regular Windows NT Server 4.0 in a few ways (see Figure 16-2), and it goes without saying that the Windows NT Server 4.0 operating system that ships with SBS is a world apart from Windows 2000 Server.

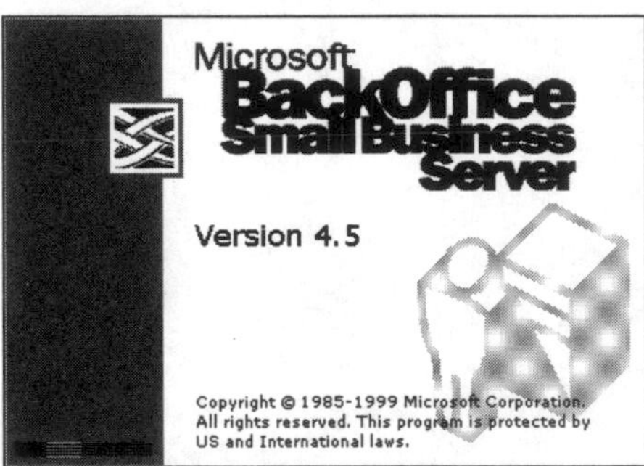

Figure 16-2: Small Business Server 4.5

First, the SBS Console is clearly an addition that isn't part of Windows NT Server 4.0 or Windows 2000 Server. In fact, the only thing that comes close to the SBS Console is the Administrative Wizards GUI-based interface in regular Windows NT Server 4.0 or the MMC in Windows 2000 Server. I discuss the SBS Console in detail later in this chapter.

Other ways in which the SBS version and Windows 2000 Server and Windows NT Server differ are as follows:

- Licensing. Windows 2000 Server, Windows NT Server, and BackOffice enable you to select either per-seat or per-server licensing. You even have a one-time opportunity to switch between the two. And — here is a lifesaver in the real world — Windows 2000 Server, Windows NT Server, and BackOffice do not implicitly lock out users after the license count you defined during setup or via Licensing in Control Panel (for per-server mode) or via Licensing (Windows 2000 Server) or License Manager (Windows NT Server) in the Administrative Tools program group (for per-seat mode) is exceeded. Not that you would break any software licensing agreement, but it's a nice touch to work with the honor system in regular Windows NT Server. Often I'll call my software vendor to purchase more licenses when the number of logons exceeds the license count, but at least staff can work until the "paper" licenses arrive in the mail the next day. The easiest way to discover that you are out of compliance with your licensing is to monitor the System Log in Event Viewer. License Manager will map log entries when either per-server or per-seat licensing violations have occurred. At that time, it behooves you to order more licenses.

  Licensing for SBS (including Window NT Server 4.0) is on a per-server basis and somewhat unique compared to other BackOffice products. The key point regarding SBS licensing is that any user attempting to log on after the maximum licenses have been exceeded will be denied access. No honor system here, rather we're talking hard-core license enforcement.

Ironically, the user attempting to log on after the number of SBS licenses at the server has been exceeded will appear to be authenticated on the network. That means the logon activity will occur normally where you enter your name and password at the domain logon dialog box. However, the moment that you attempt to map a drive or access a server-based resource such as a printer or e-mail, you will be denied. The denials come in the form of "Error #71," which is undefined except for a reference in Microsoft TechNet.

- Registry. The Windows NT Server 4.0 Registry on an SBS machine has additions, restrictions, and modifications that the Windows 2000 Server and Windows NT Server 4.0 don't.
  - Additions. Additions include Registry entries for unique SBS features such as Microsoft Fax Server and the Modem Sharing Server.
  - Restrictions. Restrictions include entries that enforce the SBS client licensing limits and SQL Server 7.0 table size limits.
  - Modifications. Many existing Registry keys are treated differently in SBS than other flavors of Windows 2000 Server, Windows NT Server, and BackOffice. For example, in SBS's CurrentControlSet key (found via HKEY_LOCAL_ MACHINE), you will find the SQL Server Executive server has a start value of 0x3, meaning it is essentially disabled until you turn the service on via Control Panel. In Windows 2000 Server with BackOffice, the SQL Server Executive would typically have a lower start value (0x2) so it automatically starts when Windows NT Server boots.

NT Service Pack 4

SBS ships with Windows NT Server 4.0 Service Pack 4, which is applied as part of the setup process. However, I'm worried that you might bring forward a Windows 2000 Server or Windows NT Server behavior that could be very destructive to SBS. As you know from your experience and your MCSE courses, the latest service pack should always be reapplied after major changes to your network operating system have occurred. Changes that qualify include upgrading or reinstalling a BackOffice application, installing a major third-party application on the server such as Oracle, and so on.

With SBS, it's important that you not perform this type of service pack reinstallation because doing so may cause errors and problems on your SBS machine. I would also caution that whenever a service pack is released, you wait until Microsoft releases either an SBS upgrade wizard to apply the service pack or a statement clarifying that you may apply it to SBS without concern.

Under any circumstances, be sure to make at least one verified backup of your SBS machine prior to any upgrade (service pack, application, whatever!).

NT Option Pack

A modified version of the Windows NT Server Option Pack ships with SBS. This is included to enable you to use Internet Information Server 4.0 and Index Server, and even play around with a few advanced goodies such as Microsoft Transaction Server and Microsoft Script Debugger.

Finally, it is worth repeating that the SBS version of Windows NT Server, while slightly modified, is really just as robust and trustworthy as regular Windows NT Server 4.0. Likewise, the underlying operating system isn't Windows 2000 Server. That is something you and your SBS customers need to remember.

Microsoft Exchange Server 5.5

By definition, Microsoft Exchange Server 5.5 is a rock-solid and very powerful e-mail, scheduling, and groupware application. Best known for its e-mail, Microsoft Exchange Server (see Figure 16-3) supports:

- **E-mail.** Both internal and external (Internet) e-mail are supported.
- **Server-based scheduling.** The scheduling function is managed at the server level by the Microsoft Exchange Server engine so that Outlook clients on an SBS network can create appointments and schedule meetings.
- **Groupware.** This is supported by public folders that enable sharing information, applications, corporate contacts, bulletin boards, and the like.
- **Support for Internet newsgroups.** Microsoft Exchange can act as a newsgroup server.
- **Updated communications functionality.** Microsoft Exchange Server has replaced Microsoft Mail (thank God!).

Luckily, Microsoft shipped SBS with Microsoft Exchange 5.5 instead of its 4.*x* predecessor. The improvements are striking, but three stand out:

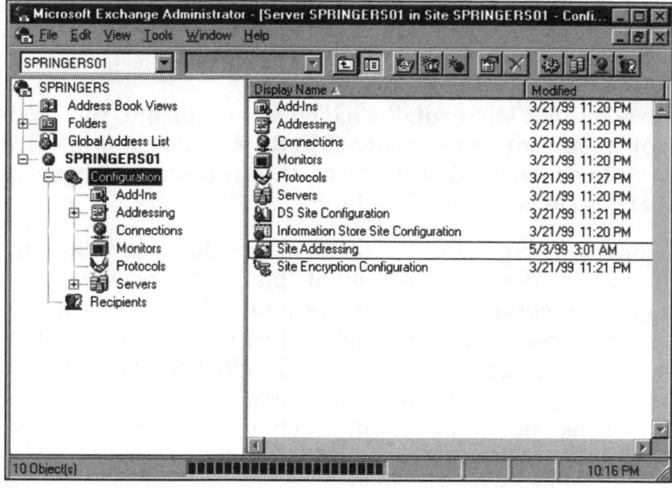

Figure 16-3: Microsoft Exchange 5.5

- **Active Server Page support.** This area, known as `*.asp` files, has emerged as a major area requiring additional work after the network is up and running.
- **Web-based Outlook solution.** Properly configured with a robust, full-time connection, this enables you to access your Microsoft Exchange Server-based e-mail from any area of the Internet using a modern WWW browser (Internet Explorer 3.*x* or higher, Netscape Navigator 3.*x* or higher). For example, if your company's Internet domain was `thepass.com` and you had correctly implemented this Outlook/Exchange solution, you would point your browser to `exchange.thepass.com/exchange` to bring up the Outlook Web client.
- **Internet Mail Service (IMS).** IMS replaced the older Internet Mail Connector and has significant improvements such as a much more robust and stable ETRN mail retrieval support. ETRN is a popular mail get/retrieve trigger that fires when a periodic dial-up connection is made to your Internet Service Provider. ETRN was dramatically improved with the release of Microsoft Exchange Server 5.5, and is the default mail retrieval method when you implement SBS with dial-up networking to an ISP and sign up with the ISP via the Internet Connection Wizard.

If you would like more information on the use of ETRN and configuring the IMS, I highly recommend that you download the Internet Connectivity White Paper at either of these locations:

```
www.microsoft.com/directaccess
www.microsoft.com/backofficesmallbiz
```

You may also find this information on the Microsoft TechNet CDs.

Microsoft Exchange has been trimmed down to fit inside SBS. At the enterprise level, you commonly place Microsoft Exchange Server on its own server machine (and a very powerful machine at that). With SBS, however, the challenge was to fit Microsoft Exchange Server and other BackOffice applications on the same server. Talk about an engineering accomplishment!

One of the ways that Microsoft Exchange Server fits into the SBS family lies in trimming its memory footprint to 8MB RAM, which is dramatically less than the RAM you would allocate at the enterprise level. Thus, Exchange inherently runs slower at an SBS site.

The SBS consulting community is divided over this next point, but I present it for your benefit. Many SBS consultants install Microsoft Exchange on a separate member server apart from the actual SBS server machine. That allows the Microsoft Exchange e-mail application to be isolated from the rest of the network. This means you could reboot the Microsoft Exchange member server without disrupting (too greatly) other network activities. Great idea if someone will pay for it, which is the other side of the argument. Just try to get the millionaire-next-door, small business owner to pony up and purchase a member server (good luck!).

A couple more Exchange insights before moving on. As of this writing, a POP3 gateway is to be released for SBS 4.5 late 1999 that will enable you to take advantage of POP e-mail configurations such as CompuServe, AOL, or Hotmail. That means you can easily retain your existing ISP without having to procure and implement your own domain name. This SBS feature is bound to be popular with the segment of the SBS community that doesn't want to reprint their business cards to reflect new e-mail addresses.

And a word about backing up that important e-mail corpus. Note that Microsoft Exchange Server is very sensitive to how backups are performed. Just running a normal backup routine from the SBS built-in backup program is insufficient. You need to run the Exchange-specific backup routine within the SBS tape backup program to ensure that the Information Store and Directory Services are backed up. Better yet, purchase a bona fide third-party tape backup solution such as Backup Exec or ArcServe.

And you can count on the first call from your SBS client, after the network is up and running, to be a complaint that e-mail isn't working. Funny how e-mail has become the most important thing in the office in the late 1990s.

SQL Server 7.0

A real diamond in the rough in SBS is SQL Server 7.0 (see Figure 16-4). It is probably the most powerful application that ships with SBS and is frequently one of the most ignored. Most small businesses considering SQL Server don't even really know what it is, much less how it might help them to run their businesses better.

That ignorance is usually corrected when they look at narrow vertical market applications that run on the SBS network. Great Plains Dynamics, SQL Server version is a great example. Many small businesses want to upgrade to the latest accounting software from Great Plains, the SQL Server version. Once that need is identified, SBS sells itself. All the SBS customer knows is that SQL Server is a database engine that drives the accounting system. And that's all they really need to know.

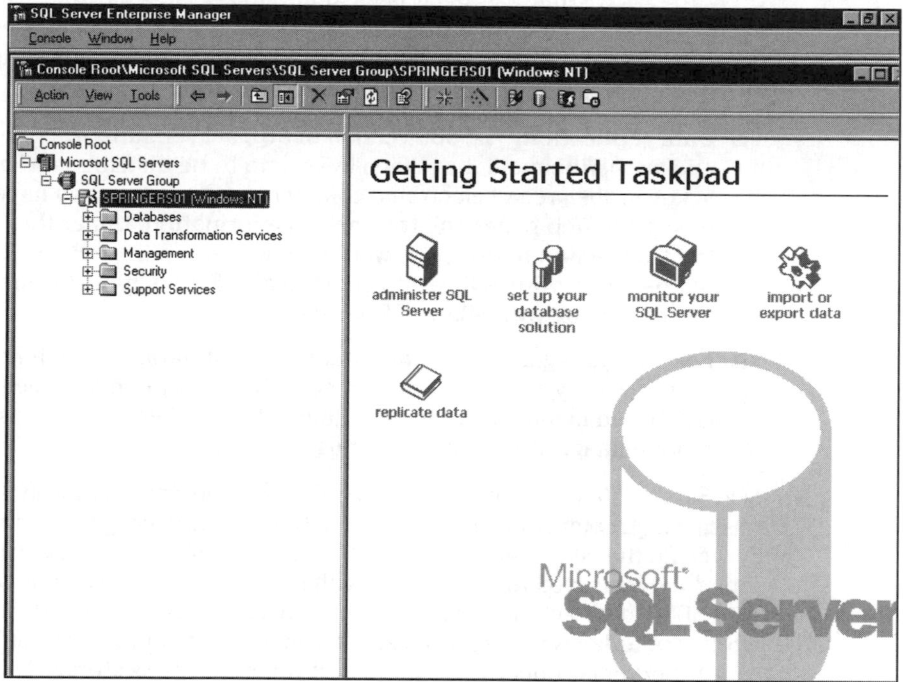

Figure 16-4: SQL Server 7.0

You, on the other hand, are probably interested in more of the meat on the bone. At its most basic definition, SQL Server is an SQL-based server engine, data warehouse, and management tool that coordinates the small business data. By that I mean SQL Server responds to SQL-language queries such as SELECT that are sent by client applications such as Great Plains Dynamics, SQL Server version. Once an SQL query is received by SQL Server, it is processed and fulfilled, with the results returned to the client applications. SQL Server is an extremely powerful relational database application, one that many MCSEs have made a great (and profitable) living from.

Key SQL Server features are as follows:

- **SQL Server performance.** I consider SQL Server to be a rock-solid database application that has the security needed to protect sensitive data.
- **SQL as an open standard.** As stated, applications such as accounting programs can hook into SQL Server. This interoperability makes SQL Server a very attractive component of SBS. SQL Server also supports numerous communication avenues such as OLE, OBDC, ActiveX, and integration with the Event Log and e-mail.

- **Internet support.** SQL Server is being used in several ways to extend the reach of the Internet to the small business, such as through its capability to interact with Internet Information Server (IIS), its support for Active Server Pages (ASP), and its role in electronic commerce sites with other Microsoft BackOffice components such as Site Server. Its role in electronic commerce is best exemplified by the Great Plains e-commerce module. This electronic commerce accounting software module requires both Site Server and SQL Server to run.
- **Data replication.** The SBS version of SQL Server supports the publish-and-subscribe metaphor that allows data to be distributed. This feature is key in the area of electronic commerce, where you may have your ISP host your Web pages and transaction information. Under this scenario, the transaction information would be housed on the ISP's SQL server and published to your SQL server periodically. Such support is included right out of the box with SBS's SQL Server.
- **Ease of management.** To the extent a robust database such as SQL Server is easy, you can use Microsoft SQL Enterprise Manager, a GUI-based management tool, to demystify SQL Server and make it more manageable by mere mortals.

SQL Server 7.0 was trimmed to fit SBS. The trimming doesn't mean there are missing SQL commands or support. You basically are using the same SQL Server 7.0 that ships with "big" BackOffice (the full-featured version). However, tables are restricted to 10GB in size with the SQL Server 7.0 edition that ships with SBS. That's actually a large number, given that much of the data businesses work with today is really plain text in a column/row table format (at least as far as SQL Server is concerned). However, if you exceed this storage limit, you can easily upgrade to the full version of SQL Server 7.0.

Microsoft Proxy Server 2.0

Out of the box, SBS provides Microsoft Proxy Server 2.0 (See Figure 16-5). Microsoft Proxy Server is best known, in layperson's terms, for its firewall and caching capabilities. Technically, it is a secure gateway to connect a LAN to the Internet with such features as follows:

- **Single point of connection to the Internet.** Instead of users "doing their own thing" and connecting in an ad hoc manner to the Internet, Microsoft Proxy Server acts as a central connection point or "gateway." This enables you to better manage Internet access and activity. Better management alone results in better security.
- **Connection capabilities.** Includes on-demand and scheduled connections. The AutoDial application enables you to set access hours and such in a dial-up Internet connection scenario.
- **Caching.** This allows popular Web pages to be stored locally on your SBS server. This feature reduces frequent connections to the Internet if the requested Web pages are found in the local cache. It also speeds user access time for cached pages, as these pages are returned at LAN speed, not Internet connection speeds.

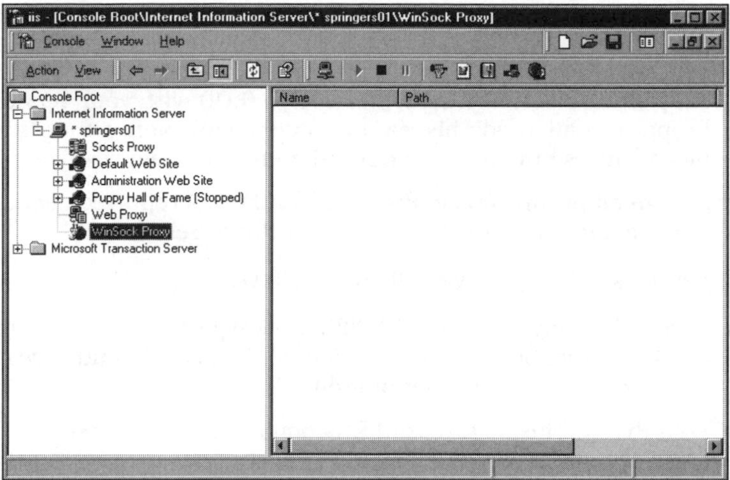

Figure 16-5: Proxy Server 2.0

Caching is one of the most popular features of Microsoft Proxy Server.

- **Internet content and access management.** You can allow rich-content Internet sites to be accessed by the browsers on your network. You can also restrict the type of sites your users may visit on the basis of protocol or specific domain name. With the proper configuration, you can also use logging to observe what sites users have visited. I've found such logging to serve as a major deterrent to misbehavior on SBS networks.
- **Full SBS integration.** Microsoft Proxy Server integrates cleanly with the SBS package. It supports the native TCP/IP protocol (and even IPX/SPX if you like). It is managed via Internet Information Server (included with SBS).
- **Year 2000 compliance.** This is actually one of the main reasons that Microsoft announced the free Proxy Server 2.0 upgrade for SBS sites. Proxy Server 1.0 had Year 2000 compliance issues that are addressed with this upgrade.
- **Packet layer security with dynamic packet filtering.** Inbound and outbound packet filtering is supported in Proxy Server 2.0.
- **Real-time security alerts.** Immediate notifications that might alert you to intrusions are now available.
- **Reverse proxy.** This allows your Web server, located behind the Proxy Server firewall, to publish to the World Wide Web without security breaches. What's the benefit of this? In the case of electronic commerce, you can have your Web server communicate with your accounting application server and enable outsiders to legitimately hit the same Web server. In short, the feature helps accommodate electronic commerce.
- **Reverse hosting.** This is as close to clustering as it gets here. Several Web servers sitting behind your Proxy Server firewall appear as a single virtual directory.

- **Server proxying.** Proxy Server listens for inbound packets destined for other servers, such as an accounting application server. The packets are forwarded to the appropriate server. This feature is great for supporting electronic data interchange (EDI) with your vendors. Properly configured, this feature would enable your vendors to make entries directly into your order entry system.
- **Improved performance.** Proxy Server 2.0 has reported caching performance gains of 40 percent over Proxy Server 1.0.

Key services in Proxy Server 2.0 are as follows:

- **WinSock Proxy.** Supports IPX/SPX, uses Windows NT Challenge/Response (CHAP) authentication, controls inbound and outbound access by port number, protocol, and user or group.
- **Web Proxy.** This feature is CERN-compatible and supports HTTP, FTP, and Gopher. It caches HTTP objects and allows data encryption.

Microsoft Internet Information Server

Microsoft Internet Information Server (IIS) 4.0 provides an easy way for SBS sites to publish content on the Internet and the firm's internal intranet. In fact, SBS has an intranet page that appears by default when users launch their browsers.

IIS is integrated with the underlying Windows NT Server 4.0 operating at the service level. IIS is increasingly used by independent software vendors (ISVs) for application support, an example of this being the reliance on IIS by Great Plains for its new electronic commerce accounting module. IIS is very powerful in its capability to support multiple virtual directories and in its security and performance. Additional support in IIS 4.0 that wasn't present in previous versions includes support for FrontPage extensions and Active Server Pages (ASPs). Finally, the ease of use for IIS can't be understated. Its Internet Service Manager allows centralized management of the following IIS services.

The key features of IIS are its World Wide Web service with its robust HTTP hosting capability.

Note that you must manually install the FTP service in SBS 4.5's IIS. In previous versions of SBS, FTP was automatically installed. That's too bad, as I've had a couple of SBS customers use FTP for large file transfers, such as CAD architectural drawings. Support for Gopher was dropped in IIS 4.0. SBS 4.0 originally shipped with IIS 3.0, which had Gopher support. When upgrading to or installing SBS 4.5, you will lose Gopher support.

Microsoft Fax Service 4.5

This application allows users to fax from the desktop using one or more (up to four) fax modems attached to the SBS machine. Faxes may be sent from any program because the fax-related functionality is that of "printing" to the fax modem on the network. Inbound faxes are received at the SBS machine and may be printed or e-mailed to one user who may distribute the faxes over the company's Exchange-based e-mail system, or even stored on a shared directory on the SBS machine. Security allows the administrator to determine who may view faxes.

Microsoft Fax Service 4.5 is managed via the Fax Server applet in Control Panel. Once it is launched, you will see the Fax Server Properties dialog box (see Figure 16-6).

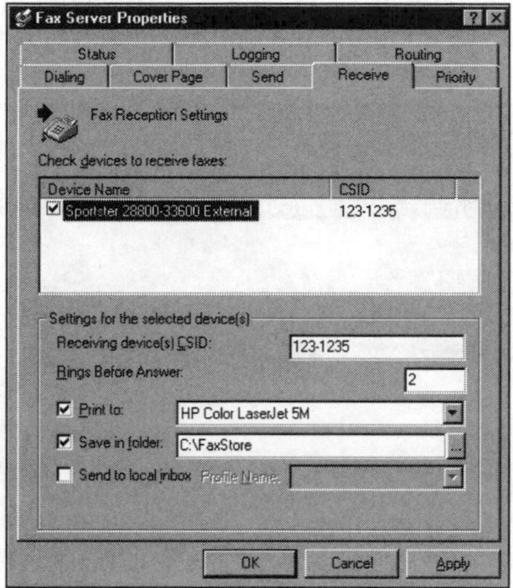

Figure 16-6: Microsoft Fax Server

Ironically, the one feature that many SBS users ask for is surprisingly absent. When faxing, users need to know if the fax arrived at its destination. Up the ante when you're discussing law firms and their unique faxing needs (law firms typically need a fax confirmation page for legal proceedings). This information is traditionally conveyed to users via a fax confirmation sheet that they receive after the fax has either been successfully sent or failed. This typically occurs in real time with the user standing by the fax machine to grab the fax confirmation report from the fax machine paper tray.

Note that Fax Server enables you to send out broadcast faxes from your desktop (that is, send faxes to many recipients). This feature is very popular with small businesses seeking to use SBS as a real marketing tool.

Microsoft Modem Sharing Server 1.0

This is a modem pooling application that is not available either with regular Windows NT Server or BackOffice. It is also one of the most valuable features for SBS customers that intend to use a dial-up connection to the Internet, take advantage of the capability to dial-in or dial-out via RAS, or use SBS's inbound/outbound faxing capabilities.

Surprisingly, many SBS customers initially plan for extensive use of the modem polling capabilities, but with the advent of digital full-time Internet connections such as DSL and ISDN, the modem sharing capability is often only used in cases where a user needs to dial a BBS, another dial-in site (such as an office building HVAC management system), or secure sites (such as Visa/MasterCard authorization centers or drug testing labs). In other words, SBS's modem sharing capability isn't as popular as you might imagine.

Up to four modems may participate in a modem pool. The modem pool is managed via the Modem Sharing applet in the Control Panel (see Figure 16-7).

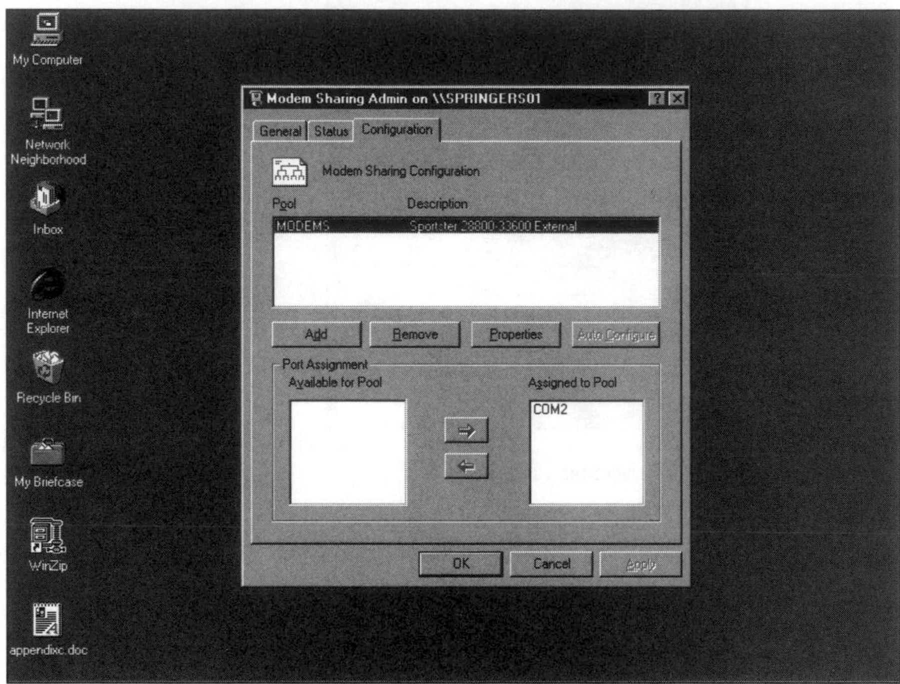

Figure 16-7: Modem Sharing applet

Note

Modem Sharing Server interacts with RAS. RAS in SBS is essentially the same RAS that is contained in regular Windows NT Server.

Microsoft Index Server 2.0

This is a more than adequate search engine right out of the SBS box (see Figure 16-8). I've used Index Server for in-class training exercises as part of the MCSE curriculum I teach as an MCT. An author who is a good friend of mine has used Index Server to organize newsgroup threads as part of his writing research so that the newsgroup information is readily searchable by keyword. I've recommended to several SBS clients that they consider using Index Server as a document management system. How? Index Server will "scan" your corpus (or collection) of documents for keywords. When you want to retrieve a document you can remember the title of, simply launch the Index Server homepage, which has a search engine attached to it, and type a keyword (such as a client name). A list of all documents with that keyword within the corpus will be displayed. Bingo — you have a free document management system. And that beats the heck out of spending over $10,000 on other third-party document management systems.

However, be advised that Index Server has practical limits. By this I mean to say that firms engaged in online electronic commerce and the like don't use this version of Index Server for their "real" online operations. Rather, firms with heavy indexing requirements beyond the capabilities of Index Server, such as online legal databases, use third-party solutions such as ProDocs.

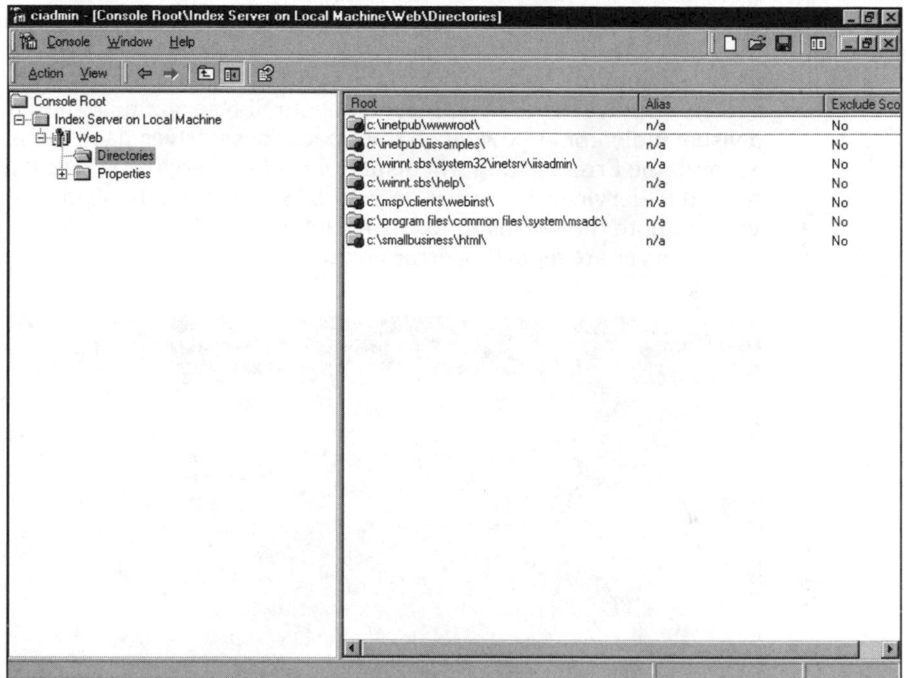

Figure 16-8: Index Server

To be frank, the best use of Index Server on an SBS network is for indexing and organizing internal company information for use on the firm's intranet. There it shines, with its basic query forms and full-text indexing features. In short, Index Server can probably meet your internal needs but has limits when interacting with external stakeholders.

SBS Console

On the server side, it all ends at the SBS Console (see Figure 16-9). This is the primary user interface for managing the SBS server. The SBS Console is analogous to the way that the MMC is used in Windows 2000 Server. You use the MMC to manage your Windows 2000 Server, and the SBS Console is used to perform the same work on an SBS server machine.

The SBS Console is actually made up of four pages.

Home

The SBS Console Home page displays general buttons that enable you to drill down to the SBS To Do List, an "About" page that displays version information and a link to the SBS Web site at Microsoft (`www.microsoft.com/backofficesmallbiz`). This is the default screen when you launch the SBS Console. The Home page has two very popular features beyond its three standard buttons. First, the Drives listing on the left side of the screen displays the drives present on your SBS server machines and is a visual indicator of how much free space these drives have remaining. Second, the Errors listing will display, in cherry red, the errors (typically related to services) that exist on your SBS server machine. In Figure 16-9, you will note the Microsoft Exchange Internet Mail Connector (IMC) and DHCP Server are reporting error conditions.

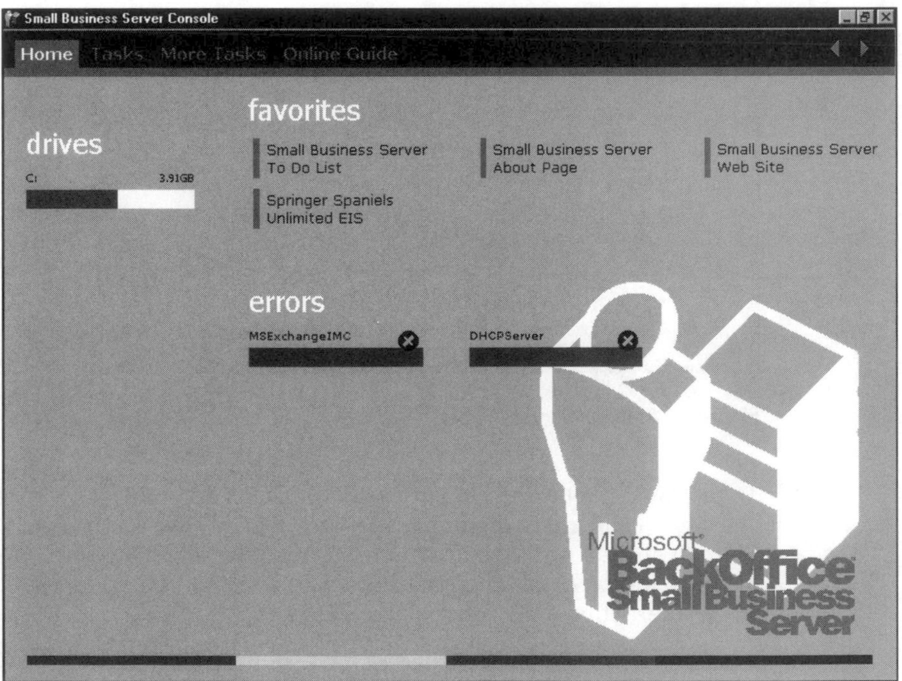

Figure 16-9: SBS Console — Home

The SBS Console is customizable so that you may add your own buttons to it! This is an increasingly popular option for ISVs writing software specifically for SBS (such as tape backup applications). Other uses include adding company-specific information, such as buttons that display sales information.

Tasks

The Tasks page (Figure 16-10) offers buttons for common tasks you would perform to manage your SBS server machine.

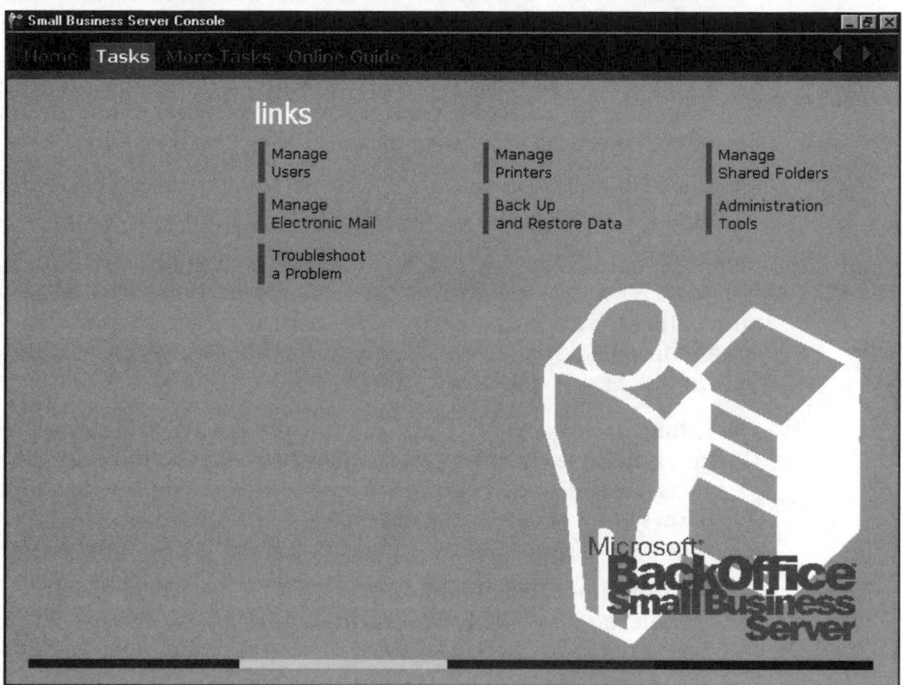

Figure 16-10: SBS Console — Tasks

These links include the following:

- **Manage Users.** This is where basic user management is performed, including adding users and modifying existing user information (for example, changing passwords).

The Manage Users page will not permit you to manage groups (for example, local or global). SBS requires that you use User Manager for Domains to accomplish that task.

- **Manage Printers.** This is where you add and manage printers.
- **Manage Shared Folders.** This is where you create and manage shared folders with share-level permissions. You cannot manage file-level permissions here.

Manage Shared Folders does not permit you to manage NTFS-level permissions. You must use Windows NT Explorer to manage NTFS-level (for example, files) permissions.

- **Manage Electronic Mail.** It is here that you check on the status of your e-mail activity. The Send/Receive Now button on the Manage Electronic Mail page is very useful for forcing a dial-up session with your ISP. Note that the Microsoft Exchange Internet Mail Connection property sheet (found in the Microsoft Exchange Administrator) offers no such easy way to force a dial-up session.
- **Back Up and Restore Data.** This selection provides several online help screens to assist you in using the built-in NT Backup program.

Please do not use the built-in tape backup program provided in SBS (and Windows NT Server 4.0 for that matter). It is difficult to set this backup application to run consistently on a timer (using the AT command, which is often unreliable), plus NT Backup doesn't have any provision for backing up live SQL Server databases. Ouch!

- **Administration Tools.** This is one of the coolest additions to SBS 4.5. You now have several powerful management tools at your beck and call to assist you in monitoring the health of your SBS network. This page allows you to configure and periodically generate SBS server health reports. Let's just say preventive medicine has now arrived in SBS 4.5!
- **Troubleshoot a Problem.** This page provides assistance in troubleshooting SBS problems from A (adding and removing software) to W (Web publishing). Yes, it's an online help system, but at least Microsoft is trying to meet SBS users' needs here.

More Tasks

The third page in the SBS Console is More Tasks (see Figure 16-11). It is here that important but less frequently performed tasks are presented. At least, that's the goal.

- **Manage E-mail Distribution Lists.** This allows you to manage Microsoft Exchange-based e-mail distribution lists, such as "Everyone."

Using Manage E-Mail Distribution Lists, you can only manipulate and manage e-mail objects that appear on Microsoft Exchange Administrator's Global Address List. This means you cannot, by default, add Internet e-mail recipients to a list created or managed by the Manage E-Mail Distribution page. That's because the Global Address List only contains internal e-mail user names unless you create a "Custom Recipient" object and an external or Internet e-mail address. Got it? If not, run this problem by your nearest Exchange guru.

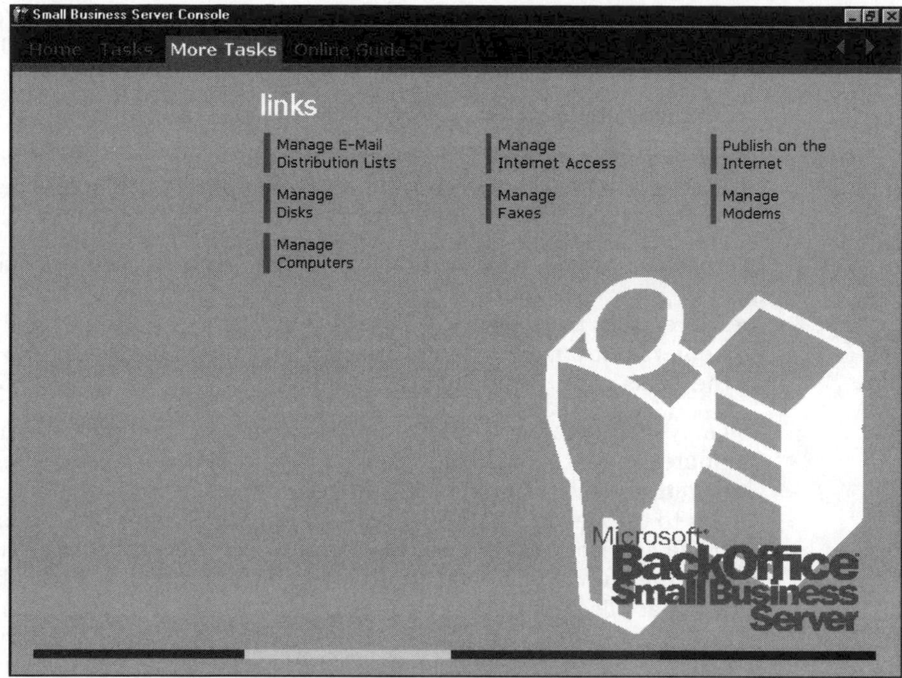

Figure 16-11: SBS Console — More Tasks

- **Manage Internet Access.** This allows you to easily set up and maintain an Internet connection using either a dial-up or full-time broadband connection approach. To be honest, this is one of the most powerful and well-designed pages in the SBS Console. It works beyond your expectations. It's nice to be surprised, eh?
- **Publish on the Internet.** You can manage both your internal (intranet) and external (Internet) Web pages from this button. The assumption is that you've created your Web page with the FrontPage application (either the 98 or 2000 version) that ships with SBS 4.5.
- **Manage Disks.** At a glance, you can see how much free space you have on each of the disks on your SBS server machine. This is similar to the SBS Console Home page Drives view, with a slight twist. On the Manage Disks page, the storage information is presented numerically in megabytes. There are also options for learning how to mirror disks, create an emergency repair disk, and troubleshoot disk problems.

- **Manage Faxes.** Not surprisingly, this page allows you to manage the faxing function on an SBS server machine. Options include controlling access to faxing and otherwise generally managing fax jobs.
- **Manage Modems.** Here is where you manage modem pools.
- **Manage Computers.** This is one of the most popular SBS Console buttons. It is here that you add a new computer to your SBS network, install the SBS client-side components, and add software to a computer.

Microsoft's design goal with the Tasks and More Tasks pages was to place the most popular tasks on the Tasks page and have less popular tasks placed on the More Tasks page. This was a completely valid goal. However, the Manage Computers button, a very popular selection, should clearly have been placed on the Tasks page, in my humble opinion.

You may modify the Add software to a computer option on the Manage Computers page to install applications of your choice on the SBS end user's workstation. This scripted push application installation capability is very similar to the way in which System Management Server (SMS) uses packages to install applications on workstations. However, several conditions must be met for the automatic application installation approach to work. First, the software application to be installed must work with the Setup Computer Wizard. For example, will the application install without user heavy user interaction? Second, you must obtain it from the software vendor or create an installation file (`.inf`) yourself for the application to be installed. Third, the Setup Computer Wizard's initialization file (`scw.ini`) must be modified with information about the application you intend to install. Finally, the Setup Computer Wizard's client optional component information file (`clioc.inf`) must be modified with information about the application you are installing.

Online Guide

It seems to me that the rich set of checklists in the Windows 2000 environment might have gotten its start from the roots of the SBS Online Guide. I know for a fact that both documentation teams are located in the same building on Microsoft's Redmond campus and often collaborate. The SBS Online Guide is much richer than previous online help systems that Microsoft has produced. It is also organized logically by function in the left pane (see Figure 16-12).

It is also possible to run the SBS Console on another machine (such as your workstation). This is known as *remote console* and is similar to running the Windows NT Server 4.0 server tools on your workstation. To implement the remote management capabilities of the SBS Console, see the NetMeeting discussion on the SBS online "Help" system.

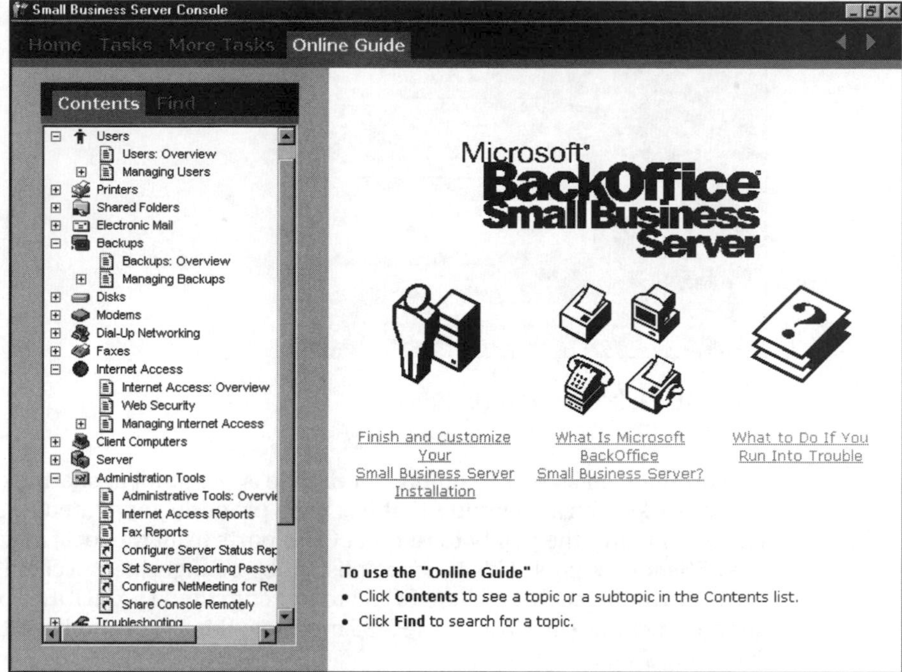

Figure 16-12: SBS Console — Online Guide

Client-side components

You are already familiar with many of the SBS client-side components such as Internet Explorer (IE) 4.*x* browser and Microsoft Outlook. Other client-side components such as the way in which Proxy Server interacts with the desktop and applications (via the Proxy selection in IE and the WSP applet in Control Panel) are the same as those found via Proxy Server in BackOffice. So far, so good. Not much by way of differences.

But two unique client-side components are worth reviewing because of their uniqueness to SBS. These are the fax client and the modem sharing client.

The fax client is best seen as a print option that appears in Windows applications after the SBS client setup disk (a.k.a. magic disk) has been run. When it is selected, you essentially "print" to the fax modem on the SBS server machine. You are then prompted for basic fax-sending information (see Figure 16-13).

Figure 16-13: Sending a fax via SBS

The other client-side SBS component of note is the modem-sharing component. When working on a computer that has been properly configured as an SBS client, you have the ability to redirect COM ports from the local machine to the SBS modem pool. This is accomplished by configuring the client's COM ports correctly, such as telling COM3 to be redirected to \MODEMS on the SBS server machine. On a Windows 98/95 machine, this is accomplished with the following steps.

STEPS:

To configure the client's COM ports

Step 1. Right-click My Computer from the desktop.

Step 2. Select the Properties menu option.

Step 3. Select the Device Manager tab sheet.

Step 4. Expand the Ports (COM & LPT) listing.

Step 5. Observe which ports have been automatically redirected. This configuration occurred when you ran the SBS Client Setup disk. Typically COM ports 3 and 4 are automatically redirected.

Step 6. Double-click the COM port of your choice that you want to redirect to the modem pool. The Modem Sharing Port (COM#) Properties dialog box appears.

Step 7. Select the Model Sharing Settings tab sheet and complete the Uniform Naming Convention (UNC) path to the modem-sharing pool on the SBS server.

The Small Business Model

The small business market differs markedly from the medium- and large-company environment with which most of us associate Windows NT Server. I can think of three ways in which these two differ:

- **Resources.** The small business doesn't have the wealth of the medium- and large-sized organization. Undoubtedly, you will be asked to make older workstations and printers functional. You'll find yourself cannibalizing older equipment to support the walking wounded.
- **Viewpoint.** Small businesses can be hostile environments to implementing new technology. Many of these businesses have gotten along just fine without computers for years. Why should they spend $5,000 to $20,000 or more to implement the SBS solution when perhaps they would rather give out that kind of money as a larger Christmas bonus? This is a tough situation, and I've found that the small business negative attitude toward SBS is often just a cry for more information. Use your skills in educating the SBS customer about when the benefits, such as better information, clearly outweigh the costs.
- **Expertise.** If you've ever wanted to be a big fish in a small pond, become an SBS consultant. It's a great feeling to know an area well and legitimately help the customer. As an SBS consultant, I've found challenges to one's expertise to be far less frequent than at the enterprise level.

Small Business Server philosophy

The SBS philosophy is akin to the small business philosophy. That is, we're all seeking the answer to the question, "How can I run my business better?" SBS is an answer to that question. I'll show you how via the SBS food chain (see Figure 16-14).

Starting from left to right, you have a small businessperson trying to run his or her business. To be brutally honest, such a person probably isn't very interested in computers, networks, SBS, and the like. The businessperson is more interested in management reports, accounting reports, and so on.

The desktop computer, again, is considered a tool to accomplish work, such as working with the accounting system. That's an important point. Unlike the MCSE types who view technology as the end-all of everything, small businesspeople tend to view technology as a tool to get more important business-related work done.

Moving right across the SBS food chain, the network is only important to the small businessperson when it doesn't work. Otherwise, it is that silent and forgotten infrastructure that is best left alone.

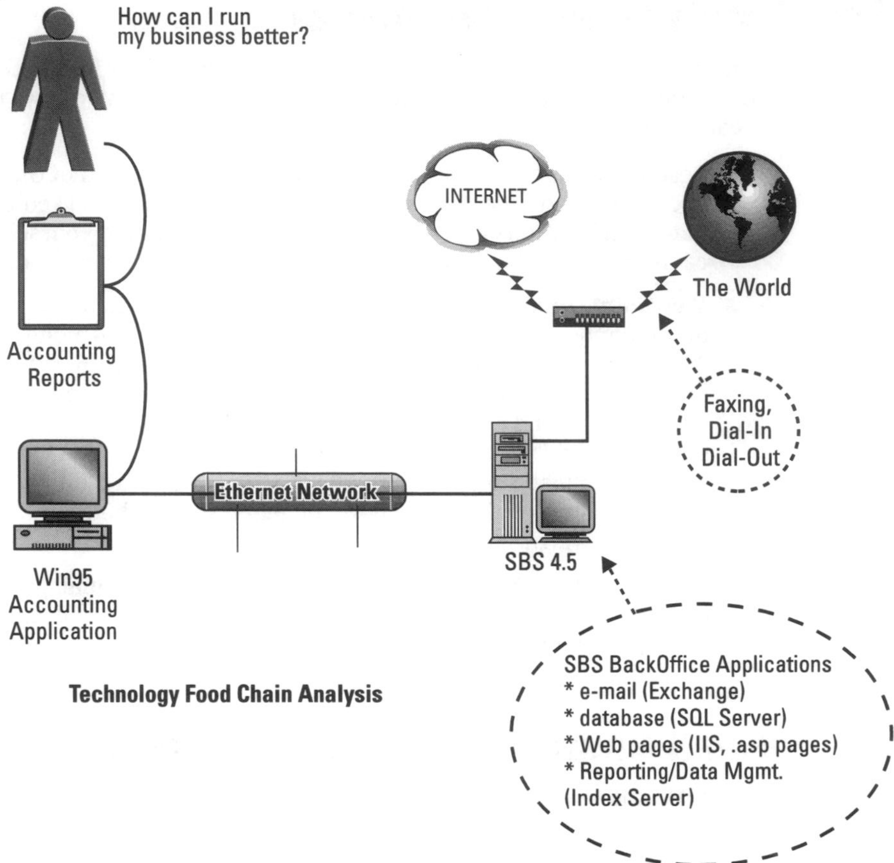

Figure 16-14: The SBS food chain

At the far right of the SBS food chain, there lies the SBS server machine and SBS itself. Here, the small businessperson sees values, for many of the reasons already stated in this chapter. The ability to send broadcast faxes from the network adds value to the small business's operations. The ability to call in from a remote site and attach to the SBS network adds value. The ability to send and receive e-mail, both internally and externally, adds value. The ability to surf the Web in a secure manner (via Proxy Server) is a great comfort and value to the small businessperson. Bottom line? The SBS food chain is a value-added process as you move from left to right. And it's the bottom line that clearly matters most to the SBS customer.

Use the SBS Console for everything! Discover why it might not work for you before you resort to the old Windows NT Server way of doing things.

Who are SBS customers?

The potential SBS customer base is enormous. In the U.S. alone, there are 22 million small businesses. That numbers dwarfs the Fortune 1000, which by definition is limited to the 1,000 largest U.S. enterprises. Approximately ¾ of these small businesses own a PC. Just under ⅓ of these small business are networked, a number that is expected to grow by nearly 50 percent in the next two years. SBS is well positioned to take advantage of this growth.

Looks can be deceiving

On the surface, SBS looks great. Many networking professionals consider SBS to be a small sibling to BackOffice. But here is where we revert to comparing and contrasting. Those who know Windows NT Server well don't necessarily know SBS. Many NT gurus have failed when trying to roll out SBS because they readily drop under the hood and use Windows NT Server tools such as User Manager for Domains instead of the SBS Console. You have been warned. Treat SBS as an entirely new product and you will do fine. In fact, I've observed that NetWare network administrators have more initial success with SBS than the NT guru crowd. Why? Because the NetWare folks are scared to death of SBS and actually read the manual, follow the rules (such as by completing the To Do List in SBS Console), and so on. The NT gurus are step skippers, because they assume they already know it all.

Here again, I must interject a few clarifying comments regarding the SBS design goals discussed in the past several pages. For new users and NetWare administrators coming over to SBS, I've found the SBS Console is great and really aids the learning process. But for good old Windows NT Server gurus with their headstrong way of doing things, the SBS Console is more of an enemy. Painfully and agonizingly, these Windows NT Server gurus begrudgingly use the SBS Console (but not at the first, second, or third time they attempt to perform a task; that would be too easy!).

SBS architecture

A quick look at the SBS architecture (see Figure 16-15): As you have learned, the "official" SBS components sit on top of the Windows NT Server 4.0 Service Pack 4 operating system. The underlying Windows NT Server 4.0 has the same kernel and user mode architecture described in Chapter 17. No difference here. After that, it gets more complex.

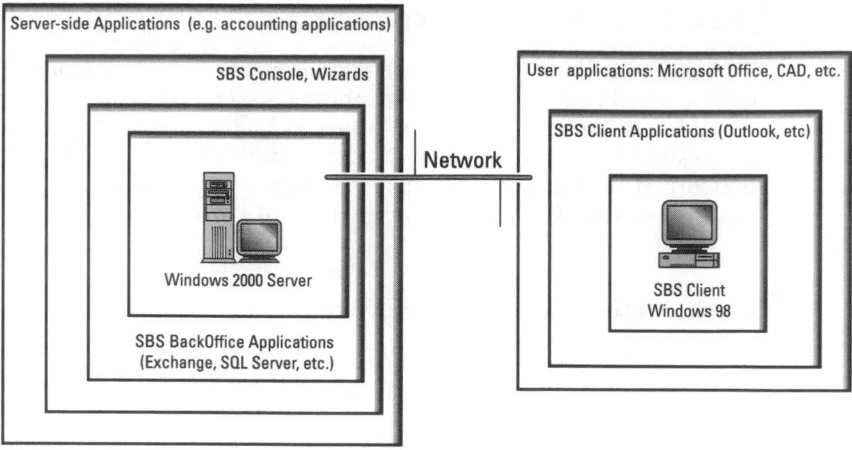

Figure 16-15: SBS architecture

The SBS BackOffice applications reside above the Windows NT Server operating system. Above that, you will find SBS tools such as the SBS Console and miscellaneous wizards. Finally, server applications such as client/server accounting packages (Great Plains Dynamics, for instance) are run.

On the SBS client side, you start with a workstation operating system such as Windows 98. On top of that, you add the SBS-specific client components such as Outlook, faxing, modem sharing, Proxy Client, and the like. Finally, the user applications such as Microsoft Office run at the workstation.

SBS Server-side Setup

With SBS 4.5, the early setup stages (identified further on as Phase A and Phase B) are currently very similar to installing Windows NT Server 4.0. Earlier versions of SBS (the 4.0 and 4.0a releases) had a modified Windows NT Server installation process that caused fits at times with SBSers such as yours truly. But after the underlying operating system is installed, the SBS setup process is markedly different from that of Windows NT Server or BackOffice.

The SBS HCL (Hardware Compatibility List) is different from the HCL for "regular" Windows NT Server. Because of that, before you commence the SBS setup, be sure to read the Readme file on SBS CD-ROM Disc 1 and the HCL in the SBS manual (it shipped with your SBS software media).

I've conveniently divided SBS setup into three phases, based on my experience with the product and, more importantly, trying to explain it the hard-core MCSE types:

- **Phase A: Windows NT Server character-based setup.** This phase could be called the "three-floppy swappy" if you were to write a country-western song about installing computer operating systems (Garth Brooks, watch out!). You'll endure one or two reboots and insert the first CD-ROM disk along the way. To be brutally honest (again), the setup process in Phase A is virtually the same for SBS 4.5 and Windows NT Server 4.0.

- **Phase B: Windows NT Server GUI-based setup.** Here you will answer questions relating to the time zone, networking protocols, services, and the like. There are minor differences between SBS 4.5 and Windows NT Server 4.0 in this setup phase. For example, if a network adapter cannot be detected, SBS installs a dummy network adapter called "MS Loopback adapter."
- **Phase C: SBS installation and setup.** It is here that the worlds of SBS 4.5 and Windows NT Server 4.0 diverge dramatically and more than one NT/2000 MCSE-type guru has gotten burned. Remember that paradigm shift I've been emphasizing in this SBS chapter? Now is your time to see it in action. Besides entering basic user and company information such as address, telephone number, and confirming the modem and networking selections (brand of modems, network adapters), the following SBS applications are installed (in order):
  - Internet Explorer 5.0 browser
  - Microsoft Management Console 1.1
  - SQL Server 7.0
  - Windows NT Option Pack
  - Proxy Server 2.0
  - Microsoft Fax Service 4.5 (a.k.a. Microsoft Fax Server)
  - Modem Sharing Service 4.5
  - Microsoft Exchange Server 5.5
  - Small Business Server Administrator
  - Client applications such as Microsoft Office 2000 (if you purchased the version of SBS 4.5 that contains Microsoft Office 2000)

Between 90 and 180 minutes will have elapsed from start to finish while installing SBS 4.5 in your server machine. Much of that time, especially in Phase C, is what I call unattended time, meaning no additional input is necessary from you (that is, autopilot installation). I'd encourage you to use that time to surf the Web for the latest news on SBS. One SBS-related site I recommend is `www.smallbizserver.com`. Speaking of time passing, at this point you've completed the core SBS 4.5 installation and are presented with the To Do List (see Figure 16-16) to apply some finishing touches.

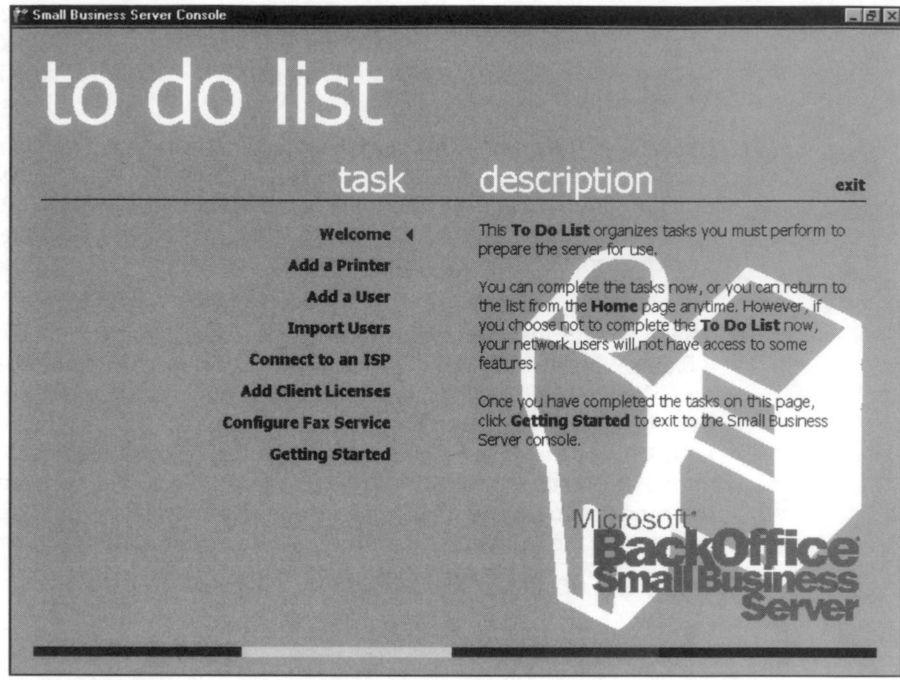

Figure 16-16: SBS To Do List

I've found that, acknowledging Microsoft's best attempts to create an ordered checklist, the To Do List typically isn't followed step by step. I do recommend that, at a minimum, you complete the Add a New Printer, Add User Licenses, and Create an Emergency Repair Disk options during the SBS server installation. I've found that the Add a New User and Set Up a Computer options are typically run hours or days later when you are truly ready to add workstations to your SBS network.

SBS Workstation-side Setup

A profound difference between regular Windows NT Server and SBS is how client workstations are configured. Unlike regular Windows NT Server, where configuring a network client typically occurs via its Network applet in Control Panel (for Windows 2000/98/95 and Windows NT Workstation), SBS uses a client installation disk. This is commonly called the "magic disk" among SBS users. Its magic is that, based on some basic SBS workstation configuration specifications you elect at the SBS server, the magic disk installs the necessary SBS networking components and applications on the SBS client machine. In fact, using the magic disk is commonly thought of as an autopilot approach versus the much more manual approach to configuring workstations to attach to a regular Windows NT Server network.

To create the magic disk as part of the SBS workstation-side setup, you will first add a user, and then be prompted to set up a computer. When setting up a user, you will be prompted for basic setup information including a given name (or "full name"), user name, job title, and password. You must then select the e-mail lists, printers, folders, and fax devices that the user will have access to (and how much access at that!). The last setup user questions relate to accessing the Internet (allowed or not allowed), ability to access the network remotely (allowed or not allowed), and granting full rights to the server computer and network resources to the user.

When asked as part of the user setup process whether the user should have full rights to the server computer and network resources, ponder the question that is really being asked of you. It is here you have the ability to make the user an administrator on your SBS network. This is of course a very powerful and dangerous thing. The default answer on the Administrative Privileges screen is no. I recommend you keep it that way.

You will create a magic disk for each user on your SBS network (it's very easy). Then, at each workstation, the `setup.exe` file on the magic disk is launched. The setup routine will verify the TCP/IP protocol is installed on the SBS workstation and the IP address is assigned dynamically. One reboot later and the SBS client applications (modem sharing client, fax client, proxy client, Internet Explorer, Outlook, and perhaps Office 2000) are installed. One final reboot and logon and you're in business, SBS style!

SBS Troubleshooting

I end this chapter with a few lessons learned in working with SBS. Again, the underlying theme is that SBS is so very different from regular Windows NT Server. Honor this above all else.

Do your software vendors support SBS?

If not, then *stop* the SBS project! I've done it twice. In both cases, it involved older releases of business accounting systems that hadn't been approved for SBS. The lesson learned here was that SBS is different. How? Look no further than the SBS subdirectory structure (see Figure 16-17).

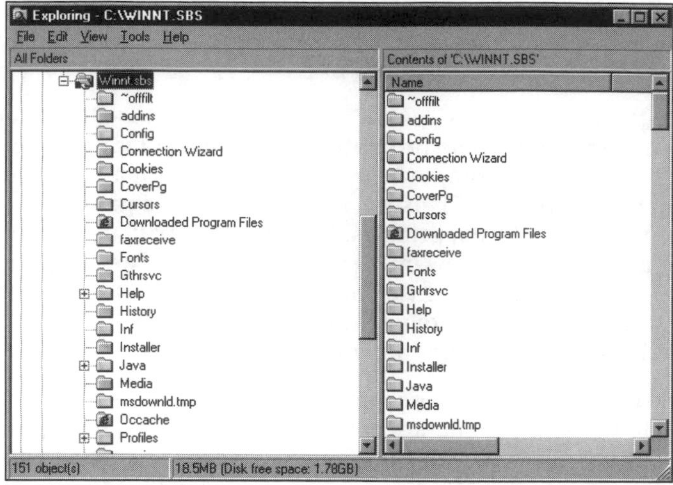

Figure 16-17: Modified Windows NT Server subdirectory (winnt.sbs) with SBS

As you may be aware, a regular Windows NT Server installation places Windows NT Server in the `\WINNT` subdirectory by default. SBS is different and places Windows NT Server in the `\WINNT.SBS` directory, which of course is a modified subdirectory name. This one change can be a point of failure in supporting your older applications. If your older application is approved for Windows NT Server 4.0, it might be expecting the subdirectory path `\WINNT` and could fail under SBS's modified path of `\WINNT.SBS`.

Modem sharing

The default modem sharing UNC share name is COMPORTS when created or viewed on the server, if the modem-sharing service is implemented post-conversion. If the modem-sharing service is implemented during the initial installation, the modem pool is correctly named MODEMS. The clients (Win95, NT4) point to the communication port share name MODEMS by default. So one lesson I've learned is that you need to check the communication port share name being used on the SBS server.

Then check the communication port share name under your client workstation that has the modem-sharing client installed on it. For Windows 98 or 95, you will need to look under the communication ports (COM ports) in Device Manager (see Figure 16-18).

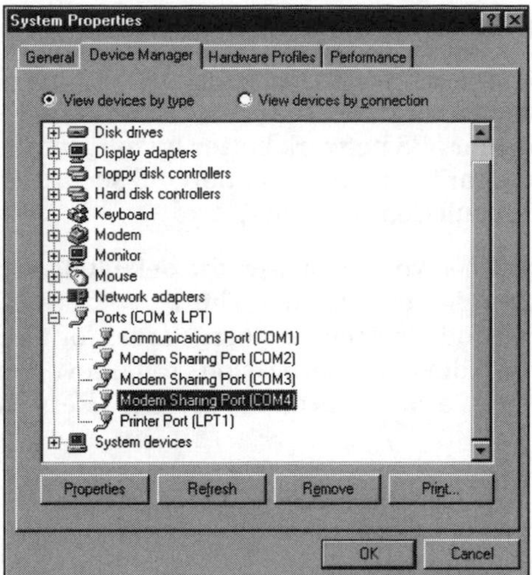

Figure 16-18: Communications ports redirected to the modem share on the SBS server

As you may know, Device Manager is accessed by selecting the property sheet for My Computer (right-click My Computer and select Properties from the secondary menu. Then select the Device Manager tab sheet). When all is said and done, you need to affirm that the communications port share name matches on both the SBS server and clients. If not, you will receive the error message shown in Figure 16-19 when trying to use the modem sharing capabilities.

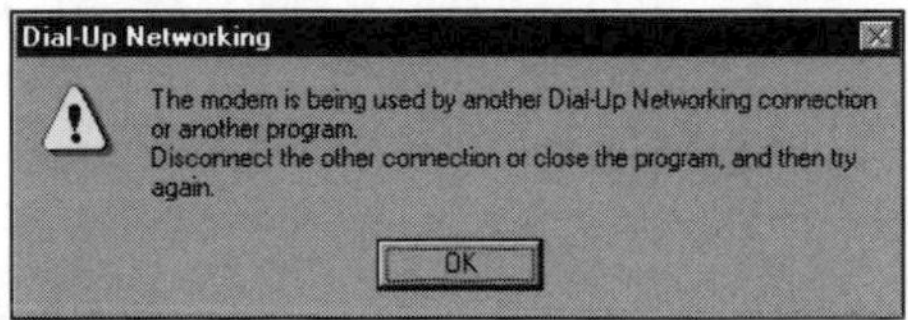

Figure 16-19: Dial-up networking error message

Harmless event logs errors

Suppose your SBS server uses a direct ISDN connection to the Internet and has no modems attached. Because SBS installs RAS whether you have a modem or not, the Event Viewer will log errors from RAS-related services at startup if you didn't set up any modems. This condition will be displayed as a harmless "A service failed to start" error message upon server startup. Not a big deal, but it can freak out novice SBS administrators. To eliminate this situation, disable both the Remote Access Connection Manager and Remote Access Server services.

Revisiting SBS security

Besides standardizing drive mappings for your user populations (say the S: drive for user directories and the T: drive for the company directory), you can manage the security of your SBS network better by following these few steps. Perhaps you share my earlier concerns about SBS security being too generous (everyone receives Full Control rights).

You need to understand that when you add a user, the default permission for any SBS user is "read" for any other user's folder. This is typically unacceptable, as small business owners demand confidential storage areas for their work. To fix that, modify the NTFS-based directory permissions to remove the (default) Read right via the Manage User Permissions on the Manage Users page in the SBS Console.

Virus detection

Remember that SBS does not have a native virus detection solution. For that, you need to consider a robust virus detection solution such as Inoculan from Computer Associates or McAfee Total Protection Suite. You might be interested to know that Computer Associates also offers Inoculan for Small Business Server for $645 suggested retail (see `www.cai.com`). The Inoculan solution is considered realtime because it constantly scans for viruses that may arrive via network file transfers, Internet e-mail and file transfers, floppy disks, and so on.

There is yet another virus detection alternative in the SBS world — Seagate's Backup Exec tape backup application, which has a modified virus detection routine wherein each file to be backed up is scanned for viruses. While not realtime, such regular scanning of files for viruses via a tape backup program is better than what SBS offers you natively out of the box: nothing!

The Future of SBS

To all appearances, SBS is here to stay. If for no other reason, SBS has allowed Microsoft to clearly delineate its networking offering for the small business from that offered to the enterprise. For today, that small business offering is SBS 4.5 based on Windows NT Server 4.0; compare that against the real reason for this book, Windows 2000 Server, which is positioned better for the enterprise.

So what does the future hold for SBS? Here is what I predict. Within 18 months of the release of Windows 2000, you can look forward to SBS 5.0, which will offer Windows 2000 Server as its underlying network operating system. I also think you'll see some of the winning features from SBS, such as ease of administration, offered in the Windows 2000 Server community for purposes such as managing branch offices. And all the usual suspects such as Exchange, IIS, IE, and perhaps NetMeeting will be improved in the next SBS release. But like you, I'll have to wait to see what really happens!

Summary

In this chapter, Small Business Server was explored and explained, starting with a basic introduction and ending with advanced topics:

- Defining Small Business Server
- Understanding the small business environment
- Identifying Small Business Server design goals and philosophy
- Planning for your Small Business Server implementation
- Installing the Small Business Server — Client components
- Using the Small Business Server To Do List
- Troubleshooting Small Business Server
- Planning for future releases of Small Business Server

Part VI

Optimizing Windows 2000 Server

Chapter 17

Analyzing and Boosting Performance

In This Chapter

- Learning why you should monitor, boost, and forecast Windows 2000 Server performance
- Defining performance analysis
- Learning about and distinguishing between quantitative and qualitative tools
- Learning the conceptual steps in performance analysis
- Learning about troubleshooting via performance analysis
- Knowing what the four most important areas to monitor in order to boost performance are
- Reasons for declines in performance

Analyzing and boosting performance is a very important part of a Windows 2000 Server professional's job. You are responsible for getting the most from your implementation of Windows 2000 Server. Installing, managing, and using Windows 2000 Server is a big investment on your part in both time and money. By analyzing and boosting performance, you can increase the return on that investment. This chapter will not only define performance analysis from both quantitative and qualitative viewpoints, but will also set the foundation for the chapters that follow in Part VI, "Optimizing Windows 2000 Server."

This chapter is for the MBA in all of us. While MBAs spend their days applying linear programming to business scenarios and mastering the inner workings of their Hewlett-Packard (HP) 12C calculators, Window 2000 Server engineers can learn a lot from the basics of quantitative analysis used by MBAs. You can apply the quantitative or scientific approach to Windows 2000 Server performance analysis and add real value to your network and its operations. To do so, consider mastering System Performance Monitor, Network Monitor, and Task Manager.

Why? Smart practitioners know that you get what you give to Windows 2000 Server. If all you do is set up and simply answer several questions posed by the Windows 2000 Server setup dialog boxes, your signature will be on public display when others follow and look closely at your network. Simple is as simple does. A network setup in a simple fashion will basically perform, but doom lurks. Once your network experiences significant growth either via user count or activity levels, system design and implementation issues often return to wreak havoc. Thus the need to study, master, and implement the performance boosting secrets discussed in this and the next few chapters in the Performance Analysis part. These secrets include third-party products that add to and help you exceed the capabilities of Microsoft's built-in performance analysis tools.

Performance Analysis

We wouldn't embark on a sailing trip without a plan, a map, and a compass in our stash of necessities. We like to know where we are headed, how long it will take, and often, whether we can get there sooner. Managing Windows 2000 Server environments is no different. Is our Windows 2000 Server performance headed in the right direction? Going south on us? Remaining stable or veering sideways? These are the types of questions we ask ourselves in the middle of the night, workaholics that we are in this exciting and demanding field of Windows 2000 Server network administration and engineering. To answer these questions, we tinker, try again, and tinker more, hoping to boost Windows 2000 Server performance and predict where our environment is headed.

Chant the following mantra: It all starts with the data. While this is a popular refrain among database administrators (DBAs), it is the data that ultimately matters when analyzing and boosting the performance of Windows 2000 Server-based networks. Data is at the center of our efforts to analyze Windows 2000 Server, so we place great importance on the type of data, the quantity of data, and the quality of data we can obtain from Windows 2000 Server. Fortunately, the computer readily generates this data for us. Thank God we don't have to record by hand like the door-to-door U.S. government census interviewers of days gone by.

Data can be collected as a one-time snapshot of our system health, or it can be systematically collected over time. As quantitative analysts, we desire and seek out large clean data sets that provide enough values for us to perform meaningful analysis and draw meaningful conclusions.

Tip

Whichever data analysis tool you use to monitor and manage your Windows 2000 Server network, you should strive to collect data consistently, frequently, and routinely. We love large data sets as the foundation of our analysis. Statistically, we refer to a large data set as a large sample size.

Built-in performance analysis tools

In Windows 2000 Server, we typically use six tools to collect and analyze our data: System Performance Monitor, Network Monitor, Task Manager, Windows 2000 System Information, Event Viewer, and Device Manager. System Performance Monitor enables us to perform sophisticated analysis via charts, logs, reports, and alerts over time (see Figure 17-1). System Performance Monitor is discussed at length in Chapter 18. Network Monitor is truly a gift in Windows 2000 Server, enabling basic networking packet analysis without having to spend $5,000 or more on a hardware-based sniffer (see Figure 17-2). Network Monitor is discussed at length in Chapter 19. Task Manager (see Figure 17-3), Windows 2000 System Information (see Figure 17-4) and Event Viewer (see Figure 17-5) are discussed extensively in Chapter 20. You can also read more about System Performance Monitor, Network Monitor, and Task Manager in the "Are You Being 'Outperformed?'" section of this chapter. Device Manager, a welcome addition to the Windows 2000 family, was discussed in Chapter 9 (see Figure 17-6).

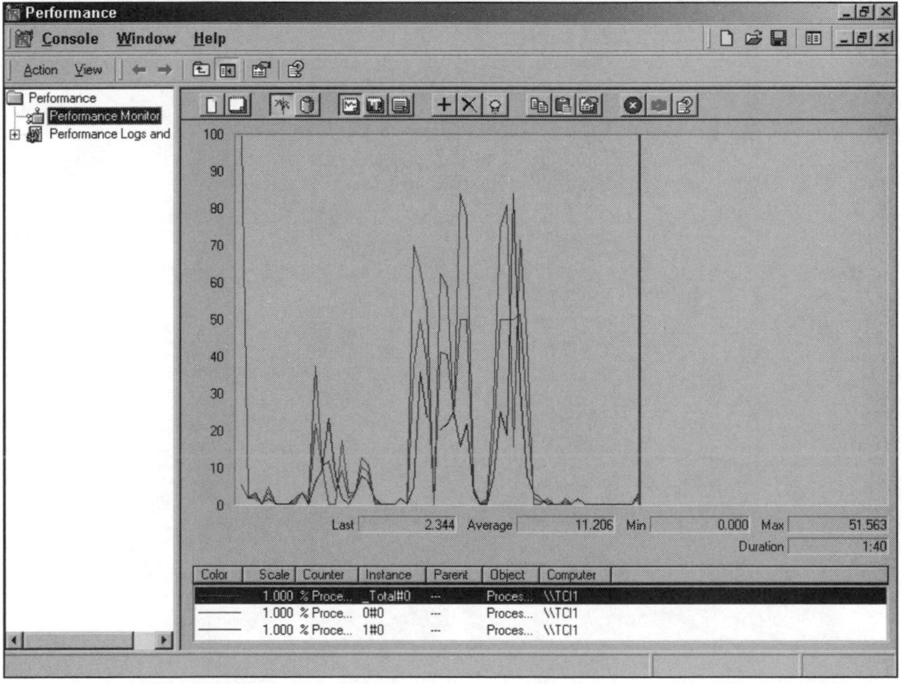

Figure 17-1: Default view of System Performance Monitor showing the Object:Processor Counter:% Processor Time

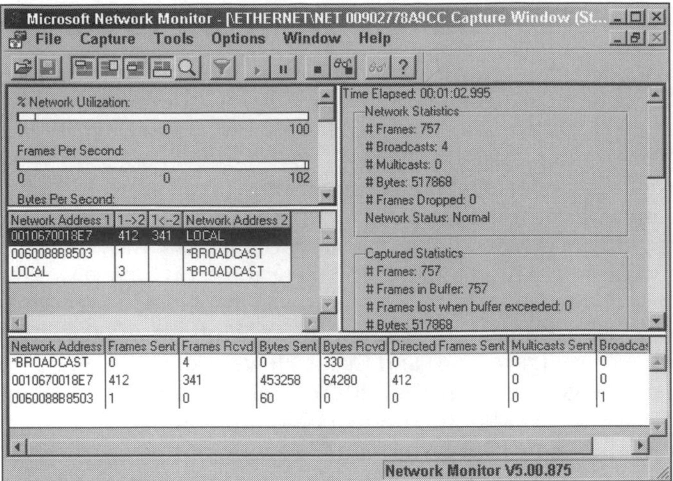

Figure 17-2: Default view of Network Monitor — Capture View window

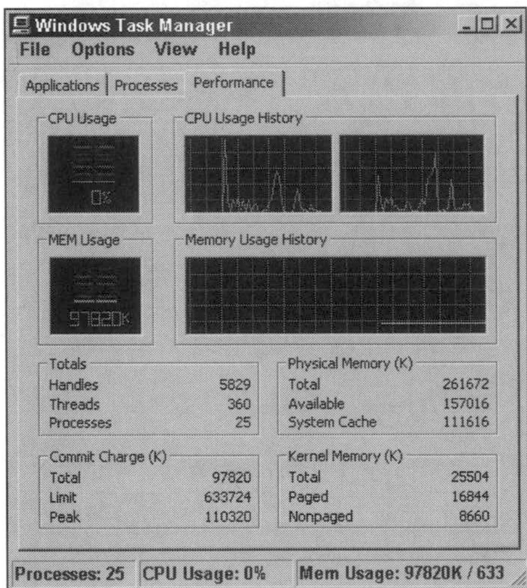

Figure 17-3: Default view of Task Manager — Performance tab sheet

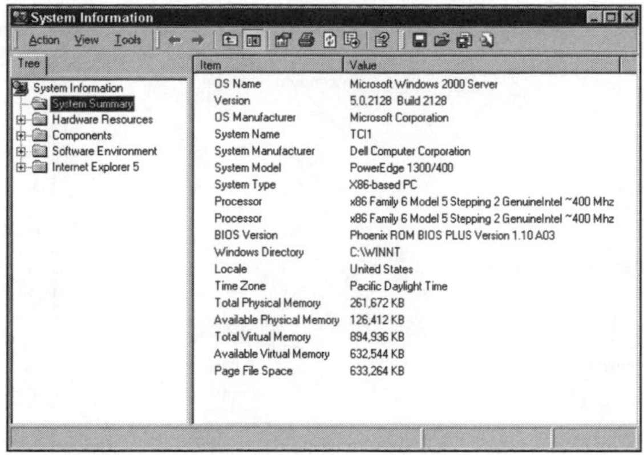

Figure 17-4: Default view of Windows 2000 System Information — System Summary

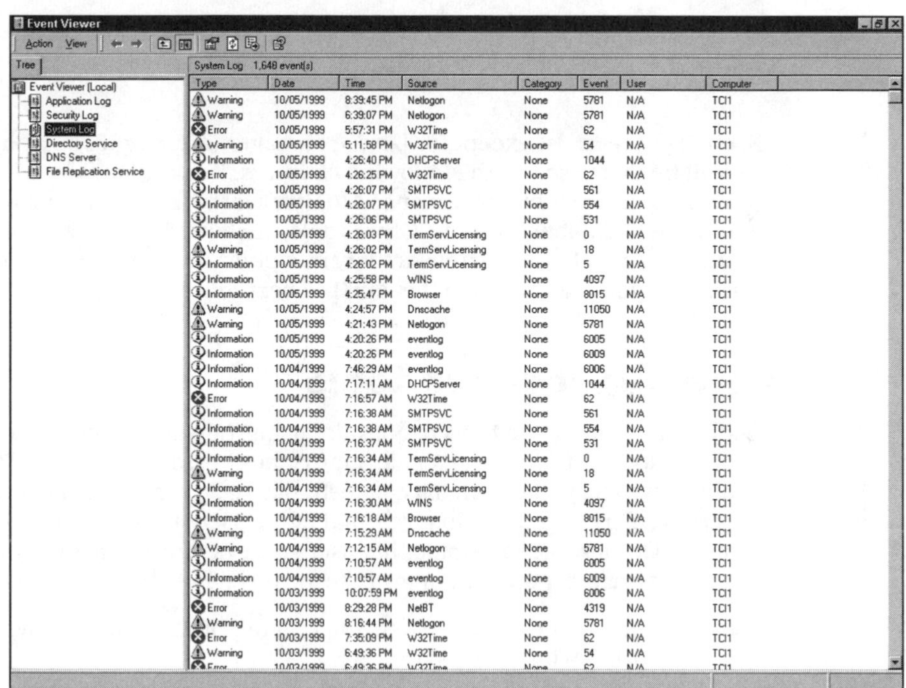

Figure 17-5: Default view of Event Viewer — System Log

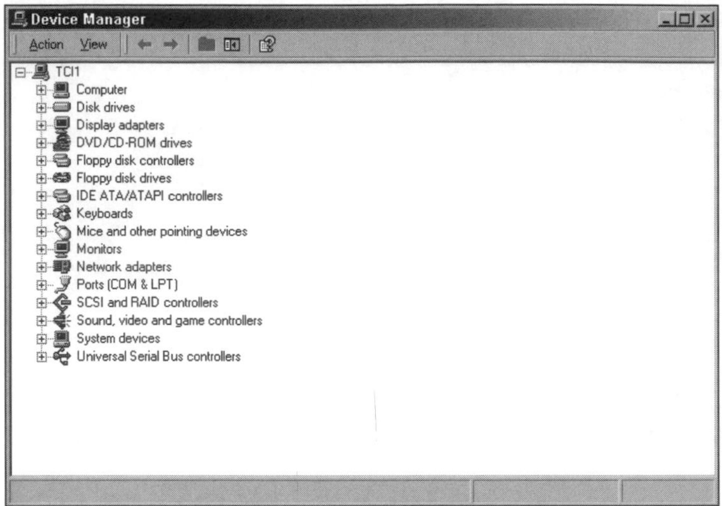

Figure 17-6: Default view of Device Manager

Each of these tools, except for Device Manager (already discussed in Chapter 9), will be discussed in the following chapters. It is critical to note that some tools such as System Performance Monitor work best when analyzing data over time to establish trends. Other tools, such as Network Monitor, typically provide a snapshot of system activity at a point in time. This distinction is critical as you read through this and the next few chapters.

More quantitative tools

Additional quantitative tools to consider using, beyond those provided with Windows 2000 Server, include approaches borrowed from the MBA and quantitative analysis community, namely, manually recording measurements, observing alert conditions in logs, conducting user surveys, and basic trend line analysis. Of these, keep in mind that user surveys directly involve your users and are, therefore, perhaps some of the most valuable tools at your disposal.

- Manually record measurements and data points of interest while monitoring Windows 2000 Server.
- Observe event log error conditions that trigger alerts (a big approach used in managing SQL Server).
- Survey users about system performance via e-mail or a paper-based survey. These survey results, when ranked on a scale (say 1 being low performance and 5 being high performance), can be charted and analyzed. It's really fun to deliver the same survey again to your users several months later and compare the results to your original survey. Using feedback from your users is one of the best performance-monitoring approaches.

- Carry out trend line analysis, frequency distribution, central tendency, regression, correlation analysis, probability distribution, seasonality, and indexing. These approaches are discussed over the next several pages.

The trend line analysis approach, while extremely powerful, is also the most difficult of these four analysis methods. Because it has a high degree of difficulty, I discuss trend line analysis at length over the next several pages. But don't be frightened by this preamble. The trend line analysis that follows may be tried at home, and I didn't hire professionals to complete the stunts.

Trend line analysis

Also known as *time series analysis*, this approach finds the best fit of a trend line applied against a plotted data set. In terms of managing Windows 2000 Server environments, that means applying the chart view in System Performance Monitor to observe data points being charted via a line graph, and then placing a ruler on your screen to create the trend line. The slope of the ruler would be the trend line and represents a line drawn equidistant from each point that has been plotted. Not surprisingly, this is a simple and effective forecasting tool for predicting system performance and is generally known as the freehand method. The mathematicians reading this book know that this handheld-ruler method is a gross oversimplification when it comes to creating a trend line, and indeed a trend line is best calculated via the least-squares method. See the quantitative methods book of your choice for a more in-depth discussion.

Frequency distribution

Imagine you are a network analyst in a large organization deploying Windows 2000 servers. You want to know what amount of RAM is available in the client machines. Table 17-1, based on data collected by Microsoft's System Management Server, was created to show a frequency distribution.

Table 17-1 Frequency Distribution Example

RAM	*Number of Clients (Frequency)*
12MB	150
16MB	200
24MB	100
32MB	50

Simple enough. You have now created the frequency distribution to help plan your technology requirements. Clearly, most of the machines have less than 24MB of RAM and may need a memory upgrade in the near future.

Central tendency — the mean, the mode, and the median

Assume you are in a large organization with WAN network traffic management problems. The organization is growing rapidly. You are curious about the nature of the network traffic. Are just a few users creating most of the network traffic? Are all users placing a similar amount of traffic on the wire? Analyzing the mean, mode, and median will accomplish this for you. The mean is simply the mathematical average calculated as the sum of the values divided by the number of observations (ten apples divided by five schoolchildren = two apples per child on average). The mode is the most frequently occurring value in a data set (following our apple example, if four schoolchildren each took one apple and the fifth school child took six apples, the mode would be one). The median is determined by placing a data set in order ranging from the largest number to the smallest number, and then choosing the values that occur in the middle of the set:

One schoolchild ate one apple

One schoolchild ate two apples

One schoolchild ate three apples

One schoolchild ate four apples

The median would be between two and three apples. The actual median would be 2.5 (you are supposed to calculate the arithmetic mean of the two middle values if there is no one middle number).

How does this apply to Windows 2000 Server performance analysis? Suppose your network traffic pattern has the characteristics shown in Table 17-2 for 11 users.

Table 17-2 Sample Network Traffic for 11 Users

Central Tendency Measurement	*Number of Data Packets*
Mean	1,500
Median	225
Mode	200

From this information, we can reliably state that one or more large users generate most of the network traffic as measured by data packets on the wire. How? When your median and mode measurements are smaller than your mean, you can assume that a few users (in this case) are supplying an inordinate amount of data packets. In the preceding information, you can easily see that the mean (or average) is considerably larger than the median or mode. The median, being a reflection of the midpoint of the data series when ordered from smallest to largest values, suggests that the data is skewed toward the smaller values. The mode, in this case, confirms this observation in that the most frequently occurring value is much smaller than the average value. Finally, looking at the data set used to create the example (see Table 17-3) proves the argument that a couple of users (Dan and Ellen) are creating most of the network traffic.

Table 17-3 User Network Traffic

Users (11)	*Network Packets Sent*
Adam	225
Betty	100
Carol	50
Dan	10,000
Ellen	5,000
Frank	250
Gary	200
Harry	225
Irene	175
Jackie	150
Kia	125
Total 11 Users	16,500 Packets

Regression

This quantitative analysis method, which seeks to define the relationship between a dependent variable and an independent variable, can be used to boost the performance of Windows 2000 Server. Assume you use Windows 2000 Server as an Internet server. Suppose you are interested in seeing how Web traffic impacts the processor utilization rate on the server. Perhaps you believe that Web activity ("hits") on your site negatively impact the processor utilization rate by causing that value to grow. You can find out by charting the dependent variable Processor:% Processor Time (this is an object:counter in System Performance Monitor that is described in Chapter 18) against the independent variable HTTP Service:Connections/sec (see Figure 17-7.)

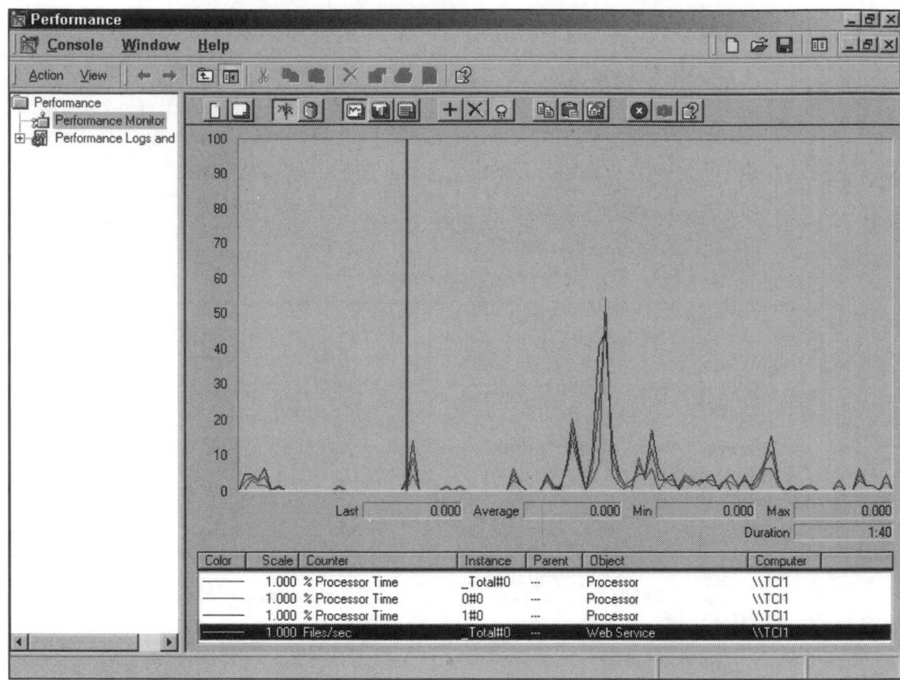

Figure 17-7: Dependent (Processor:%Processor Time) and independent (Web Service:Files/sec) variables

More hits on your Web site result in a higher processor utilization rate.

Correlation analysis

In the regression example just given, a positive correlation was discovered between Processor:% Processor Time and Web Service:Files/sec. A negative correlation between variables in Windows 2000 Server might exist when comparing two object:counters that seem to move in opposite directions when set side by side on a System Performance Monitor chart. At a basic level, the object:counters Memory:Available Bytes and Memory:Pages/sec would have a negative correlation. That is, the less available bytes of memory you have, the more paging activity will occur. These topics are discussed in greater detail in the System Performance Monitor chapter.

A negative correlation isn't necessarily bad. Do not be lulled into the fallacy that a positive correlation is good and a negative correlation is bad. Correlations merely define a relationship, whether that relationship is positive or negative. Another way to think about positive and negative correlations is to view a positive correlation as cyclical and a negative correlation as counter-cyclical.

Probability distribution

Do you work for a manager who worships the bell curve, always wondering where things fit in? Then use this quantitative analysis approach, not only to better understand the performance of your Windows 2000 Server system, but also to explain technology-related events to your manager. The cool thing about the normal curve is you can easily predict how just over ⅔ (actually 68 percent) of your end users group together when measured against what is called the first standard deviation. A standard deviation measures variability. But let's speak English. The first standard deviation is a very basic measurement and represents the behavior of 68 percent of your users on a network. We might say that 68 percent of the users are proficient in mapping drives to another server. Of that 68 percent, some are more proficient than others. A measurement taken to the second standard deviation accounts for 95.4 percent of the user population. Here we'll consider the ability to log on to the network successfully as our "task" that we believe such a large number of users could complete. However, within that population of 95.4 percent, some may log on without ever having authentication problems, while others may have to enter their name and password multiple times to log on (maybe they are poor typists!). Finally, to the third standard deviation, you can account for the behavior of 99.7 percent of the user population. For this group, it might be safe to say that 99.7 percent of the users can turn on their computers. In the underlying trend I've just described, you can see that as the bell curve encapsulates more and more of the user population, the activities and behaviors demonstrated by the users become less and less arduous. That makes sense. To cover the computing behavior of 99.7 percent of your users, you're speaking about some pretty simple tasks that nearly everyone can accomplish.

The normal curve provides a different way of thinking about network performance analysis. What if you believed and measured that 68 percent of your users use three or more applications, but 99.7 percent of your users employ at least one application?

Might you somehow try to group the 68-percent group of users (that is, to the first standard deviation), if we can identify this group easily, into its own separate collision domain? Such is the thought and logic behind switching in network management. This quaint mumbo-jumbo really does apply.

Seasonality

Do Windows 2000 servers really have seasons? Maybe so! Doesn't it make sense to remain sensitive to peak system usage when such usage occurs at specific times each year? Take Clark Nuber, the Seattle-based accounting firm that owns the consulting practice where I'm employed. Our network clearly experiences its heaviest loads during tax season (January to April). I can document the increased load using the different Windows 2000 Server performance tools discussed in this chapter, but more important, I can easily predict the increased load on Clark Nuber's network each tax season.

Needless to say, we "Clark Nuberites" have learned (sometimes the hard way) not to upset the network with upgrades or enhancements during tax season. On more than one occasion, the network couldn't handle the increased load and crashed!

Create an index

Once you've worked extensively with Windows 2000 Server and collected large data sets, then you can create meaningful measurement indexes. Here's how. Assume you've tracked several sites with System Performance Monitor for several months, periodically capturing data to a log file. At this point, you would have a sufficiently large data set. Then you want to know what a fair measure of a user's impact on paging activity is on a typical Windows 2000 server for your sites. To determine this impact, you would create an index. Suppose you looked at the average Pages/Sec (found under the Memory object) in System Performance Monitor and divided that by the average number of users on the system. Note calculating the average Pages/Sec should incorporate readings from different logon periods from different sites so that you can indeed create a generic index. If the average Pages/Sec value were 15.45 and you had 100 users on average, then the index calculation would be 15.45 / 100 = 0.1545. This index value of 0.1545 enables you to predict, on average, what paging file activity might be caused on a per-user basis. In effect, an index enables you to predict the load on your system, something that might be very useful when scaling a new system for an upgrade.

Qualitative tools too!

Performance analysis is not only a quantitative exercise, it is also a qualitative endeavor. We can map and chart Windows 2000 Server performance until the cows come home, but many of us also rely on, if not favor, our intuition and other qualitative analysis approaches. Individuals equipped with strong qualitative analysis skills may not even need to know the finer points of System Performance Monitor and other Windows 2000 Server performance analysis tools. These people simply "know" when something isn't right. Then they set out to troubleshoot the problem and fix it. This is how many CEOs run their organizations. While these leaders might not have a solid grasp of the technologies their firms use, they do know when something is out of place or not right.

Loosely defined, qualitative approaches to boost Windows 2000 Server performance include the following:

- Experience working with Windows 2000 Server
- Luck
- Intuition
- Luck
- Good judgment

- Luck
- Good advice from peers
- Luck
- A seventh sense
- Luck
- Decision making under uncertainty
- Luck
- ESP
- And finally... LUCK!

Several of us long on Windows 2000 Server work experience rely on our qualitative judgments on a day-to-day basis. We use the quantitative analysis approaches such as System Performance Monitor logging periodically or during intensive troubleshooting, but probably not in our day-to-day world. Those with strong qualitative skills often reap the rewards that accrue to the privileged in this line of work, such as higher pay and more work. Why? Because these individuals simply work more efficiently and better. Think about that the next time you team with an industry peer to troubleshoot a Windows 2000 Server problem and find yourself left behind analytically as you marvel at your companion's superior skills. Fear not, however, for the rest of us can be equally successful by employing Windows 2000 Server's built-in performance analysis tools. Stated another way, when you're short on qualitative tools, you should emphasize the quantitative tools. And of course, even our Windows 2000 Server companions with ESP can still benefit from the fundamentals of quantitative analysis.

It takes both the quantitative and qualitative approaches to successfully analyze and boost the performance of your Windows 2000 Server over the long term! In other words, it takes a combination of the quantitative tools (System Performance Monitor, Network Monitor, and Task Manager) plus the qualitative approaches you have at your disposal (experience, intuition, and a seventh sense). Both the quantitative and qualitative schools should receive attention if not equal weight. And don't you forget it!

Data = information

The central activity performed in performance analysis is to capture and analyze Windows 2000 Server data. In effect, we turn data into information. The information is used to correct Windows 2000 Server deficiencies, eliminate system bottlenecks, proactively prevent system problems before they occur, troubleshoot problems once they do occur, and plan for system upgrades and enhancements.

Are You Being "Outperformed?"

After you have arrived on the scene as the great net god, whether as consultant or full-time employee, and fixed the obvious problems, your talents often reach a fork in the road. The first fork is that of mediocrity in network management. Many in the network engineering field are content to coast once a system is up and running. That's truly what I'd call satisfying behavior: working only hard enough to satisfy management, bosses, clients, and end users. These technology peers are great readers of industry trade journals (on company time!). They also have shoes that are hardly worn because their feet are perched on their desktops while reading those trade journals.

The other fork network professionals take is to exceed everyone's expectations. In the world of Windows 2000 Server, this is accomplished by mastering tools such as System Performance Monitor, Network Monitor, and Task Manager. That is when and where you can really master the management of your Windows 2000 Server networked environment. Mastery involves cultivating the ability to identify and mitigate bottlenecks, preventing poor system performance by planning for system additions, and more planning, planning, planning.

System Performance Monitor

Mastering System Performance Monitor not only enhances your professional standing, but more important, it enables you to provide your end users with a more efficient and stable network for accomplishing their work. And that is how you and your network are ultimately evaluated: by how well your end users do their jobs using computers attached to your Windows 2000 Server network. By employing the suggestions that follow, you can proactively manage your Windows 2000 Server networks and provide solutions before encountering problems. In fact, it's been said that preventing problems is the best definition of a superior systems engineer. You don't necessarily have to provide the latest and greatest bells and whistles on your network. You do have to provide an efficient, reliable, and secure Windows 2000 Server network computing environment that users know they can trust.

Network Monitor

Mastering Network Monitor provides benefits different from System Performance Monitor. Network Monitor provides a snapshot view of network activity in the form of packet analysis. When working with Microsoft technical support at the senior systems engineer level (read "paid incident level"), it is not uncommon for a Microsoft support engineer to have you install Network Monitor and perform a capture. This capture file is then e-mailed to the engineer for analysis.

In fact, the way I learned packet analysis was by using exactly this approach. E-mailing the capture file and then discussing its contents with a Microsoft support engineer provided me with the packet analysis fundamentals lacking in many published texts. That is, except Microsoft Official Curriculum course

#689, "Windows NT Server 4.0 Enterprise Technologies," which has an excellent Network Monitor section. Realizing that Microsoft periodically updates its course offerings, I suspect the successor courses to course #689 will also teach this important topic.

If you have routers in your Windows 2000 Server network mix, you will be learning and using Network Monitor. And you will inevitably be e-mailing those packet captures to Microsoft for analysis. Count on it!

Task Manager

Task Manager is my buddy. With a deft right-mouse click on the taskbar, I can essentially assess the memory and CPU conditions of my Windows 2000 Server. Task Manager can be thought of as System Performance Monitor "light." Task Manager lives for the moment and doesn't really offer any long-term analysis capabilities. But more on that later. First, some thoughts on the conceptual framework of performance analysis.

Conceptual Steps in Performance Analysis

A few basic steps are undertaken to analyze and boost the performance of your Windows 2000 Server:

1. **Develop the model to use.** In System Performance Monitor, this means it is critical to pick the correct object:counters as part of your model. For Network Monitor, this step might refer to the duration of your packet capture and from what point on the network you capture packets.
2. **Gather data for input into the model.** This is a collection phase that involves acquiring the data. For System Performance Monitor, you log the data to a file for a reasonable amount of time. More important, this step is where we're most concerned about the first two parts of GIGO (garbage in/garbage out). Poor data accumulation results in garbage in, certainly a poor foundation to build the rest of your analysis upon. In fact, this step is analogous to my recent homebuying experience on Bainbridge Island (near Seattle). As I was writing this book, my family decided to go house-shopping. After identifying a house that met our needs, we retained a construction engineer to assess the house's fitness. Unfortunately, he reported the house was unacceptable because it was built on a wood foundation, the rule being that a house's foundation affects everything from that point forward, including resale value. With respect to Windows 2000 Server, blow this step and suffer for the remainder of your analysis period.
3. **Analyze the results.** Now the fun begins. If Steps 1 and 2 went well, you are now ready for Step 3: analyzing the results. Success at this stage will truly enable you to boost performance and optimize your Windows 2000 Server implementation. If you struggle here, see the next section on troubleshooting.

4. **Gather feedback.** Are we missing the boat with our analysis? Did Steps 1, 2, and 3 lead us to optimize the system in such a way that performance was improved, not hampered? Your ability to gather and interpret feedback will make or break your ability to become a superstar system engineer.

Troubleshooting via Performance Analysis

Everything discussed so far is meaningless if the knowledge transfer between us doesn't leave these pages. It is essential that there be a real-world outcome to the intense performance analysis discussion you and I have embarked on. Otherwise this discussion is nothing more than a pleasant academic exercise. The outcome we're both seeking is applying the performance analysis tools and tricks readily available to improve your network's performance. And that obviously includes troubleshooting.

The performance analysis tools included with Windows 2000 Server are software-based and do a better job of diagnosing virtual problems than truly physical problems. Physical problems, such as a bad cable run, are better diagnosed using a handheld cable tester.

There is no magic elixir to troubleshooting. Troubleshooting ability, by most accounts, is primarily a function of on-the-job experience, including long weekends and late nights at work. As an MCSE and MCT instructor, I've seen countless students struggle with the required Networking Essentials exam when their résumés are short and their tenures as Windows 2000 Server administrators are measured in months, not years. Students with significant industry experience enjoy an easier ride when taking the Networking Essentials exam, and not surprisingly, they have more sharply honed troubleshooting skills. Troubleshooting is something you learn with lots of on-the-job experience. The performance analysis tools provided with Windows 2000 Server are valuable not only for helping you improve the performance of your network, but also for troubleshooting problems more efficiently and effectively.

Be advised that even the best set of tools in unclean or incompetent hands will usually result in an unfavorable outcome.

Troubleshooting is not only a function of your Windows 2000 Server architectural experience, but also of your ability to swim comfortably within the Windows 2000 Server Registry. That's so you can observe and capitalize on driver dependencies and start values, track the Windows 2000 Server boot process to the point of failure, and understand stop screens. It won't hurt if you've worked with Microsoft support with the debugger utilities. But more on that in Chapter 25.

Print and review the entire Window 2000 Server Registry as soon as you install Window 2000 Server. Learn the location of important information (for example, HKEY_LOCAL_MACHINE is much more important than HKEY_CLASSES_ROOT). By studying and learning the Registry early, you will know where to go to investigate Registry values in an emergency. Don't forget to place this Registry printout in a notebook and update it periodically (quarterly, if you make significant changes or install lots of applications). I would highly recommend that you print to file and edit the information in a word processing application such as Microsoft Word. You will shorten the size of the printout considerably and make it more readable. Of course, you can always print to file as your only form of storage (and avoid printing to the printer at all). Whether you print to file or the printer, the Registry information is most valuable.

Misdiagnosing a problem is as problematic in the world of Windows 2000 Server as it is in the world of medicine. Although using System Performance Monitor, Network Monitor, and Task Manager will not assure a correct diagnosis, these tools are legitimate ways to eliminate false reads. Furthermore, some third-party performance analysis tools I'll discuss in the next few chapters can be used to supplement Windows 2000 Server's built-in tools and dramatically improve your troubleshooting efforts.

The Four Big Areas to Monitor

Quick, what are the four resource areas you should monitor in order to boost performance in Windows 2000 Server? They are memory, processor or, disk subsystem, and network subsystem.

Memory

Perhaps the simplest secret conveyed in this entire book is that adding memory will truly solve many problems in your networked environment. Looking beyond that reasoning is the idea behind analyzing memory performance. First, you probably have economic and technical constraints that prevent you from adding an infinite amount of memory to your server. Second, simply buying your way out of a problem by purchasing and installing more memory isn't fundamentally sound network engineering. Understanding the reasons for adding memory is what's important. Simply stated, we look at two forms of memory as part of our analysis: RAM and cache memory. RAM is, as we all know, volatile primary storage. Cache memory, also in RAM, is where Windows 2000 Server places files, applications, drivers, and such that are currently being accessed by the users, the operating system, and so forth. In Chapter 22, memory will be discussed in more detail with respect to specific memory object:counters used in System Performance Monitor.

Processor

My experience with analyzing the processor is that it usually isn't the cause of everyone's grief. Many suffer from processor envy, which is no doubt a function of popular advertisements creating the need for the latest and greatest Intel processor. So network engineers and administrators on the front line are often greeted with free advice from users on upgrading the processor. However, in most small- and medium-sized organizations, the processor utilization rates are well within acceptable limits. In large networked environments, a strong case can be made for faster, more powerful processors and even implementing multiple processors. These larger enterprises will be interested in learning more about Windows 2000 Server's multiple processing capabilities using the symmetric multiprocessing model.

Disk subsystem

Another tired solution that's the bane of network engineers and administrators is the "just buy a faster hard disk" approach. Easier said than done. Again, economic considerations may prevent you from just throwing money at your problems. A more intelligent approach is to analyze your disk subsystem in detail to determine exactly where the bottleneck resides. Issues to consider when analyzing the disk subsystem include

- What is your disk controller type (ranging from legacy IDE controllers to more modern Fast SCSI-2 and PCI controllers)?

Disk controller type technology changes rapidly and new innovations in system buses are introduced frequently. If you do not have a strong hardware orientation, make sure you are reading the hardware ads in popular technology trade journals and occasionally taking your technician/hardware guru buddy to lunch.

- Do your controllers have on-board processors (typically known as "bus master" controllers)?
- Do your controllers cache activity directly on the controller card, thereby bypassing the use of RAM or internal cache memory on the computer to store limited amounts of data?
- Do disk-bound applications and the associated high levels of read and write requests suggest you need to consider the fastest disk subsystem available?

Current disk device drivers: Are you implementing the latest disk subsystem drivers on your system? While this is an often overlooked duty, using current drivers can go a long way toward boosting your disk subsystem performance (and are typically available for the low price associated with downloading a driver from the vendor's Internet site).

Hardware-based RAID solutions offer significantly better performance than RAID solutions implemented via software (the software-based RAID capabilities found in Disk Administrator). That's because hardware-based RAID parity calculations are performed independently of the operating system.

Sometimes you just have to reboot! Here's one secret you won't find in any Windows 2000 Server user manual. For reasons I can't fully explain, sometimes Windows 2000 Server just freaks out and the hard disks spin excessively. When this happens, you don't even get enough processor time to freely move your mouse. The solution? Just restart the server. This condition will often disappear upon reboot. Truth be told, this "secret" is one of the best consulting freebies that I offer my clients — I often tell my clients to reboot and call me in the morning. It's usually just what the doctor ordered. I don't know if it is a function of Microsoft products more than other vendor products, but rebooting works wonders! I often say the rebooting Windows 2000 Server will solve 90 percent of your problems.

Be sure to delay rebooting your Windows 2000 Server until after work hours if possible. Users often take advantage of a reboot condition to call it a day and leave early, causing unexpected traffic jams in the parking lot!

Network subsystem

The network subsystem consists of internal and external network components such as the network adapter type, number of network adapter cards, cabling media, routers and switches, Windows 2000 Server services, and the types of applications used (SQL Server, Exchange, and other Microsoft BackOffice applications). And don't forget end users. I consider end users to be a network component because they can impact the performance of the network with their usage. How you configure Active Directory will also impact the performance of your network. A complex and unwieldy Active Directory structure can hinder rather than help your network. See Chapters 5 and 16 for more information on Active Directory.

In general, network bottlenecks are more difficult to detect and resolve than problems found in the three subsystems just discussed (memory, processor, and disk subsystem). In fact, all of the tools discussed in this and the next several chapters are typically used to resolve network bottlenecks. Additionally, physical tools are readily employed to remedy network subsystem ailments. These include cable testers and time domain reflectors (TDRs).

In fact, detection of quasi-logical/virtual and quasi-physical problems on your network may present one of your greatest challenges as a Windows 2000 Server professional. At a small site, I once fell victim to some tomfoolery introduced on the network by a 3COM switch. The device, being used primarily as a media converter between a 100MBps backbone run to the network adapter on the Windows 2000 Server and 10MBps runs to the workstations, decided to both reconfigure itself and downright break one evening when Microsoft Proxy Server 2.0 was introduced. Several hours of sleuthing later, it was determined the 100MBps downlink port had truly gone under. That is, the 100MBps port had lost its configuration. The solution? We quickly implemented a cheap 10MBps Ethernet concentrator to get everything running again. The hours spent fussing over the switch clearly eliminated all of the advantages associated with the 100MBps server backbone. But that's another topic.

Use 32-bit network adapters. Older 8-bit network adapters transfer up to 400 kilobytes per second (Kbps). Newer (and now standard) 32-bit network adapters transfer up to 1.2 Megabytes per second (MBps). If the network adapter card is too slow, it cannot effectively perform transfers of information from the computer to the network and vice versa.

Consider installing multiple network adapter cards to boost throughput). A single network adapter card can be a bottleneck in the network subsystem by virtue of its primary role in taking 32-bit parallel form data and transferring it to a serial form for placement on the wire (see Figure 17-8). Multiple network cards will boost network subsystem performance.

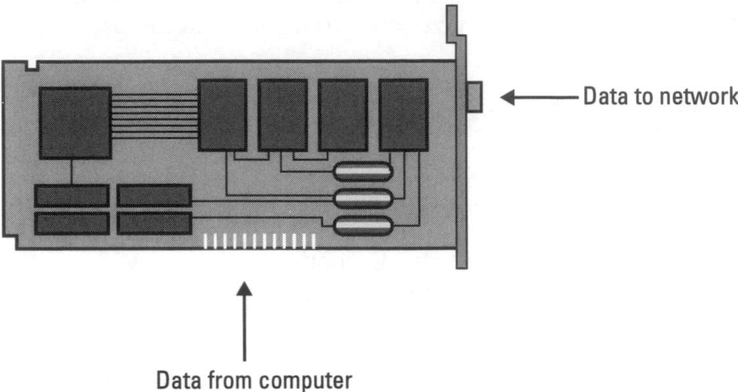

Figure 17-8: A network adapter card performing data transfer

Bind only one protocol type to each network card if possible. This enables you to perform some load balancing between network adapter cards. For example, if you have a second network cable segment for backing up the servers in your server farm to a backup server, consider binding the fast and efficient NetBEUI protocol to the network adapter cards on this segment (assuming no routing is involved). Binding multiple protocols to each network adapter can result in a performance decline on your network. Reducing excess protocols will reduce network traffic. Some types of network traffic, such as connection requests, are sent over all protocols at the same time. Now that's a traffic jam!

Try and reduce the number of protocols and networking services used on your Windows 2000 Server. Small is beautiful because overhead is reduced with a smaller networking subsystem footprint.

Use network adapters from the same manufacturer, if possible. Different manufacturers implement drivers against the lower layers of the OSI model differently. Using the same type of card from the same manufacturer results in a consistent implementation of the network subsystem component.

Networking services in Windows 2000 Server may be installed from the Add/Remove Programs applet in Control Panel. Simply select the Add/Remove Windows Components button in the Add/Remove Programs applet and complete with the Windows Components Wizard, as seen in Figure 17-9. Select the network services you want to install.

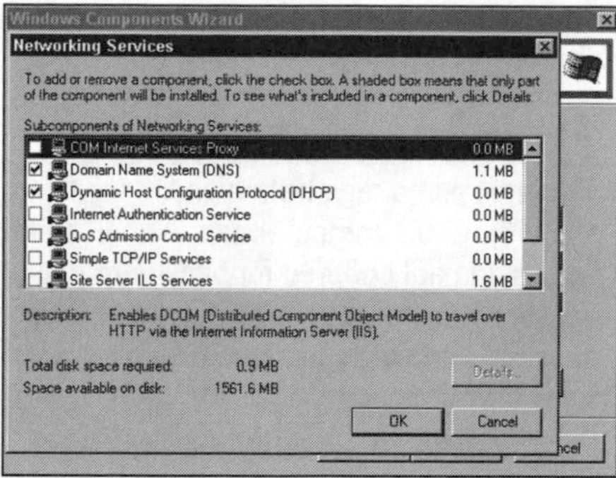

Figure 17-9: Networking Services in Windows Components Wizard

Table 17-4 is a list and description of possible network-related services that may be installed with Windows 2000 Server via the Networking Services dialog box.

Table 17-4 Windows 2000 Server Networking Services

Service Name	*Description*
COM Internet Services Proxy	This service automatically enables the Distributed Component Object Model (DCOM) to travel over HTTP via the Internet Information Server (IIS).
Domain Name System (DNS)	This is the mechanism that answers queries and updates requests for the Domain Name System (DNS) names.
Dynamic Host Configuration Protocol	This service enables a network connection to the Internet to dynamically assign a temporary IP address to a network host when the host connects to the network.
Internet Authentication Service	This service verifies authentication requests that are received via the RADIUS protocol.
QoS Admission Control Service	This service enables you to specify the quality of the network connection for each subnet. In other words, it is here that you may manage network bandwidth for QoS compliant applications.
Simple TCP/IP Services	Client program for simple network protocols, including Character Generator, Daytime, Discard, Echo, and Quote of the Day.
Site Server LDAP Services	This service provides the useful function of scanning TCP/IP stacks and updating directories with current user information.

Continued

Table 17-4 *(continued)*

Service Name	Description
Windows Internet Name Service	Dynamic name registration and resolution service that maps NetBIOS computer names to IP addresses. Note this is primarily offered for backward-compatibility reasons for applications that need to register and resolve NetBIOS-type names.

Other networking services may also be deployed via the following selections in the Windows Components Wizard:

Other Network File and Print Services	This installs File, Print Services for Macintosh, Print Services for Unix.
Certificate Services	This installs a certification authority (CA) to issue certificates for use with public key security applications. Note this certification discussion relates to security, not the MCSE-style certification.
Internet Information Services (IIS)	You would install IIS with its Web and FTP support plus FrontPage, transactions, ASPs, and database connection support here.
Management and Monitoring Tools	This installs Connection Management Components (for example, Phone Book Service), Director Service Migration Tool, Network Monitor Tools, and Simple Network Management Protocol.
Message Queuing Services	This service provides another form of reliable network communication services.
Microsoft Indexing Service	This is Microsoft Index Server with its robust full-text searching of files.
Terminal Services and Terminal Services Licensing	This is where you would install Terminal Server, a multisession remote host solution similar to WinFrame or PCAnywhere.

The bottom line on the network subsystem? You should be interested in ultimately knowing where you are today in terms of network performance (via System Performance Monitor using the Network Segment object and Network Monitor using its statistics pane), plus accurately forecasting where you will be tomorrow.

Why Performance Declines

Several reasons exist for performance declines in Windows 2000 Server. Likely suspects include memory leaks, unresolved resource conflicts, physical wear and tear on the system, and system modifications such as installing poorly behaved applications and running poorly configured applications.

The funny thing about operating system patch kits is that previously denied problems by Microsoft such as memory leaks originating from the executive services (like drivers and DLLs) are not only acknowledged, but also fixed. Memory leaks, which can be monitored by performing specific memory measurements over time, are typically corrected by simply rebooting the server periodically. That's an old trick for those of us who managed NetWare servers in the early days of NetWare 2.*x* and 3.*x*, when a monthly reboot was essential to terminate discontiguous memory.

Unresolved resource conflicts might include the dance of the fighting SCSI cards. I recently had an experience with a new workstation from a well-known hardware manufacturer where the on-board SCSI controller was fighting with the Adaptec SCSI card. Several modifications later, the conflict appeared to be resolved (by turning off the SCSI BIOS on the Adaptec card), but I could swear the boot time still remained unacceptably long, suggesting the existence of some lingering difficult-to-detect resource conflict (and yes, likely causes such as IRQ settings had been checked and resolved).

An example of a poorly configured application might be SQL Server with too much RAM allocated to it, causing a memory shortage for Windows 2000 Server. That would be likely to cause Windows 2000 Server to page excessively, resulting in lower overall system performance. Such a situation not only hurts Windows 2000 Server, but also SQL Server — the application you were trying to help with the original memory optimization scenario. I discuss RAM issues in more detail in Chapter 10. Fragmentation is another source of declining performance in Windows 2000 Server. All operating systems and secondary storage media are subject to fragmentation. This is where a file can be stored across several areas of the hard disk. That adds to read and write times and user frustration levels. Third-party products such as Executive Software's Diskeeper provide defragmentation services that optimize the secondary storage media and thus boost performance. I discussed fragmentation in more detail in Chapter 10.

Consider running the "error checking" utility Check Now found on the Tool tab of a drive's Properties sheet. Figure 17-10 shows the Check Disk dialog box that should appear. Error checking automatically checks for system errors and scans for and attempts to recover bad sectors.

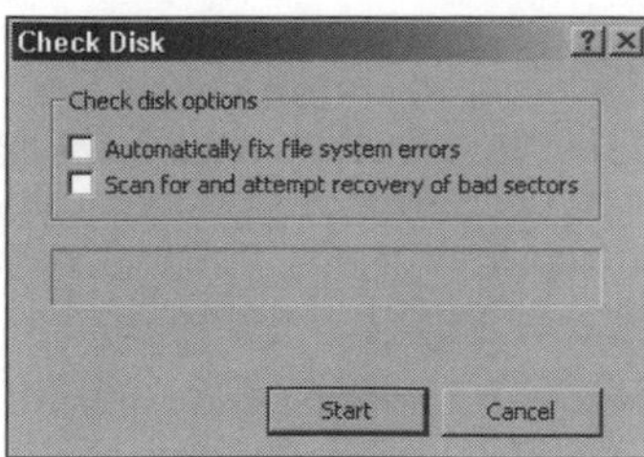

Figure 17-10: Check Disk dialog box

If you have SCSI drives, sector sparing (also known as a hotfix in NetWare) enables your system to essentially heal itself, kinda like my old VW van. That van had a way of healing itself from ailments if I just let it sit for a month or two. Sector sparing works much faster than my mystic VW van's healing magic by mapping out bad blocks on the secondary storage media and preventing further writes to that bad space.

When all else fails, you can improve performance by truly manually defragmenting your hard disk using a technique employed during my early Macintosh days. Simply store your data to backup tape (be sure to verify the fitness of your backup by performing a test restore) and reformat your hard disk. No doubt a drastic measure, but one that enables you to start fresh!

Additional ways to improve performance after you have suffered declines include

- Keeping the Recycle Bin empty.
- Deleting those pesky temporary files that many applications write to your secondary storage yet don't erase.
- Using NTFS for partitions over 400MB in size and FAT for smaller partitions under 400MB in size. However, be advised that this is a white-paper recommendation. Many Windows 2000 Server professionals frown upon the use of FAT partitions because NTFS file and folder-level security isn't available. Other Windows 2000 Server professionals like to install the operating system on a FAT partition and data and applications on an NTFS partition (see Chapter 3 for more discussion).

Lying with Performance Analysis

A must-read for MBA students is *The Honest Truth about Lying with Statistics* by Cooper B. Holmes, a primer on how to manipulate statistical analysis to meet your needs. To make a long story short, we can apply some of the same principles contained in Holmes' book to Windows 2000 Server performance analysis. For example, changing the vertical scale of data presented in System Performance Monitor can radically emphasize or deemphasize performance information, depending on your slant. If you're seeking a generous budget allotment to enhance your Windows 2000 Server network, perhaps scaling the processor utilization or network utilization counters in System Performance Monitor to show dramatic peaks and valleys will "sell" your business decision makers on your argument (see Figure 17-11).

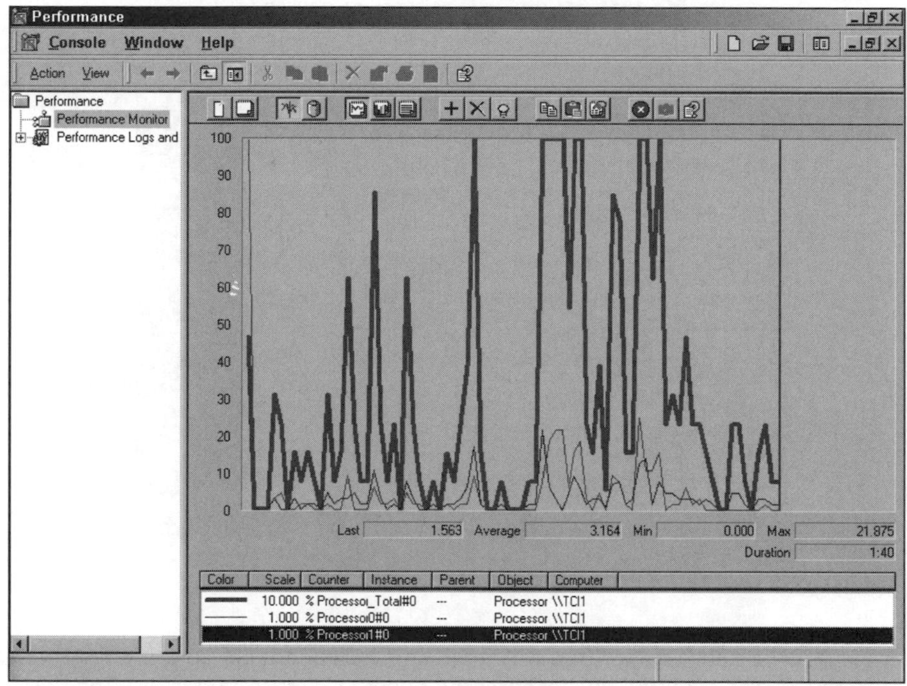

Figure 17-11: An exaggerated view of processor utilization

Performance Benchmarks

Several products enable you to establish performance benchmarks when comparing several servers running Windows 2000 Server, different applications, or different services and protocols. These tools change frequently, but perhaps your best source for such benchmarking applications is `www.zdnet.com` (the Ziff-Davis site). This site has available Socket Test Bench (STB) to test your WinSock-based communications and several other bench-test applications, including ServerBench and Winstone.

ServerBench is a popular client/server benchmarking application that runs on many popular operating systems including Windows 2000 Server, Novell NetWare, OS/2 Warp Server, and SCO UNIX (see Figure 17-12). The processor, disk, and network subsystems are all exhaustively tested by ServerBench through different tests and load levels placed on the server being tested. The bottom line? Performance is measured in transactions per second for each of the measured subsystems. These transactions reflect the activity between client and server and allow for meaningful comparisons between network operating systems and different makes of computers. Programs such as ServerBench enable you to better evaluate the performance of your Windows 2000 Servers individually and against other network operating systems you might have at your site.

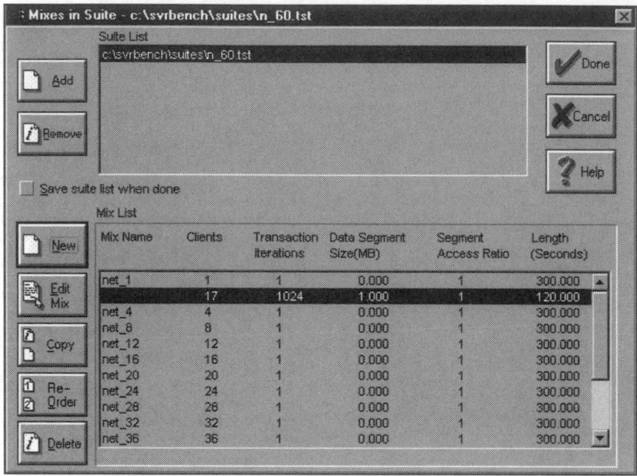

Figure 17-12: ServerBench 4.0

Be sure to perform the same ServerBench tests periodically so that you can identify any bothersome declines in system performance. Also note that a search of the Internet using popular search engines such as AltaVista will help you identify performance benchmarking applications you can use on your Windows 2000 Server network.

It's all about positive outcomes. By employing performance analysis methods and approaches to the management of Windows 2000 Server, you can see trends, observe usage patterns, detect bottlenecks, and plan for the future. You can create meaningful management reports that not only keep the appropriate decision makers informed but also identify needed equipment acquisitions and facilitate the IT budgeting process. That's a key point! Getting budget approval is the life blood of any Windows 2000 Server manager. Don't forget it!

Now — onward to System Performance Monitor!

Summary

This chapter introduced performance analysis. Specifically, it presented quantitative and qualitative methods to analyze and boost Windows 2000 Server performance. This understanding of computer network performance issues provides both the foundation for the next few chapters and your efficient and effective use of Windows 2000 Server in your organization. The following points were covered:

- Appreciating why you would monitor and forecast Windows 2000 Server performance
- Understanding and being able to define performance analysis
- Being able to distinguish between quantitative and qualitative tools
- Listing performance analysis steps
- The four most important Windows 2000 Server areas to monitor
- Understanding why performance declines in Windows 2000 Server

Chapter 18

Performance Monitor

In This Chapter

- Performance Monitor capabilities
- Performance Monitor basics
- Six quick steps to using Performance Monitor
- The five faces of Performance Monitor
- How to collect data
- In-depth analysis: memory bottlenecks, disk bottlenecks, network bottlenecks
- Analysis: file and print servers, application server

Nestled in the Administrative Tools program group you will find Performance, which launches Performance Monitor. This unassuming tool embodies many of the powers of Windows 2000 Server. By the end of this chapter, I think that you will agree that Performance Monitor is a lot more powerful than you previously thought.

Here is where the pedal meets the metal. Performance Monitor is a tool to be mastered so that you can optimize and continually improve the performance of your Windows 2000 Server network. Although Task Manager (discussed in Chapter 20) provides several measurements similar to those presented by Performance Monitor, it is the latter that enables us to track long-term trends and measurements such as those discussed in Chapter 17.

Performance Monitor is referred to as Performance, System Performance Monitor, and System Monitor in some of the Windows 2000-related documentation and in peer-group discussions. That's because in the early beta cycle of Windows NT Server 5.0 (which was renamed Windows 2000 Server), the tool known as System Monitor was really Performance Monitor. I'll use the term Performance Monitor in this chapter.

The Power of Performance Monitor

Some of the best deals about Windows 2000 Server are the no-cost utilities that are included, such as Performance Monitor. While Novell includes its own form of "performance monitor" (MONITOR.NLM) for free with NetWare, I think you will quickly agree that Windows 2000 Server's Performance Monitor, with its many capabilities, is one of the best tools you never had to pay for (see Figure 18-1).

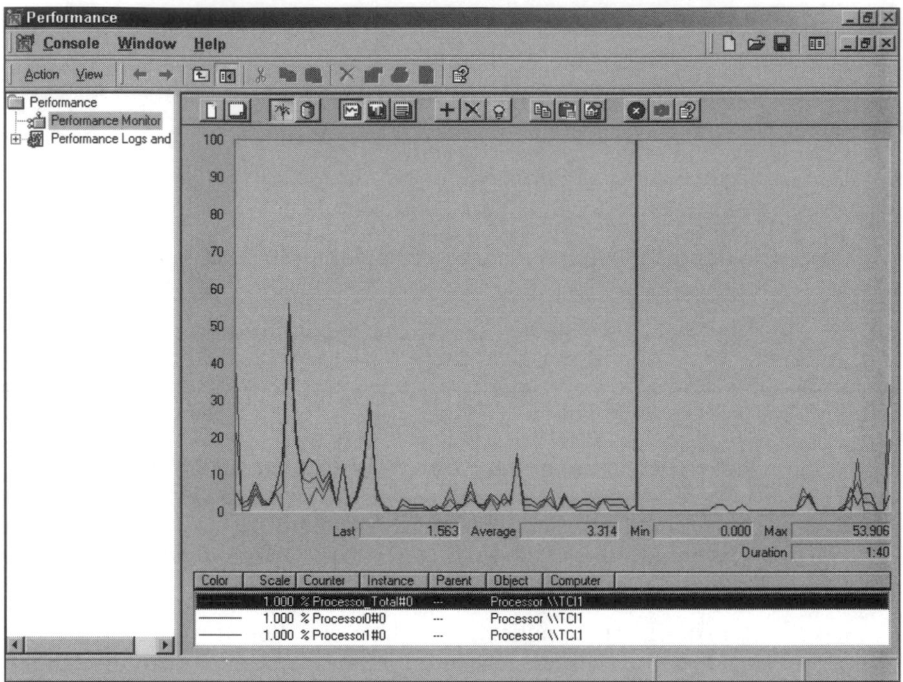

Figure 18-1: Performance Monitor

Here are some features of Performance Monitor:

- Logs and saves historical performance data
- Charts data in realtime
- Monitors server-based applications on an individual basis (with its own counters)

Tip

Using individual object and counters is a big deal when it comes to the effective rollout and management of Microsoft SQL Server. Microsoft offers several courses on Microsoft SQL Server 7.0 deployment, administration and development (see `www.microsoft.com` for more information).

- Provides several realtime and historical views of memory, server, disk, and network performance
- Enables you to observe the effects of changes to your system
- Alerts you to system-related problems immediately
- Monitors multiple servers using one session of Performance Monitor
- Runs several sessions of Performance Monitor (just try loading multiple instances of MONITOR.NLM on a NetWare server and see what happens)
- Saves specific analysis configurations via workspaces
- Exports data to other applications including Microsoft Excel and Microsoft SQL Server

Comparing Performance Monitor to NetWare MONITOR.NLM

Let's contrast Windows 2000 Server Performance Monitor with the NetWare MONITOR.NLM application (see Figure 18-2). MONITOR.NLM provides a realtime, snapshot view of how your network and server are functioning. MONITOR.NLM lives for the moment, but as we know, moments are fleeting. Serious performance analysis demands we view our data both in current snapshots and from a historical perspective. Performance Monitor enables you to do both. As an old NetWare CNE, I can attest to the value of Windows 2000 Server Performance Monitor over NetWare MONITOR.NLM. I've recommended and selected Windows 2000 Server (and Windows NT Server previously) over NetWare in several cases on the basis of Performance Monitor alone. This is truly one of the best-kept secrets about Windows 2000 Server, one that I'm about to share with you in detail.

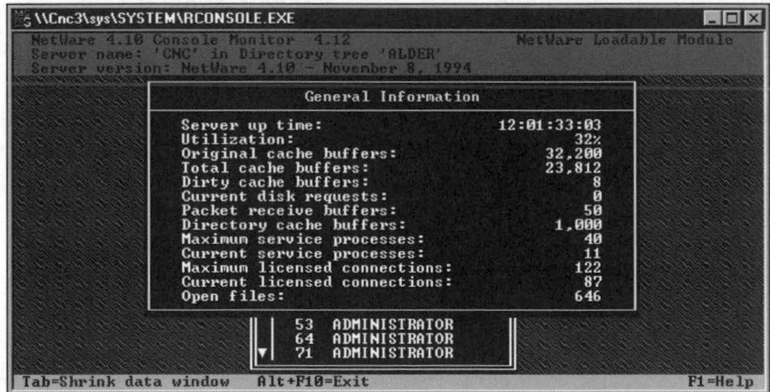

Figure 18-2: Novell NetWare MONITOR.NLM

It is essential you employ Performance Monitor for at least a bare-bones analysis so that you can monitor the health of your patient (your server and network) over its life from cradle to grave. Rest assured that time spent learning and using Performance Monitor is akin to the time you spend performing system backups: time well spent! Many network professionals have embraced Performance Monitor and employed it to its full extent. Taking full advantage of Performance Monitor, with all of its bells and whistles, is mandatory for larger LANs and WANs. Needless to say, I've found Performance Monitor to be a welcome and wonderful addition to my consulting bag of tricks. This said, welcome to performance analysis via Performance Monitor.

Performance Monitor is a strong tool for both developers and network engineers. But when you look at that long list of counters associated with numerous objects, please understand that most of the counters don't apply to those of us on the networking side of the aisle. In fact, the mission of this chapter is to present the most important Performance Monitor counters that apply to managing your Windows 2000 Server network. Developers are advised to consult the Windows 2000-related Software Developer Kit (SDK) for more information about the appropriate use of Performance Monitor counters vis-à-vis application development.

Performance Monitor basics

Most of us know Performance Monitor as an X/Y coordinate graphing application that's kinda fun. But Performance Monitor is much more than that. If all you ever wanted are pretty charts, you can achieve that small victory using a variety of Microsoft "front office" applications like Excel, PowerPoint, or even Word. For example, you could use Excel to chart the number of users on your network and possibly dupe your superiors into increasing your networking budget because your chart shows the number of users growing. That might work in the smallest of companies, but serious performance analysis requires serious use of Performance Monitor. But more on that in a moment. First, let's discuss the basics.

Performance Monitor is launched as an application from the Administrative Tools group via the Performance menu option. It runs as an MMC snap-in, so that also means you may launch Performance Monitor by simply launching an MMC and then adding the Performance snap-in. Technically speaking, launching the MMC-based Performance Monitor is accomplished with the following command line:

```
%SystemRoot%\system32\perfmon.msc /s
```

The "older" version of Performance Monitor can still be used in Windows 2000 Server (that is, the version that is not MMC-based). This older version can be launched from the command line by typing **PERFMON** at the command prompt. You will be greeted by a dialog box that tells you "Perfmon has been replaced by the Performance Monitor MMC. Click OK to start the

Performance Monitor MMC or Cancel to continue and use Perfmon." If you click cancel, you will be presented with good old Performance Monitor (the non-MMC version) from the old Windows NT Server days.

Performance Monitor works with performance objects, performance counters, and instances. An object is a major system area (such as Memory or Disk) or an application that reports to Performance Monitor (Microsoft SQL Server, Microsoft Exchange, or the like). A performance counter is a specific subset of a performance object. Performance objects typically have many performance counters. Performance counters are discrete items that can be measured. For example, the memory counter has over 32 counters ranging from % Committed Bytes in Use to Write Copies/sec. Counters have explanations, as shown at the bottom of the dialog box. Instances are the occurrence of multiple items. For example, if you have two processors, you will have two instances plus a TOTAL#0 instance that enables you to summarize the two instances (as seen in Figure 18-3). The syntax of performance objects, performance counters, and instances is object:counter:instance. Also, performance objects and performance counters are typically referred to as objects and counters (which is the language I will use in this chapter).

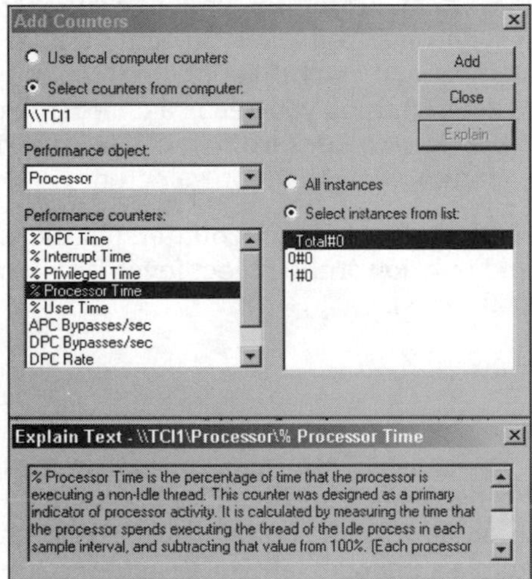

Figure 18-3: Performance objects, performance counters, and instances

Be sure to click the Explain button in the Add Counters dialog box when adding a counter to a chart. A text field will appear at the bottom of the dialog box that describes each counter in sufficient detail. The Microsoft developer, known only to God, who added this feature is a candidate for sainthood in my book!

Six quick steps to using Performance Monitor

Although I assume you are already armed with the user manuals for Windows 2000 Server, I'll quickly detail the process for using Performance Monitor. I highly recommend you study the Windows 2000 Server user manuals to better acquaint yourself with basic Performance Monitor feature sets, such as opening and saving files (stuff that I will not be addressing in this chapter).

Step 1: Select a view

Select the view in Performance Monitor that will work for you. If you are new to Performance Monitor, I'd recommend you start with the Chart view and work up to mastering and using the Log view. In the real world, I haven't found the Alert view or the Report view to be as meaningful. The Histogram view, which I will discuss later, has its 15 minutes of fame as well.

Step 2: Add objects

Add the appropriate objects, counters, and instances that you want to monitor. When you launch Performance Monitor, you may suffer from what I call the "blank spreadsheet" syndrome. You know the affliction, as you stare at (blank) cell A1 on a spreadsheet and can't think of anything to type. When Performance Monitor starts, the first thing you see is a chart (the default view) with basically nothing but y-axis values from 0 to 100. You will need to "populate" the Performance Monitor view that you selected.

If you are logging on, you may now select object:counters! In the old days of Windows NT Server, you could only log at the object level. This is a great improvement in Windows 2000 Server.

Step 3: Configure

Configure Performance Monitor by setting the time measurement interval, scaling, and so on. Properly configuring Performance Monitor is critical; it is the foundation of your performance analysis house. A bad foundation could skew your analysis in unfavorable or embarrassing ways. Remember, like a house, a bad foundation requires shimming forever to get everything right.

Setting time intervals

The default time interval for logging is 15 seconds. There are compelling reasons to change this value. Microsoft certification candidates will often change the time interval to one second to quickly generate a large data set to complete labs. At large Windows 2000 Server sites, it is common to set the default time interval to 600 seconds because creating a data point every ten minutes is acceptable for analysis purposes. When setting the time interval, just remember it depends on your needs.

Scaling

Given that many of us in the networking profession do not have advanced degrees in operations research and quantitative analysis, the scaling feature for counters in the Chart view can be perplexing. Essentially, you are trying to show a proportional relationship between different object:counters. Typically, you want to center information on the chart so you can easily detect correlations between the counters you are measuring. If you change a system setting or add another component, you can see how the relationship changes between the counters you are measuring. If these counters are centered on your chart, then sit back and enjoy being spoon-fed!

Centering

Suppose you would like to see the relationship between Memory:Available Bytes (Memory is the object, Available Bytes the counter) and Processor:% Processor Time. And if we assume that you use your Windows 2000 Server primarily as a file and print server, than we can safely assume that you typically have lots of available bytes of RAM and a low % Processor Time value, as seen in Figure 18-4 (note the default scale is set to 1.0 for the Processor:% Processor Time counter and 0.000001 for the Memory: Available Bytes counter).

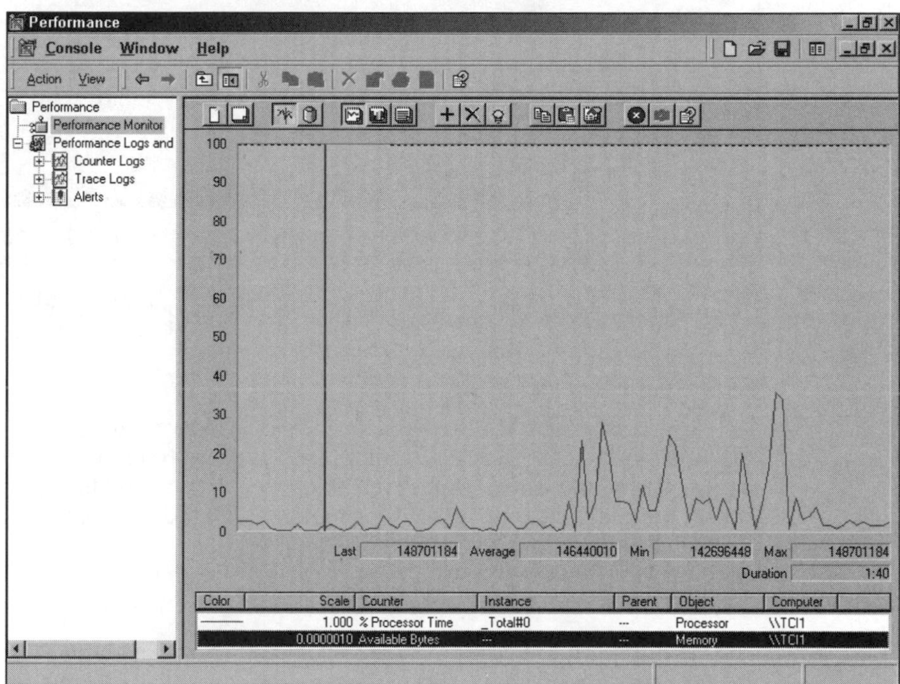

Figure 18-4: Charting Memory:Available Bytes and Processor:% Processor Time

This chart is not very meaningful from a quantitative analysis perspective because the two counters are charted at different ends of the vertical axis. Now, if we modify the scale on Memory:Available Bytes from 0.000001 to 0.0000001, this counter is charted in the center of the screen, enabling us to extrapolate a much clearer relationship between Memory:Available Bytes and Processor:% Processor Time (see Figure 18-5).

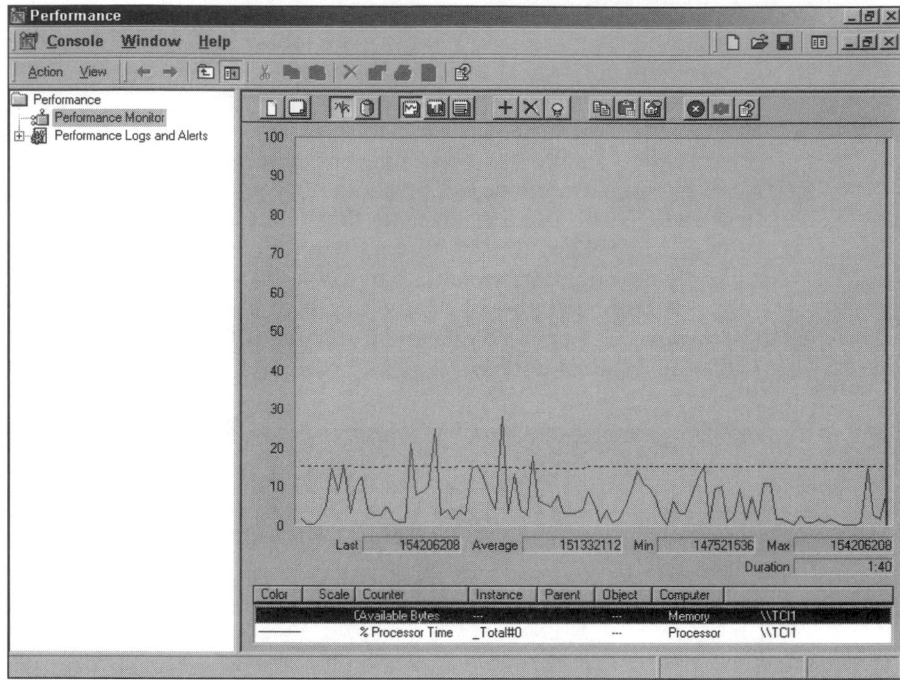

Figure 18-5: Centering Memory:Available Bytes and Processor:% Processor Time

Learning chart scaling

To learn more about scaling, you can take one of two paths. First, trial and error. Adjust the scaling for different counters to create a chart that is meaningful and easy to interpret. Then freeze these scaling settings for a period of time. Do the relationships look meaningful? Should you change the scaling of one counter to better position it on the chart and demonstrate its relationship to other counters being charted? In a few weeks and after several implementations, you will be a pro at chart scaling.

The second path to learning more about scaling is to use the Performance Monitor workspaces included with several Microsoft BackOffice applications. The best BackOffice Performance Monitor workspaces I've seen ship with Microsoft Exchange and Microsoft SQL Server. By learning from the Performance Monitor workspaces that Microsoft ships with its BackOffice applications, you are learning directly from the source. And the charts ain't bad-lookin', either!

If you have any Microsoft BackOffice applications such as Microsoft Exchange or Microsoft SQL Server, now is a good time to look at the Performance Monitor file created to monitor these respective applications. You may find these files either on the Microsoft BackOffice CD-ROM (by searching on `*.pmw` with the Windows 2000 Server Find command) or, better yet, if these applications are installed, in the Applications program group (from the desktop Start menu).

Tip

Now is also a good time for you to consider saving your Performance Monitor configuration as an MMC workspace file (`*.msc`). That way, you can recall this Performance Monitor scenario simply by opening your MMC workspace file. To do this, select Save As from the Console menu.

Step 4: Commence data collection

Next, start the data collection process so that you can build that data set! In the Chart view, data points are taken as soon as a counter is pasted on the chart. With logging, you will need to start the logging process.

Step 5: Terminate data collection

After sufficient data points have been taken, you can terminate the data collection process. This primarily applies to the logging function. We don't want to have our data log file grow forever, so we terminate logging after a set amount of time. Otherwise, like a bad B-grade movie in which alien tomatoes take over the world, our log file will take away all the available space on our Windows 2000 Server machine!

Step 6: Interpret the results

Now the fun really begins. Collecting data is meaningless unless we interpret it. Thus, we spend a great deal of time at this stage trying to assess where our Windows 2000 Server-based system is today and where it is headed. Essentially, we are looking for trends over time. This topic is covered in much greater detail later in this chapter under the "Collecting Data" and "Making Better Use of Performance Monitor" sections. You will also recall that trend analysis was discussed in Chapter 17.

The Five Faces of Performance Monitor

Performance Monitor has five views: Chart, Histogram, Alert, Log, and Report. I discuss each view, but would be remiss if I didn't share with you that I primarily use the Log and Chart views. I have had little real-world need for the Histogram, Alert, and Report views.

Chart

Easily the most popular view in Performance Monitor, data is displayed as lines or a histogram. This is what I call the medical view. Whereas medical doctors have EKG machines to closely monitor a patient's heartbeat, we have the Chart view in Performance Monitor to monitor the health, both in realtime and when reviewing logged data, of our servers and network. I've always felt really important when viewing these charts, much like a cardiologist looking at EKG reports being generated by a heart-attack patient. Many of the screenshots already displayed in this chapter show the Chart view (for example, see preceding Figure 18-5). To select the Chart view, simply select the Chart Display button on the Performance Monitor toolbar.

Histogram

Always use histogram charting in cases where the data would traditionally be displayed as a pie chart. You will recall that pie charts are drawn to show how individual slices total 100 percent, or the "whole". We can do the same with histograms when comparing the total instance of a counter against the individual counters that make up the total instance. Note that this is why Figure 18-6 is presented as a histogram chart.

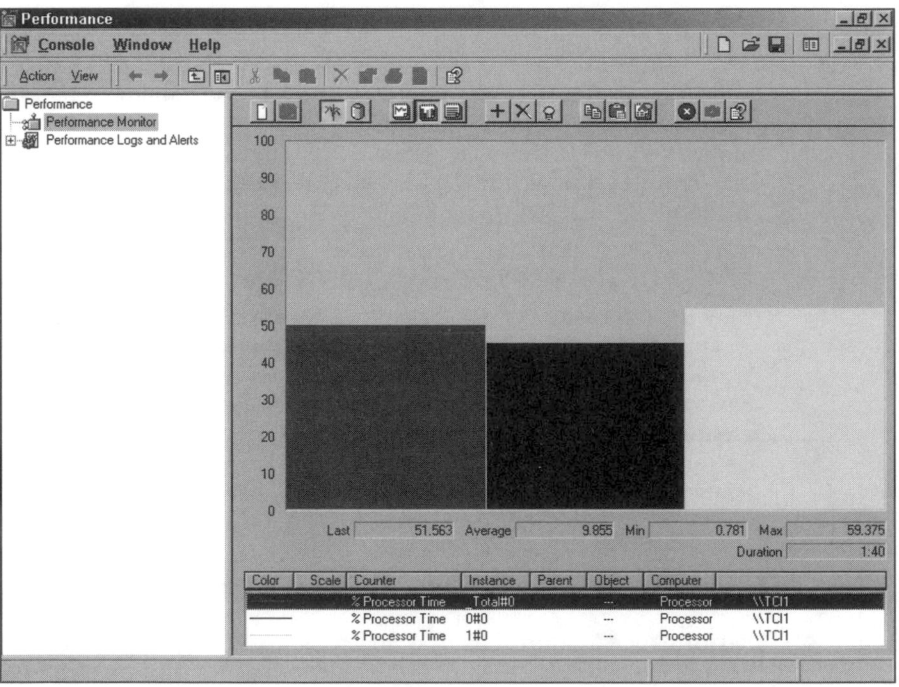

Figure 18-6: The Histogram Chart view

Test the display of your counters to see whether the line graph or histogram best reflects the counter's meaning. You will find many counters are best displayed as a histogram chart, but many Performance Monitor users never use that approach on charts because the line graph is the default.

Alert

Properly configured, the Alert view enables you to set triggers and conditions that generate alerts when certain boundaries or thresholds are met or surpassed. Alerts can be configured on a per counter (or parameter) basis.

STEPS:

To configure alerts

Step 1. From the left pane of the Performance Monitor MMC, expand Performance Monitor Logs and Alerts. Three items will be displayed: Counter Logs, Trace Logs, and Alerts.

Step 2. Select Alerts. In the right pane (that empty white space), right-click and select Create New Alert Settings from the New menu option on the secondary menu that will be displayed (see Figure 18-7).

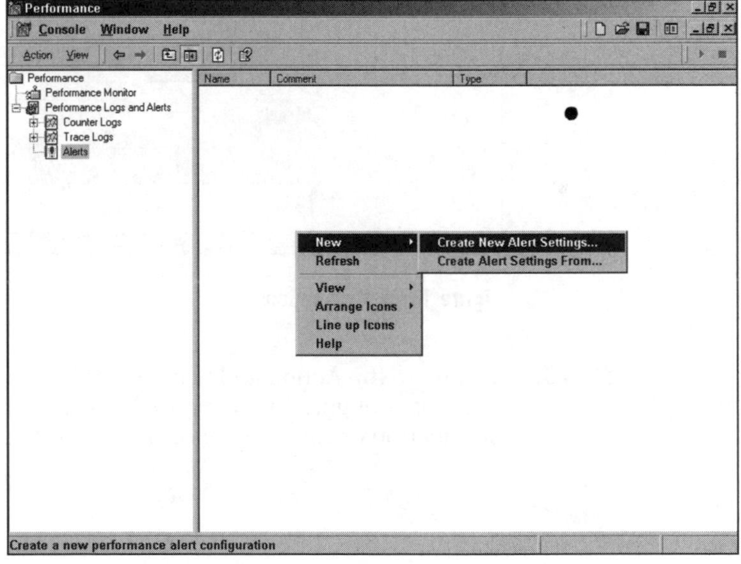

Figure 18-7: Create New Alert Settings

Continued

STEPS:

To configure alerts *(continued)*

Step 3. Give the Alert Settings a name (for example, "Main Alerts"). Click OK. A dialog box displaying the Alert Settings name will be displayed. Select the object and counter for the alert by clicking the Add button. Feel free to add a comment in the Comment field (for example, "This is the Main Alert").

Step 4. Select your Alert condition in the Alerts when value is fields ("Alert If Over 50%"). You will also need to select how often the data is sampled. By default, the data is sampled every five seconds (see Figure 18-8).

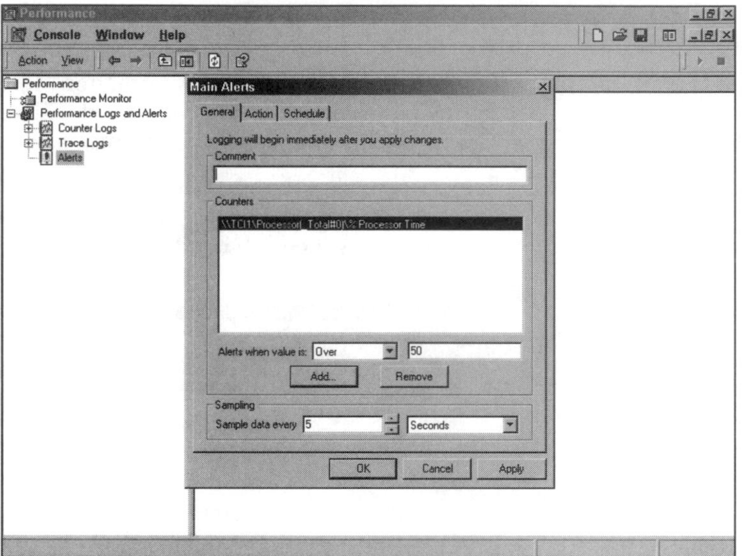

Figure 18-8: Alert options

Step 5. Complete the Action and Schedule tabs. The Action tab is where you will configure the response to an alert such as a broadcast notification or the running of an executable program.

It is not necessary to use traditional Universal Naming Convention (UNC) naming when completing the Net Name field. The NetBIOS name is sufficient.

You can configure the Alert view in Performance Monitor to electronically page you when certain conditions occur — such as every time processor utilization exceeds 90 percent. To do this, you would create a batch file that sends e-mail to you when this condition is met. You would then configure your e-mail service to page you when you receive this type of e-mail. I've seen this accomplished with third-party e-mail/pager services such as Message Flash.

Logs

What appears to be the driest aspect of Performance Monitor — logging — is actually one of the most powerful. You configure Performance Monitor to capture data in a semi-binary/semi-delimited file that can be used for performance analysis via Counter Logs (see Figure 18-9). The log files you create and save to disk will enable you to detect bottlenecks and the causes of declining system performance.

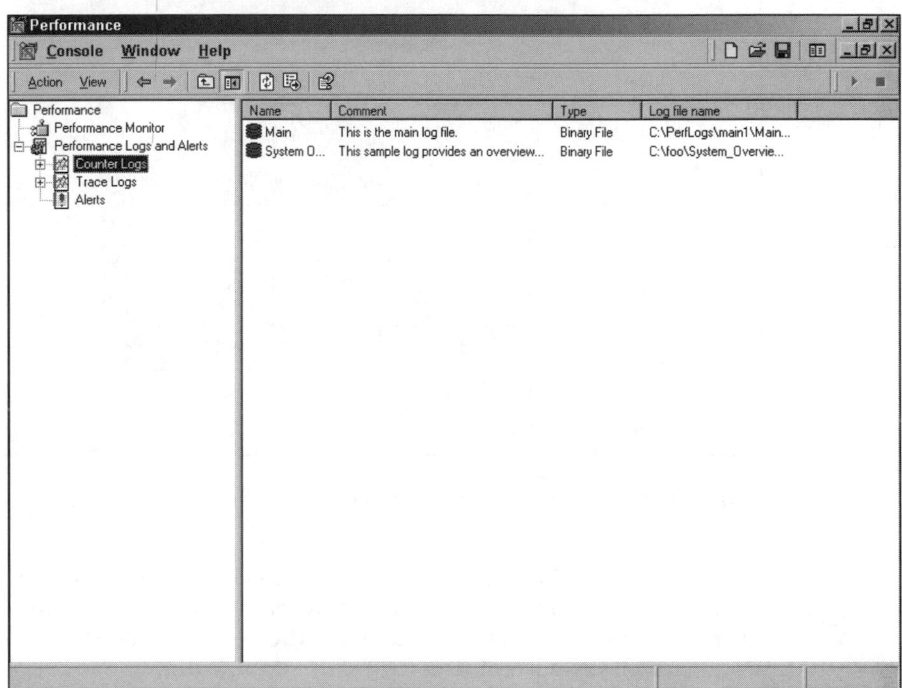

Figure 18-9: Counter Logs

A new feature in Windows 2000 Server, Trace Logs, enables you to trace infrastructure-level activity such as System activity (shown in Figure 18-10), including Process, Thread, Disk I/O, Network TCP/IP, Page faults, and File I/O. You may also trace General infrastructure activity, including

- Active Directory: Kerberos
- Active Directory: NetLogon
- Active Directory: SAM
- Local Security Authority (LSA)
- Windows NT Active Directory Service

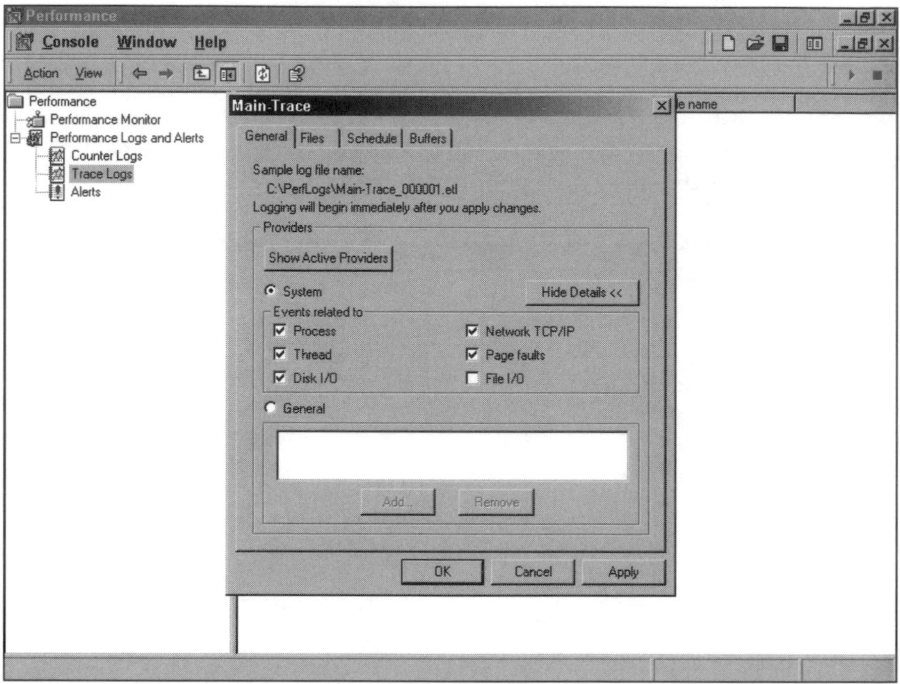

Figure 18-10: Trace Log — System Setting

In the old days of Windows NT Server 4.0, Performance Monitor ran as an application, not a service. That meant when you were logging information over a long period of time (say a week), the Performance Monitor logging would stop if the current user logged off of the Windows NT Server that was performing the logging. During my weekly visits to client sites, more than once I was surprised to see the logging I had so carefully set up and initiated was nowhere to be found. Ouch! I used the Monitor application (MONITOR.EXE) found in the Windows NT Server 4.0 Resource Kit to turn the Performance Monitor application into a service. With that, my logging activity would continue without anyone logged onto the Windows NT Server 4.0 machine. This approach worked very well.

But all that has changed with the arrival of Windows 2000 Server. This ability to treat Performance Monitor as a service and not an application is now handled via the Performance Logs and Alerts service (see Figure 18-11).

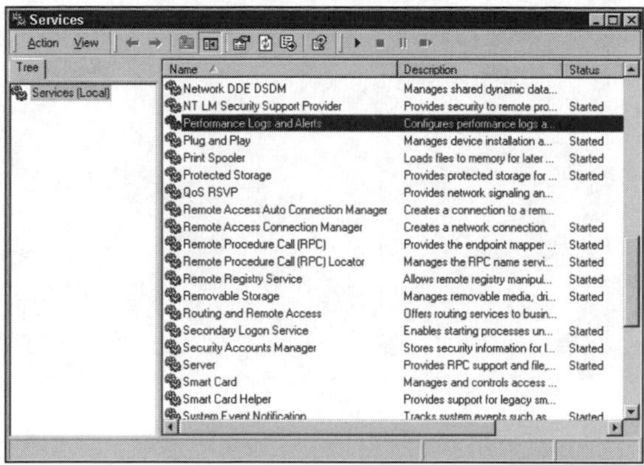

Figure 18-11: Performance Logs and Alerts service

Report

The Report view (see Figure 18-12) displays counters with their current values. Averaged counters display the average value during the time measurement interval (known as the *time window*). Instantaneous counters display ending values that are recorded at the end of the time measurement interval. Choose Report by selecting the Report Display button on the Performance Monitor toolbar.

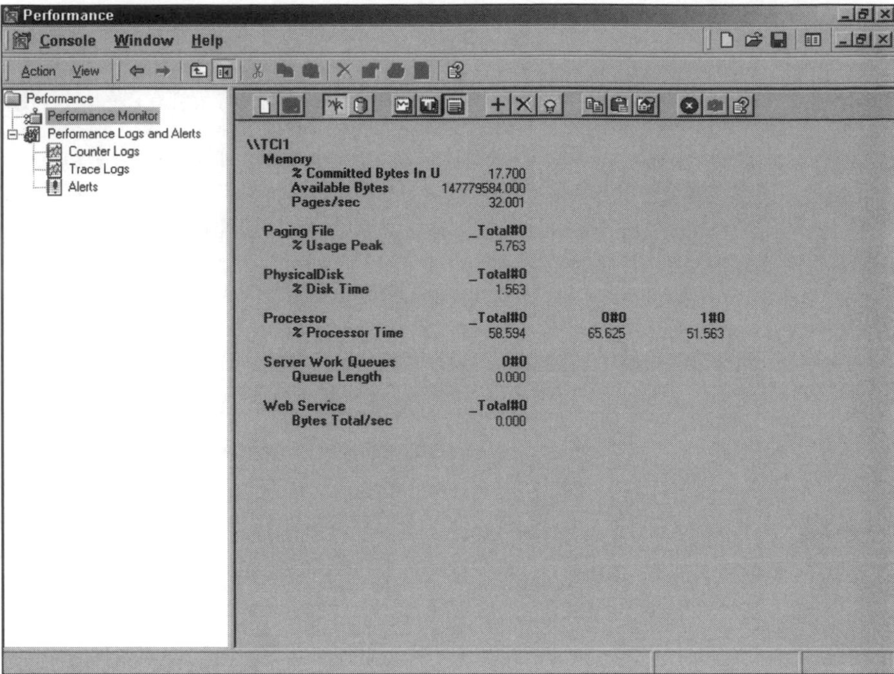

Figure 18-12: Report view

Data Collection and Interpretation

I've heard it expressed the following way by a U.S. ski team member whom I had the good fortune to know: "Getting out the door is the hardest step; the rest is duck soup." While this individual was referring to cross-country ski training, the same analogy can be applied to using Performance Monitor.

You would be amazed how many of my students from the MCSE certification world learn a lot about Performance Monitor but don't even launch it at work. Why? I'm not sure, but clearly, launching Performance Monitor from the Administrative Tools program group is the difficult part; the rest is duck soup.

Collecting data

Collecting data is obviously a critical step that must be performed correctly to ensure valid and meaningful analysis. Here are some suggested steps for you to follow so that your data is collected properly.

Step 1: Creating a baseline

You might question the value of proactively collecting data when nothing is wrong. You might say, "Don't we already have enough data in this world?" and, "I'm trying to reduce the amount of data I collect." Well, do a 180-degree turn. Collecting data proactively before system performance issues emerge gives you the easiest, cheapest, and cleanest data you will ever collect. If you start your data collection once system performance problems appear, you are looking at a dance with dirty data. That is because you have no baseline to which you can compare your current predicament. A baseline is created by capturing system-related information early in the life cycle of the system. This baseline is the basis from which all future comparisons are made. It's similar to your dental records. Your early records provide the baseline information that all future dentists will use to track your dental progress. Further, your Performance Monitor baseline and subsequent data can be used by pathologists to help determine your system's cause of death (should it die prematurely).

Change the default time interval in Performance Monitor from 15 seconds to 600 seconds for your baseline data collection. Observing a data point every ten minutes is sufficient for baseline analysis. Longer time intervals will dramatically reduce the size of your baseline data file. Just by collecting the objects I recommend next, you arrange that each data point adds approximately 30K to 50K to the size of your baseline data file. Even with this time interval recommendation, you will have a very large data file at the end of your monitoring period (especially if you perform a 7-day, 24-hour baseline capture).

Now is a good time to become familiar with the time interval setting in Performance Monitor. Consider the following exercise: Start one Performance Monitor session and chart the default object:counter (Processor:% Processor Utilization) at the default time interval. Launch a second version of Performance Monitor and, using the same object:counter, set the interval to 600 seconds. Let both of these Performance Monitor sessions run for an hour, and then compare the results. Did the longer interval of 600 seconds help or hinder the trend line associated with processor utilization activity? You be the judge.

I would highly recommend you consider storing your Performance Monitor data files on a removable hard disk. That way, you don't use precious secondary storage. Plus, if you are a Windows 2000 Server consultant, you can take the removable hard drive back to the office and analyze your client's data on your own system. In fact, you can build a library of removable drives that hold client performance data. That's something your clients will appreciate in case of a fire or flood. You will benefit directly from building such a reference library because you can easily compare the performance of one client site against the performance of another.

Step 2: Capturing baseline objects

You must select objects to create your baseline capture (see Table 18-1). The counters associated with these objects will be viewed in the future using the Chart or Report view. In addition to defining these core objects that should be captured as part of your baseline, I've rated these counters according to whether you are a beginner, power user, expert user, or a super-engineer, which should help you understand how the object applies to you. Note that this is a generic object rating that I've created based on my research and experience. Individual counters within these objects may have significantly different ratings.

Table 18-1 Core Objects to Capture via Performance Monitor Logging

Object	*Description*	*User Level*
Cache	Primary memory area that typically holds such items as recently used documents and file pages, data. This is analogous to cache memory found in NetWare-based servers. Caching file pages dramatically improves access time (no secondary storage activity!).	Power User
Logical Disk	Logical views of disk space, including disk partitions. This is how you analyze performance matters relating to contiguous secondary storage. A logical disk is assigned a drive letter.	Beginner
Memory	Enables you to analyze performance matters relating to real memory. Includes both primary (RAM) and virtual (paging file) memory.	Beginner
Network Segment	Provides the capability to monitor network activity on the specific cable segment on which the Windows 2000 Server machine is located. The counters are similar to the measurement tools provided in Network Monitor. This object is added when the Network Monitor Agent service is added to your Windows 2000 Server.	Beginner
Network Interface	Includes counters that measure bytes and packets sent and received by the network adapter card on a TCP/IP network. This object is added when you install the SNMP service on your Windows 2000 server (assuming you are using the TCP/IP protocol).	Power User

Object	Description	User Level
Objects	Relates to system software objects. Windows 2000 Server has an object view of the world and sees active system components as objects. Objects have properties and are subject to access control restrictions imposed by Windows 2000 Server security. Each object steals memory to store basic object information. Therein lies the concern — how much memory are objects stealing?	Beginner
Physical Disk	Secondary storage such as hard disks, RAID arrays. Will contain at least one (and likely more) logical partition.	Beginner
Process	A software object that is an active or running program. A process is created when a user application or a Windows 2000 Server service is run.	Beginner
Processor	The central processing unit (CPU). Given that Windows 2000 Server has a scalable architecture, this object can measure multiple CPUs. Multiple CPUs are considered instances when you are viewing a specific counter associated with this object.	Beginner
Redirector	Manages network connections between your computer and others.	Beginner
Server Work Queues	Essentially contain counters used to measure processor congestion on your Windows 2000 Server. Also used to measure how busy your server is, in terms of sending and receiving bytes from network clients.	Power User
System	Counters to measure activity on system hardware and software. For example, the System Uptime counter measures (in seconds) the total time that Windows 2000 Server has been running since the last reboot. This object includes many counters that apply to all of the processor activity on the computer.	Beginner
Thread	The basic unit of execution. Every running process contains one or more threads. Multiple threads within a process mean multithreading.	Beginner

Continued

Table 18-1 *(continued)*

Object	*Description*	*User Level*
Others	Includes specific objects related to applications such as SQL Server and Exchange. Developers are encouraged to write Performance Monitor objects to provide application-specific monitoring capabilities. To analyze the protocols discussed later in this chapter, you need to collect these additional objects: NetBEUI, NWLink IPX, TCP, and UDP.	Beginner to Super-Engineer

Step 3: Adding to your baseline

Additional data collection activity should occur on a regular basis during the life of your Windows 2000 Server system. You might collect baseline data weekly if you are a large organization or monthly if you are a smaller organization. There are two ways to collect additional data: log on to a new Performance Monitor data file or add to the existing Performance Monitor baseline data file. The choice is yours. By creating a new log file, you separate the time periods in which you collected the data. Plus, you can more easily observe the data by tiling the Performance Monitor chart of the updated data against a chart of the baseline data. See my comments near the end of this chapter under the section "Running multiple Performance Monitors" regarding running two Performance Monitor sessions.

Step 4: Creating a new baseline

Don't forget to create new baseline measurements when significant additions or subtractions are made to the system. What is the rule for starting a new baseline measurement? Think of it as Economics 101 and the demand curve. Normal activity is reflected by movements up and down the demand curve (such as when product prices are high, or demand is less). This is analogous to day-to-day system operations. However, in economics, when the fundamental or underlying relationship between consumer and product changes, there is a shift in the demand curve (such as when the introduction of new technology redefines the product). So think of a shift in the demand curve in economics as an event that's analogous to creating a new baseline measurement in Performance Monitor. Such major events might include the following:

- **A server upgrade to a new, more powerful server.** Obviously your old baseline data, based on the older server, won't be meaningful when compared against system data collected by the newer, more powerful server.
- **Additional servers.** Suppose you keep the existing server that has performed Performance Monitoring activities for a period of time, but

you add new servers to your site to take over certain functions. A good example of this is Microsoft System Management Server (SMS). Small sites often deploy SMS using a primary domain controller (PDC) running both SMS and Microsoft SQL Server. That's a BackOffice combination guaranteed to strain servers under the most ideal conditions. Assuming you collected your baseline data under this scenario, and then you acquired another two servers to spread the SMS/SQL Server load, it's now time to create a new Performance Monitor baseline measurement. In fact, Microsoft recommends that the PDC be used strictly for such activities as authentication and replication. We assume the two new servers, acting as member servers, would run SMS and SQL Server, respectively. The original baseline data is no longer meaningful when compared to any future performance data collected on your PDC. Thus the need to create a new baseline.

- **Major Capital Additions.** From an accounting point of view, we might consider creating a new baseline when we make significant capital additions to our network. For example, adding an expensive switch might forever alter (er, improve) the performance of your network. Such an addition might render your original baseline meaningless.

Interpreting your data

Not surprisingly, capturing baseline data via Performance Monitor logging is the easy part. The difficult part is analyzing the data. Therein lie the basics of quantitative analysis. Follow this discussion, and you will be a master Windows 2000 Server performance analyzer before you know it!

Logged data captured by Performance Monitor isn't very useful by itself. You must chart the counters contained within the objects, and in many cases, specific instances within the counters. Plus, for really meaningful performance analysis, you must have a solid data set, taken as samples over time. When all of these dimensions are in place, you can conduct serious data interpretation. For example, many of the object:counters to be described speak toward adequate system performance as a function of primary memory (RAM). When tracked over time and a valid baseline exists, you can easily determine at what point your system's performance took a nosedive (about the time you started using SQL Server for more purposes than serving as a data repository for SMS).

Tip

Don't underestimate your simplest, and in many ways, most important data interpreter. I'm speaking about the kind that talks back — the end user. While end users will quickly bring system performance matters to your attention, the business manager in all of us knows this is perhaps your most expensive form of system performance analysis: end users not doing their jobs efficiently and complaining about the computer system to you. Isn't it better to proactively manage your system via performance analysis with Performance Monitor than disgruntled end users?

Table 18-2 depicts a "quick and dirty" guide to analyzing your Performance Monitor log. I recommend you chart these items for the best viewing. Once that is accomplished, you will have a quick view of the health of your Windows 2000 Server and network.

Table 18-2 "Quick and Dirty" Analysis

Object	*Counter*	*User Level*
Cache	Data Map Hits %	Super-Engineer
Logical Disk	Avg. Disk Queue Length	Beginner
Memory	Pages/sec	Beginner
Network Interface	Bytes Total/sec	Power User
Objects	Processes	Beginner
Physical Disk	Avg. Disk Queue Length	Beginner
Processor	% Processor Time	Beginner
System	System Up Time	Beginner
Redirector	Bytes Total/sec	Beginner
Server	Bytes Total/sec	Beginner

Here is a description (in simple English to the extent possible) of object:counters.

Cache:Data Map Hits %

This is an advanced counter oriented toward the super-engineers who want to know the percentage of data maps in cache memory that were resolved without calling out to secondary storage to retrieve a page. In simple terms, the system found the page in primary storage. This is a good value to monitor over time, enabling you to determine if your system needs more primary storage (RAM).

Logical Disk:Avg. Disk Queue Length

This reflects the number of requests outstanding over the time measurement interval. Basically this refers to read and write requests awaiting service. This is a great value to track over time and enables you to determine how your hard disk is performing.

Memory:Pages/sec

Basically this object:counter is used to determine if you have a memory shortage. This is an excellent object:counter to track over time, as you can pinpoint deterioration (as a function of memory problems) in your system's performance if this counter value increases. Technically speaking, this counter measures the number of pages read to or written from secondary storage (disk) when Windows 2000 Server couldn't find the requested information in primary memory (RAM). This is an important counter to monitor to see if your system is generating too many hard page faults (having to go out and retrieve information from secondary storage). In surfer lingo (ocean surfing, not Web surfing), this counter is used to measure thrashing (excessive memory pressure).

Network Interface:Bytes Total/sec

This refers to the number of bytes per second that were sent and received by the Network Interface. Here we are basically observing activity at layer one of the Open Systems Interconnection (OSI) Model (see Figure 18-13). Layer one of the OSI model is known as the physical layer. In essence, this object:counter measures how busy your network interface card is, and it should be tracked over time. Analyzing this counter would enable you to determine whether you need to add extra items such as another NIC card. Note that this value is selected by instance (with the instance being your adapters).

Application	E-Mail application
Presentation	
Session	
Transport	
Network	
Data Link	
Physical	Network adapter cards

Figure 18-13: The OSI model

Objects:Processes

This reflects the number of programs running at the moment the measurement is taken. Technically speaking, it is the number of processes running on the computer when the data was collected. But don't forget that each process is essentially a program.

This value can also be calculated manually by adding up the Image Names in the Process tab sheet in the Task Manager dialog box.

Physical Disk:Avg. Disk Queue Length

This is similar in meaning to the Logical Disk:Avg. Disk Queue Length just described. The primary difference is that the instance category lists your physical disk(s).

Processor:% Processor Time

This object:counter reflects how busy the processor is. This is selected by instance (individual processors). Think of this object:counter as the percentage (or fraction) of time the processor is accomplishing meaningful work. Technically, this counter measures non-idle threads (threads where meaningful work is being accomplished). Remember that idle threads are run when no meaningful work awaits the processor (analogous to treading water in swimming!). If this value is over 75 percent on a long-term basis (measured in days and weeks), the processor is a bottleneck and should be upgraded.

If indeed the processor is a bottleneck, you can bank on the following strategies:

- **Application server.** Add multiple processors. Assuming Windows 2000 Server is being used as an application server, the applications that are running locally on the server are consuming significant processor time. Given Windows 2000 Server's symmetrical multiprocessing (SMP) architecture, you will directly benefit by adding multiple processors and having the processor load spread over several processors.
- **File and print server.** Those with NetWare backgrounds know that file and print servers typically have lower processor utilization rates than application servers. I've seen many NetWare servers with processor utilization rates hovering near zero percent! That is because the file and print server is not doing anything (literally). However, assuming you experience a processor bottleneck, as measured by Processor:% Processor Time when using Windows 2000 Server as a file and print server, then you need to add a faster processor.
- **Multiple servers.** Windows 2000 Advanced Server and Datacenter Server usher in a new era of clustering technology (see Figure 18-14). Clustering can free up the processor on a single server. Essentially, the processor load is distributed over multiple Windows 2000 Servers. Not ready to implement Windows 2000 Server–based clustering yet? Then offload some of your processes to other servers (a great BackOffice example is to place Systems Management Server on one server and SQL Server on another).

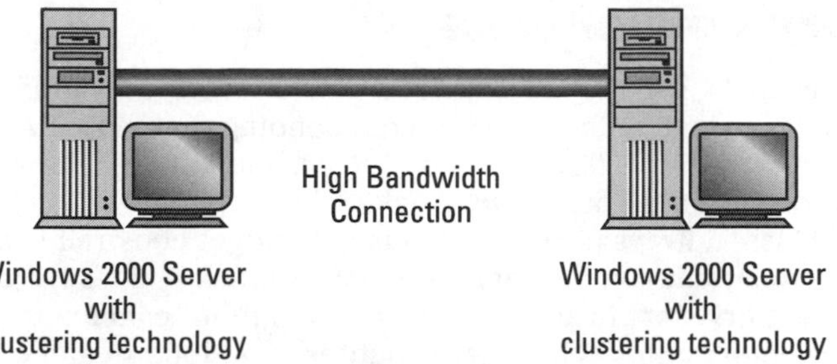

Figure 18-14: Windows 2000 Advanced Server clustering

System:System Uptime

This object:counter provides an easy answer to the question, "How long has the server been running?" This measures the elapsed time that the server has been running since the last reboot or restart. Very useful.

Redirector:Bytes Total/sec

Found in the middle to lower levels of the OSI model, the Redirector manages network connections between your computer and others on the network. This counter measures the rate that the Redirector is processing bytes. It is a measure of how busy your network-related components are (from the network adapter card up through the protocol stack).

Server:Bytes Total/sec

This relates to the server service (a process that connects the local computer to network services). This is the rate that the server is sending and receiving bytes from the network. Thus, it is a measure of how busy the server is.

Now that you're armed with a few quick and dirty object:counters for analysis at a glance, let's go under the hood of Performance Monitor and examine the details by exploring more object:counters and performing analysis in different environments.

Performing In-Depth Analysis

Let's get down to the business of in-depth baseline performance analysis. Six areas are addressed: memory, processor, disk, network, analyzing protocols, and TCP/IP. Note I assume you have or will learn and use all of the counters discussed previously in the "quick and dirty" analysis section, so I won't repeat that discussion here. Don't forget that the counters are best interpreted when analyzed over time, not from the perspective of a single snapshot.

Memory bottlenecks

Sometimes making money as a Windows 2000 Server consultant is too easy. That's because I often find myself recommending that more RAM be added to the server. Windows 2000 Server loves RAM, and adding RAM is something of an elixir for what ails your server. Snake oil salespeople aside, just adding more RAM isn't always possible because of budget constraints and possible physical constraints on the computer. Ask yourself — does the server have enough memory slots to add more memory without cannibalizing your existing memory chips? The object:counters that follow can be used to help you justify adding RAM to your server (and if you report to the CFO or controller in your organization, you will want this type of quantitative analysis provided by Performance Monitor to justify your purchases!).

Besides just adding RAM to solve your memory bottlenecks, you can increase the size of your paging file if your secondary storage permits. In fact, Windows 2000 Server allows multiple paging files, but only one paging file can be located on a given partition. And don't forget that you can boost overall Windows 2000 Server performance when you place at least one paging file on (a) partition(s) separate from the partition on which the operating system is installed.

I almost forgot the third rule of Windows 2000 Server memory bottleneck consulting (the first two being to add more RAM and increase your paging file size). The third rule is to shut down unnecessary services and remove unnecessary protocols and drivers. Take services. On my Windows 2000 Server test machine, I was running Microsoft Exchange months after I had completed my need for this BackOffice application. However, several Microsoft Exchange services start automatically. Once I disabled the Microsoft Exchange services, I noticed a huge performance gain on my test server and my available memory climbed dramatically.

Trusting applications

Don't overlook the following question. How well do you trust your Windows 2000 Server applications? Many applications are memory incontinent (a.k.a. leaky apps). Poorly developed applications don't completely close out memory resources upon exit. An example of this would be a user who repeatedly opens and closes files in a word processing application. Soon, not all of the memory is recovered when the file is closed. And you have a leaky application! The counters presented in the text that follows help you detect leaky apps. Of course, once you discover a badly behaved leaky application, you are typically told to let the appropriate application software developer know that it needs to be fixed. Big help that is in the heat of the moment. But at least you know which applications are going to give your system bad gas!

Note that two general trends to look for in detecting memory bottlenecks are how virtual memory is being used and hard page faults. Virtual memory resides on secondary storage and is thus much slower than memory in primary storage. Hard page faults occur when Windows 2000 Server can't find information in physical memory and has to perform a physical disk read operation.

Guns and butter memory management

Also, be cognizant of how the guns and butter law from economics can be applied to Windows 2000 Server memory management. Guns and butter is an economic theorem wherein an economy can produce lots of guns or a lot of butter, but typically not a lot of both without production tradeoffs. In Windows 2000 Server memory management, this discussion applies to Windows 2000 Server applications. We like our Windows 2000 Server-based applications to be efficient. Simply stated, we like our applications to use as little real memory as possible without having to page out to secondary storage to retrieve data. If an application uses too little real memory, it has to frequently retrieve data from secondary storage (a page out). However, if an application uses too much real memory, it hogs memory from other applications that might use it. Note that guns and butter has been renamed to stadiums and schools in many cities that are struggling to keep their professional sports franchises and provide adequate education for schoolchildren, Seattle and San Francisco, for example.

Memory:Available Bytes

This instantaneous counter measures the amount of available free memory. The Virtual Memory Manager in Windows 2000 Server tries to minimize the memory footprint of the operating system and processes so that it can provide the greatest amount of free memory available. Not surprisingly, we like this value to be high and to have a minimum of 8MB free. Anything below that amount and you might suffer excessive paging. In addition to adding RAM to solve problems here, you can attempt to find the process that is hogging all of the memory. See the next two counters to accomplish this.

Process:Working Set

One counter to use in your hunt for memory-hogging applications is the Process:Working Set object:counter for the instance you select (such as NOTEPAD.EXE). When the Working Set counter for NOTEPAD.EXE is high, the Available Bytes counter will be lower (these counters have an inverse relationship).

For a really cool view of the Process:Working Set counter, set the Chart view to Histogram and add the Total instance for this counter in addition to the specific application instances you are monitoring. This view enables you to see how much working set memory the application is hogging relative to all working set memory for all applications and processes.

Note that a process's working set is the amount of physical memory that Windows 2000 Server has given it.

Process:Page Faults/sec

Here is yet another counter used for detecting memory-hogging applications and processes. A bad application that can't get along with Windows 2000 Server's memory management model might well be causing a high rate of page faults (that is, retrieving data from secondary storage instead of caching frequently accessed data in real memory). To detect such an offender, select this counter and the appropriate instance (such as WORDPAD.EXE). Chart the TOTAL instance and display this scenario as a histogram chart.

An easy and informal way to detect your memory-hogging applications is to use Task Manager and view the Processes tab sheet. Visually scan the list for which processes are using the most memory. Take notes and periodically revisit this tab sheet to re-evaluate. Be advised that this is a very informal approach that might not meet your needs.

Memory:Committed Bytes

This is an easy definition. This counter refers to the amount of virtual memory that is committed as opposed to reserved. The commitment can be to physical RAM or page file space. This memory is unavailable for other purposes. We like to see this counter value remain low.

Memory:Pool Non-paged Bytes

Remember how system-critical activities couldn't be paged out to virtual memory? Then this is the counter for you! Basically, critical operating system components accomplish their tasks in this memory area. We like this counter value to remain stable.

Process:Page File Bytes

This counter, with the Total instance selected, enables you to witness the dramatic growth that occurs in page file size when there is a memory shortage. Be sure to chart this as a line in Performance Monitor and watch that positive slope once you hit a severe system memory shortage!

Memory:Pages/sec is a very important counter for this area and was defined early in the "quick and dirty" analysis section.

Now is a good time to launch Performance Monitor and create a chart with the seven counters just listed. Run this session for at least a day and see if you can, at a glance, observe some of the behaviors previously discussed regarding memory consumption. Of course as part of this exercise, I assume that you are using your server for ordinary and necessary activities (that is, generating some form of system activity) to make this exercise meaningful.

Feeling sadistic? Then set the MAXMEM parameter on your friends' Windows 2000 Server boot.ini file to reduce the amount of available physical memory. Watch them squirm when they can't figure out why performance has dropped so fast since the last reboot. The syntax is /MAXMEM=24 if you want to restrict

Windows 2000 Server to 24MB of RAM. This parameter is placed on the multi() operating system selection line. Ah, this stunt brings back memories of short-sheeting fellow campers in my youth during summer camp in the Texas hill country. Of course, use this secret in good faith. Hey—maybe spring this exercise as an advanced job interview "hands-on" test for a superstar Windows 2000 Server systems engineer. See if the candidate can detect the cause of the memory shortage.

Processor bottlenecks

Processor bottlenecks are not as common as you think. But that doesn't sell well on Madison Avenue, where ad agencies lead many of us to believe the latest Intel processor will solve all our problems. While this discussion on processor bottlenecks is important, take it with a grain of salt. Looking for a processor bottleneck is where we arrive at in performance analysis, not where we start. In the works of New Age guru Deepak Chopra, it is the journey of discovery that is important; discovery is a big part of mastering Performance Monitor. The rule is, don't assume that you have a processor bottleneck. Discover that you have a processor bottleneck.

In fact, the great challenge you face is to recognize a processor bottleneck. Keep in mind when studying the counters that follow that it's critical you run the Performance Monitor logging function during busy times. For larger organizations, you can probably justify 7/24 logging periods. For smaller organizations that basically adhere to 40-hour work weeks, consider using the AT command to automatically start and stop Performance Monitor logging during working hours.

As a processor-bottleneck sleuth, look for the likely suspects. These include CPU-bound applications as well as processes, drivers, and interrupts. CPU-bound applications are processor utilization hogs. You know the ones, like the slide show feature in the Microsoft PowerPoint application. Have you ever been giving a speech to a group using a Microsoft PowerPoint slide show and hotkeyed over to another application to demo (say SQL Server). Were you disappointed with the speed at which the other application ran? Congratulations. You've just met a CPU-bound application and it's taking advantage of your processor. Other problems are excessive interrupts from faulty hardware or a good old IRQ conflict between hardware devices.

Memory problems have a tricky way of hiding behind high processor use. Add more RAM to your Windows 2000 Server and you will often see your processor time drop dramatically. That's because page faults are reduced.

Those dazzling screen savers that ship with Windows 2000 Server are really adding to your processor load when they run. Do yourself a favor and don't use screen savers on your server. If you are concerned about your monitor suffering from screen burn, simply turn off the monitor when you aren't viewing it.

Processor:%Processor Time

The previous discussion on Processor:% Processor Time in the "quick and dirty" analysis applies to this discussion on processor bottlenecks. It is interesting to note that one of the great debates among network professionals today is what percentage of processor time is too high. In the Novell CNE program, you are taught that a sustained processor utilization rate in excess of 80 percent over a week (or greater period) suggests a processor bottleneck. Even Microsoft provides conflicting values. In the MCSE curriculum, certification candidates are instructed that a sustained %Processor Time value greater than 75 percent suggests a processor bottleneck. But the Microsoft Windows 2000 Workstation Resource Kit (for the 2000 version) states that a frequently observed 90 percent value for the % Processor Time counter is a bottleneck. "Whatevah," as they say back in Boston! Fact of the matter is that a sustained %Processor Value over 75 percent is ultimately going to be a source of trouble for you. And you guessed it. We like this counter value to stay low.

Processor:% Privileged Time

This is the time spent in Privileged mode running the Windows 2000 Server service layer, Windows 2000 Server Executive routines, and Windows 2000 Server Kernel activity. These are active or non-idle threads. We desire a low counter value here.

Processor:% User Time

This is basically just the opposite of the preceding counter. It is a way to view processor time (as a percentage) allocated to applications that are running and subsystem code that is executing. And let me take a moment to remind you that code executing in User mode *cannot* damage device drivers or the Windows 2000 Executive or Kernel. That's one of the things that make Windows 2000 Server so special. We seek a low counter value when tracking Processor:% User Time.

Here is where you have one up on your NetWare brethren. Remember an NLM (application) running under NetWare can crash the NetWare network operating system. Windows 2000 Server-based applications cannot crash the Windows 2000 Server operating system because applications run in a subsystem in User mode.

Processor:Interrupts/sec

Simply stated, the processor is subject to device interrupts. This counter is the number of interrupts per second. This is the type of counter that will be valuable to monitor over time. Hopefully, the counter value will remain at a consistent level.

System:Processor Queue Length

According to Microsoft, this is the instantaneous length of the processor queue in units of threads. Translated into English, this refers to queued threads that are waiting to be processed. If you are using a single-processor machine, then only one thread can be processed at a time by the processor. If more than two additional threads are queued, as measured by the object:counter, then you have a potential processor bottleneck.

Server Work Queues:Queue Length

Requests made to the Windows 2000 Server are work items. While work items are waiting to be processed, they are queued. This object:counter is the length of that queue. If you observe a value greater than four over a sustained period of time, you are suffering from processor congestion. We want this counter value to remain low.

Process:% Processor Time

This object:counter is the elapsed time, expressed as a percentage (%), that all of the threads of a process used the processor to execute instructions. Note that you would pick a process to measure by selecting from the list of instances. Examples of instances include SQLEXEC (if you are running SQL Server) and NOTEPAD (if you are running the Notepad application). By selecting specific instances and monitoring them over time, you can observe if the process has become an unruly beast or if it is well behaved.

Thread:% Processor Time

This object:counter is the percentage of elapsed time that a thread used the processor to execute its instructions. To effectively use this command, you select one of the threads (in the Instance field in the Add Counters dialog box in Performance Monitor). Examples of threads you might select would include thread zero if you are running Notepad (a single-threaded application) or any of threads zero to six if your are running the SQLEXEC process. This counter enables us to investigate unruly processes down to the thread level. Of course I would never admit to anyone that's how I spent my summer vacation!

Disk bottlenecks

Admit it, detecting disk bottlenecks was probably one of the first attempts at performance analysis that you undertook. You know the old trick from the Windows for Workgroups (WFW) 3.*x* days. You tiled two windows in File Manager and copied a large set of files from one hard disk to another. Then you turned on 32-bit disk access, restarted WFW, performed the same file copy exercise, and wowed your audience by showing a dramatic performance increase. It was a simple trick and a simple way to demonstrate disk bottlenecks. Today it's harder to repeat this exact trick because

Windows 2000 Server only uses 32-bit disk access, eliminating a simple bottleneck culprit.

You can use an old dog for new tricks! Take the preceding example, modify it slightly, and apply it to your Windows 2000 Server computing environment. Here is what you should do: First, add the counters discussed in this section to a Performance Monitor chart. Then perform an enormous file copy operation from one physical disk to another (c: to d: drive, c: to a: drive, or even a local drive to a network drive). Monitor the counters that follow and make appropriate observations. Then perform this exercise under the same set of circumstances at a future date (say, three months later). How do the charted counters look three months later compared to your original chart? Any declines or improvements in disk-related performance?

Detecting disk bottlenecks is also a function of the different buses on the system, such as I/O and devices. The controller card and the disk access time play into any disk bottleneck scenario. Sometimes the fix is as simple as upgrading your existing controller card or even adding another controller card for a second disk. At other times the solution is more complex, such as upgrading your motherboard so that you can employ the latest system I/O bus architectural standards. Here are some valuable counters for both the Logical and Physical Disk objects to use in your quest to detect and mitigate disk bottlenecks.

LogicalDisk:% Disk Time and PhysicalDisk:% Disk Time

Finally, a simple definition. This is the percentage of time the disk drive is busy with read and write requests. Note that these two counters are selected on an Instance basis (physical hard disk for PhysicalDisk and partitions for LogicalDisk). It is important this counter value remains low (under 50 percent could be considered acceptable).

LogicalDisk:Disk Queue Length and PhysicalDisk:Disk Queue Length

This is a snapshot of the number of requests outstanding on the disk. It refers to disk-related requests (for example, read or write). These counters are selected on a per-Instance basis. We want to avoid having this counter value exceed two (we want the counter to remain low).

LogicalDisk:Avg. Disk Bytes/Transfer and PhysicalDisk:Avg. Disk Bytes/Transfer

This is an interesting value and speaks to both the performance of your disk and the type of bus used on your computer (such as IDE or SCSI). This is the average number of bytes, during read and write operations, that are transferred to or from the disk. We want this counter value to be high, as it demonstrates efficient throughput.

LogicalDisk:Disk Bytes/sec and PhysicalDisk:Disk Bytes/sec

Similar to the preceding counter, this is the rate that the disk bytes are transferred to and from your disk. Not surprisingly, we want this counter value to be high.

Network bottlenecks

A lot of us became network professionals thinking we'd spend a great deal of time troubleshooting network bottlenecks, only to find ourselves in the midst of singing the break-fix blues. It's safe to say that when you really start to find and fix network bottlenecks, you have "arrived" as a system engineer. You've earned your wings. Performance Monitor and the counters that follow are a great place to start, but network bottlenecks are typically major problems and require the use of a network analyzer (from Network General or others). You can use the Network Monitor tool, discussed in Chapter 19, that is provided free of charge in Windows 2000 Server to assist you in your troubleshooting efforts.

Server:Bytes Total/sec

Want to know how busy your server really is? This counter measures the number of bytes sent and received from the network wire per second. Although we like this value to be high, consider adding another network adapter card to the server if it is too high. Monitoring this counter over time will enable you to decide if another network adapter card is warranted.

Server:Logon/sec

This applies to larger environments. It is the rate of all server logons.

Server:Logons Total

With this counter, you can tell how many successful or unsuccessful service, interactive, and network logons have occurred since the last time the machine was rebooted.

Network Segment:% Network Utilization

This counter repeats a value that can be found in Network Monitor: the percentage of network bandwidth in use on this network segment. Remember that with Ethernet, this value will never approach 100 percent because of the silence that is created when packet collisions occur. In fact, we like to see this value remain below 30 percent, although it can grow larger on sophisticated networks that employ switches.

Network Interface:Bytes Sent/sec

This one almost defines itself. It is the number of bytes sent via the network adapter per second. Essentially, this counter provides the rate at which bytes are being sent. It is a measure of throughput and can be measured on a per-network adapter card instance.

The counter Network Interface:Bytes Total/sec, defined in the "quick and dirty" analysis section, applies to this section on network bottlenecks.

Analyzing protocols

The Windows 2000 Server Network Monitor application or some other network analysis sniffer tool typically handles protocol analysis. However, Performance Monitor enables you to engage in some rough protocol-related analysis. Note that the first three counters are presented for both NetBEUI and NWLink IPX.

NetBEUI:Bytes Total/sec and NWLink IPX: Bytes Total/sec

This is the number of bytes sent to and received from the network, and is a throughput measure. This counter is charted by instance (representing the network adapter cards to which this protocol has been bound).

NetBEUI:Datagrams/sec and NWLink IPX:Datagrams/sec

A datagram is a connectionless packet (meaning delivery is not guaranteed). These counters measure the rate at which datagrams are sent and received. It's really reflecting the rate at which datagrams are being processed by the computer.

NetBEUI:Frames/sec and NWLink IPX:Frames/sec

This is the rate at which packets are processed by the computer. We like this value to be high, but not too high. This counter should be measured over time with an eagle eye cast on the trend line when displayed in Performance Monitor Chart view.

TCP:Segments/sec

This basically manages the rate at which TCP/IP packets are sent and received. Again, a high value is good but too high is detrimental. You can define "too high" for yourself by measuring and learning about the behavior of this counter over time.

UDP:Datagrams/sec

This is the rate at which UDP datagrams (connectionless packets) are sent and received by the computer. UDP packets are typically used in communication scenarios where reliability isn't mission critical, such as the streaming of video and sound. Because of its connectionless orientation, UDP packets are faster than TCP-based packets. In fact, UDP packets have a nasty habit of "butting in" and pushing TCP packets out of the way.

Network Interface:Output Queue Length

This value represents the backup of outbound packets at layer one of the OSI model (basically the network adapter). This counter value should remain below two.

Analysis in Different Computing Environments

In many ways, Windows 2000 Server is a "jack-of-all-trades" network operating system. In fact, I have heard it described as the minivan of NOSes, meaning it does a lot of things well and is superior in select areas. It competes strongly with NetWare in the file and print server area (see Figure 18-15). It competes head-on with the AS/400 and UNIX environments as an applications server. Depending on the way that you have implemented Windows 2000 Server in your organization, you will want to undertake the following analysis for either file and print or application server environments.

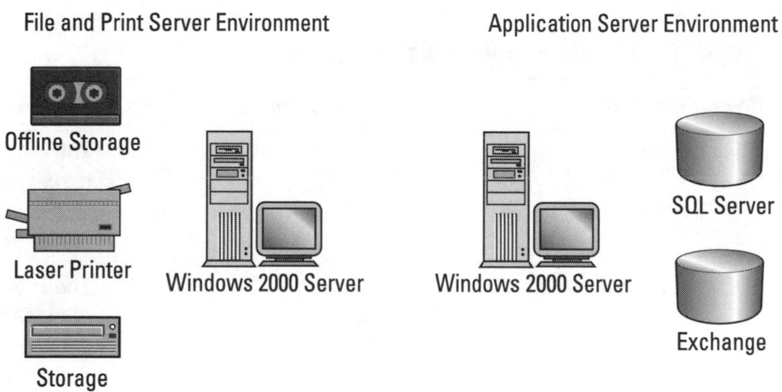

Figure 18-15: File and print server environment versus application server environment

File and print server environment analysis

In a file and print server environment, we are most concerned about server memory and the network subsystem. Our main concern with memory is caching. As always, the more memory the better, so we can cache more files.

With file and print servers, I strongly recommend you add a second network adapter when you have performance concerns in this area. I once worked with a manufacturer that had a large base of AutoCAD users. As you know, AutoCAD files are huge! Needless to say, adding a second network adapter card dramatically improved performance when it came to opening and saving AutoCAD files.

Once again, don't forget we need to track these trends over time (I repeat, an individual snapshot in time just isn't meaningful). When viewing your historical trend data, ask yourself these questions about your file and print server environment. Viewing the world this way might enable you to see the forest and not just the trees.

- How many users can your Windows 2000 Server file server support?
- Do users access the file server primarily to open and save data files?
- Do users download applications (such as by running network installations of Microsoft Word)?

The Performance Monitor counters in Table 18-3 are specifically oriented to understanding your file and print server environment. These should be tracked in addition to the "quick and dirty" and "in-depth baseline analysis" counters presented earlier.

Table 18-3 File and Print Server Counters

Workload Unit	*Performance Monitor Counter*	*Definition*
Disk activity	PhysicalDisk:% Disk Time	The time (on a percentage basis) the disk is busy with read and write requests
Average transaction size	PhysicalDisk:Avg. Disk Bytes/Transfer	The average number of bytes transferred during read and write operations
User sessions (concurrent)	Server:Server Sessions	Current server activity expressed by quantifying the number of active sessions on server

Workload Unit	***Performance Monitor Counter***	***Definition***
Network usage	Network Segment:% Network Utilization	Percentage of network bandwidth in use on a particular cable segment
Files open	Server:Files Open	On the server, the number of files currently open. A measure of server activity
Disk activity (read)	PhysicalDisk:% Disk Read Time	Percentage of time the disk is fulfilling read requests
Disk activity (write)	PhysicalDisk:% Disk Write Time	Percentage of time the disk is fulfilling write requests

Application server environment system performance

By far, our greatest concern is the processor in an application server environment. Application servers (see Table 18-4) typically run robust server-based programs such as SQL Server and other Microsoft BackOffice products. Consequently, the processor is consumed with application threads and can become a bottleneck on your network. An application server can directly benefit from adding multiple processors and distributing the workload. Memory is our second concern because the server will have memory allocated to both the operating system and the server-based applications (and services) that are running.

Table 18-4 Application Server Counters

Workload Unit	***Performance Monitor Counter***	***Definition***
Available memory	Memory:Available Bytes	The amount of real memory available
Average disk transaction size	PhysicalDisk:Avg. Disk Bytes/Transfer	The average number of bytes transferred during read and write operations

Continued

Table 18-4 *(continued)*

Workload Unit	*Performance Monitor Counter*	*Definition*
Average network transaction size	Will vary by protocol, such as NetBEUI:Frame Bytes/sec	The rate at which data bytes are processed by the computer
Cache usage	Cache:Copy Read Hits %	The percentage of Cache Read Requests that find their information in cache memory and don't need to perform a disk read
Disk activity	PhysicalDisk:% Disk Time	The time (on a percentage basis) the disk is busy with read and write requests
Network usage	Network Segment:% Network Utilization	The percentage of network bandwidth in use on a particular cable segment
Paging	Memory:Pages/sec	The number of pages read from or written to disk per second
Processor usage	Processor:% Processor Time	The processor utilization rate
User sessions (concurrent)	Server:Server Sessions	The number of current sessions on a server

Making Better Use of Performance Monitor

Now that you have created a baseline and charted the appropriate counters, it's time to discuss several ways to make better use of Performance Monitor.

Running multiple Performance Monitors

You might consider running multiple copies of Performance Monitor, each monitoring a different machine on your network. By doing so, you clearly create the data set you need to perform more detailed analysis, such as comparing and contrasting how different server machines behave. Essentially, you gather more information, allowing for more meaningful comparative analysis.

If you run multiple copies of Performance Monitor at the same time, you will most likely want to "tile" the Performance Monitor screens across your desktop so that you can observe the information in a meaningful way. I'd recommend that you tile horizontally because the Performance Monitor chart fills from left to right. Clearly, tiling vertically wouldn't be as meaningful.

If you are monitoring several machines, create a Performance Monitor Chart window for each machine being monitored. These windows can then be arranged on your desktop in an orderly manner so you can monitor these machines visually from a single desktop. Think of it as creating your own investment trading console. In the trading rooms at investment houses, numerous charts showing different financial trading indicators are displayed simultaneously on one or more CRT monitor screen. In fact, if you manage (and monitor) a large network, you might seriously consider setting up multiple CRT screens to increase the display area (and allow more Performance Monitor charts to be shown at once, as shown in Figure 18-16). Check with video card vendors such as Radius regarding the use of multiple CRTs with Windows 2000 Server.

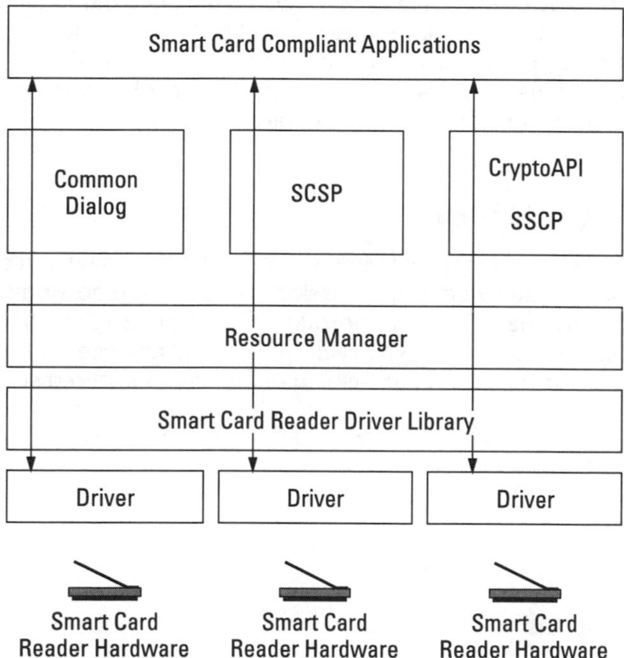

Figure 18-16: Multiple CRTs on a single machine

Don't forget that running multiple copies of Performance Monitor simultaneously on one machine enables you to dedicate that machine to performance monitoring (which is good) and avoid having each monitored machine run its own Performance Monitor session (and having each machine suffer an increased CPU load — which is bad).

Another reason to run multiple copies of Performance Monitor is that one Performance Monitor session can record a log while another Performance Monitor session reports current information on the statistics being collected in the log. In effect, you can chart counters of the objects you are logging in almost realtime. By almost, I mean that the Performance Monitor session which is doing the charting will only chart up to the point where it has conducted its initial read of the log file being created in the other Performance Monitor session. You would need to "relaunch" the Performance Monitor session that is performing the charting to have it display a later update of the other machine's logging activity. Similarly, you can run one copy of Performance Monitor to display historical logged data while another copy of Performance Monitor displays current charts with data (data you are catching in realtime). Don't forget to tile on your desktop by right-clicking the Taskbar and selecting Tile Windows Horizontally.

Consider running multiple copies of Performance Monitor to limit the size of log files during the baseline collection phase. I recently worked with a client that asked for an extensive baseline analysis of its system. The baseline file grew by nearly 50K every ten minutes. Given a baseline data collection period of seven days, it became apparent we would literally run out of available secondary storage on the first partition. The solution? Breaking the logging activity into two files using two Performance Monitor logging sessions enabled the data to be placed on two separate disk partitions.

Removing clutter

Cluttered charts in Performance Monitor are difficult to view and analyze (see Figure 18-17). You can run multiple sessions of Performance Monitor to create visually appealing charts. Each Performance Monitor session would contain a portion of the object:counters you seek to view and analyze. The point is to have several uncluttered screens instead of one very cluttered screen. Get it?

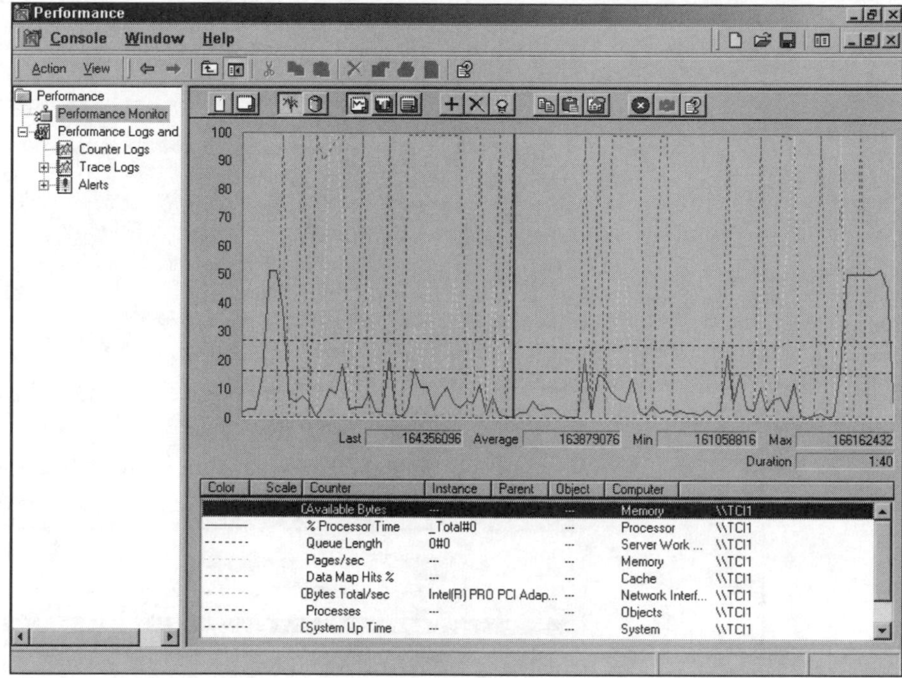

Figure 18-17: A cluttered chart in Performance Monitor

I'd recommend you limit your counters to six or fewer per chart so that you can easily see the data points being graphed (see Figure 18-18).

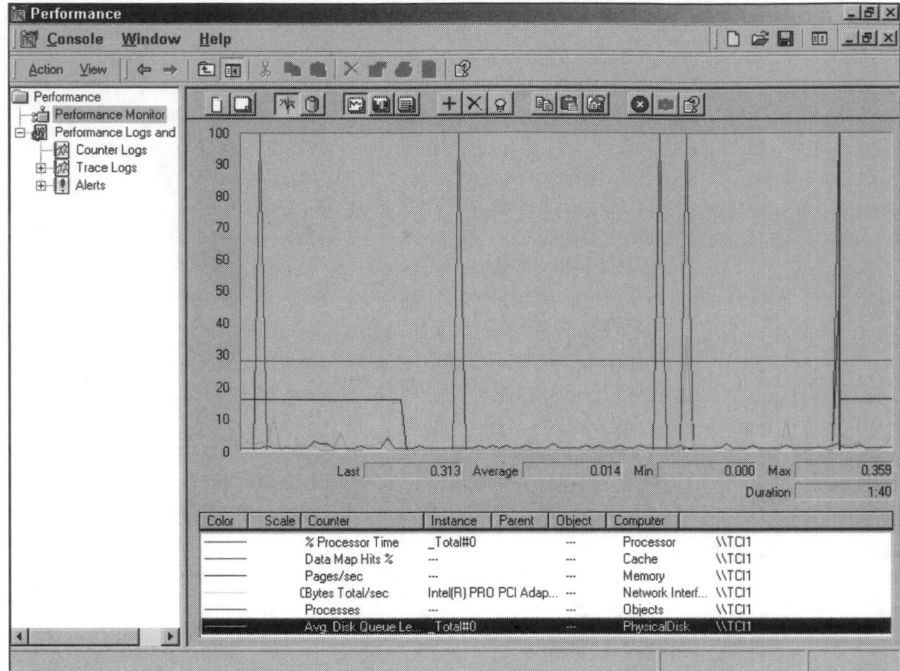

Figure 18-18: A reduced number of counters

Use the Ctrl+H keystroke when viewing charts in Performance Monitor. Performance Monitor power users know how quickly the Chart view can become cluttered. If you track more than several counters, the relatively limited chart area is impossible to read. As seen in the screen that follows, selecting a specific counter and pressing Ctrl+H simultaneously highlights the selected counter line (in bold white). The other lines retain their existing visual properties (thin, colored lines), but the highlighted line stands out dramatically in comparison. Another Ctrl+H tip is to scroll the selected counters using the up-arrow and down-arrow keys in the bottom portion of the Chart window (where the counters are listed). When you perform this scrolling action, the highlighted counter on the chart changes to reflect the counter you've selected from the list that follows. It's a great way to "hop" from counter to counter and view the chart line in bold white.

The key point to highlighting your chart information is to draw attention to specific information over other information (see Figure 18-19). By doing so, you make the chart and the information conveyed more meaningful.

Chapter 19

Network Monitor Secrets

In This Chapter

- Defining Network Monitor
- Network Monitor Basics
- Ongoing network monitoring
- Frame capture patterns
- Network analysis timing
- Network Monitor's artificial intelligence features
- Network analysis resources for continued learning
- Windows 2000 Server's Network Monitor versus System Management Server's (SMS) Network Monitor

Some areas of the technology industry are still immature. In the context of Windows 2000 Server, you will clearly see how this statement applies to Network Monitor's role in helping you manage your Windows 2000 Server network. Few network testing standards exist, and even fewer technical texts explain the finer points of packet analysis. Unfortunately, it is still the Wild West when it comes to implementing a sniffer analysis tool and analyzing frame captures.

This chapter will help you gain a deep understanding of the Network Monitoring tool included with Windows 2000 Server. By the end of this chapter, you will be more than adequately equipped to seize the day with your Network Monitor tool. Likewise, I hope your interest will have been piqued to discover more about frame trapping and packet analysis. But you are not left hanging. Several advanced resources, beyond the scope of this book, are listed for you to further study the mysterious world of network analysis via frame trapping and packet analysis.

Defining Network Monitoring

The lesson learned from the Watergate era is that power corrupts and absolute power corrupts absolutely. So you want to be very careful with

Network Monitor in Windows 2000 Server. This application is a reasonably powerful sniffer, warts and all. And a sniffer may spell trouble on your network when such a tool is used by inexperienced hands. Sniffers enable you to analyze network traffic at the packet level, potentially allowing others to trap packets and see unencrypted passwords. Let's just say that, in the wrong hands, Network Monitor absolutely corrupts.

On a positive note, Network Monitor is an advanced tool that, while too often used as a last resort in problem solving, can save your bacon big time! Network Monitor is used to provide statistics regarding network utilization and packet traffic as well as capture frames for analysis. The version of Network Monitor included with Windows 2000 Server is a crippled cousin to the full-featured version included with Microsoft System Management Server (SMS).

For comprehensive network analysis and monitoring, be sure to upgrade to SMS so that you can employ the full version of Network Monitor. In part, the reason for shipping a crippled edition of Network Monitor with Windows 2000 Server is to prevent unsavory users from trapping packets on a network-wide (actually segment-wide) basis. The crippled version of Network Monitor only allows you to capture frames sent to or from your computer (along with broadcast and multicast frames). At the end of this chapter, you will find a complete comparison between the Windows 2000 Server and SMS versions of Network Monitor.

Network Monitor basics

Network Monitor is installed either during the setup of Windows 2000 Server or from the Add/Remove Programs applet in Control Panel. In the Add/Remove Programs approach, Network Monitor is installed as Network Monitor Tools under the Management and Monitoring Tools selection in the Windows Components Wizard (see Figure 19-1).

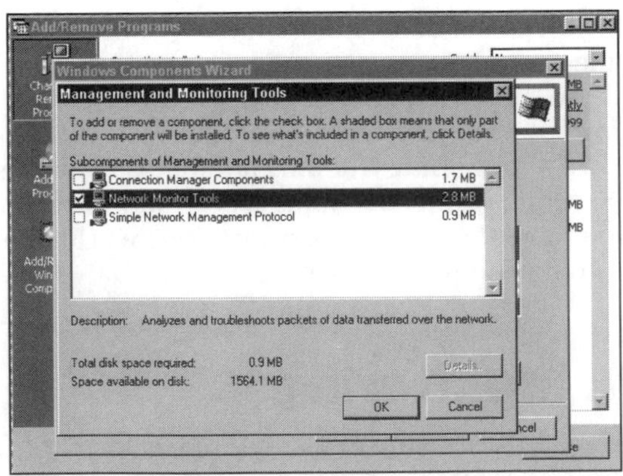

Figure 19-1: Installing Network Monitor

When starting the Network Monitor application in Windows 2000 Server (after you have installed it, of course), you select Network Monitor from the Administrative Tools program group. You will be presented with Network Monitor's default Capture window (see Figure 19-2).

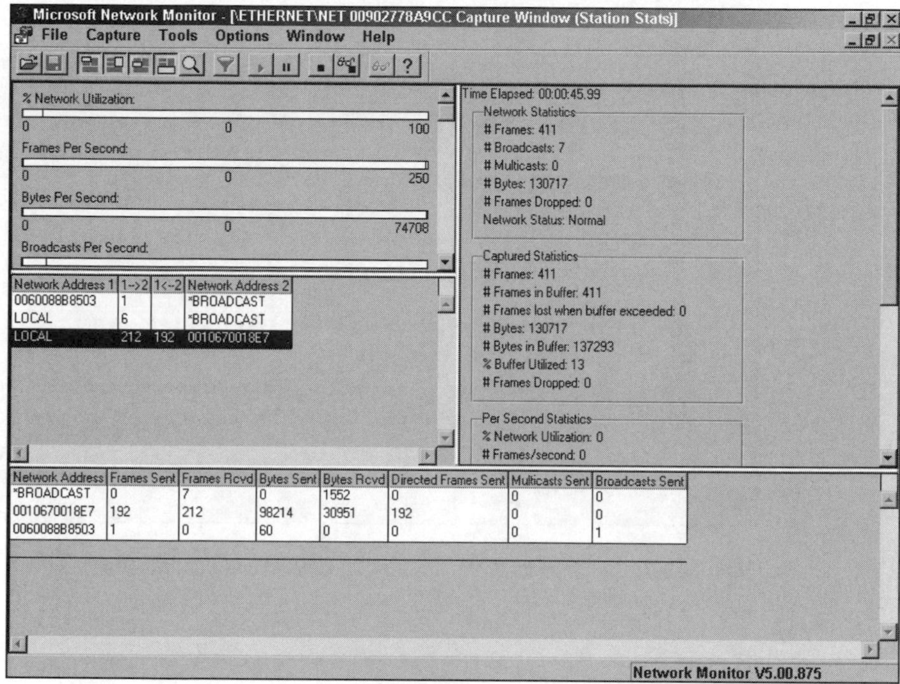

Figure 19-2: Network Monitor Capture window

Capture window components

Network Monitor provides several types of information in the Capture window (the default window at startup). The Capture window is divided into four parts (see Figure 19-3): Graph pane, Total Statistics pane, Session Statistics pane, and Station Statistics pane. Each of these four panes is discussed in the text that follows.

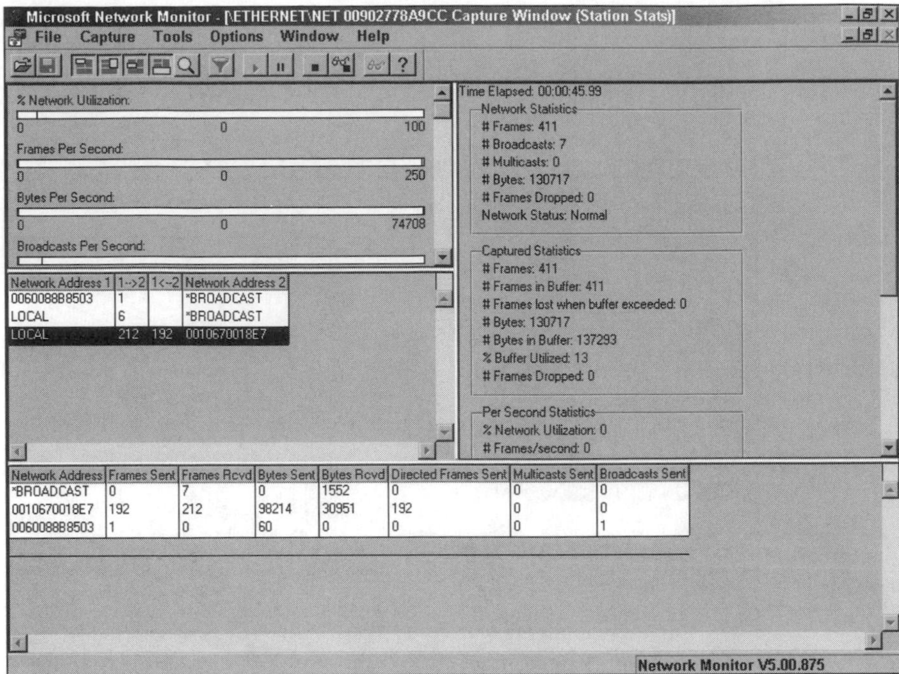

Figure 19-3: Components of the Capture window in Network Monitor

Graph

The upper left pane is the Graph pane; it depicts current activity occurring on the network in a thermometer-bar fashion.

Total statistics

The upper right pane is the Total Statistics pane, which displays total network activity detected since the capture process began. In the full-featured Network Monitor included with SMS, the frames depicted in the Total Statistics pane are the frames that are actually trapped, assuming no filtering is occurring (filtering will be discussed later in this chapter). In the crippled Network Monitor included with Windows 2000 Server, the Total Statistics pane presents network statistics for the entire network, but only traps the frames shown in the Captured Statistics area of the Total Statistics pane (again, assuming no filtering is occurring).

Session statistics

This pane, on the lower left, displays information about individual sessions occurring between two nodes. It is interesting to note that "sessions" means literal sessions wherein Network Address 1 and Network Address 2 (nodes) have negotiated and established a session.

Station statistics

This shows generic statistics about frames sent and received on a per-node basis. This pane is useful for determining at a glance who the worst offenders are on your network segment in terms of flooding the network with packets.

Capturing frames

Capturing frames is the art and science of trapping packets that will be meaningful to us. Typically, this is commenced by clicking the Start Capture button on the Network Monitor toolbar in the Capture window. This button looks very much like the Play button on a simple audiocassette recorder. You may also press the F10 key to begin a frame capture.

Network Monitor will capture frames until system memory is filled. However, you typically capture enough frames to show the condition you are trying to analyze. For example, suppose a workstation cannot successfully log onto the Windows 2000 Server network. After troubleshooting the obvious causes, such as an unconnected workstation, you decide to trap frames for more analysis. The steps are to basically have the workstation try to log onto the domain while Network Monitor is running on Windows 2000 Server.

Run the frame capture mode on Network Monitor on Windows 2000 Server from the moment you power on the workstation you intend to use for logon testing. This workstation will generate client initialization traffic from its startup (just after the power on system test or POST phase). For example, client initialization traffic might include renewing the leased IP address from the DHCP server. Do *not* wait to start capturing frames when the workstation in question is at the "Logon validation" stage (that is, showing the logon dialog box), or you will have missed some very important frame traffic that might help solve your problem.

Required hardware

To use Network Monitor, you must be physically attached to the network. This is stating the obvious, but if you are not attached to a network, you will not capture network traffic. To attach to a network, you must have some type of network adapter. This, of course, is typically a network adapter card placed in the computer and connected to the network media or cabling. If you have more than one network adapter card, you may select which one will be used with your current session of Network Monitor. You may do this via the Select a network dialog box found via the Networks menu option on the Capture menu (see Figure 19-4).

Something that isn't well known is that you may also run multiple sessions of Network Monitor simultaneously to monitor multiple network adapter cards. If you run multiple sessions of Network Monitor to accommodate multiple network adapter cards, be sure to tile the Network Monitor applications for easy viewing. To tile, right-click the taskbar and select either Tile Horizontally or Tile Vertically.

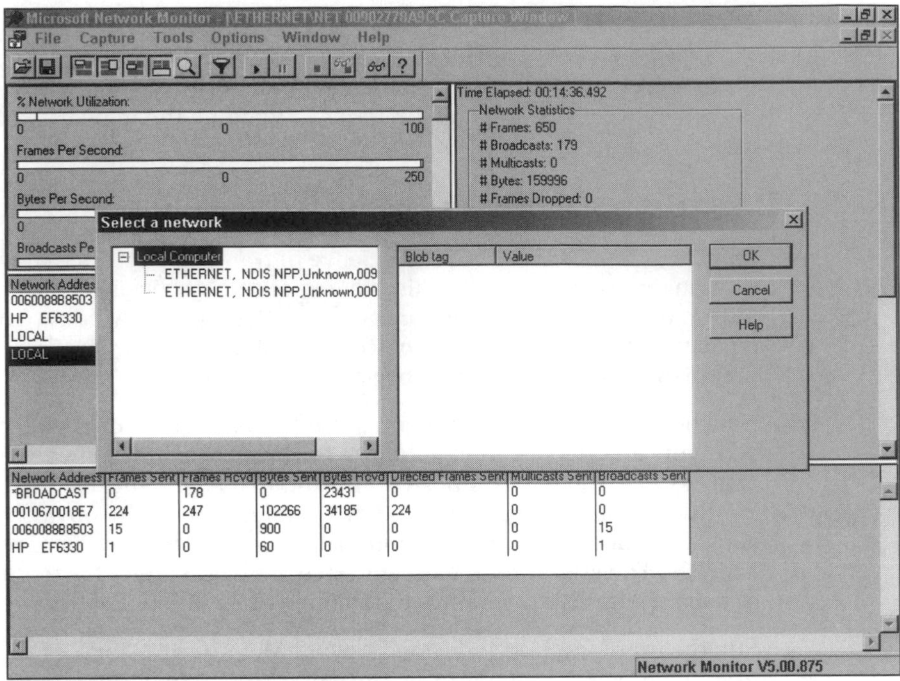

Figure 19-4: Select a network dialog box

Use an NDIS 4.0 driver on your network adapter card. If you have an NDIS 4.0 (or greater) driver installed on your network adapter card, Network Monitor captures in local mode. This means that only packets with the capturing computer's destination address are accepted. Previously, the capturing computer was placed in promiscuous mode, meaning each frame was evaluated whether it was destined for the capturing computer or not. Promiscuous mode increased processor utilization by up to 30 percent. A true bottleneck! This discussion applies to the crippled edition of Network Monitor included in Windows 2000 Server. The full version of Network Monitor contained in SMS supports captures of network-wide traffic. Note that the Hardware Compatibility List contains a list of network adapter cards successfully tested with Network Monitor.

As we approach the sunset of Windows NT Server and the dawn of Windows 2000 Server, most network adapter card manufacturers now provide NDIS drivers without any questions asked. This is especially true if you purchase leading network adapter cards from companies such as 3COM and Intel.

If you have multiple network adapter cards, be sure to use the Network Monitoring Agent option in Control Panel to describe each card. Providing a friendly name facilitates easier identification.

Analysis

Network Monitor presents the information in the Frame Viewer window in such a way that some of the analysis is already completed for you (see Figure 19-5). Assuming you are in the Capture window of Network Monitor, the Frame Viewer window is created by selecting the Stop and View Capture button on the Network Monitor toolbar (the eyeglasses button), or by selecting the Display Captured Data option from the Capture menu (or simply pressing F12).

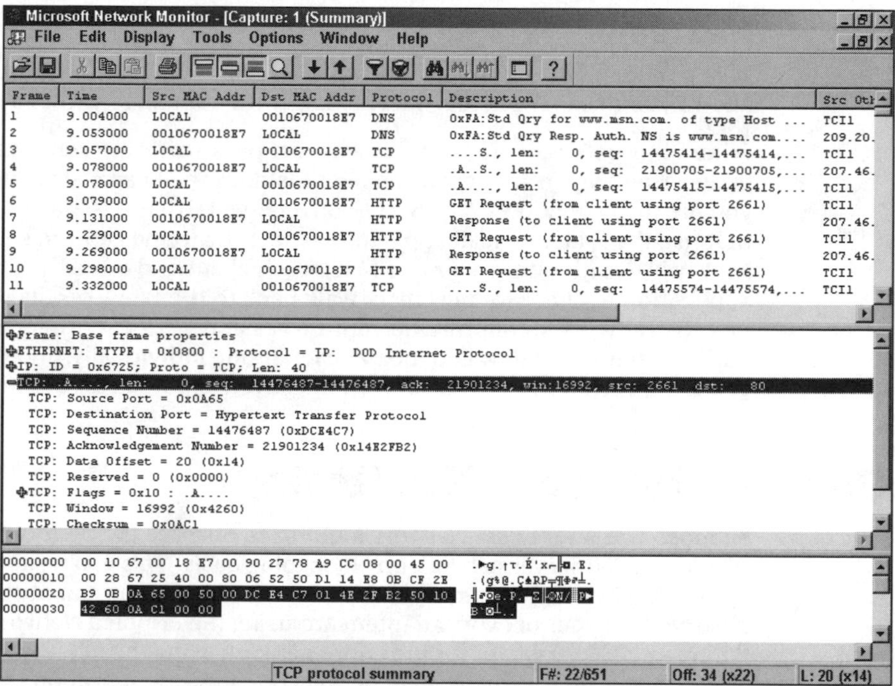

Figure 19-5: The Frame Viewer window in Network Monitor

The window is divided into three sections: Summary pane, Detail pane, and Hex pane.

Summary pane

The Summary pane lists frames captured, the elapsed time since time period zero, source and destination MAC addresses (hardware addresses from layer one and the MAC portion of layer two in the OSI model), the protocol being used, and a very useful text description. Double-clicking one of the frames creates the other two panes for this window.

Detail pane

Here is where Network Monitor really shines. The highlighted frame is presented in greater detail, showing the content of the frame and what protocols sent it, in English to assist your analysis. Even relative novices can educate themselves on the basics of packet analysis based on the layout in the Detail pane. While it's safe to say the devil is in the details, the Detail pane layout truly enables you to understand the basic structure of a packet and apply the conceptual knowledge you have of the OSI Model to the real world of network optimization via packet analysis.

Hex pane

This portion of the Capture window, on the far right in Network Monitor, allows you to see the actual data as ASCII text contained within a frame.

Where this gets exciting is when clear-text passwords are sent over the network and you trap the packets. For instance, you can see for yourself if you are using Windows 2000 Server on a network that has Macintosh clients that use the Eudora e-mail application. Start the frame capture session using Network Monitor. Walk over to a Macintosh client and force the Eudora e-mail application to check for new mail. Walk back to the Windows 2000 Server and halt the Network Monitor frame capture session. Press F12 to launch the Capture Viewer window and look at each frame individually. Soon enough, you will see the clear-text password displayed as ASCII text in the Hex pane.

Ongoing Network Monitoring

Suppose you want to use Network Monitor to observe the performance of your Windows 2000 Server network on an ongoing basis. This can be accomplished by running Network Monitor continuously. From this, you can observe (as observed via your network adapter card using the crippled Network Monitor in Windows 2000 Server; or for the entire network using the full-featured Network Monitor in Systems Management Server) the network utilization rate, frames per second, bytes per second, broadcasts per second, and multicasts per second. These are all valuable measurements to observe at a glance. In fact, to see all of these measurements at once, be sure to extend the Graph pane in Network Monitor by clicking and holding the lower Graph pane window borders and dragging downward.

Set the Capture Buffer to a small value for continuous network monitoring via Network Monitor. This is accomplished by selecting the Buffer Settings menu option under the Capture menu in Network Monitor. The smallest buffer setting available is 1.0MB, and you are encouraged to use this value for continuous network monitoring. Once the capture buffer is full, the oldest frames are dropped and the newest frames are retained. However, the network statistics values displayed in the Graph pane are still valid, as the time sample duration for calculating the statistics displayed in the Graph pane is much shorter than the time required to fill the buffer.

Using the capture trigger

One of the benefits of running a capture is the strategic and wise use of the capture trigger (see Figure 19-6), which provides the capability to trigger on conditions ranging from text pattern matches to how much buffer space has been consumed, or a combination of these two variables. Interestingly, you can specify that the trigger consider the order of operations when evaluating the pattern match and buffer space variables. You can specify that the pattern match be evaluated before the buffer space variable is considered or vice-versa. The capture trigger is found via the Trigger menu option on the Capture menu.

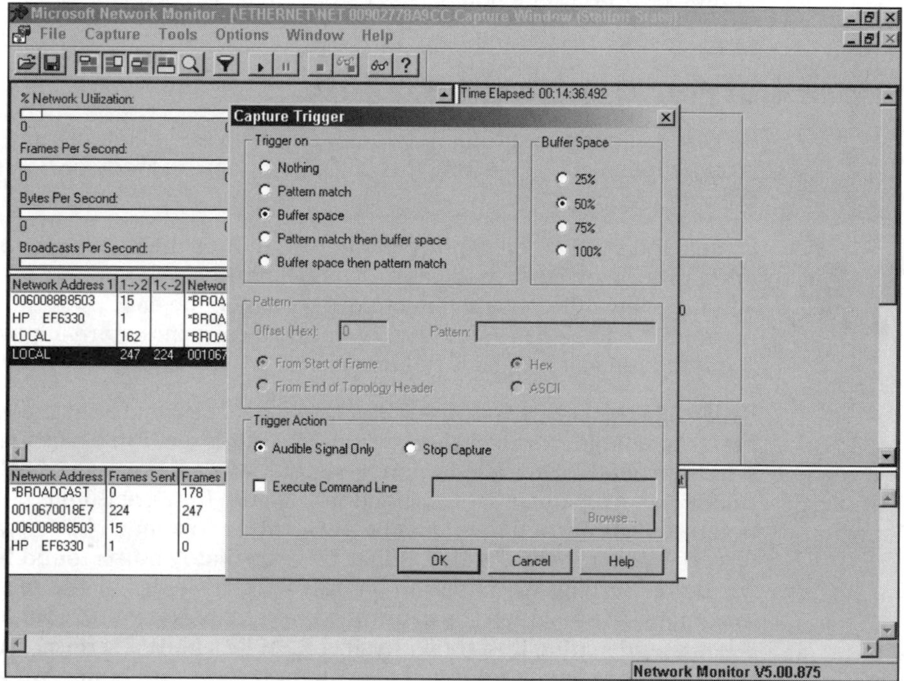

Figure 19-6: The capture trigger

This is very similar to but much weaker than the Run Program on Alert capability found in Performance Monitor, where you can specify a program that will run or a network message that will be sent to a specific machine. Unfortunately, the trigger action for Network Monitor is restricted only to executing a command line command. Also, you can't launch a program such as SQLALRTR.EXE that runs in Performance Monitor when a SQL Server object:counter is out of whack. As you may know, SQLALRTR.EXE can write an error to the error log and that can generate an e-mail message with important information that is sent to you. Instead, Network Monitor requires you to be a deft batch file programmer to achieve true functionality, or have a pager-alert e-mail program that perhaps accepts command line variables to really alert you, via pager, to an unacceptable event.

If you are only interested in monitoring the statistics in the Graph pane, then I highly recommend you consider creating an alert in Performance Monitor using the Network Segment object:counters. The alert capabilities in Performance Monitor are much stronger than those found in Network Monitor. The trigger capabilities of Network Monitor are only oriented toward text strings contained in a packet or the buffer setting value (percentage of buffer full). Thus, it isn't possible to use the trigger capabilities in Network Monitor to be alerted of unacceptable network utilization values (such as broadcast storms sending network utilization values through the roof!).

Larger capture sessions

Be sure to consider setting Network Monitor to dedicated capture mode. This is accomplished by selecting the Dedicated Capture Mode option under the Capture menu.

By selecting dedicated capture mode, you reduce the demands on the microprocessor. Dedicated capture mode allows the computer to "keep up" and drop fewer frames than might otherwise be the case. Additional screens do not have to be drawn on the computer screen, and more important, the possibility of lost frames is reduced.

Regarding the large capture session issue, don't forget to set the capture buffer to a large storage value to support your large-frame capture sessions. Windows 2000 Server allows you to set this value as high as 24.5MB using the Buffer Size drop-down menu selection from the Capture Buffer Settings dialog box (see Figure 19-7), but it can be overwritten to a much larger value (say 50MB). Note that the Capture Buffer Settings dialog box is found by selecting the Buffer Settings menu option on the Capture menu. For the record, the maximum size to which the capture buffer can be set is 1,024MB, but I would recommend setting it to total physical RAM less 8MB. Exercise caution with respect to how much RAM you allocate to the capture buffer. We want to ensure that Windows 2000 Server doesn't perform unnecessary swapping to your hard disk, which dramatically lowers overall system performance and loses frames in the capture.

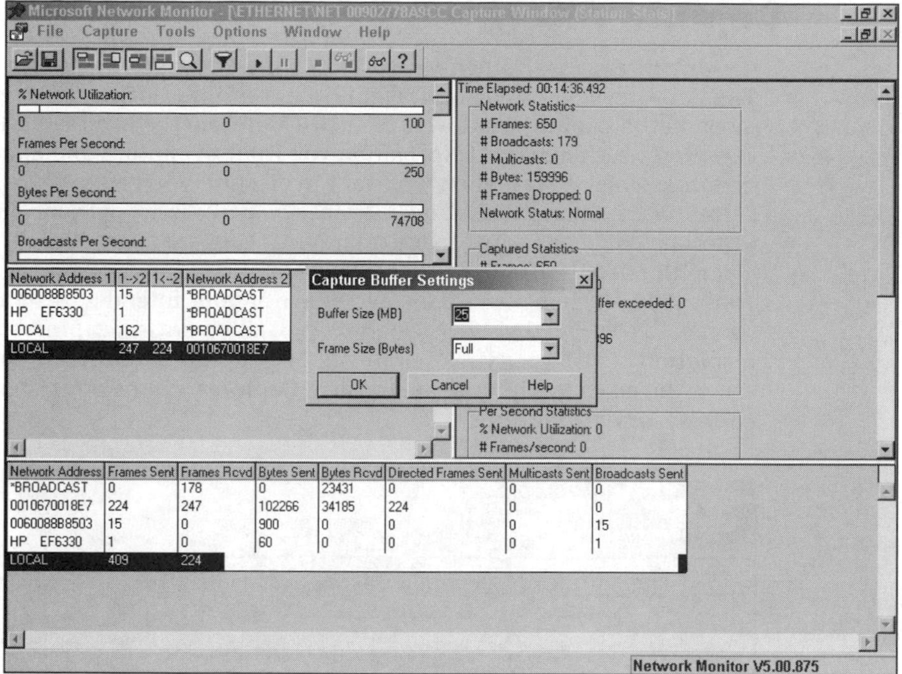

Figure 19-7: The Capture Buffer Settings dialog box

Frame size setting

Capture settings can be modified in another way. The frame size setting enables you to capture just part of the frame. Why might you use this setting? By capturing only part of the frame (the header section), you can typically still perform your network analysis without filling your capture buffer unnecessarily with the data portion of the frame. Why waste capture buffer space unless you are really sniffing the network to read data?

You cannot reduce the actual size of the frame. That, if possible, would seriously alter the implementation of the different standards (802.2, 802.3, 802.5) on your network, and that's a road you don't want to travel. You can determine how much of the frame you want to capture by setting the Frame Size (Bytes) setting in the Capture Buffer Settings dialog box (see Figure 19-7) to the size of the header section(s) you want to capture. For an Ethernet frame on a TCP/IP network, this would be approximately 60 bytes.

Capture filters

Capture filters are another way to "cut to the chase" with large captures. The Capture Filter dialog box is found via the Filter option under the Capture menu in the Capture window in Network Monitor (see Figure 19-8). By selecting which network information you want to capture and effectively dictating which information you want to discard, you can capture just a subset of the information. This is a smart way to perform frame captures, especially large ones. Too many frames in a capture might force you to get lost in the details. However, by selecting just the type of frames of interest, you will be much more focused and arrive at your intended results much sooner. Experienced network analysts typically perform captures seeking resolution of just one type of problem. The capture filter allows them to select the exact frame traffic necessary. Captures can be filtered by protocol, address, or data patterns.

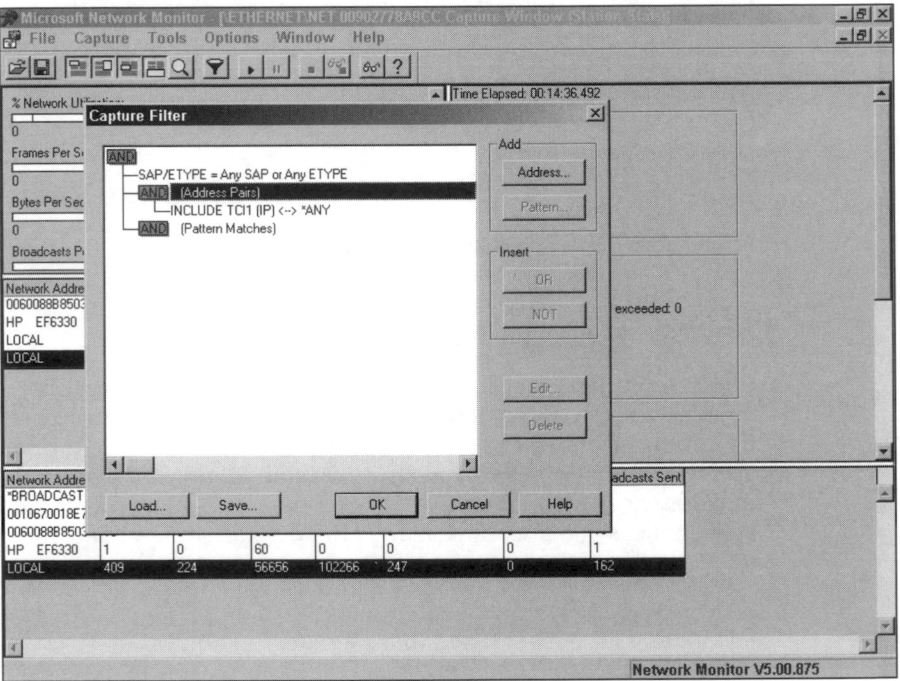

Figure 19-8: The Capture Filter dialog box

Protocols

Here the capture is defined for a set of specific protocols. The default setting for Network Monitor is to capture frames for all protocols supported by your version of Network Monitor. As you will see later in the chapter, the SMS version of Network Monitor supports several more protocols than the abbreviated edition of Network Monitor included with Windows 2000 Server. The capture settings you designate (see Figure 19-9) can be saved as a capture filter file and reused at a future date and even a different client site when appropriate. Remember that much of our packet analysis occurs on a protocol-by-protocol basis, making this capture capability especially important. Note the Capture Filter SAPS and ETYPES dialog box is displayed when you double-click or select the SAP/ETYPE = Any SAP or Any ETYPE line item in the Capture Filter dialog box and then select the Edit button. You may also double-click the SAP/ETYPE = Any SAP or Any ETYPE line item.

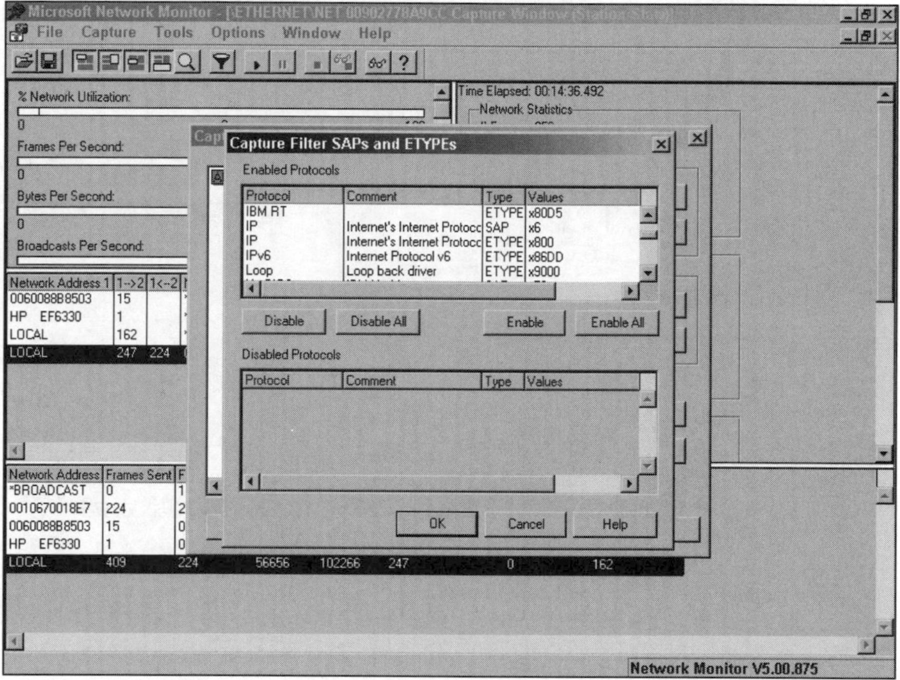

Figure 19-9: Using protocols to define your capture filter

Using capture filters helps you to preserve buffer resources. That will have an impact on both reducing the total amount of frame traffic plus increasing system responsiveness. By using capture filters for a narrowly defined frame capture scenario, you are much less likely to drop frame traffic because the computer can't keep up with the volume of frames.

Addresses

Address settings have major real-world implications for those of us who work in the industry by day (and sometimes night!). How many times has an end user complained that he or she can't connect to the network? Where do you begin to troubleshoot that problem? Start by creating a capture filter that only captures packets between that end user's workstation and the appropriate servers on your network. Why? Because, after you've defined the workstations to capture, the resulting network capture will enable you to view only the traffic between specific network nodes (or "hosts," in the language of TCP/IP). Addresses are displayed in the Address Expression dialog box, which is displayed when you select the Address Pairs line item in the Capture Filter dialog box and then click the Address button (see Figure 19-10).

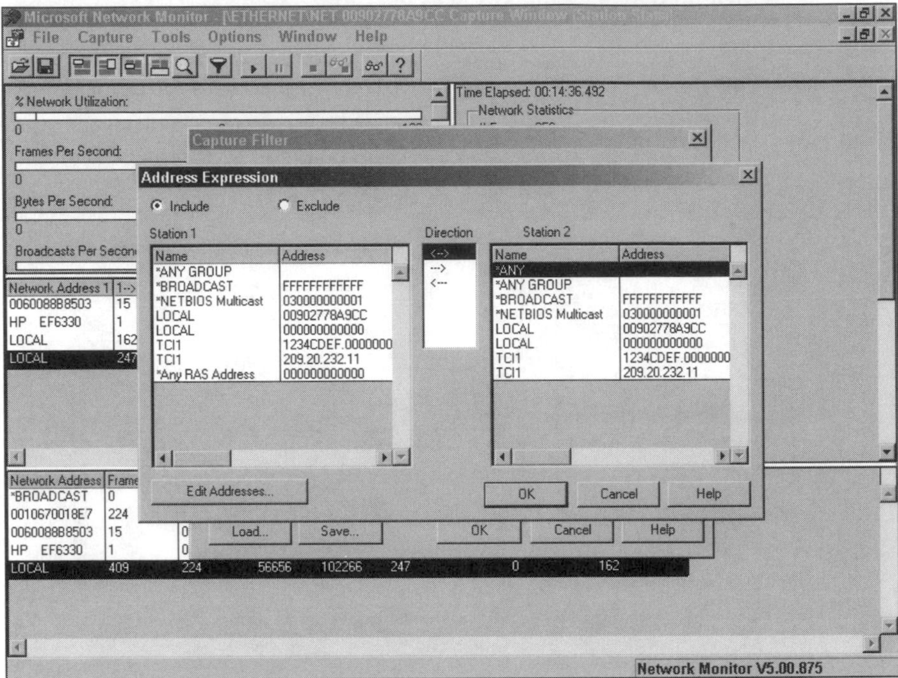

Figure 19-10: Address Expression dialog box

Note that filtering by address capabilities can be used to include or exclude specific addresses. The exclusion feature is most valuable in situations where you might not be interested in trapping frame traffic generated by the Macintosh computers in the marketing department, for example.

Data pattern

The data pattern is simply a pattern of data appearing in captured frames. It may be in either ASCII text or hexadecimal form. As will be shown, you must specify how far into the frame the data pattern will occur. This positioning via number of bytes is called an *offset*. This offset value can be specified as a number of bytes from the beginning or end of the frame.

If you are using either the Ethernet (802.2, 802.3) or Token Ring (802.5) networking standard, you are advised to specify your offset from the end of the frame. Why? These type of frames have a variable-length field in the MAC address field. That will cause confusion in your capture if you perform a data pattern capture based on an offset calculation that commences from the start of the frame. You have been warned.

Display filter

Of course, if you blow it during the capture and trap far too many frames, you can always recover via the display filter (see Figure 19-11). Actually, it is a very useful tool that lets you take a fundamentally different approach in how you capture frames. You could capture an enormous number of frames and save them as a capture file. This capture file could essentially be your baseline frame capture that is representative of network traffic on your Windows 2000 network at a given point in time. The display filter can, in laypersons' terms, be used to analyze your baseline frame capture for specific features of your network traffic at a later date, even if you didn't define your exact analysis needs at the time of capture.

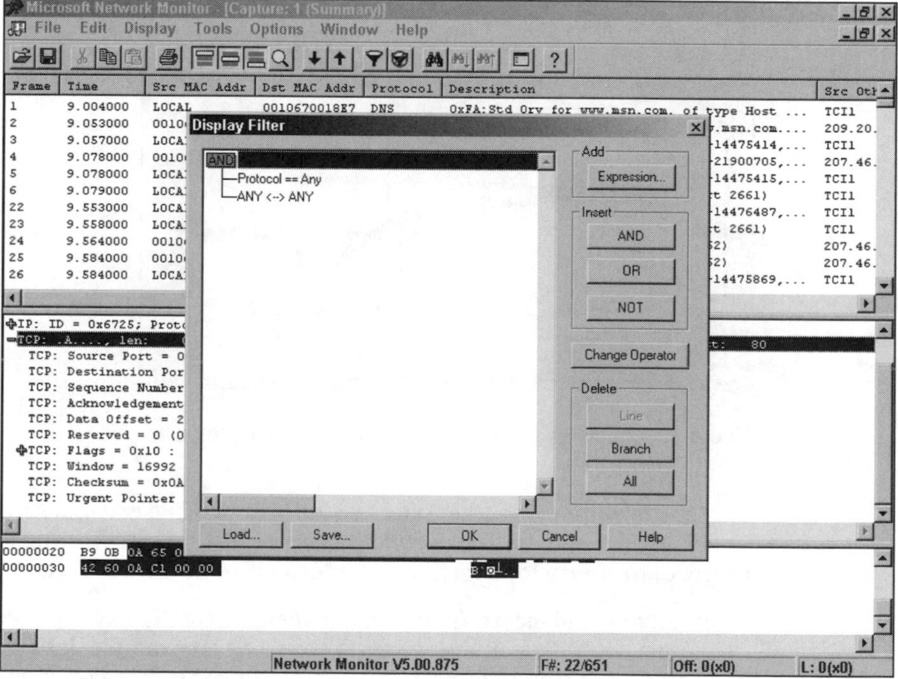

Figure 19-11: The display filter

Likewise, if you capture too many frames by mistake during one session, and you really wanted to analyze a more targeted subset of network activity, then the display filter will (here again) bail you out so that you don't have to undertake another capture session. Think of the display filter as similar, in many respects, to a query executed against SQL Server. By defining this query by address, protocol, or data properties, you can see the specific types of frames you are interested in without having to suffer through analyzing every frame in a large capture. You can extract only the specific frames of interest. As you will see, the way in which we filter frames with the display filter is very similar in nature to the capture filter previously discussed.

Designing a display filter forces you to define your end objectives, that is, what you want your resulting information to be. It's a good process in that you have to decide what you are really trying to accomplish. Of course, the good news is that you didn't have to have this sense of definition prior to running the capture; it can arrive post-capture.

One example might be to examine all IP packets with a certain protocol stack property such as MERIT Internodal but not the Locus Address Resolution property (see Figure 19-12).

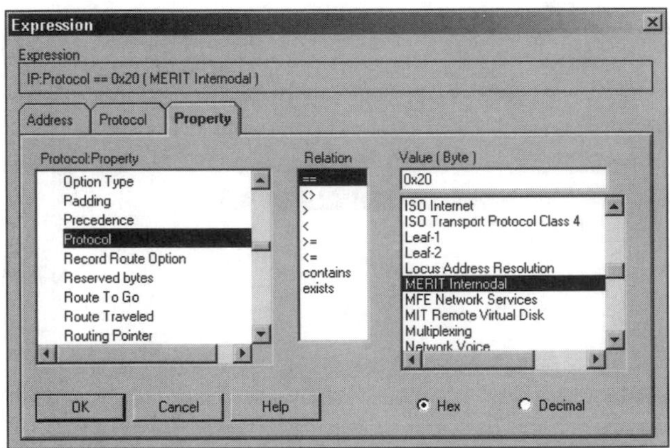

Figure 19-12: Packet activity containing only specific protocols

Another example might be to make sure your DHCP server is sending ACK or acknowledgments. That would be accomplished by selecting the ACK protocol property for DHCP and the "exists" relation (see Figure 19-13).

To creatively and masterfully design a meaningful display filter, you must first define the problem you are trying to solve. As an example, let's assume you have extensive Web-related traffic (which is pretty darn common today!) and have great difficulty establishing a session with your ISP and/or certain Web sites. You have run a large frame capture with no capture filtering (that means you captured everything). To better troubleshoot your problem, you create the display filter shown in Figure 19-14, wherein you want to display HTTP frames.

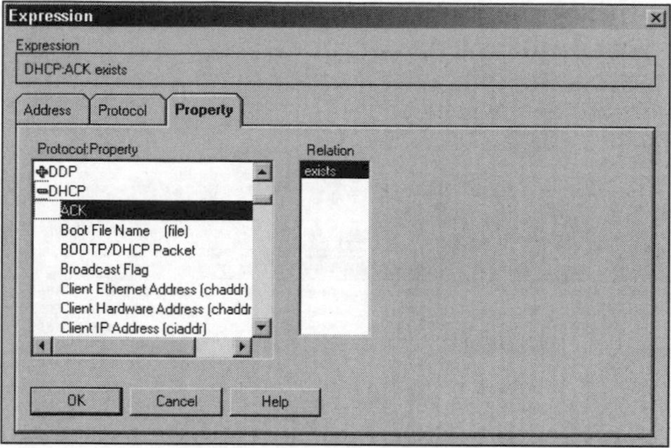

Figure 19-13: The "exists" relation in defining a display filter

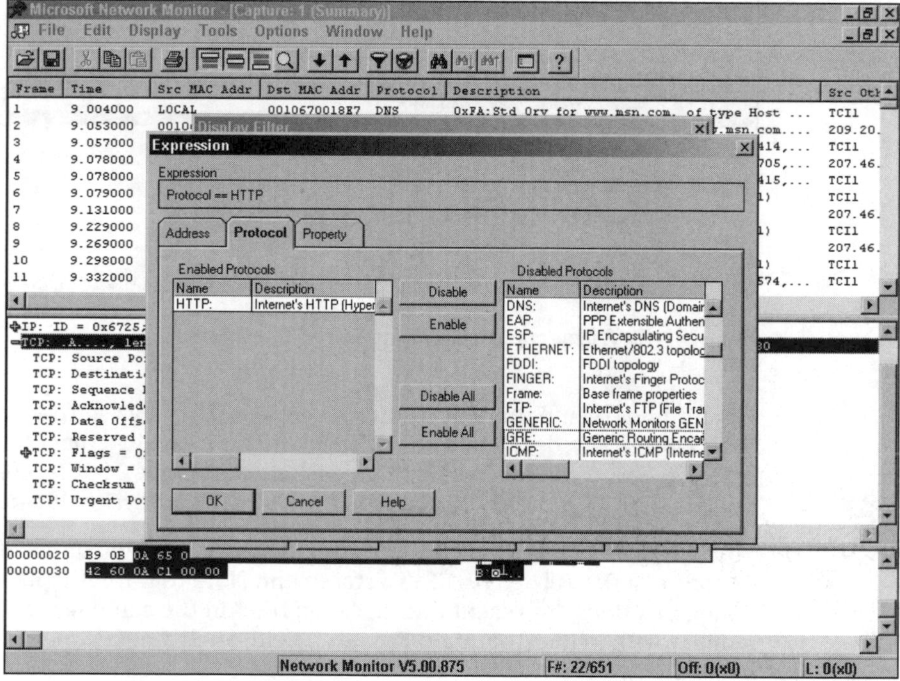

Figure 19-14: HTTP as the only enabled protocol in the display filter

Once the display filter is invoked by successively selecting OK on each display filter-related dialog box, you will be presented with only those frames that meet your criterion (see Figure 19-15). Mastering this step, that is, creating a display filter that allows you to cut to the heart of your analysis, will pay enormous dividends when you are trying to solve network traffic problems (usually under somewhat hostile conditions — that is, tense users asking when the problem will be solved!).

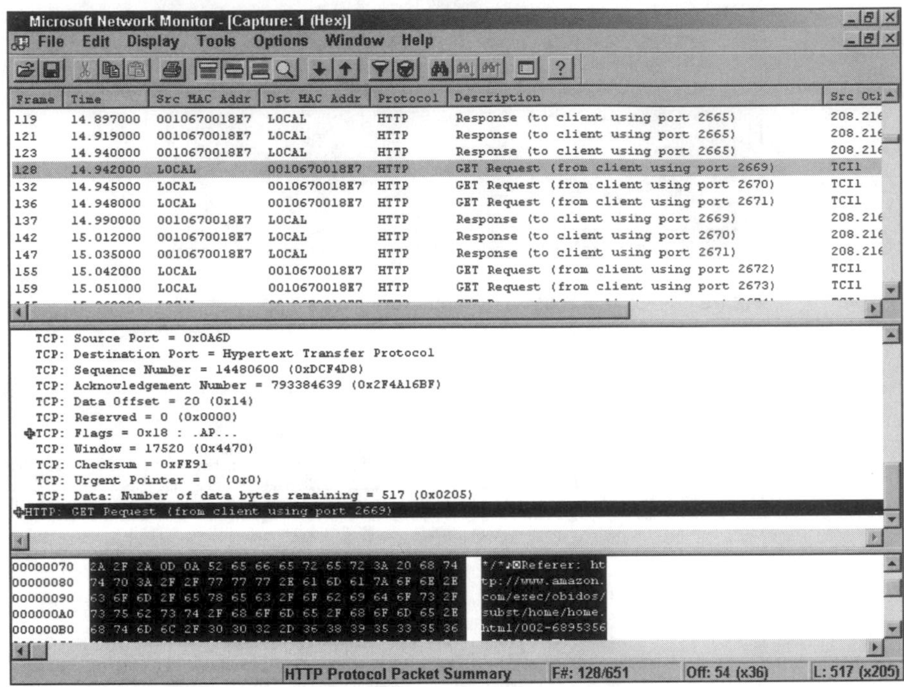

Figure 19-15: A large capture displaying only HTTP packets

Finally, understand that Microsoft presents the Display Capture dialog box, in their words, as a decision tree. Although this is logically correct in that you build up query conditions, there are visual limitations. That is, complex queries aren't especially readable in the Display Capture dialog box.

Tip

You can think of the construction of the query expression as building an out-of-control `If... Then... Else` statement. Note that the Display Capture dialog box doesn't present the "decision tree" in the same manner we are familiar with in the Operation Research field. Such a decision tree would make greater use of branches.

You must click the OK button after adding each decision statement to the Display Filter dialog box. To add a second decision statement, once again select Filter under the Display menu in the Capture Viewer window or press F8. It is important to note that multiple decision statements or queries are possible, making this a very powerful and impressive tool.

Differences between capture filter and display filter

Some fundamental and important differences exist between capture filters and display filters. These differences are as follows:

- The capture filter forces you to define your research parameters in advance. So capture filters are for those incredibly organized people who know exactly what they want; display filters are for the rest of us. The display filter is much more forgiving. My free advice? Run large unimpeded frame captures when performing network analysis and use a display filter to refine your analysis as you go.
- You can have only three address pairs in the capture filter (see Figure 19-16). Display filters do not have this limitation (see Figure 19-17). Thus, the display filter would be more useful when applied against at-large, general network frame captures when you wanted to analyze lots of sessions among lots of network nodes. I think you would find capture filters to be somewhat limiting if you were trying to undertake the same analysis.

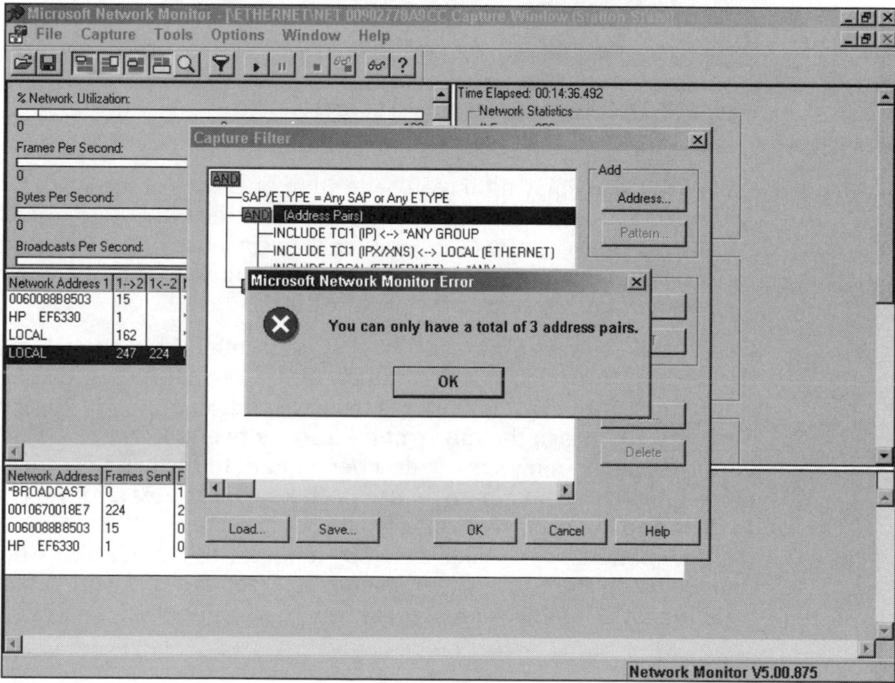

Figure 19-16: Three address pairs in the capture filter

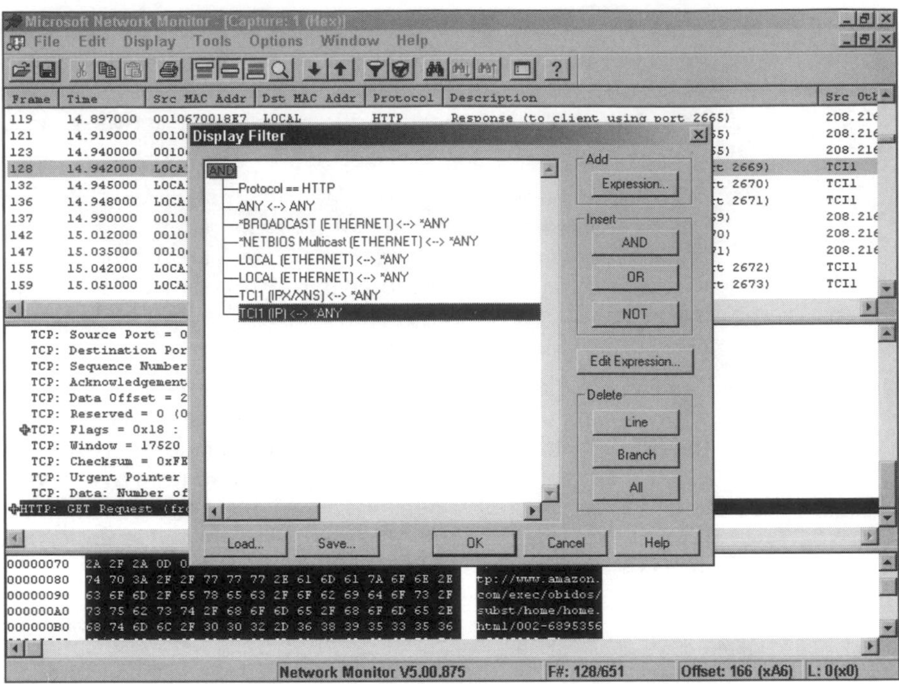

Figure 19-17: Several address pairs in the display filter

- With the display filter, you have wide open use of the AND, OR, NOT operators in constructing your decision-tree type query (see Figure 19-18). The capture filter enables generous use of the AND operator but does not enable use of the OR and NOT operators in the context of nested pattern search (see Figure 19-19).

Tip

Don't forget to save your capture session frequently, especially narrowly defined captures that you created via either the capture or display filters, for future use. These saved captures become your capture file library for solving similar problems in the future at the same site and network. In fact, you may capture frames from one site as a benchmark to evaluate captures from other sites. I highly recommend you use both long filenames and the comment field to describe the capture. Properly labeled and stored, these files are akin to a medical patient's X ray files saved by a doctor to further his or her knowledge in the future when diagnosing a related problem. A fact worth repeating: Capture files are a great way to learn network analysis.

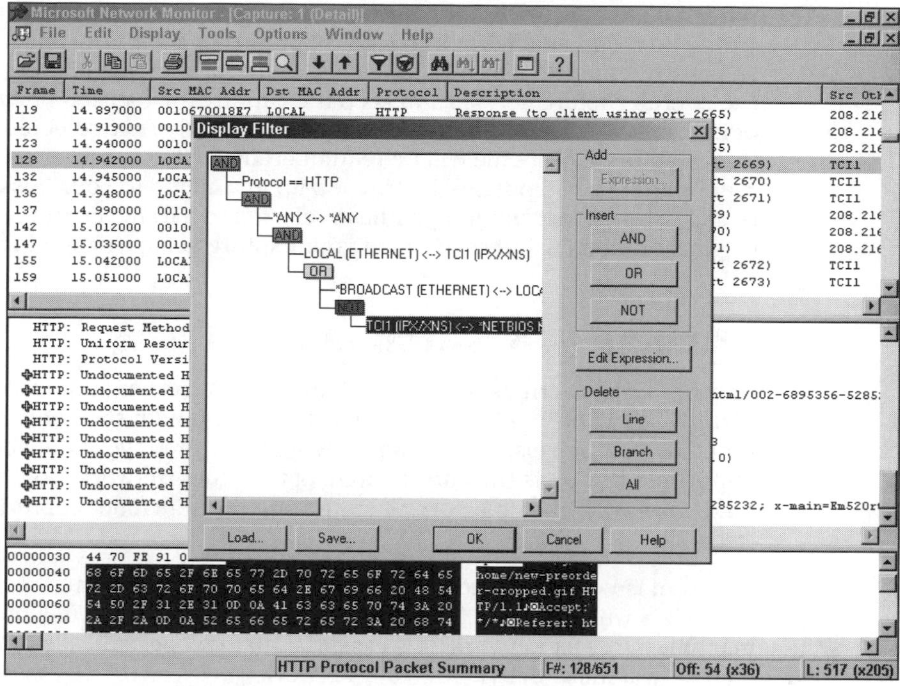

Figure 19-18: Display filter with AND, OR, NOT conditions

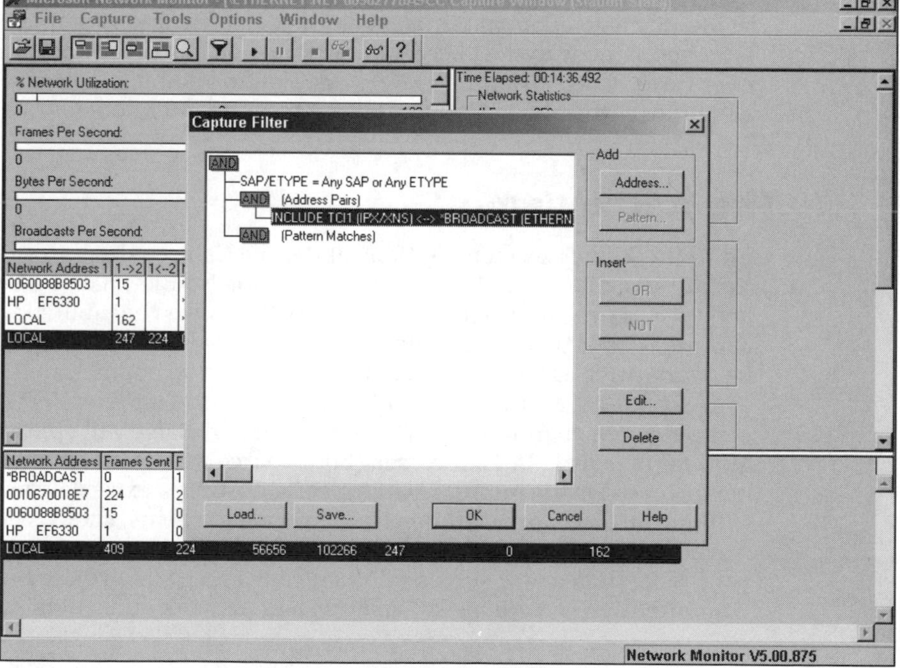

Figure 19-19: Capture filter with only the AND condition

When you save your capture, notice the Range option in the Save Data As dialog box. This enables you to save all or part of a capture. It is possible to select a tight range of frames for saving in the capture file in order to reduce the overall capture file size and keep the capture file focused on just the area of interest. When you use the range option and only save selected frames, the frames in the capture file will be renumbered starting at one. This renumbering could potentially trip you up in a memo to your boss or in front of a class as an instructor if you have referred to a frame capture via its original numbering but then saved your capture using a defined range.

Watching you watch me

Another mission-critical tool for a Windows 2000 Server administrator is the Identify Network Monitor Users menu selection (under the Tools menu). This tool tells you who else is running Network Monitor on your network. Most important, it reports the current state of the other Network Monitor running on the network. Possible current state conditions include "capturing" and "running."

Tip

This tool is your protection from weekend warriors and other computer hobbyists who "acquire" Network Monitor and install it on one of their machines on your network. It is essential that you periodically determine who is "watching" activity on your network.

At a BackOffice Professional Association (BOPA) user group meeting held at the Redmond campus of Microsoft, I once saw Network Monitor being demonstrated in great detail. When the speaker demonstrated the command to identify network monitor users on the demonstration computer that was attached directly to the Microsoft corporate network, the screen showed over three dozen instances of Network Monitor running. Now you know what all of those workaholic Microsoft developers do after hours!

The name game

Go to the Addresses menu options under the Capture drop-down menu in Network Monitor. Listed there you will see the NetBIOS name, MAC address, and type of network listed for computers that have contributed frames to the capture. The MAC address field is editable, and the default NetBIOS name can be overwritten as well. It is recommended that you not modify the MAC address but create a street-friendly name for those non-NetBIOS named computers on your network. This street-friendly name will appear in Network Monitor in lieu of MAC addresses (both source and destination) once it has been created in the Address Database. Again, this is extremely useful when working on a network with non-NetBIOS-named clients, such as Macintosh or Novell NetWare users. Employing the methods discussed here will simplify your Network Monitor screens dramatically and enable you to better focus your attention on core packet analysis and network utilization issues. You will notice that a second entry exists for each computer in the Address Database (see Figure 19-20) to reflect its address from layer three (network) of the OSI model. Under the TCP/IP protocol, it is the computer's TCP/IP network address.

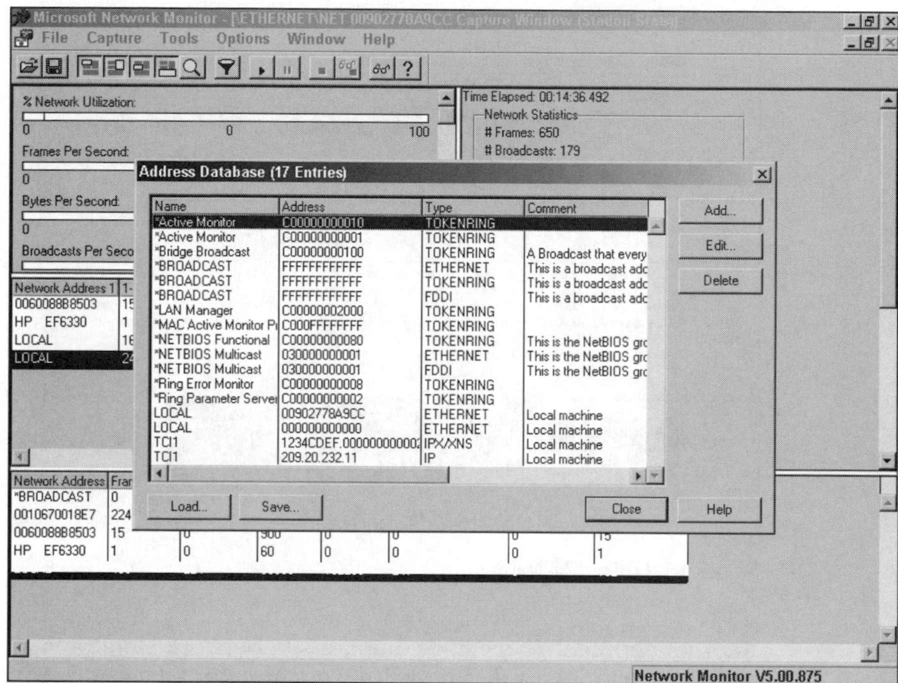

Figure 19-20: Address Database

You may edit the address information in the Address Database by selecting the Edit button. You will then be presented with the Address Information dialog box that enables you to modify the protocol type, computer name, address, and comment field. If you haven't yet done so, click the Edit button now to observe these fields.

To better understand which computers generating traffic are which, you can do two things. First, you can run the Find All Names command found in the Display Menu when the View Capture window is displayed (see Figure 19-21). Running this command adds NetBIOS-based computer names to the address database.

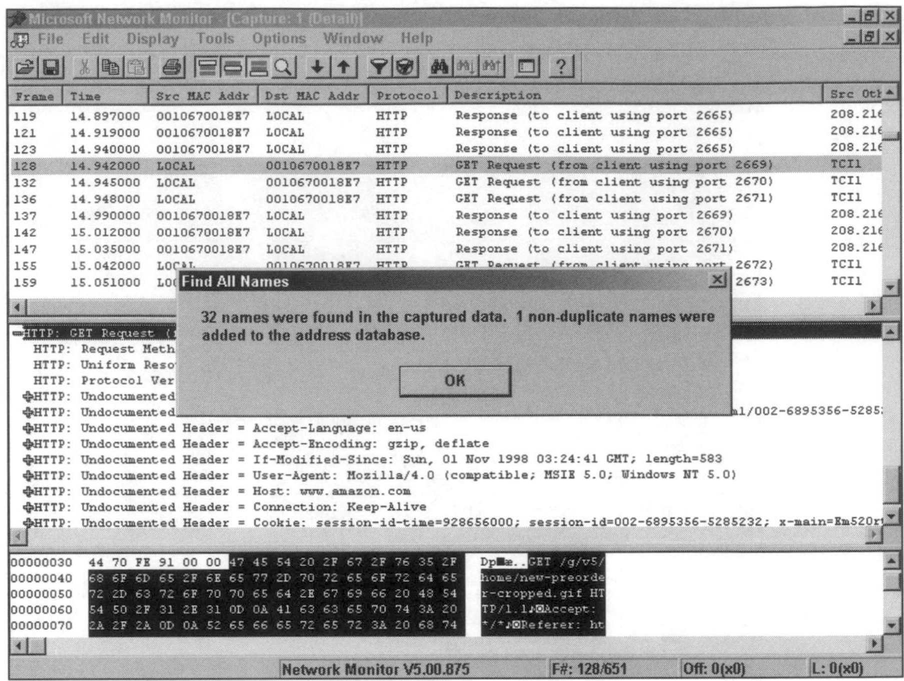

Figure 19-21: Find All Names

Another approach to naming computers in Network Monitor is to start at each computer that will run the Network Monitoring agent (including the Windows 2000 Server with Network Monitor installed). Inside the Network Monitoring Agent, you can edit the MAC address description of the network adapter. So instead of hexadecimal alphanumeric gibberish, you can identify the network card with a meaningful street name. That way, when you observe packets in the Capture view windows, the SRC MAC Addr and the DST MAC Addr (source and destination MAC addresses, respectively) will reflect the new names you assigned to the network adapters.

You can find the MAC address for a Windows 2000 (Server or Professional) or Windows 98 or 95-based PC running the TCP/IP protocol by using the following commands. For a Windows 2000 Server or Professional machine running TCP/IP, type **ipconfig /all** at the command line to see the screen shown in Figure 19-22.

For a Windows 98 or 95 computer running TCP/IP, type **winipcfg** at the command line. You will see the IP Configuration dialog box that reports MAC address information in addition to the IP address. You may recall that both the IPConfig and the Winipcfg commands were discussed at length in Part II, "TCP/IP," earlier in this book.

```
Command Prompt
C:\>ipconfig /all

Windows NT IP Configuration

        Host Name . . . . . . . . . : TCI1
        Primary Domain Name . . . . : Main.local
        Node Type . . . . . . . . . : Broadcast
        IP Routing Enabled. . . . . : No
        WINS Proxy Enabled. . . . . : No
        DNS Suffix Search List. . . : Main.local

Ethernet adapter Local Area Connection:

        Adapter Domain Name . . . . :
        DNS Servers . . . . . . . . : 209.20.130.35
                                      209.20.130.33
        Description . . . . . . . . : Intel(R) PRO/100+ PCI Adapter
        Physical Address. . . . . . : 00-90-27-78-A9-CC
        DHCP Enabled. . . . . . . . : No
        IP Address. . . . . . . . . : 209.20.232.11
        Subnet Mask . . . . . . . . : 255.255.255.0
        Default Gateway . . . . . . : 209.20.232.1

C:\>
```

Figure 19-22: The ipconfig /all command in Windows 2000 Server

If you are capturing frames from a network with Macintosh or Novell NetWare clients, however, you're potentially in for a world of trouble. "But," you ask, "how can I edit the MAC address of the network adapter card for a Macintosh or Novell NetWare client if said computers aren't running the Network Monitor Agent?" Fear not! You will have to get creative and manually populate the Address Database, as will be described.

To "discover" the MAC address on a Novell NetWare client, I recommend that you boot from a DOS-based system disk and then run the utility program on the driver disk that shipped with your network adapter card. These utility programs typically enable you to configure your network adapter card as well as learn more about the card. This includes having the MAC address reported back to you.

For MAC address discovery on 3COM cards, you typically run INSTALL.EXE on the EtherDisk network adapter card utility disk for Ethernet networks (see Figure 19-23).

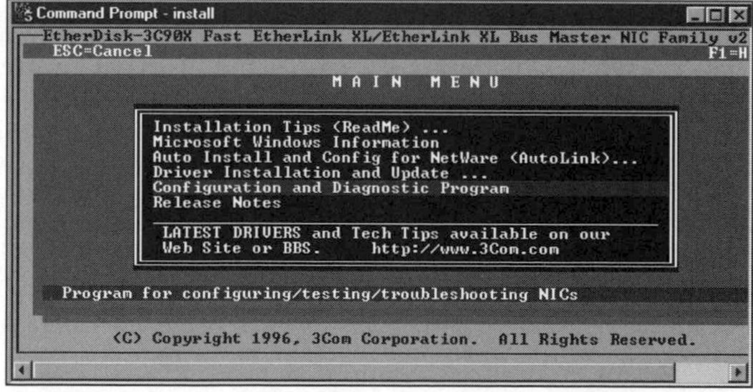

Figure 19-23: Detecting a MAC address with 3Com's Install program

There is another and possibly easier way to provide a friendly name for the MAC address in Network Monitor. Simply right-click the Session Statistics pane on Network Monitor's Capture window and select the Edit Address option on the context menu shown in Figure 19-24. Highlighting an address gives you the opportunity to edit the address name.

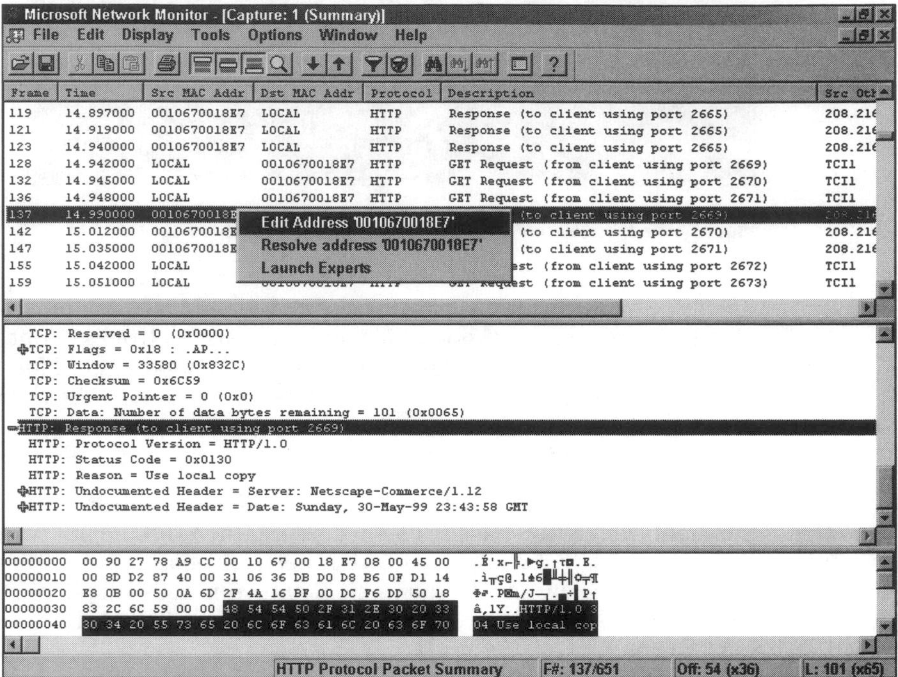

Figure 19-24: The context menu and edit address

To edit the address name, simply overwrite the default entry in the Name field of the Address Information dialog box (see Figure 19-25).

You may also right-click the Summary pane of the Display Capture window when your cursor is positioned underneath the SRC MAC Address or DST MAC Address columns. Select the Edit Address context menu option and the Address Information dialog box will appear as in the preceding figure.

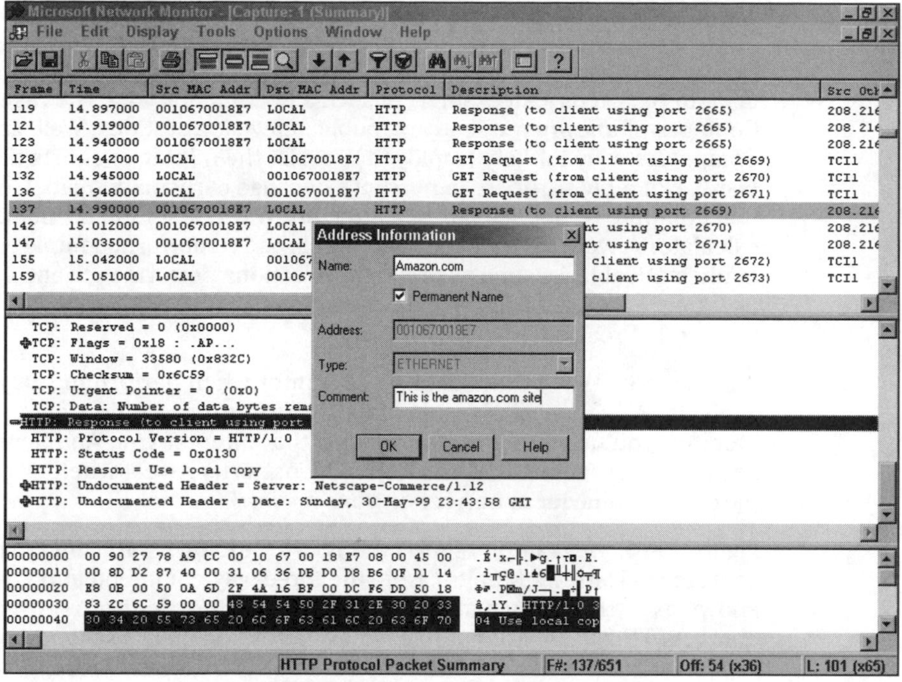

Figure 19-25: The Address Information dialog box in the context menu

Because the Address Database table is automatically populated with the registered street-friendly or NetBIOS names and addresses (both MAC and TCP/IP) of computers that contributed to the capture session, you do not have to manually make entries to this table. However, you can add computers to this database by simply selecting the Add button in the Address Database dialog box. The benefit here is to create a database that you will use on your network from day one or to add computers that haven't been automatically added to the Address Database for whatever reason. When manually adding a computer, the unique identifier is the hexadecimal MAC address or network protocol address (such as IP address). The underlying purpose of adding a computer name to your Address Database is to resolve MAC addresses to street-friendly names that you have created. This capability has a time and a place, but it is most useful when needed.

It's All in the Patterns

Ever watch any one of the documentaries about the beginnings of computers in modern society? An example of such a documentary is "The History of Computers" shown frequently on public television stations. Well, guess what! Computers were initially employed to assist the military's efforts during World War II. Not a big surprise there. That's because early mathematicians noticed that computers (the machines, not the pre-WWII definition of "human" calculators) were exceptionally well equipped to perform complex mathematical tasks such as predicting weapons performance and code breaking. Capturing frames and performing network analysis is no different from code breaking.

It is essential that you think like a computer when performing network analysis. When you analyze the data in the Capture window of Network Monitor, you must look for the *patterns* that interest you. And herein lies the key to successful network analysis. The patterns reveal whether or not a particular behavior is correct on your network.

Figure 19-26, for example, shows the TCP/IP session establishment process capture via Network Monitor. Note the three-way communication pattern, known as a "three-way handshake," in frames 26–28. In the first frame, the TCI1 contacts TCI2 in an attempt to establish a session. In the second frame, TCI2 replies to TCI1 as an acknowledgment. The third frame represents a return acknowledgment from TCI1 back to TC2, with which the session is established.

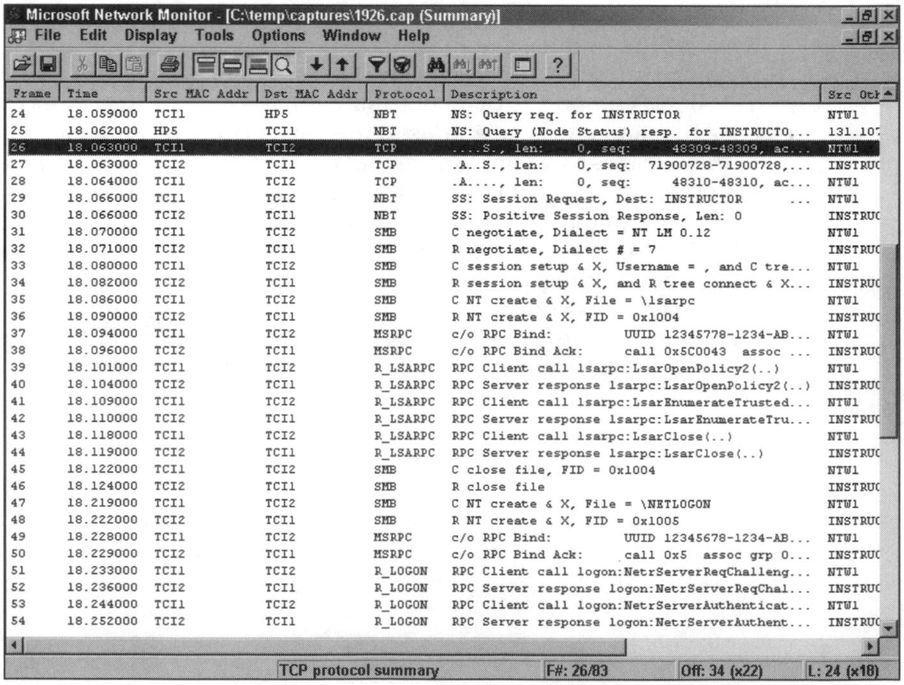

Microsoft Network Monitor - [C:\temp\captures\1926.cap (Summary)]

File Edit Display Tools Options Window Help

Frame	Time	Src MAC Addr	Dst MAC Addr	Protocol	Description	Src Oth
24	18.059000	TCI1	HP5	NBT	NS: Query req. for INSTRUCTOR	NTW1
25	18.062000	HP5	TCI1	NBT	NS: Query (Node Status) resp. for INSTRUCTO...	131.10
26	18.063000	TCI1	TCI2	TCP	....S., len: 0, seq: 48309-48309, ac...	NTW1
27	18.063000	TCI2	TCI1	TCP	.A..S., len: 0, seq: 71900728-71900728,...	INSTRUC
28	18.064000	TCI1	TCI2	TCP	.A...., len: 0, seq: 48310-48310, ac...	NTW1
29	18.066000	TCI1	TCI2	NBT	SS: Session Request, Dest: INSTRUCTOR ...	NTW1
30	18.066000	TCI2	TCI1	NBT	SS: Positive Session Response, Len: 0	INSTRUC
31	18.070000	TCI1	TCI2	SMB	C negotiate, Dialect = NT LM 0.12	NTW1
32	18.071000	TCI2	TCI1	SMB	R negotiate, Dialect # = 7	INSTRUC
33	18.080000	TCI1	TCI2	SMB	C session setup & X, Username = , and C tre...	NTW1
34	18.082000	TCI2	TCI1	SMB	R session setup & X, and R tree connect & X...	INSTRUC
35	18.086000	TCI1	TCI2	SMB	C NT create & X, File = \lsarpc	NTW1
36	18.090000	TCI2	TCI1	SMB	R NT create & X, FID = 0x1004	INSTRUC
37	18.094000	TCI1	TCI2	MSRPC	c/o RPC Bind: UUID 12345778-1234-AB...	NTW1
38	18.096000	TCI2	TCI1	MSRPC	c/o RPC Bind Ack: call 0x5C0043 assoc ...	INSTRUC
39	18.101000	TCI1	TCI2	R_LSARPC	RPC Client call lsarpc:LsarOpenPolicy2(..)	NTW1
40	18.104000	TCI2	TCI1	R_LSARPC	RPC Server response lsarpc:LsarOpenPolicy2(..)	INSTRUC
41	18.109000	TCI1	TCI2	R_LSARPC	RPC Client call lsarpc:LsarEnumerateTrusted...	NTW1
42	18.110000	TCI2	TCI1	R_LSARPC	RPC Server response lsarpc:LsarEnumerateTru...	INSTRUC
43	18.118000	TCI1	TCI2	R_LSARPC	RPC Client call lsarpc:LsarClose(..)	NTW1
44	18.119000	TCI2	TCI1	R_LSARPC	RPC Server response lsarpc:LsarClose(..)	INSTRUC
45	18.122000	TCI1	TCI2	SMB	C close file, FID = 0x1004	NTW1
46	18.124000	TCI2	TCI1	SMB	R close file	INSTRUC
47	18.219000	TCI1	TCI2	SMB	C NT create & X, File = \NETLOGON	NTW1
48	18.222000	TCI2	TCI1	SMB	R NT create & X, FID = 0x1005	INSTRUC
49	18.228000	TCI1	TCI2	MSRPC	c/o RPC Bind: UUID 12345678-1234-AB...	NTW1
50	18.229000	TCI2	TCI1	MSRPC	c/o RPC Bind Ack: call 0x5 assoc grp 0...	INSTRUC
51	18.233000	TCI1	TCI2	R_LOGON	RPC Client call logon:NetrServerReqChalleng...	NTW1
52	18.236000	TCI2	TCI1	R_LOGON	RPC Server response logon:NetrServerReqChal...	INSTRUC
53	18.244000	TCI1	TCI2	R_LOGON	RPC Client call logon:NetrServerAuthenticat...	NTW1
54	18.252000	TCI2	TCI1	R_LOGON	RPC Server response logon:NetrServerAuthent...	INSTRUC

TCP protocol summary | F#: 26/83 | Off: 34 (x22) | L: 24 (x18)

Figure 19-26: TCP/IP packet capture showing session establishment (Frames 26-28)

So what patterns can we see from this? Let's take a look:

- **The three-way handshake in a TCP/IP session.** If this pattern is absent, something is amiss on our network. Under the Description column in Figure 19-26, look at the entries for frames 26-28 (three frames). The "S," "A..S," and "A" shown from frames 26 to 28 represent the three-way handshake.
- **The "acknowledgment" of TCP as our transport-level protocol.** Remember that TCP provides guaranteed, connection-oriented service, thus the acknowledgments.
- **Additional traffic.** These acknowledgment packets, while necessary for the type of guaranteed delivery we insist upon with data transmissions, do add to our overall network traffic.

The three-way handshake is further discussed in RFC 793 (Section 3.4). It was also discussed in Part II, "TCP/IP" earlier in this book.

By looking for the patterns and behaviors present in certain types of network communications, you're well on your way to understanding network analysis. Although one can research network analysis, the only true way to learn this area is to practice it, and more important, to do it for real in a crisis situation!

Another way to enhance your network analysis is through the effective use of color. By selecting the Colors option under the Display menu while in the View Capture window, you can assign a different color to each protocol (see Figure 19-27). Depending on your needs, I recommend you assign a color to just the type of protocol activity you are seeking to observe and analyze to simplify your analysis. For example, you might have IP and IPXCP packets appear in red so that they are more visible.

One last pattern topic concerns timing. The standard approach used in network analysis is to measure the frame capture from time period zero, the moment that the frame capture commenced. This is the default setting in Network Monitor and can be modified in the Display Options dialog box found under the Display Menu of the Capture Viewer window. This is conceptually similar to the finance discipline, wherein much financial analysis performed starts at time period zero. For most of us, time period zero is a term used in finance to denote the day that you close the loan on your house. I highly recommend you keep this default setting so that you conform to this generally accepted standard of network analysis.

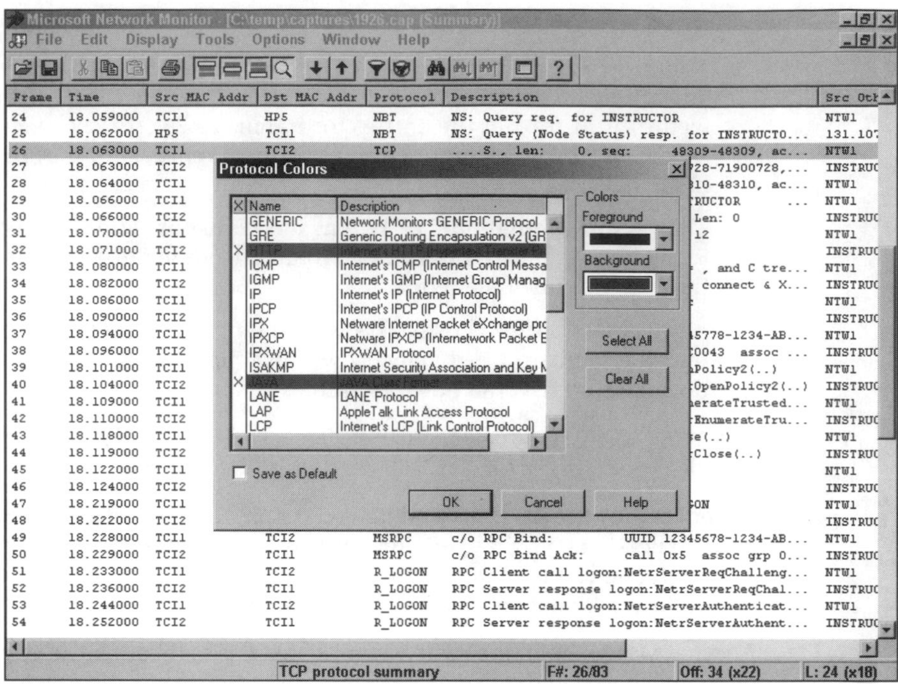

Figure 19-27: Protocol colors

Artificial Intelligence Arrives in Network Monitor

This is no tabloid headline. It's really about the sixth column of the Summary pane in the Capture Viewer window (titled Description). The default is to show the name of the last protocol for a specific captured frame. By default, the comments in the Description column match the last protocol listed in the packet. In Figure 19-28, frame 26 is highlighted and the TCP protocol, having been listed last in the Detail pane, is also listed in the Description column of the Summary pane.

I strongly recommend that you select the artificial intelligence option for the Description column. Network Monitor can display the appropriate protocol information it infers you might like to see from the query conditions you have defined in the display filter. Cool! And much more meaningful than defaulting to the last protocol in the frame of interest. Select the Auto radio button in the Display Options dialog box found under the Display menu in the Capture Viewer window (see Figure 19-29). The Auto selection allows Network Monitor to decide what to display in the Description column. Note that you can also select how the Time column is displayed with the Time options.

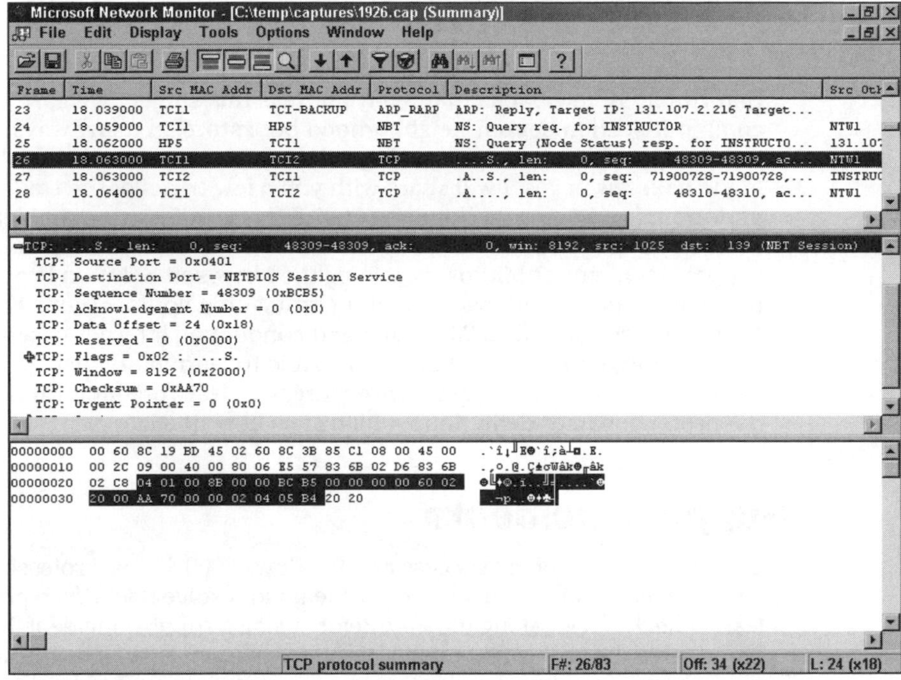

Figure 19-28: Network Monitor's Summary pane

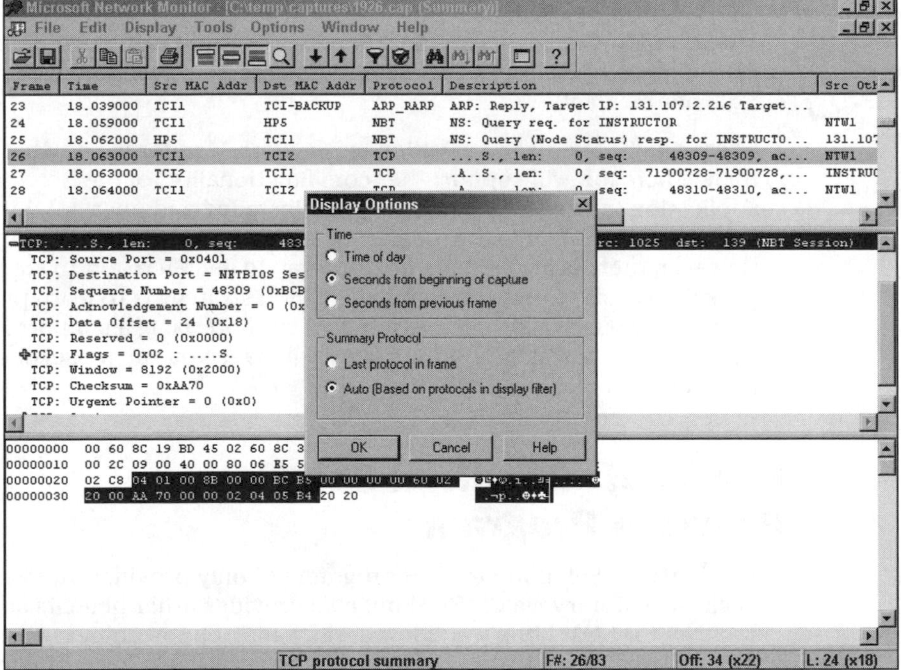

Figure 19-29: The Auto selection

I Want to Learn More!

But how does one really learn the finer points of packet analysis? Unfortunately, few books that really address this subject well are in the computer section of your neighborhood bookstore. In many ways, you are on your own in an area where learning comes in the form of on-the-job training. In the next few pages, I will share with you a few tricks of the trade for performing as a superior Windows 2000 Server professional and learning more about packet analysis along the way. These tricks include using paid support incidents at Microsoft, joining the Microsoft Solution Provider program, attending official Microsoft certification courses, consulting the Microsoft TechNet CD-ROM library, and conducting Internet-based research. Oh, did I forget to tell you that it is possible to learn more just by using Network Monitor? One way to learn more with Network Monitor is by using the protocol parser definitions, which I will describe later.

Support incidents

One of the secrets of my success as a Windows 2000 Server professional has been the use of Microsoft support incidents to resolve BackOffice problems and learn a heck of a lot along the way. Before using a support incident, I typically try to solve the problem at hand. Once it is apparent that I'll be unsuccessful, I don't throw in the towel, but rather use a support incident to be connected to a senior Microsoft support engineer. These guys and gals at Microsoft will stick with you for days until the problem is resolved. More important, they tend to turn you on to better ways to use existing tools, such as Network Monitor.

These support incidents are now free for Microsoft Certified Solution Providers as of early 1999. In the past, Microsoft charged between $150 to $200 per incident.

Interestingly, Microsoft's position on Network Monitor is not what you might think. Microsoft will support the "core functionality" of the Network Monitor application (such as its capability to be installed and operate), but "network-dependent tasks" such as true packet analysis are officially unsupported. However, there is an "undocumented" way to get Microsoft to support your packet analysis efforts. This undocumented strategy is to learn packet analysis by purchasing a Microsoft paid support using a support incident where the Microsoft support engineer will have you run a packet capture with Network Monitor.

Microsoft Certified Solution Provider Program

The Certified Solution Provider program not only provides you with the full BackOffice library via CD-ROM but also provides other benefits such as the TechNet CD-ROM library and low-cost training opportunities. All combined, this array of benefits will arm you with the knowledge base you need to tackle packet analysis and the advanced use of Network Monitor.

Official Microsoft Certification Training

As a knowledge worker, you will find that it is in your best interest to continually seek out and attend germane training to improve your skill level. One of the most consistent training channels is the Microsoft certified trainer programs. For commercial training centers, you would attend Microsoft Official Curriculum (MOC) courses at authorized technical education centers (ATECs). On the academic side, the same courses are offered at authorized academic training program (AATP) sites.

Tip

Don't overlook Microsoft's certification and training courses for learning packet analysis. Note the following comments relate to existing Windows NT Server 4.0 classes that address packet analysis and Network Monitor. As of this writing, Microsoft hasn't announced specific Windows 2000 Server classes which are dedicated to these topics (however, I'm sure such courses will be offered in the future).

Course #689, "Supporting Windows NT Server 4.0—Enterprise Technologies," and Course #692, "Microsoft Windows NT Server 4.0—Network Analysis and Optimization," are highly recommended for learning basic packet analysis in the Windows NT Server environment. Note that Course #689 is a five-day course that covers all (and more) of the material delivered in Course #692 (a two-day class). These courses are delivered at Microsoft ATECs and AATPs, the commercial training and academic training centers authorized by Microsoft. Note that these course names and titles are subject to revision based on new product releases and curriculum enhancements. Check with your Microsoft training provider for the most current version and course number for these classes. For more information on training, see `www.microsoft.com/train_cert`. I also suggest that you consider taking one or more of the instructor-led or self-study courses offered by Cisco (`www.cisco.com`). In the spirit of the analysis typically undertaken with Network Monitor, you might purchase and complete the "Managing Traffic on Cisco Routers" self-study course sold by Cisco.

I previously mentioned in passing that frame capture files are a great way to learn network analysis. Not only can you create your own capture files and create a library, but you can use and study the student sample capture files from Microsoft Certification Course #689, "Windows NT Server—Enterprise Technologies" (or its successor courses). As a student in this class, you receive a CD-ROM with numerous capture files that show everything from adding a user to a network to observing Windows 95 perform a file copy. Wouldn't that last capture file be a great way to troubleshoot a pesky problem such as when a user complains of not being able to copy a file from a Windows 95 client to a Windows 2000 Server? You bet! In all, the student CD-ROM for the #689 class provides over 30 meaningful capture files (many with the comment field completed to help you understand at a glance what each capture file is trying to demonstrate). This is truly one of the best ways to master network analysis. The Network Monitor capture files included with Microsoft's "Windows NT Server—Enterprise Technology" class are great for learning packet analysis.

Display Filter dialog box — protocol definitions

You can learn protocol definitions in the Display Filter dialog box. Study the basic protocol definitions, conditions, operators, and default values for each element of a protocol. Note that this is a very rich area of Network Monitor that will assist you greatly in trying to learn network analysis. The information conveyed in this rich, multilayered dialog box is, quite frankly, somewhat overwhelming. But the devil is in the details, and if you look closely at the default values for each part of the protocol, you have a road map to understanding and interpreting frame captures. Detailed information about virtually any networking protocol can be obtained via the Property tab sheet in the Expression dialog box selected from Display Filter (see Figure 19-30).

This is the slow and steady way to go when mastering Network Monitor. To assist and speed your efforts, however, I have listed detailed descriptions of selected protocols supported by the Windows 2000 Server version of Network Monitor in Appendix B.

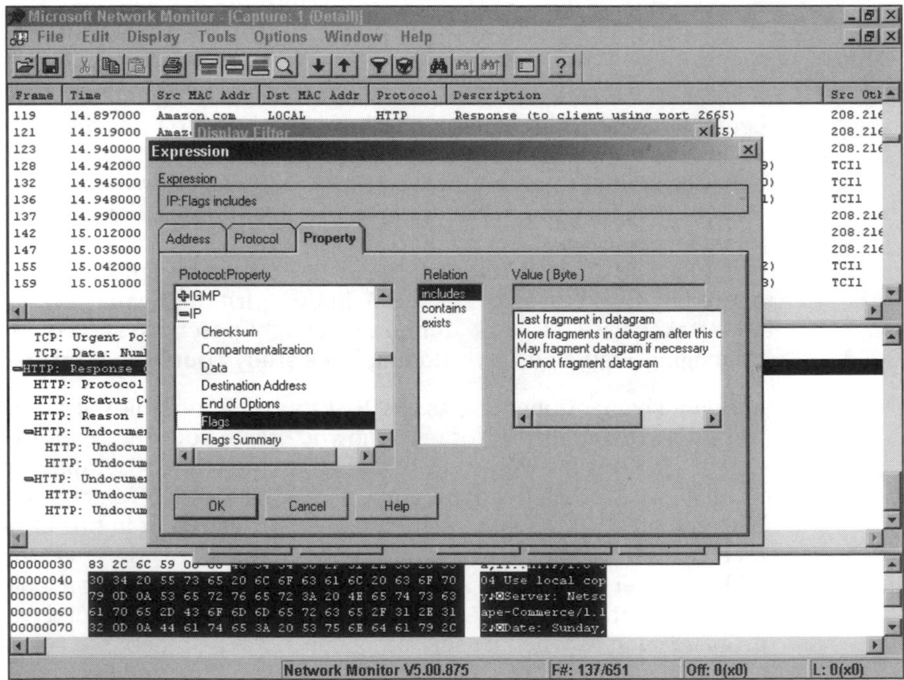

Figure 19-30: Property tab sheet

Microsoft TechNet CD-ROM

A frequently cited tool in *Windows NT Server 4.0 Secrets* (IDG Books Worldwide), Microsoft TechNet, is probably the fastest way to learn about each protocol property by searching appropriate terms. An annual subscription to TechNet is approximately $300 (U.S.), for which you receive a monthly CD-ROM library. For example, suppose you wanted to learn about the "sequence" value discussed in the TCP portion of the TCP/IP protocol stack. Note that the term "sequence" is shown in Figure 19-26 as "seq" in the Description column for frames 26-28. Here are recommended steps to successfully undertake this search.

STEPS:

To search TechNet for information on sequence value

Step 1. First, I would highly recommend you create a subset to narrow your search on Microsoft TechNet. Given our interest in learning about the sequence value in the TCP protocol in the context of Windows 2000 Server, creating and using the BackOffice (for instance, "BackOffice1") subgroup is a great place to start. Of course, if we were wrong (which we're not), we could expand the scope of the search by creating a broader subgroup or, heck, by searching the entire Microsoft TechNet CD-ROM. A subset is easily created via the Define Subset command under the Contents menu in Microsoft TechNet.

Step 2. Next, create the search query. In this case, I'm interested in the term "sequence" in the context of the TCP protocol. Thus, this query is constructed with the term "sequence" near "tcp." Note that the BackOffice1 subset from Step 1 is being used (see Figure 19-31).

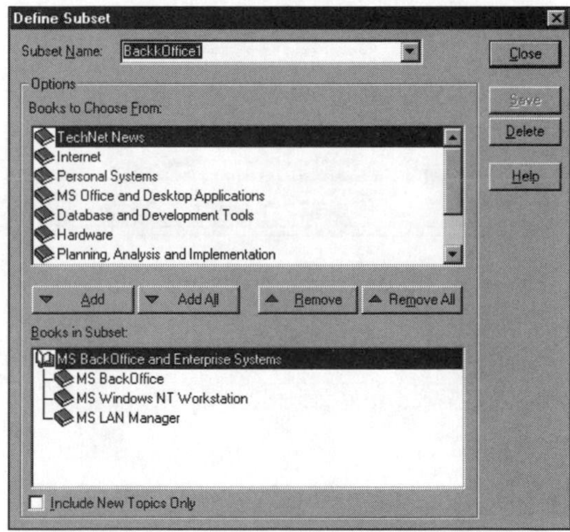

Figure 19-31: The BackOffice query window

Continued

STEPS:

To search TechNet for information on sequence value *(continued)*

Step 3. The results of this query clearly bear the fruit we are seeking. Once you have the results of your query, they will be displayed as shown in Figure 19-32. The challenge you face is to quickly select the article(s) that will provide the knowledge you need.

Make heavy use of the term "near" when constructing your searches in Microsoft TechNet. The "near" term will look for the requested terms within sixteen words of each other. This search term is much more powerful than the typical Boolean search terms "and" and "or." Take it from a daily user of Microsoft TechNet: The term "near" should be near and dear to your heart.

Step 4. Voila! After selecting the best article (see Figure 19-33), press Ctrl+D to hop quickly down to the appropriate search terms. In this case, Ctrl+D places us in a paragraph that is very descriptive and helpful in our quest to learn about the sequence number in the TCP protocol. The first article we found has a passage that sufficiently defines the term "sequence."

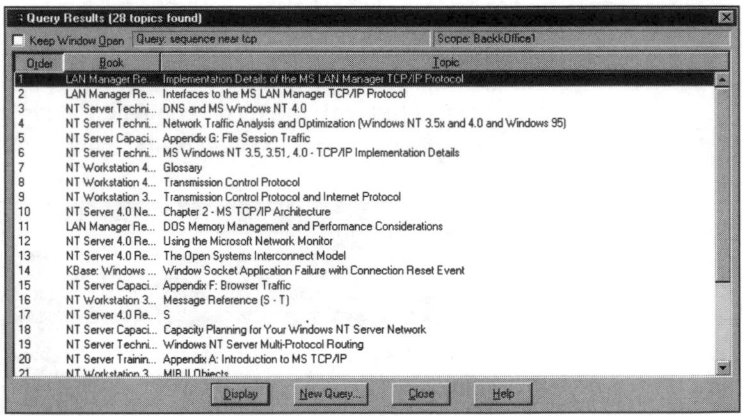

Figure 19-32: The search results in 28 hits

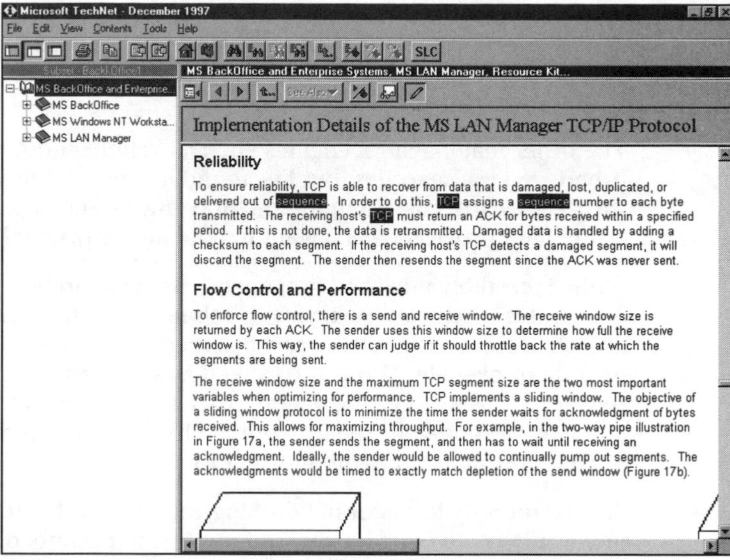

Figure 19-33: A selected article from the search results

Internet-based research

And of course, don't overlook the possibilities of the Internet when researching network analysis. Here's a quick example. You can use the Search button on the toolbar of the Internet Explorer browser and search on the general terms "network analysis" using one of the popular search engines. Using the Search button will take you to the all-in-one search engine page supported by Microsoft.

Tip

Consider using Infoseek as your Internet search engine if you think the nature of your queries will be "drill-down." Not to sound biased, but my experience has shown that Infoseek has the strongest drill-down capabilities. Notice that I didn't say Infoseek was the strongest search engine, just that it shines in this one type of structured search. What is drill down? When I recently searched on the word "network" using Infoseek, nearly four million hits were returned. Then I added the term "analysis" to my Infoseek search, and that resulted in fewer than 2,500 hits. Finally, I added the term "packets" to my search, and the results dropped to approximately 126 hits, most of which were germane to my packet analysis educational mission. If you haven't discovered the drill-down nature of Infoseek, I encourage you to repeat the same experiment I've just shared with you. Infoseek may be reached, as previously mentioned, via the Search button on Microsoft Internet Explorer, or at `www.infoseek.com`.

The other major search engines such as Yahoo! and AltaVista are great for broad, general searches, but I've found it is more difficult to drill down into the data I want. For example, the AltaVista search engine has a complex refinement process when I want to append my original search conditions.

While incredibly powerful for general, broad searches, AltaVista presents challenges when you are trying to refine and drill down into your initial search. Here, on the refine search screen, you must select which terms to include or exclude. Terms are ranked as a percentage of importance. While powerful, this search refinement process is somewhat time consuming and annoying. Feel free to see for yourself by selecting AltaVista after clicking the Search button in Microsoft Internet Explorer, or go to `www.altavista.com`.

Surfing directly to major networking vendors' Web sites is, of course, another powerful way to educate yourself on the finer points of network analysis. These Web sites typically host white papers that, while often promoting a specific product, also provide solid technical knowledge. For starters, I can recommend the sites listed in Table 19-1 as good sources of information on network analysis.

Table 19-1 Networking Analysis Resources on the Web

Vendors	*Site*	*Comments*
IBM	`www.ibm.com`	Yes — IBM. A great site for research relating to network analysis. Yes, it's true. Big Blue has got it right.
3COM	`www.3com.com`	Search on keywords such as "switches" and "routers." Used to have white papers that were truly academic (er, nonsales) in nature.
Shiva	`www.shiva.com`	This is a long-time player in computer communications including wide area connectivity.
John M. Fluke Company	`www.fluke.com`	A leading manufacturer of cable testing and network analysis devices. This site has excellent white papers.
Microsoft	`www.microsoft.com`	Of course!

Hardware devices

You may have arrived in the networking industry via the hardware break/fix and wiring/cabling industry. The experience you bring is worthwhile, and perhaps you've already performed network monitoring using hardware-based analysis tools.

One tool I have used is the Fluke One Touch Network Assistant 10/100. This device provides, in the palm of your hand, many of the same statistics we use Network Monitor for. From the main LCD panel, you can perform the tasks shown in Table 19-2.

Table 19-2 One Touch Network Assistant 10/100 Features

Feature	*Description*
AutoTest	This option performs discovery. Connectivity tests are performed so that devices are identified on your network. The devices for your cable segment are displayed via NetBIOS names and MAC addresses. I've found the node discovery to be very reliable. Like the full-featured version of Network Monitor in SMS, the Fluke Network Assistant performs router discovery. Servers are listed by type (NetWare, Windows 2000 Server). Windows 2000 servers are identified as domain controllers, member servers, and master browsers. Additional information is provided for frame type, protocol, and domain membership.
Network Health	This is very similar to performing a frame capture using the Capture windows in Network Monitor. Tests are performed for utilization, errors, collisions, broadcasts protocols, and individual station statistics. At a glance, I've found the broadcast traffic statistics to be incredibly valuable.
Cable Tests	Just try this with Network Monitor, my friend. These are the advanced cable testing functions built into the Network Assistant. Tests are included to measure the cable length, the wire pinouts on a cable (this is great for verifying the accuracy of homemade crossover cables), cable quality, and intermittent failures associated with cables.
NIC/Hub Tests	These tests determine if the network adapter card and hub are functioning properly. Here again, with the MCSE lab where I teach evening classes, this type of test has really helped in troubleshooting those annoying gotchas that students always seem to discover during a lecture. These include underperforming workstations, dead workstations, no primary domain controller error messages at logon, and other general nonsense.
Ping Station	This is exactly the same as the PING IP test at the C:> prompt in a command prompt window. This capability of the Fluke Network Assistant makes it much more than just another cable tester.

Needless to say, Fluke's Network Assistant has been invaluable in troubleshooting the MCSE lab environments that I teach in and provides a different view of network analysis. Best of all, you can print out the analysis from the Network Assistant to a printer connected to its printer port. Oh, did I forget to mention that this device is approximately $5,000? That's a little bit more than Network Monitor, which of course is included for free with Windows 2000 Server.

Books

I've eliminated many of the texts that are too focused on theoretical hooey. You want immediate results. These two books deliver and are suggested as next steps once you are familiar with Network Monitor:

- Enck, John, and Mel Beckman. *LAN to WAN Interconnection.* McGraw-Hill, 1995. This book is appropriately subtitled "For those who are familiar with one geography and perplexed by the other." Indeed, it was this book that enabled me to better understand the world of wide area networking. Better yet, this book provides excellent references to packet construction, so I know my DSOs from my DLCIs. If these two acronyms are foreign to you, it is essential that you read this book on your path to mastering network analysis.
- Buchanan, Jr., Robert. *The Art of Testing Network Systems.* Wiley Computer Publishing (John Wiley & Sons, Inc.), 1996. This book provides numerous test methodologies that are directly applicable to structuring your network analysis. Without test methodologies, you may well be tempted to perform your analysis in a willy-nilly fashion, which at a minimum will take longer to complete. I highly recommend this book.

For a long list of books that discuss network monitoring from a technical perspective, go to the online Windows NT Server documentation (this is not a joke) and select the "book" term in the network monitoring help area. Look for the chapter titled "Network Monitor Guide to Books on Networking" and you will be presented with over 33 texts to select from. Yes—you read correctly. Go back and find your old Windows NT Server and fire it up. These resources are not listed in the new documentation included with Windows 2000 Server (bummer). Good luck!

Online help

Network Monitor's online help has been dramatically improved under Windows 2000 Server. That's based on direct feedback from users who wanted to take advantage of Network Monitor but didn't know how. There are two online help systems for Network Monitor; one is superior and the other is adequate. The superior online help system for Network Monitor is found via the general online help for Windows 2000 Server (select Help from the Windows 2000 Server Start menu). This online help system contains a section titled Monitoring and Diagnostics Tools. Nested in this section is a Network Monitor chapter that contains rich information about packet analysis, including incredibly valuable checklists (see Figure 19-34). The "adequate" online help system is found via the Help menu in Network Monitor. It has only a section titled "Analyzing Network Data with Network Monitor."

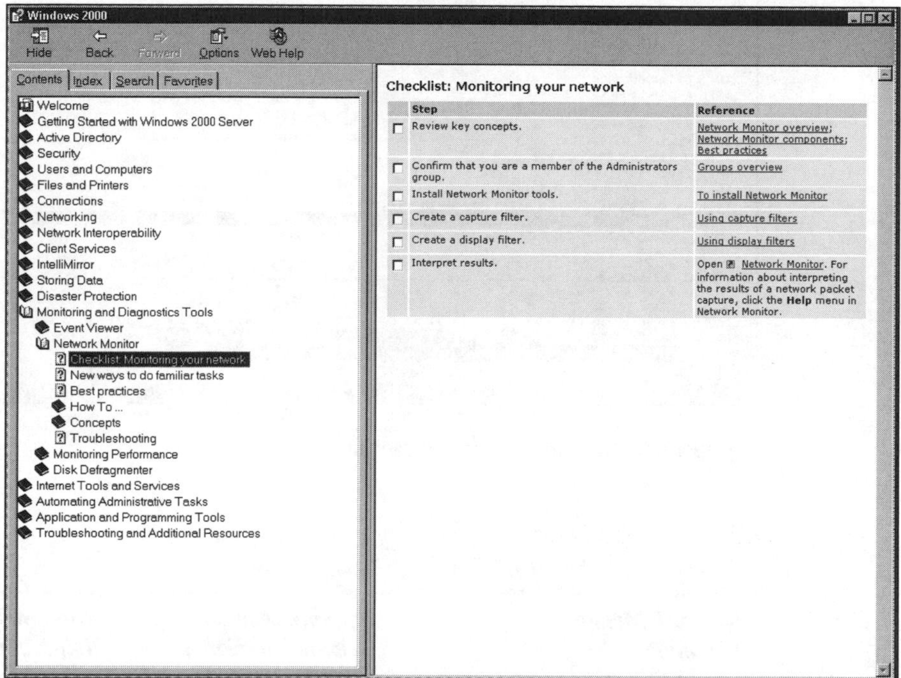

Figure 19-34: Network Monitor checklists via online help system

Comparing Network Monitors: SMS versus Windows 2000 Server

The basic differences between the crippled version of Network Monitor included with Windows 2000 Server and the full-featured version of Network Monitor found in SMS are discussed in Table 19-3. You might be interested in knowing that the version of Network Monitor included with Windows 2000 Server is also known as the "Lite Version" (see Figure 19-35).

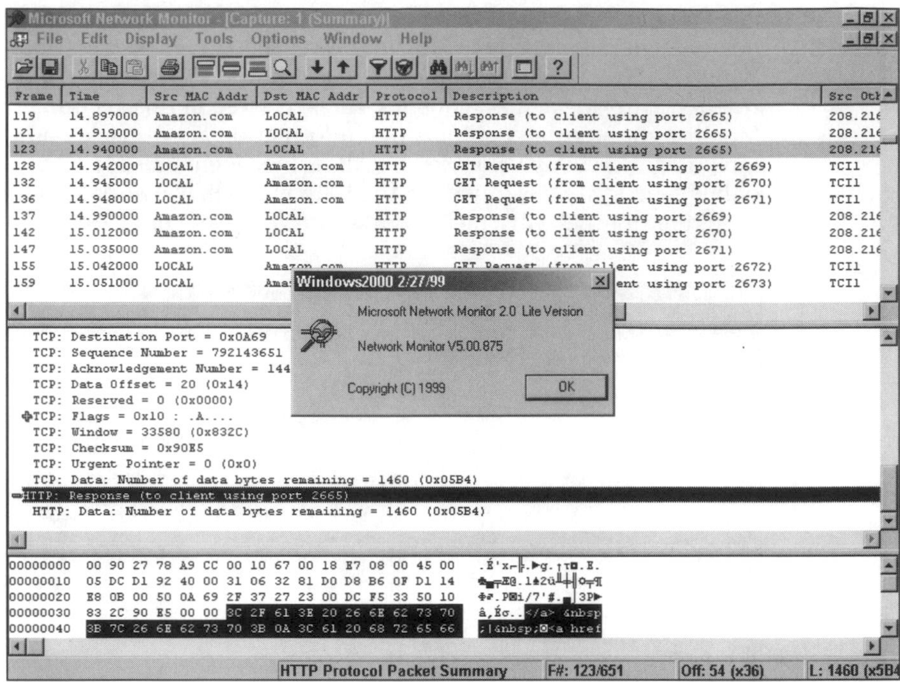

Figure 19-35: Network Monitor lite version

Table 19-3 Network Monitor Comparison

Network Monitor Capability	***Network Monitor (crippled version in Windows 2000 Server)***	***Network Monitor (full-featured version in SMS)***
"Man in the middle" — Editing and resending frames	No	Yes
Remote Capturing based on Network Monitor Agent running on other workstations	No	Yes
Capability to run Network Monitor Agent to enable other workstations running Network Monitor to capture frames at your workstation	Yes	Yes
Determining heaviest user of network resources (bandwidth)	Not built-in. Secret: Can visually determine by observing Station Statistics pane in Network Monitor.	Yes (built-in capability)

Network Monitor Capability	***Network Monitor (crippled version in Windows 2000 Server)***	***Network Monitor (full-featured version in SMS)***
Determining which protocol is using the greatest amount of bandwidth	Not built-in. Secret: Could be determined by capturing all protocols and using the Display Filter dialog box to display each protocol separately in the Frame Viewer window. This would be a rough guesstimate approach at best.	Yes (built-in capability)
Reverse resolution of a device name (NetBIOS name) being resolved to a MAC address	No. The command Resolve Addresses from Name under the Tools menu returns an error message: "Tool Unavailable: This command is available only in the version of Network Monitor provided with Microsoft Systems Management Server."	Yes
I See You and You See Me — determining which machines are running Network Monitor	Yes. Under the Tools menu, select Identify Network Monitor users.	Yes
Experts — Wizard-like helpers that assist with your packet analysis	No	Yes
Capability to find routers	No. Selecting Find Routers under the Tools menu returns an error message: "Tool Unavailable: This command is available only in the version of Network Monitor provided with Microsoft Systems Management Server."	Yes

Besides purchasing and installing SMS to obtain the full version of Network Monitor, you can obtain the full-featured version of Network Monitor by attending Microsoft certification course #689, "Supporting Windows NT Server 4.0 — Enterprise Technologies" (or its soon-to-be-announced Windows 2000-related successor course). Students are provided the same Network

Monitor as found in SMS for training and learning purposes. It is not intended to be used as a tool on your "real" network. However, just having access to the full-featured edition of Network Monitor enables you to learn and exploit its advanced capabilities. At that point, you may decide to purchase SMS and legally obtain the full version.

Summary

In this chapter you learned about the following.

- The definition of Network Monitor
- The basics of Network Monitor
- The basics of network analysis
- That Network Monitor can be configured for capturing and viewing
- That resources for learning more about Network Monitor include paid support incidents, Microsoft certification courses, Microsoft TechNet, specific books on network analysis, Internet resources, and Windows 2000 Server online help
- That, although the products are comparable, there are different features in Windows 2000 Server Network Monitor and System Management Server (SMS) Network Monitor

Chapter 20

Task Manager and Other Neat Tricks

In This Chapter

- Defining Task Manager features
- Tuning Task Manager to report the information you need
- Optimizing Windows 2000 Server via Task Manager
- Defining System Information features in Windows 2000 Server
- Learning about SQL Trace and ODBCPING
- Learning about the Microsoft Exchange RPING utility
- Viewing and analyzing event logs
- Discovering the Microsoft System Information tool
- A visit from Dr. Watson!

Windows 2000 Server contains several more performance management tools than just Performance Monitor and Network Monitor to help you manage your system. These tools include, but are clearly not limited to, Task Manager and System Information. Both of these offer a more static view of your system than discussed in the past few chapters.

But don't let the small footprint of Task Manager lull you into complacency. Behind its meek appearance, Task Manager serves a useful purpose. By the end of this chapter, I think you will agree that Task Manager is much more important than you ever imagined. In fact, Task Manager reports some measurements that both Performance Monitor and Network Monitor can only dream about reporting. System Information (previously known as WinMSD) is an old friend and is the reincarnation of MSD from the DOS era. The primary difference between System Information and WinMSD (Windows NT Server era) and MSD (MS-DOS era) is that System Information is MMC-based, stable under Windows 2000, and reports much more information than its Windows NT Server or MS-DOS predecessors.

I'll show you the Systems Properties sheet and neat little tools included with SQL Server and Microsoft Exchange to assist with your performance management activities. And don't forget the event logs contained in Event Viewer. You have my personal assurance that you will interact frequently with the event logs as you journey toward the perfectly optimized Windows 2000 Server configuration.

One of the best-kept secrets is to actually install Microsoft Office on your Windows 2000 server to dramatically improve the monitoring of your system. That is so that you can use Microsoft System Information contained within Excel. But more on that wonderful trick later.

At the end the chapter, we'll get a house call from our friend, Dr. Watson. Now, let's discuss Task Manager.

Introducing Task Manager

Remember attending college and how important "exact" details seemed? Take the quantitative mathematics series in business school which emphasized statistics and corporate financial analysis. Exact mathematical calculations performed as part of the financial analysis to theoretically purchase a stock seemed so doggone necessary. Let me ask you a question several years hence. When you recently met with your life insurance agent, did you perform the same rigorous mathematics as you allocated your retirement fund between high-risk, growth, and conservative investment vehicles? Of course not, even with something as important as that. Most likely, you sat on your sofa and barked something like 30 percent to aggressive, 40 percent to high-growth, and 30 percent to conservative. Case closed and investment made.

This reflects how most of us live in the real world on a day-to-day basis. Intuition, combined with a reasonable amount of information, guides our decisions, including how we manage our Windows 2000 Server networks. Intuition in network managers is clearly gained through experience or by being blessed with superior intelligence. Efficiently gathering reasonable amounts of information in Windows 2000 Server is the goal. Thankfully, much of the quick-and-dirty information we need is just a simple right-click away via Task Manager. Let's face it! Task Manager is probably sufficient to provide enough system-based information to meet your casual Windows 2000 Server decision making needs (see Figure 20-1).

Task Manager is my buddy and I make no bones about it. I use Task Manager on a day-to-day basis as outlined in the text that follows. Access Task Manager by right-clicking while the cursor is on the Windows 2000 Server taskbar.

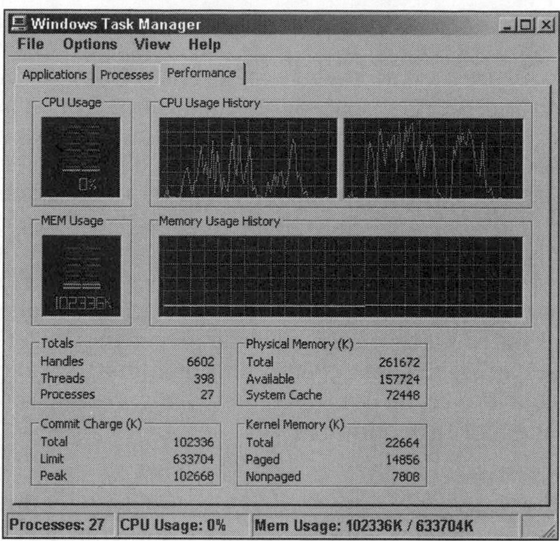

Figure 20-1: Windows 2000 Server Task Manager — Performance tab sheet

- **The Applications tab sheet.** Use the Applications tab sheet (Figure 20-2) to identify which applications are running and what the status of each is. In particular, I'm interested in the "Not responding status." It is those applications that are not responding that I deftly annihilate with a swift click on the End Task button.

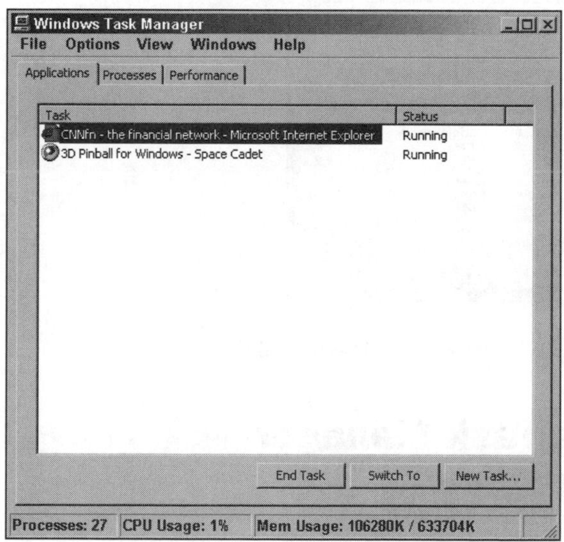

Figure 20-2: The Applications tab sheet in Task Manager

- **The Performance tab sheet.** The Performance tab sheet is your mini-Performance Monitor (see Figure 20-1). At a glance, you can get a quick view of the CPU usage on your server and a sense of how memory is being used. This tab sheet is most useful when I encounter a badly behaved application or process. Periodically, I know my system is running slow because acceptable response times drops and end users start calling. Looking at the Performance tab sheet typically confirms my beliefs. Microsoft Exchange is perhaps the one BackOffice application that is still really finding its feet. Exchange-related processes (such as DSX.EXE — a process related to Exchange Directory Services) have a way of freaking out on occasion, resulting in 100 percent processor utilization rates on your server plus no available memory. Not only does the Performance tab sheet confirm this nightmare, but I can terminate this bad dream, as described previously, via the Application tab sheet and the End Task button.
- **The Processes tab sheet.** The Processes tab sheet, while used less frequently, is invaluable when we seek to identify the offending process down to the file name (see Figure 20-3). Take my Microsoft Exchange example. The DSX.EXE process once really did consume the CPU time on my Windows 2000 Server. The solution? I went to the Processes tab sheet, quickly identified the problematic "Image Name" (Microsoft's term for process or application in column one of the Processes tab sheet) and killed it by clicking the End Process button. Yahoo! Problem solved.

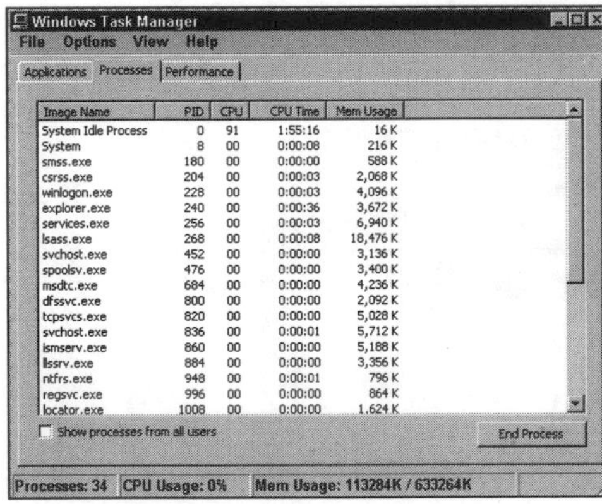

Figure 20-3: The Processes tab sheet in Task Manager

Configuring Task Manager — Applications view

The Applications view is the simplest and most common view found in Task Manager. It is the view that you typically use to determine whether an application is running or not responding. This is usually the screen where you kill your non-running applications. Even though the interface for the Applications tab is simple, it underscores a major point about Windows 2000

Server compared to previous Windows desktop releases (such as Windows For Workgroups). That is, you can kill a crashed application without having to reboot the server. Remember that applications run in a protected memory area separate from the Windows 2000 Server kernel.

One feature that is extremely helpful on a day-to-day basis is the Context menu (see Figure 20-4). From the Context menu, you may end a task. To access a Context menu for an application, simply right-click while an application name has the focus (that is, you have the mouse pointer placed over the application name).

Another possible use for the Applications view in Task Manager is to start a launch of another application by selecting the New Task (Run) menu option under the File menu.

The New Task (Run) is available by right-clicking anywhere on an unoccupied area of the Applications tab sheet.

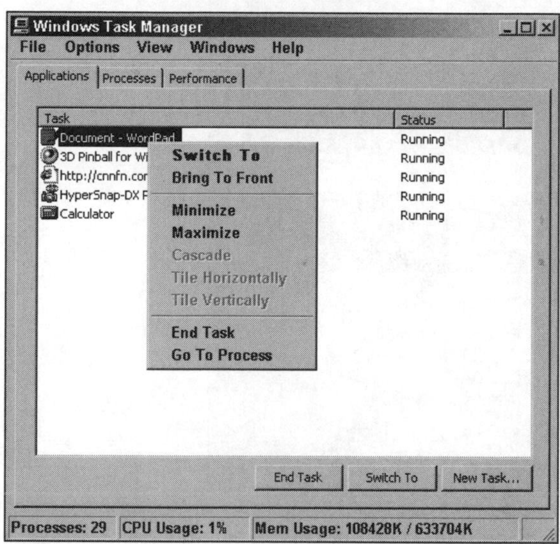

Figure 20-4: A context menu in Task Manager

Configuring Task Manager — Performance view

This is the "heartbeat" display in Task Manager. It is, at a glance, perhaps the best view to show a manager. Even basic computer users can understand the two major features of this view: CPU Usage and MEM Usage.

CPU Usage

CPU Usage is similar to two object:counters in Performance Monitor — Processor:% Processor Time and System:% Total Processor Time. Note that

CPU Usage doesn't measure Idle threads. To see Idle threads, you would need to view the System Idle Process row on the Processes tab sheet in Task Manager (remember that Windows 2000 Server uses Idle threads as something of a sleep mode for the CPU).

MEM Usage

MEM Usage not only reflects the kilobytes of virtual memory used, but can also be tracked via the Memory:Committed bytes object:counter in Performance Monitor.

Task Manager does something with its Performance view that can only be accomplished in Performance Monitor when two copies of Performance Monitor are running. That special feature is to display the same counter simultaneously as a histogram and a graph (see Figure 20-5).

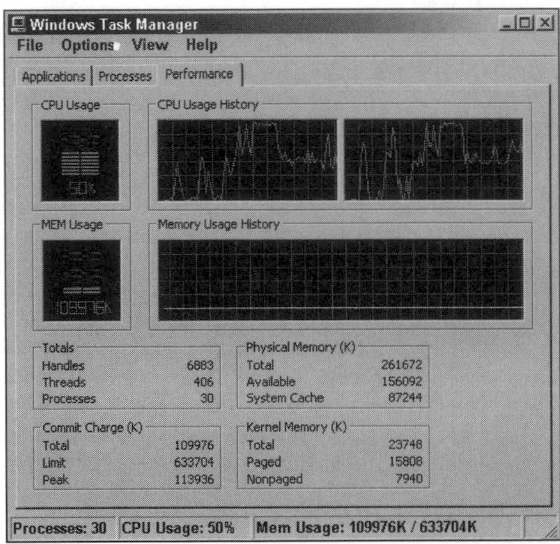

Figure 20-5: The Performance tab sheet histogram, graph, and table formats

Totals

This section refers to several types of system objects including handles, threads, and processes. Because system objects take up space in nonpaged memory that is managed by the operating system, we are indeed concerned about these numbers. Too many active system objects typically result in bottlenecks at the processor or in memory use.

- **Total handles.** Handles essentially refer to system objects such as open files. Technically, it means the object handles present in all active processes.
- **Total threads.** Reflects executing threads or, stated another way, the number of threads running. This measurement is akin to the Process:Thread Count_ Total in Performance Monitor.

- **Total processes.** A process, in my eyes, can simply be thought of as an application. This number reflects Idle processes that basically run when the CPU is sleeping.

Physical Memory

This is easy. Total refers to the total RAM installed on the computer running Windows 2000 Server. It is measured in kilobytes. Not surprisingly, "Available" refers to the available RAM in kilobytes. File Cache refers to the total memory that has been allocated to the file cache.

Commit Charge

This generically refers to memory allocated to the operating system and programs. This includes both physical RAM and virtual memory. Total refers to the memory (both real and virtual) that is currently in use. Limit refers to the upper limits of all memory combined before the paging file size would have to be increased. Peak refers to highest memory in use during the current session.

Kernel Memory

First, it is important to understand that kernel refers to memory in use by the operating system in kernel mode. Figure 20-6 demonstrates the differences between Kernel mode and User mode in Windows 2000 Server.

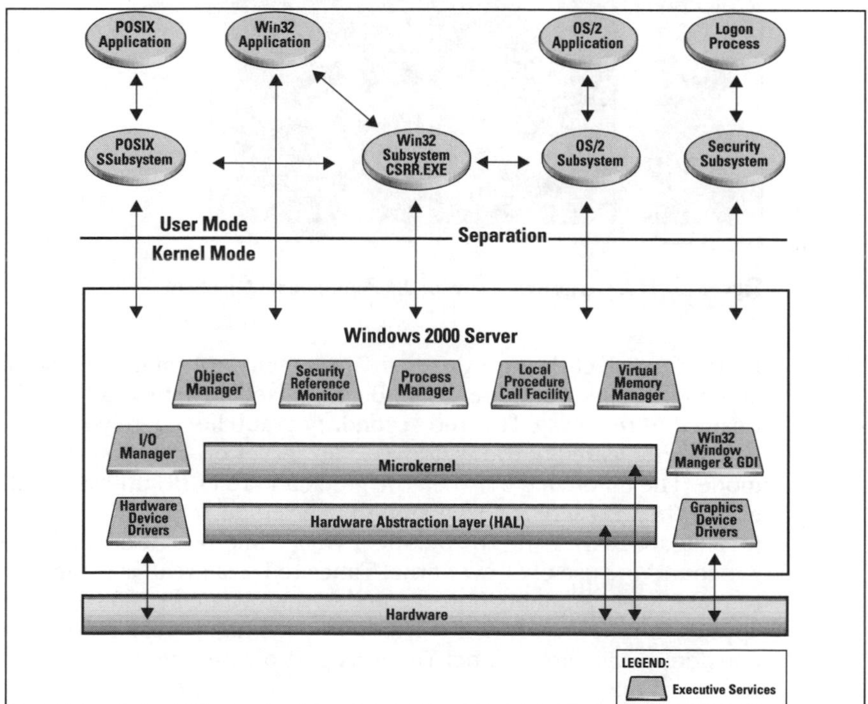

Figure 20-6: Windows 2000 Server User and Kernel modes

Basically, Windows 2000 Server Executive-related services run in Kernel mode. Total refers to both the paged and nonpaged memory in use. Paged refers to the operating system's page pool. Nonpaged, not surprisingly, refers to the nonpaged memory dedicated to the operating system.

Double-click anywhere on the Performance tab sheet in Windows 2000 Server Task Manager, and the CPU Usage and MEM Usage real-time charts will expand to fill the entire Task Manager window (see Figure 20-7). This will eliminate the extra descriptions, such as Totals, Physical Memory, Commit Charge, and Kernel Memory, and give you just the charts. You may resize this window to consume the entire screen or just a small portion of it. When this window is resized to cover your desktop, it looks very much like another tool we're familiar with: Performance Monitor (that is, if all we charted on Performance Monitor was the CPU utilization rate).

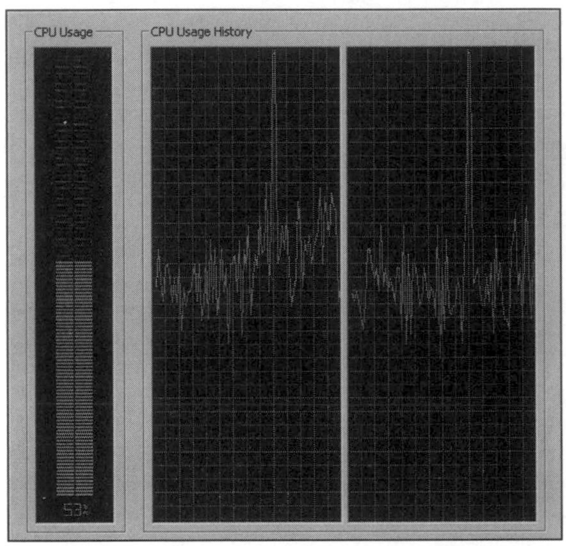

Figure 20-7: An "exploded" view of the Performance tab sheet

Be sure to select the Show Kernel Times menu option under the View menu. You might think it's the return of Big Red (NetWare) in your Task Manager CPU Usage, but rest easy. This red secondary graph line merely reflects the CPU activity dedicated to the Windows 2000 Server operating system in Kernel mode. The difference between the green and red CPU utilization chart lines reflect the CPU activity dedicated to User mode activities such as applications (see Figure 20-8). From the perspective of a Microsoft Certified Trainer (MCT), I've found the use of Show Kernel Times to be of great assistance when trying to teach eager students how the underlying Windows 2000 architecture applies to the real world. If you're a trainer, I highly recommend that you consider using Show Kernel Times as part of your lectures.

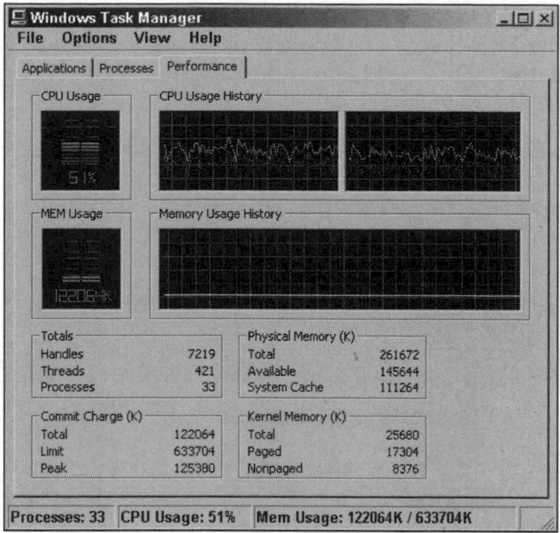

Figure 20-8: Show Kernel Times in Performance view

Configuring Task Manager — Processes view

Task Manager can be richly configured to reflect many different Windows 2000 Server system conditions. Fully configured, Task Manager in the Processes view would display 23 columns of information and look similar to Figure 20-9.

Windows Task Manager

File Options View Help

Applications Processes Performance

Image Name	PID	Username	Session ID	CPU	CPU Time	Mem Usage	Peak Mem Usage	Mem Delta	Page Faults	PF Delta	VM Size	Paged Pool
System Idle Process	0	SYSTEM	0	94	1:59:02	16 K	16 K	0 K	1	0	0 K	0 K
System	8	SYSTEM	0	00	0:00:08	216 K	636 K	0 K	1,921	0	24 K	0 K
smss.exe	180	SYSTEM	0	00	0:00:00	588 K	2,244 K	0 K	680	0	276 K	6 K
csrss.exe	204	SYSTEM	0	00	0:00:03	2,068 K	2,156 K	0 K	939	0	1,284 K	34 K
winlogon.exe	228	SYSTEM	0	00	0:00:03	4,096 K	8,108 K	0 K	5,987	0	4,980 K	35 K
explorer.exe	240	Administrator	0	00	0:00:36	4,164 K	9,016 K	0 K	47,205	1	5,224 K	57 K
services.exe	256	SYSTEM	0	00	0:00:04	6,932 K	7,292 K	0 K	2,194	0	2,852 K	35 K
lsass.exe	268	SYSTEM	0	00	0:00:08	18,476 K	18,644 K	0 K	8,927	0	14,548 K	51 K
svchost.exe	452	SYSTEM	0	00	0:00:00	3,136 K	3,144 K	0 K	835	0	1,132 K	19 K
spoolsv.exe	476	SYSTEM	0	00	0:00:00	3,400 K	3,480 K	0 K	1,026	0	1,320 K	22 K
msdtc.exe	684	SYSTEM	0	00	0:00:00	4,236 K	4,276 K	0 K	1,183	0	1,468 K	23 K
dfssvc.exe	800	SYSTEM	0	00	0:00:00	2,092 K	2,096 K	0 K	558	0	632 K	13 K
tcpsvcs.exe	820	SYSTEM	0	00	0:00:00	5,028 K	5,032 K	0 K	1,526	0	2,632 K	26 K
svchost.exe	836	SYSTEM	0	00	0:00:01	5,720 K	5,736 K	0 K	1,730	0	1,724 K	35 K
ismserv.exe	860	SYSTEM	0	00	0:00:00	5,188 K	5,204 K	0 K	1,623	0	1,832 K	32 K
llssrv.exe	884	SYSTEM	0	00	0:00:00	3,356 K	3,464 K	0 K	1,015	0	1,348 K	17 K
ntfrs.exe	948	SYSTEM	0	00	0:00:01	820 K	9,572 K	0 K	8,307	0	10,224 K	22 K
regsvc.exe	996	SYSTEM	0	00	0:00:00	864 K	872 K	0 K	225	0	236 K	7 K
locator.exe	1008	SYSTEM	0	00	0:00:00	1,624 K	1,624 K	0 K	403	0	580 K	15 K
mstask.exe	1024	SYSTEM	0	00	0:00:00	2,396 K	2,416 K	0 K	637	0	644 K	21 K
termsrv.exe	1076	SYSTEM	0	00	0:00:00	3,188 K	3,200 K	0 K	912	0	1,768 K	21 K
lserver.exe	1132	SYSTEM	0	00	0:00:00	5,432 K	5,596 K	0 K	1,572	0	3,432 K	23 K
wins.exe	1176	SYSTEM	0	00	0:00:00	2,860 K	2,864 K	0 K	840	0	2,204 K	19 K
dns.exe	1192	SYSTEM	0	00	0:00:00	3,316 K	3,320 K	0 K	886	0	1,244 K	21 K
inetinfo.exe	1224	SYSTEM	0	00	0:00:06	8,784 K	8,972 K	0 K	2,534	0	5,628 K	46 K
hsdx.exe	1436	Administrator	0	00	0:00:04	264 K	6,088 K	(956) K	12,491	68	2,900 K	25 K
mdm.exe	1760	Administrator	0	00	0:00:00	2,292 K	2,456 K	0 K	690	0	652 K	17 K
taskmgr.exe	1848	Administrator	0	00	0:00:01	1,356 K	2,076 K	8 K	881	2	592 K	20 K
svchost.exe	2000	SYSTEM	0	00	0:00:00	3,028 K	3,040 K	0 K	763	0	1,560 K	25 K
netmon.exe	2096	Administrator	0	00	0:00:03	1,740 K	10,708 K	0 K	24,437	0	2,080 K	29 K

Show processes from all users

End Process

Processes: 34 CPU Usage: 2% Mem Usage: 112228K / 633264K

Figure 20-9: Process columns displayed on one screen

You might be interested to know this is a significant change from Windows NT Server, when the Processes view could only be configured to display 16 columns of information. This is yet another example of how Windows 2000 Server is a dramatic improvement over Windows NT Server.

Each column reports important system information. To add columns when in the Processes view, first select the View drop-down menu and click the Select Columns menu option (see Figure 20-10). Then single-click the checkbox for each column you want to add to the Task Manager Processes view.

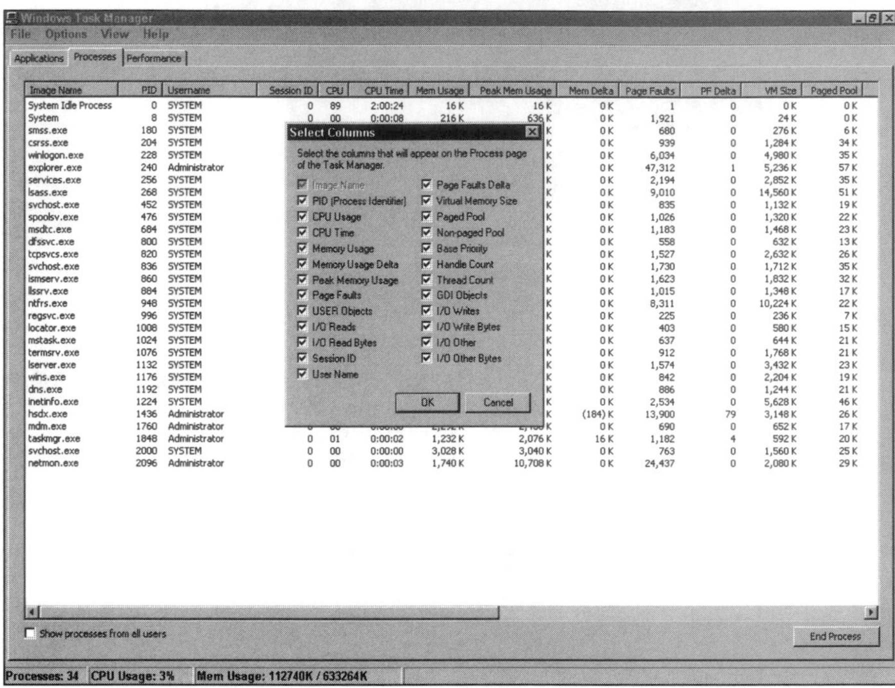

Figure 20-10: The Select Columns dialog box

"So what," you remark. "What do all of these columns really do for me?" Your answer is in Table 20-1.

Table 20-1 Task Manager Processes Column Definitions

Column	*Comments*	*Relation to Performance Monitor (Process Object)*
Image Name	This must always be selected and is the process name.	It is similar to selecting one of the instances in the Instances box of Performance Monitor after you have selected a specific object:counter.

Column	*Comments*	*Relation to Performance Monitor (Process Object)*
PID (Process Identifier)	This is the Process ID number that a running process receives. One use of this column is to better understand and see in action the nature of processes and threads discussed halfway through Course #687, "Windows NT Server — Core Technologies" certification course (or its successor). In the certification class, processes are identified in the context of running multiple processes on a single computer or a process being single- or multithreaded. The conceptual discussion also includes priority boosting of processes and threads (we actually handle this vis-à-vis the Set Priority context menu option, discussed later in this chapter). Because the certification exam will hold you responsible for understanding and identifying processes running on Windows 2000 Server, it is highly recommended that you take a moment to consider the importance of the PID column.	This is the ID Process counter associated with the Process object. Note that Process IDs are assigned on a session basis. The ID number will change, for example, the next time you reboot Windows 2000 Server. Process ID in Performance Monitor maps directly to the PID column in Task Manager. In Performance Monitor, display Process:ID Process in the report format. This value looks silly when plotted in the Performance Monitor Chart view. That's because it is an identifier, not a performance value.

Continued

Table 20-1 *(continued)*

Column	*Comments*	*Relation to Performance Monitor (Process Object)*
CPU Usage (Displayed as CPU)	This is the percentage of processor utilization time since the last update interval. The update interval is discussed later in this chapter.	This is the same as %Processor Time.
CPU Time	Measured in seconds, this is the total CPU time used by a process since its activities commenced.	There is no equivalent measurement in Performance Monitor.
Memory Usage (Mem Usage)	Measured in kilobytes, this is the quantity of main memory used.	This is the same as the Working Set performance counter.
Memory Usage Delta (Mem Delta)	The word delta, in statistics, refers to change, and its usage is no different here. This process measure refers to the memory use change since the last update interval. It is interesting to note that negative values (a decline in memory usage) can be reflected in Task Manager, but not in a like manner in Performance Monitor.	None.
Page Faults	This is cool. For a given process, this refers to how many times a page fault occurred. That means the data wasn't in memory and had to be retrieved from the hard disk, which of course is much slower. This is a cumulative value from the time the process commenced.	None. You might be tempted to use the Page Faults/sec counter found in the Process object, but that would be misleading and have you comparing apples to oranges. Page Faults/sec is calculated as a rate per second, but Page Faults in Task Manager is, of course, a cumulative value.
Page Faults Delta (PF Delta)	This reflects the difference or change in the number of page faults since the last update interval.	There is no equivalent measure in Performance Monitor.

Column	*Comments*	*Relation to Performance Monitor (Process Object)*
Virtual Memory in Size (VM Size)	Want to know how much of the paging file your process is consuming? Then this is your measure. Note that the information is reported in kilobytes.	Refer to the counter Page File Bytes under the Process object in Performance Monitor for an equivalent measure.
Paged Pool	Reflects how much user memory a process is using. Remember that paged pool memory is the virtual memory that is available and can be paged to disk. It contains user memory (all) and system memory (some). The measurement is in kilobytes.	See the Page File Bytes counter (same as in the preceding item).
Nonpaged Pool (NP Pool)	This is the nonpaged pool or system memory used by a process. By definition, this memory is not paged to disk. The measurement is in kilobytes.	See the Pool Nonpaged Bytes counter under the Process object in Performance Monitor.
Base Priority	This measurement ties into the previous discussion about how threads are explained in the Windows NT Server Core Technologies course (don't worry, the topics also apply to Windows 2000 Server). This value, the base priority, is set by the process itself, not Windows 2000 Server. The role of Windows 2000 Server is to adjust the process's threads within a range of the base priority. These ranges are described when setting base priorities via Task Manager is discussed.	Select the Priority Base counter in the Process object.

Continued

Table 20-1 *(continued)*

Column	*Comments*	*Relation to Performance Monitor (Process Object)*
Handle Count	Reflects the number of object handles in the process's object table. In English, this refers to the process's capability to access an object. When an object is accessed, a handle is created as a token. This identifies who has a connection to the token object. At a very deep level in security auditing in Windows 2000 Server, we are interested in who is accessing objects. Handles provide the method for monitoring such accesses. An alternative definition of handles is the "the number of system objects."	See the Handle Count counter under the Process object.
Thread Count	This is simple. It is the threads running in a process. Note that 16-bit applications are only going to have one process because they are single-threaded.	See the Thread Count counter under the Process object.
USER Objects	Reports information on objects active in user mode.	N/A
GDI Objects	Reports information on graphic display interface related objects.	N/A
Peak Memory Usage	This is the peak amount of memory that a process has used since the process was launched. This measurement is new in Windows 2000 Server.	N/A

Column	*Comments*	*Relation to Performance Monitor (Process Object)*
I/O Reads	This is the read input/output activity generated by the process. This includes but is not limited to device, network and file activity. This measurement is new in Windows 2000 Server.	See the IO Read Operations/sec counter under the Process object.
I/O Read Bytes	This reflects the volume of bytes read in I/O activity generated by the process. This includes but is not limited to device, network and file I/O activity. This measurement is new in Windows 2000 Server.	See the IO Read Bytes/sec counter under the Process object.
I/O Writes	This reflects write I/O activity created by the process. This includes but is not limited to device, network and file I/O activity. This measurement is new in Windows 2000 Server.	See the IO Write Operations/sec counter under the Process object.
I/O Write Bytes	This reflects the volume of bytes written in I/O activity generated by the process. This includes, but is not limited to, device, network, and file I/O activity. This measurement is new in Windows 2000 Server.	See the IO Write Bytes/sec counter under the Process object.
I/O Other	This measures general I/O activity that is neither read nor write in nature (for example, a control function). This measurement is new in Windows 2000 Server.	See the IO Other Operations/sec counter under the Process object.
I/O Other Bytes	This reflects the volume of bytes transferred in I/O operations that are neither read nor write in nature. This measurement is new in Windows 2000 Server.	See the IO Other Bytes/sec counter under the Process object.

See Appendix C for descriptions of common image names displayed in Task Manager.

How to look important with no money down — or how I justified my job using Task Manager! Had enough bulk mail in your e-mail in-box lately promising fantastic returns for little or no effort? Here is one more. Depending on your work situation, you may or may not have a need to justify your existence on occasion. So when those downsizing bean counters are nipping at your paycheck, fight back! Take a Windows 2000 Server and run Task Manager in the Processes view with all of the columns loaded up. Watch the cell values dance as Windows 2000 Server performs normal operations. This activity gives the illusion of important activity (okay, it is important activity) and makes your role look indispensable! Don't forget the "secret" to magic; sometimes keeping your job is illusion!

Once you have adjusted the Task Manager window to the size you want, it is easy to automatically have the Processes tab sheet display as many of the measurement columns as possible. This is accomplished by using the column autoresize feature in Task Manager. This feature is similar to that found in Excel. Simply place the cursor over the column separator vertical bar along the title line. The cursor will change shapes and look something like a Danforth anchor used in boating (see Figure 20-11). When this Danforth anchor-like symbol is present, double-click while still on the vertical separator bar and the column will automatically adjust to the smallest width possible that still accurately displays the column information. The results are impressive when you do this for the entire set of columns in Task Manager. On a 17" monitor, I was able to get nearly all columns of information to display at once on the Processes tab sheet.

Getting prioritized

Task Manager can be used to set CPU processing priorities for an application or process in Windows 2000 Server. This is accomplished very easily by selecting a process in the Processes tab sheet in Task Manager and displaying the context menu via a right-click (see Figure 20-12). You can change the base priority of a process to one of several options: Realtime, High, AboveNormal, Normal, BelowNormal, and Low. These changes are only temporary and last for the current session that the process is running.

To change an application's base priority so that the changes are retained each time the application is launched, perform the following: On the properties sheet for an application's executable file (`.exe`), use the command lines discussed in Table 20-2.

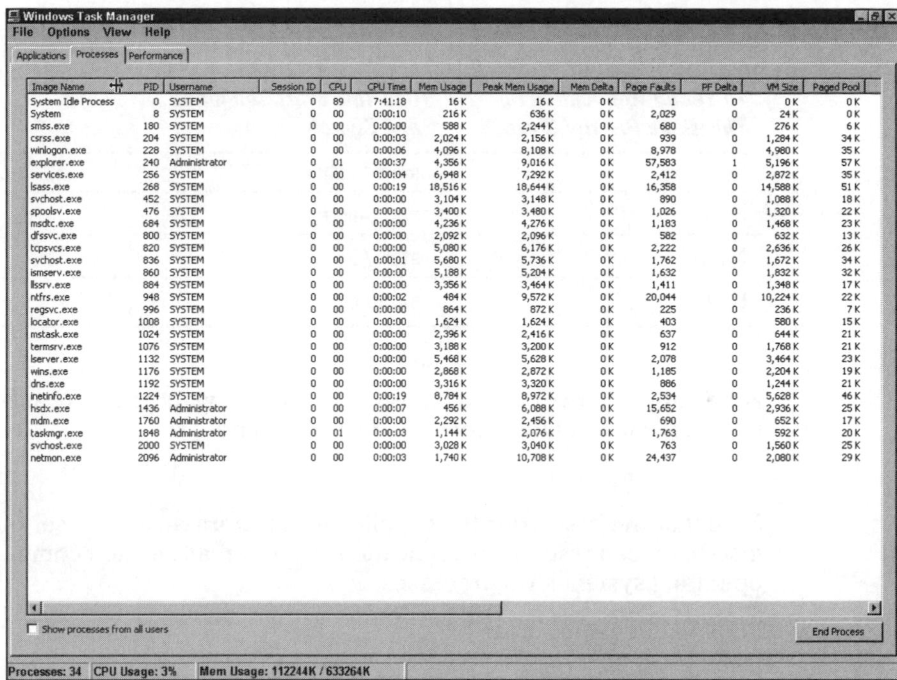

Figure 20-11: Customizing the number of displayed columns

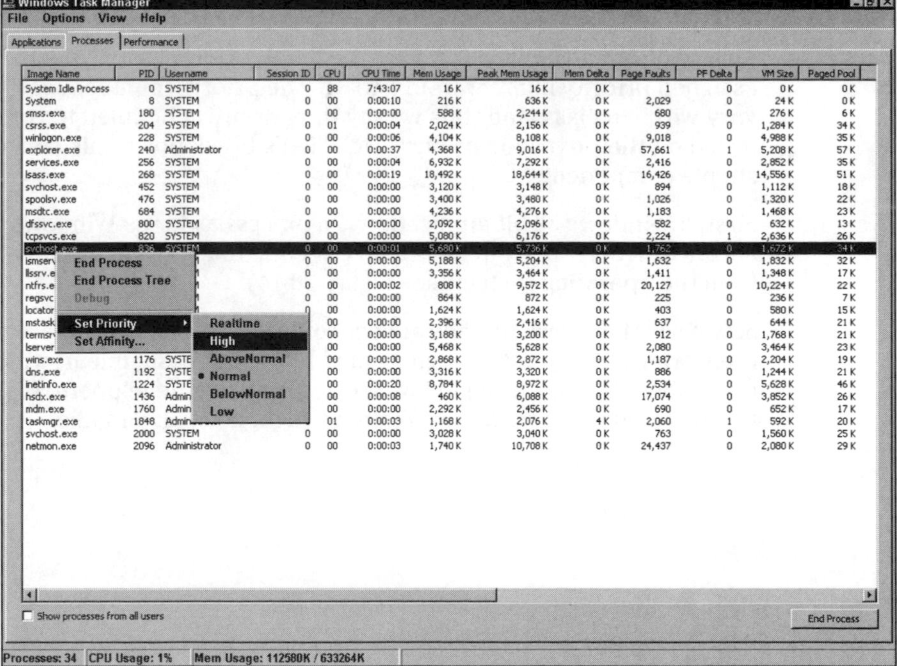

Figure 20-12: Setting a priority

Table 20-2 Setting Application Priority Classes via Command Lines

To Set an Application to This Base Priority Class	*Use This Start Command and Switch*
Realtime	start /realtime
High	start /high
Normal	start /normal
Low	start /low

For example, if the application is Excel and you want to set a base priority for this application of high, then use this command:

```
Start /high excel.exe
```

Note that the base priority of applications is normal. In fact, serious system instability can result if an application is set to realtime and competes with operating system-level processes.

But what does this mean?

Windows 2000 Server uses the microkernel to manage the prioritization threads with respect to processing. So what is the microkernel? It rests atop the hardware abstraction layer (HAL) and is affectionately referred to as the heart and soul of Windows 2000 Server, as shown in the diagram of the Windows 2000 Server architecture (see Figure 20-13).

Threads from an application are scheduled for processor time based upon an assigned priority number from 1 to 31. The priority number assigned can vary within a class, and thus we say threads are scheduled for processing based on their dynamic priority. Huh? Let's break down this concept into simple components.

First, a Windows 32-bit application is a *process* as far as Windows 2000 Server is concerned. Next, a *thread* is a unit of code that can get a slice of CPU time from the operating system (see Figure 20-14).

So we see that these threads are scheduled for processor time according to their priority. A priority is determined by a class assignment, which is a range of numbers that are assigned by the application's developers. A process can belong to one of four classes: realtime, high, normal, and idle.

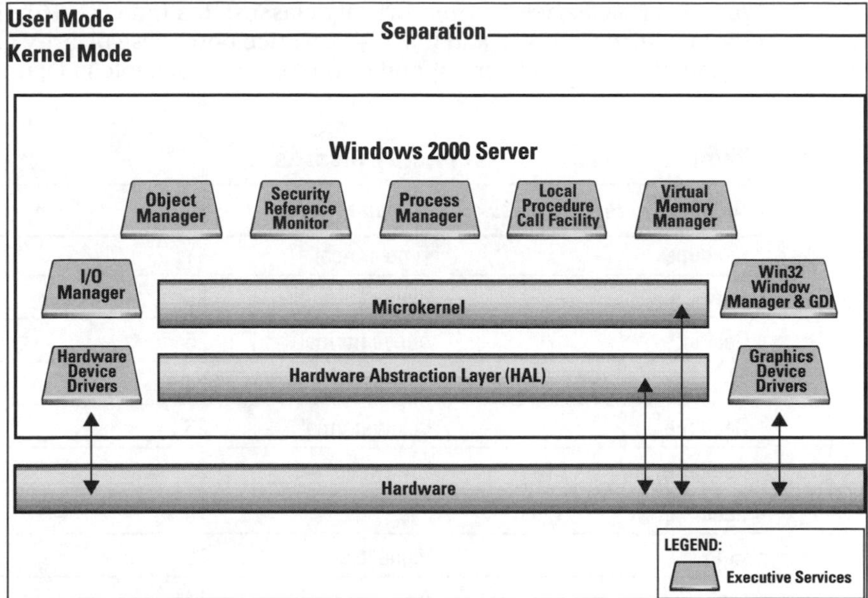

Figure 20-13: Windows 2000 Server architecture

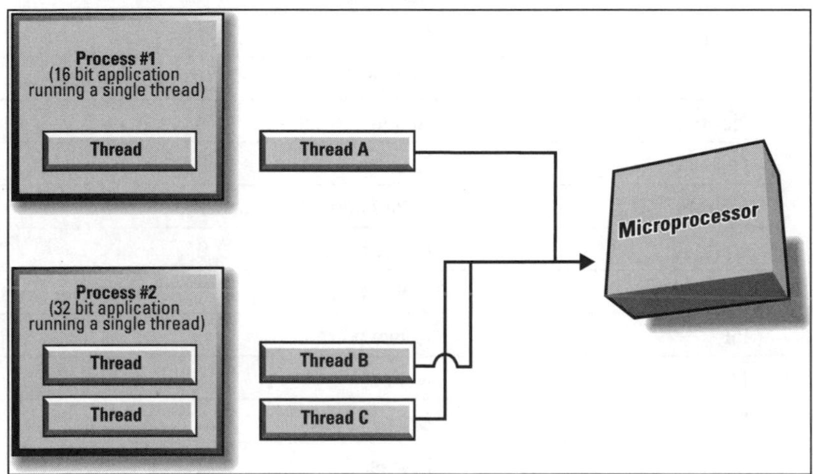

Figure 20-14: Processes and threads

Windows 2000 Server has four priority classes: Realtime (31–16), High (15–11), Normal (10–6), and Idle (6–1). Notice how these priority classes outlined in Table 20-3 correspond to the options available in Figure 20-12.

Table 20-3 Application Priority Classes

Application Priority Class	*Thread Priority*	*Base*
Realtime	Time critical	31
Realtime	Highest	26
Realtime	Above normal	25
Realtime	Normal	24
Realtime	Below normal	23
Realtime	Lowest	22
Realtime	Idle	16
High	Highest	15
High	Above normal	14
High	Normal	13
High	Below normal	12
High	Low	11
Normal	Highest	10
Normal	Above normal	9
Normal	Normal	8
Normal	Below normal	7
Normal	Lowest	6
Idle	Highest	6 (overlaps with Normal-Lowest)
Idle	Above normal	5
Idle	Normal	4
Idle	Below normal	3
Idle	Lowest	2
Idle	Idle	1

Windows 2000 Server can vary the process's priority within a class. Take Normal, for example. Normal is a priority class with a range of 6 to 10. The base priority of a process or application in the Normal class is 8 (which is the midpoint between the class range of 6 and 10). To efficiently schedule CPU resources, Windows 2000 Server will "dynamically" boost the priority of a thread within the base class of its process (+/– 2). This is normal and helps balance the competing demands on the processor (see Figure 20-15).

You can, or course, modify the base priority of a process in Windows 2000 Server. This was shown in Figure 20-12. It can also be accomplished in a similar way via Windows 2000 System Properties under the Advanced tab. Select the Performance Options button and optimize performance for either applications or background services.

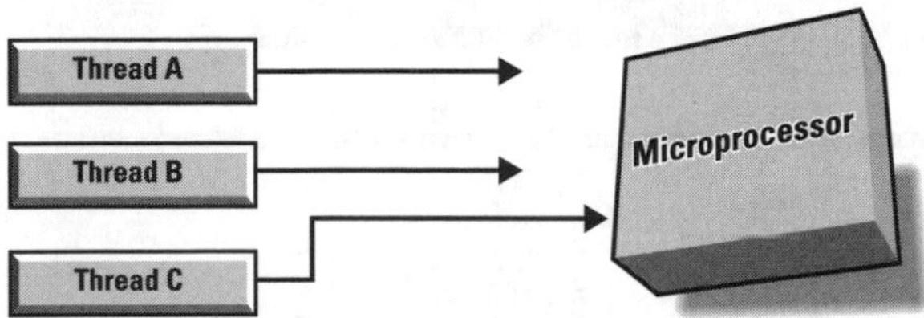

Figure 20-15: Thread boosting

Converting image names to real names

One of the biggest problems I encountered for *the longest time* was how to identify the application that the process name was associated with. This problem severely limited my effective use of the Processes view of Task Manager. And believe me, I had major needs to use Task Manager effectively, like the time a File and Print Services for NetWare (FPNW) application was being overpowered in a large-client environment. My specific need was to identify the image names or, in lay terms, the process names associated with FPNW. Once identified, I could experiment with boosting the process's priority so that it was guaranteed more processor time and thus higher performance (but, of course, hopefully without incurring any system instabilities).

Here is how you can identify what image name is associated with which application. The best way is to simply search your drives using the Find command accessed via the Start button in Windows 2000 Server. Alternative ways to find out more information on a specific image name include searching on the image name with a broad query applied against Microsoft TechNet or one of the powerful search engines on the Internet (see the text that follows).

In this example using the Find command, we will seek to better identify IEXPLORE.EXE and demystify what it really is.

STEPS:

To discover the true identity of IEXPLORE.EXE

Step 1. Notice the image name IEXPLORE.EXE in the Processes tab sheet of Task Manager (see Figure 20-16). You can easily perform these steps to better identify any image name; we are simply using IEXPLORE.EXE as an example.

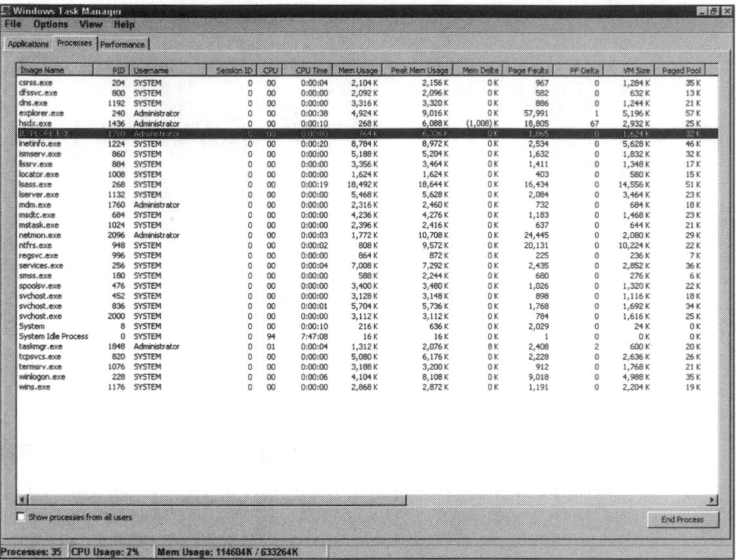

Figure 20-16: The IEXPLORE.EXE image name

Step 2. Using the Search button accessed from the Start button, select the For File and Folders menu option. Type IEXPLORE.EXE in the Search for files or folders names field. Then click the Search Now button. Hint: It is recommended that you first search the drive(s) that contain the Windows 2000 Server operating system and/or related applications. You may either search by a specific drive identifier such as [C] for the C: drive or search on "My Computer" to search all local drives. It has been my experience that many of the image names I'm interested in are indeed Windows 2000 Server operating system-related, so by first searching on the drive that contains the operating system, I save search time. The results from our search on IEXPLORE.EXE are shown in Figure 20-17.

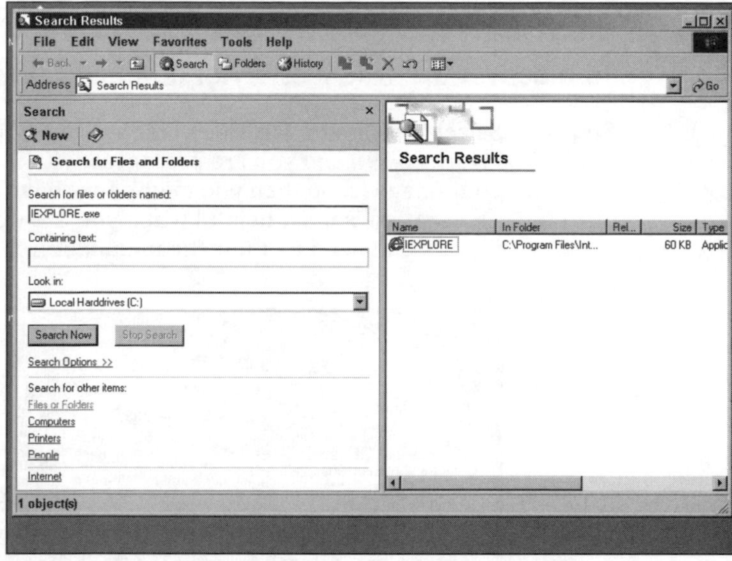

Figure 20-17: Using Find File to find IEXPLORE.EXE

Step 3. Right-click the file named IEXPLORE.EXE (or whatever file you have searched on). Select the Properties menu option on the context menu (see Figure 20-18).

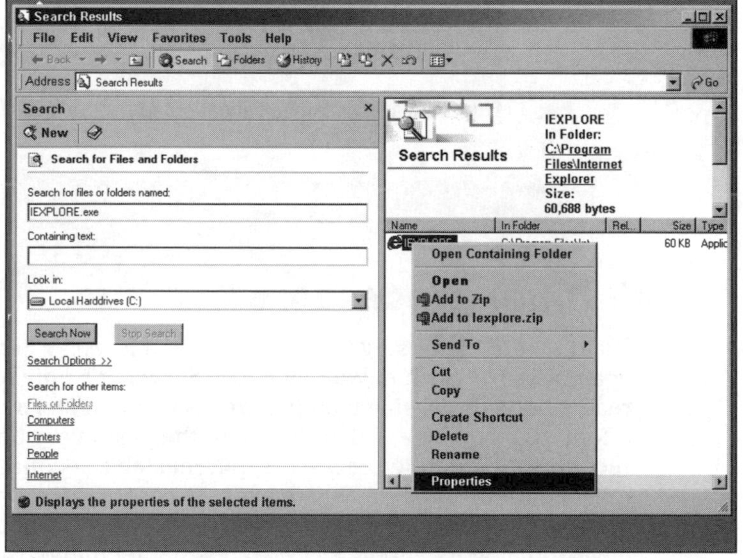

Figure 20-18: Selecting properties for IEXPLORE.EXE

Continued

STEPS:

To discover the true identity of IEXPLORE.EXE *(continued)*

Step 4. Select the Version tab sheet on the Properties dialog box (see Figure 20-19), and you are presented with more information about your image name than you might ever have imagined. This information is most helpful when you are working with third-party drivers and need to know the manufacturer of the file.

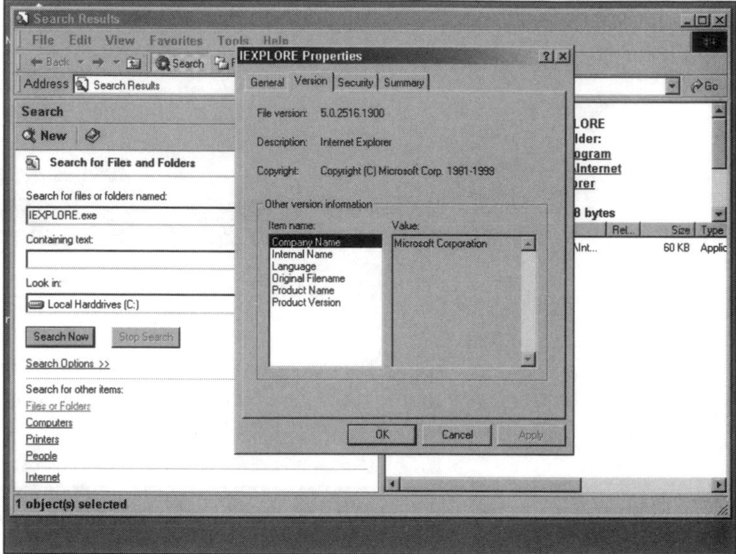

Figure 20-19: Version tab sheet properties for IEXPLORE.EXE

Multiple processors

I said it in the later stages of the life of Windows NT Server 4.0 and I'll say it again with the birth of Windows 2000 Server. It's only recently that one can read a book discussing multiple processors and feel a real connection to such a topic. By that I mean that though in the past every book seemed to recommend multiple processors, purchasing a second processor wasn't realistic for most of us, only the largest corporate networks. But that's all changed with the arrival of the new century! That's because Moore's Law is alive and at work. Moore's Law states that technology prices will drop and processing power will increase over time (prices will drop by half every 18 months). Dell servers (low-end PowerEdges such as the Model 1300) can be purchased with dual processors for under $3,000 as of mid-1999.

Tip

Today, a computer equipped with multiple processors is often deployed in even the smallest of server environments and high-end workstation environments. In fact, it is my sincere recommendation that you deploy Windows 2000 Server on nothing less than a dual-processor machine. Between you and me, on the test machine that I planned to use as a server for the purposes of writing this book, I quickly discovered that its single processor wouldn't cut it. I quickly purchased a dual-processor Dell server and learned that a dual processor is the minimum performance point for Windows 2000 Server. For what's it's worth, installing Windows 2000 Server literally took one hour less on my dual-processor machine than my old single-processor machine. Now that's performance!

Task Manager was constructed with multiple processors in mind. The Performance tab sheet can display the activity of each processor on separate CPU History windows. This has been displayed to you in every screen shot of the Performance tab in this chapter. You will note that the two graph panes (one on the left, the other on the right) represent a chart of each of the two processors.

Task Manager enables you to assign which processors may execute which application (or process). To understand the benefit of this feature, you need to understand how Windows 2000 Server processes threads on a multiple-processor machine. First, Windows 2000 Server supports up to eight processors. Second, the microkernel in Windows 2000 Server distributes thread-based activity across the processors (based on the priorities assigned to the threads). Thus, 32-bit applications with multiple threads of execution will have threads processed over more than one processor.

Windows 2000 Server uses soft affinity to try to distribute the processing load equally over all processors. This is known as symmetric multiprocessing (SMP) and reflects the current design and implementation paradigm in the computing community. This is truly Windows 2000 Server's way of trying to treat each processor equally. You could think of it as "separate but equal." Technically, this is called soft affinity, which assumes all processors are equal and can access the same physical memory.

But back in the days when knights were bold and kings owned all thegold, the computing community used asymmetrical multiprocessing implementations to distribute processes via assignments to specific processors. This approach is known as processor affinity and can be implemented in Windows 2000 Server via the context menu on the Processes tab sheet in Task Manager (see Figure 20-20).

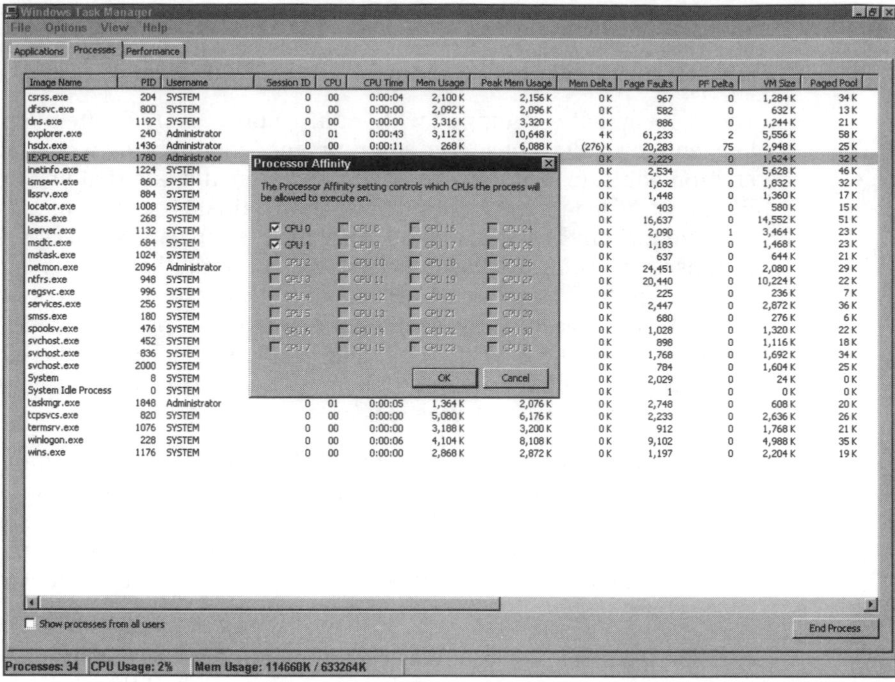

Figure 20-20: Task Manager's Processor Affinity menu

You can then select which processor(s) this application or process will be executed on. With forethought and planning, you could create a Windows 2000 Server computing scenario whereby each application had one processor to itself and didn't have to share. However, conventional thinking is that your entire system will suffer a performance decrease because the other applications will be forced to compete for the limited resources of the remaining processors. And Windows 2000 Server does such a great job of distributing the load equally over your bed of processors in an SMP scenario—why mess with success? Think of it as an automatic gearbox on an automobile. Real muscle-car owners typically prefer automatic transmissions to manual transmissions because the car does a better job than the human driver of shifting under acceleration. That's why you would typically leave well enough alone and allow Window NT Server's soft affinity approach to work unimpeded. It can probably do a better job automatically than you can manually.

System Information Is a Winner!

System Information (a.k.a. WinMSD) is one of the other goodies that I promised to describe for you in addition to Task Manager. It is distinctly different from Task Manager. System Information is a static snapshot of system health, with an emphasis on devices. It is also a portal to other system information tools including the Windows Report Tool. In contrast, Task Manager presents a dynamic view of processor activity, memory consumption, and currently running applications and processes. In this section, we will review each of the following MMC objects in System Information: System Summary, Hardware Resources, Components, and Software Environment.

This version of System Information is much more accurate and reliable than its distant DOS-based MSD cousin. Perhaps you remember when MSD was introduced as part of MS-DOS, not too long ago. It was the greatest thing since sliced bread, enabling you not only to troubleshoot interrupt conflicts but also to decide, via the MSD memory map, in what order device drivers should be loaded, low or high, in your CONFIG.SYS file. Life was great as long as you ran MSD in a strict or true DOS session. But if you launched Windows and then tried to run good old MSD, you not only got a warning screen that the results of MSD may be unreliable, but you were able to witness these unreliable results firsthand. Don't believe me? Then just go upstairs to your attic and pull out that old 386-based PC running MS-DOS 5.0 and WFW. Create an interrupt conflict somehow (maybe put in a second sound card). Then, under WFW, launch MSD and attempt to resolve the interrupt conflict. Let's just say I wish you well, my friend.

To launch System Information, type the command **winmsd** in the Run dialog box in Windows 2000 Server (see Figure 20-21).

The WinMSD command launches the System Information MMC shown in Figure 20-22. This application has changed dramatically since it was known as WinMSD in the old Windows NT Server days. I'll show you the ways in which it has changed.

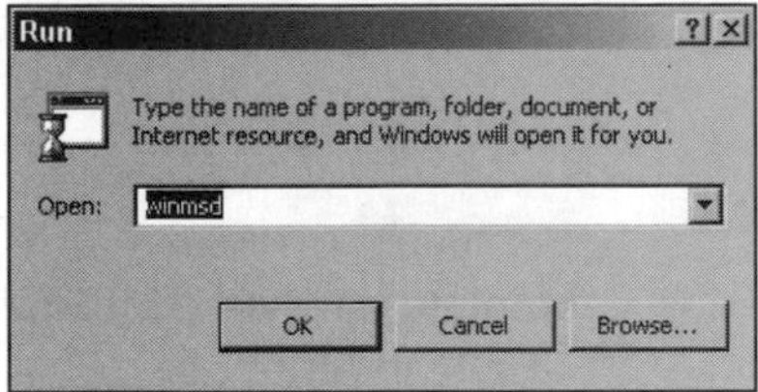

Figure 20-21: The WinMSD command

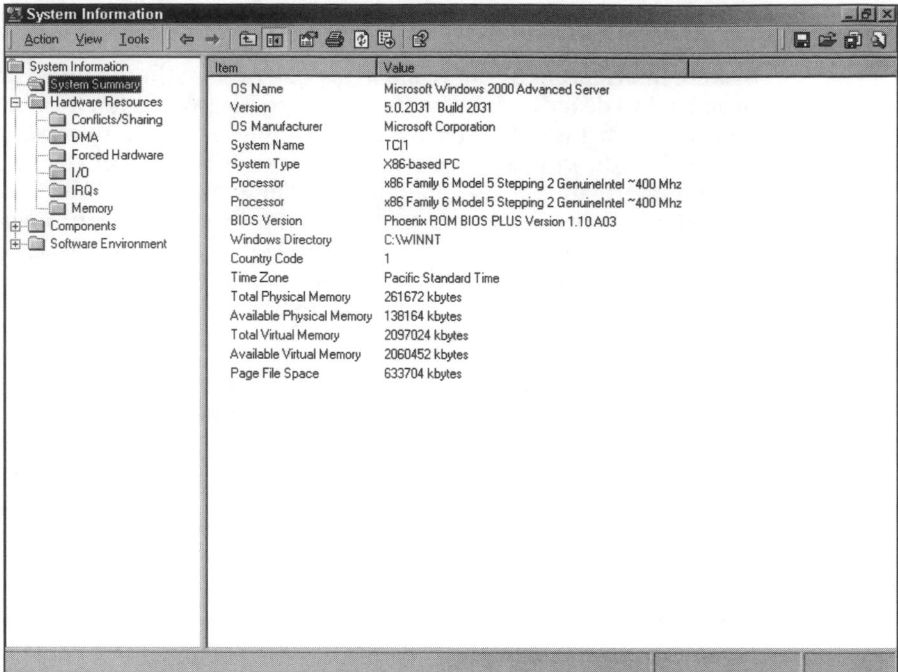

Figure 20-22: System Information

System Summary

At a glance, on System Summary, you can tell what version of Windows 2000 Server you are running. This might seem like a silly thing to do, but out on the server farm, it's easy to become confused. Such confusion can be resolved with System Summary.

I've made a habit of running System Information and looking at System Summary so that I can tell what service pack has been applied to Windows 2000 Server. Service Pack version information is shown in the Version field.

Hardware Resources

The Hardware Resources view reports complete hardware information, helpful in troubleshooting see Figure 20-23), including

- Conflicts/Sharing
- DMA
- Forced Hardware

- I/O
- IRQs
- Memory

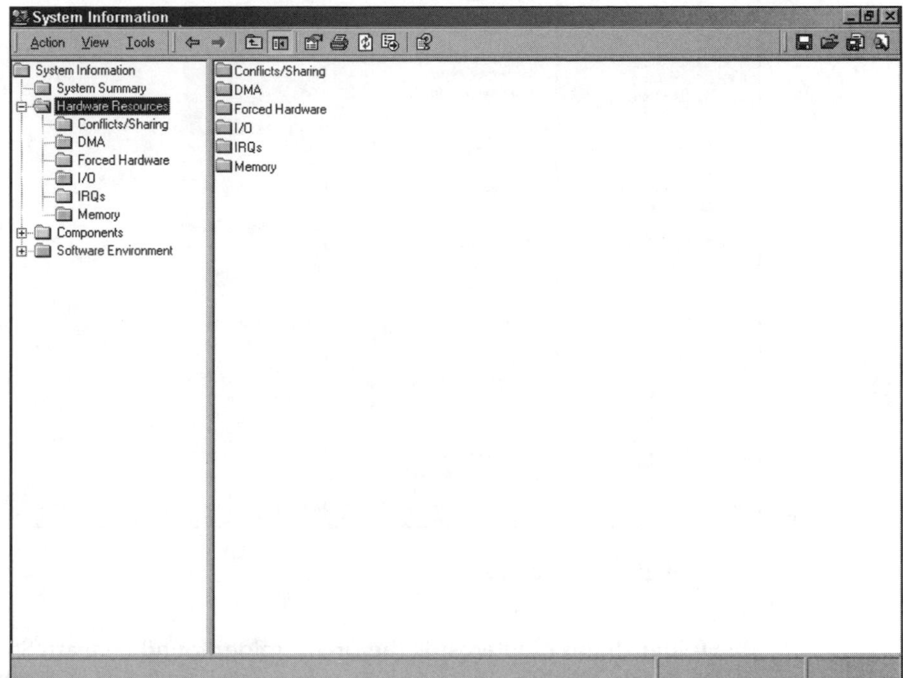

Figure 20-23: Hardware Resources view

Components

The Components view reports detailed component information for computer system components ranging from multimedia to USB (see Figure 20-24). Again, this information is very helpful when troubleshooting.

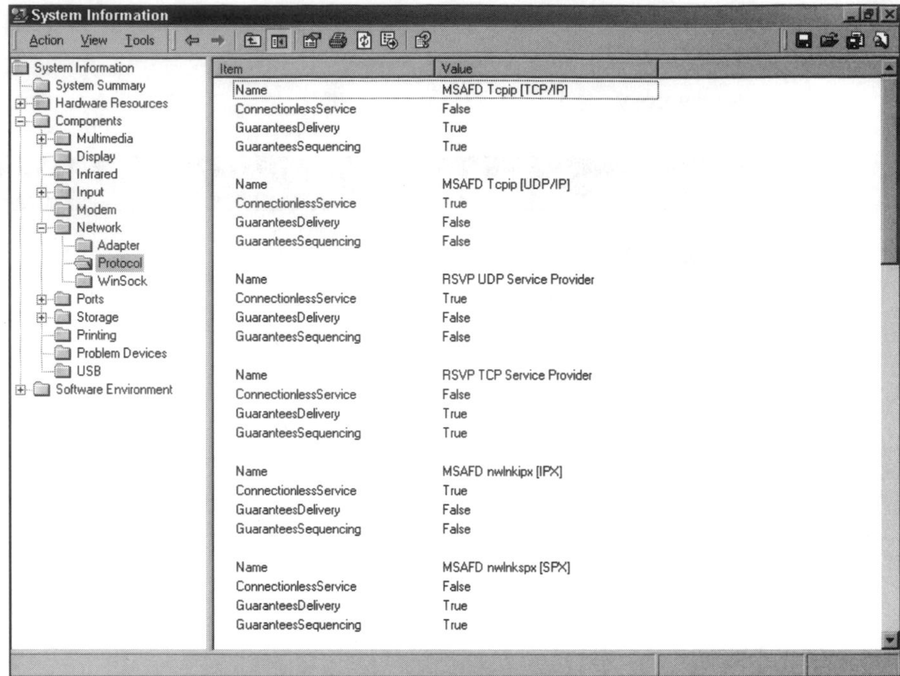

Figure 20-24: Components view

One folder that is of interest is the Drives folder found beneath Storage in the Components. It is here that you can obtain detailed drive information, such as the drive manufacturer and model (see Figure 20-25). I've found this useful when working with Dell or Compaq technical support engineers and they ask for such information.

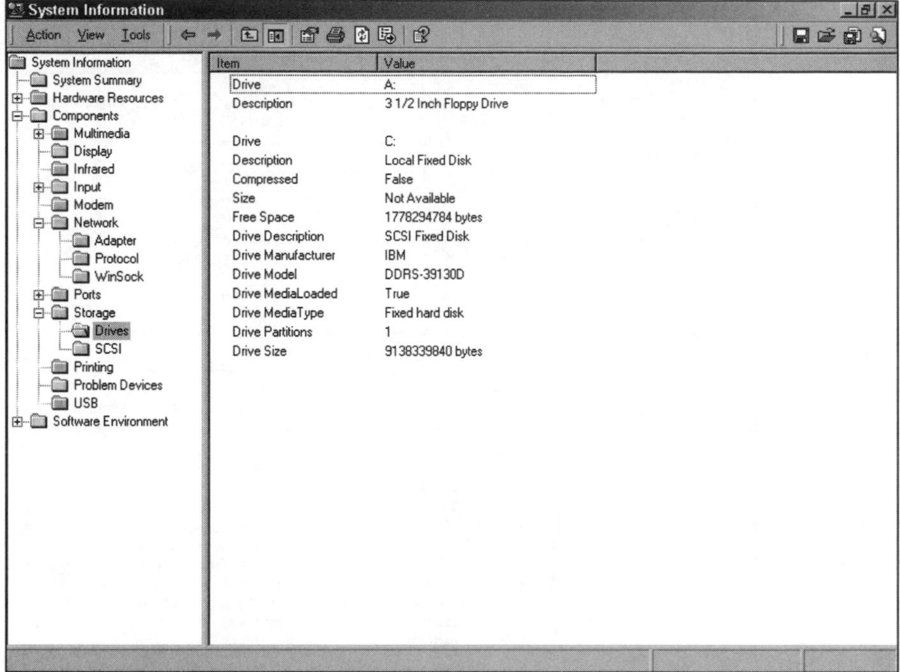

Figure 20-25: Drives folder

Software Environment

Here in the Software Environment view in System Information, you can view important software-based environmental information, such as drivers loaded, environmental variables network connections, and services, just to name a few of the folders (see Figure 20-26).

Drivers

The Drivers view allows you to see, in a detailed manner, the device drivers that exist on your Windows 2000 Server (see Figure 20-26). I've found myself here most often when working with Technical Support at...(you pick the vendor: Microsoft, Dell, Compaq).

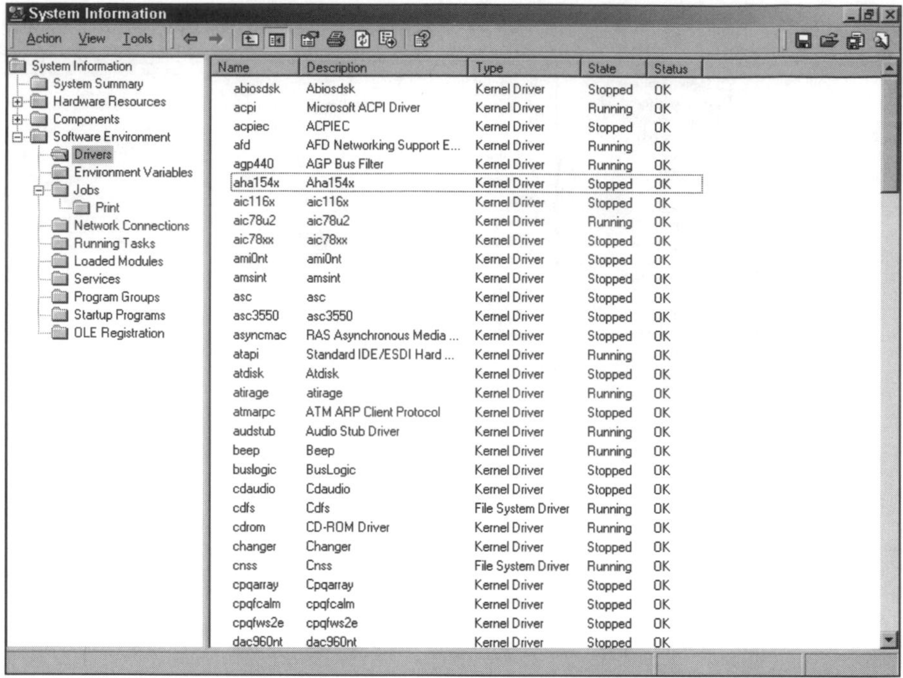

Figure 20-26: Drivers view

Environmental Variables

If you install or otherwise maintain third-party applications running on Windows 2000 Server, you'll most likely need the Environmental Variables view. For example, Great Plains Dynamics, a popular accounting software application which uses Microsoft SQL Server, requires that you make adjustments to the operating environment of the computer system on which it runs. Such adjustments can typically be viewed via Environmental Variables (see Figure 20-27).

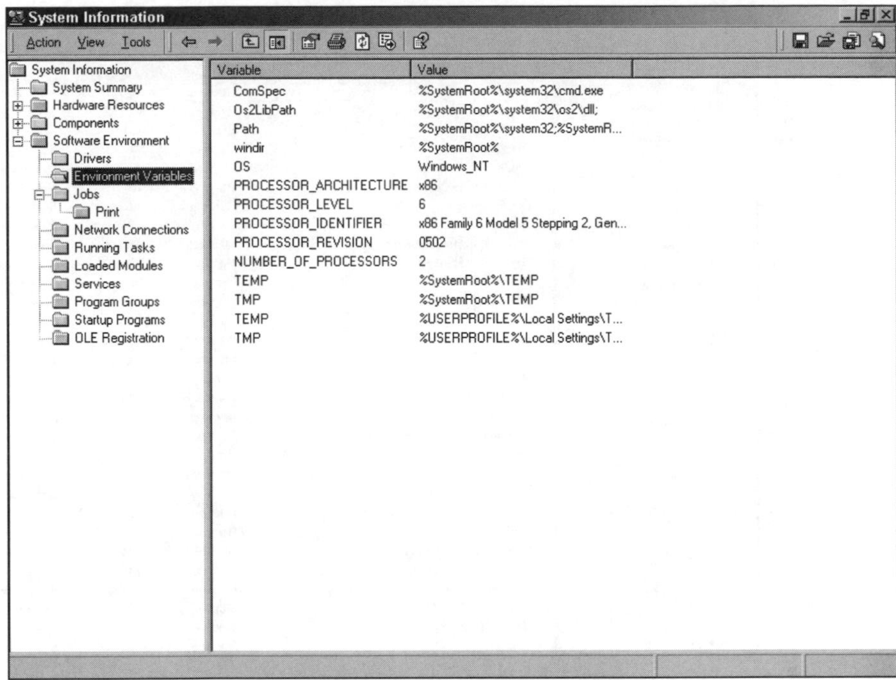

Figure 20-27: Environmental Variables view

Services

Perhaps you've noticed one thing about services in Windows 2000 Server compared to the old Windows NT Server days: there are a lot more of them! Such is the case because Windows 2000 Server is a more complex environment than its predecessor releases (Windows NT Server 4.*x*, 3.*x*). The Services view in System Information (see Figure 20-28) is again a friend indeed in the time of troubleshooting need.

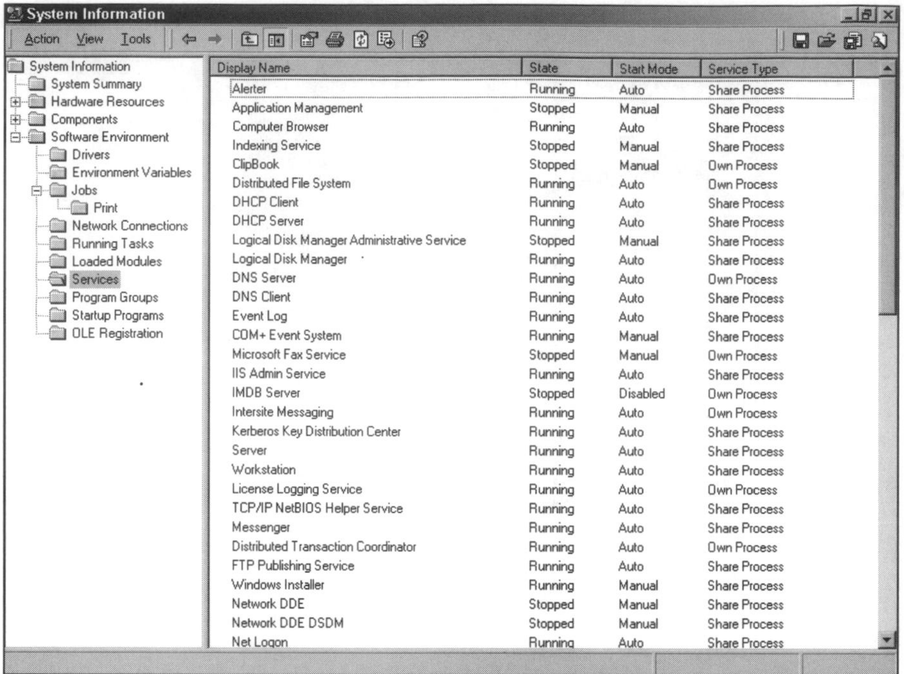

Figure 20-28: Services view

System Information portal

A different perspective on System Information can be drawn from the burgeoning Internet community, namely, the portal concept. America Online (AOL) and Microsoft's MSN Web sites are different portals or entry points to the Internet. Similarly, System Information is the Windows 2000 Server system's health portal. It's an often-overlooked feature.

By clicking the Tools menu in System Information and then expanding the Windows menu option, you will see the portal menu, which offers no less than ten Windows 2000 Server system-related tools, all from one menu (see Figure 20-29).

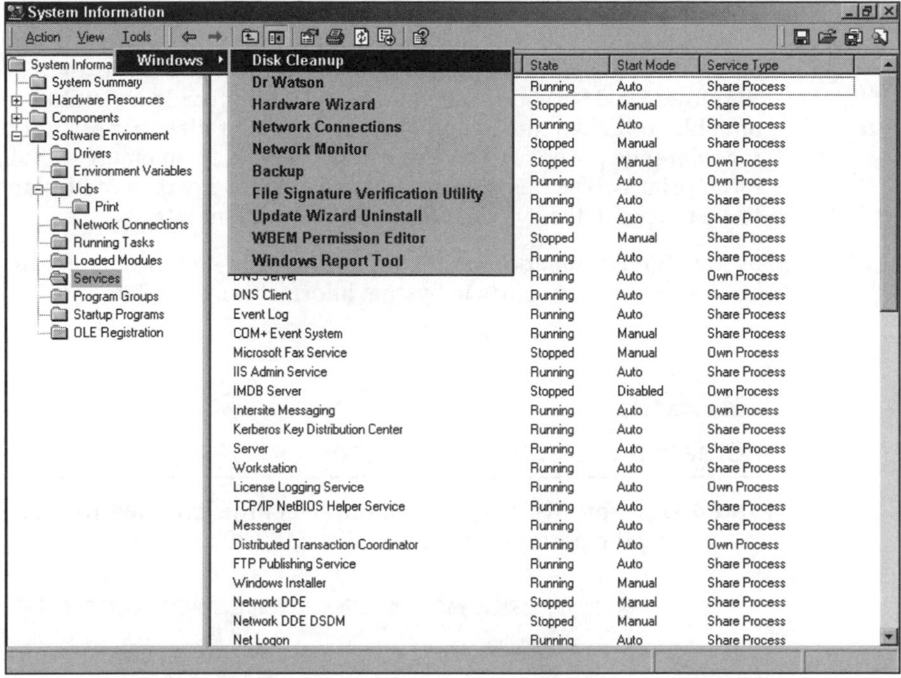

Figure 20-29: System Information portal menu

I strongly recommend that you consider using System Information as your "portal" on a daily basis by making a shortcut of this tool on your desktop.

I discuss many of the portal menu options (Figure 20-29) in different sections of this book. For example, Network Monitor was discussed in Chapter 19. I will next discuss the Windows Report Tool, and Dr. Watson at the end of this chapter.

Reporting meaningful system information

Time to get back to business basics for a moment. Remember the theme that surfaces occasionally in this book regarding the business use of Windows 2000 Server with business applications, the business decisions makers with whom you must interact, and even the business of implementing Windows 2000 Server in businesses? Well, allow me to add one additional business component: business-style reporting. Anyone in business loves reports, and if you're in the Windows 2000 Server consulting business, you have the means to provide such reports for both your own system management and client's benefit.

I've made a good living and kept well-organized system reports by habitually printing out the full report set for all of the system information contained on all tabs found in System Information. By completing this exercise for each Windows 2000 Server at each site for which I provide consulting services, I am able to build detailed and informative client files that are not only great for reference purposes, but extremely valuable in an emergency. In fact, I often print two copies of these reports: one for my off-site files and another to be placed in the system notebook at the client site.

System Information doesn't let you down when it comes to creating reports. To create system reports in System Information, complete the following steps.

STEPS:

Creating a system report

Step 1. From System Information, select the Windows Report Tool from the portal menu (see in Figure 20-30).

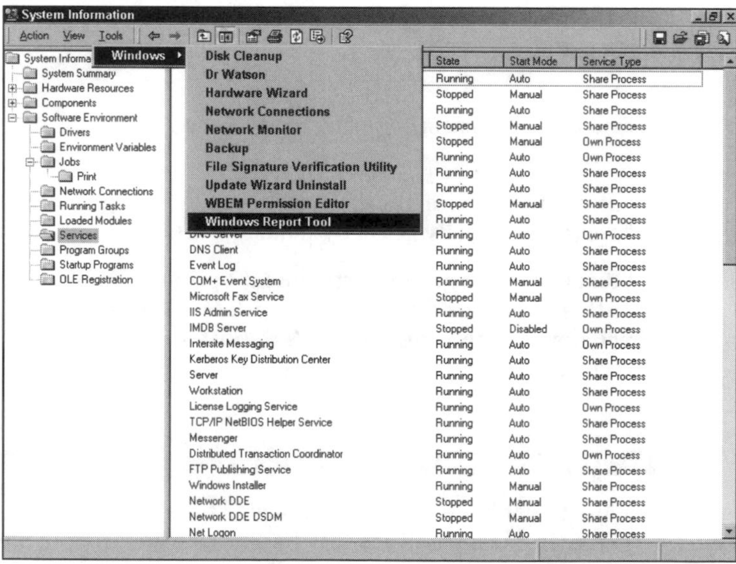

Figure 20-30: Windows Report Tool menu option

The Windows Report Tool will be displayed. Complete the Problem description, Expected results and Steps to reproduce the problem fields (see Figure 20-31).

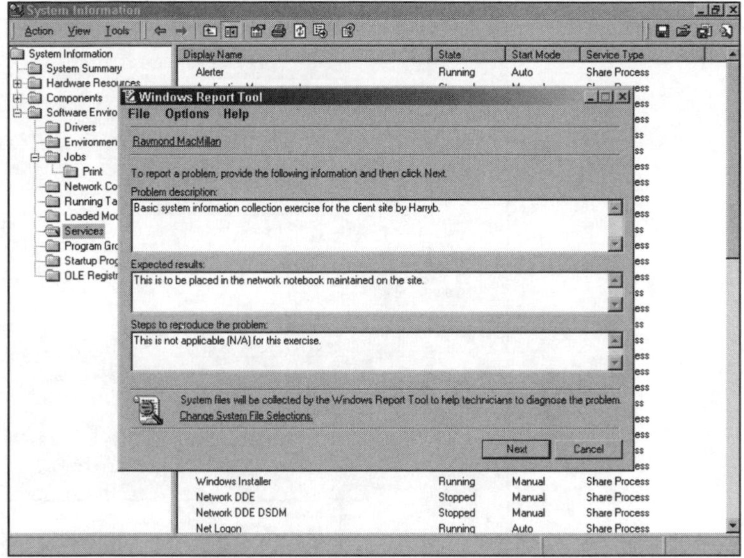

Figure 20-31: Windows Report Tool dialog box

Step 2. Click the Change System File Selections hyperlink at the bottom left of the Windows Report Tool. Windows 2000 Server system information will be collected and the Collected Information dialog box will be displayed. Select all checkboxes in the Files to copy dialog box area for the purposes of the system information collection exercise (see Figure 20-32). You can select all of the report by simply clicking the Select All button.

Continued

STEPS:

Creating a system report *(continued)*

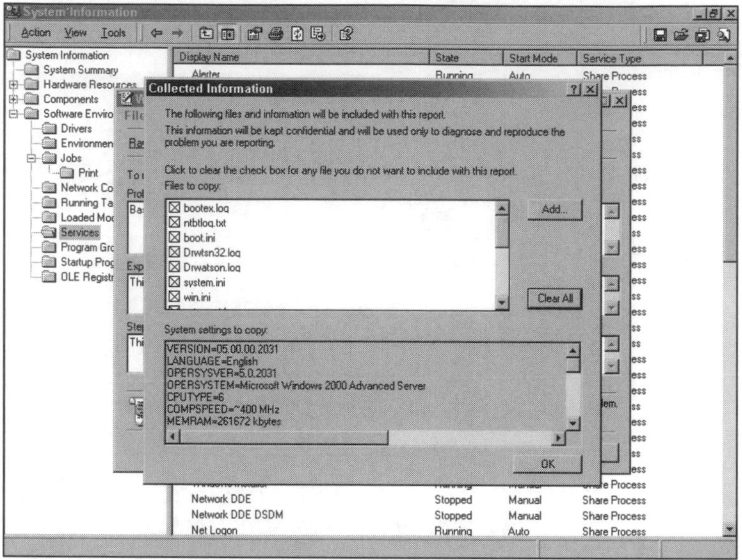

Figure 20-32: Collected Information dialog box

Step 3. Click OK to close the Collected Information dialog box.

Step 4. Click Next on the Windows Report Tool dialog box. The Save As dialog box will appear asking for a file name. Provide a file name such as "System Report December 1999" and click Save.

Step 5. The Creating report information file status bar will appear for several minutes and display the report creation process.

Step 6. After the reports have been created, you will need to close the Windows Report Tool by clicking Cancel.

I highly recommend you consider creating such a comprehensive system report in December 1999 (just before the year 2000 rolls over) so you have a static view of your system and how it looked prior to the year 2000. It's a just-in-case kinda thing to do!

System Properties

The good old System Properties dialog box is still with us from the Windows NT Server days (see Figure 20-33).

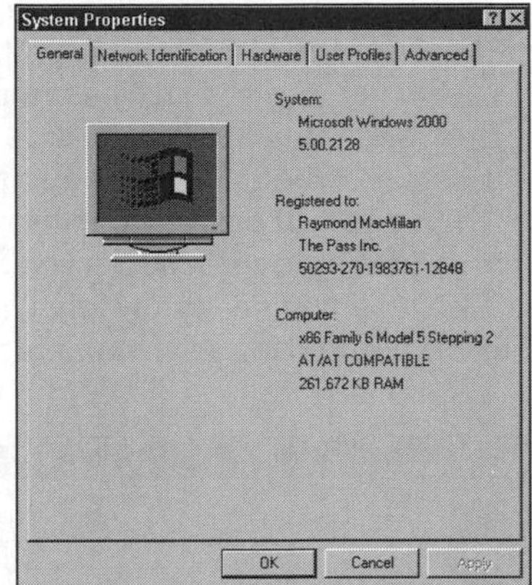

Figure 20-33: System Properties dialog box

System Properties has five tab sheets: General, Network Identification, Hardware, User Profiles, and Advanced:

- **General.** This tab sheet reports general information such as the registered owner.
- **Network Identification.** This tab sheet reports the computer and domain name.
- **Hardware.** This tab sheet provides access to the Hardware Wizard, Device Manager and Hardware Profiles. Device Manager is a wonderful new addition to Windows 2000 Server that has long been available in the Windows 95/98 worlds.
- **User Profiles.** This tab sheet contains user profile information.
- **Advanced.** This tab sheet contains a Performance Option where you set the foreground/background application response and paging file size. It also contains an Environmental Variable option where you may edit environmental variables. The third option, Startup and Recovery, allows you to select the default startup menu option and invoke certain Recover features such as writing a dump file.

Tip

Be sure to deselect the Automatically reboot checkbox on the Startup and Recovery screen. It is selected by default, but heaven forbid your server continuously reboots over a long holiday weekend without you around should said server encounter a fatal and reproducible blue screen of death!

SQL Trace

As we ascend the OSI model, we typically become more interested in application performance, not just OS-level performance. Given that BackOffice is largely responsible for a huge chunk of Windows 2000 Server's sales, I thought you might like to know about a BackOffice-based tool that can be used for monitoring performance, albeit at the application level. SQL Trace (see Figure 20-34) ships with SQL Server and is a GUI-based utility that tracks SQL Server database activity. How does this apply to Windows 2000 Server, you ask? In many ways. If your server is being used as an applications server primarily running SQL Server, then you will be very concerned about the interaction of SQL Server, its users, and Windows 2000 Server. SQL Trace is simply another tool to arm yourself with as you seek the Holy Grail of eternally optimized Windows 2000 Server computing environments.

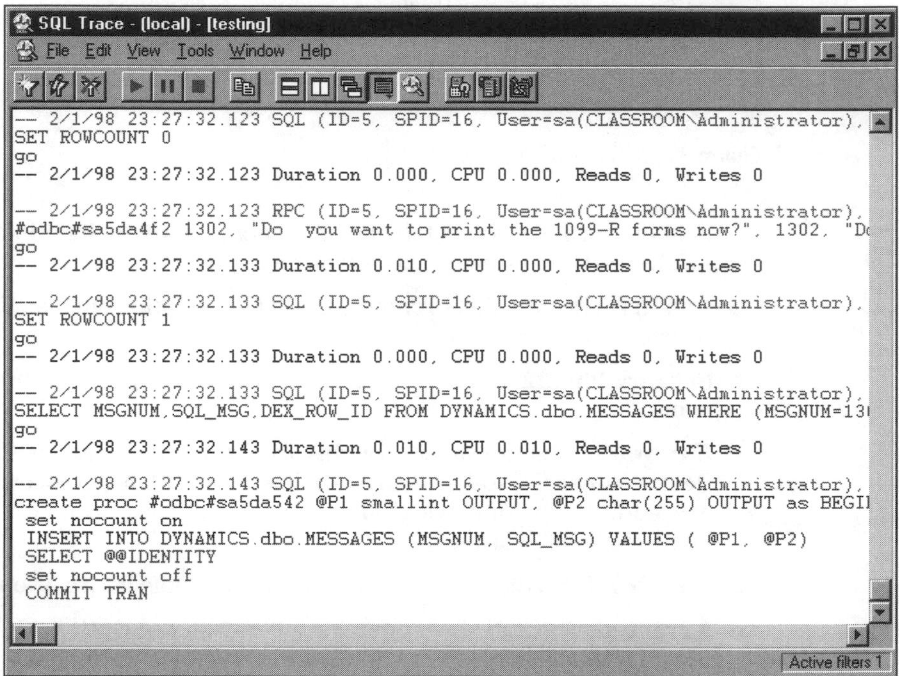

Figure 20-34: SQL Trace

SQL Trace is typically used to monitor connections between users and SQL Server, along with SQL statements and RPC activity in SQL Server. These events report a start and end time, CPU utilization, and read and write activity. Believe me, SQL Trace is a tool worth having in your BackOffice back pocket.

SQL Server ODBCPING and Exchange RPING

Another SQL Server tool, ODBCPING (see Figure 20-35) enables you to test ODBC connectivity between nodes. It is intended for use with SQL Server, but it can test ODBC connectivity in a more general sense as well. Typically, this tool is used by software vendors such as Great Plains Accounting to test its Dynamics accounting application's communications with SQL Server via ODBC.

```
Command Prompt
Microsoft(R) Windows NT(TM)
(C) Copyright 1985-1996 Microsoft Corp.

C:\>odbcping
usage: odbcping [-S Server | -D DSN] [-U Login Id] [-P Password]
C:\>
C:\>odbcping -s harryb -u sa -p

CONNECTED TO SQL SERVER

ODBC SQL Server Driver Version: 02.65.0213

SQL Server Version: Microsoft SQL Server  6.50 - 6.50.213 (Intel X86)
        Jul 23 1996 19:16:49
        Copyright (c) 1988-1996 Microsoft Corporation

C:\>
```

Figure 20-35: Meet ODBCPING

Another BackOffice buddy is the RPING utility included with Microsoft Exchange (see Figure 20-36). This utility, run on two machines simultaneously, enables you to test the strength and validity of Remote Procedure Calls (RPC) communications. I have used this tool while trying to set up a second Microsoft Exchange Server in an existing Exchange site. In this case, Exchange server setup kept failing when the first Exchange server was trying to perform its directory synchronization with the second Exchange server being set up. RPING was used to verify that we indeed had problems deeper than Microsoft Exchange itself. We proved that the RPC communications were failing between the two servers. Because Microsoft Exchange relies heavily on RPC-based communications for its site communications, our discovery of failing RPC communications proved to be vital. In fact, the site was ultimately reconfigured to have only one Exchange server, thus eliminating our RPC communication failure problem.

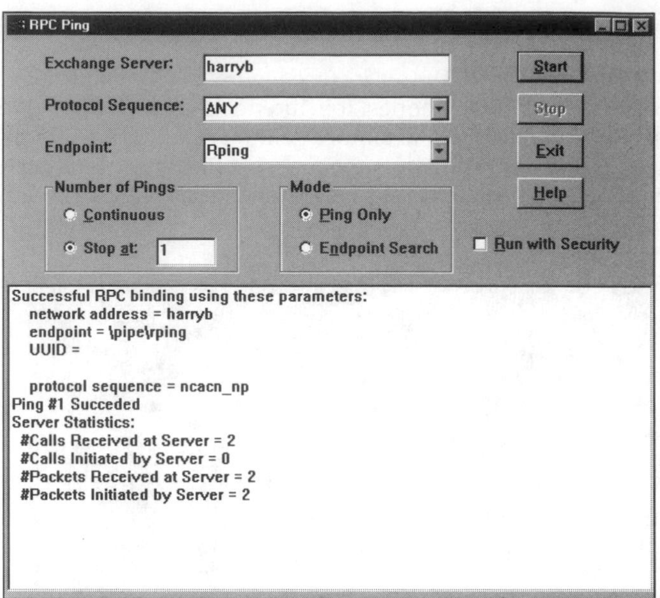

Figure 20-36: The RPING utility

Event Logs

I would be remiss if I didn't discuss event logs in the context of performance. Suffice it to say, event logs are a frequently visited area (FVA) in Windows 2000 Server as you undertake performance-enhancing steps. Often, after you make an adjustment to the system, you will restart the system via a reboot. There is usually no better place than the event logs to check and see the outcome of your performance-enhancing adjustments. More likely, you will be warned via an error message at startup that something somewhere failed to start. You attention will then be directed to Event Viewer (see Figure 20-37). Don't say I didn't tell you — you have now been told.

The Directory Service, DNS Server, and File Replication Service logs are new to Event Viewer in Windows 2000 Server. These didn't exist under Windows NT Server.

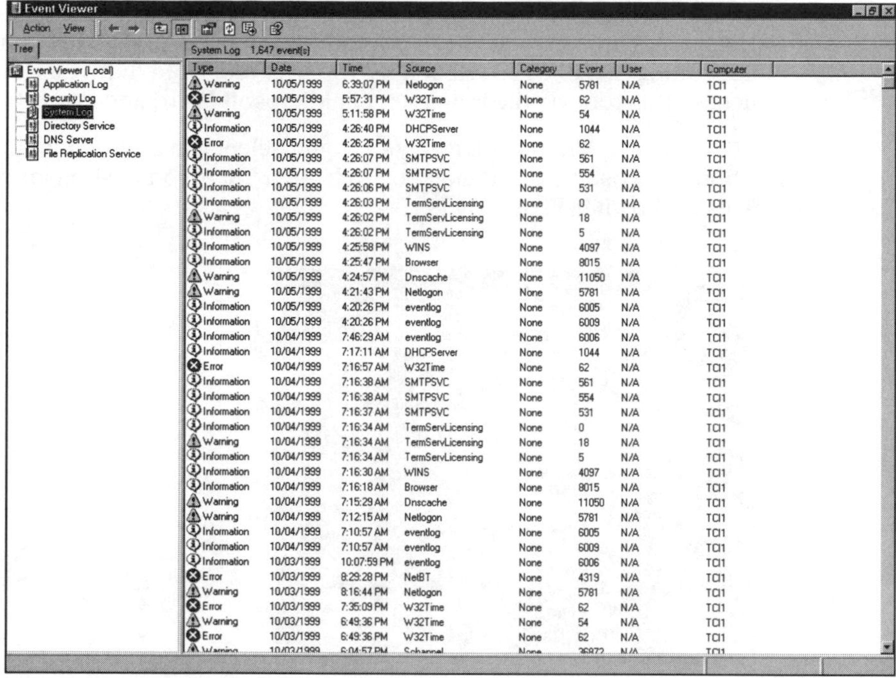

Figure 20-37: Event Viewer

Microsoft Office — Microsoft System Information

Remember at the start of the chapter I suggested the rather oddball idea of installing Microsoft Office on your Windows 2000 Server machine? Have I forgotten many of the Windows 2000 Server planning basics I discussed in Chapter 1, where I emphasize that servers should be used as servers, not server/workstation combinations? In other words, am I suggesting that you would type Microsoft Word documents right at your Windows 2000 Server machine? No, I'm not. It is not my intention to have you actually perform work on the Windows 2000 Server machine any more than necessary. I'm interested in having you install Microsoft Office so that you're able to access the Microsoft System Information application from any of the major Office applications, such as Microsoft Excel. In fact, I'll use Excel as my sample application to show you Microsoft System Information, a robust system reporting tool.

This tool, accessed via the About Microsoft Excel menu option under the Help menu in Microsoft Excel, is a little-known tool that I keep in my consulting bag of tricks. Hopefully you will, too! Note that you can also access this tool via the Help menu in Microsoft Word and PowerPoint.

In the case of Microsoft Excel, you would select the System Info button in the About Microsoft Excel dialog box to launch Microsoft System Information. This is shown in Figure 20-38.

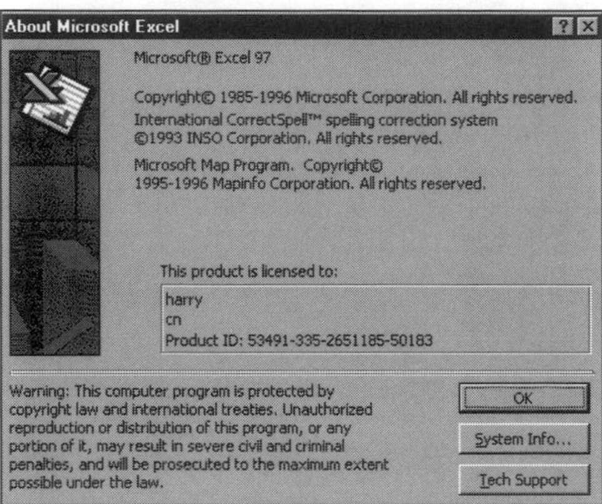

Figure 20-38: About Microsoft Excel

Note that Microsoft System Information accessed via a Microsoft Application tool is a different application than System Information, discussed earlier in this chapter.

Microsoft System Information is a tool that provides facts pertaining to both user mode operations (applications) and kernel mode operations (Windows 2000 Server executive). This tool reports on the following:

- **Microsoft System Information.** Basic system information (see Figure 20-39) such as dynamic swap file settings. This sheet is useful at a glance.
- **System Dynamic Link Libraries (DLLs).** This is the only place in Windows 2000 Server where you can conveniently observe DLLs installed on your system (see Figure 20-40). It is here that a DLL's version number, creation date, size, build number, and load status are reported. This is an exceedingly important area as you try to optimize your system and implement the latest DLL for the benefit of any application or operating system feature. Needless to say, it is also very important for troubleshooting purposes. Incorrectly managed, an overwritten or missing DLL can bring your system to a crashing halt. For more information about managing DLLs at the application level, see the Windows 95 and Windows 98 *Secrets* books co-written by my colleague Brian Livingston (IDG Books Worldwide).

- **The Font, Proofing, Graphic Filters, Text Converters, and OLE Registrations.** These relate to how applications are currently configured on your machine and are beyond the scope of this book. The Display, Audio, and Video selections relate to information that is essentially reported via Display and Multimedia Property boxes accessed from the Control Panel.

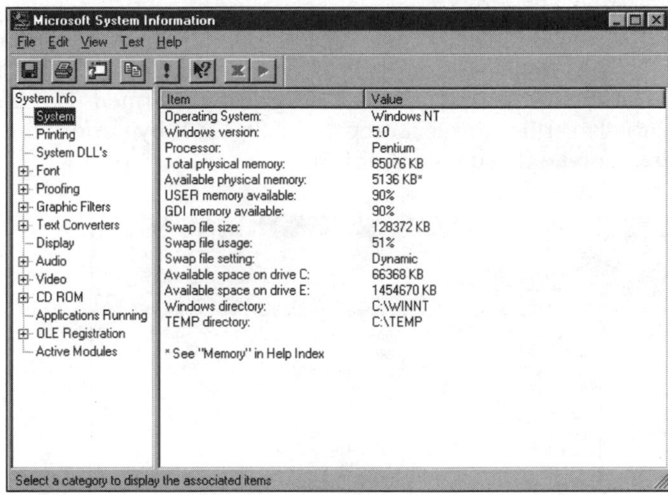

Figure 20-39: Microsoft System Information

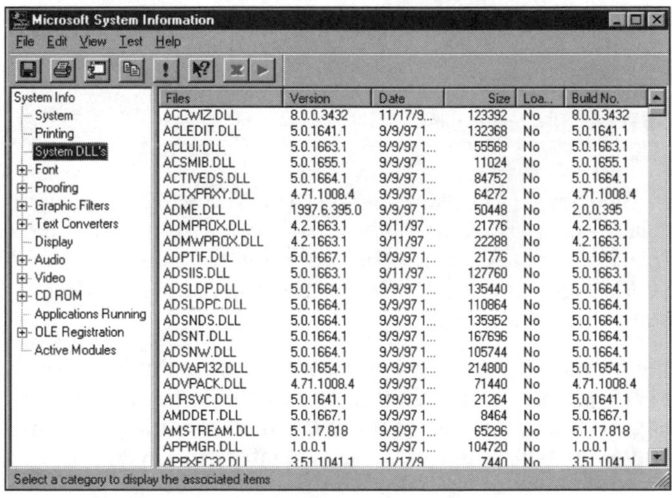

Figure 20-40: The System DLLs view

- **The CD-ROM selection.** This is the only place in Windows 2000 Server to perform a read/write performance test involving the transfer rate and accuracy of your CD-ROM player. To do this, place a CD-ROM in your CD-ROM player and double-click the CD-ROM selection on the left side of Microsoft System Information. The test can take up to a minute to complete. After you double-click the CD-ROM selection in the left pane, the test results will be displayed on the right pane, typically within one minute. These results (see Figure 20-41) display information about the sample transfer file that was used, the total file size, and its transfer rate. This is very useful when measuring the performance of your CD-ROM reader. Note the integrity test that was also performed. This second test essentially verifies the accuracy of the first test by performing tests against another file on the CD-ROM.

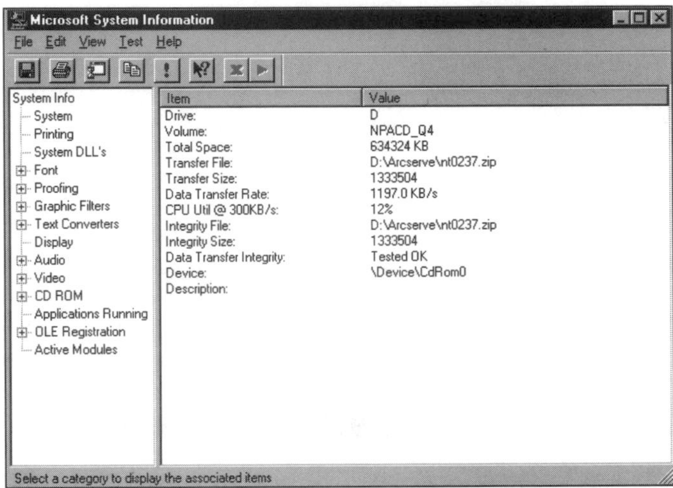

Figure 20-41: CD-ROM test results

Windows 2000 Server Disk Management (via the MMC) (see Figure 20-42) and CD-ROM Drive properties (see Figure 20-43) are proof that you cannot run a similar transfer rate test using other common tools in Windows 2000 Server. Both Disk Management and My Computer disk properties do not allow for such a test to be performed.

- Active Modules. This view in Microsoft System Information (see Figure 20-44) displays information that supplements the Processes view in Task Manager. In fact, it provides more detailed module information than displayed in Task Manager, as shown later. However, this information is static and relates to such items as the file build date, file location, size, and whether a module is 16-bit or not. The term "active," while not meaning dynamic, does mean that the modules displayed were active at the time the Active Modules command was executed. Task Manager via the Processes page is designed to report dynamic information such as CPU usage. Active Modules reports different information than the Processes tab sheet in Task Manager (see Figure 20-45).

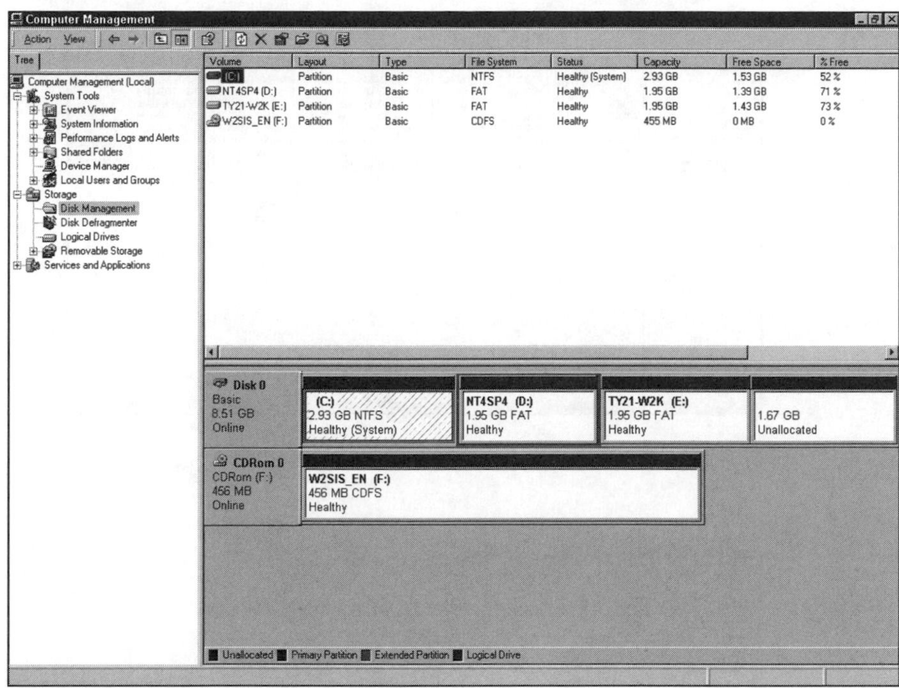

Figure 20-42: Disk Management

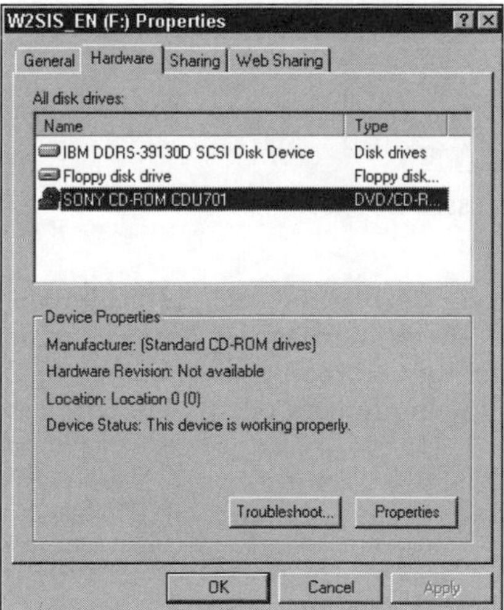

Figure 20-43: CD-ROM Properties

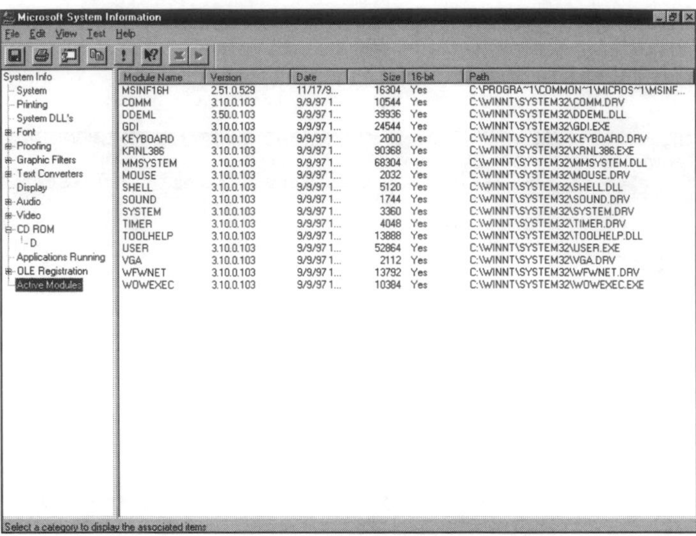

Figure 20-44: Active Modules in Microsoft System Information

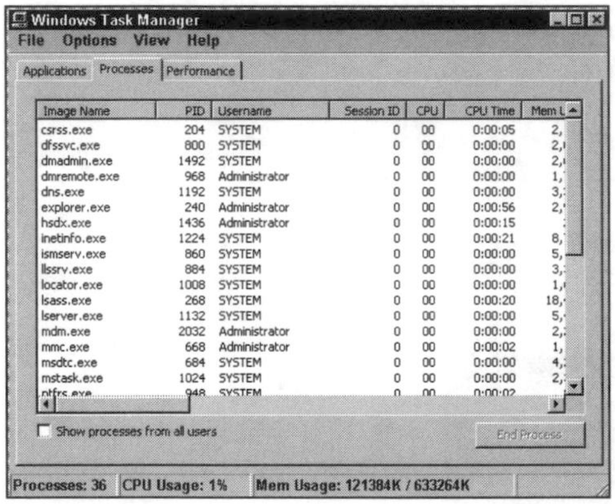

Figure 20-45: The Task Manager Processes tab sheet

Note that it's a nice touch to have the modules' file paths displayed on the far right of the Active Modules window in Microsoft System Information (see Figure 20-46). We can thus quickly get more information on a module by going to the subdirectory containing the module and displaying the properties for that file (see Figure 20-47).

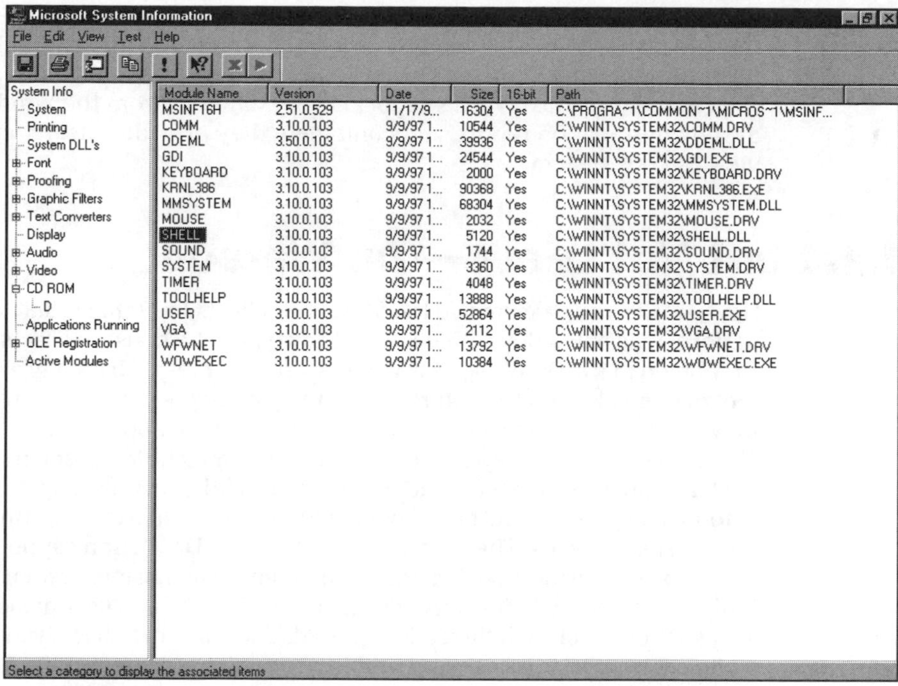

Figure 20-46: The path to SHELL.DLL displayed in the Active Modules view of Microsoft System Information

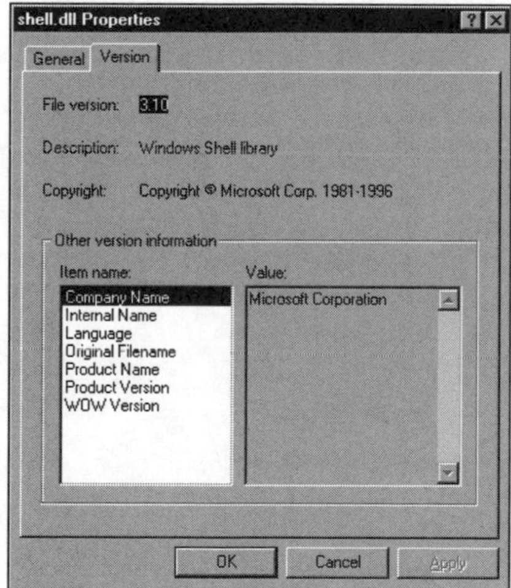

Figure 20-47: The Properties sheet for SHELL.DLL

Be sure to print out the full system report (select the Print command from the File menu) from Microsoft System Information and place it in the same file in which you store the printout from Windows 2000 System Information (discussed previously). This report is very different from the Windows 2000 System Information report, and combined, they provide a nearly exhaustive view of your system.

Last but Not Least — Dr. Watson

Hey — make a mistake and go too far in your efforts to optimize and boost the performance of Windows 2000 Server and you'll get a house call from Dr. Watson! Dr. Watson (a.k.a. Dr. Watson for Windows 2000 Server) is basically a diagnostic tool that enables you to capture information about the crash (see Figure 20-48). Dr. Watson typically launches when you encounter an application or Windows 2000 Server executive-layer error. You may also launch Dr. Watson from the portal menu in System Information (discussed earlier in this chapter). Dr. Watson automatically runs in the background and captures important information when your system crashes. The type of information that Dr. Watson captures includes exception information, such as exception number and name. System information is also captured, including machine name, OS version, and user name. Finally, a snapshot dump of each thread is captured. This information is given to Microsoft technical support to assist your problem resolution efforts.

While you can turn off Dr. Watson on your Windows 2000 Server at the following Registry location — `\HKEY _LOCAL _MACHINE\SOFTWARE\Microsoft\Windows NT\CurrentVersion \AeDebug:Auto` — there is really no compelling reason to do so. Note you would set the default auto value from 1 to 0. You might recall that, back in the Windows 3.1 desktop days, you had to explicitly turn on Dr. Watson for it to work.

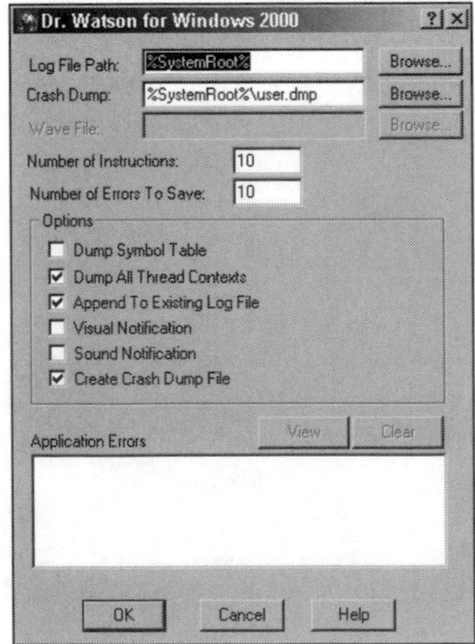

Figure 20-48: Dr. Watson for Windows 2000 Server

Summary

In this chapter, you

- Defined Task Manager features
- Tuned Task Manager to report the information you need
- Optimized Windows 2000 Server via Task Manager
- Defined System Information features
- Learned about SQL Trace and ODBCPING
- Learned about the Microsoft Exchange RPING utility
- Analyzed event logs
- Discovered the Microsoft System Information tool
- Had a visit from Dr. Watson!

Chapter 21

Troubleshooting Secrets

In This Chapter

- Learning formal troubleshooting steps
- Listing troubleshooting resources
- Defining troubleshooting
- Conducting a walkthrough of a troubleshooting example and developing your troubleshooting methodology
- Learning and applying the one-hour rule
- Calculating the value of downtime
- Using Windows 2000 troubleshooters
- Mastering Recovery Console
- Mastering the emergency repair process
- Analyzing blue screens

We finally arrive at the troubleshooting section!

Microsoft reported in its legacy MCSE Course 689, "Windows NT Server Enterprise Technologies," that over 58 percent of success in troubleshooting is experience-based, whether that prior knowledge derives from general computer systems knowledge or knowledge of the specific problem you face. The remaining troubleshooting success factors include luck, research efforts, and your inherent native problem-solving capabilities. Of course, reading and actively using books such as *Windows 2000 Server Secrets* only increases your odds of success when performing troubleshooting. It's also important to appreciate that developing your troubleshooting skill set is a lifelong journey, not an end that is attained and forgotten.

Troubleshooting skills, while developed primarily through experience, can be supplemented with outside reading, training, and drawing on your other skill sets. If you are short on experience with Windows 2000 Server, that doesn't necessarily mean that you will come up short when trying to solve problems. Heck, even that liberal arts degree you hold might just give that angle everyone else is overlooking in certain Windows 2000 Server troubleshooting scenarios. And while you can cite studies that indicate you need this much experience to successfully perform certain tasks and troubleshoot Windows 2000 Server, I prefer the Nike advertising slogan — "Just do it." That is, don't let your inexperience necessarily prevent you from gaining more experience.

Troubleshooting Steps

Like performance analysis, troubleshooting involves identifiable steps. These steps are similar conceptually to the steps you take in performance analysis (discussed in the past few chapters). In other words, you do the "basics" used in solving all problems: identification, assessment, solution planning, testing and verification, and documentation. Consider these troubleshooting steps as the foundation to guide your troubleshooting efforts.

STEPS:

To troubleshoot problems

Step 1. **Identify the problem.** Can you successfully identify the problem as a software or hardware problem?

Step 2. **Perform diagnosis.** Separate symptom from cause. Is the system acting out for some underlying, fundamental reason? Will addressing the symptoms do anything toward resolving the cause of those symptoms?

Step 3. **Develop and implement the solution.** Not surprisingly, this step is often repeated again and again.

Step 4. **Verify that the solution works.** This is the proverbial feedback loop that assures us of success. Solutions typically need to be tested several times and under different conditions. Fixing a Windows 2000 Server-specific problem might break a Novell NetWare connection in a mixed server environment.

Step 5. **Document the solution.** Too often, Windows 2000 Server professionals (including myself) successfully implement a wonderful solution, only to forget the finer problem-solving points at a future date when confronting the same scenario. In effect, we have to relearn the solution. Obviously, taking a few extra minutes to document each and every solution from our troubleshooting exploits can return huge dividends posthaste!

Microsoft promotes a troubleshooting methodology called D.E.T.E.C.T. (another legacy MCSE course, "Windows NT Server 4.0 Enterprise Technologies," pages 447–448, Microsoft Corporation). This method, created by a group of Microsoft technical support engineers, provides a suggested strategy for systems engineers to pursue when solving Windows NT Server problems. Note that these same steps apply equally well to Windows 2000 Server (since we're really talkin' methodology here, eh?). D.E.T.E.C.T. is:

D	Discover the problem
E	Explore the boundaries
T	Track possible approaches
E	Execute the approach
C	Check for success
T	Tie up loose ends

To expand on this sequence:

D **Discover the problem.** Speak with users at the user level, not the technical level. Try to find out what software they use (release versions if possible) and if their hardware is on the Hardware Compatibility List (HCL). What are the symptoms that the problem is displaying?

E **Explore the boundaries.** Can you and/or the user identify what changes have occurred since the system was last reported to work correctly? Can you identify what software was running when the problem occurred?

Tip

Here is an important dimension: Is the problem reproducible? Being able to reproduce the problem is an essential step in troubleshooting those tough ones that defy easy explanations and solutions. If you can't reproduce the problem, typically you are in for a long haul.

T **Track possible approaches.** This is just the documentation argument in sheep's clothing. You can learn from this incident and avoid the old inefficient trial-and-error approach by tracking the troubleshooting steps that you undertake.

E **Execute an approach.** Aside from managing expectations so that the different parties involved are not bothered if the first resolution attempt fails, you should already be thinking about plan B if the first approach fails. Don't forget that you should back up critical system and application files prior to executing a task (or series of tasks) to solve your problem.

C **Check for success.** Assuming you solved the problem, can the user be taught to correct the problem if it should reappear?

T **Tie up loose ends.** Share the results with others once the case is closed.

What is significant about the past several pages is that many different troubleshooting approaches exist, but virtually all follow a simple underlying model, as shown in Figure 21-1.

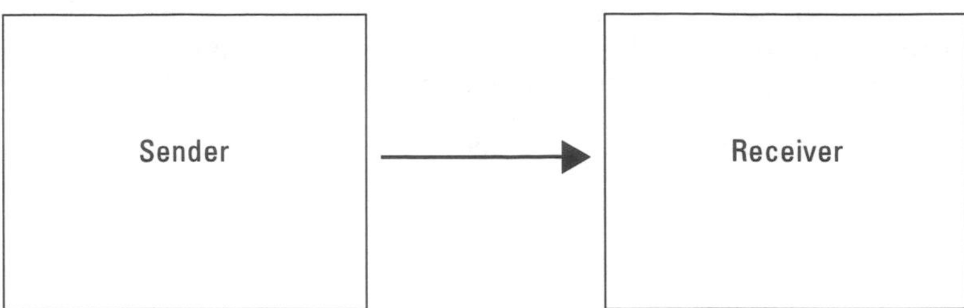

Figure 21-1: Input — Processing — Output model

Having troubleshooting steps to follow methodically is clearly the first step toward successfully troubleshooting your way out of Windows 2000 Server-related system problems. And don't worry. You're bound to encounter problems along the way with Windows 2000 Server. The good news is that these problems are what keep Windows 2000 Server professionals employed. In fact, I've heard comments from peers that they are hopeful the software industry never figures everything out, lest the resulting layoffs of systems engineers and network administrators send the industry and leading economic indicators into a tailspin!

I discuss many of the Windows 2000 Server tools for troubleshooting, such as WinMSD, in prior chapters. However, I finish this section on performance analysis and troubleshooting by discussing the merits of a structured approach to troubleshooting and what additional tools might benefit you in your quest for a happy and healthy Windows 2000 network.

Defining Troubleshooting

One definition of troubleshooting is when expensive MCSE-type consultants live, breathe, and bill hours to fix your network problems. Think about it. Many of us started in the field as $15/hour temps and woke up one day to discover that we were charging a lot more money for our time. We also discovered that the nature of our work changed dramatically. This is known as climbing the technology value chain. Whereas a $15/hour temp is allowed to discover the answer via learning, playing, and making mistakes, the $100/hour consultant is called in to troubleshoot problems and know the answers. In fact, a dear friend elected to avoid the stresses and strains of the high-end consulting market and stay at his modest $35/hour rate as a fully qualified MCP so that he might enjoy the journey of life much more. Of course, this discussion doesn't just apply to outside consultants. What senior manager doesn't occasionally wax nostalgic for the early carefree career stage of yearning and learning? (Of course, it's unlikely this same manager dwells too long on those painful entry-level salaries.)

The more you charge or make in the technology profession, the more troubleshooting duties you assume. You also have more stress!

Another definition of troubleshooting involves those tasks that fall into the pager-management category. If you're a network administrator or engineer, you know this all too well. Active pagers equal troubleshooting duties dead ahead. In this section, I cover methodology, the one-hour rule, and downtime value calculations.

A methodology

For many, troubleshooting is a methodology. Here, the carpenter's phrase, "measure twice, cut once" applies with a twist. Certainly a Windows 2000 Server professional should think twice and act once under any circumstances. Perhaps you, like me, have worked too many Saturdays in your career correcting mistakes on projects you started on late Friday afternoon. Lamenting "if I could only undo that" is a frequent cry for those new to the industry. Unfortunately, Windows 2000 Server has fewer undo capabilities than you might expect. The "Last Known Good" boot option is typically your best undo hope. I discuss Last Known Good later in this chapter.

Save yourself heartache and heartburn by following the golden rule of troubleshooting: Change only one variable at a time. Changing only one variable at a time and then testing for success or failure enables you to document your troubleshooting efforts effectively.

An example serves to bring meaning to this issue. In fact, it is recommended you complete portions of this example on a spare Windows 2000 Server to better understand how to troubleshoot your server environment methodically.

In the world of TCP/IP, it often is necessary to tweak and fine-tune TCP/IP addresses as you implement and manage your network. Suppose you have a TCP/IP configuration on a Windows 2000 Server running Microsoft Proxy Server, as shown in Figure 21-2.

Users Clint, Teresa, and Diane complain that they can't surf the Internet from their Internet Explorer applications on their Windows 98 workstations. You check the TCP/IP configuration for each network adapter card on Proxy Server and discover the settings shown in Figures 21-3 and 21-4. Note that it is essential to look closely at the IP values in these figures, for they and they alone hold the key to solving our riddle. And don't be concerned if you remain bewildered and befuddled at this point, as I give you the correct answer soon.

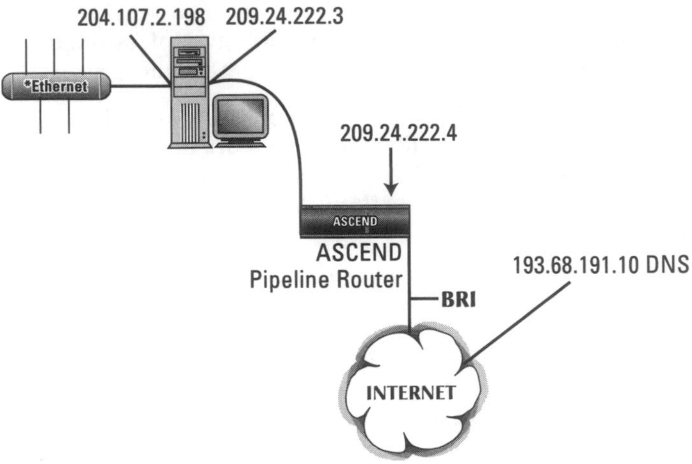

Figure 21-2: A sample network using the TCP/IP protocol and Proxy Server

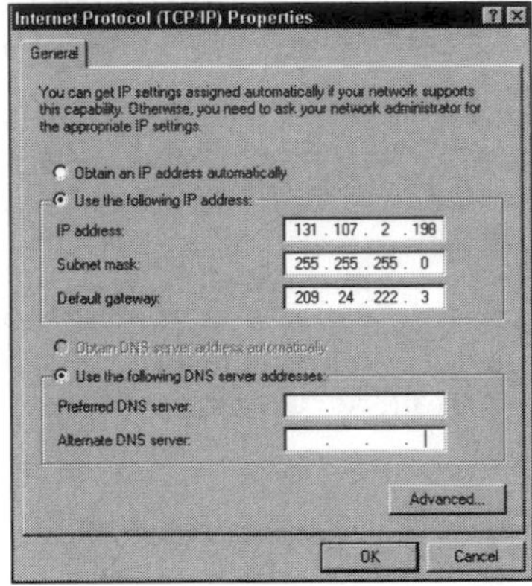

Figure 21-3: The TCP/IP configuration for the internal LAN network adapter card (a.k.a. "first NIC") on the Proxy Server

You now have enough information to solve the problem. Hint: Two TCP/IP configuration problems exist, but only one is causing the users to fail in their efforts to surf the Web via Internet Explorer. The other, noncritical, configuration issue — while it should be corrected — is more of an academic issue as far as Proxy Server is concerned (but it can create problems for your Cisco routers). Now take a few minutes to solve the problem. The challenge is that you only need to change one variable to arrive at the solution. By changing one variable and testing the results, you can discover the correct answer — that is, what variable you need to change to allow Proxy Server to function correctly.

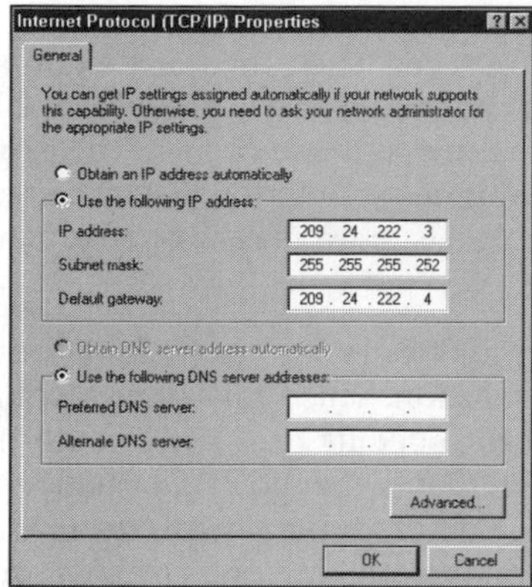

Figure 21-4: The TCP/IP configuration for the external LAN network adapter card (a.k.a. "second NIC") on the Proxy Server

First, let's evaluate the IP address for the internal network adapter card. This card has an IP node address of 131.107.2.198, yet a subnet mask of 255.255.255.0 (which of course suggests a Class C license). The IP node address is out of range for a Class C license, because the first octet position has a value of 131. Class C licenses require that node addresses commence with the number 192 or higher in the first octet position. Could this be causing the problem? Change the IP address for the node (and ultimately the IP addresses for all nodes on this subnet) to 204 so that you are within the Class C addressing range (see Figure 21-5).

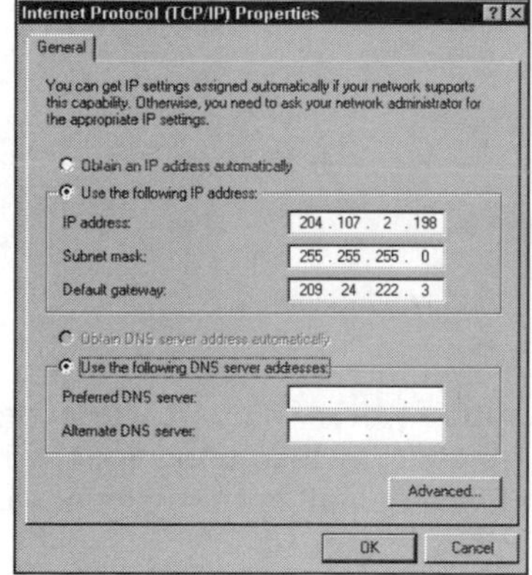

Figure 21-5: Changing the first octet value from 131 to 204

I highly recommend that you reboot after making troubleshooting modifications to your Windows 2000 Server. The preceding example is a perfect point. Although officially it is not necessary in Windows 2000 Server to reboot after changing an IP node address, those of us in the profession know that the dynamic binding capabilities of Windows 2000 Server demand a reboot to really work right. So the rule is, always reboot after making changes.

Assuming you've rebooted Windows 2000 Server after making the preceding changes, it is important to test the solution. This first change, while fixing one noncritical problem, doesn't fix the specific problem of external Internet access via Proxy Server. The problem that is fixed by that change affects your real routers, such as the Cisco 4500. Routers typically are designed to adhere to the traditional minimum and maximum starting octet values for each IP class (Class A starts at 0, Class B starts at 128, and Class C starts at 192). See Chapter 7 for more information.

So in the formal troubleshooting approach, we try again. For our second test, let's delete the existing Default gateway address and leave the field blank on the internal network adapter (see Figure 21-6).

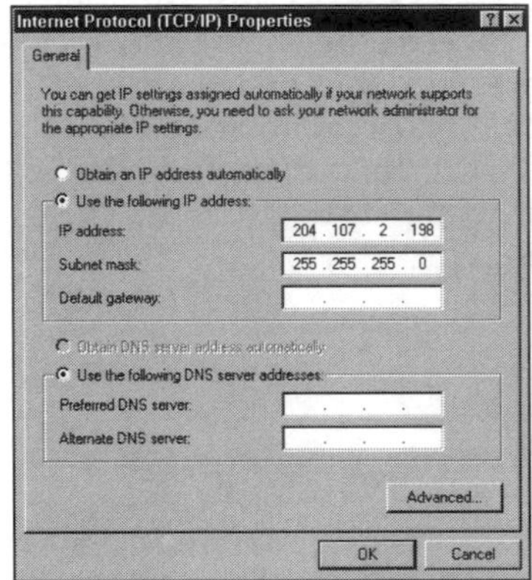

Figure 21-6: Deleting the existing Default gateway address

After rebooting, we discover this solution works. Why? It works because Proxy Server doesn't require a default gateway field entry for the internal network adapter card. In fact, providing a default gateway value, as you've discovered in this example, causes Proxy Server to fail.

So what did you learn about methodology from this exercise? When troubleshooting, change one variable at a time and test. Trust me.

The one-hour rule

Experience has shown that our less-experienced brethren have a higher propensity for going "heads down." Heads down occurs when you are troubleshooting a problem and you either get tunnel vision or lose perspective on time. Tunnel vision is the trap of not considering external factors that might be causing your problem. Many times external factors are causing your grief. Too often, we look at our Windows 2000 Server environments from a myopic viewpoint. However, elements beyond our control may well be impacting our situation.

In any case, it is essential to limit your core troubleshooting efforts to just one hour before stepping back from the situation and calling in help and reinforcements. My favorite approach is to get into a Windows 2000 Server problem for an hour. If I can't solve it or assure myself that I'm reasonably close, then I'm on the telephone with Microsoft Technical Support or at least conferring with another peer in the Windows 2000 Server community. Be sure to use your fellow professionals from the industry as resources.

Cultivate peer relationships in the Windows 2000 Server field. Soon you will be on your local Windows 2000 Server "prayer chain," providing and receiving advice to help solve Windows 2000 Server problems. Remember that a prayer chain is used by churches to call members when someone has fallen ill to get the power of prayer working to heal the stricken. In this case, as part of my one-hour rule, I start calling my Windows 2000 Server prayer chain shortly after I've allowed myself an hour to try and solve a problem. And remember to take a fellow Windows 2000 Server professional to lunch and develop your troubleshooting resources. It's the best investment you can make in the troubleshooting area.

Another variation on the one-hour rule is that you need to keep in perspective the value of your time relative to the value of the problem you are solving. If you earn $52,000 per year as a Windows 2000 Server network administrator, then your time could be worth as much as $31.25 per hour ($25 per hour plus 25 percent for benefits). Consider your value when you look up and see you've spent a half day troubleshooting that pesky LPT1 port on your Windows 2000 Server when a new multifunction I/O card costing under $75.00 can solve the problem immediately.

So circling back to our earlier discussion, how does this correlate to your experience in the industry? I've observed that "newbies" tend to take on Windows 2000 Server troubleshooting as a personal crusade. They have something to prove, and their budding egos sometimes force them to go stupid and heads down. Six hours later, although they may have resolved a TCP/IP configuration problem similar to our exercise earlier in the chapter, it probably could have been solved within one or two hours if they consulted outside resources. You will find no more (painfully) honest statement in this book.

Area code changes

Many regions are undergoing area code changes to account for the tremendous demand for analog and digital telecommunications services. Pagers, fax devices, cellular telephones, and additional telephone lines at work and home are, as many of you know, rapidly depleting the availability of telephone numbers within area codes. You might think that this problem only impacts voice telephone lines, but ISDN service is also affected. We learned this observation the hard way when a regional area code recently was split into three new area codes. When that change occurred, my client's Exchange-based e-mail system, and more specifically, the Internet Connector, stopped working. Having battled with Exchange on this particular server recently, I started my troubleshooting efforts there. Slowly and methodologically, I worked my way up to the ISDN router. Sure enough, the area code change required a simple modification to the ISDN router's image file. Problem solved, but I would have rather watched two NFL football games that Sunday than spend six hours troubleshooting this problem.

A stronger consideration of external factors would have eliminated hours of unsuccessful troubleshooting. Be sure to monitor scheduled area code changes if you utilize external communication services, such as ISDN lines.

Year 2000 issues

Look for Year 2000 issues as a possible source of problems in the near future. Although Windows 2000 Server doesn't have any specific Year 2000 issues to confront, you may be impacted if you use terminal emulation gateways, such as SNA Server from the Microsoft BackOffice family. The legacy machines you attach to may have underlying Year 2000-related problems. Thus, those problems become your problems in the Windows 2000 Server environment. Also, I have seen many clients with heavy metal machines convert to Windows 2000 Server to avoid having to address their legacy COBOL code. What a nice cop-out!

Workstation side, not server side

Another myopic misdirection is to become so focused on the server side that you forget the entire second half of the equation: the workstation side. I've got war stories galore here, including the construction accounting software package that actually ran fine on the server but had deeply disguised DLL conflicts on the workstation side. One of my tools of choice in troubleshooting workstation-side problems is good old System Editor (`sysedit`). I realize that this tool, which reports back basic `autoexec.bat`, `config.sys`, and `*.ini` information, isn't as cool as it was in the era of local Registry databases in Windows 95 and Windows 98. However, System Editor helps when an application has installed workstation components and created environment settings in the `config.sys` file. System Editor displays this file promptly, enabling me to arrive at a better solution.

The point is to think outside of the proverbial box. If you're not getting it fixed on the server side, take a walk over to the workstation side. You just may be surprised to find that's where the problem is!

The value of downtime

Another reality check to consider when troubleshooting is the value of downtime in your organization. By considering this, you might decide to take a markedly different approach to solving your problems. Simply stated, $50 per hour in downtime is different from $5K in downtime per hour or $50K per hour in downtime. To calculate downtime, use the information in Table 21-1.

Table 21-1 Calculating Downtime

Number of Employees	*Scenario A: Professional Services Firm with $100/Hour Bill Rate (Average)*	*Scenario B: Manufacturing Firm with Annual Sales of $100 Million*
50	$5,000 per hour of downtime	
1,000		$48,000 per hour of downtime ($100 million divided by 2,080 hours)

Assuming that the lost hours are not absorbed into future work periods — that is, the work can't be made up — these figures are daunting. In Table 21-1, we also assume that Windows 2000 Server-related downtime prevents people from working. In reality, you might apply a correction factor in your downtime calculations that better reflects Windows 2000 Server's real role in an organization. For example, with the manufacturing concern I describe, perhaps productivity is cut in half when the Windows 2000 Server fails, and thus the cost of downtime per hour really is $24,000.

Don't create such a large correction factor that you underestimate how workers respond to computer downtime. Although your staff cost accountants can determine accurately what processes are negatively impacted by system downtime, our friends from the sociology world correctly tell us that many workers use system downtime as an excuse to stop working and perhaps go home. Think about it. In an office environment, have you ever observed workers taking advantage of computer downtime to return overdue telephone calls? Many workers simply say the computer system has crashed and they can't work.

Another example is using a word processor during downtime. Many organizations have word processing applications such as Microsoft Word installed on a network drive both to save space on local workstation drives and possibly to reduce the number of necessary licenses. When the system is down under this scenario, Microsoft Word is inaccessible. However, WordPad is available and ready for local use if your client workstations run Windows 95/98, Windows 2000 Professional, or Windows NT Workstation. WordPad can save its files as `*.doc`, which actually is Microsoft Word version 6.0. At a later date, your users indeed may use Microsoft Word to edit these WordPad documents.

These two examples — not taking advantage of system downtime or using local applets — are as much a cultural issue as a technical issue. That said, issues such as this need to be managed or you will suffer high system downtime costs.

Given the high cost of system downtime, it is safe to say two things. Those of us in the IT profession are "cheap money," and once you recognize the high cost of downtime, you might employ more expensive troubleshooting methods than you previously considered.

By cheap money, I mean the following. Let's say that you are a Windows 2000 Server consultant billing at $125 per hour and you have a situation wherein the client is on the cheap (a.k.a. a "nickel and dimer"). Perhaps you have heard that they want to take many of the tasks for a Windows 2000 Server conversion "in house" — that is, have the staff perform many of the conversion duties without your input and participation. While you might agree readily to such an arrangement, several problems may arise here that, while saving money up front, can be very costly later.

The first problem is that you lose control of the project. Windows 2000 Server tinkering, modifications, and adjustments occur as in-house activities (well-intentioned, of course) without your knowledge. Second, suppose the project involves multiple sites over a Windows 2000 Server WAN. By forgoing the opportunity to learn each site, you risk not having your "head" in the system — that is, not having the Windows 2000 Server system committed to memory. And this is where matters get expensive when the system goes down. Without your head fully into the system, you have to relearn it. That takes time and costs money. So truly, you are cheap money as a consultant when you begin to speak of system downtime costs that start at $5,000 per hour for a modest-sized firm and approach $50,000 per hour for a $100 million manufacturer.

System downtime costs dictate how you approach troubleshooting. As I have shown, system downtime is surprisingly expensive. Even if you are in a small organization, you can calculate system downtime costs that easily approach hundreds of dollars per hour. So doesn't it make sense to use your best troubleshooting tools sooner rather than later?

The Troubleshooting Quilt

As you know, a quilt results from the combined efforts of many people trying to reach a common end, typically an attractive and functional quilt. Troubleshooting is similar in that it generally requires a variety of people making their own contributions toward reaching a completion: a solution to a problem. In this section, I want to look at some of the patches in the troubleshooting quilt, including the troubleshooting map, learning curve analysis, box canyon avoidance, and time management.

A troubleshooting map

Like writing a book, troubleshooting is better performed — and certainly more efficient — if you work from an outline or map. In fact, it's been my experience that you should reserve the conference room and use the mounted whiteboard to create your troubleshooting map. Just getting out of the computer room or server closet is often the dose of troubleshooting elixir that many need to take. I suppose being in a room physically removed from the Windows 2000 Server machines allows you to calm down and think with a clear and level head.

Secret

By creating a troubleshooting map on a whiteboard, you can involve the business managers in your efforts. Many business types are accustomed to mapping out scenarios in conference rooms; it's a comfort zone. By involving business managers in problem resolution, you not only benefit from some fresh blood — and fresh insights — but you also foster positive relations between the technical and business communities in your Windows 2000 Server environment. That relationship building is especially important when your Windows 2000 Server troubleshooting efforts take longer than expected.

By creating your troubleshooting map on a whiteboard and perhaps involving the business managers in your efforts, you can sell them on the solution(s) and, more important, achieve their buyoff on your strategies. Countless studies and maybe your own work experience have shown that when you have buyoff from the stakeholders, your likelihood of success is much higher. Do as you like with these suggestions, my friend, but I highly recommend you give 'em a shot.

And don't forget that good relations among the technical and professional staffs and management is worth a lot when your technology budget is reviewed (and hopefully approved) for the next fiscal year. Given the importance of your technology budget in a Windows 2000 Server environment, perhaps reserving the conference room for some planning on the whiteboard isn't such a bad idea after all. Plus, given that IT is often a cost center in an organization, you can use all the management friends you can get.

Learning curve analysis

Often, when confronted with a troubleshooting-related matter in Windows 2000 Server, you need to confront the limitations of your skill set and honestly assess if you are qualified to remedy the maladies negatively impacting your network. Table 21-2 presents a decision-making model that enables you to assess when you should attempt to solve the problem and when you should employ the skills of outside experts.

Table 21-2 Defining the Learning Curve

Nature of Problem	***Your Skills***	***Learning Curve***	***Proposed Solution***
Simple	High	Low	You solve the problem.
Occurs often, not difficult	Moderate	Adequate	You solve the problem after some learning and troubleshooting. Benefits include good use of learning time, because this type of problem occurs often. Once you learn and troubleshoot the solution, it will be much easier to solve again in the future.
Occurs infrequently, problem is "middle of the road" between simple and difficult	Low to moderate	Medium to high	Perhaps teaming with a Windows 2000 Server consultant or expert makes sense here. You can have the consultant demonstrate the solution so that perhaps you can solve the problem independently or with telephone support in the future.
Once in a lifetime, incredibly difficult	Nonexistent	Very high	Farm it out. Retain an expert to solve the problem and perhaps try to explain it to you. Don't worry if you can't understand it.

For the first two situations, it is probably a good use of your time to troubleshoot the problem. For the last two, help clearly is needed to minimize system downtime and organization pain associated with Windows 2000 Server problems that fall into those classes.

Early on in your troubleshooting efforts, assess the nature of the Windows 2000 Server problem you are trying to solve and determine whether you can arrive at the solution individually or you need to engage additional help to fortify your resolution efforts. Make the call as soon as you can.

Avoiding box canyons

How many times in a complex troubleshooting scenario have you started to perform the same steps or action again and again? Kinda like when you lose something at home and you start searching already-scoured areas repeatedly. Doesn't seem very rational, does it? Of course not. However, we fussy Windows 2000 Server network engineers do exactly that in the heat of the troubleshooting battle.

One proven way to correct this self-defeating behavior is to dictate into a low-cost microcassette tape recorder each and every step you take from minute one. This record enables you to revisit your approach and determine whether a troubleshooting path was pursued or not and the nature of the outcome.

You or a staff secretary can transcribe these convenient microcassette tapes so that you can review the steps via a hard-copy printout. I recommend dictation over simply handwriting your troubleshooting steps out for one simple reason: burnout. People often write by hand the troubleshooting steps taken for the first several steps or even the first several hours. But as hours become days, burnout causes a breakdown in this manual system. Steps are missed or skipped altogether. Dictation is a relatively painless way to document your troubleshooting efforts, and there is hope that you can capture each and every step from start to finish.

Another side benefit from dictation is the document trail you create to resolve billing disputes if you are a consultant. It seems like once per year in my practice, a billing is disputed to the extent that all parties resort to their files to seek both truth and resolution. Even though these billing dispute problems occur infrequently, they are monsters when they do. Fortunately, I've been able to prevail more often than not by having extensive documentation of the Windows 2000 Server system. This documentation includes troubleshooting notes that I typically capture via dictation. When you're talking about invoices in the $10,000 to $30,000 range, saying that dictation of your troubleshooting steps pays for itself is an understatement.

As an aside, I have found dictation to be an invaluable tool when troubleshooting TCP/IP-related problems due to the sheer details involved in any TCP/IP scenario. Correct me if I'm wrong, but it is easy to get confused when trying to keep multiple subnets clear in your head during the heat of a troubleshooting battle. Sometimes, after many hours at the helm, it's even difficult to communicate verbally about what IP address goes to what router port and what client machine.

So much troubleshooting, so little time

Many of us who are Windows 2000 Server professionals make a good living by providing services to professionals who are too busy to do it themselves. Here is what I mean. Many technology professionals want to, and given a reasonable amount of time, can troubleshoot and resolve Windows 2000 Server problems. But given the constraints imposed on each of us by Father Time, we find there simply are not enough hours to do everything we set out to do. Hiring out certain areas such as troubleshooting makes a lot of sense, especially if you consider troubleshooting something of a black hole when it comes to time management. Have you ever been troubleshooting a problem that started on Monday and looked up at the clock to find it was Saturday afternoon? Did you ever notice your other work start to pile up in stacks as your head got into a massive troubleshooting problem?

Remember that on-the-job success is measured as a whole. Don't get lost in the troubleshooting black hole at the expense of performing poorly in other job areas.

Another time issue with respect to troubleshooting involves core competencies. Many want to and even enjoy troubleshooting Windows 2000 Server problems. But for many other Windows 2000 Server professionals, the cost is far too high. An example is the professional headhunter I know who also works as a part-time Windows 2000 Server administrator at his firm. His role, as a commissioned-based recruiter, is to find and place talent. That's his core competency and greatest contribution to the firm. However, this individual tends to get sucked into Windows 2000 Server troubleshooting time robbers. When that happens, he stops performing his job and, I guess, starts performing his hobby. And while he is a competent Windows 2000 Server administrator, let's just say his talents are more efficiently allocated toward recruiting.

Even if you have stellar Windows 2000 Server troubleshooting skills, perhaps you were promoted and now run the IT department. You had best acknowledge the fact that your role has changed and delegate the Windows 2000 Server troubleshooting tasks to a more junior, more current, and less expensive staffer. The moral of this discussion? Assess if you are the best person to troubleshoot your Windows 2000 Server problem from the standpoints of both core competency and use of time.

Hardware versus Software — What a Paradox!

Many nights have been spent debating whether a problem is hardware or software related. And the debate isn't getting any easier with Windows 2000 Server now performing hardware-like functions such as routing. Viewed from the other side, hardware also is changing. Intel's microprocessors now assume more and more software functions, such as multimedia management. Even motherboards contribute to the debate. Is the culprit the on-board video card or the new video driver? Is it harder to troubleshoot an on-board video card than the old-fashioned video adapter cards (which can be changed out readily)?

If you're strong on one side, let's say software, and you've diligently been troubleshooting a hardware/software problem where the solution escapes you, then the solution is probably emerging from the other side or your weaker half. I know from experience with Windows 2000 Server that if I try and try to solve a problem from my vantage point (my strengths in software far outweigh my break-fix hardware skill set), then it is usually the other side of the coin causing my grief. More than one bad network adapter card has disguised itself as a software-based network problem in my experience. It all depends where you're coming from.

It's worth repeating a point from earlier in the chapter. Be sure to take peers from the industry to lunch occasionally. You can bet several break-fix technicians are on my short list of frequent lunch guests. It's one of my tricks of the trade when troubleshooting hardware and software problems.

Let's Get Technical!

So far, I've spent the first part of this chapter discussing the all-important foundation of troubleshooting. Now, let's direct our attention to the more technical aspects of troubleshooting.

The most basic activity to commence the Windows 2000 Server session is to boot the machine on which Windows 2000 Server is installed. It is from this point forward that problems might occur. In fact, one of the very first troubleshooting questions you were taught to ask is, "Can you boot the machine?"

To see and learn what the boot process is all about, I recommend that you edit your `BOOT.INI` file, typically found in `C:\Documents and settings\Administrator\Recent` (this file was previously in the root folder of C:\ in Windows NT Server 4.0). Add the `/sos` command to the `multi` or `scsi` line(s) found underneath the `[operating system]` section.

The `/sos` option (see Figure 21-7) displays each driver on your monitor during Window 2000 Servers startup phase. Seeing what drivers load is an exercise in learning more about your Windows 2000 Server. Call it Zen, but by knowing more about Windows 2000 Server, you become one with Windows 2000 Server.

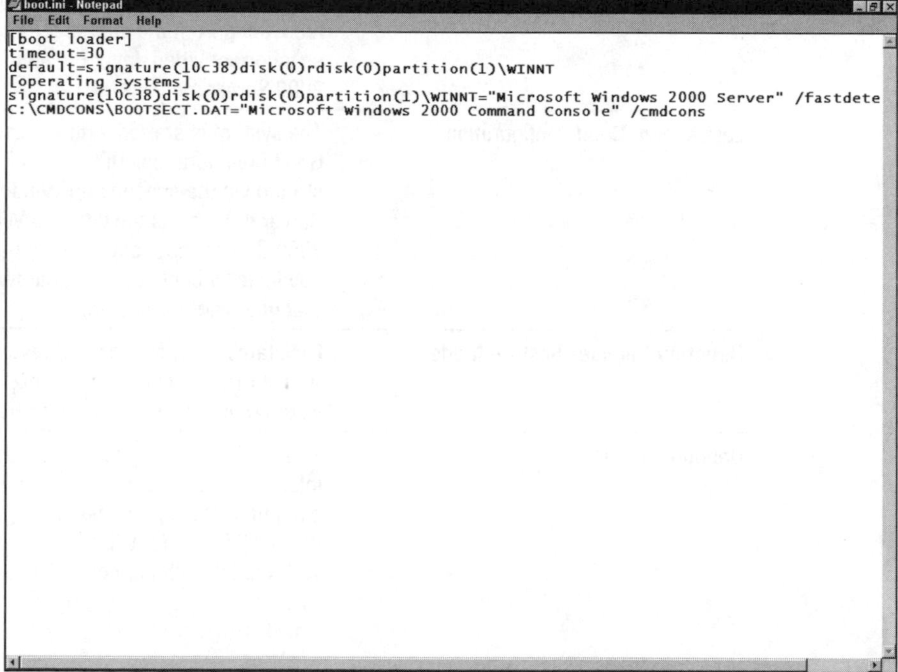

Figure 21-7: BOOT.INI and the `/sos` option

Bye-bye BOOT.INI switches

Other than the use of /sos in the boot.ini file, Microsoft has redesigned the Windows 2000 Server startup configurations. The shift is away from the numerous BOOT.INI switches you can use in Windows NT Server 4.0 to the Advanced Startup Options Menu, accessed by pressing F8 at startup, that you're familiar with from your experience with Windows 9*x*. Table 21-3 shows the advanced startup options.

Table 21-3 Advanced Startup Options

Menu Option	*Description*
Safe Mode	Basic drivers are loaded.
Safe Mode with Networking	Safe mode drivers plus basic networking functionality.
Safe Mode with Command Prompt	Basic drivers are loaded and command prompt is displayed.
Enable Boot Logging	Initiates startup-related logging to a text file.
Enable VGA Mode	The basic VGA driver is loaded. This was the /basevideo switch in the BOOT.INI file in Windows NT Server 4.0. Very useful for recovering from the improper installation of an incorrect video driver on your Windows 2000 Server machine.
Last Known Good Configuration	The system is started with the Last Known Good Configuration. This was selected at startup via the spacebar in Windows NT Server 4.0. This is the ultimate Windows 2000 Server undo feature. Very useful when you install a badly behaved hardware driver that you want to remove.
Directory Services Restore Mode	Facilitates maintenance and restoration of the Active Directory and the sysvol (the system volume) on the domain controllers.
Debugging Mode	This enables debugging and sends debugging information across a serial cable to another computer. This option was configured in the BOOT.INI file under Windows NT Server 4.0 with the following options: /debug, /baudrate:, /debugport=com, /nodebug.

Another few words on Last Known Good Configuration are in order. The Last Known Good Configuration option is a true friend indeed. This option has bailed me out of trouble — on numerous occasions dating back to the legacy Windows NT Server 4.0 days — when I installed a badly behaved driver that directly accessed the hardware (such as early drivers for Iomega's Jaz drive and the Connectix QuickCam video camera used for CUSEEME). Selecting the Last Known Good Configuration, which acts very much like the `Undo` command in Microsoft Word or Excel, truly undoes the damage I've caused and provides just the built-in recoverability I'm seeking in an operating system.

The Last Known Good Configuration uses the most recent control set that was created at the last successful logon (see Figure 21-8). It is important to know that, once you've logged on to Windows 2000 Server successfully, the Last Known Good Configuration option is updated and you inherit the changes that you made in the last session. Beware.

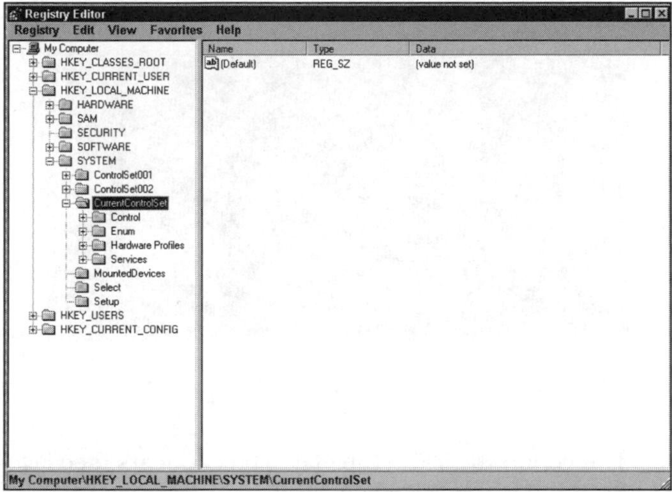

Figure 21-8: Control sets in the Registry

If you ever wanted to know which Control set Windows 2000 Server is using at startup, simply observe the following Registry key: `HKEY_LOCAL_MACHINE\SYSTEM\Select`. You can see entries for Current, Default, Failed, and LastKnownGood. If the Current entry is 0X00000001 (1), then ControlSet001 is being used at startup. If LastKnownGood has a value of 0X00000002(2), then ControlSet002 is being used. This is very valuable when you need to know which control set to edit service start values in to disable a badly behaved service as part of your troubleshooting efforts. Believe me, you most likely are on the telephone with Microsoft Support at this point!

Recovery Console

Windows 2000 Server has a great new feature for performing command-line troubleshooting: Recovery Console. This tool enables you to start and stop services, read and write data on local NTFS drives, and format hard disks. You must install it from the Windows 2000 Server CD-ROM using the following steps.

STEPS:

Installing Recovery Console

Step 1. From the command line of the I386 directory of your Windows 2000 CD-ROM, type the following command: **winnt32 /cmdcons**. This is shown in Figure 21-9.

Figure 21-9: Winnt32 /cmdcons

Step 2. The Windows 2000 Setup dialog box appears (see Figure 21-10). Read the message and click Yes to install Recovery Console.

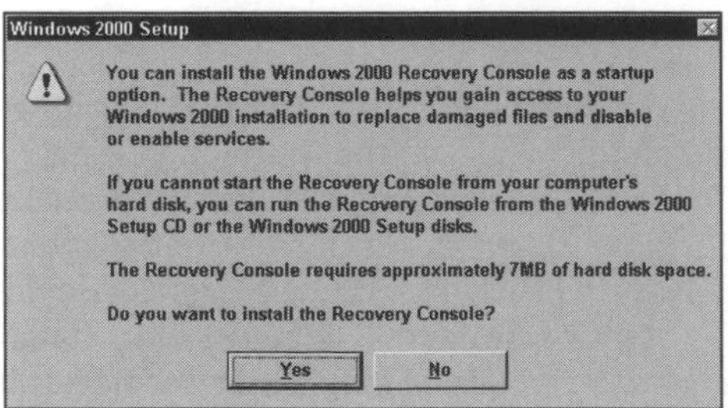

Figure 21-10: Windows 2000 Setup — Recovery Console

Step 3. Setup copies the Recovery Console files to your disk and you receive a Microsoft Windows 2000 Server Setup notice that the setup was successful (see Figure 21-11). Click OK.

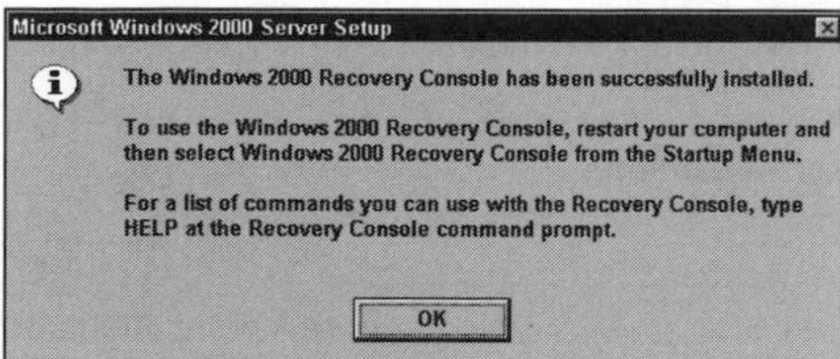

Figure 21-11: Recovery Console setup completed

The Recovery Console creates the folder `c:\cmdcons` on your Windows 2000 Server machine. This program may be launched from the Start menu. Note that Recovery Console also may be launched from the Windows 2000 setup disks or CD-ROM to help facilitate your troubleshooting efforts. The following commands shown in Table 21-4 may be used with Recovery Console. Note that these commands are similar to, if not the same as, the old MS-DOS command with which you are familiar.

Table 21-4 Recovery Console Commands

Recovery Console Command	*Description*
`cd`	This is the change directory command.
`chkdsk`	This is the check disk command.
`cls`	This is the clear screen command.
`del`	This is the delete command.
`dir`	This is the directory command.
`disable`	This may be used to disable a service or device driver.
`enable`	This may be used to enable a service or device driver.
`exit`	This exits the Recovery Console and enables you to restart your computer.
`fdisk`	This is the format disk command.
`fixboot`	This creates and writes a new partition boot sector onto the system partition.
`fixmbr`	This is similar to the `/mbr` command with the fdisk command. This repairs the master boot record for the partition boot sector.

Continued

Table 21-4 *(continued)*

Recovery Console Command	*Description*
`format`	This is the format command.
`help`	This is the help command.
`logon`	This enables you to log onto a Windows 2000 installation.
`map`	This displays a list of drive letter mappings.
`md`	This is the make directory command.
`more`	This is used to display a text file.
`rd`	This is the remove directory command.
`ren`	This is the rename command.
`systemroot`	This assigns the system root variable to the current folder.
`type`	This is used for displaying a text file.

Recovery Console also may be invoked as part of the emergency repair process discussed later in the chapter.

System start values

Another troubleshooting strength you should cultivate is the ability to interpret and modify the system start values for services and devices. Basically, the Registry entries for services and devices have a start value. The start values, listed in Table 21-5, show possible start values.

Table 21-5 Possible Start Values

Possible Driver Start Values	*Description*
0	Loaded but not initialized during the Boot Loader phase of the Windows 2000 Server startup cycle.
1	Loaded and initialized during the middle part of the Kernel phase.
2	Loaded and initialized at the end of the Kernel phase. Also loaded at the end of the Logon phase when the Service Controller (SCREG.EXE) makes a last pass through the Registry.
3	Loaded as required as the drivers initialize.
4	Disabled.

Using the information in Table 21-5 and the earlier discussion on how to determine what your current control set is (that is, from where your starting configuration is being derived), you can ascertain what service or device is using which start value (see Figure 21-12).

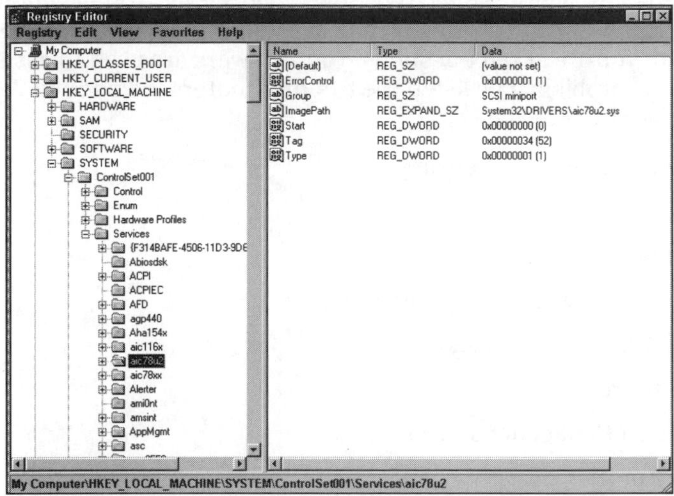

Figure 21-12: aic78u2 start is "0"

If you interpret the "0" start value with the information in Table 21-5, you can say that aic78u2 is loaded but not initialized. If you work with Microsoft Support to troubleshoot a startup problem, they might very well request that you set this start value to "4" to disable it and get it out of the picture.

If you troubleshoot Windows 2000 Server at this level, be sure to keep a list of the service and device name, its original start value, and the changed start value. Later, when you discover the offending service or device — via checking start values one at a time — you want to return the other, non-problematic services and devices back to their original start values.

How to Get Out of Trouble

Some of the most popular books of our time are "how to" books. You name the topic, and a "how to" book has been published on it. Perhaps the popularity of these books is their often practical and pragmatic advice for those seeking answers. In that spirit, this section starts to wrap up our excursion of the last few chapters on performance analysis and troubleshooting by offering you sage advice on how to get out of trouble with Windows 2000 Server. My offerings include Windows 2000 Server's new troubleshooters, replacing files via the `EXPAND` command, and using the Windows 2000 Server emergency repair disk and process. Last, I provide advice on how to flee the country if nothing else works.

Troubleshooters

Certainly a source of frustration for the user education group at Microsoft is the proverbial challenge of creating meaningful and truly helpful online help. Progress has been made with Windows 2000 Server and the introduction of *troubleshooters*. Simply stated, Windows 2000 Server troubleshooters assist you in diagnosing and solving technical problems. When a troubleshooter is launched, you are asked questions. Your answers are used to assist you in solving the problem. I've listed the troubleshooters included in Windows 2000 Server here:

- Client Services for Netware
- DHCP
- Display
- Group Policy and Active Directory
- Domain Name Services
- Hardware
- Internet Connections (ISP)
- Modem
- MS-DOS Programs
- Multimedia and games
- Networking (TCP/IP)
- Print
- Remote Access (RAS)
- Sound
- Startup and shutdown
- STOP Errors
- System setup
- Server management
- Windows 3.*x* programs
- WINS

Using a troubleshooter is easy. Follow these steps from the Windows 2000 Server online help system.

STEPS:

Using a troubleshooter

Step 1. From the Start menu, launch Help.

Step 2. On the Contents tab, double-click Troubleshooting and Other Resources.

Step 3. Double-click the Troubleshooting book that appears in the left pane.

Step 4. Double-click Troubleshooting overview.

Step 5. Select Troubleshooters. A list of troubleshooters appears in the right pane.

Step 6. Select the troubleshooter of your choice (for example, Group Policy and Active Directory).

Step 7. Answer each troubleshooter screen and click Next (see Figure 21-13).

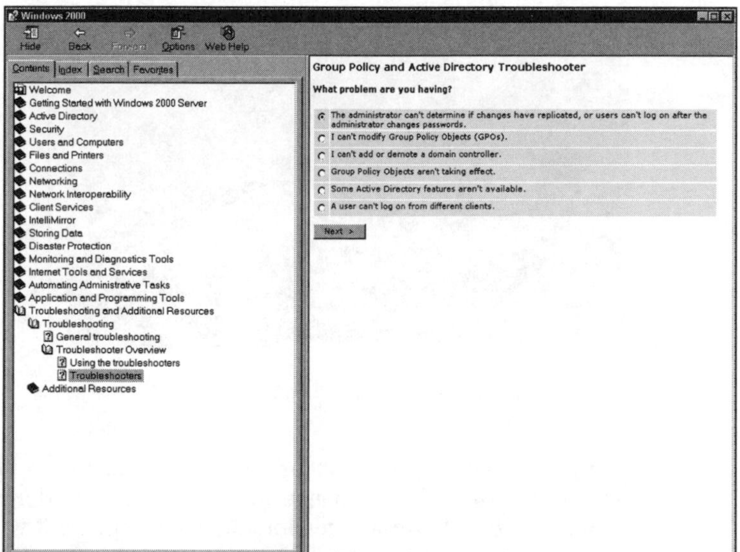

Figure 21-13: Using a troubleshooter

Step 8. Complete each troubleshooting screen until your problem is resolved, you give up, or you call for technical support.

Remember, troubleshooters in their present form are another troubleshooting tool for you to use, but they aren't perfect. Consider it another arrow in your troubleshooting quiver.

Expanding your way out of trouble — The case of the missing system files

Although it's unlikely this would be a daily dilemma, there are times (typically when advised by Microsoft Technical Support), when you will replace a corrupt system file from the Windows 2000 Server CD-ROM. Files on the CD-ROM are stored in a compressed format and need to be expanded. The `EXPAND` command (see Figure 21-14) officially is known as the Microsoft File Expansion Utility Version 5.00.

The `EXPAND` command is used to decompress files on the Windows 2000 Server CD-ROM so that you may replace an already installed file. The `-r` switch is necessary as compressed files typically have a shortened file extension on the CD-ROM (the file `*.sys` is stored as `*.sy_`).

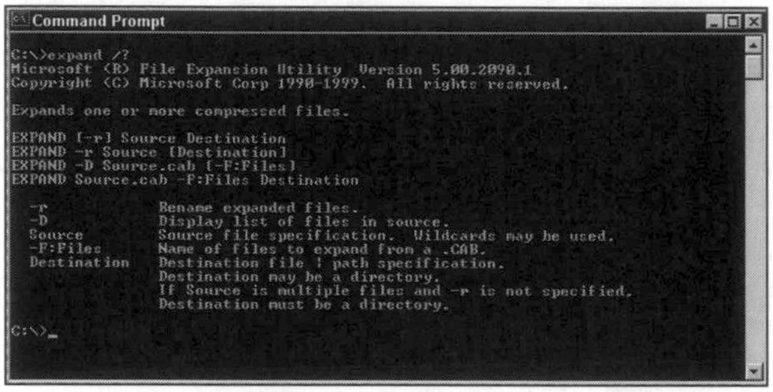

```
Command Prompt

C:\>expand /?
Microsoft (R) File Expansion Utility  Version 5.00.2090.1
Copyright (C) Microsoft Corp 1990-1999.  All rights reserved.

Expands one or more compressed files.

EXPAND [-r] Source Destination
EXPAND -r Source [Destination]
EXPAND -D Source.cab [-F:Files]
EXPAND Source.cab -F:Files Destination

  -r            Rename expanded files.
  -D            Display list of files in source.
  Source        Source file specification.  Wildcards may be used.
  -F:Files      Name of files to expand from a .CAB.
  Destination   Destination file | path specification.
                Destination may be a directory.
                If Source is multiple files and -r is not specified.
                Destination must be a directory.

C:\>_
```

Figure 21-14: The `EXPAND` command

Did you know that system files and drivers may be replaced even while they are in use? How? Simple. Once such files are loaded in memory, it is possible to rename the driver in question and then replace it with a fresh copy from the Windows 2000 Server CD-ROM. Here is how you accomplish that.

STEPS:

To rename and replace a driver

Step 1. Let's assume the corrupted file is `winmsd.exe`, which is Microsoft Windows 2000 Diagnostics (version 5.0.2) that ships with Windows 2000 Server (a.k.a. System Information). This file needs to be replaced in its existing subdirectory: `\WINNT\system32`. The file currently is loaded and in use.

Step 2. Rename the file to `winmsd.foo` (see Figure 21-15).

Step 3. Copy the file `winmsd.ex_` from the Windows 2000 CD-ROM. (This file is located in the I386 subdirectory.) Place the file in the same subdirectory as the original `winmsd.exe` file: `\WINNT\system32`.

Step 4. Use the `EXPAND` command to decompress the file (see Figure 21-16).

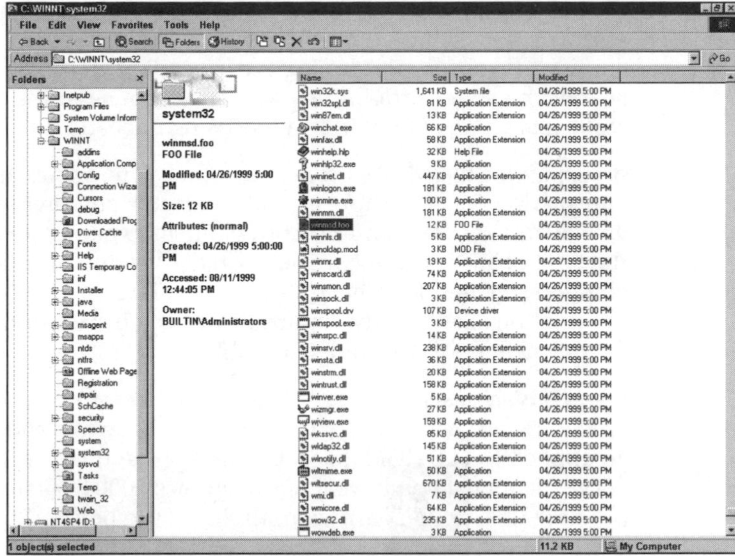

Figure 21-15: Renaming `winmsd.exe` to `winmsd.foo`

Figure 21-16: The `EXPAND` command

Step 5. You are finished. Depending on the file you've modified, you will need to restart the computer so that the changes may take effect. Simple application files don't typically require a restart, but operating system files do. You now may "trash" (oops, recycle) the old, corrupted file.

Note that it has been my experience that the preceding steps typically are performed in conjunction with recommendations from Microsoft Technical Support. If you are performing the preceding Steps 1–5, you should have very specific reasons for doing so. I do not recommend that you attempt these steps just for the fun of it. In advertising lingo, do not try this at home.

An expanded file, via its Properties sheet, reports much more property information than a compressed file. In fact, a compressed file doesn't report its File Version, Description, Copyright, and specific Item Name information—the type of information contained on the Version tab sheet. (That's because compressed files don't have Version tab sheets.) This type of detailed information is especially important when you are working with Microsoft Technical Support to resolve a problem.

If you haven't used the `EXPAND` command before, now is a good time to try it. I recommend that you expand a relatively safe file, such as a `readme` file from an application CD-ROM disc, such as Microsoft Office, to your Windows 2000 Server. In fact, if you have a test Windows 2000 Server that you use to practice with as you earn your MCSE, all the better.

So far, everything discussed with respect to the `EXPAND -R` command assumes that the system is running and you can get to the corrupted file in question. However, if the system is not running and you encounter a corrupted file or driver that prevents you from logging on successfully, you might again think it's time to update your résumé and run for the nearest exit. But first try one more thing, assuming you have an NTFS partition. Install a fresh copy of Windows 2000 Server to another subdirectory on your NTFS partition and then replace the corrupted file or driver in the location of the original Windows 2000 Server installation. If you have a FAT partition, you can boot from a system disk and simply copy over the necessary files.

911—Keep a current emergency repair disk

Even if you didn't create an emergency repair disk (ERD) while installing Windows 2000 Server, you may do so at any time by running Backup (from the System Tools program groups in Accessories) and select the Emergency Repair Disk menu option (see Figure 21-17).

The Emergency Repair Disk menu option in Backup can be used either to create or update your ERD. It essentially copies the updated system information found in the `\\WINNT\REPAIR` directory (see Figure 21-18).

It is essential that you periodically update your ERD so that it maintains current system-related information in the event that you should suffer problems with your Windows 2000 Server installation. I typically update the ERD for my clients when I make my house call visits to inspect their networks. At a minimum, I try to perform this ERD update once per month. Major updates—such as adding a service pack to your Windows 2000 Server or new drivers—justify an update to your ERD regardless of when the last backup occurred.

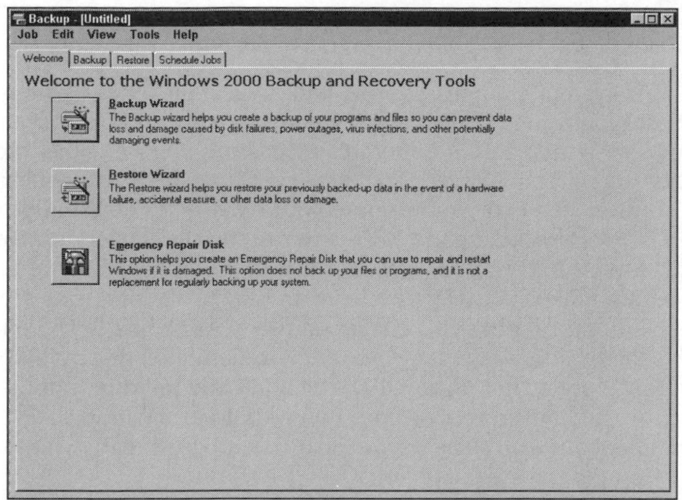

Figure 21-17: Emergency Repair Disk

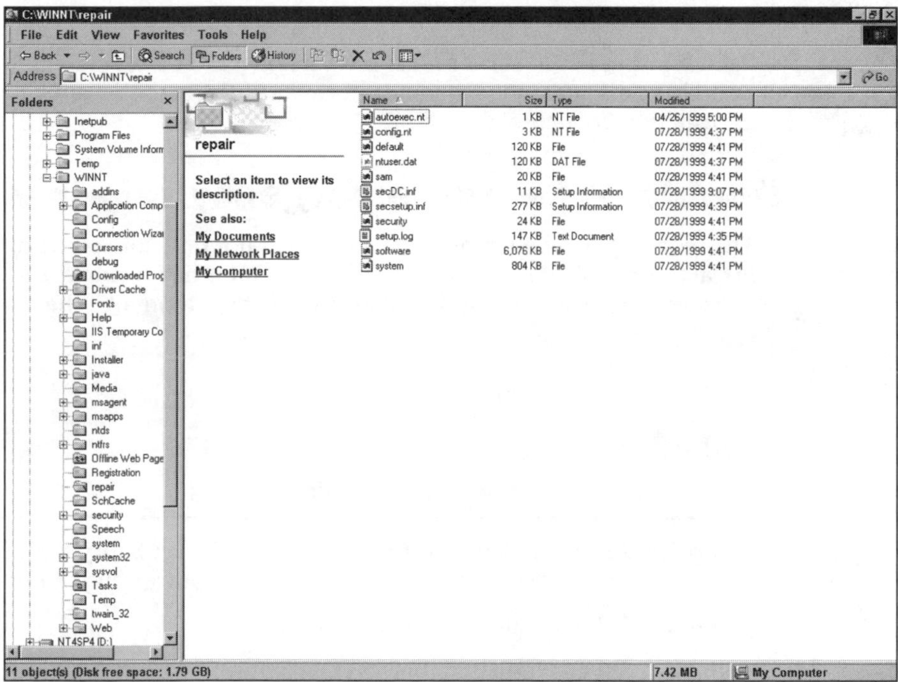

Figure 21-18: The WINNT\repair directory

If you don't update your ERD periodically and it is used to recover from a Windows 2000 Server dilemma, you face the prospect of going two steps backward. That's because the ERD reapplies historical system information such as for the Security Account Manager (SAM) found on the existing ERD that may not contain the last users added to your system (since the last ERD was created).

After major system changes to your Windows 2000 Server, be sure to do at least one of following things before you update your ERD. First, reboot and test the new configuration. Can you successfully log on? Does the new configuration on your Windows 2000 Server operate at a level that satisfies you? If so, then go ahead and update your existing ERD. What you are trying to avoid is overwriting a good ERD with potentially flawed information. Second, I have a better idea. Why not just create a new ERD and archive your existing ERD? That way you have an ERD update history archived on successive floppies, plus you address a really weak link in the entire Windows 2000 Server recovery chain: the reliance on floppy disk-based media. Don't forget that floppy disks periodically fail due to moisture, destruction, and other acts of God. Given that your Windows 2000 Server network is only as strong as its weakest link, do you really want this weak link to be an old floppy disk? No!

However, with this multifloppy scenario, be sure to limit the number of floppies in your rotation. Perhaps three floppies can work, giving you child, parent, and grandparent versions of the ERD. And of course be sure to label each floppy clearly with the ERD creation date.

Each Windows 2000 Server must have its own ERD. These disks are not interchangeable among machines because of the machine-specific information contained on the ERD.

Double 911 — the emergency repair process

The emergency repair process is a lifesaver not only for recovering a corrupt installation of Windows 2000 Server, but also for narrowing the search for and remedying corrupt files and drivers. Here is how to invoke the emergency repair process.

STEPS:

To invoke the emergency repair process

Step 1. Insert the Microsoft Windows 2000 Server Setup Boot Disk 1 (a.k.a. Setup Disk 1) in the floppy drive and power on your computer.

Step 2. When requested, insert Disk 2.

Step 3. When requested, insert Disk 3.

Step 4. When requested, insert Disk 4.

Step 5. When you see the Windows 2000 Setup Welcome Screen, select "R" for the repair option. The Welcome Screen appears as:

```
Windows 2000 Server Setup
===================
Welcome to Setup.
```

```
Windows 2000 Server Setup
Welcome to Setup.
This portion of the Setup program prepares Microsoft(r) Windows
2000(tm) to run on your computer.
*     To setup Windows 2000 now, press ENTER.
*     To repair a Windows 2000 installation, press R.
*     To quit Setup without installing Windows 2000, press F3.
ENTER=Continue  R=Repair  F3=Quit
```

Step 6. Insert the Windows 2000 Server CD-ROM Disk when requested. Press ENTER.

Step 7. Next, select the appropriate actions from the Repair screen. In this case, press R to commence the emergency repair process.

```
Windows 2000 Server Setup
====================
Windows 2000 Repair Options:
* To repair a Windows 2000 installation by using the Recovery Console,
press C.
* To repair a Windows 2000 installation by using the emergency repair
process, press R.
If the repair options do not successfully repair your system, run
Windows 2000 Setup again.
```

Step 8. Another Windows 2000 Server Setup screen appears enabling you to select between a manual and fast repair option.

```
Windows 2000 Server Setup
====================
This operation will attempt to repair your Windows 2000 system.
Depending on the type of damage present, this operation may or may not
be successful. If the system is not successfully repaired, restart
Setup and choose the option to recover a destroyed system or system
disk.
Select one of the following repair options.
* Manual Repair: To choose from a list of repair options, press M.
* Fast Repair: To perform all repair options, select F.
```

Step 9. Assuming you select "M" for manual repair, you see the following screen.

```
Windows 2000 Server Setup
====================
As part of the repair process, Setup will perform each optional task
selected below.
To have Setup perform the selected tasks, press ENTER.
To change the selections, use the UP or DOWN ARROW keys to select an
item, and then press ENTER.
[X] Inspect startup environment
[X] Verify Windows 2000 system files
[X] Inspect boot sector
 Continue (perform selected tasks)
```

Note that each option is selected (as denoted by the "X"). Table 21-6 provides an explanation of each emergency repair option.

Table 21-6 Emergency Repair Options

Emergency Repair Option	*Description*
Inspect startup environment	Used when you know you have Windows 2000 Server installed on your system but there is no startup menu option to select it. Basically modifies the `BOOT.INI` file. Requests that you insert the emergency repair disk you created when you installed Windows 2000 Server (and have hopefully updated periodically).
Verify Windows 2000 system files	Simply stated, this option verifies the existence and integrity of all Windows 2000 system files. If you provide the confirmation, damaged files are replaced on a case-by-case basis. You even can have all damaged files replaced automatically without having a confirmation required for each file.
Inspect boot sector	A new boot sector is copied to your disk. This is a good option to use if the Windows 2000 Server boot sector is damaged by errant use of the MS-DOS `sys.com` command. By running this command, you preserve dual-boot capabilities.

You are prompted to insert the emergency repair disk (ERD) depending on the options that you select. For example, with the "Inspect registry files" option, you are prompted to elect which portions of the Registry you want to replace. This replacement Registry information is taken from the ERD.

Be sure to verify the security on the files and directories that may be affected by the repair process just described. The repair process sets the security on impacted files and subdirectories back to a default installation state. That may or may not be how you maintained your system prior to running the repair processes.

If you already haven't done so, take a moment to observe the security settings on files and folders contained in the `\%SYSTEMROOT\WINNT` directory. This is accomplished by selecting the folder or file about which you seek to observe security information, and then selecting the secondary menu (via a right-click). Next, select either Sharing or Properties, and then the Security option. You then can observe the security that currently is applied to that file or folder.

After making systemic or significant changes to your Windows 2000 Server environment, such as running the emergency repair process and having files replaced, it is essential you reapply the appropriate Windows 2000 Server service packs as they are released by Microsoft. I say "appropriate" because Microsoft is somewhat inconsistent with respect to its service packs. Some service pack life cycles are inclusive; that is, you only need to apply the latest service pack and all prior or predecessor patches and fixes are brought forward. However, some service pack histories are more bothersome. For example, with Microsoft Exchange 4.*x*, it was necessary to apply Service Pack 2 prior to applying Service Pack 4. So not only should you reapply the service packs as needed, but be darn sure to do so in the correct order.

Finally, I share with you the ultimate way to get out of trouble: keep an updated passport. You laugh now at such a suggestion, but wait until we meet offshore from the Florida Keys under the palm trees one day, my friend!

Examining STOP Screens

The dreaded ARGGH! The infamous blue screen. It's *Revenge of the Nerds, Part Three*. All are appropriate descriptions of the fatal error STOP screen. And stop means STOP in all capitals. You ain't goin' no further, my friend, when Windows 2000 Server generates one of these babies.

STOP screens can be created a variety of ways. By far, the easiest way is to have a badly behaved device driver *not* make your day. I've been there and done that. Both you and I can crash Windows 2000 Server by installing one of a handful of known bad hardware drivers. Boom. STOP screen generated at startup. The technical reasons for this are that said drivers are supporting devices that aren't natively supported by HAL. Well, if you leave it up to third-party ISVs to write the perfect driver to run under Windows 2000 Server, you're bound to have an occasional STOP screen.

The most common causes of STOP screens are hardware-related errors. That's because these drivers are granted access by the Windows 2000 Server kernel to "touch" the hardware. And it is possible for bad things to happen when the hardware is touched by dirty hands... er, drivers. Other specific causes of STOP screens include corrupted system files and/or a corrupted file system.

So just what are STOP screens really? They are divided into three sections: top, middle, and lower (see Figure 21-19).

```
*** STOP: 0x0000001E (0xC0000005, 0xF24A447A, 0x00000001, 0x00000000)
KMODE_EXCEPTION_NOT_HANDLED

*** Address F24A447A base at F24A0000, DateStamp 35825ef8d - wdmaud.sys

If this is the first time you've seen this Stop error screen, restart your
computer. If this screen appears again, follow these steps:

Check to be sure you have adequate disk space. If a driver is identified in
the Stop message, disable the driver or check with the manufacturer for
driver updates. Try changing video adapters.

Check with your hardware vendor for any BIOS updates. Disable BIOS memory
options such as caching or shadowing. If you need to use Safe Mode to
remove or disable components, restart your computer, press F8 to select
Advanced Startup Options, and then select Safe Mode.

Refer to your Getting Started manual for more information on troubleshooting
Stop errors.

Kernel Debugger Using: COM2 (Port 0x2f8, Baud Rate 19200)
Beginning dump of physical memory
Physical memory dump complete. Contact your system administrator or
technical support group.
```

Figure 21-19: Blue screen

1. The top portion of the screen provides error code and related parameter information. First, you naturally see the word STOP. Next you see the error code, which also is known as the bug check code.
2. The middle portion of the screen displays recommended user actions.
3. Kernel Debugger and memory dump information is presented at the bottom of the screen.

Although STOP screens seem to convey lots of information that might be overwhelming to the uninitiated, fear not. The STOP screens have improved dramatically under Windows 2000 Server! Now back to business. Not surprisingly, the next step is to run, not walk, to the nearest telephone and recite these lines of information to Microsoft Technical Support. Rest assured, the good guys and gals in tech support will get it from there—with your hands-on assistance, of course.

Here are a few common STOP screens that you likely will encounter as a Windows 2000 Server practitioner. These messages are broken into several different categories under Phase 0 (see Table 21-7) and Phase 1 (see Table 21-8). Note that during Phase 0, interrupts are disabled and only a few Windows 2000 Server Executive components are loaded. An example of this is the Hardware Abstraction Layer (HAL). Phase 1 of the Executive initialization results in a system that is fully operational with the Windows 2000 Server subcomponents having completed full initialization.

Table 21-7 Phase 0 Initialization STOP Messages

STOP Message	*Meaning*
0x0031	PHASE0_INITIALIZATION_FAILED
0x005C	HAL_INITIALIZATION_FAILED

STOP Message	Meaning
0x005D	HEAP_INITIALIZATION_FAILED
0x005E	OBJECT INITIALIZATION_FAILED
0x005F	SECURITY_INITIALIZATION_FAILED
0x0060	PROCESS_INITIALIZATION_FAILED

The common workaround for a Phase 0 STOP message is to run the hardware manufacturer's diagnostic program (for example, Dell's Server Assistant).

Table 21-8 Phase 1 Initialization STOP Messages

STOP Message	Meaning
0x0032	PHASE1_INITIALIZATION_FAILED
0x0061	HAL1_INITIALIZATION_FAILED
0x0062	OBJECT1_INITIALIZATION_FAILED
0x0063	SECURITY1_INITIALIZATION_FAILED
0x0064	SYMBOLIC_INITIALIZATION_FAILED
0x0065	MEMORY1_INITIALIZATION_FAILED
0x0066	CACHE_INITIALIZAITON_FAILED
0x0067	CONFIG_INITIALIZATION_FAILED
0x0068	FILE_INITIALIZATION_FAILED
0x0069	IO1_INITIALIZATION_FAILED
0x006A	LPC_INITIALIZATION_FAILED
0x006B	PROCESS1_INITIALIZATION_FAILED
0x006C	REFMON_INITIALIZATION_FAILED
0x006D	SESSION1_INITIALIZATION_FAILED
0x006E	SESSION2_INITIALIZATION_FAILED
0x006F	SESSION3_INITIALIZATION_FAILED
0x0070	SESSION4_INITIALIZATION_FAILED
0x0071	SESSION5_INITIALIZATION_FAILED

Microsoft's initial recommendation for a Phase 1 STOP error is to reinstall Windows 2000 Server.

The Microsoft Windows 2000 Server Resource Kit is another source of information for you in your hunt to resolve STOP messages. Microsoft TechNet also is a good source of definitions on STOP messages.

So what to do with STOP screens?

The next step to resolve STOP-related problems is to jump into system debugging, also known as the art of searching for and eliminating fatal errors. The following discussion is intended to introduce you to debugging terms. After that, you'll be armed and ready for action. Note that in reality you will perform debugging activity in conjunction with Microsoft Support.

Let's set aside our engineering hats and put on our developer hats. These terms are important in understanding how debugging devices work.

Symbol file

Developers build code. This code comes in two flavors: checked and free. Checked code contains debugging code that helps the developers; but alas, it runs slower. Free code is speedy and dangerous. It doesn't contain the necessary debugging code to help developers debug their coding efforts. However, with less overhead to deal with, free code-based applications run much faster. Windows 2000 Server, when viewed from a code perspective (that is, the many millions of lines of code) has the best of both worlds by combining speed, debugging capabilities, and less overhead. In effect, the source code for Windows 2000 Server tastes great and is less filling; it is a combination of checked and free versions. Important: You know the symbol files in one of two ways. The first way is through the Symbols subdirectory underneath the I386 directory on the Windows 2000 Server CD-ROM. The second way that you probably are familiar with symbols is the way in which service packs historically have been applied to Windows 2000 Server. Remember those extra steps described in the `readme.txt` file of a service pack release that detail how to install the symbols? In a service pack, installing the updated symbols file is for the benefit of your debugging efforts.

Structured exception handling

Active at all times in Windows 2000 Server, structured exception handling provides the capabilities to trap exceptions for possible later manipulation. If the exception is handled via structured exception handling, the application may continue unimpeded.

Local debugging

Using a null-modem cable, the host computer is connected to a target computer for local debugging.

Remote debugging

Via Remote Access Services (RAS), you can set up a remote debugging session with Microsoft Technical Support. This is considered deep diagnostics.

Troubleshooting via the Registry

Of course, during your career as a Windows 2000 professional, it will be essential to master the Registry. Not surprisingly, the Registry is a huge area. Typically, troubleshooting via the Registry is performed under the guidance and watchful eye of Microsoft Technical Support. However, there are other ways to learn the Registry.

I've learned to swim around the Registry by drawing on the tips and experience of highly qualified Microsoft Certified Trainers during my days as an MCSE candidate. Another approach I've employed is to draw on tips from the Microsoft newsgroups found at `www.microsoft.com`. Although some of the information on these newsgroups is suspect, pay close attention to the offerings from the "Most Valuable Players" (MVPs).

Troubleshooting Resources

Remember that troubleshooting is part method, part luck, and part research. Strong research demands great resources. A world of tools is available to help you troubleshoot, including the Internet, books, Microsoft TechNet, journals, newspapers, training, and other professional resources, such as trade associations.

The Internet: The Web and newsgroups

Here we sit, turning the corner on a new century and millennium for that matter, and we're equipped with a research tool that simply was unimaginable even a few years ago back in the early networking days (the LAN Manager and NetWare 1.*x* days). That tool, of course, is the Internet. Recall that in Chapter 10 I discuss configuring Windows 2000 Server to connect to the Internet. Here, the context of the Internet discussion is slightly different and relates to research.

Using the World Wide Web, newsgroups, e-mail, and the powerful search engines, you often can resolve your problems for little or no cost. The only investment you must make is time. But many feel that time spent researching a solution to a problem is time well spent.

The Microsoft site at `www.microsoft.com` provides the Windows 2000 Server fan a wealth of information. The search engine dedicated strictly to searching the Microsoft site enables you to tap into the online knowledge base (which contains some information separate from the CD-ROM version, discussed later).

The newsgroups supported at www.microsoft.com provide an abundance of information, plus offer you the opportunity to contribute your own expertise. As when investing, however, you are warned to exercise care when disseminating information obtained from public newsgroups. The information often is worth exactly what you paid for it (nothing). Let the buyer beware! Also, the newsgroups sometimes are dominated by anti-Microsoft postings. While occasionally amusing, these irrelevant postings are severe time wasters.

Books to help you

Of course this book was written with you in mind, so I hope that *Windows 2000 Server Secrets* will be a well-worn, doodled, and tattered companion residing atop your Windows 2000 Server. But don't overlook the Windows 2000 Resource Kits. You will want to purchase the server-related and workstation-related editions, as both kits contain relevant information that pertains to both the server and workstation environments.

I highly recommend you keep the legacy resource kits from previous versions of Windows NT Server for two reasons. First, the older books often contain useful subject matter that has been deleted from updated releases. Second, the resource kits enable you to successfully administer older sites you are bound to see as a Windows 2000 Server professional. What I wouldn't give for a copy of the original Windows 3.1 Resource Kit (yes, that old Windows circa 1990).

In fact, this book you are reading assumes that you own and frequently refer to the Windows 2000 Resource Kits. When combined, you've armed yourself with the referral resources necessary to enjoy success as a Windows 2000 Server professional.

Microsoft TechNet

Be sure to use Microsoft TechNet. This is a monthly CD-ROM subscription service that contains countless articles on Microsoft products including Windows 2000 Server, the Knowledge Base with extensive references to Windows 2000 Server, articles and presentations, and resource kits and training materials for Windows 2000 Server and other Microsoft products. It costs approximately $300/annually.

Keep old versions of TechNet on your shelf (see Figure 21-20). TechNet is updated each month, so older drivers and articles are removed to make room for new entries. By keeping your old TechNet releases, you can keep a surprisingly valuable library at your fingertips.

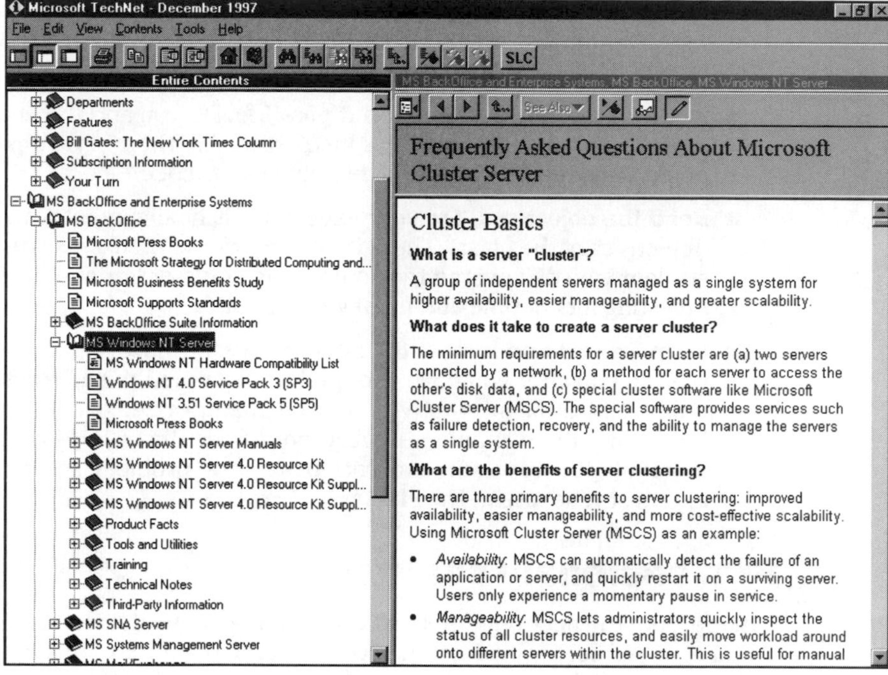

Figure 21-20: Microsoft TechNet

And speaking of articles and the like, don't forget the weekly trade rags. Publications such as *InfoWorld* offer a wealth of advice. Make these publications a regular part of your weekend reading.

Training and education

Because you are a knowledge worker, clearly one of your best avenues to develop strong troubleshooting skills is to increase your knowledge. Knowledge, obviously, is multidimensional. Many acquire knowledge via experience (a.k.a. the "School of Hard Knocks"). Others prefer a mix of education in the knowledge equation. Therein lies another resource for you to consider: education. If you put on your manager hat, perhaps you can step back and develop your own sense of how important additional education is in developing your technical skills and troubleshooting talents.

Education comes in many forms, ranging from instructor-led to self-study. To discover formal training avenues authorized by Microsoft, visit `www.microsoft.com/services`. To see an example of an online training opportunity, you may surf to `www.spu.edu` and learn about the online MCSE program that I instruct (in my spare time!).

When selecting an educational avenue to hone our troubleshooting skills, I highly recommended that you consider three things to maximize your return — considering the time and money you are asked to invest:

- **Attend a sample class session if possible.** Do you and the instructor get along? Can you learn from this instructor? Are there style differences that might negatively impact your learning experience?
- **Read the objectives.** Are your expectations in alignment with the objectives of the class? There is nothing worse than a dissatisfied student who discovered the course wasn't his or her cup of tea (after investing lots of time and money to attend).
- **Shop around and look at the alternatives.** Perhaps self-study doesn't look so bad after you have shopped and sampled the instructor-led and online education alternatives. Are the unauthorized training centers a better fit for you and your pocketbook? Does the training center have any tools to screen students with behavioral problems, or can anyone and everyone attend the classes?

Professional resources

Aside from the peer relationships that you may have developed as a Windows NT Server professional, professional resources are available to help you troubleshoot your problems.

Microsoft Certified Solutions Providers

Consider engaging the services of a Microsoft Solution Provider. Calling the Certified Solution Provider program at 1-800-SOLPROV enables you to communicate your needs, location, and budget to the representative, who then forwards your request as a lead to three or four qualified Solution Providers in your area. While not a perfect avenue for finding and engaging competent professionals, the Microsoft Solution Provider program does provide you a better approach than just using the Yellow Pages. Solution Providers receive the latest Microsoft software for learning and testing purposes. Solution Providers also are required to employ a minimum number of Microsoft Certified Professionals. Again, not a perfect approach, but the Solution Provider program does create a base standard to which its members must adhere.

Microsoft Consulting Services

Some clients implementing Windows 2000 Server want to go right to the source. Microsoft Consulting Services, with billing rates comparable to the Big Six accounting firms, dispatches Microsoft employees to work with you. While this approach is an expensive option to say the least, it is the best option for many organizations (typically larger organizations). There is nothing like having a representative from the software company that developed Windows 2000 Server side by side with you solving complex implementation problems. Kinda makes you feel as if you're feeding Microsoft a bowl of its own dog food. Contact Microsoft Consulting Services at 425-882-8080. Telephone support is available starting at $195/hour. I have some dear friends who work for Microsoft Consulting Services. Tell them Harry sent ya!

BackOffice Professional Association (BOPA), Network Professional Association (NPA)

These two trade organizations rate one and two respectively in providing and connecting you with the professional resources necessary to solve your Windows 2000 Server problems. The BOPA may be contacted at `www.bopa.org`. The NPA may be contacted at `www.npa.org`.

Secret

Be sure to save those business cards from peers and sales engineers that you meet at conferences and trade shows. Often the sales engineers from specific vendors provide a certain amount of free support (a.k.a. presales engineering) if you call so that they can earn your approval and goodwill.

Microsoft support incidents

And don't overlook the easiest path to escalated Windows 2000 Server support: incident support. What previously cost $200 per incident is, as of this writing, free! Take advantage of it.

From the Backroom to the Boardroom

Mind if I borrow from the Grateful Dead for a moment? What a long, strange, and interesting trip it's been to be a technology professional in the 1990s. From the rise and fall of NetWare to the emerging dominance of Windows 2000 Server, it's been quite a ride. But some things have remained constant throughout, including the need for top-notch troubleshooting skills. With the release of Windows 2000 Server, it is even more apparent that these skills are needed, watched for, and utilized. That's because the technology professional standing behind each Windows 2000 Server deployed is no longer viewed as a backroom technician. The fact of the matter is that Windows 2000 Server professionals now have the full attention of the executive staff, if only for the reasons this chapter outlines. One point is the staggering cost of downtime. Even nontechnical executives understand that. And as more and more Windows 2000 Servers are deployed in mission-critical, enterprise-wide roles, more boardroom executives are relying on your superior troubleshooting skills to keep these things up and running! Best of luck to you and thanks for reading this book.

Summary

And so this chapter and this book come to an end. This end, appropriately, is the topic of troubleshooting. Assuming you have set up and are using your Windows 2000 Server network, troubleshooting is where most of the work ahead will be. In this chapter, you did the following:

- Used formal troubleshooting steps
- Learned about troubleshooting resources
- Applied the one-hour rule
- Performed downtime value calculations
- Learned about using troubleshooters and Master Console
- Learned about the importance of maintaining a current Emergency Repair Disk (ERD)
- Analyzed STOP errors

Appendix A

Performance Monitor Objects

As discussed in Chapter 18, this appendix provides you with selected Performance Monitor object:counter definitions. I've only provided the core object:counters here, in the interest of time and space, but also according to their importance. To be honest, most of the object:counters I have omitted are not used by Windows 2000 Server administrators and engineers. What I've attempted to do is only list the definitions and explanations for the object:counters you are likely to use in the management of your Windows 2000 Server network. However, exceptions and additions exist. The objects for which counters are defined in this appendix include the following:

- Cache
- Logical Disk
- Memory
- Network Interface
- Network Segment
- Objects
- Physical Disk
- Process
- Processor
- Redirector
- Server Work Queues
- System
- Thread

Third-party ISVs have long taken advantage of Performance Monitor in several ways. First, during the software application development cycle, ISVs use Performance Monitor to monitor the health and performance of the Windows 2000 Server machine and network. This not only enables them to see that their development environment is either running optimally or similar to that of their customers, but it also enables them to see how their software applications are impacting the system. Second, the ISVs typically write object:counters that are unique to their software application, which they run as part of Performance Monitor. Here again, this enables them to monitor and optimize their software application during the development cycle. But perhaps most important, by creating application-specific object:counters, ISVs expose a wealth of monitoring and optimization possibilities for you, the customer. For example, when you purchase and install Microsoft SQL Server, several object:counters specific to this application are added to Performance Monitor. When using and developing with SQL Server, you benefit greatly from these SQL Server-specific object:counters in the management of your database applications and your network.

For descriptions of object:counters not listed here, simply click the explain button for the object:counter of your choice in the Add Counters dialog box.

Table A-1 Performance Monitor Object Types

Object	*Object Counter*	*Description*
Cache	Async Copy Reads/sec	Measures the frequency of reads from cache pages involving a memory copy of the data from the cache to the application's buffer. Application regains control immediately even if the disk must be accessed to retrieve the page.
Cache	Async Data Maps/sec	Measures the frequency at which an application, using a file system such as NTFS to map a page of a file into the cache, reads the page and does not wait for the cache to retrieve the page if not found in main memory.
Cache	Async Fast Reads/sec	Measures the frequency of reads from cache pages that bypass the installed file system and retrieve the data directly from the cache. Typically, the file I/O requests invoke the appropriate file system to retrieve data from a file, but this path permits direct retrieval of cache data without file system involvement if the data is in the cache. Even if the data is not in the cache, one invocation of the file system is avoided. If the data is not in the cache, the request (application program call) does not wait until the data is retrieved from disk, but gets control immediately.

Object	***Object Counter***	***Description***
Cache	Async MDL Reads/sec	Measures the frequency of reads from cache pages using a Memory Descriptor List (MDL) to access the pages. Note that the MDL contains the physical address of each page in the transfer, thus permitting direct memory access (DMA) of the pages. If the accessed page(s) are not found in main memory, the calling application program does *not* wait for the pages to fault in from disk.
Cache	Async Pin Reads/sec	This measures the frequency of reading data into the cache preparatory to writing the data back to disk. Pages read in this fashion are pinned in memory at the completion of the read. File system regains control immediately even if the disk must be accessed to retrieve the page. A page's physical address is not altered while pinned.
Cache	Copy Read Hits %	Displays the percentage of cache Copy Read requests that hit the cache. Stated another way, does not require a disk read in order to provide access to the page in the cache. Copy Read is a file read operation that is satisfied by a memory copy from a cache page to the application's buffer. The LAN redirector and disk file systems use this method for retrieving cache information, as does the LAN server for small transfers.
Cache	Copy Reads/sec	Measures the frequency of reads from cache pages that involve a memory copy of the data from the cache to the application's buffer. The LAN redirector uses this method for retrieving cache information, as does the LAN server for small transfers.
Cache	Data Flush Pages/sec	Measures the frequency of the number of pages that the cache flushes to disk as a result of a request to flush or to satisfy a write-through file write request. More than one page can be transferred on each flush operation.

Continued

Table A-1 *(continued)*

Object	*Object Counter*	*Description*
Cache	Data Flushes/sec	This is the frequency that the cache flushes its contents to disk as the result of a request to flush or to satisfy a write-through file write request. One page or more can be transferred on each flush operation.
Cache	Data Map Hits %	This is the percentage of data maps in the cache that can be resolved without having to retrieve a page from the disk — in other words, the page is already in physical memory.
Cache	Data Map Pins/sec	This is the frequency of data maps in the cache that results in pinning a page in main memory, an action usually preparatory to writing to the file on disk. A page's physical address in main memory and virtual address in the cache are not altered while pinned.
Cache	Data Maps/sec	This is the frequency at which a file system such as NTFS maps a file page into the cache to read the page.
Cache	Fast Read Not Possible/sec	This is the frequency of attempts by an Application Program Interface (API) function call to bypass the file system to get at cache data that cannot be honored without invoking the file system.
Cache	Fast Read Resource Misses/sec	This is the frequency of cache misses necessitated by the lack of available resources to satisfy the request.
Cache	Fast Reads/sec	This is the frequency of reads from cache pages that bypass the installed file system and retrieve the data directly from the cache. Typically, file I/O requests invoke the appropriate file system to retrieve data from a file, but this path permits direct retrieval of cache data without file system involvement if the data is in the cache.

Object	***Object Counter***	***Description***
Cache	Lazy Write Flushes/sec	Lazy writing is the process of updating the disk after the page is changed in memory, so that the application making the change to the file does not have to wait for the disk write to complete before proceeding. It is possible for more than one page to be transferred on each write operation.
Cache	Lazy Write Pages/sec	This is the frequency with which the cache's lazy write thread is written to disk. Lazy writing is the process of updating the disk after the page is changed in memory, so that the application making the change to the file does not have to wait for the disk write to complete before proceeding. It is possible for more than one page to be transferred on a single disk write operation.
Cache	MDL Read Hits %	This is the percentage of cache memory descriptor list (MDL) read requests that have hit the cache — that is, that do not require disk accesses in order to provide memory access to the page(s) in the cache.
Cache	MDL Reads/sec	This is the frequency of reads from cache pages that use a memory descriptor list (MDL) to access the data. The MDL contains the physical address of each page involved in the transfer and thus can employ a hardware direct memory access (DMA) device to effect the copy. Note that a LAN server uses this method for large transfers out of the server.
Cache	Pin Read Hits %	This is the percentage of cache Pin Read requests that have hit the cache, that is, that do not require a disk read in order to provide access to the page in the cache. A page's physical address in the cache is not altered while pinned. Note that a LAN redirector uses this method for retrieving cache information, as does the LAN server for small transfers and disk file systems.

Continued

Table A-1 *(continued)*

Object	*Object Counter*	*Description*
Cache	Pin Reads/sec	This is the frequency of reading data into the cache preparatory to writing the data back to disk. Pages read in this fashion are pinned in memory at the completion of the read. A page's physical address in the cache is not altered while it is pinned.
Cache	Sync Copy Reads/sec	This is the frequency of reads from cache pages that involve a memory copy of the data from the cache to the application's buffer. A file system does not regain control until the copy operation is complete, even if the disk must be accessed to retrieve the page.
Cache	Sync Data Maps/sec	This is the frequency that a file system such as NTFS maps a page of a file into the cache to read the page and requests to wait for the cache to retrieve the page if it is not in main memory.
Cache	Sync Fast Reads/sec	This is the frequency of reads from cache pages that bypass the installed file system and retrieve the data directly from the cache. Typically, file I/O requests invoke the appropriate file system to retrieve data from a file, but this path permits direct retrieval of cache data without file system involvement if the data is in the cache. Whether or not data is in the cache, one invocation of the file system is avoided. If the data is not in the cache, the request (application program call) waits until the data is retrieved from disk.
Cache	Sync MDL Reads/sec	This is the frequency of reads from cache pages that use a memory descriptor list (MDL) to access the pages. The MDL contains the physical address of each page in the transfer, thus permitting direct memory access (DMA) of the pages. If accessed page(s) are not in main memory, then the caller waits for the pages to fault in from the disk.

Object	***Object Counter***	***Description***
Cache	Sync Pin Reads/sec	This is the frequency of reading data into the cache preparatory to writing the data back to disk. Pages read in this fashion are pinned in memory at read completion. The file system does not regain control until the page is pinned in the cache, in particular, if the disk must be accessed to retrieve the page. While pinned, a page's physical address in the cache is not altered.
LogicalDisk	% Disk Read Time	This is the percentage of elapsed time the selected disk drive is busy servicing read requests.
LogicalDisk	% Disk Time	This is the percentage of elapsed time the selected disk drive is busy servicing read or write requests.
LogicalDisk	% Disk Write Time	This is the percentage of elapsed time the selected disk drive is busy servicing write requests.
LogicalDisk	% Free Space	This is the ratio of the free space available on the logical disk unit to the total usable space provided by the selected logical disk drive.
LogicalDisk	Avg. Disk Bytes/Read	This is the average number of bytes transferred from the disk during read operations.
LogicalDisk	Avg. Disk Bytes/Transfer	This is the average number of bytes transferred to or from the disk during write or read operations.
LogicalDisk	Avg. Disk Bytes/Write	This is the average number of bytes transferred to the disk during write operations.
LogicalDisk	Avg. Disk sec/Read	This is the average time in seconds of a data read from the disk.
LogicalDisk	Avg. Disk sec/Transfer	This is the average time in seconds of the disk transfer.
LogicalDisk	Avg. Disk sec/Write	This is the average time in seconds of a write of data to the disk.
LogicalDisk	Disk Bytes/sec	This is the rate at which bytes are transferred to or from the disk during write or read operations.

Continued

Table A-1 *(continued)*

Object	***Object Counter***	***Description***
LogicalDisk	Current Disk Queue Length	This is the number of outstanding requests on the disk at the time the performance data is collected, including requests in service at the time of the snapshot. It is one instantaneous length or discrete value, not an average over the time interval. Multispindle disk devices can have multiple requests active at one time, but other concurrent requests await service. This counter reflects a transitory high or low queue length, but if there is a sustained load on the disk drive, it is likely that this will be high consistently. Requests experience delays proportionate to the length of this queue minus the number of spindles on the disks. Look for a difference averaging less than 2 for good performance.
LogicalDisk	Disk Read Bytes/sec	This is the rate at which bytes are transferred from the disk during read operations.
LogicalDisk	Disk Reads/sec	This is the rate of read operations performed against the disk.
LogicalDisk	Disk Transfers/sec	This is the rate of read and write operations on the disk.
LogicalDisk	Disk Write Bytes/sec	This is the rate at which bytes are transferred to the disk during write operations.
LogicalDisk	Disk Writes/sec	This is the rate of write operations on the disk.
LogicalDisk	Free Megabytes	This displays the unallocated space on the disk drive in megabytes.
Memory	Available Bytes	This displays the size of the virtual memory currently on the Zeroed, Free, and Standby lists. Zeroed and Free memory is ready for use, with Zeroed memory cleared to zeros. Standby memory is memory removed from a process' working set, but is still available. Notice that this is an instantaneous count, not an average over the time interval.

Object	*Object Counter*	*Description*
Memory	Cache Bytes	This measures the number of bytes currently in use by the system cache. The system cache is used to buffer data retrieved from disk or LAN. The system cache uses memory not in use by active processes in the computer.
Memory	Cache Bytes Peak	This measures the maximum number of bytes used by the system cache. The system cache is used to buffer data retrieved from disk or LAN. It uses memory not in use by active processes in the computer.
Memory	Cache Faults/sec	This measures the rate at which the cache manager does not find a file's page in the immediate cache and must ask the memory manager to locate the page elsewhere in memory or on the disk so that it can be loaded into the immediate cache.
Memory	Commit Limit	This is the size (in bytes) of virtual memory that can be committed without having to extend the paging file(s). If the paging file(s) can be extended, this is a soft limit.
Memory	Committed Bytes	This displays the size of virtual memory (in bytes) that is committed (as opposed to simply reserved). Committed memory must have backing (disk) storage available or must be assured never to need disk storage, because main memory is large enough to hold it. This is an instantaneous count, not an average over the time interval.
Memory	Demand Zero Faults/sec	This is the rate of page faults for pages that must be filled with zeros before the fault is satisfied. If the Zeroed list is not empty, you can resolve the fault by removing a page from the Zeroed list.
Memory	Free System Page Table Entries	This is the number of Page Table Entries not currently in use by the system.

Continued

Table A-1 *(continued)*

Object	*Object Counter*	*Description*
Memory	Page Faults/sec	This is the rate of page faults in the processor. A page fault occurs when a process refers to a virtual memory page that is not in its Working Set in main memory. A page fault does not cause the page to be fetched from disk if that page is on the Standby list, and hence already in main memory, or if it is in use by another process with which the page is shared.
Memory	Page Reads/sec	This is the rate of the number of times the disk is read to retrieve pages of virtual memory necessary to resolve page faults. Multiple pages can be read during a disk read operation.
Memory	Page Writes/sec	This is the rate of the number of times that pages are written to the disk because they were changed since last retrieved. Each such write operation may transfer a number of pages.
Memory	Pages Input/sec	This is the rate of the number of pages read from the disk to resolve memory references to pages that were not in memory at the time of the reference. This counter includes paging traffic on behalf of the system cache to access file data for applications. This is an important counter to observe if you are concerned about excessive memory pressure (that is, thrashing) and the excessive paging that may result.
Memory	Pages Output/sec	This is the rate of the number of pages that are written to disk because the pages have been modified in main memory.

Object	*Object Counter*	*Description*
Memory	Pages/sec	This is the rate of the number of pages read from the disk or written to the disk to resolve memory references to pages that were not in memory at the time of the reference. This is the sum of Pages Input/sec and Pages Output/sec. This counter includes paging traffic on behalf of the system cache to access file data for applications. This is the primary counter to observe if you are concerned about excessive memory pressure (that is, thrashing) and the excessive paging that may result.
Memory	Pool Nonpaged Allocs	This is the number of calls to allocate space in the system Nonpaged Pool. Nonpaged Pool is a system memory area where space is acquired by operating system components as they accomplish their appointed tasks. Nonpaged Pool pages cannot be paged out to the paging file; instead, they remain in main memory as long as they are allocated.
Memory	Pool Nonpaged Bytes	This is the number of bytes in the Nonpaged Pool, which is a system memory area where space is acquired by operating system components as they accomplish their appointed tasks. Nonpaged Pool pages cannot be paged out to the paging file; instead, they remain in main memory as long as they are allocated.
Memory	Pool Paged Allocs	This is the number of calls to allocate space in the system Paged Pool. Paged Pool is a system memory area where space is acquired by operating system components as they accomplish their appointed tasks. Paged Pool pages can be paged out to the paging file when not accessed by the system for sustained periods of time.

Continued

Table A-1 *(continued)*

Object	***Object Counter***	***Description***
Memory	Pool Paged Bytes	This is the number of bytes in the Paged Pool, which is a system memory area where space is acquired by operating system components as they accomplish their appointed tasks. Paged Pool pages can be paged out to the paging file when not accessed by the system for sustained periods of time.
Memory	Pool Paged Resident Bytes	This is the size of Paged Pool resident in core memory. This is the actual cost of the Paged Pool allocation, because this is actively in use and using real physical memory.
Memory	System Cache Resident Bytes	This is the number of bytes currently resident in the global disk cache.
Memory	System Code Resident Bytes	This is the number of bytes of System Code Total Bytes currently resident in core memory. This is the code working set of the pageable executive. In addition, there are another ~300K bytes of nonpaged kernel code.
Memory	System Code Total Bytes	This is the number of bytes of pageable pages in `NTOSKRNL.EXE`, `HAL.DLL`, and the boot drivers and file systems loaded by `NTLDR/OSLOADER`.
Memory	System Driver Resident Bytes	This is the number of System Driver Total Bytes currently resident in core memory. This number is the code working set of the pageable drivers. In addition to this, there are another ~700K bytes of nonpaged driver code.
Memory	System Driver Total Bytes	This is the number of bytes of pageable pages in all other loaded device drivers.
Memory	Transition Faults/sec	This is the number of page faults resolved by recovering pages that were in transition — that is, written to disk at the time of the page fault. The pages are recovered without additional disk activity.

Object	***Object Counter***	***Description***
Memory	Write Copies/sec	This is the number of page faults that are satisfied by making a copy of a page when an attempt to write to the page is made. This is an economical way of sharing data because the copy of the page is made only on an attempt to write to the page; otherwise, the page is shared.
Network Interface	Bytes Received/sec	This is the rate at which bytes are received on the interface, including framing characters.
Network Interface	Bytes Sent/sec	This is the rate at which bytes are sent on the interface, including framing characters.
Network Interface	Bytes Total/sec	This is the rate at which bytes are sent and received on the interface, including framing characters.
Network Interface	Current Bandwidth	This is an estimate of the interface's current bandwidth in bits per second (bps). For interfaces that do not vary in bandwidth or for those where no accurate estimate can be made, this value is the nominal bandwidth.
Network Interface	Output Queue Length	This is the length of the output packet queue (in packets.) If this is longer than 2, delays are experienced, and the bottleneck should be found and eliminated if possible.
Network Interface	Packets Outbound Discarded	This is the number of outbound packets that are discarded — even though no errors are detected — to prevent their transmission. One possible reason for discarding such a packet is to free up buffer space.
Network Interface	Packets Outbound	This is the number of outbound packets that cannot be transmitted because of errors.
Network Interface	Packets Received Discarded	This is the number of inbound packets that are discarded — even though no errors are detected — to prevent delivering them to a higher-layer protocol. One possible reason for discarding such a packet is to free up buffer space.

Continued

Table A-1 *(continued)*

Object	*Object Counter*	*Description*
Network Interface	Packets Received Errors	This is the number of inbound packets that contain errors, preventing them from being delivered to a higher-layer protocol.
Network Interface	Packets Received Non-Unicast/sec	This is the rate at which non-unicast (that is, subnet broadcast or subnet multicast) packets are delivered to a higher-layer protocol.
Network Interface	Packets Received Unicast/sec	This is the rate at which unicast (subnet) packets are delivered to a higher-layer protocol.
Network Interface	Packets Received Unknown	This is the number of packets received, via the interface, that were discarded because of an unknown or unsupported protocol.
Network Interface	Packets Received/sec	This is the rate at which packets are received on the network interface.
Network Interface	Packets Sent Non-Unicast/sec	This is the rate at which higher-level protocols request packets to be transmitted to non-unicast (that is, subnet broadcast or subnet multicast) addresses. The rate includes the packets that are discarded or not sent.
Network Interface	Packets Sent Unicast/sec	This is the rate at which higher-level protocols request packets to be transmitted to subnet-unicast addresses. The rate includes the packets that are discarded or not sent.
Network Interface	Packets Sent/sec	This is the rate at which packets are sent on the network interface.
Network Interface	Packets/sec	This is the rate at which packets are sent and received on the network interface.
Network Segment	% Broadcast Frames	This is the percentage of network bandwidth that is made up of broadcast traffic on this network segment.
Network Segment	% Multicast Frames	This is the percentage of network bandwidth that is made up of multicast traffic on this network segment.

Object	*Object Counter*	*Description*
Network Segment	% Network Utilization	This is the percentage of network bandwidth in use on this network segment.
Network Segment	Broadcast Frames Received/sec	This is the number of broadcast frames received per second on this network segment.
Network Segment	Multicast Frames Received/sec	This is the number of multicast frames received per second on this network segment.
Network Segment	Total Bytes Received/sec	This is the number of bytes received per second on this network segment.
Network Segment	Total Frames Received/sec	This is the total number of frames received per second on this network segment.
Objects	Events	This is the number of events in the computer at the time of data collection. This is an instantaneous count, not an average over the time interval. An event is used when two or more threads have to synchronize execution.
Objects	Mutexes	This counts the number of mutexes in the computer at the time of data collection. This is an instantaneous count, not an average over the time interval. Threads use mutexes to ensure that only one thread is executing some section of code.
Objects	Processes	This is the number of processes in the computer at the time of data collection. It is an instantaneous count, not an average over the time interval. Each process represents the running of a program.
Objects	Sections	This is the number of sections in the computer at the time of data collection. This is an instantaneous count, not an average over the time interval. A section is a portion of virtual memory created by a process for storing data. A process may share sections with other processes.

Continued

Table A-1 *(continued)*

Object	***Object Counter***	***Description***
Objects	Semaphores	This is the number of semaphores in the computer at the time of data collection. This is an instantaneous count, not an average over the time interval. Threads use semaphores to obtain exclusive access to data structures they share with other threads.
Objects	Threads	This is the number of threads in the computer at the time of data collection. This is an instantaneous count, not an average over the time interval. A thread is the basic executable entity that can execute instructions in a processor.
PhysicalDisk	% Disk Read Time	This is the percentage of elapsed time that the selected disk drive is servicing read requests.
PhysicalDisk	% Disk Time	This is the percentage of elapsed time that the selected disk drive is servicing read or write requests.
PhysicalDisk	% Disk Write Time	This is the percentage of elapsed time that the selected disk drive is servicing write requests.
PhysicalDisk	Avg. Disk Bytes/Read	This is the average number of bytes transferred from the disk during read operations.
PhysicalDisk	Avg. Disk Bytes/Transfer	This is the average number of bytes transferred to or from the disk during write or read operations.
PhysicalDisk	Avg. Disk Bytes/Write	This is the average number of bytes transferred to the disk during write operations.
PhysicalDisk	Avg. Disk sec/Read	This is the average time in seconds of a read of data from the disk.
PhysicalDisk	Avg. Disk sec/Transfer	This is the time, measured in seconds, of the average disk transfer.

Object	***Object Counter***	***Description***
PhysicalDisk	Avg. Disk sec/Write	This is the average time in seconds of a write of data to the disk.
PhysicalDisk	Disk Bytes/sec	This is the rate bytes are transferred to or from the disk during write or read operations.
PhysicalDisk	Current Disk Queue Length	This is the number of requests outstanding on the disk at the time the performance data is collected. It includes requests in service at the time of the snapshot. It is an instantaneous length, not an average over the time interval. Multispindle disk devices can have multiple requests active at one time, but other concurrent requests await service. Note that this counter may reflect a transitory high or low queue length, but if there is a sustained load on the disk drive, it is likely that this will be high consistently. Requests experience delays proportionate to the length of this queue minus the number of spindles on the disks. For good performance, this difference should average less than 2.
PhysicalDisk	Disk Read Bytes/sec	This is the rate at which bytes are transferred from the disk during read operations.
PhysicalDisk	Disk Reads/sec	This is the rate of read operations on the disk.
PhysicalDisk	Disk Transfers/sec	This is the rate of read and write operations on the disk.
PhysicalDisk	Disk Write Bytes/sec	This is the rate at which bytes are transferred to the disk during write operations.
PhysicalDisk	Disk Writes/sec	This is the rate of write operations on the disk.

Continued

Table A-1 *(continued)*

Object	*Object Counter*	*Description*
Process	% Privileged Time	This is the percentage of elapsed time that this process' threads spend executing code in Privileged mode. If a Windows NT system service is called, the service often runs in Privileged mode to gain access to system-private data. Such data is protected from access by threads executing in User mode. Calls to the system may be explicit or they may be implicit, such as when a page fault or an interrupt occurs. Note that Windows NT, unlike earlier operating systems, uses process boundaries for subsystem protection in addition to the traditional protection of User and Privileged modes. Therefore, some work done by Windows NT on behalf of your application may appear in other subsystem processes in addition to the Privileged Time in your process.
Process	% Processor Time	This is the percentage of elapsed time that all of the threads of this process used the microprocessor to execute instructions. An instruction is the basic unit of execution in a computer, a thread is the object that executes instructions, and a process is the object created when a program is run. Code executed to handle certain hardware interrupts or trap conditions may be counted for this process.

Object	***Object Counter***	***Description***
Process	% User Time	This is the percentage of elapsed time that this process' threads spend executing code in User mode. Applications execute in User mode, as do subsystems such as the window manager and the graphics engine. Code executing in User mode cannot damage the integrity of the Windows NT Executive, Kernel, and device drivers. Windows NT uses process boundaries for subsystem protection in addition to the traditional protection of User and Privileged modes (unlike some early operating systems). Therefore, some work done by Windows NT on behalf of your application may appear in other subsystem processes in addition to the Privileged Time in your process.
Process	Elapsed Time	This is the total elapsed time (in seconds) that this process is running.
Process	Handle Count	This is the total number of handles currently open by this process. This number is the sum of the handles currently open by each thread in this process.
Process	ID Process	Simply stated, this is the unique identifier of this process. ID Process numbers are reused, so they only identify a process for the lifetime of that process.
Process	Page Faults/sec	This is the rate of page faults by the threads executing in this process. A page fault occurs when a thread refers to a virtual memory page that is not in its working set in main memory. This doesn't cause the page to be fetched from disk if it is on the standby list and already in main memory, or if it is in use by another process with which the page is shared.

Continued

Table A-1 *(continued)*

Object	*Object Counter*	*Description*
Process	Page File Bytes	This is the current number of bytes that this process uses in the paging file(s). Note that paging files are used to store pages of memory used by the process that are not contained in other files. All processes share paging files, and lack of space in paging files can prevent other processes from allocating memory.
Process	Page File Bytes Peak	This is the maximum number of bytes that this process uses in the paging file(s). Paging files are used to store pages of memory used by the process that are not contained in other files. All processes share paging files, and lack of space in paging files can prevent other processes from allocating memory.
Process	Pool Nonpaged Bytes	This is the number of bytes in the Nonpaged Pool, which is a system memory area where space is acquired by operating system components as they accomplish their appointed tasks. Nonpaged Pool pages cannot be paged out to the paging file; instead, they remain in main memory as long as they are allocated.
Process	Pool Paged Bytes	This is the number of bytes in the Paged Pool, which is a system memory area where space is acquired by operating system components as they accomplish their appointed tasks. Paged Pool pages can be paged out to the paging file when not accessed by the system for sustained periods of time.
Process	Priority Base	This is the current base priority of this process. Threads within a process can raise and lower their own base priority relative to the process' base priority.

Object	***Object Counter***	***Description***
Process	Private Bytes	This is the current number of bytes that this process allocates that cannot be shared with other processes.
Process	Thread Count	This is the number of threads currently active in this process. An instruction is the basic unit of execution in a processor, and a thread is the object that executes instructions. Every running process has at least one thread.
Process	Virtual Bytes	This is the current size in bytes of the virtual address space that the process is using. Use of virtual address space does not imply corresponding use of either disk or main memory pages. Virtual space is finite, and by using too much, the process may limit its ability to load libraries.
Process	Virtual Bytes Peak	This is the maximum number of bytes of virtual address space that the process uses at any one time. Use of virtual address space does not imply corresponding use of either disk or main memory pages. Virtual space is finite, and by using too much, the process may limit its ability to load libraries.
Process	Working Set	This is the current number of bytes in the Working Set of this process. The Working Set is the set of memory pages touched recently by the threads in the process. If free memory in the computer is above a threshold, pages are left in the Working Set of a process even if they are not in use. When free memory falls below a threshold, pages are trimmed from Working Sets. If they are needed, they are soft-faulted back into the Working Set before they leave main memory.

Continued

Table A-1 *(continued)*

Object	*Object Counter*	*Description*
Process	Working Set Peak	This is the maximum number of bytes in the Working Set of this process at any point in time. The Working Set is the set of memory pages touched recently by the threads in the process. If free memory in the computer is above a threshold, pages are left in the Working Set of a process even if they are not in use. When free memory falls below a threshold, pages are trimmed from Working Sets. If they are needed they are soft-faulted back into the Working Set before they leave main memory.
Processor	% DPC Time	This is the percentage of elapsed time that the processor spends in Deferred Procedure Calls. When a hardware device interrupts the processor, the Interrupt Handler may elect to execute the majority of its work in a DPC. DPCs run at lower priority than interrupts and so permit interrupts to occur while DPC is executed. Deferred Procedure Calls are executed in Privileged mode, so this is a component of Processor: % Privileged Time. This counter can help determine the source of excessive time being spent in Privileged mode.
Processor	% Interrupt Time	This is the percentage of elapsed time that the processor spends handling hardware interrupts. When a hardware device interrupts the processor, the Interrupt Handler executes to handle the condition, usually by signaling I/O completion and possibly issuing another pending I/O request. Some of this work may be done in a Deferred Procedure Call (see % DPC Time). However, time spent in DPCs is not counted as time in interrupts. Interrupts are executed in Privileged mode, so this is a component of Processor: % Privileged Time. This counter can help determine the source of excessive time being spent in Privileged mode.

Object	***Object Counter***	***Description***
Processor	% Privileged Time	This is the percentage of processor time spent in Privileged mode in non-Idle threads. The Windows NT service layer, the Executive routines, and the Windows NT Kernel execute in Privileged mode. Device drivers for most devices, other than graphics adapters and printers, also execute in Privileged mode. Windows NT uses process boundaries for subsystem protection, in addition to the traditional protection of User and Privileged modes (unlike some early operating systems). Thus, some work accomplished by Windows NT on your application's behalf may appear in other subsystem processes in addition to the Privileged Time in your process.
Processor	% Processor Time	This is the percentage of the elapsed time that a processor is busy executing a non-Idle thread. You can view this as the fraction of the time spent doing useful work. Each processor is assigned an Idle thread in the Idle process that consumes those unproductive processor cycles not used by any other threads.
Processor	% User Time	This is the percentage of processor time spent in User mode in non-Idle threads. All application code and subsystem code executes in User mode. The graphics engine, graphics device drivers, printer device drivers, and window manager also execute in User mode. Code executing in User mode cannot damage the integrity of the Windows NT Executive, Kernel, and device drivers. Unlike some early operating systems, Windows NT uses process boundaries for subsystem protection in addition to the traditional protection of User and Privileged modes. Therefore, some work done by Windows NT on behalf of your application may appear in other subsystem processes in addition to the Privileged Time in your process.

Continued

Table A-1 *(continued)*

Object	***Object Counter***	***Description***
Processor	APC Bypasses/sec	This is the rate at which kernel APC interrupts are short-circuited.
Processor	DPC Bypasses/sec	This is the rate at which Dispatch interrupts are short-circuited.
Processor	DPC Rate	This is the average rate at which DPC objects are queued to this processor's DPC queue per clock tick.
Processor	DPCs Queued/sec	This is the rate at which DPC objects are queued to this processor's DPC queue.
Processor	Interrupts/sec	This is the number of device interrupts that the processor experiences. A device interrupts the processor when it completes a task or when it otherwise requires attention. Normal thread execution is suspended during interrupts. An interrupt may cause the processor to switch to another, higher-priority thread. Clock interrupts are frequent and periodic and create a background of interrupt activity.
Redirector	Bytes Received/sec	This is the rate of bytes coming in to the redirector from the network. It includes all application data, as well as network protocol information, such as packet headers.
Redirector	Bytes Total/sec	This is the rate at which the redirector processes data bytes. This includes all application and file data, in addition to protocol information, such as packet headers.
Redirector	Bytes Transmitted/sec	This is the rate at which bytes leave the redirector to the network. It includes all application data, as well as network protocol information, such as packet headers.
Redirector	Connects Core	This is the number of connections to servers running the original MS-Net SMB protocol, including MS-Net itself, Xenix, and Vax.

Object	***Object Counter***	***Description***
Redirector	Connects Lan Manager 2.0	This is the number of connections to Lan Manager 2.0 servers, including LMX servers.
Redirector	Connects Lan Manager 2.1	This is the number of connections to Lan Manager 2.1 servers, including LMX servers.
Redirector	Connects Windows NT	This is the number of connections to Windows NT computers.
Redirector	Current Commands	This is the number of requests to the redirector that currently are queued for service. If this number is much larger than the number of installed network adapter cards, the network(s) and/or server(s) being accessed will be bottlenecked seriously.
Redirector	File Data Operations/sec	This is the rate at which the redirector processes data operations. One operation includes (hopefully) many bytes. I say "hopefully" here because each operation has overhead. This enables you to determine the efficiency of this path by dividing the Bytes/sec by this counter to determine the average number of bytes transferred per operation.
Redirector	File Read Operations/sec	This is the rate at which applications ask the redirector for data. Each call to a file system or similar Application Program Interface (API) call counts as one operation.
Redirector	File Write Operations/sec	This is the rate at which applications send data to the redirector. Each call to a file system or similar Application Program Interface (API) call counts as one operation.
Redirector	Network Errors/sec	This is the number of serious unexpected errors, which generally indicate that the redirector and one or more servers are having serious communication difficulties. For example, an SMB (server manager block) protocol error generates a Network Error. These errors result in an entry in the system Event Log, so look there for details.

Continued

Table A-1 *(continued)*

Object	*Object Counter*	*Description*
Redirector	Packets Receive/sec	This is the rate at which the redirector receives packets (also called SMBs or server message blocks). Network transmissions are divided into packets. The average number of bytes received in a packet can be obtained by dividing Bytes Received/sec by this counter. Some packets received may not contain incoming data; for example, an acknowledgment to a write made by the redirector counts as an incoming packet.
Redirector	Packets Transmitted/sec	This is the rate at which the redirector sends packets (also called SMBs or server message blocks). Network transmissions are divided into packets. It is the average number of bytes transmitted in a packet. This value can also be obtained by dividing Bytes Transmitted/sec by this counter.
Redirector	Packets/sec	This is the rate at which the redirector processes data packets. One packet typically includes many bytes. You may determine the efficiency of this path by dividing the Bytes/sec by this counter to determine the average number of bytes transferred per packet. You may divide this counter by Operations/sec to determine the average number of packets per operation.
Redirector	Read Bytes Cache/sec	This is the rate at which applications on your computer access the cache using the redirector. Many data requests may be satisfied merely by retrieving the data from the system cache on your own computer if it happens to have been used recently and there is room to keep it in the cache. Requests that miss the cache cause a page fault (see Read Bytes Paging/sec).

Object	***Object Counter***	***Description***
Redirector	Read Bytes Network/sec	It is the rate at which applications read data across the network. For some reason, the data is not in the system cache, and these bytes actually come across the network. Dividing this number by Bytes Received/sec indicates the efficiency of data coming in from the network, because all of these bytes are real application data (see Bytes Received/sec).
Redirector	Read Bytes Non-Paging/sec	These are the bytes read by the redirector in response to normal file requests by an application when these bytes are redirected to come from another computer. In addition to file requests, this counter includes other methods of reading across the network, such as Named Pipes and Transactions. This counter doesn't count network protocol information; it counts application data.
Redirector	Read Bytes Paging/sec	This is the rate at which the redirector attempts to read bytes in response to page faults. Page faults are caused by loading of modules (such as programs and libraries), by a miss in the cache (see Read Bytes Cache/sec), or by files directly mapped into the address space of applications (a high-performance feature of Windows NT).
Redirector	Read Operations Random/sec	This is the rate at which, on a file-by-file basis, non-sequential reads are made. If a read is made using a particular file handle and then is followed by another read that is not contiguous, this counter increases by one increment.
Redirector	Read Packets Small/sec	This is the rate at which reads less than one-fourth of the server's negotiated buffer size are made by applications. Too many of these can indicate a waste of buffers on the server. This counter is increased by one increment for each read, but packets are not counted.

Continued

Table A-1 *(continued)*

Object	***Object Counter***	***Description***
Redirector	Read Packets/sec	This is the rate at which read packets are placed on the network. Each time a single packet is sent with a request to read data remotely, this counter is increased by one increment.
Redirector	Reads Denied/sec	This is the rate at which the server is unable to accommodate requests for Raw Reads. When a read is much larger than the server's negotiated buffer size, the redirector requests a Raw Read which, if granted, permits the transfer of the data without a lot of protocol overhead on each packet. Consequently, the server must lock out other requests, so the request is denied if the server is really busy.
Redirector	Reads Large/sec	This is the rate at which reads over twice the server's negotiated buffer size are made by applications. Too many of these can place a strain on server resources. This counter increases by one increment for each read. It does not count packets.
Redirector	Server Disconnects	This is the number of times that a server disconnects your redirector (see Server Reconnects).
Redirector	Server Reconnects	This is the number of times that your redirector reconnects to a server in order to complete a new active request. The server may disconnect you if you remain inactive for too long. Locally, even if all your remote files are closed, the redirector keeps your connections intact for (nominally) 10 minutes. Inactive connections are called Dormant Connections. Reconnecting is expensive in terms of time.
Redirector	Server Sessions	This is the number of active security objects that the redirector manages. For example, a logon to a server followed by a network access to the same server establishes one connection, but two sessions.

Object	***Object Counter***	***Description***
Redirector	Server Sessions Hung	This is the number of active sessions that are timed out and unable to proceed due to a lack of response from the remote server.
Redirector	Write Bytes Cache/sec	This is the rate at which applications on your computer write to the cache using the redirector. Your computer may retain the data in the cache for further modification before writing it to the network. This saves network traffic. Each write of a byte into the cache is counted here.
Redirector	Write Bytes Network/sec	This is the rate at which your applications write data across the network. Either the system cache was bypassed, as for Named Pipes or Transactions, or the cache wrote the bytes to make room for other data. Dividing this counter by Bytes Transmitted/ sec indicates the efficiency of data written to the network, because all of these bytes are real application data (see Bytes Transmitted/sec).
Redirector	Write Bytes Non-Paging/sec	This is the rate of the bytes that are written by the redirector in response to normal file outputs by an application when they are redirected to go to another computer. In addition to file requests, this counter includes other methods of writing across the network, such as Named Pipes and Transactions. This counter counts application data, not network protocol information.
Redirector	Write Bytes Paging/sec	This is the rate at which the redirector attempts to write bytes changed in the pages used by applications. The program data changed by modules (such as programs and libraries) that were loaded over the network are "paged out" when no longer needed. Other output pages come from the cache (see Write Bytes Cache/sec).

Continued

Table A-1 *(continued)*

Object	***Object Counter***	***Description***
Redirector	Write Operations Random/sec	This is the rate at which, on a file-by-file basis, non-sequential writes are made. If a write is made using a particular file handle and then is followed by another write that is not contiguous, this counter is increased by one increment.
Redirector	Write Packets Small/sec	This is the rate at which writes are made by applications that are less than one-fourth of the server's negotiated buffer size. Many of these writes can indicate a waste of buffers on the server. This counter is increased by one for each write, not packet.
Redirector	Write Packets/sec	This is the rate at which writes are sent to the network. Every time that a single packet is sent with a request to write remote data, this counter is increased by one increment.
Redirector	Writes Denied/sec	This is the rate at which the server is unable to accommodate requests for Raw Writes. When a write is much larger than the server's negotiated buffer size, the redirector requests a Raw Write which, if granted, permits the transfer of the data without a lot of protocol overhead on each packet. The server must lock out other requests, so the request is denied if the server is really busy.
Redirector	Writes Large/sec	This is the rate at which writes are made by applications that are over twice the server's negotiated buffer size. Many of these writes can place a strain on server resources. This counter is increased by one increment for each write, not packets.
Server Work Queues	Active Threads	This is the number of threads presently working on a request for a CPU. The operating system keeps this number as low as possible to minimize unnecessary context switching. This is an instantaneous count for the CPU, not an average over time.

Object	Object Counter	Description
Server Work Queues	Available Threads	This is the number of server threads the CPU is not working on currently. The server dynamically adjusts the number of threads to maximize server performance.
Server Work Queues	Available Work Items	Every request from a client is represented in the server as a work item, and the server maintains a pool of available work items per CPU to speed processing. This is the instantaneous number of available work items for this CPU. A sustained near-zero value indicates the need to increase the MinFreeWorkItems Registry value for the server service. This value always is 0 in the Blocking Queue instance.
Server Work Queues	Borrowed Work Items	Every request from a client is represented in the server as a work item, and the server maintains a pool of available work items per CPU to speed processing. When a CPU runs out of work items, it borrows a free work item from another CPU. An increasing value of this running counter may indicate the need to increase the MaxWorkItems or MinFreeWorkItems Registry values for the server service. This value always is 0 in the Blocking Queue instance.
Server Work Queues	Bytes Received/sec	This is the rate at which the server receives bytes from the network clients on this CPU. This value is a measure of how busy the server is.
Server Work Queues	Bytes Sent/sec	This is the rate at which the server sends bytes on the network to clients, measured by CPU. This value is a measure of how busy the server is.
Server Work Queues	Bytes Transferred/sec	This is the rate at which the server sends and receives bytes with the network clients on this CPU. This value is a measure of how busy the server is.
Server Work Queues	Context Blocks Queued/sec	This is the rate at which work context blocks are placed on the server's FSP queue to await server action.

Continued

Table A-1 *(continued)*

Object	*Object Counter*	*Description*
Server Work Queues	Current Clients	This is the instantaneous count of the clients serviced by this CPU. The server actively balances the client load across all of the CPUs in the system. This value always is 0 in the Blocking Queue instance.
Server Work Queues	Queue Length	This is the current length of the server work queue for this CPU. A sustained queue length greater than four may indicate processor congestion. This is an instantaneous count, not an average over time.
Server Work Queues	Read Bytes/sec	This is the rate at which the server reads data from files for the clients on this CPU. This value is a measure of how busy the server is.
Server Work Queues	Read Operations/sec	This is the rate at which the server performs file read operations and is a measure of how busy the server is. This value always is 0 in the Blocking Queue instance.
Server Work Queues	Total Bytes/sec	This is the rate at which the server reads and writes data to and from the files for the clients on this CPU. This value is a measure of how busy the server is.
Server Work Queues	Total Operations/sec	This is the rate at which the server performs file read and file write operations for the clients on this CPU. This value is a measure of how busy the server is. This value always is 0 in the Blocking Queue instance.
Server Work Queues	Work Item Shortages	Every request from a client is represented in the server as a work item, and the server maintains a pool of available work items per CPU to speed processing. A sustained value greater than zero indicates the need to increase the MaxWorkItems Registry value for the Server service. This value always is 0 in the Blocking Queue instance.

Object	***Object Counter***	***Description***
Server Work Queues	Write Bytes/sec	This is the rate at which the server writes data to files for the clients on this CPU. This value is a measure of how busy the server is.
Server Work Queues	Write Operations/sec	This is the rate at which the server performs file write operations for the clients on this CPU. This value is a measure of how busy the server is. This value always is 0 in the Blocking Queue instance.
System	% Total DPC Time	This is the sum of % DPC Time of all processors divided by the number of processors in the system (see Processor: % DPC Time).
System	% Total Interrupt Time	This is the sum of % Interrupt Time of all processors divided by the number of processors in the system (see Processor: % Interrupt Time).
System	% Total Privileged Time	This is the average percentage of time spent in Privileged mode by all processors. On a multiprocessor system, if all processors are always in Privileged mode, this is 100%; if one-fourth of the processors are in Privileged mode, this is 25%. When a Windows NT system service is called, the service often runs in Privileged mode in order to gain access to system-private data. Such data is protected from access by threads executing in User mode. Calls to the system may be explicit, or they may be implicit — such as when a page fault or an interrupt occurs. Windows NT uses process boundaries for subsystem protection in addition to the traditional protection of User and Privileged modes (unlike some early operating systems). Thus, some work done by Windows NT on behalf of an application may appear in other subsystem processes in addition to the Privileged Time in the application process.

Continued

Table A-1 *(continued)*

Object	*Object Counter*	*Description*
System	% Total Processor	This is the average percentage of time that all of the processors on the system are busy executing non-Idle threads. On a multiprocessor system, if all of the processors are always busy, this is 100%; if all of the processors are busy half the time, this is 50%; and if all processors are busy one-fourth of the time, this is 25%. You can view this number as the fraction of the time spent doing useful work. Each processor is assigned an Idle thread in the Idle process which consumes those unproductive processor cycles not used by any other threads.
System	% Total User Time	This is the average percentage of time spent in User mode by all processors. On a multiprocessor system, if all processors are always in User mode, this is 100%; if all processors are in User mode half the time, this is 50%; and if all the processors are in User mode one-fourth the time, this is 25%. Applications execute in User mode, as do subsystems such as the window manager and the graphics engine. Code executing in User mode cannot damage the integrity of the Windows NT Executive, Kernel, and device drivers. Unlike some early operating systems, Windows NT uses process boundaries for subsystem protection in addition to the traditional protection of User and Privileged modes. Therefore, some work done by Windows NT on behalf of an application may appear in other subsystem processes in addition to the Privileged Time in the application process.
System	Alignment Fixups/sec	This is the rate of alignment faults fixed by the system.

Object	***Object Counter***	***Description***
System	Context Switches/sec	This is the rate of switches from one thread to another. Thread switches can occur either inside of a single process or across processes. A thread switch may be caused either by one thread asking another for information, or by a thread being preempted by another, higher-priority thread becoming ready to run. Unlike some early operating systems, Windows NT uses process boundaries for subsystem protection in addition to the traditional protection of User and Privileged modes. Therefore, some work done by Windows NT on behalf of an application may appear in other subsystem processes in addition to the Privileged Time in the application. Switching to the subsystem process causes one Context Switch in the application thread. Switching back causes another Context Switch in the subsystem thread.
System	Exception Dispatches/sec	This is the rate of exceptions dispatched by the system.
System	File Control Bytes/sec	This is the aggregate of bytes transferred for all file system operations that are neither reads nor writes. These operations usually include file system control requests or requests for information about device characteristics or status.
System	File Control Operations/sec	This is the aggregate of all file system operations that are neither reads nor writes. File Control Operations/sec usually include file system control requests or requests for information about device characteristics or status.
System	File Data Operations/sec	This is the rate at which the computer issues read and write operations to file system devices. It does not include file control operations.
System	File Read Bytes/sec	This is the aggregate of the bytes transferred for all of the file system read operations on the computer.

Continued

Table A-1 *(continued)*

Object	*Object Counter*	*Description*
System	File Read Operations/sec	This is the aggregate of all of the file system read operations on the computer.
System	File Write Bytes/sec	This is the aggregate of the bytes transferred for all of the file system write operations on the computer.
System	File Write Operations/sec	This is the aggregate of all of the file system write operations on the computer.
System	Floating Emulations/sec	This is the rate of floating emulations performed by the system.
System	Processor Queue Length	It is the instantaneous length of the processor queue in units of threads. This counter is always 0 unless you are monitoring a thread counter, too. All processors use a single queue in which threads wait for processor cycles. This length does not include the threads that are executing currently. A sustained processor queue length greater than 2 generally indicates processor congestion. This is an instantaneous count, not an average over the time interval.
System	System Calls	This is the frequency of calls to Windows NT system service routines. These routines perform all of the basic scheduling and synchronization of activities on the computer and provide access to nongraphical devices, memory management, and namespace management.
System	System Up Time	This is the total time (in seconds) that the computer has been operational since it was started last.
System	Total Interrupts/sec	This is the rate at which the computer receives and services hardware interrupts. Some devices that may generate interrupts are the system timer, the mouse, data communication lines, and network interface cards. This counter indicates how busy these devices are on a computer-wide basis (see Processor: Interrupts/sec).

Object	*Object Counter*	*Description*
Thread	% Privileged Time	This is the percentage of elapsed time that this thread spends executing code in Privileged mode. When a Windows NT system service is called, the service often runs in Privileged mode in order to gain access to system-private data. Such data is protected from access by threads executing in User mode. Calls to the system may be explicit, or they may be implicit — such as when a page fault or an interrupt occurs. Windows NT uses process boundaries for subsystem protection in addition to the traditional protection of User and Privileged modes (unlike some early operating systems). Therefore, some work performed by Windows NT on behalf of your application may appear in other subsystem processes in addition to the Privileged Time in your process.
Thread	% Processor Time	This is the percentage of elapsed time that this thread uses the processor to execute instructions. An instruction is the basic unit of execution in a processor, and a thread is the object that executes instructions. Code executed to handle certain hardware interrupts or trap conditions may be counted for this thread.
Thread	% User Time	This is the percentage of elapsed time that this thread spends executing code in User mode. Applications execute in User mode, as do subsystems such as the window manager and the graphics engine. Code executing in User mode cannot damage the integrity of the Windows NT Executive, Kernel, and device drivers. Unlike some early operating systems, Windows NT uses process boundaries for subsystem protection in addition to the traditional protection of User and Privileged modes. Therefore, some work done by Windows NT on behalf of your application may appear in other subsystem processes in addition to the Privileged Time in your process.

Continued

Table A-1 *(continued)*

Object	*Object Counter*	*Description*
Thread	Context Switches/sec	This is the rate of switches from one thread to another. Thread switches can occur either inside of a single process or across processes. A thread switch may be caused either by one thread asking another for information, or by a thread being preempted by another, higher-priority thread becoming ready to run. Unlike some early operating systems, Windows NT uses process boundaries for subsystem protection in addition to the traditional protection of User and Privileged modes. Therefore, some work done by Windows NT on behalf of an application may appear in other subsystem processes in addition to the Privileged Time in the application. Switching to the subsystem process causes one Context Switch in the application thread. Switching back causes another Context Switch in the subsystem thread.
Thread	Elapsed Time	This is the total elapsed time (in seconds) that this thread has been running.
Thread	ID Process	This is a unique identifier of this process. ID Process numbers are reused, so they only identify a process for the lifetime of that process.
Thread	ID Thread	This is a unique identifier of this thread. ID Thread numbers are reused, so they only identify a thread for the lifetime of that thread.
Thread	Priority Base	This is the current base priority of this thread. The system may raise the thread's dynamic priority above the base priority if the thread is handling user input, or the system may lower it toward the base priority if the thread becomes computer bound.

Object	***Object Counter***	***Description***
Thread	Priority Current	This is the current dynamic priority of this thread. The system may raise the thread's dynamic priority above the base priority if the thread is handling user input, or the system may lower it toward the base priority if the thread becomes computer bound.
Thread	Start Address	This is the starting virtual address for this thread.
Thread	Thread State	This is the current state of the thread. It is 0 for Initialized, 1 for Ready, 2 for Running, 3 for Standby, 4 for Terminated, 5 for Wait, 6 for Transition, and 7 for Unknown. A Running thread is using a processor; a Standby thread is about to use one. A Ready thread wants to use a processor, but is waiting for a processor because none are free. A thread in Transition is waiting for a resource in order to execute — for example, waiting for its execution stack to be paged in from disk. A Waiting thread has no use for the processor because it is waiting for a peripheral operation to complete or a resource to become free.
Thread	Thread Wait Reason	This is only applicable when the thread is in the Wait State (see Thread State). It is 0 or 7 when the thread is waiting for the Executive, 1 or 8 for a Free Page, 2 or 9 for a Page In, 3 or 10 for a Pool Allocation, 4 or 11 for an Execution Delay, 5 or 12 for a Suspended Condition, 6 or 13 for a User Request, 14 for an Event Pair High, 15 for an Event Pair Low, 16 for an LPC Receive, 17 for an LPC Reply, 18 for Virtual Memory, and 19 for a Page Out. 20 and higher have not been assigned at the time of this writing. Event Pairs are used to communicate with protected subsystems (see Context Switches).

Appendix B

Protocol Definitions

These selected protocol definitions are extremely helpful in learning the finer points of network protocols. This information is exposed under Network Monitor's Display Capture dialog box. While only selected protocols are displayed here in the interest of space, you may be interested in using Network Monitor and learning more about other definitions.

Data Type	***Legend***
●	Byte
❍	Array of Bytes
❑	Word
■	Array of Words
▲	Dword
✓	Array of DWords
×	Large Integer
◗	Date & Time
✚	Address
◆	No Value
Version Control Legend*	
Property with asterisk (*)	New in Windows 2000
Property in *italics*	Was in Windows NT, but not Windows 2000

*Note: Some property names have both of these characteristics, which means that the values changed from Windows NT to Windows 2000.

Protocol Name/Properties	Relations								
	=	<>	>	<	>=	<=	*Contains*	*Exists*	*Includes*
ARP_RARP (Address Resolution Protocol/ Reverse Address Resolution Protocol)	○	○							
*Address Length Flags						○	◆	●	
*ARP								◆	
ARP	○						○	◆	
*ATM ARP								◆	
Frame Padding							○	◆	
Hardware Address Length	●	●	●	●	●	●	○	◆	
*Hardware Type	■	■	■	■	■	■	○	◆	
Opcode	■	■	■	■	■	■	○	◆	
Protocol Address Length	●	●	●	●	●	●	○	◆	
*Protocol Type	■	■	■	■	■	■	○	◆	
*RARP Protocol							◆		
RARP Protocol	○						○	◆	
Sender's Hardware Address	+						○	◆	
Sender's Protocol Address	+						○	◆	
*Senders ATM Address Length	●	●	●	●	●	●	○	◆	
*Senders E.164 Address Length	●	●	●	●	●	●	○	◆	
*Source ATM Address	○						○	◆	
*Source E.164 Address	○						○	◆	
*Target ATM Address	○						○	◆	
*Target E.164 Address	○						○	◆	
Target's Hardware Address	+						○	◆	
Target's Protocol Address	+						○	◆	

Protocol Name/Properties	***Relations***								
	=	<>	>	<	>=	<=	***Contains***	***Exists***	***Includes***
*Targets E.164 Address Length	●	●	●	●	●	●	❍	◆	
Hardware Address Space	■	■	■	■	■	■	❍	◆	
Protocol Address Space	■	■	■	■	■	■	❍	◆	
IP (Internet Protocol)	❍	❍							
Checksum	■	■	■	■	■	■	❍	◆	
Compartmentalization	■	■	■	■	■	■	❍	◆	
Data							❍	◆	
Delay	●	●	●	●	●	●	❍	◆	
Destination Address	+						❍	◆	
End of Options	●	●	●	●	●	●	❍	◆	
Flags						❍	◆	●	
Flags Summary	●	●	●	●	●	●	❍	◆	
Fragment Offset	■	■	■	■	■	■	❍	◆	
Fragmented Datagram Data							❍	◆	
Gateway	+						❍	◆	
Handling Restrictions	❍						❍	◆	
Header Length	●	●	●	●	●	●	❍	◆	
Identification	■	■	■	■	■	■	❍	◆	
*Internet Timestamp Option							❍	◆	
Internet Timestamp Option	●	●	●	●	●	●	❍	◆	
Invalid Option	●	●	●	●	●	●	❍	◆	
*Malformed Option							❍	◆	
*Loose Source Routing Option							❍	◆	
Loose Source Routing Option	●	●	●	●	●	●	❍	◆	
Missed Stations	●	●	●	●	●	●	❍	◆	
Next Slot Pointer	●	●	●	●	●	●	❍	◆	
No Operation	●	●	●	●	●	●	❍	◆	
*Option Data							❍	◆	

Continued

Protocol Name/Properties	***Relations*** *(continued)*							
	<>	>	<	>=	<=	***Contains***	***Exists***	***Includes***
Option Fields								
Option Length	●	●	●	●	●	●	○	◆
*Option Type	●	●	●	●	●	●	○	◆
Padding							○	◆
Precedence	●	●	●	●	●	●	○	◆
Protocol	●	●	●	●	●	●	○	◆
*Record Route Option							○	◆
Record Route Option	●	●	●	●	●	●	○	◆
Reliability	●	●	●	●	●	●	○	◆
*Reserved Bytes							○	◆
Reserved Bytes	●	●	●	●	●	●	○	◆
*Route To Go						○	◆	
Route To Go	●	●	●	●	●	●	○	◆
*Route Traveled							○	◆
Route Traveled	●	●	●	●	●	●	○	◆
Routing Pointer	●	●	●	●	●	●	○	◆
Security Level	■	■	■	■	■	■	○	◆
*Security Option							○	◆
Security Option	●	●	●	●	●	●	○	◆
Service Type	●	●	●	●	●	●	○	◆
Source Address	+						○	◆
Stream Identifier	■	■	■	■	■	■	○	◆
*Stream Option							○	◆
Stream Option	●	●	●	●	●	●	○	◆
*Strict Source Routing Option							○	◆
Strict Source Routing Option	●	●	●	●	●	●	○	◆
*Summary								◆
Summary	○						○	◆
Throughput	●	●	●	●	●	●	○	◆

Protocol Name/Properties	Relations							
	<>	>	<	>=	<=	Contains	Exists	Includes
Time Options	●	●	●	●	●	●	○	◆
Time Point	▲	▲	▲	▲	▲	▲	○	◆
Time Pointer	●	●	●	●	●	●	○	◆
Time Route	▲	▲	▲	▲	▲	▲	○	◆
Time to Live	●	●	●	●	●	●	○	◆
Total Length	■	■	■	■	■	■	○	◆
Transmission Control Code	●	●	●	●	●	●	○	◆
Version	●	●	●	●	●	●	○	◆
NBT (NetBIOS over TCP/IP)	○	○						
Adapter Address	+						○	◆
Additional Record Count	■	■	■	■	■	■	○	◆
Answer Count	■	■	■	■	■	■	○	◆
ASCII Name	○						○	◆
*Called Name							○	◆
Called Name	○						○	◆
*Calling Name							○	◆
Calling Name	○						○	◆
Datagram Flags	●	●	●	●	●	●	○	◆
Datagram ID	■	■	■	■	■	■	○	◆
Datagram Length	■	■	■	■	■	■	○	◆
Datagram Packet Type	●	●	●	●	●	●	○	◆
Destination Name							○	◆
*DS								◆
DS	○						○	◆
DS Data							○	◆
DS First/More Packet Flags						○	◆	●
Duration	■	■	■	■	■	■	○	◆
Error Code	●	●	●	●	●	●	○	◆

Continued

Protocol Name/Properties	***Relations*** *(continued)*							
	<>	>	<	>=	<=	***Contains***	***Exists***	***Includes***
Flags Summary	■	■	■	■	■	■	○	◆
Frame Padding							○	◆
Free NCBS	■	■	■	■	■	■	○	◆
FRMRS Received	■	■	■	■	■	■	○	◆
FRMRS Transmitted	■	■	■	■	■	■	○	◆
Group Name Flag						○	◆	■
Iframe Receive Errors	■	■	■	■	■	■	○	◆
Iframe Transmit Errors	■	■	■	■	■	■	○	◆
Lanman Destination Name							○	◆
Lanman Source Name							○	◆
Length Extensions						○	◆	●
Max Config Sessions	■	■	■	■	■	■	○	◆
Max Datagram	■	■	■	■	■	■	○	◆
Max NCBS	■	■	■	■	■	■	○	◆
Max Sessions	■	■	■	■	■	■	○	◆
Name Flags						○	◆	■
Name Service Count	■	■	■	■	■	■	○	◆
Name Service Flags						○	◆	■
*NBT Summary								◆
NBT Summary	○						○	◆
NCBS	■	■	■	■	■	■	○	◆
No Receive Buffers	■	■	■	■	■	■	○	◆
No Transmit Buffers	■	■	■	■	■	■	○	◆
*NS								◆
NS	○						○	◆
Number of Names	●	●	●	●	●	●	○	◆
Opcode	■	■	■	■	■	■	○	◆
Opcode Reply Flag						○	◆	■

Protocol Name/Properties	***Relations***							
	<>	>	<	>=	<=	***Contains***	***Exists***	***Includes***
Owner IP Address	✚						○	◆
Owner Node Type	■	■	■	■	■	■	○	◆
Packet Flags	●	●	●	●	●	●	○	◆
Packet Length	■	■	■	■	■	■	○	◆
Packet Offset	■	■	■	■	■	■	○	◆
Packet Size	■	■	■	■	■	■	○	◆
Packet Type	●	●	●	●	●	●	○	◆
Pending Sessions	■	■	■	■	■	■	○	◆
Question Class	■	■	■	■	■	■	○	◆
Question Count	■	■	■	■	■	■	○	◆
Question Name							○	◆
Question Type	■	■	■	■	■	■	○	◆
RDATA Length	■	■	■	■	■	■	○	◆
Received	▲	▲	▲	▲	▲	▲	○	◆
Reserved	■	■	■	■	■	■	○	◆
Reserved Flags	●	●	●	●	●	●	○	◆
*Reserved Packet Flags	●	●	●	●	●	●	○	◆
Reserved Packet Flags			●	●				
Reserved Record Class	●	●	●	●	●	●	○	◆
Resource Record Flags	■	■	■	■	■	■	○	◆
Resource Record Name							○	◆
Resource Record Type	■	■	■	■	■	■	○	◆
Result Code	■	■	■	■	■	■	○	◆
Retarget IP Address	✚						○	◆
Retarget Port	■	■	■	■	■	■	○	◆
Session Service Error Code	●	●	●	●	●	●	○	◆
Source End-Node Type	●	●	●	●	●	●	○	◆
Source IP Address	✚						○	◆

Continued

Protocol Name/Properties	***Relations*** *(continued)*								
	<>	<	>	<=	>=	***Contains***	***Exists***	***Includes***	
Source Name							○	◆	
Source Port	■	■	■	■	■	■	○	◆	
*SS								◆	
SS	○						○	◆	
SS Data							○	◆	
*SS: Session Message Cont.								◆	
SS: Session Message Cont.	○						○	◆	
T1 Timeouts	■	■	■	■	■	■	○	◆	
Ti Timeouts	■	■	■	■	■	■	○	◆	
Time to Live	▲	▲	▲	▲	▲	▲	○	◆	
Transmitted	▲	▲	▲	▲	▲	▲	○	◆	
Transaction ID	■	■	■	■	■	■	○	◆	
Transmit Aborts	■	■	■	■	■	■	○	◆	
Version Major	●	●	●	●	●	●	○	◆	
Version Minor	●	●	●	●	●	●	○	◆	
Netlogon (MS Netlogon Broadcasts)	○	○							
Allowable Account Control Bit							○	◆	▲
*Allowable Account Control Bits Summary	▲	▲	▲	▲	▲	▲	○	◆	
Allowable Account Control Bits Summary						○	◆	▲	
Computer Name						○	◆		
Database Index	▲	▲	▲	▲	▲	▲	○	◆	
Date and Time	▲	▲	▲	▲	▲	▲	○	◆	
*DB Change Info Summary							◆		
DB Change Info Summary	○						○	◆	
DB Count	▲	▲	▲	▲	▲	▲	○	◆	
Domain Name						○	◆		
Domain SID	○						○	◆	
Domain SID Size	▲	▲	▲	▲	▲	▲	○	◆	
Large Serial Number	×	×	×	×	×	×	○	◆	

Protocol Name/Properties	***Relations***							
	<>	>	<	>=	<=	***Contains***	***Exists***	***Includes***
LM20 Token	■	■	■	■	■	■	❍	◆
LMNT Token	■	■	■	■	■	■	❍	◆
Logon Server Name							❍	◆
Low Serial Number	▲	▲	▲	▲	▲	▲	❍	◆
Mailslot Name							❍	◆
NT Date and Time	×	×	×	×	×	×	❍	◆
NT Version	▲	▲	▲	▲	▲	▲	❍	◆
Opcode	■	■	■	■	■	■	❍	◆
Pad	●	●	●	●	●	●	❍	◆
Primary DC Name							❍	◆
Pulse	▲	▲	▲	▲	▲	▲	❍	◆
Random	▲	▲	▲	▲	▲	▲	❍	◆
Request Count	■	■	■	■	■	■	❍	◆
Script Name							❍	◆
*Signature	●	●	●	●	●	●	❍	◆
Signature	■	■	■	■	■	■	❍	◆
*Summary								◆
Summary	❍						❍	◆
Unicode Computer Name							❍	◆
Unicode Domain Name							❍	◆
Unicode Logon Server							❍	◆
Unicode Primary DC Name							❍	◆
Unicode User Name							❍	◆
Update Type	■	■	■	■	■	■	❍	◆
User Name							❍	◆
Workstation Major Version	●	●	●	●	●	●	❍	◆
Workstation Minor Version	●	●	●	●	●	●	❍	◆
Workstation OS Version	●	●	●	●	●	●	❍	◆
SMB (Server Message Block Protocol)	❍	❍						

Continued

Protocol Name/Properties	***Relations*** *(continued)*							
	<>	>	<	>=	<=	***Contains***	***Exists***	***Includes***
Access Mask Standard Flags						❍	◆	▲
Access Mask Summary	▲	▲	▲	▲	▲	▲	❍	◆
Access Mask Token Specific Flag						❍	◆	▲
Access Mode	■	■	■	■	■	■	❍	◆
Account Name							❍	◆
ACE							❍	◆
ACE Count	■	■	■	■	■	■	❍	◆
ACE Flags						❍	◆	●
ACE Flags Summary	●	●	●	●	●	●	❍	◆
ACE Size	■	■	■	■	■	■	❍	◆
ACE Type	●	●	●	●	●	●	❍	◆
ACL Size	■	■	■	■	■	■	❍	◆
Action Taken	■	■	■	■	■	■	❍	◆
Action Taken Flags	■	■	■	■	■	■	❍	◆
Allocation	▲	▲	▲	▲	▲	▲	❍	◆
Available Allocation Units (NT)	×	×	×	×	×	×	❍	◆
Bad SMB Error Code	■	■	■	■	■	■	❍	◆
Block Mode	■	■	■	■	■	■	❍	◆
Block Mode Flags						❍	◆	■
Blocking	●	●	●	●	●	●	❍	◆
Blocks Per Unit	▲	▲	▲	▲	▲	▲	❍	◆
Blocks Per Unit (WORD)	■	■	■	■	■	■	❍	◆
Boolean IS Directory	●	●	●	●	●	●	❍	◆
Boolean Volume Supports Object	●	●	●	●	●	●	❍	◆
Buffer Length	▲	▲	▲	▲	▲	▲	❍	◆
Byte Count	■	■	■	■	■	■	❍	◆
Byte Parameters						❍	❍	◆
Bytes Left	■	■	■	■	■	■	❍	◆
Bytes Per Block	■	■	■	■	■	■	❍	◆

Protocol Name/Properties	Relations								
	=	<>	<	>	>=	<=	Contains	Exists	Includes
Bytes Per Block (NT)	▲	▲	▲	▲	▲	▲	❍	◆	
Bytes Remaining in Message	■	■	■	■	■	■	❍	◆	
Bytes Remaining in Pipe	■	■	■	■	■	■	❍	◆	
Caching Mode	■	■	■	■	■	■	❍	◆	
Capabilities	▲	▲	▲	▲	▲	▲	❍	◆	
Capabilities Flags						❍	◆	▲	
Change Count	■	■	■	■	■	■	❍	◆	
Change Time	◗	◗	◗	◗	◗	◗	❍	◆	
Command	●	●	●	●	●	●	❍	◆	
Common Header	❍						❍	◆	
Computer Name	❍						❍	◆	
Copy Flags	■	■	■	■	■	■	❍	◆	
Create Action	▲	▲	▲	▲	▲	▲	❍	◆	
Create Disposition	▲	▲	▲	▲	▲	▲	❍	◆	
Create Flags Dword	▲	▲	▲	▲	▲	▲	❍	◆	
Create Flags flags						❍	◆	▲	
Create Options	▲	▲	▲	▲	▲	▲	❍	◆	
Create Option Bits						❍	◆	▲	
Creation Time	◗	◗	◗	◗	◗	◗	❍	◆	
Data							❍	◆	
Data Bytes	■	■	■	■	■	■	❍	◆	
Data Count	▲	▲	▲	▲	▲	▲	❍	◆	
Data Displacement	■	■	■	■	■	■	❍	◆	
Data Displacement (NT)	▲	▲	▲	▲	▲	▲	❍	◆	
Data Length	■	■	■	■	■	■	❍	◆	
Data Offset	▲	▲	▲	▲	▲	▲	❍	◆	
Data Offset	■	■	■	■	■	■	❍	◆	
Desired Access	▲	▲	▲	▲	▲	▲	❍	◆	
Desired Access Flags						❍	◆	▲	

Continued

Protocol Name/Properties	***Relations*** *(continued)*							
	<>	>	<	>=	<=	***Contains***	***Exists***	***Includes***
Destination Mode	■	■	■	■	■	■	❍	◆
Destination Name	❍						❍	◆
Destination Tree ID (TID2)	■	■	■	■	■	■	❍	◆
Destination Type	■	■	■	■	■	■	❍	◆
Device State	■	■	■	■	■	■	❍	◆
DFS 8.3 Filename							❍	◆
*DFS Expanded Name							❍	◆
DFS Filename							❍	◆
DFS Max Referral Level	■	■	■	■	■	■	❍	◆
DFS Number of Referrals	■	■	■	■	■	■	❍	◆
*DFS Number of Expanded Names	■	■	■	■	■	■	❍	◆
DFS Path Consumed	■	■	■	■	■	■	❍	◆
DFS Proximity	▲	▲	▲	▲	▲	▲	❍	◆
DFS Request Filename							❍	◆
DFS Server Function	▲	▲	▲	▲	▲	▲	❍	◆
DFS Server Function Flags						❍	◆	▲
*DFS Server Site GUID	❍						❍	◆
DFS Server Type	■	■	■	■	■	■	❍	◆
DFS Sharename							❍	◆
*DFS Special Name							❍	◆
DFS Strip Path	■	■	■	■	■	■	❍	◆
DFS Time to Live	■	■	■	■	■	■	❍	◆
DFS Version 1 Referral							❍	◆
DFS Version 2 Referral							❍	◆
*DFS Version 3 Referral							❍	◆
DFS Version Number	■	■	■	■	■	■	❍	◆
Dialect Strings	❍						❍	◆
Dialect Strings Understood	❍						❍	◆
Directory Entry	❍						❍	◆

Protocol Name/Properties	***Relations***								
	=	<>	>	<	>=	<=	***Contains***	***Exists***	***Includes***
Disconnect Flag	■	■	■	■	■	■	○	◆	
Discretionary ACL (DACL)							○	◆	
Domain Name							○	◆	
DOS Error Code	■	■	■	■	■	■	○	◆	
EA Offset Error	■	■	■	■	■	■	○	◆	
EA Size	▲	▲	▲	▲	▲	▲	○	◆	
Echo Reverb	■	■	■	■	■	■	○	◆	
Echo Sequence	■	■	■	■	■	■	○	◆	
Encrypted Password	○						○	◆	
Encryption Key	●	●	●	●	●	●	○	◆	
Encryption Key Length	●	●	●	●	●	●	○	◆	
Encryption Key Offset	■	■	■	■	■	■	○	◆	
End of File	×	×	×	×	×	×	○	◆	
End of Search	■	■	■	■	■	■	○	◆	
Error Class	●	●	●	●	●	●	○	◆	
Error Code	■	■	■	■	■	■	○	◆	
Errored Path							○	◆	
Exist Action	■	■	■	■	■	■	○	◆	
Extended Attribute List	■	■	■	■	■	■	○	◆	
Extended Attributes	■	■	■	■	■	■	○	◆	
Extended OS Error Code	■	■	■	■	■	■	○	◆	
File Allocation Size	×	×	×	×	×	×	○	◆	
File Attribute Flags						○	◆	▲	
File Attributes						○	◆	▲	
File Attributes	■	■	■	■	■	■	○	◆	
File Creation Time	◗	◗	◗	◗	◗	◗	○	◆	
File Creation Time (sec)	◗	◗	◗	◗	◗	◗	○	◆	
File ID (FID)	■	■	■	■	■	■	○	◆	
File Index	▲	▲	▲	▲	▲	▲	○	◆	

Continued

Protocol Name/Properties	Relations (continued)							
	<>	>	<	>=	<=	Contains	Exists	Includes
File Name							○	◆
File Name Length	▲	▲	▲	▲	▲	▲	○	◆
File Offset	▲	▲	▲	▲	▲	▲	○	◆
File Offset (NT)	×	×	×	×	×	×	○	◆
File Offset, High	▲	▲	▲	▲	▲	▲	○	◆
File Share Access	▲	▲	▲	▲	▲	▲	○	◆
File Size	▲	▲	▲	▲	▲	▲	○	◆
File System Info						○	◆	▲
File System Info Summary	▲	▲	▲	▲	▲	▲	○	◆
File Type	■	■	■	■	■	■	○	◆
Files Copied	▲	▲	▲	▲	▲	▲	○	◆
Find Count	■	■	■	■	■	■	○	◆
Find Entry	▲	▲	▲	▲	▲	▲	○	◆
Find Flags	■	■	■	■	■	■	○	◆
Find Flags Detail						○	◆	■
Find Handle	■	■	■	■	■	■	○	◆
Find Key	○						○	◆
Find Key (client)	○						○	◆
Find Key (server)	○						○	◆
Find Key ID	●	●	●	●	●	●	○	◆
Find Key Length	■	■	■	■	■	■	○	◆
Find Resume Key	▲	▲	▲	▲	▲	▲	○	◆
Flags						○	◆	●
Flags Summary	●	●	●	●	●	●	○	◆
Flags 2						○	◆	■
Flags2 Summary	■	■	■	■	■	■	○	◆
Free Allocation Units	▲	▲	▲	▲	▲	▲	○	◆
Free Units (WORD)	■	■	■	■	■	■	○	◆
FSCTL Function	■	■	■	■	■	■	○	◆

Protocol Name/Properties	***Relations***							
	<>	>	<	>=	<=	***Contains***	***Exists***	***Includes***
FSCTL Method	■	■	■	■	■	■	○	◆
Group ID	■	■	■	■	■	■	○	◆
Group SID							○	◆
Guest Logon	■	■	■	■	■	■	○	◆
Hard Error Code	■	■	■	■	■	■	○	◆
I/O Bytes	■	■	■	■	■	■	○	◆
Impersonation Level	▲	▲	▲	▲	▲	▲	○	◆
Info Level	■	■	■	■	■	■	○	◆
Instance Count	●	●	●	●	●	●	○	◆
IOCTL Category	■	■	■	■	■	■	○	◆
IOCTL Data	●	●	●	●	●	●	○	◆
IOCTL Function	■	■	■	■	■	■	○	◆
IOCTL Parameters	●	●	●	●	●	●	○	◆
IPX Group ID	■	■	■	■	■	■	○	◆
IPX Key	▲	▲	▲	▲	▲	▲	○	◆
IPX Sequence Num	■	■	■	■	■	■	○	◆
IPX Session ID	■	■	■	■	■	■	○	◆
Kerberos Ticket	○						○	◆
Lanman Destination Name							○	◆
Lanman Source Name							○	◆
Last Access Time	◗	◗	◗	◗	◗	◗	○	◆
Last Access Time (sec)	◗	◗	◗	◗	◗	◗	○	◆
Last Modify Time	◗	◗	◗	◗	◗	◗	○	◆
Last Modify Time (sec)	◗	◗	◗	◗	◗	◗	○	◆
Last Name	■	■	■	■	■	■	○	◆
Last Write Time	◗	◗	◗	◗	◗	◗	○	◆
Locality	■	■	■	■	■	■	○	◆
Lock Bytes	▲	▲	▲	▲	▲	▲	○	◆
Lock Length	▲	▲	▲	▲	▲	▲	○	◆

Continued

Protocol Name/Properties	Relations (continued)							
	<>	>	<	>=	<=	Contains	Exists	Includes
Lock Length (NT)	×	×	×	×	×	×	❍	◆
Lock Range	❍						❍	◆
Lock Status	■	■	■	■	■	■	❍	◆
Lock Type	■	■	■	■	■	■	❍	◆
Lock Type Flags						❍	◆	■
Mailslot Class	■	■	■	■	■	■	❍	◆
Mailslot Opcode	■	■	■	■	■	■	❍	◆
Major Version	●	●	●	●	●	●	❍	◆
Max Buffer Size	■	■	■	■	■	■	❍	◆
Max Component Name Length	▲	▲	▲	▲	▲	▲	❍	◆
Max Count	■	■	■	■	■	■	❍	◆
Max Data Bytes	■	■	■	■	■	■	❍	◆
Max Data Count	▲	▲	▲	▲	▲	▲	❍	◆
Max MPX Requests	■	■	■	■	■	■	❍	◆
Max Parameter Count	▲	▲	▲	▲	▲	▲	❍	◆
Max Parm Bytes	■	■	■	■	■	■	❍	◆
Max Print Jobs	■	■	■	■	■	■	❍	◆
Max Raw Size	▲	▲	▲	▲	▲	▲	❍	◆
Max Setup Words	●	●	●	●	●	●	❍	◆
Max Setup Words	■	■	■	■	■	■	❍	◆
Max Transmit Size	■	■	■	■	■	■	❍	◆
Max VCs	■	■	■	■	■	■	❍	◆
Min Count	■	■	■	■	■	■	❍	◆
Minor Version	●	●	●	●	●	●	❍	◆
Multiplex ID (MID)	■	■	■	■	■	■	❍	◆
Name Length	●	●	●	●	●	●	❍	◆
Name Length (NT)	■	■	■	■	■	■	❍	◆
Native FS	●	●	●	●	●	●	❍	◆
Native Lanman							❍	◆

Protocol Name/Properties	***Relations***							
	<>	>	<	>=	<=	***Contains***	***Exists***	***Includes***
Native OS							❍	◆
Negotiate Encryption Key	❍						❍	◆
New Path							❍	◆
Next Offset	■	■	■	■	■	■	❍	◆
No-Exist Action	■	■	■	■	■	■	❍	◆
Notify Completion Filter	▲	▲	▲	▲	▲	▲	❍	◆
Notify Completion Filter Flags						❍	◆	▲
Notify Watch Tree	●	●	●	●	●	●	❍	◆
NT File Attributes	▲	▲	▲	▲	▲	▲	❍	◆
NT IOCTL Function Code	▲	▲	▲	▲	▲	▲	❍	◆
NT Last Access Time	◗	◗	◗	◗	◗	◗	❍	◆
NT Max Buffer Size	▲	▲	▲	▲	▲	▲	❍	◆
NT Status Code	▲	▲	▲	▲	▲	▲	❍	◆
NT Status Code System Error	■	■	■	■	■	■	❍	◆
NT Status Code System Information	■	■	■	■	■	■	❍	◆
NT Status Code System Success	■	■	■	■	■	■	❍	◆
NT Status Code System Warning	■	■	■	■	■	■	❍	◆
NT Status Customer Code	●	●	●	●	●	●	❍	◆
NT Status Facility	■	■	■	■	■	■	❍	◆
NT Status Reserved Bit	●	●	●	●	●	●	❍	◆
NT Status Severity Code	●	●	●	●	●	●	❍	◆
NT Transact Flags	■	■	■	■	■	■	❍	◆
Number of Locks	■	■	■	■	■	■	❍	◆
Number of Print Jobs	■	■	■	■	■	■	❍	◆
Number of Unlocks	■	■	■	■	■	■	❍	◆
Open Flags						❍	◆	■
Open Flags Summary	■	■	■	■	■	■	❍	◆
Open Function	■	■	■	■	■	■	❍	◆
Open Mode	■	■	■	■	■	■	❍	◆

Continued

Protocol Name/Properties	Relations (continued)							
	<>	>	<	>=	<=	*Contains*	*Exists*	*Includes*
Open Mode FCB Open	■	■	■	■	■	■	○	◆
Open Mode File Access						○	◆	■
Open Mode Files Sharing	■	■	■	■	■	■	○	◆
Open Timeout	▲	▲	▲	▲	▲	▲	○	◆
Oplock Level	●	●	●	●	●	●	○	◆
Optional Support	■	■	■	■	■	■	○	◆
Optional Support Flags						○	◆	■
Originator Name	○						○	◆
Owner SID							○	◆
Parameter Bytes	■	■	■	■	■	■	○	◆
Parameter Count	▲	▲	▲	▲	▲	▲	○	◆
Parameter Displacement	▲	▲	▲	▲	▲	▲	○	◆
Parameter Displacement	■	■	■	■	■	■	○	◆
Parameter Offset	▲	▲	▲	▲	▲	▲	○	◆
Parameter Offset	■	■	■	■	■	■	○	◆
Password	●	●	●	●	●	●	○	◆
Password Length	■	■	■	■	■	■	○	◆
Path NameX	○						○	◆
Pipe Endpoint	●	●	●	●	●	●	○	◆
Pipe Function	■	■	■	■	■	■	○	◆
Pipe Status	■	■	■	■	■	■	○	◆
Pipe Type	●	●	●	●	●	●	○	◆
Print Job Info	●	●	●	●	●	●	○	◆
Print Job Status	●	●	●	●	●	●	○	◆
Print Job Time	■	■	■	■	■	■	○	◆
Process High ID	■	■	■	■	■	■	○	◆
Process ID (PID)	■	■	■	■	■	■	○	◆
Protocol Index	■	■	■	■	■	■	○	◆
QFS Info Level	■	■	■	■	■	■	○	◆

Protocol Name/Properties	Relations							
	<>	>	<	>=	<=	Contains	Exists	Includes
Query Mode						❍	◆	■
Query Mode	■	■	■	■	■	■	❍	◆
Read Mode	●	●	●	●	●	●	❍	◆
Read-Ahead	■	■	■	■	■	■	❍	◆
Recognized as FSCTL	●	●	●	●	●	●	❍	◆
Rename Flags	■	■	■	■	■	■	❍	◆
Rename Flags						❍	◆	■
Reserved Byte	●	●	●	●	●	●	❍	◆
Reserved Dword	▲	▲	▲	▲	▲	▲	❍	◆
Reserved Word	❑						❍	◆
RMX Error Code	■	■	■	■	■	■	❍	◆
Root Dir FID	▲	▲	▲	▲	▲	▲	❍	◆
Search Attributes	■	■	■	■	■	■	❍	◆
Search Count	■	■	■	■	■	■	❍	◆
Search Path							❍	◆
Security Descriptor Control Summary						❍	◆	■
Security Descriptor Control Summary								
Security Flag Bits						❍	◆	●
Security Flags								
Security Identifier Authority	❍						❍	◆
Security Identifier Offset to the Group SID	▲	▲	▲	▲	▲	▲	❍	◆
Security Identifier Offset to the Owner SID	▲	▲	▲	▲	▲	▲	❍	◆
Security Identifier Sub Authority	✓						❍	◆
Security Identifier Sub Authority Count	●	●	●	●	●	●	❍	◆
Security Information	■	■	■	■	■	■	❍	◆
Security Information Flags						❍	◆	■
Security Mode						❍	◆	●
Security Mode Summary (NT)	●	●	●	●	●	●	❍	◆
Security Mode Summary (WORD)	■	■	■	■	■	■	❍	◆

Continued

Protocol Name/Properties	*Relations (continued)*							
	<>	>	<	>=	<=	*Contains*	*Exists*	*Includes*
Security Object Revision	❍						❍	◆
Seek Mode	■	■	■	■	■	■	○	◆
Server Announce Opcode	■	■	■	■	■	■	○	◆
Server Announce Rate	■	■	■	■	■	■	○	◆
Server Comment	❍						○	◆
Server Error Code	■	■	■	■	■	■	○	◆
Server Time	◗	◗	◗	◗	◗	◗	○	◆
Server Time	■	■	■	■	■	■	○	◆
Server Time Zone	■	■	■	■	■	■	○	◆
Service Flags						❍	◆	▲
Service Flags Summary	▲	▲	▲	▲	▲	▲	○	◆
Service Name	❍						○	◆
Session Key	▲	▲	▲	▲	▲	▲	○	◆
Set File Info Level	■	■	■	■	■	■	○	◆
Setup Action	■	■	■	■	■	■	○	◆
Setup Count	●	●	●	●	●	●	○	◆
Setup Words	❍						○	◆
Sharing Bits						❍	◆	▲
Short File Name							○	◆
Short Name Length	●	●	●	●	●	●	○	◆
Signature	▲	▲	▲	▲	▲	▲	○	◆
SMB Status	▲	▲	▲	▲	▲	▲	○	◆
Source Mode	■	■	■	■	■	■	○	◆
Spool Header Size	■	■	■	■	■	■	○	◆
Spool Mode	■	■	■	■	■	■	○	◆
Spool Restart Index	■	■	■	■	■	■	○	◆
Spool Start Index	■	■	■	■	■	■	○	◆
Summary	❍						○	◆
Supported Services	■	■	■	■	■	■	○	◆

Protocol Name/Properties	*Relations*							
	<>	>	<	>=	<=	*Contains*	*Exists*	*Includes*
System ACL (SACL)	▲	▲	▲	▲	▲	▲	❍	◆
T2 I/O Flags						❍	◆	■
T2 I/O Flags Summary	■	■	■	■	■	■	❍	◆
Total Allocation Units	▲	▲	▲	▲	▲	▲	❍	◆
Total Allocation Units (NT)	×	×	×	×	×	×	❍	◆
Total Data Bytes	■	■	■	■	■	■	❍	◆
Total Data Count	▲	▲	▲	▲	▲	▲	❍	◆
Total Parameter Count	▲	▲	▲	▲	▲	▲	❍	◆
Total Parm Bytes	■	■	■	■	■	■	❍	◆
Total Units (WORD)	■	■	■	■	■	■	❍	◆
Transact Flags Summary						❍	◆	■
Transact Flags Summary	■	■	■	■	■	■	❍	◆
Transact Function	■	■	■	■	■	■	❍	◆
Transact Timeout	▲	▲	▲	▲	▲	▲	❍	◆
Transact2 Function	■	■	■	■	■	■	❍	◆
Transaction Data	❍						❍	◆
Transaction Parameters	❍						❍	◆
Transaction Priority	■	■	■	■	■	■	❍	◆
Tree Copy	■	■	■	■	■	■	❍	◆
Tree ID (TID)	■	■	■	■	■	■	❍	◆
Unicode Password Length	■	■	■	■	■	■	❍	◆
Unique File ID	▲	▲	▲	▲	▲	▲	❍	◆
Unlock Range	❍						❍	◆
User ID (UID)	■	■	■	■	■	■	❍	◆
VC Number	■	■	■	■	■	■	❍	◆
Verify	■	■	■	■	■	■	❍	◆
Volume Creation Time	◗	◗	◗	◗	◗	◗	❍	◆
Volume Name							❍	◆
Volume Name Size	■	■	■	■	■	■	❍	◆

Continued

Protocol Name/Properties	***Relations*** *(continued)*							
	<>	>	<	>=	<=	***Contains***	***Exists***	***Includes***
Volume Serial Number	▲	▲	▲	▲	▲	▲	❍	◆
Volume Time	◗	◗	◗	◗	◗	◗	❍	◆
Word Count	●	●	●	●	●	●	❍	◆
Word Count	●	●	●	●	●	●	❍	◆
Word Parameters	❑						❍	◆
Write Mode	■	■	■	■	■	■	❍	◆
Write Mode Flags						❍	◆	■
TCP (Transmission Control Protocol)	❍	❍						
Acknowledgement Number	▲	▲	▲	▲	▲	▲	❍	◆
Checksum	■	■	■	■	■	■	❍	◆
Data							❍	◆
Data Offset	●	●	●	●	●	●	❍	◆
Destination Port	■	■	■	■	■	■	❍	◆
Flags	●	●	●	●	●	●	❍	◆
Frame Padding							❍	◆
Invalid Option	■	■	■	■	■	■	❍	◆
*Left Edge of Block	▲	▲	▲	▲	▲	▲	❍	◆
*Malformed Option							❍	◆
*Maximum Segment Size							❍	◆
*Maximum Segment Size Option							❍	◆
*Option Data	❍						❍	◆
Option End	●	●	●	●	●	●	❍	◆
Option Kind (Maximum Segment Size)	●	●	●	●	●	●	❍	◆
Option Length	●	●	●	●	●	●	❍	◆
Option MaxSegSize	●	●	●	●	●	●	❍	◆
Option Nop	●	●	●	●	●	●	❍	◆
*Option Padding							❍	◆
*Option Type	●	●	●	●	●	●	❍	◆
Option Value	■	■	■	■	■	■	❍	◆

Protocol Name/Properties	***Relations***							
	<>	>	<	>=	<=	*Contains*	*Exists*	*Includes*
Options							○	◆
Padding	■	■	■	■	■	■	○	◆
*Reply Timestamp	▲	▲	▲	▲	▲	▲	○	◆
Reserved	■	■	■	■	■	■	○	◆
*Right Edge of Block	▲	▲	▲	▲	▲	▲	○	◆
*SACK Option							○	◆
*SACK Permitted Option							○	◆
Sequence Number	▲	▲	▲	▲	▲	▲	○	◆
Source Port	■	■	■	■	■	■	○	◆
*Summary								◆
Summary	○						○	◆
TCP Flags						○	◆	●
*Timestamp							○	◆
*Timestamps Option	▲	▲	▲	▲	▲	▲	○	◆
Unknown Option							○	◆
*Unrecognized Option							○	◆
Urgent Pointer	■	■	■	■	■	■	○	◆
Window	■	■	■	■	■	■	○	◆
*Window Scale	●	●	●	●	●	●	○	◆
*Window Scale Option							○	◆

Appendix C

Common Image Names in Task Manager

This appendix provides the descriptions of common image names displayed when you select the Processes tab sheet in Windows 2000 Server's Task Manager (see Table C-1). These descriptions enable you to understand better what the file does. More important, knowing the description of the Task Manager image name enables you to conduct more research on that image name on the Web or on Microsoft TechNet.

Table C-1 Task Manager Image Names

Image Name	*Vendor (Company Name)*	*Real Name (Description)*	*Original Filename*	*Location*	*Version*
smss.exe	Microsoft	Windows 2000 Session Manager	smss.exe	\%SYSTEM ROOT%\ system 32	5.00.2015.1
csrss.exe	Microsoft	Client Server Runtime Process	CSRSS.exe	\%SYSTEM ROOT%\ system32	5.00.2010.1
winlogon.exe	Microsoft	Windows 2000 Logon Application	WINLOGON.EXE	\%SYSTEM ROOT%\ system32	5.00.2023.1
services.exe	Microsoft	Services and Controller Application	Services.exe	\%SYSTEM ROOT%\ system32	5.00.2023.1
lsass.exe	Microsoft	LSA Executable and Server DLL	lsasrv.dll and lsass.exe	\%SYSTEM ROOT%\ system32	5.00.2029.1
svchost.exe	Microsoft	Generic Host Process for Win32 Services	svchost.exe	\%SYSTEM ROOT%\ system32	5.00.2008.1
spoolsv.exe	Microsoft	Spooler SubSystem Application	Spoolsv.exe	\%SYSTEM ROOT%\ system32	5.00.2016.1
mstask.exe	Microsoft	Task Scheduler Engine	mstask.exe	\%SYSTEM ROOT%\ system32	4.71.2022.1

Image Name	*Vendor (Company Name)*	*Real Name (Description)*	*Original Filename*	*Location*	*Version*
explorer.exe	Microsoft	Windows 2000 Explorer	Explorer.exe	\%SYSTEM ROOT%	5.0.2516.1900
msiexec.exe	Microsoft	Windows Installer – Unicode	msiexec.exe	\%SYSTEM ROOT%\ system32	1.01.0213.0
taskmgr.exe	Microsoft	Windows 2000 Task Manager	Taskmgr.exe	\%SYSTEM ROOT%\ system32	5.00.2010.1

Appendix D

About the CD-ROM

CD-ROM Contents

The CD-ROM included with this book contains the following materials:

- Adobe Acrobat Reader
- An electronic version of this book, *Windows 2000 Server Secrets*, in `.pdf` format
- Hotfix Control
- Ping Plotter
- Micro House Technical Library (Demo)
- WinZip 7.0

Installing and Using Items on the CD-ROM

The following sections describe each product and include detailed instructions for installation and use.

Adobe Acrobat Reader

Adobe Acrobat Reader is a helpful program that will enable you to view the electronic version of this book in the same page format as the actual book.

To install and run Adobe Acrobat Reader and view the electronic version of this book, follow these steps:

1. Start Windows Explorer (if you're using Windows 95/98) or Windows NT/2000 Explorer (if you're using Windows NT/2000), and then open the `Adobe Acrobat` folder on the CD-ROM.
2. In the `Adobe Acrobat` folder, double-click `rs40eng.exe` and follow the instructions presented onscreen for installing Adobe Acrobat Reader.
3. To view the electronic version of this book after you have installed Adobe Acrobat Reader, start Windows Explorer (if you're using Windows 95/98) or Windows NT/2000 Explorer (if you're using Windows NT/2000), and then open the `Windows 2000 Server Secrets` PDF folder on the CD-ROM.

In the `Windows 2000 Server Secrets` PDF folder, double-click the chapter or appendix file you want to view. All documents in this folder end with a `.pdf` extension.

Hotfix Control

Hotfix Control is an application that allows you to track which hotfixes and service packs have been applied to a Windows NT Server machine. This functionality is not natively provided by Microsoft Windows 2000 Server.

To install Hotfix Control, follow these steps:

1. Log into your Windows 2000 system as a user with administrative privileges.
2. Copy the contents of the `Hotfix Control` folder on the CD-ROM to a folder on your hard disk.

Double-click the `hotfxctl.exe` file to run Hotfix Control.

Ping Plotter

Ping Plotter is an application that traces packet paths across the LAN and WANs by identifying each hop taken by the packet. It is also useful for maintaining WAN connections by periodically sending out packets via the Ping command.

To install Ping Plotter, follow these steps:

1. Log into your Windows 2000 system as a user with administrative privileges.
2. Copy the `pngplt_2.exe` file from the `Ping Plotter` folder on the CD-ROM to your hard disk.
3. Double-click the `pngplt_2.exe` file.
4. Complete the steps in the Setup wizard.

Micro House Technical Library (Demo)

Micro House Technical Library is a useful CD-ROM-based set of encyclopedias that contains hardware-configuration information. This evaluation copy of Micro House Technical Library includes only the encyclopedia of I/O cards. Use this evaluation copy to determine whether or not you want to purchase the full version of the Micro House Technical Library.

To install and access the Micro House Technical Library, follow these steps:

1. Start Windows Explorer (if you're using Windows 95/98) or Windows NT/2000 Explorer (if you're using Windows NT/2000), and then open the `Micro House Tech Lib` folder on the CD-ROM.
2. In the `Micro House Tech Lib` folder, double-click `MTLTrial.exe` and follow the instructions presented onscreen for installing the Micro House Technical Library.
3. To run the Micro House Technical Library, select Start ⇨ Programs ⇨ MH Tech Library ⇨ MTL Demo Edition.

WinZip 7.0

WinZip 7.0, by Nico Mak Computing, Inc., is a popular file/folder compression and decompression application. It is typically used to transfer large files as e-mail attachments or on a floppy disk.

To install WinZip 7.0, follow these steps:

1. Log into your Windows 2000 system as a user with administrative privileges.
2. Double-click the `Setup.exe` file in the `Winzip70` folder on your CD-ROM.
3. Complete the steps in the Setup wizard.

Index

B

D

E

F

G

H

J

K

N

O

P

Q

R

T

X

Y

Z

IDG Books Worldwide, Inc. End-User License Agreement

READ THIS. You should carefully read these terms and conditions before opening the software packet(s) included with this book ("Book"). This is a license agreement ("Agreement") between you and IDG Books Worldwide, Inc. ("IDGB"). By opening the accompanying software packet(s), you acknowledge that you have read and accept the following terms and conditions. If you do not agree and do not want to be bound by such terms and conditions, promptly return the Book and the unopened software packet(s) to the place you obtained them for a full refund.

1. **License Grant.** IDGB grants to you (either an individual or entity) a nonexclusive license to use one copy of the enclosed software program(s) (collectively, the "Software") solely for your own personal or business purposes on a single computer (whether a standard computer or a workstation component of a multiuser network). The Software is in use on a computer when it is loaded into temporary memory (RAM) or installed into permanent memory (hard disk, CD-ROM, or other storage device). IDGB reserves all rights not expressly granted herein.

2. **Ownership**. IDGB is the owner of all right, title, and interest, including copyright, in and to the compilation of the Software recorded on the disk(s) or CD-ROM ("Software Media"). Copyright to the individual programs recorded on the Software Media is owned by the author or other authorized copyright owner of each program. Ownership of the Software and all proprietary rights relating thereto remain with IDGB and its licensers.

3. **Restrictions On Use and Transfer**.

   (a) You may only (i) make one copy of the Software for backup or archival purposes, or (ii) transfer the Software to a single hard disk, provided that you keep the original for backup or archival purposes. You may not (i) rent or lease the Software, (ii) copy or reproduce the Software through a LAN or other network system or through any computer subscriber system or bulletin-board system, or (iii) modify, adapt, or create derivative works based on the Software.

   (b) You may not reverse engineer, decompile, or disassemble the Software. You may transfer the Software and user documentation on a permanent basis, provided that the transferee agrees to accept the terms and conditions of this Agreement and you retain no copies. If the Software is an update or has been updated, any transfer must include the most recent update and all prior versions.

4. **Restrictions on Use of Individual Programs**. You must follow the individual requirements and restrictions detailed for each individual program in Appendix D of this Book. These limitations are also contained in the individual license agreements recorded on the Software Media. These limitations may include a requirement that after using the program for a specified period of time, the user must pay a registration fee or

discontinue use. By opening the Software packet(s), you will be agreeing to abide by the licenses and restrictions for these individual programs that are detailed in Appendix D and on the Software Media. None of the material on this Software Media or listed in this Book may ever be redistributed, in original or modified form, for commercial purposes.

5. **Limited Warranty.**

   (a) IDGB warrants that the Software and Software Media are free from defects in materials and workmanship under normal use for a period of sixty (60) days from the date of purchase of this Book. If IDGB receives notification within the warranty period of defects in materials or workmanship, IDGB will replace the defective Software Media.

   (b) **IDGB AND THE AUTHOR OF THE BOOK DISCLAIM ALL OTHER WARRANTIES, EXPRESS OR IMPLIED, INCLUDING WITHOUT LIMITATION IMPLIED WARRANTIES OF MERCHANTABILITY AND FITNESS FOR A PARTICULAR PURPOSE, WITH RESPECT TO THE SOFTWARE, THE PROGRAMS, THE SOURCE CODE CONTAINED THEREIN, AND/OR THE TECHNIQUES DESCRIBED IN THIS BOOK. IDGB DOES NOT WARRANT THAT THE FUNCTIONS CONTAINED IN THE SOFTWARE WILL MEET YOUR REQUIREMENTS OR THAT THE OPERATION OF THE SOFTWARE WILL BE ERROR FREE.**

   (c) This limited warranty gives you specific legal rights, and you may have other rights that vary from jurisdiction to jurisdiction.

6. **Remedies.**

   (a) IDGB's entire liability and your exclusive remedy for defects in materials and workmanship shall be limited to replacement of the Software Media, which may be returned to IDGB with a copy of your receipt at the following address: Software Media Fulfillment Department, Attn.: *Windows 2000 Server Secrets*, IDG Books Worldwide, Inc., 7260 Shadeland Station, Ste. 100, Indianapolis, IN 46256, or call 1-800-762-2974. Please allow three to four weeks for delivery. This Limited Warranty is void if failure of the Software Media has resulted from accident, abuse, or misapplication. Any replacement Software Media will be warranted for the remainder of the original warranty period or thirty (30) days, whichever is longer.

   (b) In no event shall IDGB or the author be liable for any damages whatsoever (including without limitation damages for loss of business profits, business interruption, loss of business information, or any other pecuniary loss) arising from the use of or inability to use the Book or the Software, even if IDGB has been advised of the possibility of such damages.

   (c) Because some jurisdictions do not allow the exclusion or limitation of liability for consequential or incidental damages, the above limitation or exclusion may not apply to you.

7. **U.S. Government Restricted Rights.** Use, duplication, or disclosure of the Software by the U.S. Government is subject to restrictions stated in paragraph (c)(1)(ii) of the Rights in Technical Data and Computer Software clause of DFARS 252.227-7013, and in subparagraphs (a) through (d) of the Commercial Computer — Restricted Rights clause at FAR 52.227-19, and in similar clauses in the NASA FAR supplement, when applicable.

8. **General.** This Agreement constitutes the entire understanding of the parties and revokes and supersedes all prior agreements, oral or written, between them and may not be modified or amended except in a writing signed by both parties hereto that specifically refers to this Agreement. This Agreement shall take precedence over any other documents that may be in conflict herewith. If any one or more provisions contained in this Agreement are held by any court or tribunal to be invalid, illegal, or otherwise unenforceable, each and every other provision shall remain in full force and effect.

my2cents.idgbooks.com

Register This Book — And Win!

Visit **http://my2cents.idgbooks.com** to register this book and we'll automatically enter you in our fantastic monthly prize giveaway. It's also your opportunity to give us feedback: let us know what you thought of this book and how you would like to see other topics covered.

Discover IDG Books Online!

The IDG Books Online Web site is your online resource for tackling technology — at home and at the office. Frequently updated, the IDG Books Online Web site features exclusive software, insider information, online books, and live events!

10 Productive & Career-Enhancing Things You Can Do at www.idgbooks.com

- Nab source code for your own programming projects.
- Download software.
- Read Web exclusives: special articles and book excerpts by IDG Books Worldwide authors.
- Take advantage of resources to help you advance your career as a Novell or Microsoft professional.
- Buy IDG Books Worldwide titles or find a convenient bookstore that carries them.
- Register your book and win a prize.
- Chat live online with authors.
- Sign up for regular e-mail updates about our latest books.
- Suggest a book you'd like to read or write.
- Give us your 2¢ about our books and about our Web site.

You say you're not on the Web yet? It's easy to get started with IDG Books' *Discover the Internet,* available at local retailers everywhere.

Installation Instructions

Each software item on the *Windows 2000 Server Secrets* CD-ROM is located in its own folder. To install a particular piece of software, open its folder with My Computer or Internet Explorer. What you do next depends on what you find in the software's folder:

1. First, look for a `ReadMe.txt` file or a `.doc` or `.htm` document. If this is present, it should contain installation instructions and other useful information.
2. If the folder contains an executable (`.exe`) file, this is usually an installation program. Often it will be called `Setup.exe` or `Install.exe`, but in some cases the filename reflects an abbreviated version of the software's name and version number. Run the `.exe` file to start the installation process.
3. In the case of some simple software, the `.exe` file probably is the software — no real installation step is required. You can run the software from the CD to try it out. If you like it, copy it to your hard disk and create a Start menu shortcut for it.

The `ReadMe.txt` file in the CD-ROM's root directory may contain additional installation information, so be sure to check it.

For a listing of the software on the CD-ROM, see Appendix D.